# of Economics, Policy and Development

'This is welcome collection of IG's ideas and musings over a long period. Here is the key to economic policymaking not only for India over the last fifty years but in the larger international context as well.'

—**Lord Meghnad Desai**, Professor Emeritus, London School of Economics

'Two of India's foremost economists and thinkers, Y.V. Reddy and Deena Khatkhate, have done singular service to the present and future generations of our country by putting together this extraordinary collection of essays by I.G. Patel. As is well known, IG's contribution to India's development planning and evolution of economic policy over several decades after independence was unparalleled in its sweep, clarity and intensity. I strongly recommend this book to all academics, policymakers and other professionals who are interested in knowing more about India's past and its future potential.'

—**Bimal Jalan**, Former Governor, Reserve Bank of India

'Dr I.G. Patel was one of our superstars on economic policy. This beautifully edited volume of his writings shows why. Read and enjoy.'

—**Jagdish Bhagwati**, University Professor, Economics Department, Columbia University

'Dr I.G. Patel was one of the outstanding national and international public servants of the post-war era. He was a fine economist, of great experience and extraordinarily wise. He combined strong analytical insight with a deep understanding of institutional and political practicalities. He contributed greatly to higher education, notably as Director of my own institution, the LSE. And he was loved and admired by all who had the good fortune to work with him. His writings reflect his wisdom and experience and there is much to learn for all concerned with the principles and practice of economic policy. We should be very grateful to Dr Deena Khatkate and Dr Y.V. Reddy for gathering together and editing these important writings from a man of special distinction.'

—**Nicholas Stern**, I.G. Patel Professor of Economics and Government, London School of Economics (Baron Stern of Brentford)

'This collection of lucid essays provides a fascinating insight into the evolving thinking of I.G. Patel on some of the great questions facing practical economists. The breadth of his interests and the prescience of many of his ideas are truly impressive.'

—**Mervyn King**, The Governor, Bank of England

# of Economics, Policy and Development

An Intellectual Journey by

I.G. PATEL

EDITED BY
Deena Khatkhate
Y.V. Reddy

OXFORD
UNIVERSITY PRESS

OXFORD
UNIVERSITY PRESS

Oxford University Press is a department of the University of Oxford. It furthers the University's objective of excellence in research, scholarship, and education by publishing worldwide. Oxford is a registered trademark of Oxford University Press in the UK and in certain other countries

Published in India by
Oxford University Press
YMCA Library Building, 1 Jai Singh Road, New Delhi 110001, India

First Edition published in 2012
Second impression 2012

ISBN 13: 978-0-19-807898-2
ISBN 10: 0-19-807898-6

Typeset in Minion Pro 10.5/12.5
by Le Studio Graphique, Gurgaon 122 001

Contents

List of Tables and Figures ix
Acknowledgements xi
Introduction by Deena Khatkhate xiii

PART I

Monetary and Credit Policy

1. Demand for Money during Periods of Inflation and Stabilization 3
2. Nature and Significance of Monetary Policy and Its Instruments 32
3. Selective Credit Controls in Underdeveloped Economies 44
4. Some Thoughts on Monetary and Credit Policy 56
5. Monetary Policy Revisited 64
6. Communication Policy of Central Banks 85

PART II

Gold Policy

7. India's Elasticity of Demand for Gold 97
8. On Turning Gold into Base Metal 113

Part III

Economic Development and Planning

9. Exports by Countries in Process of Industrialization 121
10. The Challenge for the Newly Industrializing Countries 138
11. Capital Formation in the Private Corporate Sector 142
12. Physical Planning 148
13. The Second Five Year Plan: A Tentative Framework 155
14. The Role of the Public Sector in a Small Open Economy 192
15. The First Five Year Plan of China (1953–1957): An Appraisal 201

Part IV

Growth, Equity and Social Justice

16. The Socialist Legacy 223
17. Growth, Modernization, Self-reliance and Social Justice 232
18. Equity in a Modern Society 241
19. The Idea of India as an Ideal 248

Part V

Economic Reform and Policy in India

20. The Vision for a New India 265
21. India's Economic Reforms and Development 280
22. Current Unease with Indian Economic Reform 289

Part VI

Banking and the Financial System

23. Role of Banks and Financial Institutions in Corporate Finance 299
24. Capital Market Regulation 307

PART VII

International Aspects

25. The Role of PL-480 Supplies in the Development of India 319
26. Trade and Payments Policy for a Developing Economy 333
27. Lessons from the Monetary Events of 1971 354
28. Indebtedness of Developing Countries 365
29. A New International Economic Order? 370
30. The Adjustment Problem 385
31. Protectionism: Its Causes and Manifestations 392

PART VIII

Miscellany

32. Professor A.C. Pigou: A Memoir 405
33. The Adam Smith Perspective 412
34. Advising the Advisers 418

Epilogue by Y.V. Reddy 423
About the Author and Editors 445
Index 447

Tables and Figures

Tables

1.1	Indices of Changes in Money Supply, Prices, and the Velocity of Circulation of Money in Germany	15
1.2	Indices of Money Supply, Prices, and the Velocity of Circulation of Money in Austria	21
1.3	Inflation and Money Supply in Belgium	24
1.4	Belgian Government's Budgetary Position	25
1.5	Daily Averages of the Number of Registered Unemployed in Belgium	25
1.6	Index Numbers of Employment in Industry in Belgium	25
7.1	Two Alternative Forms of Relative Price of Gold	102
9.1	Projections of India's Exports	125
13.1	Net National Output of India at Current and Constant Prices	158
13.2	Growth in National Income in Selected Countries	159
13.3	Estimated Total Investment Required for Achieving the Targets in Industries and Mining	169
13.4	Tentative Breakdown of the Net Investment of Rs 6,000 crore	175
13.5	Tentative Breakdown of the Net Investment of Rs 4,200 crore in the Public Sector	176
13.6	Tentative Breakdown of the Net Investment of Rs 2,500 crore in the Private Sector	176
13.7	Index of Wholesale Prices in India	177
13.8	Domestic Product of India	178

13.9 Additional Employment We May Count on in the Second Plan 181
13.10 Occupational Pattern, India 182
13.11 Rough Approximation of the Budgetary Position of the Centre and the States Combined 185
13.12 Budgetary Position over the Second Plan 186
15.1 Increase in the Production of Mass Consumed Commodities 205
15.2 Pattern of Investment 210

Figures

7.1 Demand for Gold in India: Correlation Chart (Equation 1) 104
7.2 Demand for Gold in India: Correlation Chart (Equation 2) 105

Acknowledgements

The editors profusely thank Alaknanda Patel and Rehana Patel for graciously authorizing them to include assorted papers and articles by late Dr I.G. Patel in this volume. They wish to place on record Alaknanda Patel's invaluable guidance in locating, assembling, and authenticating the papers. They appreciate the preparatory work for the volume done by M.N. Sane, Sandhya Gajjar and Priyal Chokshi, by collecting Dr Patel's published and unpublished papers and addresses with care and good understanding from scattered sources. Thanks are also due to D.G. Patel for graciously compiling the manuscript papers included in the volume. Arthur Monteiro made an excellent typescript for publication, which is acknowledged by the editors.

Acknowledgements are also due to Sunil Nagpal for the valuable services rendered with devotion and diligence, at all stages of the book, in all respects. The services rendered by B. Sudhakar Reddy are also appreciated.

Above all, the editors express gratitude to the Oxford University Press team for their outstanding support through the various stages of production in bringing out this volume.

The editors and the publisher acknowledge with thanks the following for permission to include the extracts/essays in this volume:

International Monetary Fund for 'Monetary Policy in Post-war Years', *IMF Staff Papers*, Vol. III, No. 1, 1953, © International Monetary Fund, Washington, DC, USA.

International Monetary Fund for 'Selective Credit Controls in Underdeveloped Economies', *IMF Staff Papers*, Vol. IV, No. 1, September 1954, © International Monetary Fund, Washington, DC, USA.

Reserve Bank of India Bulletin for 'Some Thoughts on Monetary and Credit Policy', February 1979.

Reserve Bank of India for 'Monetary Policy Revisited'. Published as a booklet, 1988.

Economic Weekly for 'India's Elasticity of Demand for Gold', 11 February 2006.

Economic Weekly for 'On Turning Gold into Base Metal', Special Number, July 1958.

Oxford University Press for 'Exports by Countries in Process of Industrialization', in *New Directions for World Trade*, A Chatham House Report, London, 1964.

Reserve Bank of India for 'The Role of the Public Sector in a Small Open Economy', June 1979.

Economic Weekly for 'The Socialist Legacy', Special Number, July 1964.

Institute of Social Sciences for 'The Idea of India as an Ideal: Can Our Dreams Come True', New Delhi, November 2005.

Economic and Political Weekly for 'India's Economic Reforms and Development', 30 May 1998.

Reserve Bank of India Bulletin for 'Role of Banks and Financial Institutions in Corporate Finance', September–October 1979.

Per Jacobsson Foundation for 'Lessons from the Monetary Events of 1971', September 1972.

Indian Economic Review for 'A New International Economic Order?', Vol. 9, No. 1, January–June 1974.

Springer Science and Business Media and Martinus Nijhoff Publishers for 'The Adjustment Problem', *Trade Policies for a Better Future: The Leutwiler Report, the GATT and the Uruguay Round*, Dordrecht, 1987.

Economic Weekly for 'Professor A.C. Pigou: A Memoir', 5 March 1960.

Economic and Political Weekly, Annual for 'Advising the Advisers', January 1956.

Introduction

> Things are always at their best in their beginning.
> —Blaise Pascal

I.G. Patel was one of the lustrous stars of the new generation of economists in post-independence India who could think strategically with deep insights into India's economic problems and design economic policy to deal with, if not solve them, to the satisfaction of all. One of credos of I.G. Patel (hereafter IG) was, "The route to the rational is not always direct", which underlay his approach to economic policy as he could interpret it in terms of economic theory and cultural overtones of the Indian society. Two social scientists who observed what IG achieved through his own lens, noted perceptively that

> The middle path IG tended to seek in several conflicting situations was not a heroic position. It invited charges of conservatism and ad-hocism. But mediation too required a certain quiet courage; in IG's case, the role was discharged with a clear sense of direction and with much tactical skill, subtlety, and wit. (Guhan and Shroff 1986, p. xi)

IG as a policymaker was greatly influenced by his teacher at Cambridge, Joan Robinson, the Grand Dame of pure economic theory, who hortatively told him: "An economic model cannot tell much more than what we tell it" (Patel 1986, pp. 29–30). IG himself improved upon Joan Robinson's dictum. "After all," he said in his book of articles, "it is not internal consistency but consistency with the facts of life which distinguishes an operational from a pedagogic or propagandist model of growth" (Patel 1986, p. 38).

He revelled in his role as a policy adviser, which was lauded perceptively by two leading members of the Indian Civil Service when they pleaded for a professional economist to manage economic policy. One of them argued strongly that "The analytical grasp of economists needs to be combined with the pragmatism of an economic administrator" (Jha 1986, p. 322). Another was even more explicit in stating that

> Specialists, whether they be doctors, engineers, scientists or economists, while very useful as advisers, do not, as a rule, make good administrators. IG's greatness lies in the successful transition he made from an academic economist to an economic administrator. He used economic theory but was wise enough to modify it for the real world. He needed neither economic nor administrative advisers; he combined the functions of both in himself.... Not only have I had the opportunity of watching his work at close quarters, but I owe a personal debt to him, as much of such success as I might have had in my economic incarnation was due to him (Nehru 1986, p. 317).

IG's stellar academic achievements inducted him into the Political Economy Club of Keynes in Cambridge because Keynes was impressed by his talent for thinking fundamentally on economic issues. IG was the first non-European secretary of the exclusive club. His versatile intellectual personality roaming with equal ease in his writings and economic adviser's role on the national scene as well as internationally were all inextricably linked with the personal life he lived since he was a young prodigy. His experience thus has an important bearing on why despite all his competence in economic and monetary theory as revealed in his early papers written while in the International Monetary Fund (IMF) as a young economist just out of his teens, he switched on to being an economic policymaker. A proper understanding of his career choice, and a major part of his later writings in the economic policy domain, can only be comprehended in terms of his life story which defined his belief system.

His voyage to UK for pursuing higher education at the Cambridge University in 1944 gave him, as he put it,

> Time to ruminate about the past and to dream and prepare for the future. I knew from personal experience by then that it is not poverty but insecurity that demeans and degrades.... Faced with insecurity, change and ambition, people seek some comfort and solace in a sense of belonging, in having some firm roots—whether in the family, or the caste, or the community.... But they are debilitating too. And how does one nurture a sense of nationhood in the midst of such myriad of loyalties? (Patel 2002, p. 8)

IG often used to tell friends and family members that he was prompted by the surrounding social and political institutionalism to do something that would be of some help and advantage to people in squalor and poverty. It was this mental make-up that led IG to venture, when he was only 17 years old, to write a paper on "Economic Consequences of the Caste System". He argued there that

> no student of Indian economics can afford to overlook the influence which our social environment exercised upon our economic life.... Caste system, like all other social organisms, has steadily evolved and has undergone changes with consequent variations in its reaction to our economic life. (unpublished)

Though much of his cogitation has been overtaken by the dynamics of social values and their political manifestation, it reveals more eloquently what guided IG in moulding his professional career.

IG's wider vision of his life's mission beyond mere preoccupation with economic theory received an intellectual impetus from Professor A.C. Pigou's teaching at Cambridge. "One had felt, of course," IG elaborates in his memoir of Pigou (more in Chapter32), the impact of Professor Pigou's mind and heart even before meeting him. The decision whether to specialize in economics or not had turned largely on the glow one felt on reading his *The Economics of Welfare* (1932, p. 5), more particularly the earlier pages where he forcefully explains the rationale. "It is not wonder but rather the social enthusiasm which revolts from the sordidness of mean streets and the lessons of withered lives, that is the beginning of social science" (Pigou). Pigou's other book *Economics in Practice* (1935) had a message, loud and clear, for the sensitive mind of IG who was on the same wavelength as Pigou through his own life experience. There Pigou says,

> Now the academic economist discussing economic life often suffers from the same handicap.... He cannot write realistically because he lacks the necessary personal experience: and if he does not attempt to write realistically, but confines himself to analysis of a general character from which detail is excluded, his task is half-finished. Therefore—I am giving now advice that I myself have notoriously failed to follow—it is up to the economist, when he is young and his mind is plastic, to take whatever opportunities he can find for direct acquaintance with the life of men and women in factory and field; to understand machinery; to see for himself at first hand how businesses are organized and run. (Pigou 1935, p. 12)

Growing up in an impoverished country, Pigou's dictum touched a deep chord in IG and in consequence, he defined his life's mission to "provide practical answers to questions that arise in real life by application in limited contexts such as substitution or shifting incidence or cost-benefit ratios" (Patel 1986, p. 43).

The green shoots of his ultimate profile as economic policy thinker rather than a pure theorist were clearly discernible in his PhD dissertation at Cambridge in 1949 under Austin Robinson as his supervisor and Richard Kahn and Tapan Hollond as examiners. He was sceptical about looking at economic policy only on the basis of facts or logic. He believed in culture as an influential factor in development as well. "The study of Japan for my thesis led me to emphasize social and cultural factors in development.... Work habits and consumption remained culture-specific" (Patel 2002, pp. 21–2).

IG argued that India could certainly gain by more introspection about our history and national culture. This theme resonated in the subsequent work of Michio Morishima (1982, pp. 52–3), who regarded Japanese economic success as a confluence of Japanese ethos and Western technology. IG foreshadowed the contemporary "culture matters" school of developmental economists (Harrison and Huntington 2000). These perceptions came in useful in course of his tenure as a policymaker since he could take a broader view of his role, enabling him to accommodate or modify purely speculative economic considerations in the context of India's history, sociology and culture.

With a clear and enlightened vision of the mission in his life, IG promptly followed the advice of his first boss and mentor in the IMF, the legendary policy economist E.M. Bernstein, that he should be a practical economist after his experience at the IMF, and return to his country.

Before assuming his new role as a policymaker who could "cut to the chase in policy debates before others on the opposite side could even comprehend the nature of issues under scrutiny" (Dasgupta 2005, p. 210), IG left his rich legacy in economic theory with important research papers. His first analytical paper, apart from his thesis referred to earlier, was "India's Elasticity of Demand for Gold" in which he used co-relation analysis with an ingenious use of variables. Its publication would have established IG as a pioneer, had he not refused to publish it in the prestigious *IMF Staff Papers* despite the urging of J.J. Polak, his director. IG's "Selective Credit Controls in Underdeveloped Economies" and "Nature and Significance of Monetary Policy and its Instruments", published in the *IMF Staff Papers*, were equally original and well ahead of their time, as also his published articles with E.M. Bernstein on "Economic Development with Stability" and "Inflation and Economic Development" where the novel concepts of safe limit of deficit financing and wage–price spiral were introduced. IG wrote several papers which were published in journals and conference volumes, later reproduced in his two books, *Essays in Economic Policy and Economic Growth* and *Economic Reforms and Global Change*.

IG's intellectual persona was shaped and seasoned by the life he lived and what it signified for his conscious self is well epitomized in the review by Bhabatosh Datta, a well-known economist, of IG's book *Essays in Economic Policy and Economic Growth* (*Economic Times* 1987). In Datta's view,

> IG Patel has been over a period of more than three decades that rare kind of economist who can both think and act. His grip over economic theory and over the complex facts of economic life is remarkable.... If Mr. Patel emphasized anything, it is the need for modesty in applying theorizing as against the attempt to jump from the esoteric to the practical.... Social decisions are taken in an ambiance of imperfect knowledge and decision-makers other than economists make worse mistakes than economists.

This perception of IG's intellectual accomplishments and the evaluation that ensues from it fits in perfectly with B.K. Nehru's judgement from the prism of a civil servant, referred to earlier, that IG used economic theory in his advice but not without reassessing it in the context of the real world we live in.

It is necessary to throw light on the criterion adopted by the editors in selecting articles for this volume. First, there is an inflection point in IG as an economist. His papers on money and finance, highly theoretical, were written at the start of his career. They show that he brought in full force his deep grasp of economic theory, using econometric techniques with innovative skills. This phase was most prominent during his tenure at the IMF, with its research output which compared with the best anywhere in the field. Second, after his departure from the IMF, he changed the trajectory of his professional interest from theory to policy while modifying economic theory to solve the problems of his country and other similarly situated countries where neo-classical theories of static equilibrium were inapplicable. In his quest for adjusting economic theory to the requirements of development, he drew lessons from the Keynesian macroeconomics and Joan Robinson's seminal extension of the Keynesian short-period in which the production capacity is given to the developing countries where labour remains unemployed because of the shortage of production capacity. In the process, IG's economic contributions shifted to the area where economic policy had to reflect the reality he was confronted with. For this reason, IG's later contributions were policy oriented, but fully backed with relevant economic analysis. Many of IG's papers included in this volume fall in this category and as such will hopefully enlighten the readers about how the macroeconomic theory, predominant in developed countries assumed new meaning and dimensions in the context of economic development. Third, IG's papers will enable the readers to see the logic of certain interventionist policies the adoption of which was unavoidable in India during the period 1950–1960 and why that logic lost its rationale after the developing countries learnt by doing during the course of development to face competition in order to raise efficiency of production of goods and services. All this has a contemporary relevance with salutary lessons for policymakers. Fourth, the essays in each part are presented in a chronological order. This would reflect how IG's ideas evolved due to the challenges he faced in his profession, and the way he handled them. Finally, most of the essays in this volume being addresses or speeches are printed as spoken with only essential editing.

IG's unpublished manuscripts are a veritable treasure trove and to make them available to a wider readership is the leitmotif of this volume. These articles contain a tapestry of ideas in economics in regard to money, finance, trade, balance of payments, economic development, and monetary policy. It is a firm belief of the editors of this volume that they would enable the readers to perceive that some of IG's ideas are still relevant with different nuances to which they are attuned and resonate in the contemporary Indian and global settings.

The book is divided into eight parts which contain in all 34 chapters. An attempt is made in this introduction to focus selectively on some of the most important chapters in which IG's analysis of issues was novel, prescient and at times controversial. The first chapter, "Demand for Money during Periods of Inflation and Stabilization", may appear on the surface familiar and jejune but it contains deep insights and one wonders how the author could put forth ideas which seemed to contravene the Fund's theology. He argues, for instance, that

> it is desirable to expand the money supply, even while attempting to halt an inflation, if we are not to stumble into a "stabilization crisis".... During a period of hyperinflation, legal currency is often replaced by foreign currency or by other extra-legal auxiliary currencies in which people have more confidence, or by pure barter. Insofar as stabilization reverses this process and induces people to replace barter or other currencies with the use of legal currency, there is a legitimate need for monetary expansion during stabilization. The same is true if people endeavour to increase the proportion of their income which they save with the advent of stabilization, other things being equal.

IG applies the same expansionary approach when "people accumulate excessive stock of goods, machinery, etc. during inflation or in other words, the heritage of latent deflation". Both these ideas, unconventional as they might seem, were what India followed under the rubric of "safe deficit" financing or non-inflationary level of deficit financing since the Second Plan, which has echoes even today in policy debates in India.

In Chapter 2, "Nature and Significance of Monetary Policy and Its Instruments", which is a bowdlerized version of his paper "Monetary Policy in Post-war Years", the author brings out in the open how monetary policy as it was implemented in the pre-war years was revived in a different form in the post-war period in tune with the shape of the economies in many countries. He argues here that,

> Leaving aside the use of surplus money and a more active use of existing money (that is, an increase in the velocity of circulation of money), the growth of effective demand requires additional means of payment. By controlling the supply of new money, monetary policy can check the growth of effective demand. The growth of such demand can consist of two elements: growth in prices and growth in production. The supreme test of monetary policy lies in its ability to control the supply of money in such a way that the growth in prices is checked without retarding the growth in production.

Indeed, this echoes the perennial debate in India whether restrictive monetary policy retards growth in all circumstances. IG then proceeds to make a distinction between money creation through budget deficit and external stimulus resulting from a rise in foreign exchange reserves.

Chapter 3, "Selective Credit Controls in Underdeveloped Economies", is a seminal piece where a case for selective credit policies rests on the argument that the financial intermediation process does not by itself ensure the socially optimum use of resources. IG's was the first attempt to present a cohesive, consistent and convincing case for selective credit controls on the basis of the economic calculus in economies which are in the initial stages of development. Unfortunately, India's central bank took no cognizance of this paper in articulating its selective credit controls which were neither "selective" nor "controls" as credit rarely flowed to the targeted sectors.

IG assumes a rather debatable role in Chapter 5, "Monetary Policy Revisited". He argues, even in contradiction of his theoretical and empirical ideas on monetary policy in his youth, that there are basic differences between industrial and developing countries, which ought to lead to different postures as regards the design, purpose and actual implementation of monetary policy. He states, as if from the vantage viewpoint of a central banker, that

> As far as monetary policy is concerned, it can at best have a subordinate and supporting role in both sets of countries, and there is little reason to think that it can be more effective in one group of countries than in another. Economic logic knows no national frontiers and it often transcends institutional frontiers as well.

Still more provocative is his view that

> If there is a greater danger in developing countries, it is that of giving to the Central Bank an exaggerated role under which it assumes rather hyperactive poses to demonstrate to its masters that it is doing something.... At the same time, however, it has a very important developmental role. It also has an important role in terms of analysis and advice on matters relating to inflation and balance-of-payments adjustment; and its part of advice can often best be transmitted by analysis of monetary and financial aggregates and by persuading governments to adopt procedures such as monetary target setting which facilitate focusing on the interactions between budgetary, monetary and foreign exchange policy.

Though these are non-Friedmanian views, they would evoke spirited protests even from the Keynesian economists. Particularly in contemporary India, where the Reserve Bank's independence, both *de jure* and *de facto* is a lively policy issue, the assertion to the contrary by the former Governor of the Reserve Bank of India of IG's stature would unexpectedly add pungency to the debate.

However, more important than an unconventional and subjective posture of IG on the independence of the central bank are the more fundamental theoretical issues that are involved in the debate, as pinpointed by J.R. Hicks, who wrote that

> The issue with which we have been concerned is political—even constitutional—as well as economic. There is a technical economic problem of the instrument, but it is tied up with the political problem which Keynesian economics, so it seems to me, has refused to face, while the monetarists who have seen it, have not faced the political implications. For myself, I would face it. I think I should say that monetary regulation is a major function of government, but we should emphasize that if it is to be exercised that decisively, it needs to be separated, in what is in fact the constitutional sense, from other functions. We need to remember the ancient doctrine of the separation of powers. The judicial function in a well-ordered state is recognized to be a function of government, but it is better that a function is separated. So it is with the monetary function. It is far too responsible a function. (Hicks 1977, pp. 132–3)

Anand Chandavarkar, however, would prefer to call it "a separation of authority rather than a separation of power because the monetary function is a shared function of the executive and the central bank" (1996, p. 220). However, the central question in the debate on independence of the central bank is whether there could be an authority without a power and if there is not, then a separate monetary authority is invariably equivalent to a separate power. All these issues have been amplified covering different disciplines—economics, politics and constitutional law—only to highlight the issues of the central bank's independence in a liberalized Indian economy, in contrast to the semi-planned one before 1991 when there was no monetary policy as a separate entity.

On gold policy, IG's methodical study of "India's Elasticity of Demand for Gold"(Chapter 7) was original at the time it was written and has policy implications even today. I can do no better than give the relevant extracts from a scholarly and erudite introductory essay by Chandavarkar, which sums up IG's contribution in regard to gold policy in India. As regards the elasticity of demand for gold in India, IG's results suggested that the demand for gold was highly responsive to changes in the relative price,

> Historically price has been a more important explanatory variable than income, allowing for the fact that the shortcomings of the data used tend to overestimate the price-effect and underestimate the income-effect and that the effect of a certain increase in income may not be symmetrical to the same decline in income. The assumption of linearity of the underlying relation also implies that over the period considered, no factors other than price and income supervened, assumptions which were recognized to be questionable, particularly the changes in the distribution of income induced by changes in the terms of trade between agricultural and non-agricultural occupations. (Chandavarkar 2006, pp. 112–13)

IG addressed the core issue of mobilization of the stock of hoarded gold and flow of smuggled gold into the "sinews of economic growth", given the demand for gold in Chapter 8, "On Turning Gold into Base Metal", published eight years after his paper on the elasticity of demand for gold. As Chandavarkar puts it, IG's central idea is to evaluate

> Alternative modes of transferring private gold to official reserves, viz., open market purchases by the government; issue of bonds redeemable in rupees against delivery of gold and/or to be subscribed and redeemed in gold; and acquisition by compulsion. [IG was, however,] emphatic that gold bonds would either prove a flop or make for a stronger entrenchment of tax evasion and smuggling of gold. (Chandavarkar 1996, p. 124)

IG reverted to this theme of mobilization in a private communication on Chandavarkar's article on gold hoarding in the *Oxford Economic Papers* (1961, pp. 137–48) and endorsed its conceptual framework, including the disconnect between Keynesian liquidity preference and gold hoarding (2006, p. 124). IG's analysis of gold issues retains its validity even in the changed context of the Indian economy.

In Chapter 9, "Exports by Countries in Process of Industrialization", IG deals with a very important aspect of economic development of developing countries in a manner not too much obsessed with the dirigistic policies which were most prominent in the developing world during the latter half of the twentieth century. He succinctly argues that while export promotion is imperative, there are reasons for emphasizing export policies as distinct from policies which promote growth in general. While recognizing the inevitability of resorting to a very tight regime of import and exchange restrictions, he is careful enough to point up to a need for special care to ensure that industries that compete with imports do not claim a disproportionate share of scarce resources to the detriment of export industries. This was refreshing as in the early stages of the debate, where import substitution was a hobbyhorse of economists of the structuralist school of development. But the most novel idea IG espoused was that developing countries have much to gain by promoting trade among themselves both by specialization in creating new industries and by mutual liberalization of trade (on a discriminatory basis vis-à-vis more advanced countries) even in non-essential items. This idea could have acquired greater cogency if IG had linked it with servicing of foreign debt to promote trade among developing countries.

IG's confrontational position with the private corporate sector in India in Chapter 11, "Capital Formation in the Private Corporate Sector", is quite hard-hitting to unravel some of the misconceptions that the Indian corporate sector thrived on. In India's mixed economy that ruled the roost until 1991, the private sector was, no doubt, given a step-motherly treatment by the fiscal and monetary policy but it was no excuse to slur over the corporate sector's own errors of commission and omission. IG rightly castigates the private sector for underplaying the role of public investment as an important determinant of the growth of private investment.

More telling is IG's counterpoint to the corporate sector's whining that the contribution of the organized manufacturing industry to the gross national product has declined. He proved the fallacy of this claim by showing that the corporate sector measured its contribution in current and not constant prices. In the latter case, its share would have actually risen than fallen. The entire discussion on investment in the corporate sector reflects IG's rich insights into the financial structure of the corporate structure and its bearing on its efficiency.

IG's thoughts on planning cover a wide swathe in the context of India mainly but also in relation to China and a small open economy like Fiji—two extremes in terms of size and population. The most characteristic aspect of his thinking on economic planning is his ideological neutrality in analysing the issues involved and the contours of policies pursued to achieve the stated objectives. IG's approach to economic issues is clearly reflected in what he told a journalist at the London School of Economics, who pressed him to declare himself in ideological terms. He said in his inimitable style,

> I would call myself an old-fashioned socialist. I could as well have said that I was an old-fashioned liberal. What I meant was that I was not a Marxist-socialist opposed to markets and private property. But I was not a card-carrying capitalist either, and was supportive of certain values like compassion and justice in all social and economic arrangements. This was and still remains the mainstream intellectual and indeed political opinion in India. (Patel 2002, pp. 193–4)

IG lived up to this epistemological ethos in his narrative on planning and collateral economic policies, as will be elucidated below.

P.C. Mahalanobis was the principal architect of physical planning in India, which formed the cornerstone of the planning process beginning from the Second Five Year Plan. But it is a little-known fact that IG, despite being a non-mathematical economist, crystallized thinking on physical planning as in Chapter 12. "Physical Planning", IG argues,

> is that an overall view of the requirements of different projects and sectors must be taken by the planning authority in advance so as to determine both the constituents of the plan and the steps to be taken to ensure its smooth implementation.

But IG did not ignore, as most of the proponents of physical planning like Mahalanobis and Pitamber Pant did, that the physical balances hardly balance in plan implementation, however carefully and skilfully it was designed. He points out that

> No plan, however well construed, can make it possible to avoid shortages and surpluses altogether. This is so not only because of the imperfect instruments of predictions available to a planning authority and the uncertainties that inevitably exist in any society but also for the more fundamental reason that every society has to act within certain restraints during a given period ahead. These restraints are both physical and institutional.

What was even more prophetic was IG's assertion that "If physical planning cannot eliminate altogether the problem of shortages and surpluses, it cannot provide an escape from the necessity of financial planning either." This gave the lie directly to the much-touted slogan in the euphoric phase of planning in India that "What is physically feasible is financially possible."

IG almost intuitively came to the logic of flawed physical planning as an intrinsic part of socialist planning—India's physical plan as designed by Mahalanobis was a stylized version of the Soviet model—which Janos Kornai intellectualized in his theoretical work on socialist planning in 1980s. Kornai, faced with the problematic of how the imbalances could be removed or shortages surmounted, theorized that "... the production units in the socialist system were getting wrong price signals so that demand and supply could rarely be matched" (2006, p. 299). In retrospect, it seems rather tragic that if the government had taken note of IG's cautionary wisdom, much of the chaotic planning and its tragic consequences for Indian society could have been averted.

In regard to his assessment of the prospects of the public sector in a small open economy like Fiji (Chapter 14), IG emphasizes at length that economic policies in such economies need not always be based on economic logic; they have to focus on economic geography as the small size of the economy does not warrant certain projects which might well be feasible in a large economy. He also rules out overprotection of industry as a general rule. In particular, it should avoid "heavy or capital-intensive industries which require a minimum size far beyond the absorptive capacity of the local market for efficient operation" (Chapter 14). He also pleads for "industrialization which is considerable in the longer run even for small island economies like that of Fiji".

It is perhaps less comprehended today, when the Chinese economy is roaring away with speed, that China's First Five Year Plan, 1953–1957 (Chapter 15) overlapped more or less with India's First Five Year Plan. The comparison and contrast IG poses is interesting not because there were several similarities in the pattern of plans but also logic in a way, despite the fact that the political system under which the Chinese plan was conceived and projected and the agency adopted were vastly different. The national income and saving–investment data were "guesstimates" in China as they were in India. But a striking feature of the Chinese plan was that it focused on the gross value of output as against India's net value of output. There were many other conundrums in regard to statistics. It is somewhat surprising that even with all this, IG concludes that "a large part of the difference between the percentage increase in the total output in China and in India would be statistical rather than real". Another rather provocative observation of his is that "it is claimed that the *production* of some of the main items of mass consumption is substantial and will increase". Admittedly, there is some catch in the Chinese data which IG took at face value. It is a historical fact well acknowledged that towards the end of the 1950s and early 1960s, China had a great famine which resulted in a massive destruction of human lives. Here one can recall Amartya Sen's profound insights on famine. He argues that if there was a democracy where everything was debated openly in the media and the political process was transparent, the famine would have been less devastating (Sen 1999, p. 187).

There were also some queer features of the Chinese plan. As IG rightly points out,

> Nothing is said, for example, about the manner in which the resources needed for the Plan are to be raised beyond the statement that it would be possible to raise funds on the required scale in view of the fact that the Chinese people no longer have to bear the burden of exploitation by landlords and by capitalists at home and abroad.

But what about the party nomenclature in communist states which exploited people and was a willing partner in mass annihilation of the people by starving them? The way IG discusses both the Chinese and the Indian Five Year Plans, it is clear that they were differently similar in many respects!

IG's views on socialism, a legacy from Nehru's aspirational and at times misleading thinking, are very interesting not because he ever agreed with Nehru's basic proposition on socialism. For him, Nehru's tango in his shifting positions on socialism unwittingly minimized the damage to the Indian economy. In the early stages, Nehru "dwells on the necessity and even the propriety and prevalence of confiscation and on the impossibility of ushering in socialism by the sudden passing of a few laws". But he soon changed his view almost to the opposite pole. IG's own position is well summed up in Chapter 16,

> It was Alfred Marshall who said that ideas were the most "real" of the gifts that each generation receives from its predecessors. But at the level of the idea, the socialism of the Nehru era has emerged as a rather weak and hollow reed in which one can blow almost any kind of music. In its concrete achievements, the socialism of the Nehru era can certainly lay claim to a respectable degree of public ownership of the means of production in the sphere of basic industries. But amidst the vast ocean of property in land, buildings, commerce, small industry and a major part of industry as well, the prevailing tone of social behaviour is unmistakeably

> that of acquisitiveness and private profit.... One can say, if one is so inclined, that socialism has come to stay in India. But so has capitalism.

One can play on this theme, justifying the Indian socialism with Indian characteristics!

IG's thoughts on equality and equity were ahead of his time. He perceptively remarks,

> There is now general support for a package of macroeconomic and microeconomic market-friendly policies which is conducive to efficiency and growth. If some countries remain poor, it is because they are mired in wrong interventionist policies so that it is policy reform and not aid that they really need. (Chapter 18)

Even more profound were his views that

> There is thus certainly some sense in noting that equity in a modern society means something much less than equality and is, in fact, currently advocated only in some minimalist sense.... In the ultimate analysis, equity, like liberty, in all modern societies that aspire to be democratic, has to be defined in the rough and tumble of the political arena.

This has been a subject close to the hearts of policymakers, particularly in India in recent years. One of the foremost authorities on the subject has now come to the same conclusion on this controversial issue as IG did almost 20 years ago,

> Contrary to the common presumption among the intellectuals and policymakers, rising economic inequalities, if and when they arise during the rapid growth process, are not necessarily inequitable. On the contrary, more often than not, they are likely to be associated with the advancement of equity in society through a variety of channels.... The common presumption is based on a single-dimensional view of equity, which focuses on income and wealth generating processes while ignoring other relevant factors that are more amenable to policy choices without adversely impacting the growth process. Such choices can shape and influence social perceptions of equity in distribution. (Tendulkar 2010, p. 87)

A similar argument but with more emphasis on the political regime which denies proper implementation of income distribution policies was made by other economists. Economic transformation of the poor societies, thus, is more a non-economic problem, which is not amenable to purely economic nostrums. Adding the trappings to economic strategy, however well articulated or motivated, if divorced from the nature of the regime which is supposed to make it operational, would only end in a maze of policies conducive neither to the desired change in income distribution nor to social transformation.

Chapter 20, "The Vision for a New India" is based on IG's valedictory remarks at the annual session of the Associated Chamber of Commerce

(ASSOCHAM) in 1991, a few months after the Narasimha Rao government with Manmohan Singh as the finance minister came out with a paradigm-changing economic policy in India which radically changed the Indian economy. It may be considered as a most controversial address in view of its critique of that policy. IG, for instance, is emphatic that

> I think it is correct to say that as far as macroeconomic management is concerned our understanding in India has always been good.... Even as regards the exchange rate, since 1971 we have managed our exchange rate is sound. If we had to devalue by a big step I don't think it was because we did not follow the right policies regarding the exchange rate in the preceding twenty years. It was only because, again for political reasons, we allowed the situation to develop so badly so fast that ... a drastic step had to be taken ...

The scepticism that would assail the readers of IG's essay is why then the Indian economy since 1991 with a radically different macroeconomic policy with a drastic devaluation of the rupee, a market-oriented monetary policy and burying the old façade of licensing and industrial policy regime was totally transformed not only in relation to its past but also in relation to other nations like China and other emerging countries. At the aggregate level, the growth rate during 1988–2006 was 6.3 per cent, compared with 4.8 per cent during 1981–1988. During the period from 2003–2004 to 2005–2007, the country's GDP at factor cost grew at the impressive rate of 8.6 per cent, which was never before achieved. As astounding has been

> The growth in trade, an integral part of India's growth story. To put the matter dramatically, merchandise exports in 1990–91 were \$18.1 billion; in 2005–06, growth in exports over the preceding year exceeded this amount. The acceleration in the growth of trade in recent years has been spectacular. Exports took nine years to double from their level in 1990–91. In recent period, they doubled in one-third of that time: from \$52.7 billion in 2002–3 to \$102.7 billion in 2005–06; service exports more than doubled from \$26.9 billion in 2003–4 to \$60.6 billion in 2005–6. (Panagariya 2008, p. 289)

Does this not imply that macroeconomic as well as microeconomic policies were far different from the period prior to 1991?

While looking at the Indian economy in the perspective of the East Asian countries, IG predicted that to reach the per capita income level of Thailand, Malaysia and Korea in 1991, India would take

> twenty-five years, which is, let us say, my lifetime ... which means it must grow every year at 6 per cent, which means, given the population rise at 2 per cent your real income must grow at 8 per cent per annum ... So when I say that it is my dream ... it is a very large dream. (Chapter 20)

IG would have been pleasantly surprised if he were alive today to see the Indian economy recording an average 7.5–8.0 per cent growth and it is likely to surge to 9 to 10 per cent soon; and to know that even his "very large dream" is small in today's context.

IG's narrative on "Current Unease with Indian Economic Reform" (Chapter 22) mentions seven reasons for his unease but only two are discussed below to see if they are justified in today's India. There is not yet a decisive impact, first, on growth and employment and, second, on corruption. What do the data on the ground speak on the first? The growth picture has been noted earlier. As regards employment,

> The Planning Commission's estimates of annual increment in economy-wide employment indicate strong growth from a low of three million in the crisis year, 1991–92, to an average of six million in each of the next two years and then rising further to 7.2 million in 1994–95. Since labour is the principal asset possessed by the poor, this surge in employment opportunities is likely to be associated with a favourable trend in living standards and poverty. Not only was unemployment on a downward trajectory, but real wages have tended to rise too. Though they first declined in the crisis years, they rose by 5.6 per cent in 1992–93 and by 3.6 per cent in 1993–94 as the economy recovered from the crisis in response to reform (Acharya 2006, p. 167).

Acharya's findings are amply fortified by the quinquennial National Sample Survey.

As regards the second, it is hardly disputed that though economic policy-related corruption discretionary controls on prices, trade, industrial licensing, etc., has declined after liberalization, it is one of degree and the Indian society continues to reek with rampant corruption. As Milton Friedman visualized long ago, the amount of corruption and its reach depend upon the domain of the state which is, however, specific to the social conditions, institutional environment, cultural traits and political traditions. One can find a parable for this in the Indian social structure as narrated by an Indian anthropologist, Prakash Reddy (Khatkhate 2008, p. 239).

Apart from this, corruption is a by-product of the arbitrariness of power wielded by the political authorities in India. It has been conclusively demonstrated that this political unaccountability arises from the nature of the Indian political process. Paradoxically, the Indian political system operates in such a way that at one extreme economic policy has punishment as its basis but without any sanction for enforcing it and, at the other, incentive as its basis without any inbuilt mechanism to reward for success. It is this ambivalent nature of economic policy which inclines politicians whether in power or out of power to opportunism. Looking around today's India, the sorry spectacle of corruption due to political, legal and constitutional factors is simply mind-boggling. So corruption is not an economic phenomenon but a hydra-headed monster, which can be buried only when the whole political process is changed.

Chapter 25, "The Role of PL-480 Supplies in the Development of India", speaks for IG's perspicacity in looking at the transfer of food surpluses under title I of PL-480 agreement with the US government, not merely as a supplement to the domestic supply of food grains, essential for India's economic growth without inflationary pressures, but also as an instrument to accelerate the pace of growth. IG's main role, apart from the macroeconomic management of the country, was also to facilitate much-needed aid to India. He was quick to perceive that the domestic saving gap, despite narrowing at a snail's pace, was no substitute for the foreign exchange gap, which needed to be bolstered for smooth development. That was also the period when there was an animated debate among Indian economists and politicians whether the use of PL-480 surpluses aggravated domestic inflationary pressures from the way those surpluses were financed and also whether they would damagingly dwarf domestic production of food grains, making India a perennial supplicant for foreign aid. IG strongly endorsed P.N. Rosenstein-Rodan's memorandum submitted to the Government of India that "in countries with well-worked out development plan, a reasonable assumption would be to consider two-thirds of surplus product sales as investment and the rest as consumption aid". However, this was all based on *a priori* reasoning, as IG himself was aware. IG's foresight and judicious approach were backed by the theoretical and empirical work of economists who vindicated that the real effects of food surplus disposal were positive and the monetary impact of the use of surpluses emanating from the manner in which their imports were financed was neutral.

IG's analysis of trade and payments policy for developing countries (Chapter 26) takes us back to the 1960s to see the development woes of the poor, struggling countries, when their balance-of-payments position acted as a special and distinct constraint on their continuing growth. He argues with an underpinning of economic theory that

> The policy implications of this phenomenon and the truly gigantic nature of the task of overcoming this bottleneck over a reasonable period are not generally appreciated. Many of the concrete measures required in this connection run counter to accepted norms of international trade and payments behaviour. Some would appear as establishing a double standard of morality among nations. But the double standard is also more apparent than real. Problems of international trade in the world as we find it, cannot, after all, be approached in terms of some abstract model which seeks to maximize some abstract concept of world welfare in which each nation has an equal claim to share. There exists already a will to cooperation in the development of the less developed countries; and while an extension of this cooperation in the field of international trade would not at all be easy, especially as it cannot be expressed through simple rules of thumb, the need for such cooperation is nonetheless vital. All this, however, does not amount to throwing overboard all the accepted norms in the field of commercial and payments policy—much less

> a retreat from economics in the planning and programming of development. The very fact that there are more than one developing countries would also dictate that the policies of any developing country cannot be divorced from the interest of others equally beset with difficulties; and this consideration would tend to restore the validity of many of the liberal principles of trade and payments at least insofar as relations between the developing countries are concerned.

In Chapter 27, "Lessons from the Monetary Events of 1971", IG's analysis is a throwback to the old debate. Following the maelstrom of exchange rate crisis in the wake of the US dropping the dollar–gold link, convertibility was suspended and the currency parities were realigned, for the first time after the foundation of the IMF at the Bretton Woods and the agreed rules of policies to restore the international imbalances were set out. He particularly looks at these events from the viewpoint of the developing countries. To him, the significance of the 1971 agreement was

> a welcome recognition of the importance of their being fully involved in the discussion on international monetary reform. But there are enough pointers to further dangers to their interests which would require vigilance on their part. In the meanwhile, there is nothing in the events of 1971 to suggest that the developing countries should give up their general suspicion of frequent changes in the exchange rates for major currencies or of any Calvinistic attitude towards the financing of external deficits.

Nearly four decades later, the whole international scene has been totally transformed. The dollar eminence, though still the important reserve currency as of yore, has dramatically faded, with the Chinese yuan dominating the debate on the question of currency realignment. The fixed exchange rate regime has been replaced by managed floating rates. The substitution of G-7 by G-20, in the deliberations of which some leading emerging countries like China, India, Brazil and South Africa are prominent, has led to their more effective role. The developed countries no longer occupy the magisterial position in the IMF and the World Bank. The developing countries have built up hugely their foreign exchange reserves, which not only avoided their being at the mercy of the multilateral institutions and the industrial countries, but also placed them in the vanguard to steer international currency and payment policies away from their one-sided track to a commonly agreed highway to a more equitable world.

The indebtedness of the developing countries until the 1980s was a formidable problem for a variety of reasons. For one thing, domestic savings of development-aspiring countries was grossly inadequate in relation to the required investment to achieve a respectable rate of growth of GDP. The severity of the foreign debt problem was augmented by the difficulties faced by the developing countries to increase exports in sufficient amount to pay for servicing it. IG was insightful enough to see that the difficulties in repayment of interest and the principal became intractable because of tied aid, under which the aid recipient country was required to import goods from the lending country regardless of their quality or price. On the other hand, repayments were made in foreign exchange. As IG averred, "This aid (tied aid) prima facie is not equitable because any foreign currency you get in terms of aid is worth less than what you have to earn in order to make repayment in the same currency" (Chapter 28). Obviously the solution is to remove the asymmetry in tied aid. In other words, the repayment of debt should as well be tied to exports to the lending country. This burden of the foreign debt borne by the developing countries is no longer a serious issue in the twenty-first century. The whole global economic landscape has changed now so radically that the emerging developing countries, except for the extremely poor countries in Africa, now save much more than they invest and most of the import of capital in these countries is capital inflows in search of profit—public and private and direct foreign investment. India is even more fortunate that its foreign debt burden as a proportion of its GDP is relatively small and can be managed without much ado. Of course, IG's diagnosis helps to put the issue in the historical context.

IG's admirable perception of all this comes home to roost with developing countries which not only surmounted their earlier institutional, structural and endemic economic constraints but also occupy today the front row of the table along with the industrial countries as almost equal partners in articulating trade and payments policies to the common interests of the global economy.

IG visualizes the crux of the adjustment problem and policies to resolve them in the simple but fundamental economic principle. As he puts it,

> The challenge lies in responding to the change by allowing or inducing resources to shift where new opportunities for more efficient use are emerging. And the so-called adjustment problem is nothing but the problem of ensuring that the desirable shift in resources is not hindered (that is, rigidities are removed) and in fact induced, encouraged and expedited. (Chapter 30)

More tellingly, IG prescribes this rule, to an equal degree, to all nations, developed and developing, without any distinction with regard to the stage of economic development or internal and international trade. He proceeds in the same chapter,

> By the same token, if there has to be any caveat or qualification in regard to these propositions, they have to have the same rationale whether one is speaking of internal trade and competition or international trade and competition. For the notion that any particular nation can score points at the expense of another nation by restricting trade has hardly any validity in theory or as a practical proposition. The consequences of restricting international trade are felt essentially internally and they affect both overall economic efficiency and *inter se* distribution of costs and

benefits (that is, income) in much the same way as restricting competition between two purely domestic producers.

IG's prescription is again simple economic commonsense, that "for enlightened and limited or selective intervention in support of competitive trends as opposed to myopic intervention for the purely negative type which tries to push back the incentive for efficiency forever".

IG, of course, based his views on first principles; and in today's globalized world with greater interdependence among nations and with much lesser clout exercised by the industrialized countries, these have come home with a vengeance. Protectionism is on the wane, the developing countries, particularly the emerging ones, are competing in the international markets on a more level playing field, the close and careful watch by the World Trade Organization over trade among nations and readiness to discipline if its writ on trade is flouted by any country, IG's prophecy is coming true even in India where he played a strategic role in a very difficult period of its quest for industrialization.

This rather extensive introduction to IG's volume, I am sure, would give readers with an enquiring spirit and a sense of history of ideas in money, finance and economic development in general and their manifestation in the Indian experience in particular, as well as a foretaste of IG's intellectual smorgasbord despite its selectivity. It should be instructive to them that IG's versatility and insight had a pervasive sweep with a certain degree of vision, idealism and a clear message. His admirable intellectual repertoire is untarnished with any soupcon of argumentativeness or shallow passion.

To conclude this, I must express my gratitude to late Anand Chandavarkar, an economist of repute, who spared time despite his persistent ill-health to help me select articles from IG's manuscripts and to make searching comments on the introduction with his characteristic thoroughness.

DEENA KHATKHATE

References

Acharya, S. 2006, *Essays on Macroeconomic Policy and Growth in India*. New Delhi: Oxford University Press.

Chandavarkar, A. 1996, *Central Banking in Developing Countries*. London: Macmillan.

Chandavarkar, A. 2006, "I.G. Patel on India's Gold Problem: An Introductory Essay", *Economic and Political Weekly*, 11 February.

Dasgupta, P. 2005, "I.G. Patel as I Knew Him", *Economic and Political Weekly*, 6 August.

Datta, B. 1987, "Essays in Economic Policy and Economic Growth, by I.G. Patel: A Review", *Economic Times*, 1 January.

Guhan, S. and M. Shroff (eds). 1986, *Essays on Economic Progress and Welfare: In Honour of I.G. Patel.* New Delhi: Oxford University Press.

Harrison, E. Lawrence and Samuel P. Huntington (eds). 2000, *Culture Matters: How Values Shape Human Progress.* New York: Basic Books.

Hicks, John R. 1977, *Economic Perspectives: Further Essays on Money and Growth.* Oxford: Clarendon Press.

Jha, L.K. 1986, "Economists in Government: A Symposium", in S. Guhan and M. Shroff (eds), *Essays on Economic Progress and Welfare: In Honour of I.G. Patel.* New Delhi: Oxford University Press.

Khatkhate, D. 2008, "Indian State Corrupts Absolutely", in *Ruminations of a Gadfly.* New Delhi: Academic Foundation.

Kornai, Janos. 2006, *By Force of Thought: Irregular Memoirs of an Intellectual Journey.* Cambridge, Mass: MIT Press.

Morishima, M. 1982, *Why Has Japan Succeeded? Western Technology and Japanese Ethos.* London: Cambridge University Press.

Nehru, B.K. 1986, "Economists in Government: A Symposium", in S. Guhan and M. Shroff (eds), *Essays on Economic Progress and Welfare: In Honour of I.G. Patel.* New Delhi: Oxford University Press.

Panagariya, A. 2008, *India: The Emerging Giant.* New York: Oxford University Press.

Patel, I.G. 1986, *Essays in Economic Policy and Economic Growth.* London: Macmillan.

———. 2002, *Glimpses of Indian Economic Policy: Insider's View.* New Delhi: Oxford University Press.

Pigou, A.C. 1932, *The Economics of Welfare.* London: Macmillan.

———. 1935, *Economics in Practice.* London: Macmillan.

Sen, A. 1999, *Poverty and Famines: An Essay on Entitlement and Deprivation.* New Delhi: Oxford University Press.

Tendulkar, S. 2010, "Inequality and Equity during Rapid Economic Process", in S. Acharya and Rakesh Mohan (eds), *India's Economy: Performance and Challenges—Essays in Honour of Montek Singh Ahluwalia.* New Delhi: Oxford University Press.

Part I

Monetary and Credit Policy

CHAPTER 1

Demand for Money during Periods of Inflation and Stabilization*

Introduction

The purpose of this paper is to investigate the circumstances under which an expansionist monetary policy is appropriate to the stabilization of the price level in an inflation-ridden economy. Since inflation is generally associated with increase in the quantity of money in circulation, it is often argued that if prices are to be stabilized, the injection of new money in the economy should be stopped first. But with the advent of stabilization, people may desire to hold a larger proportion of their income in the form of money; and if no new money is created, this would lead to a "stabilization crisis"—the stringency of money supply will bring in its wake a fall in prices and production. An expansionist monetary policy, on the other hand, may avert a possible crisis without defeating the aim of stabilizing the price level. Under what circumstances is such a phenomenon likely to develop? And how should new money be created, when necessary, during stabilization without sowing the seeds of a new inflation?

There is, of course, no unique answer to such a question—inflation is a phenomenon with many phases and a variety of different manifestations. What will happen during the period of stabilization depends very much on the type or stage of the inflation at which we propose to halt it. It is necessary, therefore, for our purpose to analyse what happens to people's desire for holding a part of their income in the form of money during the different phases of an inflation, bearing in mind also the peculiarities of the various

* This paper was prepared for the International Monetary Fund, Research Department, October 1950; unpublished.

economies which may be so bedevilled. This is done in Section I. This is followed in Section II by an analysis of what may happen during the period of stabilization, and a discussion of the monetary policy appropriate to this period. In Section III, the actual experience of three countries, Germany and Austria during the 1920s, and Belgium during the last decade during inflation and stabilization is examined with a view to checking the results of our a priori reasoning. And finally, in Section IV, we make some general concluding remarks.

What we are investigating here chiefly is the people's desire to hold a part of their income in the form of money. However, the need for more money in an economy does not spring only from an increased preference for liquidity. An increase in real production will also necessitate more money, if everything else remains unchanged. Thus, in the discussion below, changes in production will also be kept in mind.

One terminological point may be cleared up at this stage. What is meant exactly by liquidity preference or the desire to hold a certain proportion of income in the form of money? Between one income receipt and another, an individual does not hold all his income in the form of money. At the beginning of the income period, all his income is held in the form of money; but as he proceeds to spend it, a smaller and smaller part of his total income for the whole period remains with him as money or cash balances at the end of each subsequent day. If we take an average of the fraction of the income he had in money form at the end of each day of the period, we get the proportion of the income held by him in the form of money on the average during the period. And a similar proportion for the community as a whole can be worked out also. Our definition does not require us to distinguish between what are sometimes called "idle" and "active" balances, or between balances for "transaction and other purposes". Suffice it to say that a desire to increase the proportion of income held in the form of money may take any of these forms: (1) an increase in the average propensity to save without a change in the manner in which savings are distributed between money and other assets (this would transfer some of the so-called active balances to idle balances); (2) an increased preference for holding savings in the form of money rather than other assets; or (3) a desire to slow up the normal rate of purchase from day-to-day over the given period. How these changes in people's desires will work themselves out and how they will change the actual relationship between national income and money holdings will be analysed in detail in Sections I and II.

When liquidity preference or the desire to hold a certain part of income in the form of money is defined in this manner, it becomes very similar to the concept of the income (or circular) velocity of circulation of money. If the latter is defined as the average number of times that a unit of money enters (or leaves) the cash balances of ultimate income recipients during a period, the two concepts become reciprocals of each other. An increase in liquidity preference will manifest itself as a decline in the velocity of circulation, ceteris paribus, in any ex post calculation, and vice versa. We shall use, therefore, both these forms of expression in the following discussion. They both have their advantages—it is preferable to speak of liquidity preference where people's motivations are concerned (that is, ex ante analysis) and of the velocity of circulation of money where we deal with situations ex post.

The Velocity of Circulation of Money during Inflation

It is not very easy to say when exactly a process of expansion becomes inflationary. But let us imagine that we are dealing with a relatively simple situation in which the government initiates expansion by creating new money to finance some new development or reconstruction or war project. It is not directly relevant for our purpose here to give a detailed account of the mechanics of inflation. In what follows, therefore, a great deal is taken for granted about the causes and course of an inflation. So long as there are some employed resources, and bottlenecks in production do not appear, this would lead to an increase in production rather than in prices. Prices may, however, rise even before "full employment" is reached if the workers enforce higher wages, or if bottlenecks develop in some lines of production. But prices would not initially rise as fast as the money supply, and the real value of money balances would increase along with increase in production. Part of the additional money serves as a medium of exchange for the greater volume of production.

But at this stage, the real value of money balances may rise further increased by a decline in the velocity of circulation of money. As more and more factors of production become employed, and as the per capita income of the community increases, there is likely to be an increase in the average propensity to save insofar as people take time to change their habitual mode of living. And if the part of savings that people store in the form of money remains the same, this amounts to an increase in their preference for liquidity. This is particularly true if the previous unemployment of resources is of a chronic character as in undeveloped peasant communities where consumption habits are fairly rigid, and where a large part of savings is held in the form of money.

Apart from this, if the community has experienced reasonable stability in the price level and exchange rate in the past, the initial increase in the price level in the early phases of expansion may encourage hoarding of money for speculative reasons. People may reduce stocks or defer consumption in the expectation of a fall in prices in the future. For a country on a free exchange standard, the rise in prices may mean a fall in the exchange rate of its currency; and if this fall is deemed to be temporary, people at home and abroad will demand more domestic currency in terms of foreign exchange.

Even after "full employment" is reached and production can no longer be increased, it is possible for the government to go on adding to the money supply without raising prices in the same proportion. If imports are not freely available due to war or exchange control, and if rationing and price control limit consumption at home, a large part of the increased money increase may remain unspent. The consequent decline in the velocity of circulation merely represents repressed consumption or latent inflation. Thus, in the early phases of an inflation, the velocity of circulation of money is likely to decline. But if inflationary pressures continue to operate, we may soon get the familiar spiral of wages chasing prices and prices chasing wages. The upward pressure on wages may become difficult to resist. Alternatively, it may become increasingly difficult to maintain controls effectively; and if they are relaxed, prices may begin to rise and call forth an increase in wages. And when inflation enters this phase, we begin to get an increase in the velocity of circulation of money, and a consequent decline in the real value of monetary balances.

This is so, in the first place, because people will now wish to keep a smaller proportion of their income in the form of money in order to offset the earlier increase in their cash holdings. Once higher employment has lasted for a sufficient length of time, people will adjust their standard of living to their current incomes, and the propensity to save will fall. Those who speculated on the prospects of a fall in the price level or an appreciation of the exchange rate will have been disappointed, and they will not want to dishoard their cash balances to cut their losses. And if the government chooses to let the latent inflation work itself out, another part of the existing cash balances will be activated.

But if this were the end of the story, the increase in the velocity of circulation would not go very far. For once the abnormal idle balances of the past have marked their way into effective demand and current income, and have pushed inflation some stages further, the normal desire of the people to hold cash balances in relation to current income will be restored. Indeed, in undeveloped countries where speculation or controls are not widespread, there may not be a significant increase in the velocity of circulation of money because there would not be a significant abnormal accumulation of cash in the earlier stages.

However, if inflation continues apace, some new forces will come into operation and cut down people's preference for liquidity. First, when prices are expected to rise more or less continuously, people's propensity to save will fall. It is not worthwhile saving when the real value of savings is expected to decline continuously. This factor would not be very significant for poor agricultural countries where most people live from hand to mouth.

Apart from this, people may try to reduce the proportion of their savings they generally keep in the form of money because it would be more attractive to hold savings in the form of goods or real assets which are likely to appreciate in value. But in some types of economies, there are limits beyond which this process also cannot go. Where savings are in any case small, a shift in the form in which part of them is held has little significance. Again, such a shift is more profitable if made in favour of instruments of production or real assets such as houses rather than non-durable consumption goods. But backward or highly specialized countries which depend on imports for their requirements of capital goods or components of houses, etc., do not offer much scope for such a shift. Inflation-ridden economies generally have a balance-of-payments problem; and imports would not be very freely available to facilitate hoarding or over-accumulation of stocks.

What about the money balances people hold in order to carry on their day-to-day transactions? Will they hold less money in relation to their income if prices continue to rise? This is, no doubt, possible; but the way in which it can happen is complicated enough to deserve careful analysis. If people expect prices to rise between one income receipt and another, they may try to spend all their income as soon as they receive it, rather than distribute it at different points of time over the entire period. The scramble for goods will deplete the stocks of shopkeepers and producers faster than is the case normally during the income period. If in spite of this they do not raise their prices and if they hoard the money returned to them by consumers till the next production period, there would be no change in the velocity of circulation of money for the community as a whole. If, however, the shopkeepers and producers respond by immediately raising prices, the expenditure of the consumers will return to the shopkeepers and producers very early in the period; but the stock of commodities put on the market by them for the period as a whole will not be sold entirely at that stage. There would be a shift in real income from consumers to sellers; and the latter class can buy up the unexhausted stocks from one another at higher prices. The total number of transactions in the community would remain the same as in the previous period; but each transaction being at a higher price, money would have circulated more rapidly. The desire of the people to hold a smaller proportion of their income in the form of money will manifest itself by raising prices and money incomes rather than by changing the quantity of money. And this process can go on, increasing the velocity of circulation of money, and reducing the real value of money balances.

It is clear from the conditions set out in the preceding paragraph that such a process cannot go very far. For one thing, we have to have something like a hyperinflation before prices rise so frequently that people begin to expect a change within one income period. Even in an advanced stage of inflation we would not expect more than three or four bouts of wage-price inflation in a year; whereas an income period for a large mass of people is no longer than a week or a month—except, perhaps, in the case of predominantly agricultural communities. Secondly, certain inconvenience is always involved in a scramble for goods in order to get rid of money fast, and this would deter people from such a course to some extent. Again, the continuation of this process requires a continuous shift in real income away from consumers; and where most of the consumers live on a subsistence level, such a shift is bound to be resisted soon. It is not relevant to our purpose here to show how this may be done; suffice it to say that an increase in the velocity of circulation for reasons under consideration here cannot occur without inducing a shift in the distribution of income. Lastly, it is not very probable that the number of transactions during the period would remain the same. If sellers put up their prices when their stocks are depleted too fast in the beginning of the income period, it is partly due to the fear of an increase in the cost of restocking due to a rise in the price of labour or raw materials. If so, their increased money income would not be spent entirely on purchasing from each other the goods not bought by the consumers. A part of their higher money income would be stored up for hiring labour, etc., at higher prices during the next income period. This means that during the period under consideration, stocks would be accumulated, and the number of transactions would have fallen. Thus, although each transaction is at a higher price level, the velocity of circulation of money does not increase as much as we might think at first sight.

Needless to say, this does not amount to saying that there are limits beyond which an inflation cannot develop—all that is implied is that there are limits to the extent to which an inflation can be fed by an increase in the velocity of circulation as against an increase in the quantity of money. But if, somehow, we do get a hyperinflationary situation, the velocity of circulation may rise and the real value of money balances may decline for still other reasons.

If a runaway inflation continues, people's confidence in the currency may be so much undermined that it may lose its importance not only as a store of value, but also as a means of payment and a unit of account. More and more transactions will be carried on without the means of local currency—that is, by pure barter, or with the help of some foreign currency or some illegal or semi-legal currency introduced by non-governmental agencies with a valid or fictitious promise of stable value or convertibility in a stable currency. When prices are rising continuously, people may refuse to accept local legal tender for payments; foreign coins may be imported; and even cost accounting and price policies may be uncertain in terms of some other currency. This may be looked upon as a decline in the number of transactions in which legal money enters, and this would mean a rise in prices in terms of this currency faster than an increase in the supply of such money. Alternatively, we can say that the legal note circulation underestimates the actual money supply to the extent of the circulation of foreign or other currency.

Besides, when we have reached such a chaotic state of affairs with a variety of currencies circulating, and people inclined to prefer pure barter, we are also likely to get an actual decline in physical production. Without a generally acceptable means of payments, the production system is bound to be paralysed; and this means an increase in prices faster than the increase in money supply, irrespective of any change in the velocity of circulation of money.

Stabilization and Velocity of Circulation of Money

It is quite clear by now that what happens during the period of stabilization of prices would depend very much on the stage at which we attempt to halt an inflation. In order to analyse now what sort of monetary policy is appropriate to the task of stabilization, we would distinguish between the various stages of inflation, beginning with the most virulent type. Needless to say, such distinctions are not hard and fast; in any real situation, many elements may exist together. But for the sake of analytical convenience, we would adopt here some stratification of a hypothetical inflation.

(1) The most advanced stage of inflation is one in which the legal currency is falling into disuse as a means of exchange and a unit of account, and is being replaced by barter, foreign exchange of a "mushroom" currency, and when production is falling. It may be that a political change or the prospects of a foreign loan or the introduction of stability in the exchange rate or the introduction of new legal currency restores people's confidence in the future value of domestic currency.

In these circumstances, prices will be stabilized and people will wish to substitute other currencies in use for legal currency and stop the practice of barter. The old stock of legal currency was sufficient to finance only a relatively small number of transactions at the prevailing prices. But if the same amount of money is to finance a large number of transactions, monetary stringency will develop, and prices will fall. In other words, creation of more money is quite compatible with stabilization if it merely replaces other currencies or barter in use. Besides, once some generally acceptable means of exchange is introduced, production will increase; and new money may be created to make this possible without defeating the stabilization programme.

(2) But let us suppose next that inflation has reached only the penultimate stage in which people try to spend their income as soon as they receive it.

Now with the advent of stabilization, people will no longer fear an increase in prices between one income receipt and another, and they will try to revert to a more even distribution of their income during the period. But from our earlier analysis it is clear that this will result in a decline in the velocity of circulation only if the shopkeepers and producers cut their prices when their stocks are not exhausted as fast as they were in the earlier period. This would bring about a shift in real income from shopkeepers and producers to consumers; and if the consumers come to expect a further reduction in price and postpone their purchases, we may get a stabilization crisis unless more money is injected into the system. But it is difficult to see why the shopkeepers and producers should cut their prices in the first instance merely because people distribute their expenditure more evenly. It may be that they cut prices a little because in the earlier period they had marked them up much above cost to compensate themselves for any rise in labour or raw material costs. If with stabilization these prices do not go up, they can mark down the prices a little; and if this leads people to expect a further fall in prices, we may get a crisis. It may also be that a change in the distribution of expenditures over time is interpreted by businessmen as an actual decline in demand; and this will also give rise to a deflationist psychology. But there is no certainty that businessmen would get panicky and cause a reduction in the velocity of circulation by cutting down prices unless more money is created. Apart from this, if expectations do lead to excessive stocks, the remedy may not be to lend money to producers to enable them to hold these stocks—the producers themselves may be victims of the general deflationist psychology and, therefore, unwilling to borrow. It would be necessary then to counter this tendency by creating money for more direct purposes such as financing of public works or generous unemployment benefits, etc.

It may be that a crisis develops because the workers demand higher wages despite stable prices in order to make good the loss in real income they generally suffered during the inflation. But to create credit to enable employers to meet this demand would be to start inflation all over again. If for any reason, such redistribution is desired, it should be brought about slowly by fiscal measures and by persuading employers to accept a lower rate of profit.

(3) Let us see next what happens if stabilization occurs at a still earlier stage of inflation when people's propensity to save is falling, and when savings are held more in the form of goods and income-earning assets rather than in the form of money.

With stabilization, people's propensity to save will rise to its more normal level; and, other things being equal, this would necessitate additional money if a deflation or crisis is to be avoided. Again, with stabilization people regain confidence in their currency, and the incentive to maintain abnormally large stocks of raw materials, machinery and consumers' goods on the part of everyone will disappear. The process of liquidation of stocks will imply a fall in current expenditure below the level sufficient to sustain current prices and output and a crisis may develop. Accordingly, the propping up of current expenditure by creating more money may be necessary.

In fact, we have a situation here which may be called "latent deflation" or the reverse of "latent inflation"; and it is possible to argue that if the extent is not very great, it is best or healthy to let it work itself out by allowing some fall in prices—and perhaps production. The crisis need not be of long duration if the stocks are exhausted soon. And it will cure some of the structural disequilibrium engendered by the preceding inflation. Stabilization is not simply a matter of keeping the general price level stable, but also of restoring a structure of relative prices which would make further expansion possible. The reduction in demand will be relatively greater in the case of producers' goods, and this will help in shifting resources away from their production. The fall in the price of consumers' goods helps to shift real income from producers to wage earners and fixed-income earners. And this is a step in the right direction both in itself and insofar as it shifts the distribution of resources by shifting the pattern of demand. It also implies a fall in the propensity to save insofar as income shifts from the rich to the poor; and this will tend to make the decline in expenditure smaller than otherwise.

The trouble about such a policy of letting the latent deflation work itself out, or of not offsetting the decline in expenditure consequent on destocking, is that this may lead to secondary reactions which may further deepen the crisis, for example, the normal multiplier reaction. But this can be offset by instituting at once a generous payment of unemployment benefits to be financed by means of credit creation. But care will have to be taken to see that such benefits are not on a scale that deters the mobility of labour in the direction required. Another sort of cumulative reaction may set in through people's expectations. But here again, if more credit is created, the policy should be properly selective if structural adjustments are not to be retarded. The problem of letting the "latent deflation" work itself out without allowing secondary reactions to usher in a cumulative decline is, therefore, a very complex one—how much new credit should be created, and what should be the criteria for its selectiveness will differ from country to country, and will depend largely on the government's ability to administer and inspire confidence in its stabilization programme.

It may be that during the inflation the flight from local currency as a store of value takes the form of holding more foreign exchange—either for the sake of safety or in order to profit from the anticipated exchange depreciation or as a means of evading payment of taxes. With stabilization, these foreign exchange holdings may also be offered in exchange for local currency. Should the government create more money in order to absorb them? It is clear that such a policy would not add to the inflationary pressure only if the people are willing to hold local currency or lend it to the government to the full extent of their foreign exchange conversions. The government, therefore, would be better advised to buy foreign exchange from its nationals with its own bonds rather than with newly created money. The situation is not substantially different if the government's foreign exchange reserves increase as a result of favourable export conditions resulting from stable prices—although here it may be more practicable to let the money supply increase automatically and counteract this by budgetary policies.

(4) But let us now turn to stabilization at a still earlier stage of inflation—one in which prices are rising faster than the money supply because the idle balances of the past are being activated. At this stage, there seems to be no reason why the process of stabilization should require an increase in money supply—or, to put it alternatively, why a stabilization crisis should develop if new money is not created. The government may choose to let the latent inflation of the past work itself out by allowing prices to rise. But even if stabilization is attempted at a higher price level, any further increase in money supply is inadmissible. The government cannot continue with its programme of deficit financing without destroying the stability of the price level. It must take advantage of the rise in prices and money incomes to create a budget surplus on current account to cover any deficit it may be having on its capital account—that is, on account of its long-term investment programme. If this is not thought possible due to the paralysing effects of taxation on production, the government has to curtail its outlay on development, or let latent inflation and money supply grow once again by keeping on the controls over consumption, imports, and perhaps even investment.

However, if stabilization is attempted when the latent inflation has already worked itself out, the government or the banking system might be justified in creating credit to counteract the deflationary effect of any import surplus the country may be having on current account. But this credit creation does not expand the total money supply; it merely offsets the increase in the local currency assets of the monetary authorities. And if stabilization occurs before the latent inflation has worked itself out, it is arguable that even this compensatory action should not be undertaken. An import surplus will help absorb the dissaving of past idle balances; and to create more compensatory credit at this stage would merely amount to letting the latent inflation run its course. Nor is the situation changed if the country is able to negotiate large foreign loans at the time. The foreign loans will enable the country to run a bigger import surplus on current account without depleting its foreign exchange reserves; and the government can implement its development programme without having to curtail the supply of goods to the community by higher taxes, or without having to let the latent inflation grow once again. But so far as credit policy is concerned, this situation is not different from the one in which a smaller import surplus on current account is maintained by depleting the country's foreign exchange reserves.

(5) It is necessary to consider one more situation that may arise after stabilization. The high volume of investment during the inflation and perhaps also during the first phases of stabilization may increase productivity in the community. This, after all, is the justification of a development programme and foreign loans. Factors such as surplus farm labour or arid land which were hitherto unemployable will become employable because the scarcity of cooperating factors such as skill, capital goods, water, fertilizer, power, etc., is diminished. The growth of production may bring about a subsequent decline in prices but this does not need to be countered by credit creation. On the other hand, it may well be that the increased production potential cannot be utilized fully by private initiative; and the government may decide to undertake investment on its own account by means of credit creation. It may also be that for some reason a downward adjustment in prices is not possible, and the expansion of output by entrepreneurs can take place only at the existing price level. Once again, we are in a situation where money supply and output can increase without raising prices. The injection of more money here would be justified not because it averts a stabilization crisis, but because it prevents the opportunity of increasing employment and output from running to waste.

In the preceding sections we studied what happens during stabilization at various stages of inflation, when a stabilization crisis is likely to develop if more money is not injected in the system, when such an injection would be unnecessary or harmful, and where it would be beneficial for reasons other than averting a crisis. At this stage, we would not try to summarize these various considerations. It is better first to test by reference to the actual experience of certain countries what significance should be attached to the various a priori considerations suggested above. We will, therefore, turn to this part of our study now.

A Historical Survey of Monetary Policy during Stabilization

In this section, the actual experience of three countries during inflation and stabilization is studied.

We have not dealt with many countries, and have kept our discussion of the three countries studied rather brief. The reason is that every country's experience has so many special features of its own that we should miss the wood for the trees if we allowed ourselves to become bogged down in details. Besides, in one respect there has been a great change in the psychology of the people during the last decade. Prior to World War II, it was generally expected that a boom would be followed by a slump, and a period of rapidly rising prices by one of falling prices. But with the growing consciousness of the need for avoiding crises and unemployment, people's expectations would not be the same now. And since, as we have already seen, so much depends upon people's expectations, the experience of the past is not the surest guide to the future. Lastly, when we speak of changes in people's liquidity preference, we are interested in finding out why and how much does the ratio of money supply to total money income change during inflation and stabilization. But data relating to money income are not available for most countries except for the recent past; our appraisal of their experience, therefore, would be largely qualitative rather than quantitative. And in this type of appraisal, there is the added danger of blurring the general outline of events by raising the dust of more or less irrelevant controversies.

German Inflation and Stabilization, 1913–1926

Inflation. The German inflation began during World War I, and was brought to a dramatic halt in November 1923. We are not concerned here with the causes and course of this inflation. But attention must be drawn to such of its features as are relevant to the proper appraisal of the German experience during the period of stabilization.

For our purposes, it is not necessary to comment on the astronomical heights reached by the German price level. But Table 1.1 is compiled so as to reveal the different phases of the German inflation.

Throughout World War I, and up to the signing of the Treaty of Versailles in July 1919, we have only a relatively mild form of inflation—that is, mild in comparison to what was yet to come. Prices do not rise as fast as the money supply, and the real value of money balances increases.

But from July 1919 to February 1920 prices rose sharply and faster than money supply. This was due mainly to the "flight from the mark", that is, to the increased demand for foreign exchange induced by the misgivings about the future of Germany created by the Treaty. The fear of revolutionary developments at home, and the desire to avoid payment of the heavy taxes with which the government intended to balance the budget, also contributed to the same phenomenon.

But from February 1920 to May 1921, German prices seem to have declined despite a 50 per cent increase in money supply. The velocity of circulation also apparently declined (see Table 1.1), and at the end of this period, the real value of money balances was virtually the same as it was in 1913. But this picture may be more apparent than real, for during the same

Table 1.1 Indices of Changes in Money Supply, Prices, and the Velocity of Circulation of Money in Germany
(1913 = 1)

	Currency in Circulation	*Wholesale Prices*	*Estimated Velocity of Circulation of Money*
	(1)	(2)	(3) = (2)/(1)
October 1918	4.4	2.3	0.52
July 1919	7.0	3.4	0.49
February 1920	8.6	16.8	1.9
May 1921	12.9	13.1	1.0
July 1922	32.1	100.6	3.1
June 1923	2749.0	19,385	7.0
October 1923	413 million	7,095 million	17.0

Source: Compiled from data given in *Economics of Inflation* by C. Bresciani-Turroni, London, 1937, chapter I, p. 442.

Notes: (1) "Currency in Circulation" means the notes of Reichsbank and of the private banks of issue, the notes of the Reich; the notes issued by the Loan Offices which were created on 4 August 1914, and metallic money.

(2) "Wholesale Prices" refers to the monthly average of such prices. We have not given the cost-of-living indices because they are not available for the whole of our period. But reference is made in the text whenever the cost-of-living index reveals a significantly different trend from the index of wholesale prices.

(3) The calculations of the velocity of circulation given here are, of course, approximate estimates. They are based on the assumption that only the quantity of money and the velocity of its circulation changed, and that the number of transactions remained the same. The assumption is, of course, unreal and is necessitated by the fact that we have no knowledge of German national income during the years. But it may be noted that on this assumption, the index of the velocity of circulation of money is merely an index of the ratio of wholesale prices to the money supply. It follows also that the reciprocal of the index of the velocity of circulation gives us the change in the real value of the money supply as compared to the base year.

period the cost of living increased by some 40 per cent. Part of the money created, however, had no inflationary effect because it was in response to the desire of certain people to sell foreign exchange in return of marks which were subsequently held in the form of idle balances. Confidence was reviving, and it would still have been possible to save the mark if the German government had established a balanced budget instead of covering 60 per cent of its expenses by the issue of Treasury bills (financial year 1920–1921).

From May 1921 to November 1923 prices rose very steeply and the real value of money balances declined. People spent their income as soon as they got it, and the velocity of circulation increased sharply. During the last phase of the hyperinflation, the German mark was repudiated both as a unit of exchange and account and as a store of value. However, it should be noted that Table 1.1 does not give a correct picture of the increase in the quantity of money or of changes in the velocity of circulation. In addition to the mark itself, various foreign currencies and local pseudo-currencies were used increasingly. Some two thousand kinds of "emergency" or "mushroom" money were in use in Germany before the stabilization, and their total value was estimated variously at from 1 billion to 4 billion gold marks. Another circumstance that should be borne in mind in understanding why prices rose faster than money supply is the decline in production which took place. In December 1921, 1.6 per cent of the trade union members were completely unemployed, and another 1.5 per cent were on short time; but by November 1923 these percentages had increased to 23.4 and 47.3, respectively.[1] According to an index computed by the Frankfurter Zeitung, by October 1923 the quality of production had fallen to 64 per cent of the April 1921 figure. In addition, farmers, retailers, and other producers were accumulating stock by withholding supplies from the market.

Stabilization. It was at this point that the stabilization of the mark was attempted. Thus, on 15 October 1923 a new "Rentenbank" was established, and it was authorized to issue a new currency unit called the "Rentenmark". On 20 November 1923 the value of the paper mark was stabilized at the rate of 4,200 billion marks per US dollar, that is, 1,000 billion paper marks per gold mark. The new Rentenmark was given the value of one gold mark. Such was the chaos caused by the inflation that these measures had a dramatic effect on the confidence of the people in the new currency; and the exchange rate and the price level were almost immediately stabilized. In order to understand exactly what happened during the period of stabilization, we must review the events up until the middle of 1926 when Germany was lifted out of an acute depression by the English coal strike. And it could give us a clearer picture of "the stabilization crisis" and the role of monetary policy, if we divide the period from November 1923 to June 1926 into several phases.

1. The first phase includes the months from November 1923 to April 1924. During this period prices fell a little,[2] and the exchange rate remained stable despite a substantial increase in the issue of paper marks and Rentenmarks. Although on 16 November the discounting of Treasury bills by the Reichsbank was stopped, thus terminating the creation of paper money

[1] See *International Abstract of Economic Statistics, 1919–1939*, International Conference of Economic Services, London, 1934, pages 78–97.

[2] The official index number of wholesale prices fell from 139.0 in November 1923 to 124.1 in April 1924. The data on prices, production, employment, etc., since 1923 are taken from *International Statistics*, op. cit.

for government account. This does not mean, however, that there was no budget deficit. The Government received credits from the Rentenbank in Rentenmarks; and these were drawn upon to meet the budget deficit, the creation of paper money for commercial purposes continued. The quantity of paper marks in circulation increased from 93 trillion on 16 November 1923 to 5,690 trillion on 31 March 1924. At the same time, some 1,760 million (1 million = 10 lakh) of Rentenmarks were also added to the circulation.

During these early months, Germany showed no signs of crisis. In fact, production recovered from the paralyzed state in which it had been. And this increase in production explains partly why prices did not rise despite the increase in money supply. The number of workers working short time, which was 1.8 million in November, fell to 90,133 by 15 March 1924; and the number of workers completely unemployed and in receipt of unemployment benefit was 988,752 on 15 March 1924, compared with 1.3 million a month earlier. The quality of production also showed considerable improvement. The index of "production in important industries" showed a 50 per cent increase in the first four months of 1924.

But the increase in money supply was non-inflationary during this period, for other reasons. A considerable part of it was merely used for substituting Rentenmarks and paper marks for the various kinds of auxiliary monies. It is estimated that some 1,100 million to 1,200 million Rentenmarks were created for this purpose. Besides, the creation of paper marks by the Reichsbank enabled people to replace their foreign exchange holdings with German money. This was reflected in changes in the "other assets" of the Reichsbank, which increased from 18.8 million gold marks on 15 November 1923 to 702.3 million on 30 June 1924.

It is interesting to note, however, that in Germany stabilization was accompanied by a great increase in the domestic money supply. And in the first few months there were no signs of a crisis. It is pertinent to our problem to ask how much of this increase in money supply was due to the increased liquidity preference of the German people with the restoration of confidence. It is clear from the figures given above that almost all the new Rentenmarks created during this first phase can be accounted for by factors other than the desire to hold a higher proportion of income in money form—that is, by the conversion of foreign exchange and various terms of auxiliary money in use into domestic legal currency. Even the enormous increase in paper marks was due in part to the increase in production and the decline in the volume of barter transactions. Unfortunately, no precise figures of national income or savings or inventories are available to tell us whether a part of the new money supply was also necessitated by people's increased preference for money as against consumption or other forms of holding wealth. What is certain is that German experience at this time points to the need for additional money even after stabilization—but mainly for reasons other than increase in liquidity preference inspired by the return of confidence. Nor should it be forgotten that the increase in money supply at this stage was not entirely harmless, as it threatened to unleash a new inflation very soon.

Symptoms of a new inflation began to develop in February and March of 1924 as a result of the liberal credit policy. There was such a large demand for imports that the Reichsbank had to ration foreign exchange very severely. The exchange rate showed some signs of weakness, and prices began to move up. Accordingly, on 7 April the Reichsbank decided to restrict credit to the level which prevailed at the end of March. And to prevent speculative borrowing, loans were made payable in terms of the original gold mark value. By this time, the budget was also balanced, thereby closing an important part of the inflationary gap.

2. Once these restrictive practices were adopted, the German economy experienced a minor stabilization crisis. But this phase lasted only from April to August 1924; and the crisis was by no means acute. The number of unemployed persons increased by only 43,000; production in "important industries" fell by some 10 per cent; and wholesale prices moved down about 7 per cent between April and July of 1924. There was an increase in interest rates and in the number of bankruptcies; but these changes stimulated Germany's exports to such an extent that the deficit in the balance of trade was replaced by a surplus.

The refusal to increase Central Bank credits meant that other banks had to reduce the scale of their credit operations. However, the amount of legal money in circulation increased during this period, mainly due to the replacement of private foreign exchange holdings with German currency.

3. But after the London Agreement on the Dawes Plan, on 30 August foreign capital began to flow into Germany, and she once again entered a period of recovery. This lasted till the summer of 1925.

There was a fall in unemployment, interest rates, and the number of bankruptcies. The index number of production rose by some 20 per cent, and prices rose slightly. At the same time, the credits granted by the central bank and by other banks and the quantity of legal money in circulation expanded.

4. This state of affairs came to an end in the summer of 1925, and was followed by a period of acute crisis. The number of employed workers, which in June 1925 was 195,099, rose to more than a million on 15 December of the same year, and reached the peak figure of 3 million by March 1926. Meanwhile, industrial production (in "important industries") fell by 15 per cent, while the index of wholesale prices fell only from 142 to 132, and money wage rates actually increased a little. The total amount of notes in circulation also increased by 6 per cent during the nine months following June 1925.

At the beginning of this crisis, there was acute monetary stringency. The resources of the great banks were for the most part employed in supporting certain big industrial groups. These banks, fearing for their liquidity, initiated a rigorous policy of credit restriction, and thus compelled many industries, particularly the capital goods industries, to dismiss some of their workers. It is not relevant to our purpose to discuss how this stringency in the money supply was relieved.

But why was this stringency felt at all? And, would it have been wise to have prevented it by means of a liberal credit policy? During the inflation, a large part of the liquid resources of firms were invested in excessive stocks and fixed capital equivalent. Any attempt to recover them was found to be deflationary. And to create more credit at this stage would have meant postponing adjustment in the economy. In addition, after stabilization, there was constant upward pressure on money wages and rents. The classes which suffered during the inflation were trying to recoup their losses. For some time, employers succeeded in countering the demand for higher wages by enforcing longer hours of work. But there are obvious limits to longer hours; and employers sooner or later had to meet the demands for higher wages by increasing the productivity of labour. But this required a change in the nature of the equipment of German industry: the large amounts of misdirected and more or less unproductive equipment acquired during the inflation had to be replaced with new machines, etc. And for a country which had gone through such an acute inflation, such a process of modernization would have involved some unemployment in any case. Admittedly, the volume of unemployment was far in excess of the irreducible minimum attendant on such a process of adjustment or of cutting out the dead wood of redundant stocks, etc. Much of it was due to the secondary cumulative decline in demand; and a policy of monetary expansion might have prevented it. But it is difficult to draw the line between what was inevitable and what was not.

Austrian Inflation and Stabilization

Inflation Table 1.2 shows the course of inflation and stabilization in Austria after 1914. During World War I, the inflation proceeded at a relatively moderate pace; and it was only after the third quarter of 1921 that a hyperinflationary situation developed. The period of stabilization began in September 1922, although during the next two years prices still showed a relatively moderate rise which was not checked until 1925.

Unlike Germany, the process of inflation in Austria cannot be conveniently divided into two clear-cut stages—one in which the real value of the money supply is increasing, and the other in which it is declining. Up to the spring of 1916 money circulation increased faster than prices. But this relationship was reversed during the next three-and-a-half years. This was particularly true of the year 1919 in which food prices went up due to famine, and when other prices were also affected by the general shrinkage in production resulting from the disruption of the Austro-Hungarian Empire. But once again, during 1920 money supply increased faster than the price level, mainly because production was recovering after the initial chaos of the new regime. In December 1920 the real value of money balances was virtually the same as in the pre-war period.

But from June 1921 to August 1922, prices rose much faster than money supply; and at the same time there was a sharp increase in the velocity of circulation of money—a familiar phenomenon during periods of hyperinflation. To some extent, the increase in money supply was greater during this period than is indicated by Table 1.2, for as in Germany, an increasing amount of foreign currency was being used as a medium of exchange and as a unit of account. But even disregarding this, the decline in the real value of money balances in Austria was not so great as in Germany. Nevertheless, complaints about the shortage of cash needed to meet the ever larger payments were quite common in this period. But this rise in prices at a rate faster than the increase in money supply was not merely due to the desire of the people to make purchases as soon as they got their income; it was also due to their desire to convert more and more of their cash balances into foreign exchange thereby precipitating exchange depreciation. In fact, by this time, it was this exchange depreciation which was the prime cause of the rise in prices, and actually led the price increases in the last phase of the inflation. People had got into the habit of quoting prices in terms of foreign currencies. And the increase in money circulation was mainly due to the increase in government expenditure occasioned by the rise in prices. In other words, where the flight of capital abroad is checked, we need not expect inflation and the decline in the real value of money balances (in August 1922 the real value of money balances was roughly 36 per cent of its pre-war level) to go as far as they did in Austria, other things being equal.

Stabilization During the period of stabilization (September 1922–1925) a number of important events occurred. These can be summarized as follows. In July 1922, a rigorous exchange control was instituted in order to prevent further exchange depreciation. The central bank adopted a more restrictive policy with respect to the discounting of certain types of financial bills, thereby discouraging the demand for foreign exchange for hoarding or speculative purposes. This, together with the confidence inspired by the prospects of foreign loans and the help of the League of Nations in reorganizing Austrian finances, led to the stabilization of foreign exchange in September 1922. But the government still had to finance its budget deficit by means of credit creation, and the money supply still increased rapidly. As stated above, the prices also continued to rise after stabilization of the exchange, but at a comparatively moderate rate. During

Table 1.2 Indices of Money Supply, Prices, and the Velocity of Circulation of Money in Austria (1913 = 1)

	Quantity of Paper Money	*Prices of Goods*	*Estimated Velocity of Circulation of Money*
	(1)	*(2)*	*(3) = (2)/(1)*
	Austria-Hungary		
January 1915	2.02	1.34	0.66
July 1916	3.34	3.96	1.19
November 1918	13.17	16.40	1.24
	Austrian Republic		
January 1920	26.5	49.2	1.86
December 1920	61.3	62.2	1.01
December 1921	348	450	1.29
June 1922	1,110	1,789	1.61
August 1922	2,707	7,422	2.74
December 1922	8,160	11,683	1.43
December 1923	14,251	13,600	0.95

Source: Bresciani-Turroni, op. cit., page 161.

Notes: (1) The Velocity of Circulation of Money is calculated here in the same way as in the case of Germany and is subject to the same reservations, cf. Note 3, Table 1.1.

(2) Data for the years 1924 and 1925 are not given in the table for want of a comparable series. But from a chart given in the League of Nations publication *The Course and Control of Inflation, A Review of Monetary Experience in Europe after World War I*, page 102, the following trend can be deduced:

Indices of Currency in Circulation and Prices in Austria (December 1922 = 100)

	Money Supply	*Prices*
December 1923	175	125
December 1924	205	150
December 1925	210	150

August–December 1922, the money supply was trebled, but prices rose by only 60 per cent. This was due to three reasons: (1) Part of the money increase was nominal insofar as it was in substitution for other currencies in use; (2) Employers had already marked up selling prices far above cost in anticipation of further depreciation of the currency, but when this did not materialize they could afford not to raise prices despite the increase in consumer purchasing power; and (3) Buyers' resistance increased, not only because of the stocks which they had accumulated during the inflation, but also because of the expectation of a fall in prices. As a matter of fact, business became so slack soon after stabilization that despite continued credit creation, unemployment increased. In December 1922, there were 117,000 unemployed people on relief, as against 31,000 in August of the same year. It would seem then that "crisis" can develop after hyperinflation despite generous credit creation during the stabilization period.

But by the beginning of 1923, the government was able to cover its expenditure without credit creation mainly by borrowing from non-bank investors. Yet the credit creation of earlier months was threatening to unleash a new inflation, and even as late as 1923 additional money was being created, although at a reduced rate. Consequently, prices continued to rise, although at a slower rate than the money supply. By December 1923 the real value of money balances was virtually restored to the pre-war level. It should be noted that the increase in money supply which occurred in 1923 was almost entirely due to the conversion of foreign exchange and was accordingly reflected in the increase in the Central Bank's foreign exchange reserves. From 7 January 1923 to 31 December 1923 the bank's foreign exchange reserves increased by 2,686 billion paper crowns and the note circulation by 3,072 billion paper crowns. Most of the foreign exchange thus converted was reinvested in Austrian government loans. However, this was due primarily to a revision of government policy in favour of persons who had evaded payment of taxes, since a substantial part of foreign exchange held at that time was obtained illegally and represented tax evasions.

In 1924, money supply was still increasing although at a slower rate. But this time there was a corresponding rise in prices. The main reason for this was the rise in wage rates. It was only in the following year, 1925, that prices virtually stopped rising; but by this time the money supply was also stabilized. It is interesting to note that from December 1923 to December 1925 both the money supply and prices rose by 20 per cent.

On the whole, it seems that in Austria the increase in money supply was halted only gradually after stabilization of the exchange rate; and prices followed this movement at such a rate that the real value of the money supply was restored by the end of 1923. Austria experienced no serious crisis during this period; and from such evidence as we have, production seems to have increased more or less steadily. This lends countenance to the view that further credit creation is essential to enable people to replenish their money balances after a period of hyperinflation if a stabilization crisis is to be avoided.

This conclusion, however, is subject to the following reservations: (1) Stabilization in Austria was followed by a moderate recession, in spite of a generous credit policy. (2) Much of the new money was created for purposes other than to enable people to hold larger cash balances. (3) Even during the inflation, Austria had still not completed the task of reconstructing her economy. This, together with the substantial inflow of foreign capital, led to a significant increase in production after stabilization. In such an expanding economy, not only is there a need for more money, but there is also a greater ease in correcting maladjustments caused by inflation without enduring the pangs of crisis. (4) And lastly, the Austrian experience would suggest that even when monetary expansion is necessary to enable people to build up their money balances to more normal levels, this will, in all probability, push up prices still further. The fact is, complete stability in the price level and expansion of the money supply may be incompatible even when there is genuine need for more money in some sectors of the economy. Money is not something which can be injected in precise amounts at various points in the system, and in any practical situation there is always grave danger of overshooting the mark.

Inflation and Stabilization in Belgium during the Decade of the 1940s

The experience of Belgium during the decade of the 1940s has great significance for our problem. Unlike Austria and Germany after World War I, Belgium did not suffer from hyperinflation during the last decade. But as in most belligerent countries, World War II witnessed in Belgium the development of both an active and a latent inflation. And Belgium is one of the few countries in which inflation was brought to a halt by slow stages—at least temporarily. What is more, monetary policy—which is the chief concern of this paper—has played a vital part in this process. Indeed, in Belgium, inflation seems to have given way to a moderate recession in activity; and it is very pertinent, therefore, to inquire what light is shed on our problem by events in Belgium during the last ten years.

Tables 1.3 through 1.6 summarize the relevant developments in Belgium. Adequate data for the war years are not currently available; but since we are interested mainly in events since the liberation, this is not a serious deficiency.

During the occupation, production in Belgium declined, and national income was below the pre-war level despite a sharp rise in prices. Money supply increased more rapidly than prices and national income; and in 1943, the ratio of money supply to national income was roughly three times as high as in 1938—indicating the extent to which latent inflation had developed.

These large idle balances were to be liquidated by the monetary purge of September 1944. It is not relevant to our purpose to go into the details of this reform. But its immediate effect was to reduce the money supply in Belgium by more than one-half—the remainder being blocked permanently or temporarily. This, however, did not mean the end of Belgian inflation, since other inflationary pressures operating concurrently

Table 1.3 Inflation and Money Supply in Belgium

Year	*National Income*	*Industrial Production*	*Total Money Supply (Net)*	*Retail Prices*	*Liquidity Index*
	(1)	*(2)*	*(3)*	*(4)*	*(5)*
1937	65.3	100	43.1	100	104
1938	65.2	81	41.2	104	100
1939	65.2	86	44.0	105	98
1940	(40)	–	54.8	116	174
1941	46	–	73.7	–	199
1942	(50)	–	99.4	–	243
1943	55	–	127.1	–	284
1944	(55)	–	68.3	–	240
1945	(110)	31	125.6	350	119
1946	190	74	138.1	333	99
1947	215	86	143.2	339	100
1948	244	93	151.7	389	93
1949	249	94	160.1	378	99

Notes: (1) Refers to National Income at Factor Cost in billions of Belgian Francs. Figures in parentheses are estimates made ad hoc by Horsefield, cf. RD-848, page 13. Others are taken from National Income Statistics, Statistical Office of the UN.

(2) Indices: 1937 =100. Source: IFS.

(3) In billions of Belgian Francs. Figures refer to the end of the calendar year. Source: IFS.

(4) Indices: 1937 = 100. Source: IFS.

(5) Defined as the index of (money supply)/(national income), but with 1938 = 100. The money supply for a given year used for calculating this index is not the same as given in Column 3. During a given year, the total money supply is taken to equal the average of the money supply at the beginning and the end of that year. cf. Horsefield, RD-578, Part II, pages 20–22.

had yet to be eliminated. In 1945, the money supply increased by roughly Bfr 60 billion mainly because of the government's budget deficit, which was roughly equal to the increase in money supply. This deficit resulted from heavy expenditures on reconstruction of transport and other facilities damaged during the hostilities and large outlays for the support of Allied armies during combat and redeployment. Unfortunately, we have no data on the movement of prices and production in 1944 and 1945; but the fact that the national income in 1945 was thrice as high as in 1943 indicates that both prices and production must have increased. On the other hand, the money supply in 1945 was on the average below the 1943 level, due to the currency reform of 1944; and the velocity of circulation of money was consequently more than double that of 1943. But since all this was largely

Table 1.4 Belgian Government's Budgetary Position (in millions of Belgian Francs)

	1945	*1946*	*1947*	*1948*	*1949*
Expenditures:					
Ordinary	28,412	31,883	36,055	43,793	54,856
Resulting from war	44,541	22,746	22,176	19,376	13,136
Extraordinary	7,696	22,535	13,809	8,120	15,757
Total	80,649	77,164	72,040	71,289	83,748
Receipts:					
Ordinary	21,202	42,242	46,395	61,357	64,115
Resulting from war	46	4,184	541	1,492	1,253
Extraordinary	30	14,229	6,895	677	754
Total	21,278	60,655	53,831	63,526	66,122
Balance, total	−59,371	−16,509	−18,209	−7,76.3	−17,626

Notes: Data for 1945–1947 are taken from 'European Recovery Program: Belgium and Luxembourg', Country Study by ECA, February 1949, page 30. These figures differ from official Belgian statistics because of certain technical modifications. The figures for 1948 and 1949 refer to fiscal years, and are taken from the *Annual Report of the National Bank of Belgium*, 1950, page 24.

Table 1.5 Daily Averages of the Number of Registered Unemployed in Belgium

1946 monthly average	48,035	19,257	67,292
1947 monthly average	35,639	31,921	67,560
1948 monthly average	80,959	48,244	129,203
1949 monthly average	173,988	60,908	234,896
1949 first quarter	173,000	–	–
1950 first quarter	205,000	–	–

Source: Banque de Bruxelles, *Quarterly Survey*, 1950, No. I, page 34; and United Nations, *Economic Bulletin for Europe*, 1950, Vol. 2, No. I, page 5.

Table 1.6 Index Numbers of Employment in Industry in Belgium (1937 = 100)

1947	117	1948 fourth quarter	100
1948	120	1949 first quarter	97
1949	112	1949 second quarter	96
		1949 third quarter	92
		1949 fourth quarter	90
		1950 first quarter	88

Source: *Economic Bulletin for Europe*, 1950, op. cit., Vol. 2, No. I, page 46.

the result of an arbitrary decision of the government—viz., the currency reform—it does not tell us anything about the spontaneous changes in people's desire to hold cash during a period of inflation.

During the next two years (1946 and 1947) Belgium almost succeeded in achieving internal economic stability. Industrial production in 1947 was roughly three times the 1945 level, and was actually higher than the 1938 figure. The recovery in agriculture was not so great, production being still below the pre-war level. The government budget was still far from being balanced; but the deficit was considerably reduced—to Bfr 16.5 billion in 1946 and Bfr 18.2 billion in 1947. To counteract the inflationary effect of the deficit, Belgium allowed imports to exceed exports by a substantial margin—the import surplus on trade account being approximately Bfr 30 billion in 1946 and again in 1947 (see IFS, August 1950, page 44). These surpluses were principally financed by loans from the US, Canada, and Sweden, by Allied payments for military expenditures, and arrears of investment accruing to Belgium during the war. In order to maximize the anti-inflationary effects of these surpluses, the government deliberately encouraged the import of consumer goods and of goods for replenishing inventories. At the same time, steps were taken to prevent excessive expansion of the money supply. The discount rate was slowly raised from 1½ per cent to 3½ per cent (August 1947), and the banks were required to hold from 50 to 65 per cent of their assets in the form of Treasury obligations, the practical effect of which was that they have been unable to increase their advances to industry as from about the end of 1946. During these two years, therefore, the money supply increased by only 14 per cent, or by about Bfr 17.6 billion. Prices actually fell, as did the ratio of money supply to national income, which declined to the pre-war (1938) level.

But if Belgium was approaching internal stability during these two years, there were no manifestations yet of anything like a "stabilization crisis". Production was increasing rapidly, and there was very little unemployment. Moreover, it cannot be argued that the increase in money supply averted a possible crisis due to the increase in people's desire to hold cash balances. As has been noted above, the increase in money supply was less than the increase in production, and the liquidity index was actually allowed to fall. This is easy to explain when we consider the special circumstances prevailing in Belgium. The Belgian inflation was brought to a halt by the gradual reconstruction of the national economy. There were no excessive stocks to be liquidated as in the case of countries which witnessed a continuous rise in prices even after their productive capacity was fully employed. Again, at a time when a large part of the rest of the world was still grappling with inflationary pressures, internal stability in a country like Belgium depending heavily on its foreign trade would not induce expectations of a continuous fall in prices. Nor was it likely that the propensity to save would rise significantly with the advent of internal stability in a country which was just returning to its normal level of consumption after a prolonged period of enforced hardship. Fears for the future awakened by the cold war would also develop a psychology of living for the moment. Besides, despite the monetary purge of 1944, the money supply prior to the movement towards internal stability was in excess of the normal requirements of the people, when judged by pre-war standards.

Unfortunately, this internal stability proved temporary, and in 1948 there was open price inflation. Retail prices in 1948 advanced some 15 per cent above the 1947 level, despite a substantial increase in production and a reduction in the budget deficit and in credits to other European countries. This was due in part to the removal of subsidies and to the psychology of "living for the moment" engendered by the international political situation. But the rise in the price of Belgian imports also contributed to the inflation. Accordingly, the stringent monetary policy was continued, with the result that the ratio of money supply to national income fell below the pre-war level. (Actually, if in Table 1.3 we had used national income at market prices instead of national income at factor cost, the ratio of money supply to national income would show an even greater decline during 1948, because of the removal of subsidies.)

As one would expect, the monetary stringency manifested itself in rising unemployment. The figures for Belgian unemployment are difficult to interpret. It is arguable that although unemployment in 1948 was twice as high as in 1947, this was largely due to the voluntary withdrawal of women, old people, etc., from the labour force. In the immediate post-war period, when the Belgian standard of living was below its pre-war level, a large number of persons who would normally be outside the labour force had to seek employment; and this was encouraged by the government's appeal to the people's patriotism to reconstruct the economy. But with the subsequent increase in production, such people would probably prefer to relinquish their employment, although they might still remain on the register for unemployed persons in order to be eligible for social security benefits. Insofar as this was true, we should characterize the situation in 1946–1947 as one of over-full employment rather than speak of unemployment in 1948.

But whatever may be true of 1948 as a whole, there can be no doubt that beginning with the fourth quarter of that year Belgium had a significant amount of unemployment. In 1949, the number of fully unemployed persons was about five times as large as in 1947, and in the first quarter of 1950 unemployment was 17 per cent above the corresponding level in the first quarter of 1949. Even if we look at the level of employment in industry alone, there has been a steady decline since the fourth quarter of 1948, and this despite the repatriation of some foreign workers who were previously unemployed.

The question naturally arises if this unemployment can be explained in part in terms of a "stabilization crisis". We have already seen that in 1948 money balances were allowed to fall below the normal requirements in relation to national income (as measured by pre-war or 1938 standards). We would expect that people would try to meet this monetary stringency by a process of liquidating their stocks of goods. This would bring about a fall in prices and a rise in unemployment until the ratio of money supply to national income increased sufficiently. Something like this did happen in Belgium in 1949. It is generally recognized that one cause of the rise in unemployment in this year was the process of liquidating stocks. Prices fell, and the liquidity index was restored to more normal levels. A partial recognition of the logic of this argument can also be seen in the fact that the National Bank of Belgium attempted to mitigate the monetary stringency by lowering the bank rate from 5 per cent to 3.25 per cent, as from 6 October 1949. The government's budget deficit was larger in this year due to the increased burden of unemployment benefits. But it is arguable that a more prompt and vigorous policy of credit expansion for public works or other programmes could have avoided the secondary unemployment resulting from the initial decline in expenditure.

Nevertheless, part of the unemployment in Belgium springs from legitimate sources and cannot be laid at the door of a stringent monetary policy. The substantial increase in Belgian production since 1944 with the help of improved imported machinery would in any case create some technological unemployment. And the end of the sellers' market abroad meant that Belgian industry had to embark on a campaign for higher productivity by reorganization, cutting down absenteeism or the use of inefficient labour, etc. Again, with the cessation of Marshall aid in the offing, the Belgian economy had also to undertake some shift of resources, thereby causing frictional unemployment. One reason why the authorities did not follow an expansionist policy was the fear that it would postpone the basic readjustments which were needed. Again, part of the reason why liquidation of stocks was undertaken in 1949 had little to do with the need for building up adequate money balances. The recession in America and the falling prices of manufactured goods created in the minds of Belgian producers a pessimistic attitude toward future sales, and hastened the liquidation of stocks.

Thus, the experience of Belgium points not only to the need for creating more money during stabilization in order to avert a serious crisis, but also to the extreme difficulty of implementing such a policy without incurring the risks of renewed inflation. Belgium did not emerge from the war time inflation with the real value of her money supply depleted—quite the contrary. There was no question, therefore, in the immediate post-war years of the need for an expansionist monetary policy to avert a possible crisis. Even in 1948 when the re-emergence of inflation did reduce the ratio of money supply to national income below the normal level, it is doubtful if an expansionist monetary policy would have been appropriate at that stage, since the inflation might well have got out of hand. In 1949, as has already been suggested, the incidence of unemployment could have been reduced by a proper expansionist policy. But there were several other non-monetary factors in the situation; and it would be futile to dogmatize about the degree of success that an expansionist monetary policy would have achieved.

Concluding Remarks

What conclusions can we draw from the discussion in the earlier sections? We have seen that in a variety of circumstances it is desirable to expand the money supply, even while attempting to halt an inflation, if we are not to stumble into a "stabilization crisis". But we also found that the problem is complex and that in some cases monetary expansion can be positively harmful to the process of stabilization itself. These various points can now be summarized as follows:

(1) During a period of hyperinflation, legal currency is often replaced by foreign currency or by other extra-legal auxiliary currencies in which people have more confidence, or by pure barter. Insofar as stabilization reverses this process and induces people to replace barter or other currencies with the use of legal currency, there is a legitimate need for monetary expansion during stabilization.

(2) The same is true if people endeavour to increase the proportion of their income which they save with the advent of stabilization, other things being equal.

(3) But perhaps the most important factor to reckon with is the accumulation of excessive stocks of goods, machinery, etc., during the inflation—or in other words, the heritage of latent deflation. With the advent of stabilization there will de a tendency to convert these stocks into liquid assets and this will induce a fall in prices and production. It is arguable that up to a point it is desirable to let the latent deflation work itself out and thus correct some of the structural maladjustment caused during the inflation. But even in that case new money should be created to neutralize the secondary reactions of the initial decline in expenditure. Obviously, such a two-faced policy raises difficult administrative problems, since it requires a good deal of selectiveness in the field of credit policy and may even involve some direct controls.

(4) A stabilization crisis may be threatened by adverse expectations. In this case, people may be unwilling to borrow even if the banks are

willing to expand credit. If so, the government will be required to create credit in order to finance its own investment programme.[3]

(5) More money should be created during stabilization if production increases with the return of confidence. This may be so merely because production was paralysed during the last phases of inflation or because the fruits of high investment activity during the inflation become manifest now or because stabilization is accompanied by an inflow of capital from abroad.

(6) However, even when an expansion of the money supply is necessary for any of these reasons, there is always the risk of overshooting the mark and permitting prices to rise somewhat also. In other words, if money balances need to be increased in real terms after stabilization, this is not likely to happen by money supply increasing and prices remaining stable, but by money supply rising faster than prices. This is so because monetary policy is general in character and does not admit of precise application at various points in the economy. Alternatively, the expansion of money supply may have to be combined with some direct controls and the re-emergence of some latent inflation.

(7) During an inflation people may have acquired large holdings of gold and foreign exchange either as a store of value or for purposes of tax evasion or in order to earn speculative profits. If with stabilization people wish to convert these into local currency, there is no harm in increasing the money supply for that purpose so long as the additional money is likely to be held in the form of idle balances. Otherwise; the creation of more money for that purpose would be detrimental to stabilization.

(8) The creation of more money will also be harmful if stabilization is attempted at a time when the real value of money balances is declining because of the activation of the idle balances of the past—that is, at a time when the latent inflation of the past is working itself out or has just worked itself out, other things being equal.

What should be done in any given situation depends on which of the elements mentioned above are present and whether the authorities are prepared to administer effectively certain additional measures of direct control which may be necessary to strike a balance between the harmful and the beneficial effects of monetary expansion. It may well be that the maintenance of international competitive power, for example, requires a certain amount of unemployment and stringency in the monetary supply—if the

[3] It is possible, of course, that where the government does not enjoy the confidence of the investing public, such measures may not prove very successful.

alternative policies of devaluation or high taxation or direct controls are not thought feasible. All that can be attempted in a general discussion like this is to lay bare some of the broad phenomena that bear on the demand for money during the stabilization period.

CHAPTER 2

Nature and Significance of Monetary Policy and Its Instruments*

After a decade or so of comparative disuse, a number of countries have in recent years turned increasingly to an active use of monetary policy. There is nothing monotheistic about this revival. It is generally appreciated that monetary techniques can be fully effective only in combination with proper budgetary and other policies.

Monetary policy itself is being revived in a form somewhat different from the one familiar in the pre-war days. In addition to the simple classical techniques of discount rate changes and open market operations, central banks have added a variety of new and complex weapons to their armoury. The underlying economic situation has changed in many countries, and now that the usefulness of monetary policy in general is widely recognized, the chief point of interest about its recent revival is the manner in which it is being adapted to the present needs of different countries. Granted the need for its active use, the question that becomes important is the choice of the proper techniques for the purpose.

In this analysis of monetary policy during the years since World War II, attention will first be directed to the factors that led to the comparative neglect of monetary policy during the 1940s and to the forces responsible

* Adapted from the paper originally published as 'Monetary Policy in Post-war Years', *IMF Staff Papers*, Vol. III, No. 1, 1953, © International Monetary Fund, Washington, DC, USA. The views expressed in this paper belongs solely to the author. Nothing contained in this paper should be reported as representing IMF policy or the views of the IMF, its executive board, member governments, or any other entity mentioned herein.

for its revival in recent years. Then a brief general survey of the different monetary techniques and their comparative usefulness will be given.[1]

The Changing Emphasis on Monetary Policy

The depressed condition of the 1930s had established low interest rates everywhere; and during World War II rates were reduced still further in most countries. The gigantic task of war finance had made direct controls and heavy taxes absolutely necessary, and it was felt that under these circumstances, little more could be gained by monetary incentives or restraints. But the de-emphasis on monetary policy persisted for a few years even after the end of the war. Most countries had inherited abundant surplus money from the war. If monetary policy is successful mainly in checking the growth of new money, it cannot be of much use so long as people have large amounts of surplus old money. Concern about the cost of the public debt, a desire to maintain low housing costs, and concern about a possible post-war recession added to the bias toward cheap money. Even when the dreaded depression failed to appear, it was felt that the need for rapid recovery after the destruction and dislocation caused by the war required easy money conditions.

In addition to these considerations, there were certain ideological and theoretical factors that led to the abeyance of monetary policy. "The euthanasia of the rentier" by keeping interest rates low had come to be a popular theme. At the same time, it was thought unjust to raise interest rates on government securities and thus inflict capital losses on people who had been persuaded to buy government bonds by promises of future rewards. On the theoretical plane, the ideas of the 1930s had cast doubts on the ability of interest rate changes to influence significantly either savings or investment. Even insofar as monetary policy affects investment, it was felt that this influence is general in character, that is, not selective enough. Monetary policy can bring about some contraction or expansion of effective demand in general. But most countries had emerged from the war with structural distortions which required expansion in certain directions even when contraction in other directions was called for. In shaping demand in particular sectors, monetary policy was not deemed discriminating enough.

The renewed emphasis on monetary policy in recent years is partly the result of a change in circumstances; but it is also the product of a reassessment of the importance of monetary policy and of the adaptation of monetary policy itself to different needs and circumstances. For a variety of reasons, the wartime latent inflation has disappeared in most

[1] This paper was prepared in the autumn of 1952. Developments since then are not discussed here.

countries; and experience has shown that monetary policy itself has a part to play in removing or absorbing surplus money. This is even truer when latent inflation takes the form of excessive liquid assets in the community. Moreover, the fears of a recession have proved largely unreal and most countries have crossed the hump of economic recovery. Government budgets have swollen in response to the rise in prices, with the result that the cost of the public debt does not loom so large in the total fiscal picture as it did a few years ago. Also, after a point, all economic policies begin to show diminishing returns, so that policies hitherto neglected become relatively more useful. This had happened to monetary policy in relation to fiscal policy or direct controls in several countries, and the proper blend of economic policy has required a little more use of monetary policy. The ideological fervour for egalitarianism has also abated from its post-war peak.

On the theoretical side, it is now recognized that, whatever its limitations in a period of depressed demand, monetary policy can be quite effective in curtailing demand. It does not consist of merely varying interest rates or the cost of credit; it can directly influence the supply or availability of credit. Changes in interest rates may be required as adjuncts to other types of monetary control even if they are not of sufficient importance in themselves. Nor does monetary policy have to resign itself to measures of a generally restrictive character. The availability and terms of credit can be regulated selectively. In this respect, World War II has actually added a new dimension to monetary policy. In the general environment of direct controls, monetary policy itself became imbued with direct and selective overtones; and in the post-war years, this type of technique has been further refined.

The final impetus came with the Korea War, although even before then monetary policy was by no means totally in abeyance. The revival of inflationary pressures after the outbreak of that war and the prospect of an end to American assistance made it urgent for most West European countries to curtail demand at home. As long as economic recovery at home was rapid, and large-scale US assistance was forthcoming, it was easy to overlook the direct connection between external imbalance and the internal supply of money, but this connection was underlined by the inflationary boom after the war began.

Techniques of Monetary Policy

It is not easy to delimit precisely the area in which monetary policy operates. Broadly speaking, the task of monetary policy is to regulate the amount of money or means of payment offered for goods and services. Leaving aside the use of surplus money and a more active use of existing money (that is, an increase in the velocity of circulation of money), the growth of effective demand requires additional means of payment. By controlling the supply of new money, monetary policy can check the growth of effective demand.[2] The growth of such demand can consist of two elements: growth in prices and growth in production. The supreme test of monetary policy lies in its ability to control the supply of money in such a way that the growth in prices is checked without retarding the growth in production.

In technically advanced societies, bank credit forms a large part of the supply of money. The primary task of monetary policy, therefore, is to control the volume of bank credit. Indeed, in a narrow sense this is the entire task of monetary policy. But apart from obtaining credit from the banks, a society can increase, in a variety of ways, the means of payment at its disposal. At any given time business and individuals hold certain assets which can be converted into money, for example, time deposits, savings bank deposits, short-term or long-term government securities, etc. The distribution by the people of their assets between money and other assets depends, among other things, on the current and expected rate of interest on the other assets, and on the current and expected prices of the securities, goods, and services bought against money. If monetary policy includes the determination of the rate of interest on various more or less liquid assets, it clearly shades off into debt management policy. Apart from this, the supply of money can be increased through the operations of the government budget and the foreign trade transactions of the country. Monetary authorities are not necessarily passive in relation to the government or the agencies responsible for the management of foreign trade. But the area of monetary policy here impinges on fiscal and foreign exchange policy. In the remarks that follow on the techniques of monetary policy, attention will be centred on the control over commercial bank credit. However, the following facets of monetary policy will also be briefly examined: (1) control over idle surplus money; (2) control over a more active use of money; (3) control over a shift from near-money assets to money; (4) control over the creation of money by the government; and (5) control over the creation of money through the foreign sector.

Control over Bank Credit

The choice of proper techniques for preventing an undue expansion of bank credit depends to a large extent on the general economic conditions in a country, the nature of the banking system, and the traditions that have grown over time. The orthodox weapon is the discount rate of the central bank. Raising the discount rate, however, may not significantly curtail bank

[2] Although monetary policy can influence the process of both an increase and a decrease in effective demand, the emphasis here is on the former because of its greater relevance today.

credit, for various reasons: The demand for credit may be insensitive to its cost, in view of fears about rising prices or shortages; the cost of credit to private borrowers may not increase, if the banks are in a liquid position or are able to secure liquid funds without using the rediscount facilities of the central bank, for example, by disposing of their holdings of government securities which earn a lower rate than the discount rate. In connection with the elasticity of demand for bank credit, however, it should be remembered that in some countries banks grant medium- and long-term as well as short-term credit, and that in such countries the cost of credit may have a greater restraining significance than in other countries. The expectations about rising prices are in part determined by the confidence of the public in the ability of the authorities to pursue a vigorous monetary policy. And if the limitation of discount rate policy arises from the possibility of the banks' attaining liquidity by using some of their other assets, it can be offset to some extent by allowing other rates of interest (say, on short-term government securities) to rise.

Even when the demand for credit is not responsive to its cost, there may be some advantage in raising the discount rate. In most countries this would, traditionally, be followed by raising the cost of bank credit irrespective of the need to borrow from the central bank.[3] The higher yield on their loans would enable banks to offer a higher rate on time deposits, and this would have some effect, however small, on the rate at which such near-money assets are converted into money by the public. To the extent that the rationale of a tighter policy toward bank credit lies in the balance-of-payments position, the favourable effect of a rise in money market rates on capital movements must also be taken into consideration. In any event, the limited effectiveness of higher discount rates does not invalidate their use unless they have some undesired effects. The only such undesired effect that is likely to arise is that if the interest rate on short-term government securities has to be raised significantly in order to make a higher discount rate effective, it may not be worth the additional cost to the Treasury.

Apart from raising directly the cost of credit, monetary policy can curtail the availability of bank credit. The classical technique for this purpose is the open market operations of the central bank. The essence of these operations (in the context of inflation) is to transfer some bank deposits to the central bank by the sale of government securities to banks or the general public. The impact on the liquidity of banks is voluntary or indirect in the sense that it depends on the willingness of the public or the banks to exchange

[3] If the banks were trying to maximize profits, they would raise the rates on their loans in any case if the demand for bank loans were inelastic. But in practice the rates of banks are sluggish and in some countries they are related, by custom, to the discount rate.

liquid funds for government securities. But if the interest on government securities has to rise considerably to invoke a sufficient response to such policy, this technique may not be desirable. The central bank may be able to reduce the liquidity of banks without depressing the securities market too much under certain favourable circumstances, for example, if there is an inflow of foreign capital or a temporary windfall to the community from better terms of trade. In some countries such as West Germany, the scope for open market operations is limited by the absence of a sizeable amount of government securities in the portfolio of the central bank. Theoretically, this difficulty can be overcome by creating new securities for the purpose; but in practice, when there is a general shortage of capital and the demand for credit is brisk, it is doubtful that this policy would succeed in the absence of some official pressure on the banks to absorb government securities.

The availability of credit can be directly influenced by compulsory reserve requirements, that is, by transferring bank deposits to the central bank directly and without any cost to the government. This technique requires a fine differentiation in the reserves required for different banks if the banking system lacks uniformity, as is likely in any large country with a decentralized banking structure. Another limitation of this technique arises from the need to take into account the profit position of banks; non-earning assets cannot be imposed ruthlessly on banks, even if they are in a position to raise the cost of their ordinary loans. The chief merit of reserve requirements lies in their comparative simplicity and in the degree of decentralization they imply in deciding which types of credit will be curtailed.

Raising reserve requirements within practicable limits can, however, be somewhat ineffective under certain circumstances. If the banks hold large amounts of government securities, they can monetize them and thus create excess reserves for themselves. In most countries, banks have a traditional regard for distributing their assets in a certain way; they will not allow their holdings of short-term or long-term government securities to fall below a certain proportion of their deposits. In such cases moderate changes in reserve requirements may be sufficient to prevent any building up of excess reserves through monetization of the public debt. Where such traditions do not exist or where the actual reserves in government securities are above the traditional level, some additional steps are necessary.

If the banks are trying to circumvent reserve requirements by disposing of their excess holdings of short-term government securities, a higher rate on such securities may be offered as an incentive to hold them. If any reasonable incentive proves insufficient in view of the greater earnings on private loans, some degree of compulsion may be called for. This may take the form of compulsory reserve requirements expressed in terms of such securities, the funding of such securities into long-term bonds, or the compulsory renewal of old short-term securities as they mature. Whether this result is obtained by legislation or the moral pressure of the monetary authorities would depend, of course, on the country's traditions.

If the banks are trying to create extra reserves by selling off their long-term government securities, the task of the monetary authorities is simpler. Unless the central bank is willing to support the bond market, bond prices must fall if the banks try to sell bonds to non-bank investors, and the banks must suffer a capital loss. This loss would greatly offset the desirability of shifting from government to private loans even if the interest on the latter is significantly higher; the higher interest would be realized on a lower amount, and for many years it would merely be reimbursement for the capital loss. The banks cannot be sure that during those years demand for private loans would be sustained and that they would be able to buy back the bonds in future at the same low price they had realized on them. Even if the banks are prepared to take a capital loss, or if this loss is not great in view of the willingness of non-bank investors to absorb government bonds, the banks would be expanding private loans without any expansion of the money supply, since the purchase of securities from banks by non-bank investors would imply a fall in bank deposits. Thus, if the banks by trying to sell government bonds seek to circumvent the attempt to control the availability of bank credit, the central bank need only step out of the market and let bond prices fall. If such a course is deemed undesirable, recourse can be had to still higher reserve requirements or compulsory reserves in government bonds, or restrictions on the negotiability of bonds held by banks, or some direct controls discussed below.

Banks can circumvent the restrictive influence of higher reserve requirements even if they do not have surplus reserves of government securities to dispose of. If the central bank is prepared to offer its rediscount facilities, the banks can increase their ability to lend merely by having greater recourse to the central bank, provided they do not reject such recourse as a matter of tradition. Where conventions about keeping borrowing from the central bank within a certain ratio of banks' total loans are not strong, and as long as required reserves are only a portion of total liabilities, this is clearly possible. In such circumstances, the central bank would be constrained to raise the discount rate to prohibitive heights, or to tighten its rediscount facilities by imposing severe tests regarding the type of paper it would rediscount, or simply by establishing ceilings to the total rediscounts offered to each bank. The central bank can control the availability of bank credit in a direct manner by placing a limit on the total credit any bank can give or on the total credit any customer can obtain. This type of control involves discretion and administrative authority on the part of the central bank; and the degree of intervention implied in the affairs of private banks may not be desirable or politically acceptable everywhere. If the cost structure in the economy were rising, such a policy would call for frequent revisions of quotas. Also, one of the merits of monetary policy in general is its simplicity and freedom from direct interference from authorities. There may be something to be said for direct monetary controls in contrast to direct allocation of materials or direct controls over prices, but both are open to common objections, up to a point.

The techniques of monetary policy discussed so far influence the cost or availability of credit in general. But if, as was suggested earlier, the conditions in an economy are such that expansion in some directions is desirable even as credit in some fields needs to be curtailed, some degree of selectiveness must be introduced in monetary control. To put it differently, if the supreme test of monetary policy lies in its ability to prevent the growth of prices without retarding the growth in production, it may be necessary to control in different ways the supply of money to different sectors of the economy.

In theory, some of the techniques of monetary policy discussed above can be applied in a selective manner. But this is not true of all. Thus, the discount rate can be different for different bills. If the desire is to discourage imports or imports from certain areas, a penalty discount rate for import bills may be fixed. This can be done indirectly by prescribing different criteria for rediscounts for different bills. How significant such measures are likely to be is another matter; the banks can always rediscount eligible loans in order to enable them to increase other loans, and slight differences in the cost of financing imports may not be very effective. Again, if the availability of credit is controlled by direct means such as rediscount ceilings or ceilings to total loans by a bank or total loans to a customer, selectiveness can be introduced by making some exceptions. The central bank may even require prior approval for all bank loans or all bank loans in excess of certain amounts. But at this stage the degree of direct interference and centralization of bureaucratic decisions is increased. Selection presupposes a straitjacket of direct intervention. On the other hand, if simple and indirect techniques like open market operations or reserve requirements supplemented by necessary changes in government rates of interest are used, it is not easy to see how these can be used selectively: The only degree of selectiveness possible in such cases is that induced by moral suasion, exhortations or appeals to the banks' sense of social responsibility. When the banks find that the demand for loans is greater than what they can supply, the priorities that they would set up may be influenced by the wishes of the central bank. But the banks may have their own private loyalties and may even insist on their pound of flesh by simply raising the charges on their loans and letting that do the rationing—at least to some extent. If this happens, the government may have to fix legislatively the cost of credit to certain essential links in the economy. Perhaps the best course is to keep deliberate selectiveness to a minimum and to correct the generally restrictive environment at chosen points by non-monetary devices—such as subsidies, etc.,—or by direct assistance from the central bank. Even the simplest type of monetary technique does not restrict all expenditures in the same proportion. Higher interest rates would curtail some investments more than others, and the banks would ration credit to customers in the light of the soundness of the purpose for which it is sought. If the criteria of the market are not deemed desirable, the instruments of intervention need not be only monetary ones.

There is one type of selective credit control which has a somewhat different rationale from that implied above. If fluctuations in effective demand are centred around certain sensitive areas, and if these areas are particularly susceptible to changes in credit conditions, a decisive influence on aggregate demand may be achieved by controlling credit conditions in a few selected fields, which would minimize the need for introducing changes in credit in general. This is partly the justification for control over housing and durable consumers' goods credit in the United States. In this case a few types of credit may be intensively controlled by prescribing the duration, amount and cost of such credit, not because such credit is particularly nefarious in itself but because it occupies a key position in the economy. Strictly speaking, this type of selective control is not aimed at bank credit only; it applies to a specific type of credit from all sources—from retailers, banks, mortgage houses, etc. It creates, therefore, a more onerous problem of supervision.

While the foregoing survey of the techniques available for controlling bank credit is by no means exhaustive, an extensive study of all the possible refinements is not necessary in an introductory survey. Therefore, consideration may now be given, briefly, to other aspects of monetary policy.

Latent Inflation and Velocity of Circulation

Control over the supply of new money would lose part of its meaning if the public had accumulated surplus balances of money. Such latent inflation can be eliminated in a variety of ways: by allowing prices to rise, by developing large import surpluses, or by budget surpluses.

Alternatively, part of the excess money can be declared worthless, or it can be rendered inactive by *force majeure* or by offering some incentives until production grows and catches up with the available supply of money. An alternative to cancelling part of the money supply is to withdraw money from circulation temporarily by compulsory blocking of loans or by floating loans to which the public can subscribe voluntarily. The second alternative corresponds to open market operations and has the same limitations.[4] The success of a policy of temporary blocking depends on the ability of the government and the central bank to release old money only as production revives and to keep the supply of new money to a minimum. Otherwise, the temporary withdrawal of money would merely conceal the real process by which latent inflation is worked off, that is, by higher prices or import surpluses.

Latent inflation can also take the form of excess liquid assets rather than of surplus money. Insofar as these liquid assets are held by the banking system, they would present difficulties in controlling bank credit, as pointed out above. The liquid assets held by the general public can be dealt with by import surpluses or capital levies or by allowing prices to rise. Or the public may be induced to hold their liquid assets until there is an increase in real output. The only way that the monetary authorities can control these assets, short of a compulsory scaling down of obligations or a restricting of the negotiability of the assets, is to offer higher rates of interest. Thus, time deposits and savings deposits may be absorbed into long-term government debt. Also, short-term government securities may be funded into long-term debt. The rationale of trying to convert the near-money assets into funded debt is that it reduces the overall liquidity of these assets. If bond rates are allowed to fluctuate, the bonds cannot be liquidated without a capital loss, and this may be a deterrent to any shift from liquid assets to money. But people have to walk into this trap voluntarily, and it may be that no practicable incentive in the form of higher bond yields would induce them to do so. Ultimately, the question is how far interest rates can influence the public's propensity to spend. Nor is it always possible to brandish the hatchet of capital losses vigorously; the psychology of once-bitten-twice-shy would haunt governments which do not all expect to die in the short run. Indeed, many governments have tied their hands in this respect by offering certain amounts of special bonds guaranteed against capital loss to individuals.

Even when the amount of money and of other liquid assets is restored to its "normal" relationship with national income and even if the supply of new money is controlled as far as practicable, effective demand can grow if the public starts turning over money more rapidly or draws on near-money assets. Monetary policy can do little directly to check the increase in the velocity of circulation of money. However, such an increase is likely to take place when confidence in the future value of money is at low ebb and is, in fact, often associated with growth in money supply permitted by a weak monetary policy. A vigorous monetary policy may therefore keep to

[4] In fact, it is more difficult politically for a government to put the proceeds of new loans in cold storage than it is for a central bank to keep idle the funds it raises by open market operations.

a minimum the danger of an activation of the use of money. The problem of countering a shift from near-money assets to money is the same in kind, whether such assets are generally excessive or are temporarily regarded as rather large.

Creation of Money through the Budget and External Trade

New money would be created if the deficit in the government budget were financed by borrowing from the central bank, and to a lesser extent if it were financed by borrowing from other banks. By use of the various devices discussed above, monetary policy can prevent the secondary inflationary impact[5] of such bank-financed deficits. But the task of preventing the primary inflationary impact of such deficits lies outside the field of monetary policy. The central bank may be able to keep its credit to the government within narrow limits, but in the ultimate analysis it cannot exercise sovereign influence over the government budget. Various legal requirements concerning the composition of the central bank's assets may assist in sustaining the fiscal rectitude of the government. But beyond this, the ability of the central bank to limit its credit to the government (or to semi-government agencies) is a matter of tradition, personalities, and the sense of responsibility on the part of the ultimate repositories of power in the land.

Similar considerations apply to the creation of money through the foreign sector. Any increase in the money supply of a country that has a surplus on current account will depend on how this surplus is financed. If it is financed by private credit extended to foreigners, there need be no creation of money unless the credit comes from the expansion of bank loans rather than from the current savings of the public; but at any rate, there would be a reduction in the liquidity of the banks corresponding to the increase in the money supply. If the export surplus is financed by government grants or credits or by the accumulation of foreign exchange by the government, the problem becomes essentially a budgetary one. The government may finance the external surplus from normal budgetary sources, that is, by raising tax revenue or by borrowing the public's genuine savings. This may happen if the government is giving away the export surplus to foreigners (free grants) or if it is giving credits to foreign governments. It may happen even if the government is accumulating foreign exchange corresponding to the export surplus. But in any event, there would be no net creation of money. However, if the central bank (or the banking system) is obliged to finance the export surplus, there would be a net creation of money. Once

[5] That is, any expansion of bank credit arising from the improvement in their liquidity.

again the central bank can counteract the secondary inflationary impact of such an export surplus by normal monetary technique; but the primary inflationary impact can be curtailed only with non-monetary policies, that is, by eliminating the export surplus or by finding local currency for it by budgetary devices. Thus, the task here of controlling the amount of money is one of fiscal and foreign exchange policies rather than monetary policy. The central bank can refuse to provide local currency beyond a limit against foreign exchange or against foreign credit balances only by virtue of traditions, etc., in the society. However, in only a few countries are central banks embarrassed in the exercise of their anti-inflationary functions by export surpluses. The more real threat to monetary policy comes from reckless fiscal policies.

CHAPTER 3

Selective Credit Controls in Underdeveloped Economies*

It is often felt that credit policy in a developing economy should be selective. Monetary management should not merely aim at a general restraint or spur to economic activity; it should also try to influence different economic activities in different ways. A number of devices have accordingly been adopted in recent years, particularly in Latin America, to provide specific encouragement or discouragement to certain types of investment and expenditure.

Selective credit controls are intended to encourage or discourage specific types of investment and expenditure by influencing the lending policy of banks and similar credit institutions.[1] In evaluating the usefulness of these controls and of the different techniques for selectiveness, it is necessary first to define the basic objectives to be fulfilled.

A policy of selective credit control may be adopted, for example, as an adjunct to a well-balanced development programme. The basic problems in an underdeveloped country are to achieve a high level of savings and investment and to ensure that the funds available for investment are

* Originally published as 'Selective Credit Controls in Underdeveloped Economies', *IMF Staff Papers*, Vol. IV, No. 1, September 1954, © International Monetary Fund, Washington, DC, USA. The views expressed in this paper belongs solely to the author. Nothing contained in this paper should be reported as representing IMF policy or the views of the IMF, its executive board, member governments, or any other entity mentioned herein.

[1] Selective credit controls may be applied to banks as well as to other lenders, such as insurance companies and savings or mortgage banks. However, lenders other than banks are for the most part disregarded in this discussion.

directed to socially desirable channels. It is often contended that there is an institutional bias in underdeveloped countries in favour of investment in construction and trade to the detriment of more productive alternatives available in industry and agriculture. The traditional regard for short-term "self-liquidating" loans on the part of the banks encourages purely commercial activities as distinguished from production; and in the absence of adequate facilities for medium-term or long-term credit some of the existing opportunities for increasing production are wasted. Selective credit controls may also be necessary to protect the interests of certain ill-organized sectors of the economy, whose credit needs are not satisfied by existing institutions. Attempts to develop an economy are often accompanied by egalitarian measures, such as the division of large estates among small peasant proprietors, and such measures often create new ill-organized areas with special credit needs. Another justification for selective credit control as a long-term policy arises from the urge to diversify the economic structure.

These conditions are undoubtedly significant in many underdeveloped countries. Nonetheless, selective credit controls have only a limited role to play in the process of well-balanced development. Their ultimate objective is to ensure that bank credit is used in accordance with a certain order of priorities. If these priorities do not correspond to the lending policy of the banks but are in conformity with the investment preferences of borrowers, it is enough to control the banks; and this is a comparatively easy task. But if selective credit controls are intended to modify the investment decisions of borrowers as well as to alter the lending policy of banks, it becomes necessary to check on the actual use made of bank credit. More often than not, the bias in favour of "undesirable" investment or expenditure is on the part of borrowers as well as lenders; and this situation requires something more than selective credit controls.

A distinction should also be made between attempts to encourage a better use of existing investment opportunities and efforts to create new investment opportunities by suitable assistance. If production of certain types is to be encouraged in the interests of diversification or for other reasons, some assistance or protection may be necessary in the short run. But preferential credit arrangements can only be the first step in such a policy. Unless attempts are made simultaneously to remove the other bottlenecks in production and to divert demand, if necessary, to the desired lines of production, selective credit controls will lead only to bad debts and hidden subsidies. As a device for forcing the pace of development in certain lines, selective credit controls should not be allowed to divert attention from more basic solutions or difficulties.

Apart from this, only some of the investment in a community is financed by bank credit. A large part of the investment which is self-financed or financed through the capital market or through private borrowing would be left untouched by efforts to modify the pattern of bank credit. What is more, the possibility of substitution between bank borrowing and other finance would reduce the significance of any selective controls over banks. It is arguable that these considerations are not so important in underdeveloped countries, where capital markets are generally non-existent and where much reliance is placed on credit institutions for most short-term as well as long-term credit needs. It is also true that in a developing economy the total volume of credit is likely to expand in the course of time, and that monetary authorities have better chances of success in channelling an expansion of credit along the desired lines than in changing the distribution of a given amount of credit. Nevertheless, a large part of the investment activity going on at any time must remain outside the purview of selective credit controls.

Selective credit control may be adopted less as a long-term objective than in response to some short-term difficulties, for example, during a period of active inflation. It is now generally recognized that inflation creates balance-of-payments difficulties and encourages too much unproductive investment in inventories, luxury construction, etc. The introduction of selective credit controls in many Latin American countries in recent years has been motivated largely by the desire to minimize these adverse consequences of inflation. The reasons for adopting a policy of selective credit control during a period of active inflation, however, need careful consideration.

It may be hoped, for example, that selective credit controls would enable a country to achieve a supposedly higher rate of savings and investment through inflation without any serious misdirection of resources or without serious balance-of-payments difficulties. The need for exercising a general restraint on credit, it might be argued, would be obviated insofar as all "undesirable" credit is eliminated by selective controls over credit for construction, imports, inventories, etc.

It is not necessary to discuss here the general case for or against inflation as a means of financing development. Nor is it necessary to show why any attempt to prescribe the purposes for which bank credit could be used is bound to be futile as long as credit for ostensibly desirable purposes is available without any restraint. But even if the assumption is made that selective credit controls are effective in curtailing certain types of investment or expenditure, it does not follow that the resources so released will be automatically transferred to more productive uses. The reason for excessive investment in inventories and real estate during inflation may well be that such investment constitutes, in the short run, the major practicable channel for private enterprise. Even if other opportunities for additional investment are available, a period of inflation with the inevitable social tension and uncertainty may not provide the right atmosphere for such productive investment. If this is the case, selective credit controls will only reduce the general level of expenditure and as such the pace of inflation. But if this result is acceptable, it could be achieved more easily by straightforward or general credit controls. It is difficult to see how selective credit controls can offer any justification for pursuing a deliberately inflationary policy.

Alternatively, selective credit controls may be adopted to prevent inflation from getting out of hand. Even if it is not possible to avoid a certain degree of inflationary pressure, as a result of budgetary difficulties, for example, it may be desirable to prevent a secondary expansion of bank credit. This can be done by general credit controls. But if the inflation is very mild and if the expansion in credit is likely to be concentrated in certain areas, such as credit for imports, it may be sufficient to control credit conditions on a selective basis. In short, selective credit controls may serve as a useful substitute for general credit controls in a very mild inflation.

Another circumstance in which selective credit controls can be particularly useful is during the process of stabilization. After a period of prolonged inflation, the only way to restore confidence in the currency may be to bring the expansion of credit to a halt. If the measures taken to achieve this are very restrictive, some genuine needs for credit may not be met and there may be adverse repercussions on production. On the other hand, if some increase in credit is permitted, it may still be necessary to ensure that the credit is used for the right purposes. Selective exceptions to the highly restrictive general credit controls may be quite effective in these circumstances.

To sum up: in considering the usefulness of selective credit controls, certain distinctions must be kept in mind. Are they used as long-term devices or as short-term expedients? If they are used as an adjunct to the long-term process of development, is the intention to influence the lending policy of banks, or to alter the investment preferences of borrowers, or to create new investment opportunities? In the short run, are they employed as exceptions to a tight money regime, or as a means of exercising a general restraint on credit, or as a way of obviating the need for any restraint on the overall supply of credit?

Techniques of Selective Credit Control

An active use of credit policy rests on the assumption that the general level of effective demand, and consequently the general level of prices and production, can be influenced by modifying the availability and cost of credit. In attempting to encourage or discourage specific types of activity, selective credit controls assume further that the pattern of investment and production can be influenced by differentiating between the cost and availability of credit to different sectors.

Apart from exhortations and moral suasion, selectiveness can be introduced in credit policy in two ways. The allocation of bank credit may be influenced directly by stipulating the loans that can be made, the amounts, the rates of interest, the duration, the type that is not desirable, the amount of collateral, etc. Alternatively, if the central bank actively assists or controls the banking system, such assistance or controls may be exercised selectively, so as to influence indirectly the behaviour of the banks. For example, rediscount rates or rediscount ceilings may be different for different types of loans; where reserve requirements are imposed, some selective exceptions may be made. In short, the cost and availability of bank credit to different sectors can be differentiated by direct regulation or by indirect inducements to the banking system in terms of the cost and availability of liquid funds. By and large, the direct type of selective control entails a greater administrative burden for monetary authorities.

Selective Credit Control as a Long-term Objective

If the credit needs of the community are not met adequately by existing institutions, the government can set up new or specialized credit institutions. Almost all Latin American countries in recent years have set up such institutions to meet the special needs of agriculture or of new industries. Whatever the defects in the actual operation of these institutions, the basic idea in setting them up is undoubtedly sound. In the extreme case, governments can impose their own pattern on loans by centralizing much of the credit activity in official or semi-official agencies. Such a result can be achieved in part if governmental credit agencies appropriate for themselves the entire growth potential in credit. If reserve requirements and credit ceilings make it virtually impossible for private banks to expand credit, there is, so to speak, a nationalization of banking at the margin. Many of the smaller Latin American countries have already moved to a position where the desire for selectiveness has led to an increasing concentration of credit facilities in official entities. However, if private banks are to be assigned a significant role in the economy, it becomes necessary to influence their decisions.

The traditional fears of private banks concerning medium-term or long-term loans of a productive character may be allayed by appropriate government guarantees or rediscount facilities. A more fruitful approach may be to explore the possibility of joint loans by the commercial banks and the state-managed development finance institutes. Thus a five-year loan for the purchase of industrial machinery may be made jointly, with the provision that the bank's share will be paid back in the first year or two and can be transferred to the development institute. If the commercial banks do not have the technical staff to appraise the soundness of new schemes, the cooperation of a government agency will help to create the necessary confidence. And the banks' knowledge of particular customers and of their other activities will facilitate a better supervision of the loan.

If it is not possible to induce banks to make productive loans on an adequate scale, some measure of compulsion may be used. For example, ceilings may be established for certain types of loans so as to encourage diversion of funds into desired channels. Such a policy, however, is hardly desirable as a long-term objective. With the general growth of the economy, the ceilings have to be revised from time to time; and insofar as all banks do not grow at the same rate, any approach through absolute ceilings may create some injustice. Apart from this, any categorization of bank loans is bound to be arbitrary to some extent. A loan for commercial purposes, for example, cannot be distinguished easily from a loan to industry for raw material requirements. The monetary authorities would have a burdensome administrative task of deciding whether particular loans conform to the classification laid down by law.

Alternatively, commercial banks may be required to distribute their assets in a certain manner. For example, it may be obligatory for banks to hold at least 10 per cent of their assets in government securities. The government can use the proceeds of such loans for financing official credit institutes. But clearly, such a measure reduces rather than modifies the role of the banks. Stipulations may be made about other aspects of a bank's portfolio, requiring, for example, that loans to agriculture and industry shall not fall below a certain proportion. Here again, the problem arises of establishing uniform standards for the classification of loans; and the consequent interference and supervision by monetary authorities may not be desirable as a permanent or long-term feature.

Another technique which offers a compromise between compulsion and encouragement involves higher reserve requirements with specific exemptions. Assume that the banks keep all their cash as deposits with the central bank, and that a ratio of cash to deposits of 10 per cent is regarded as safe or necessary by the banks to meet their normal requirements. The banks, however, may be required to hold, say, 20 per cent of their deposits as reserves, with the provision that at least half of the required reserves must be kept as deposits with the central bank and the remainder held in the form of certain preferred assets or securities. This technique has been adopted in Mexico.

The reason why this arrangement induces banks to change the composition of their loans in favour of the preferred category is easy to see. Other things being equal, the volume of their loans would be increased if their lending were concentrated on the preferred type of asset that constitutes a part of the required reserves.

The technique under consideration has the great advantage of administrative simplicity. The basic reserve requirements, although high, need not be so high as to prevent banks from expanding their activity as their deposits grow; and there is no compulsion on the part of the banks to increase their loans in any set proportion. Consequently, the central bank is not required to scrutinize all the loan operations of banks. It merely has to ensure that the loans which it accepts as part of required reserves actually conform to the prescribed type.

On the other hand, the selective impact of higher reserve requirements with specific exemptions may not be as great as appears at first sight. When banks make loans, they need additional cash for two reasons. Part of the loan may be taken out in cash by the borrower; and the part which remains as an increment to deposits kept at that bank or other banks requires more cash as a normal backing or in view of legal requirements. In underdeveloped countries, where the ratio of currency to money supply is very high, the first drain on cash reserves is by far the more important, unless legal reserve requirements are very stringent. This tends to reduce the discriminatory significance of any provisions concerning reserve requirements.

It is also arguable that even if the banks are able to increase their loans more by concentrating on preferred types, they may not do so. It will be a matter of indifference to the bank whether it lends four units for one purpose or five units for another purpose, if it can charge a higher rate of interest for the first category of loan. However, such a discriminatory interest rate policy can be discouraged if the central bank prescribes maximum rates of interest for non-preferred categories of loan. Apart from this, if the banks prefer to continue lending for less desirable purposes, their total loans will in any case be smaller, inasmuch as required reserves will be higher on the average. This will enable official credit agencies to increase their encouragement to the desired lines.

Selectiveness may be introduced through reserve requirements in a number of ways. If required reserves are related to deposits, some preferred assets may simply be deducted before calculating required reserves. Alternatively, required reserves may be related to bank assets rather than to deposits, and different requirements may be set for different assets.[2] It is not necessary, however, to comment on all these variations.

On the whole, if selective credit controls are intended to correct a long-term bias in the lending policy of banks, techniques adequate for the purpose can be devised.

[2] See *Monetary Policy and the Management of the Public Debt* (Joint Committee on the Economic Report, Washington, DC, 1952), Part I, pp. 485 et seq.

Selective Credit Control as a Short-term Expedient

Some of the techniques discussed above can be useful as purely short-term expedients. It is obvious, for example, that if a tight rein is kept on credit expansion by rigid credit ceilings or stringent reserve requirements, the special needs of some sectors can be satisfied by selective exemptions. Whenever quantitative limits are placed on the total credit that a bank can give to any one customer (for example, in Paraguay) or to all its customers, it is generally provided that these limits may be exceeded in specific cases with the prior approval of the central bank. Such a selective approach can be effective when it is combined with highly restrictive general credit controls. There is no reason why the banks should want to flout the wishes of the central bank, and there will be better supervision of the end-use of credit when the few selective exemptions are scrutinized individually.

The situation is quite different, however, when selective techniques are adopted in an inflationary situation without any attempt to control the general expansion in credit. This can be shown easily by an examination of some of the expedients used for the purpose.

In most countries, the monetary authorities rely primarily on recommendations to the banks for avoiding credit for certain purposes. But such exhortations are not likely to be very effective even when they are sanctified in the form of a semi-legal decree. The banks have no incentive to comply with such requests; and even if some of them are imbued with a sense of social discipline, compliance places them at a disadvantage in relation to less scrupulous banks. The environment in many underdeveloped countries is hardly such as to sustain any concerted self-restraint on the part of the banks. Even if the banks respect the wishes of the monetary authorities, they are not able to control the end-use of their credit to any great extent. As long as inflation continues and the banks are in a liquid position, they will lend rather freely for ostensible purposes that are not frowned upon; and they will not be able to prevent the use of loans for purposes different from those intended by them. In the absence of other sanctions, selection by exhortation is likely to produce complacency rather than results.

The central bank may attempt to influence the banks indirectly by a selective rediscount policy. It may refuse to rediscount certain types of credit or it may charge higher rates of interest for certain rediscounts. The limitations of such a policy are also obvious, however. Banks can rediscount eligible paper in order to extend credit in undesirable fields. During a period of inflation, the banks need not rely much on central bank rediscounting for expanding credit if the central bank is already providing reserves, for example, by financing budget deficits. And even if the banks are influenced by discriminatory rediscount facilities, they are in no better position to control the end-use of their credit.

One measure frequently adopted and which seeks to influence bank lending indirectly, viz., prior deposit requirements for imports, is of special interest. Underdeveloped countries are particularly susceptible to balance-of-payments difficulties under inflationary conditions, the excess demand tending mainly to increase imports. In addition, the constant expectation of devaluation leads to excessive stockpiling of imports. In order to curtail the demand for imports (or to ease the pressure on exchange controls), special credit requirements are often imposed in relation to imports. One that is frequently imposed requires an importer to deposit with the central bank at the time of applying for an import licence, that is, in advance of the purchase of foreign exchange, a part of the local currency equivalent of his imports. An import licence is generally required at the time of placing an order abroad, even before the goods are shipped, whereas the payment to the supplier and the purchase of foreign exchange for the purpose can in some cases be deferred until the goods are shipped or even received. The prior deposit requirement, therefore, creates an artificial need for credit on the part of the importer. The importer may be able to borrow the sum required from a bank; but insofar as the deposit is transferred to the central bank, there will be an equal decline in the reserves of the banking system.

It is evident that prior deposit requirements of this kind for importers will have some anti-inflationary effect. If an artificial need for credit is created, and if bank reserves are reduced to the full extent of any increase in bank credit to meet this need, the liquidity of the banks is reduced effectively. Such an indirect way of curtailing the ability of the banks to expand credit has the great advantage of administrative simplicity.

It is not clear, however, that the restrictive effect will be felt primarily in the demand for imports. As far as the importers are concerned, the only unfavourable development is the increased need for borrowing in relation to a certain amount of imports. But the additional interest cost of such borrowing is likely to be only a minor deterrent in a period of inflation. The banks certainly have an incentive to avoid loans for financing prior deposit requirements for imports. Such loans tie up their reserves more than other loans. However, the banks are not in a position to decide the extent to which their loans are used for one purpose rather than another. As long as part of their loans (or current deposits) is used for meeting prior deposit requirements for imports, the banks will suffer the same immobilization of reserves. It seems, therefore, that such deposit requirements are more useful as generally restrictive measures than as devices for curtailing imports.

The effects of prior deposit requirements for imports as a generally restrictive device are of a once-and-for-all character, however. The restrictive effect comes into operation when the requirements are introduced and whenever there is a subsequent increase in imports. If the banks have sufficient excess reserves or if such reserves are being created continuously, even the once-and-for-all effect will not be of much significance.

The prior deposit requirement for imports cannot be employed in the absence of a system of import licensing. In such cases, banks may be required to keep an advance deposit with the central bank against letters of credit covering imports; and the deposit requirement may differ according to the type of import covered by the letters of credit. In principle, this device is similar to differential reserve requirements against different types of bank assets. If an importer cannot substitute for a letter of credit other means of payment, such as direct cash payments, the requirement of a prior deposit may prove effective in curtailing the demand for undesirable imports. The banks may, as was argued earlier, prefer to acquire assets other than letters of credit for importers; and even if they do not alter their lending policy because of inertia or irrationality, or because they are able to charge differential rates of interest, some general restraint on credit will be exercised.

It is arguable that, on the whole, it would be better if the banks did not modify their lending policy in response to prior deposit requirements for imports, for the prior deposit requirements would then at least have an immediate general anti-inflationary effect. If instead the banks should avoid credit for imports so as to make larger loans for other purposes, the inflationary pressures would be increased, and it would become even more difficult to avoid balance-of-payments difficulties at a later stage. In short, it may be advisable to treat prior deposit requirements for imports as a useful means of curbing inflationary pressures in general rather than as a device for curbing the demand for imports in particular. If this view is correct, their desirability would depend on a comparison with the probable effects of straightforward reserve requirements.

Another approach to selectiveness during an inflation, which deserves some attention, is margin requirements for certain types of collateral. Banks generally require some collateral against their loans, which in underdeveloped countries often consists of inventories, real estate, land, gold, or foreign exchange, that is, precisely the type of asset whose accumulation needs to be discouraged. The monetary authorities may require that loans secured against certain types of collateral shall not exceed a certain proportion (say, 80 per cent) of the value of such collateral. In the extreme case, some types of asset, such as gold, may be declared ineligible as collateral.

Such a provision poses an obvious problem of enforcement. The valuation of real estate or land must remain arbitrary to some extent, and any overvaluation would tend to nullify the effect of margin requirements. Again, such requirements are not selective enough. If inventories in general are excessive, some inventories are nonetheless essential. For small merchants and producers without other assets, inventories may be the only collateral available (or acceptable to the banks), and they would have a legitimate grievance if inventories were ruled out as collateral. In theory, this difficulty can be overcome by selective exemptions for small borrowers. But this may defeat the purpose as far as large borrowers are concerned. The banks would be less reluctant to increase their unsecured loans to big borrowers, especially when they know that their loans against inventories or real estate are over-secured. In order to be effective, margin requirements for collateral require that the banks should not increase the proportion of unsecured loans beyond a point, and that the substitution between different types of collateral by borrowers can be made only to a limited extent.

Even when margin requirements for certain types of collateral are an effective deterrent to credit expansion, the question still remains whether their usefulness lies primarily in their generally restrictive effect or in the selective character of the restraint exercised by them. Insofar as the amount of credit tends to be related to the amount of collateral, margin requirements of this kind act essentially like reserve requirements. By reducing the base for bank borrowing, so to speak, they act as a general deterrent to the expansion of bank credit. Faced with the prospect of smaller accommodation from banks, borrowers would curtail their expenditure. But it does not follow that the reduction in expenditure would fall entirely or primarily on inventories or luxury construction. It is arguable that investment in inventories or luxury construction would become relatively less attractive insofar as their usefulness as collateral is diminished. But apart from this consideration, margin requirements would achieve little more than straightforward credit restraints, such as credit ceilings and reserve requirements, which are easier to administer.

These comments on margin requirements are made having in mind particularly the possibility of excessive "new" investment in certain lines. During an inflation bank credit is used also to create a speculative boom in the market for existing assets, such as land, houses, etc., with these assets themselves serving as collateral for the credit. That high margin requirements may serve a useful purpose in curbing such speculation has been shown by the experience of the United States in connection with securities.

Summary

All these considerations show that any attempt to generalize about the effectiveness or desirability of selective credit controls is bound to be misleading. They are adopted for a variety of reasons and under different sets of circumstances. They may be adopted during a period of active inflation in the hope of minimizing the distortions introduced by inflation into the pattern of investment. Alternatively, if a tight money policy is pursued to bring inflation to a halt, it may be felt desirable to protect certain forms of investment from the generally restrictive trend. These cases should be distinguished from selective credit controls applied in an environment of monetary stability in response to certain long-term objectives or structural needs.

If selective credit controls are applied in the hope that there can be inflation, and the supposedly higher level of investment resulting therefrom without any misdirection of resources, they are likely to prove disappointing. On the other hand, they can be quite useful as temporary correctives during a determined effort at stabilization or as long-term devices to aid the process of well-balanced development. The techniques for introducing selectiveness on a long-term basis would, of course, differ from those suitable as short-term expedients.

In some cases, selective credit controls may be adopted as an economical way of influencing the general level of demand rather than as a means of influencing certain types of demand. If fluctuations in effective demand are concentrated in certain sensitive areas, and if these areas are particularly susceptible to changes in credit conditions, a decisive influence on aggregate demand may be exercised by controlling credit conditions in a few strategic fields only. This is in part the rationale of the control of durable consumer goods and housing credit in the United States. It is arguable that some of the techniques adopted recently in Latin America for influencing particular types of demand are, in fact, more useful for exercising a general restraint on credit. In judging the usefulness of selective credit controls, this aspect of the problem should also be borne in mind.

CHAPTER 4

Some Thoughts on Monetary and Credit Policy*

I think there is general agreement in India now that inflation is harmful both from the growth and equity points of view. Not long ago, there were at least some businessmen who advocated inflation as a deliberate policy to promote higher savings and investment and thus accelerate the pace of development. I have a sneaking suspicion that they were motivated in this by the belief that in the struggle for keeping ahead in relative price terms, which is at the heart of the process of inflation, businessmen and owners of all means of production such as land and equipment would come on top. But we know now from experience that inflation has many disruptive consequences, including those on industrial relations and the ability to replace and modernize obsolete or old equipment. Where much of organized industry uses locally produced raw materials, the prices of which are generally more volatile, it is not at all clear who comes on top during a period of rising prices.

Perhaps most of us would also agree that with the best will in the world, some increase in prices over the years may be unavoidable in the present national and international climate. But this makes it all the more important to strive our utmost to avoid inflation; for as in the case of pursuit of virtue or avoidance of vice, while complete success is seldom possible, there is no automatic limit below which we may not sink. Now that we have managed to achieve reasonable stability of prices for almost two years and broken the vicious circle of self-fulfilling expectations of rapidly and steadily rising prices, it would be the height of imprudence to let off our guard and to

* Address as Governor of the Reserve Bank of India at the 71st Annual General Meeting of the Indian Merchants' Chamber, Bombay, on 24 February 1979; subsequently published in the *Reserve Bank of India Bulletin*, February 1979.

surrender the hard-earned ground that would be that much more difficult to recover.

The war against inflation, of course, has to be fought on many fronts; on our farms and in factories in terms of higher production as well as greater productivity; around negotiating tables where wage agreements are arrived at; at meetings where guaranteed or minimum prices for agricultural commodities are settled; and in board rooms and elsewhere where administered prices, generally of industrial goods, are determined in a virtually oligopolistic market. But inflation cannot also be fought without an active monetary and credit policy.

It has become fashionable of late to contrast the large increase in money supply during the last two years with the comparative stability in prices and to conclude that in our conditions an increase in money supply at a rate faster than the increase in production does not lead to a rise in prices; and it is not uncommon to be told that we need not take a squeamish or alarmist view of even sizeable increases in money supply. I am afraid this country of ours, great and blessed as it is, enjoys no such divine dispensation of immunity from monetary laws which are, after all, only reasonable approximations to the laws of supply and demand which at least businessmen should not belittle or deride.

There should really be no mystery about the behaviour of prices in the face of a rapid rise in money supply in the recent past. What should be related to changes in money supply is not the increase in production but the increase in marketed supplies; and the latter increase much faster than the former in the event of good harvests. Marketed supplies have also been augmented by large imports. And the very tendency for prices to fall in some areas and get stabilized in general sets in motion expectations which reduce hoarding and the velocity of circulation of money. But what tends to be forgotten is that the reverse is also true—and for the same reasons. When harvests are not so good, prices tend to rise at a rate much faster than what one might conclude from trends in money supply. That is why so many statistical enquiries in this country have shown that while the short-term correlation between money supply and prices and production may not be good, over a period the relationship is very striking indeed.

I would, however, agree that in assessing the potential effects of an increase in money supply, the factors responsible for the increase have also to be taken into account. Thus, to the extent that money supply increase reflects building up of publicly controlled stocks of essential consumer goods or increase in foreign exchange reserves that can be quickly drawn upon to import essential requirements, the potential inflationary consequences are that much easier to avoid. But let it also be said then that from this point of view, one has to be more careful about increases in money supply resulting from unduly large budgetary deficits *and* from excessive credit expansion in favour of trade and industry. Nor should we assume that building up of buffer stocks or addition to foreign exchange reserves or for that matter budgetary deficits must necessarily lead to a corresponding increase in money supply. The objective of policy should be to mop up in the form of time deposits and the like at least a large part of the extra incomes corresponding to the higher sale of agricultural produce or the large receipt of remittances or the deficit in the budget so that the initial money-creating impact is to that extent neutralized.

Let me, therefore, say categorically that money supply does matter; and it makes sense always to ask whether it is increasing rapidly enough or too rapidly. It makes sense also to compare money supply trends with trends in production and also with trends in the recent past, making due allowance for other relevant factors. What must, however, be also said is that money supply is only an indicator of the demand pressures on the economy and you cannot increase or decrease money supply in some simple fashion as if you are turning on or turning off a tap of water. One has got to look at the underlying causes leading to an increase in money supply such as the forces making for a deficit in the budget or a surplus in external accounts and the factors that determine the net private demand for credit, which again have to be analysed in terms of savings patterns, assets preference and expectations regarding price changes and the like. Ultimately, money supply (and its velocity) can be influenced only by influencing these underlying factors and not by some simple manipulations of the balance sheets of the banking system just as fever can be brought down by attacking the root causes of infection and not by trying to manipulate the thermometer. As already implied at the outset, the fight against an excessive increase in money supply has also to be part of the general fight against inflation which has to be waged on other fronts as well. The pursuit of a sound monetary or credit policy, therefore, is not as simple or mechanical a matter as might be implied by the deceptive simplicity of the Quantity Theory of Money. As Mrs Joan Robinson told us long ago, "The Quantity Theory is not telling us anything; we are telling it."

In actual practice, monetary authorities face a number of dilemmas partly because not all the factors that influence money supply are under their control and in part because some of these factors are not easy to control anyway in the short run. And in the absence of quick or complete control, expectations are set in motion which make it more difficult to influence even the generally more amenable variables. If, for example, unavoidable budgetary deficits or foreign exchange surpluses tend to increase money supply to an extent which virtually exhausts the scope for reasonable monetary expansion, should the monetary authorities not meet the genuine needs of trade and industry? Or, should it meet these needs and thus consciously create—or be a party to the creation of—money supply in excess of safe limits? To put it differently, if budgetary and external account transactions generate extra purchasing power, on whom should the responsibility for mobilizing it be squarely put: on the banking system or on trade and industry both of which are direct beneficiaries of at least part of the extra purchasing power? If put together they are not able to mop up the extra purchasing power to the required extent, is it a lesser evil to create credit rather than to risk a curtailment of production? Or again, if one takes the easy way out in the short run, will not the mobilization efforts be further inhibited? Granted that there is legitimate scope for money or credit expansion or "deficit financing" in the aggregate, is there any way in which the legitimate share of the public and the private sector in it can be correctly defined and apportioned?

A similar problem or dilemma arises when prices tend to rise for what businessmen can with some justification claim are reasons beyond their control. Should one allow for these increases in reckoning their legitimate credit needs, or would this simply feed the fires of inflation? There are no simple answers to these questions; but they illustrate at least the difficulty of even defining what might be the correct monetary or credit policy at any given time. Compromises between different objectives become unavoidable in such an environment.

The task of monetary policy in India is rendered more difficult also by a number of institutional practices that have developed over recent years. Changes in interest rates are the main weapon in the armoury of monetary policy. But in India, interest rates have come to assume a certain degree of rigidity. At the same time, they also tend to get compartmentalized by convention or administrative decisions so that interest rate policy tends to lack flexibility and depth as well as pervasiveness. Thus, after the nationalization of banks, term deposits with banks have become a major instrument for mobilizing the savings of a vast section of society. This naturally creates resistance to any sharp change in deposit rates: they cannot be increased sharply out of fear that public opinion may not permit a corresponding reduction when circumstances are reversed, and vice versa. For reasons of promoting investment in industry and agriculture, and of late for helping the weaker sections, the emphasis in public policy is generally on keeping long-term rates low; and this makes it difficult to follow a flexible policy even in regard to short-term rates. The fact that the capital market is fairly compartmentalized or fragmented thanks to "captive" investors like banks and other financial institutions, as far as government securities are concerned, and other administrative controls on who can borrow, how much and at what rates of interest, makes it even more difficult to follow a consistent, let alone a flexible interest rate policy.

Even the other powerful instrument of monetary policy, viz., reserve requirements, has been put so much to the service of long-term developmental needs that little room for manoeuvre is left for modulating short-term trends. This leaves only selective credit controls where also the margin requirements have tended to get frozen at high levels and moral suasion, which even in a predominantly nationalized banking system is a difficult art to practise. Add to this the fact that under our system of cash credit limits which are generally high enough to permit almost chronic under-utilization, it is difficult for the banks with the best will in the world to bring about a turnaround over a short period. It has been urged by a number of experts for a long time that the cash credit system should be replaced with a loans system or by the discounting of bills if the quantum of credit is to be related more strictly to the genuine needs of industry and trade. It is medium- and large-scale trade and industry that has resisted this rational change; and I very much hope that this attitude will change as a result of efforts of Chambers like yours.

The existence of parallel or black markets and unorganized markets in money and credit also makes monetary policy that much more difficult to pursue in India. About the only factor which seems to help us in the pursuit of an appropriate monetary policy, in comparison with most other countries, is our policy of virtual isolation from international capital markets.

I have emphasized this environment which inhibits the pursuit of a very active monetary policy in India to make it clear that the complaints one often hears about trade and industry suffering from too restrictive a monetary or credit policy are difficult to take at face value. The truth of the matter is that we need more instruments and some reorientation of the general policy framework if monetary policy in India is to have a real bite.

To turn now to some of the longer-term aspects of monetary and credit policy, the fact that the commanding heights on the financial scene are now virtually all occupied by the public sector has, while securing major advantages for the nation, raised new questions that have yet to be fully resolved. A major question is a proper line of demarcation between the responsibility of the banking system for the provision of long-term finance as distinct from meeting the needs of working capital. Since the banks now mobilize a large volume of term deposits, it is reasonable to expect them to provide long-term loans to industry and agriculture in addition to subscription to government bonds. But should there not be a limit to the total of such long-term exposure? I am afraid it would not be appropriate to define this limit on the analogy of the nature of the deposits banks mobilize and stipulate that short-term deposits should be used for working capital and term deposits for long-term finance. Apart from definitional problems, in a growing volume of deposits what is likely to be withdrawn and what is not is not an easy question to answer. In theory, the answer has to be need based; but that raises a whole set of questions regarding needs.

Another familiar but vexing problem is that of drawing a correct line of responsibility between the budget and the financial institutions. How much of policy-determined buffer stocks should be financed by banks and how much by budgetary resources? Granted that banks must finance a part of public investment, can the responsibility of the banks be defined more precisely by laying down some precise guidelines? It is not surprising that harassed state governments appoint commissioners or special officers to deal with financial institutions. Nor is it surprising that they try to bring even cooperative institutions more and more under their control for the same purpose. But all this places a responsibility of adjudicating and monitoring on monetary authorities which is difficult to discharge for want of both adequate and clearly assigned authority as well as guidelines or principles which are credible as well as sensible. But an attempt nevertheless has to be made.

It is, I think, against this general background that there has been emphasis on credit planning for some time, that is, on allocation of credit as well as on the total quantum of expansion that can safely be permitted. The Planning Commission has also rightly been emphasizing that the annual budgetary plans should be dovetailed with credit plans of financial institutions. This is an enormous but necessary task which assumes, apart from timely information, a certain acceptance of discipline on the part of all concerned. One must also avoid the danger that plans often have of introducing one-way rigidity: if more resources are needed, there is the presumption that they must be somehow provided; but if more resources are not forthcoming, it is not easy to cut down earlier allocations. But even apart from the danger of a tendency towards over-expansion, it would be better first to outline some general principles or guidelines based on rational or analytical considerations regarding the respective roles of fiscal agencies and financial institutions. Otherwise, credit planning which proceeds entirely from needs and seeks to ration available funds on some ad hoc notions of what is unavoidable or of immediate priority would lead to protracted and difficult negotiations.

Similar problems arise even in relation to bank credit to private organized industry. You will recall that the Dehejia Committee was set up in 1969 to define what part of the needs of organized industry should be met from internal resources and what part from banks. Later, the Tandon Committee attempted to define norms for working capital requirements. When it comes to term loans, the question of priorities in accordance with Plan targets becomes equally relevant. There is also the need to ensure that large and privileged borrowers do not corner an unduly high share of available credit resources. It is in order to ensure that all these norms and guidelines or objectives are properly observed or realized that we have subjected now for quite some time—in fact since 1965—large credit limits to prior authorization from the Reserve Bank. Recently, we have reviewed and liberalized the scheme; and I can assure you that we have tightened our internal monitoring system to ensure that no unreasonable delays take place. The delays often take place because of lack of timely and complete information; and we have circulated a list of the most common shortcomings in this regard to ensure better compliance by banks as well as industry. We have also set up machinery for introducing necessary flexibility from time to time in the norms that we apply. We need your cooperation in complying with the requirements of information; and we on our part will consider any suggestions you have for the improvement of the scheme. But please remember that the scheme will be there as it is an essential and indeed a minimum component of credit planning. Remember also that it applies to you as well as to the public sector. I am afraid even the banks also have not fully understood the need for this scheme; and this often creates problems for their customers as many subsequent delays could be avoided if the banks properly instruct their clients at the outset. I have heard from many industrial managers that they have in fact found the scheme useful as a means of economizing on unnecessary inventories and hence on interest charges. I trust that it is for associations like this Chamber to make it clear to its members that observance of financial discipline is a social as well as private virtue.

Speaking in more general terms, there has to be at least one qualification to what we often hear nowadays, viz., that we need to pursue in this country the policy of a higher rate of economic growth without being bogged down by any doctrinaire considerations. If we don't like an ideal, we sometimes call it an ideology; and if we do not like an objective, we sometimes call it a doctrine. But by whatever name we call it, there has to be a general framework of values within which all our endeavours have to be rooted. From this point of view, the accent of our policy has to be not only on growth but also on greater equality, on the poorest and the hitherto neglected receiving the highest priority, on Antyodaya, on Unto the Last, if you like.

That is why monetary and credit policy also has to play an active role in reducing inequality—not only as between individuals but also as between regions, groups and the different communities that have historically enjoyed opportunities on a different scale. That is why we have to set targets for rural credit, for branches in rural areas, for credit to priority sectors, for an appropriate share for the poor and the scheduled castes or tribes even in the priority sectors, for weaker groups who should get credit at differential rates, for promotion of employment and similar other objectives that satisfy not only the criterion of equality but also help to integrate emotionally our nation where a thousand flowers do indeed bloom but many of whom wilt even before their prime. All this does mean some curtailment—not absolutely but relatively—in the predominant share that organized industry and trade has hitherto enjoyed in bank credit. And you as leaders of business opinion must accept this as a challenge and not as a threat.

We have no illusions that by adopting merely targets for credit to the weaker sections, we shall put them on the path to self-reliance and an assured means of livelihood. A great deal of effort is needed to create new investment opportunities for them, to train them and educate them in new processes, to help them with marketing facilities and in many other ways; for credit alone cannot achieve anything. Equally, even to the poor and the weak, credit can only be given for worthwhile projects which can yield sufficient livelihood as well as surplus for repayment. There can be no real progress unless credit is truly creative and revolving. In all this, the business community can play a very useful role in partnership, if necessary, with the banking system.

CHAPTER 5

Monetary Policy Revisited*

Preliminary Remarks

I should perhaps begin with a confession. My main reason for visiting once again the mystical territory of Central Banking is a personal one. It was more than six years ago that I left the Central Banking scene. You will, therefore, appreciate that I am suffering somewhat from the onset of the seven-year itch. During much of the past several years, I have lived in the United Kingdom where, as in most industrial countries, there has been much talk of the revival of monetary policy in a climate of some fundamental changes in technology and ideology, if not in economic perception and circumstance. The resultant changes in economic policy and in the general economic climate, however, seem to have changed the context in which monetary policy has to operate to such an extent that, paradoxically, the faith in monetary policy is already beginning to wane to some extent. Is some consensus on the role of monetary policy likely to emerge from the dust and din of recent controversies?

At any rate, does the recent experience of industrial countries have any relevance to developing countries? One cannot dismiss this question as irrelevant simply because there are obvious differences between industrial and developing countries as indeed among each of the two groups of countries. Economic phenomena have a way of raising their ugly head in all kinds of places, at all odd times; and there is, if you like, the tendency to follow the trend in the rich or, in a minority of cases, to shun such a

* Speech given at the London School of Economics and Political Science, the 41st International Banking Summer School, organized by the Reserve Bank of India, New Delhi, September 1988; subsequently published as a booklet by the Reserve Bank of India in 1988.

trend perversely. Distressingly, and often enough, such imitation begins when the trend among the more successful is already beginning to bend. Keynes may or may not have been right when he said that practical men, who believe themselves to be quite exempt from any intellectual influences, are usually the slave of some defunct economist. But practical men are prone certainly to the herd instinct, either because misery loves company or, perhaps, because there is safety in numbers. There have also been of late far-reaching monetary developments at least in some of the developing countries, particularly in the debt-ridden countries. It might be interesting, therefore, at the present juncture to look at the evolution of monetary policy in recent years with one eye so to speak on the developed countries and the other on developing ones.

Trends in Industrial Countries

Shifts in monetary policy, like those in all economic policy, are a reflection of changing ideology, perception and objective circumstances. The precise line of demarcation between theory, philosophy and objective or exogenous phenomena is difficult to draw. But at the risk of some oversimplification one can outline the recent conjuncture in the United Kingdom and in most industrial countries as follows:

(i) *Inflation* has come to occupy the *pride of place among the objectives* of economic policy. I doubt if practical men ever define their preference function or even admit that there is such a thing as a trade-off between different objectives. But clearly, there has been a shift of emphasis: from achievement of full employment to control of inflation—a shift, I hasten to add, which is not of so much relevance to developing countries where the control of inflation has been more or less a perennial preoccupation and where the problem of employment has always been seen as an aspect of long-term economic growth rather than of short-term economic management. As far as the trade-off between growth and control of inflation is concerned, there has, I think, been common ground now for quite some time in developing as well as developed countries that there is no trade-off here but a virtuous circle where growth and control of inflation mutually reinforce each other.

(ii) Again, at the level of objectives, *emphasis* has *shifted from short-term management to longer-term growth* in industrialized countries: from demand management to supply-side economics, if you like, or from macro to micro economic management—although I think it is a mistake to reduce problems of growth to the level merely of efficiency in the allocation of given resources as is commonly implied in microeconomic management. The term "supply-side economics", to my mind, captures better the essence of the process of growth. But here again, the developing countries at any rate should have no difficulty in understanding the shift. Basically, the emphasis in supply-side economics is the same as what economists in developing countries have long emphasized, viz., problems of development, which consist largely of removing rigidities and reducing structural weaknesses while maintaining a proper environment of incentives for work, enterprise, saving, investment and economic efficiency in general.

(iii) *Paradoxically*, the *reduction in emphasis on short-term demand management* (which is often described as the final negation of Keynesianism) *seems to apply asymmetrically* only in one direction: while it is vigorously asserted that you cannot increase activity or employment by raising demand, there is equally firm belief that inflation can be curtailed by controlling demand. As far as anti-inflationary policies are concerned, there is no difference between so-called Monetarists and Keynesians as to the need for reducing demand; the difference, if at all, is about the instruments or policies to be applied for reducing demand. And even here, the ideological belief of so-called Monetarists in the need for reducing the size of the public sector in practice leads to greater reliance on fiscal policy through a reduction in the public sector borrowing requirement than on any change in monetary policy. Indeed, it is possible to argue that it is not just President Reagan who has been a Keynesian in practice for following an expansionary fiscal policy. Mrs Thatcher has been a Keynesian too in that she has relied essentially on fiscal policy to rein in demand and inflation, whereas monetary policy despite all the fanfare and monetary targeting for a while has been a minor sideshow or shadow play. There is certainly a moral here for developing countries.

(iv) Again, while a great deal of homage is paid to *monetary policy* and monetary management in industrialized countries, this is essentially in the context of inflation or the exchange rate, and not *in the context of growth*. Monetary policy has little or no place in the lexicon of supply-side economics. This is not surprising as the financial system in developed countries, if anything, is a little too sophisticated and overdeveloped. But developing countries can hardly afford to take this stance. Central Banks in India and Nigeria have an important role to play in promoting development. You have explored this area in other sessions and I do not want to say much about this today. But apart from the role of the Central Bank in promoting the growth of a diversified financial structure, in creating confidence in it through various devices like supervision and deposit insurance or financial pump-priming and in influencing lending in healthy and desirable directions, there are other considerations more directly related to the traditional concerns of monetary policy which are relevant here.

It is arguable, for example, that in developing countries, where entrepreneurship is weak and capacity to assume and assess risks very limited, there is a strong case for a greater degree of stability in the interest rate structure as indeed in the exchange rate at least in real terms. This may mean that a *good monetary policy* in developing countries may well be one of *great self-restraint.*

Equally, while real interest rates on an average have to be positive to stimulate savings as well as to ration investment efficiently, it has to be recognized that too high a real rate of interest may be totally out of line with the profitability of available investment opportunities in the short run, so that it might choke off not just risk capital but all or most of investment. Alternatively, it could breed losses on a scale that would necessitate neutralizing high interest charges by subsidies in other forms. *Short-term monetary policy* in developing countries cannot thus be pursued without *due regard for* these *longer-term considerations.*

(v) Apart from the primacy of controlling inflation and reducing the size of the government, there has been a general preference among industrialized countries for the free operation of market forces and resistance to government intervention or regulation of all kinds. This has been the inspiration for the abolition of exchange controls and for the deregulation of the financial system which, together with the profound improvement in information technology, have led to a number of financial innovations like securitization of borrowing by major national and international firms. These developments have had a serious impact on the conduct of monetary policy in industrial countries. Thus the general belief in the free and unfettered operation of market forces means that monetary authorities have for all practical purposes discarded several of their traditional instruments. The Bank of England, for example, has given up the use of reserve requirements and no longer tries to influence the quantum of credit directly through rationing its own refinance, or to moderate particular areas of credit like mortgage finance. For all practical purposes, it relies only on the price of its refinance, that is, on interest rates at the short-end, although occasionally it has relied on what is rather infelicitously called over-funding—which I presume is nothing other than our old friend open-market operations in another guise. Even in Italy, where the tradition of more detailed direct control of bank credit was more established, there has been a rapid advance towards controls of a more general nature.

It is true that in response to the greater exposure to risks when interest rates and exchange rates change more often and more sharply, there has been a renewed attempt to prescribe capital adequacy requirements. But on the whole, even *monetary targeting* has become more of *a ritual* than a reality and monetary policy has operated through changes in interest rates which soon get reflected in changes in exchange rates so that it becomes difficult to follow any kind of harmonious monetary and exchange rate policy in one country without some harmonization of monetary and exchange rate policy at least among countries among which capital moves freely. Since such harmonization is far from being a reality and cannot in any case be perfect, and since expectations play a major role in the determination of interest and exchange rates in integrated financial markets, both interest rates and exchange rates have become very volatile and are often out of line with longer-term parameters of desirability. Is there any moral in this for developing countries? Can they or should they rely on monetary targeting? Should they abandon all instruments of monetary policy other than the interest rate? How can they best reconcile monetary and exchange rate policy?

(vi) It is interesting to note that, apart from the ideology of laissez-faire and developments in financial markets, some of the *theoretical refinements of recent years* also argue in favour of a less active role for monetary policy. It is clearly not possible to note here all the theoretical strands in any great detail. But three developments may be noted. In the ultimate analysis, the *Friedmanite* advocacy of a *fixed and firm rule* of monetary expansion is based not so much on belief in any particular functional relationship between money supply and national income as on lack of belief in any monetary authority having the ability to determine how much monetary expansion may be needed from time to time—lack of belief, in other words, in fine-tuning or evening out of short-period fluctuations. Whether or not one believes that a fixed and firm rate of monetary expansion is feasible, let alone desirable, there is undoubtedly merit in the point that several kinds of short-term fluctuations are better left alone or dealt with by means other than monetary policy. As we shall notice later, it is possible to put more burden on monetary policy than it can bear and it is important to remind ourselves, particularly in developing countries, of the *dangers of fine-tuning* and of the merits of a more or less *steady course* over time in the interest of creating a stable climate of expectations.

On a theoretical plane, another recent development is the hypothesis of rational expectations which is pretty nihilistic as far as its implications for policy are concerned. If policy measures are fully anticipated and their impact correctly foreseen, there is little or no scope for policy as private operators will so adjust their behaviour as to neutralize anything that goes against their own preferences. Whatever may be the logical validity of proceeding from such a hypothesis or its realism, the fact remains that policies are not made in a climate of passive acceptance and that expectations and anticipations play an important part. In order to generate the right expectations and establish credibility, a monetary authority may be tempted to announce some predetermined target or rule. But when something can be fully anticipated, it can be got around also. Monetary authorities are thus constrained to create an air of mystery around them, to keep their options open but their mouths shut, to pronounce the virtues of discretionary and, therefore, discrete policy changes. But this creates the risk of disbelief or of setting in motion perverse expectations. There is no escape from this dilemma.

The third strand of theoretical nature which may be noted goes back in a way to *the Radcliffe Committee Report* and relates to the fact that money is only one among many financial assets each differing only marginally from others in respect of yield and liquidity or credit and market risk. Current developments such as globalization of capital markets, securitization of loans and other financial innovations have vastly increased the range and substitutability of financial instruments so that monetary policy which influences only one end of the spectrum, viz., commercial banks, cannot be very effective in influencing the general liquidity of the economy and the level of aggregate demand except insofar as it raises the general level of interest rates. But apart from the limited impact of changes in interest rates on demand, the impact of monetary policy on interest rates in general is also diluted by the range of financial markets and instruments. Although these considerations may appear to be less relevant for developing countries, where financial innovations have not reached the same proportions, there are other institutional factors like informal credit markets, extensive black economy and external leakages which argue the other way.

The foregoing brief review of recent developments in monetary theory and practice in developed countries suggests that despite the apparent revival of monetary policy in these countries, the reality perhaps is that monetary policy has been relegated to a more modest role in the industrialized world. It is at any rate confined to what might be called harmonization of interest rate and exchange rate policy which as yet remains difficult of achievement. The primary responsibility for the control of inflation, which has undoubtedly been achieved, has been that of fiscal policy assisted at times by overvalued exchange rates and often by high rates of unemployment and measures to reduce trade union power.

Currently, and speaking only of the UK, there are, nevertheless, several question marks about the future evolution of economic policy. Should not the current boom in consumer credit be more directly controlled, say, through restrictions on mortgage credit? Is not excessive reliance on interest rate policy pushing up the exchange rate to the detriment of the balance-of-payments and Britain's competitive power and, therefore, undermining future levels of employment? Even without this future threat to employment, the recent modest increase in employment seems to be resulting in wage settlements exceeding productivity growth so that, together with the large increase in consumer credit, there is a resurgence of inflationary pressures. What is the appropriate response to this? A return to deflation of the 1979–1981 variety? Some kind of incomes policy? A further reduction in government expenditure? A reversal of cuts in direct taxes or an increase in indirect taxes? A more direct and more interventionist monetary policy? Or indeed, a further move to emasculate monetary policy, say, by questioning even the need for the Central Bank to offer any refinance or to be a lender of last resort in a financial emergency? It is not our purpose to try and answer these questions with reference to the UK. The point to note, before we have a closer look at monetary policy in developing countries, is that even in developed countries the jury is still out and the appropriate policy mix has yet to settle down.

If there is any strong, surviving strand, it is to emphasize longer-term or real factors such as productivity or efficiency, savings and incentives and enterprise as distinguished from monetary or financial manipulation. This is, in fact, music to the ears of orthodox development economists or even classical economists. But alas, the financial web is very much around us, and is absolutely essential. The only question is whether financial and other markets can be made so to behave as not to distort unduly the nexus between current market prices and desirable as well as feasible longer-term adjustment. But our knowledge of what a desirable and feasible adjustment might be, and what might bring it about, will never be certain or perfect. Does this argue for a less interventionist monetary policy, smoothing out, on an average, excessive variations but leaving trends alone, without worrying about whether such trends are consistent with fundamental forces? Or is a more interventionist but harmonized policy in order to reinforce what might be perceived as basic or fundamental trends? This is still an unresolved question for the developed world, and is by no means irrelevant for the developing countries.

Monetary Policy in Developing Countries

We may now turn to developing countries and the lessons for monetary policy they can draw from the recent experience of their own and that of developed countries. The discussion will be organized around: (a) value and importance of monetary targeting; (b) use of a flexible interest rate policy as distinct from a policy of administered interest rates; (c) importance of quantitative and selective instruments and other forms of direct credit controls; (d) value of monetary policy in absorbing shocks; (e) interaction between monetary and exchange policy; (f) recent stabilization efforts, particularly after rapidly accelerating inflation; and (g) transition from extensive public ownership and economic controls to greater freedom.

Monetary Targeting

It is now generally accepted that the primary role of monetary policy in developing countries is to facilitate economic growth with a reasonable stability in prices. Stability is sometimes construed to include external viability also. But balance-of-payments is more a constraint than an objective; and it makes sense to interpret stability broadly as control of inflation or keeping the general price level from rising by more than a few percentage points per year, say, by more than 4 or 5 per cent per year. Regarding a rise of this order as reasonable has no intrinsic merit, although it is sometimes argued that it is necessary to permit required changes in relative prices. In truth, it is only recognition of reality as in practice very few countries manage to do as well. But once, more and more countries achieve low rates of inflation, it should be feasible to aim at even lower rates; and it has to be regarded as a major achievement of recent years that it is no longer considered unthinkable to aim at zero rate of inflation on an average such as what has prevailed in fact over much of the industrial era.

For achieving stability, it is generally considered necessary to keep the growth of money supply in step with the demand for it, which is assumed to be uniquely related to national income, at any rate over the medium term and when due allowance is made for secular changes such as those arising from growing monetization of the economy. This line of reasoning has led in practice to some version of monetary targeting in developed as well as developing countries, often encouraged by stabilization programmes initiated under IMF or World Bank auspices. As early as 1953, an IMF mission to India had recommended such a practice which has recently found support also from the Chakravarty Committee set up to review the working of monetary policy in India.

Despite the general support and indeed practice of monetary targeting as a necessary instrument for achieving and maintaining stability, criticism of this approach is also heard often; and in practice, departures from monetary targets are so common as to warrant the suspicion that monetary targets are of no more than cosmetic value at best. Some of the criticism of monetary targeting, however, is certainly beside the mark. It can be easily shown, for example, that the velocity of circulation of money or the income elasticity of demand for money is not constant over relatively short periods of time. But there is some relationship which can be calculated as being reasonably stable over a period and it can be assumed, at least as a first approximation, that it is what is likely to prevail in the near future. No one in the realm of practical politics recommends a strict monetary target—a la Friedman or otherwise. Most such targets are set as a range and there is always the admonition that monetary targets must be kept under review. The Chakravarty Committee thus speaks of monetary targets with a feedback. What needs perhaps to be emphasized is that monetary targeting should not lead to constant tinkering with monetary policy so as to counteract every deviation from the target set. Such tinkering or fine-tuning can be destabilizing and counterproductive. But systematic and large deviations from monetary targets already set should serve as a signal for reviewing policy.

The criticism that monetary targeting, while necessary, is not sufficient is of course valid, and it was echoed long ago by Joan Robinson when she said pithily that the Quantity Theory is not telling us anything, we are telling it. If money supply is deemed to be excessive, it is not enough to say, reduce it. One has to analyse how the excess comes about—whether it originates from the budget or from the external sector or from the operations of the private sector. Apart from that, one has to chart the consequences of the precise measures adopted to remove the excess. To put it differently, monetary targeting makes sense only if the permissible increase in money supply is correctly distributed between the legitimate claims of the budget, the private sector and the country's need for foreign exchange reserves. But surely advocates of monetary targeting are aware of this and in fact monetary or credit budgeting is generally attempted on a disaggregated basis. Indeed, it can be claimed as a merit of monetary targeting that it focuses attention on a proper mix of budgetary, monetary and foreign exchange policy.

This is not to say that it is easy to apportion the permissible increase in money supply between the budget, the private sector and the external sector. One can say that as an economy grows and its external trade expands, it will need more foreign exchange reserves and this should have the first priority in the allocation of the permissible increase in money supply. I have not encountered any exercise in monetary targeting that explicitly states this. Much of the debate centres on allocation between the public and the private sector. The bias in developed countries now is to underplay the needs of the public sector—witness the drive to reduce and even to eliminate the public sector in the United Kingdom. In most developing countries there is a tendency to put the needs of the public sector before those of the private sector—witness the Chakravarty Committee which lists among the functions of the Reserve Bank the provision of the urgent needs of the government without any reference to the competing claims of the private sector. And yet, the Chakravarty Committee has to recognize that the Reserve Bank cannot perform its developmental role properly unless it assumes responsibility for the establishment of a diversified financial structure that supports the borrowing and lending needs of the private sector. Part of this responsibility can be discharged by the Central Bank directly providing resources to credit institutions that support the private sector. But I doubt if any *a priori* rule about how much of a Central Bank's assets should be in foreign exchange reserves and how much in claims on government and how much in claims on the private sector including claims on developmental financial institutions can be laid down. The nearest one can come to it is to say that the relative importance of the public and private sector in national productive investment should be borne in mind and some room must be left for the accumulation of foreign exchange reserves.

I find it difficult also to believe that it is a decisive objection to monetary targeting to point out that it is difficult to prescribe a precise boundary for "money" when there are so many near substitutes for money. It is also true that money which is easy to control (for example, reserve money) may not be in the most stable relationship with national money income. But the point is that as long as monetary targeting is used only as a significant indicator and not as a rigid framework, there is nothing wrong in watching trends in money supply as variously defined and interpreting the trends in the light of all the facts currently available. Indeed, any sensible economic analysis which must precede any policy decision must include the analysis of monetary and financial developments; and analysis implies, at least in part, comparison with some standard or target.

The criticism of monetary targeting I find more acceptable is the one which starts by pointing out that monetary targets at best are intermediate targets and the policy response to them has to be discretionary rather than rule based. If this is so, why bother about intermediate targets instead of looking at the ultimate targets or constraints for signals or indications? If the objective is price stability and external viability, one can look simply at trends in prices and balance-of-payments and analyse them and wield such instruments of policy as may appear relevant in the light of this analysis. Indeed, concentrating too much on an intermediate target like stocks of money is not just second-best; it may even be misleading as it may narrow the focus on monetary factors and lead to the overlooking of other factors. For example, current pressures on prices may be the result of interruptions in key supplies, or due to wages exceeding productivity increases, or due to some external shock rather than the result of excessive demand resulting from excessive credit creation. A strictly monetary response in such cases, as we hope to argue later, may be worse than useless.

There is a great deal of merit in this line of reasoning. But let us also remember that it only reminds us that mere analysis of monetary trends and setting of monetary targets may not be sufficient. It does not say they are not necessary. Undoubtedly, it is useful to remind ourselves that the starting point should be the final goals of price stability and balance-of-payments viability and not some intermediate and approximate indicators such as money supply which may be relevant as a part of the analysis as well as of the cure but are never the full story. To put it differently, one should speak of monetary targeting only in a minor key. Strident tones are seldom appropriate when we speak of monetary policy in any case.

There is another valid criticism of monetary targeting which is of an analytical character, viz., that for an indication of inflationary pressures and their cure, it is better to think in terms of the familiar Keynesian categories of budget deficits, current account deficits, and the difference between private savings and investment. In other words, the significant question is not the allocation of the permissible increase in money supply between the public and the private sector (abstracting for the moment from the external sector). The significant question is the allocation of available savings, or who crowds out whose investment and how. Merely talking of money creation or money supply obscures this fact. From the economic point of view what is most relevant is whether the budget deficit in the sense of the budget's claim on the community's savings is too large or too small and not whether, given the size of this deficit too large or too small a portion of this is financed by the Central Bank or by the banking system as a whole. If the Central Bank is not accommodating, interest rates will rise and crowd out private investment to accommodate the unduly large budget deficit. If the Central Bank is accommodating, the crowding out will take place through the inflation tax which will divert available savings under duress to the public sector. In either case, the damage done by fiscal imprudence will remain. It is, I think, important to emphasize that if the basic budgetary position is not right, it cannot be set right by monetary policy. It has to be set right by action on the fiscal front itself. But if the fiscal front is set right, so to speak, monetary policy can be relaxed. Given fiscal prudence, an active monetary policy is not necessary. (Without such prudence, it is of little avail.) In most developing countries, inflationary pressures arise from the operations of the budget rather than from any upsurge in credit to the private sector. Monetary policy cannot really correct this situation—it can at best bring home more effectively the consequences of imprudent public finance. Whether it does so through rocketing interest rates or rising prices is not of much comfort or consequence except perhaps to ideologues.

Having said this, it is as well to remember that where interest rates are controlled or administered and where the Central Bank virtually underwrites budgetary deficits as is the case in almost all developing countries, the savings and investment approach and the monetary targeting approach come to virtually the same thing. And the monetary approach has at least the advantage that monetary data are more readily available so that they are a better or more feasible basis for *ex ante* planning as well as for monitoring. I would, therefore, advocate analysis in savings/investment terms in addition to monetary targeting rather than instead of it.

But monetary targeting in the ultimate analysis is as good as the integrity with which such targets are set and adhered to. Can the Central Bank and the government come to a reasonable understanding on how much deficit financing is reasonable and can the government be made to stick to its part of the bargain? If experience is any guide, the answer to this must largely be in the negative. The danger, therefore, is that having set the targets, the subservient partner is often made to dance unnecessarily and unproductively to the tune of excess money creation which is vainly sought to be controlled by an activist monetary policy which at best can control the secondary effects of excessive budget deficits. Each exercise of an activist monetary policy becomes irreversible in practice because as long as budgetary policy is inflationary, any relaxation of monetary restraint will be open to criticism. The result is that there is a kind of ratchet effect whereby interest rates, reserve requirements and all the rest keep going up and monetary instruments in effect become blunt and arbitrary in their impact on private investment and activity. And yet, the monetary authority, which is flattered into being assigned a major role in maintaining stability, is made to flex its muscles in vain and to make more or less empty gestures of action most of the time. It would be better to make it clear that the major responsibility for maintaining stability in developing countries is that of fiscal policy and that monetary policy at best has a subordinate role. Its actions, therefore, should be muted and more self-restrained.

Can monetary authorities in developing countries be given greater leeway to control budgetary trends? I doubt if Central Banks in developing countries can be even moderately independent. To prescribe rules for budgetary behaviour such as ceilings on government debt or limits on Central Bank support to government securities is hardly likely to work either. Even if practicable, such steps may hinder the orderly development of a market for government securities. In the ultimate analysis, there is no alternative to the good sense of the people in power and the pressure of public opinion. It might nevertheless be desirable at least to try and set some norms for the government budget and for debt management. Thus, as a minimum, there should be no borrowing to finance current expenditure. Commercial banks should not be forced to take up government securities beyond a certain proportion of their liabilities and this proportion should not be changed except after relatively long intervals. This proportion is generally fixed in response to prudential considerations. But it may also keep in mind the legitimate share of the public sector in available savings and may, for example, be related to interest-bearing deposits and be fixed, bearing in mind the proportion that such deposits bear to total financial savings and the government's share in investment. It is also worth considering whether norms cannot be fixed for Central Bank support for government securities—such norms are implicit in monetary targeting in any case, and it may be worthwhile to make them explicit over a number of years ahead. But in the ultimate analysis, norms are norms and cannot be binding particularly in countries where the market for government securities outside the banking system is rather thin; and the credibility of norms will depend on how closely they are observed.

Interest Rate Policy

Two questions are central in any discussion of interest rate policy in developing countries. First, on an average and over a longer term, how high should the real rate of interest be in order to best provide the maximum possible incentive for savings without unduly inhibiting investment? And second, should the system of administered interest rates that prevail in most developing countries be given up in order to restore to interest rates their normal function of correcting short-term or medium-term fluctuations in demand? Much confusion often arises in discussions of interest rate policy from failure to distinguish between these two aspects.

There is, of course, no model or formulae which can give us the correct long-term equilibrium real rate of interest for any country at any given time. Wisdom on this matter is often confined to asserting that the real rate of interest should be positive or/and to arguing each time the question comes up as a practical matter that it should be raised because currently there is imbalance between supply and demand for savings as evidenced by the general scarcity of resources in the system. The admonition to keep real interest rates positive on an average, while valid, does not tell us much. For it does not tell us how high is high enough and no more. Any opinion expressed on this matter is highly subjective, and I for one would put my money on a real rate of interest of about 3 per cent per annum—maybe because I consider it sufficient that the real value of savings should double in about twenty-five years. As for appealing always to the scarcity of capital as some of our international institutions do, the argument surely is a dangerous one as it would imply raising interest rates every time one looks at them.

One question that is not often discussed is that of risk. If we are to talk of a long-term equilibrium real rate of interest, it is presumably inclusive of some risk premium for the lenders. It is precisely this problem of reducing the risk premium that is most germane in developing countries. Surely, if risks are reduced at great administrative and other expense by deposit insurance and nationalization of banks and the like, this should be taken account of in determining the rates to be offered to the savers. Equally, the Central Bank can reduce credit risk for financial agencies such as banks by providing training facilities as well as by laying down some norms for assessing the credit-worthiness of firms as well as of individual credit proposals.

But apart from credit risk, there is the market risk that arises from variability in interest rates; and it is not often emphasized that in developing countries, where there is greater aversion to risk as well as less ability to assess risks, there is a strong case for avoiding excessive variability in interest rates as an instrument for stabilization—an argument which is often behind the prevalence of administered interest rates in developing countries. I remember that in my childhood we were all taught that money doubles every twelve years as if it was on par with the proposition that two plus two equals four. I learnt later that in all personal loans at least within the family, a 6 per cent compound rate was paid even when nothing was put down on paper. A fixed rate of interest even in nominal terms was thus accepted as one of the constraints of an orderly social life. Unfortunately, the element of "stability" is often lost sight of in much discussion of stabilization nowadays.

Apart from this general consideration, the standard arguments about the relative ineffectiveness of interest rates remain. I find it difficult to believe that governments would be less profligate because they have to pay higher rates of interest. Nor can I believe that outside banks and other financial institutions there could be much of a market for government securities in most developing countries. For financial prudence, no kind of monetary policy or interstate policy can be a substitute. As for curtailing credit to the private sector in times of inflationary expectations, changes in interest rates will have to be very large to be effective; and unfortunately, once raised, interest rates are difficult to bring down in most developing countries. Without ruling out some use of the interest rate instrument, I am on the whole inclined to urge caution in its use.

The concept of competition in interest rates—which administered rates generally rule out—should also be embraced with great caution. There is more likely to be collusion rather than competition in developing countries where the financial structure is generally rather thin. Despite the blandishment of many, this situation is not likely to be remedied by a large presence of foreign banks as I doubt if they would bring much money from abroad—and the little they bring will be denominated as a debt in some foreign currency so that it is akin to short-term borrowing abroad. This is the one kind of foreign borrowing that should be avoided as it is the one that can abandon you most speedily and convert a balance-of-payments difficulty into an immediate crisis.

This is not to say that a system of administered rates needs to be totally inflexible or that it cannot admit competition in certain areas or indeed that it may need no simplification. Like all controls, administered interest rates also tend to multiply; and it is certainly true that the system should be reviewed from time to time with a view to ensuring that the relatively fixed points are few and the most crucial ones. I would thus feel that stability in interest rates in real terms for small savings and for term rates of banks is more important among the rates offered to savers. For borrowers, perhaps a maximum for bank lending is the most relevant.

There is one more point that needs to be made on interest rates and that is to emphasize that interest is a cost and its use in controlling inflation has at least some of the weakness that we attach to indirect taxes as a means of controlling inflation. Businessmen always make this point. But its obvious validity is seldom recognized by policymakers, presumably because interest cost is not reflected in most indices of wholesale or consumer prices.

It would, of course, be reflected if we had an index of production cost for industry—and sooner or later, it must get reflected in other indices as well. In the UK, in fact, where mortgage costs are reflected in consumer price indices, this effect of interest rate changes seldom escapes notice. But it needs to be noticed in developing countries as well.

Quantitative and Direct Controls

Given our contention that the practice of monetary targeting can be moderately useful as long as the more basic factors affecting prices and balance-of-payments are kept in mind and given our disinclination to endorse a very active use of the interest rate weapon, we would certainly not advocate that Central Banks in developing countries should follow the Bank of England and give up all quantitative and direct controls such as those exercised through reserve requirements for banks and at times by way of restrictions on particular types of credit or indeed on total bank credit. But equally, given our general view that the major culprit in generating inflationary pressures in developing countries is the public sector, we would not favour an over-active use of monetary policy of any kind as there is danger of monetary authorities creating a great deal of uncertainty and disturbance by heroic gestures of fighting the wrong battles in order to please their errant masters.

A flexible use of reserve requirements can help in minimizing the secondary impact of excessive fiscal deficits, and it can also help stave off private speculative booms. I would, however, emphasize once again, bearing the Indian situation in mind, that what should be used flexibly is the Cash Reserve Ratio and not the Statutory Liquidity Requirement, which must be kept stable over long periods to reflect its longer-term rationale, or prudential reserves, and a legitimate share for the government in the longer-term savings that it helps the banking system to mobilize. In a sense, marginal reserve requirements would have a greater impact in the short run, but there is often an undesirable tendency to keep them on for ever or to translate them into average terms (which comes to the same thing for the system as a whole) lest any reversal might be criticized as ill timed or inflationary. The device of making marginal reserve requirements time bound (or terminated for each bank when it reaches some previously announced target) is worthy of consideration.

The effectiveness of changes in reserve requirements will to some extent be felt through changes in interest rates, as even in a regime of administered rates of interest some interest rates will be determined freely in some of the credit markets like the informal or the black economy markets. But this does not mean that administered interest rates dilute the impact of quantitative restrictions. I have never understood why limiting the supply of credit—whether to the government or to the private sector—cannot in itself be sufficient to curtail the aggregate demand and why this latter effect should work only through interest rates. If we are operating in imperfect markets, there is no point in relying on traditional perfect market paradigms for explanations as long as we remember also that imperfection of competition is not total absence of competition either.

Direct credit controls either over credit as a whole or for particular purposes are less likely to stick in practice except insofar as they translate themselves into general tightening of credit. Also, in the absence of any credible system of punishment for violation, the effectiveness of direct controls depends essentially on moral suasion. But moral suasion can be a moderately effective measure provided it is used in moderation and provided the Central Bank maintains effective personal contacts with other financial institutions; and while I would use direct controls very sparingly, I would not rule out regular dialogues between the Central Bank and the major financial institutions to work out some general credit guidelines even on an informal basis. I would only urge that such guidelines should not be given too frequently; not more than once a year as a rule, and preferably only as urgently required as, otherwise, there is danger of too much activity on the part of the Central Bank.

There is also the danger that in order to make its credit policy more effective, the Central Bank is led on to interference in matters which are better left alone or allowed to evolve without interference. Does the system of overdraft or credit ceilings for individual borrowers make it difficult to apply credit ceilings for each bank? Then do away with the system of overdrafts and replace it with bills. Are changes in interest rates not very effective in controlling bank credit for working capital requirements? Then institute a system of credit control under which bank credit for working capital is given only in accordance with certain formulae. Is it difficult to ensure that banks reserve a part of their credit potential for priority borrowers? Then institute a system of prior authorization for credit above certain limits for non-priority users. Without trying to be dogmatic, one can say that developing countries can learn something here from the experience of developed countries which have replaced very detailed controls with more general guidelines and have encouraged greater competition while making it clear that the Central Bank or the government will not bail out all financial institutions as a rule when they suffer from the risks inherent in competition.

Monetary Policy and Periodic Shocks

How effective can monetary policy be when the upward pressure on prices comes from the supply side? The standard example of such pressure is the cost-push or the wage-push pressure, that is, the pressure for wages to rise more than is warranted by increases in productivity. Such pressure exists even in developing countries more than is recognized. But the traditional wisdom that such pressure can be resisted by a non-accommodating monetary policy has little validity even in developed countries. There is enough substitutability for money as well as stretchability in the use of money which can frustrate restrictive monetary policies for resisting supply-side pressures—unless such restrictions are carried to extreme lengths. A monetary remedy for chaining the trade union giant seems to me to be a case of overkill. It is not monetary policy so much as direct curbs on unreasonable trade union behaviour and the general public support for resisting unreasonable trade union pressure that have been responsible for the reduction in wage-push pressures in the UK in recent years; and the loud advocacy of monetarism should not be allowed to obscure the fact that its price in terms of unemployment has been heavy. Indeed, with only a modest increase in employment, there is already evidence of wages outpacing productivity once again.

Similar reasoning applies to variations in crops in developing countries from good years to bad. It is better to counteract such variations directly by imports or public procurement policies rather than attempt to counteract them with monetary policy. In predominantly agricultural economies which produce most of their food, marketable supplies increase and decrease much more than variations in total grain or food production and monetary targeting must bear this in mind. But one should not imagine that if pressures on prices are allowed to develop by not releasing more supplies in a bad year for an essential commodity like food grains, they can be counteracted by monetary policy.

A supply shock such as that administered by the sudden rise in oil prices also needs to be absorbed by more direct measures. A worsening in terms of trade which is likely to continue requires adjustments of a more basic nature—to reduce domestic consumption or/and investment while reallocating investment priorities; and to the extent that this is not immediately feasible, to rely on such medium-term external financing as might be feasible. Monetary policy at best can underpin an adequate policy response on a number of fronts but can bear little burden on its own. In the reverse situation where developing countries benefit from a favourable external factor—like a boom in commodity prices—a similar comprehensive policy response will be needed, including perhaps export taxes or compulsory levies set aside for the benefit of producers in leaner years.

Monetary and Exchange Policy

Developing countries, which generally maintain exchange controls, do not have to contend with monetary and exchange rate policies becoming inseparable as a result of capital movements highly sensitive to changes in interest rates and to the current climate of expectations. I for one would not advocate abolition of exchange controls for most developing countries; and even those countries which might abolish exchange controls will not find foreign capital flowing to them in the current climate in response to changes in interest rates or expectations.

On the other hand, most developing countries maintain what are akin to fixed exchange rates in the sense that changes in the exchange rate for their currency reflect relative changes in the value of major currencies except when discrete policy changes are made. In such a situation, as under the Gold Standard, imbalances in external accounts translate themselves fully and automatically into changes in domestic money supply. Should not developing countries seek to minimize these external disturbances by allowing their exchange rates to fluctuate freely or to alter them more frequently in response to market trends (that is, trends in their reserves)? In their case, the existence of exchange controls (which are fortified at least in one direction by the current sentiment of international bankers) gives them at least a somewhat greater degree of independence from external developments. Can this independence be strengthened by greater flexibility in their exchange rate regimes? There are technical problems in exchange markets functioning freely and well in developing countries; and we all know that changes in nominal interest or exchange rates do not bring about basic adjustment without following appropriate policies on a wide front. But there is, I feel, greater need at least for discussion of an appropriate mix of monetary and exchange rate policy in developing countries which need not be the same as in developed countries.

Stabilization Programmes

There has been of late a great deal of debate and experimentation with stabilization programmes in developing countries, particularly in the debt-ridden developing countries in Latin America. Much of the debate and discussion has centred round programmes prescribed by the IMF, the central part of which has been insistence on monetary targeting. Insofar as we see some practical value in monetary targeting, we cannot object to IMF programmes in principle. Nor do I think it is valid to criticize the IMF for some of the cruel dilemmas involved in any programme of stabilization such as the conflict in the short run between growth and stability or the conflict between desirable social goals and budgetary restraint and so on. If there are better answers for resolving such conflicts, surely the countries concerned should know them better than the IMF, and I doubt if the IMF would have insisted on its own version of detailed budgetary and other policies as long as the basic parameters of monetary targeting were satisfied.

What the IMF can be criticized for are, I think, two things. First, its faith in monetary targeting was too absolute. Surely any transgression of monetary targets—and quarterly ones at that—is a reason for reviewing policy, but not for stopping IMF assistance and thus creating a further crisis of confidence. Second, and perhaps more important, to begin with at any rate the Fund took too moralistic a view towards the developing countries only. The argument seemed to be that even if difficulties arise for reasons beyond your control, you have to adjust as long as these difficulties or circumstances are not likely to be reversed. But surely this general argument could have been strengthened by advocating strongly that the adjustment can only be made sensibly over a period. In the meanwhile, therefore, there had to be much greater official concessionary finance than was forthcoming. The private banks also were guilty and should have been made to pay for their sins from the outset. After all, it was the private international banks that had canvassed the view that they could finance balance-of-payments disequilibria when the going was good and had argued vigorously against official flows. They could not be allowed to assume moral tones and to talk of contemplating reduction of obligations as being the ultimate sin of "moral hazard". The IMF and the Central Banks and Treasuries of developed countries talked for a long time as befits a cartel of financiers rather than as a body of world statesmen. But that is the politics of the world economy for us, which unfortunately is not likely to change.

One moral of recent experience in developing countries is that once inflation is allowed to accelerate, it is difficult to bring it under control except by heroic measures. Time was when Brazil and Israel were praised for their financial genius in making inflation a toothless tiger by universal indexation. That happy trip on an ever-accelerating escalator is no more fashionable now than those other trips of the late 1960s and early 1970s.

Even the more recent burst of enthusiasm for a Brazilian innovation—the so-called heterodox shock—has, I think, faded somewhat. There is, of course, some truth in the proposition that there is such a thing as inertial inflation—inflation, that is, which continues and accelerates on its own momentum of expectations once it has been on for some time. To break this self-perpetuating chain, something drastic like a currency reform and total re-fixation of prices and wages with a subsequent freeze without any indexation may well be necessary. But if the "heterodox" was intended to be contrasted with "orthodox", experience clearly indicated that there is no such contrast. Even when heroic measures like currency reform and total restructuring of prices are necessary, they would stick only if at the same time orthodox measures are taken to correct the budgetary imbalance and to rein in the unions and the speculators. There is, in other words, no magic solution to hyperinflation any more than there is to inflation—only more problems including the problem of correctly guessing the changing needs for liquidity when high inflation rates are suddenly brought down. Experience shows that the demand for money often increases with stabilization so that unless this is met (contrary to the orthodox canons of stabilization) a crisis may result causing much loss of output and employment. But it is not easy to guess the extent of the change in the demand for money; and the danger of overshooting or setting in wrong expectations in view of past bitter experience of the people cannot be overestimated even when one acts correctly. When it comes to inflation, perhaps the best wisdom can be summed up in two propositions: small is beautiful; and two plus two makes four.

Liberalization

An interesting chapter that is unfolding in many developing countries currently is that of liberalization from a regime of extensive controls to greater reliance on market forces. This general shift has embraced not just the developed world or the socialist world but also many of the developing countries like India which have had a mixed pattern of ownership with a heavy bias in favour of public control or intervention. An interesting question in all these countries at the present juncture is the role that financial liberalization can play as part of the total process of liberalization. It is difficult to generalize on a question like this where the institutional and other specifics of each country are of obvious importance. But a few general remarks, with a country like India in mind, may be in order.

One cannot assume extremist positions like that of Professor Friedman in favour of a fixed and firm rule of monetary expression, let alone that of Professor Hayek who would remove the Central Bank's monopoly of currency creation. Nor can one perhaps endorse the more or less exclusive use of interest rates as the chief monetary instrument or the abolition of exchange controls. But one could argue that there is need not just for diversification among financial institutions but also for a degree of deregulation and competition leading to greater financial innovations. Thus banks may be encouraged to go in for mortgage finance or long-term industrial finance; industrial banks and unit trusts and provident funds can also diversify their portfolios; and indeed more private banks, private unit trusts or private industrial and other financial institutions encouraged.

Insofar as a climate for stability cannot be created without restructuring of the government budget and insofar as losses of public sector enterprises are a major problem, it may not be realistic to think in terms of "privatization" as in developed economies. But it may be worth exploring if public enterprises could not be delinked from the budget and permitted access to the market or/and made the responsibility of public financial institutions which apply financial criteria. Generally speaking, the spirit of liberalization will also imply that even public financial institutions, including the Central Bank, should be freed from routine governmental intervention and that this should be reflected in appropriate managerial and constitutional structures. The financial institutions themselves should avoid policies and procedures which give too much discretionary powers to individual officers as an overly interventionist approach is as undesirable for financial institutions as it is for the government. After all, abuses of power and corruption or politicization and being overburdened with too many objectives can and do characterize financial institutions as much as they do most other institutions.

Summing Up

It is clearly not possible to sum up a rather long and somewhat discursive argument. But a few points may be noted for ease of discussion. Developments in industrialized countries are of significance to developing countries and some of them may well be echoed with profit by them. At the same time, the policy mix in developed countries has not yet settled down. The rhetoric of policy does not always correspond with reality and there are luxuries of oversimplification that poor countries can ill afford. As far as monetary policy is concerned, it can at best have a subordinate and supporting role in both sets of countries, and there is little reason to think that it can be more effective in one group of countries than in another. Economic logic knows no national frontiers and it often transcends institutional frontiers as well.

If there is a greater danger in developing countries, it is that of giving to the Central Bank an exaggerated role under which it assumes rather hyperactive poses to demonstrate to its masters that it is doing something. The Central Bank cannot take the washing of the Finance Minister or for that matter the washing of the supply-side shocks. At the same time, it has a very important developmental role. It also has an important role in terms of analysis and advice on matters relating to inflation and balance-of-payments adjustment; and its part of advice can often best be transmitted by analysis of monetary and financial aggregates and by persuading governments to adopt procedures such as monetary target setting which facilitate focusing on the interactions between budgetary, monetary and foreign exchange policy.

In the ultimate analysis, monetary authorities cannot do much better than emphasize that their own role is only modest; that when it comes to inflation, it is best to resist in the first place; that two plus two never make five when it comes to allocation of national resources in the short run; but that it is possible to have two plus two make five in the long run if proper supply-side policies are followed which include regard for savings and efficiency in investment as much as a proper framework of incentives for work, investment and enterprise. Alas, so dismal is the science of economics that two plus two can also make three when wrong policies are followed; and the dividing line between the right and the wrong in economics is never very sharp or stable!

CHAPTER 6

Communication Policy of Central Banks*

I am indeed grateful to Governor Reddy for his kind invitation to participate in this symposium and to interact with Governors and finance officers from our neighbouring countries. Such gatherings for informal exchange of views are of immense importance. The Central Banking community is a very special community. Even when governments may not be on speaking terms, Central Bank Governors communicate and indeed cooperate and are proverbially very cordial and hospitable towards each other. This is a great national asset and is particularly valuable for regions like South Asia which seek to transcend the suspicion of decades and move towards much greater regional integration.

During my time at the Reserve Bank from 1977 to 1982 there were two or three annual occasions I greatly valued. One was the meeting of the Governors of Central Banks participating in the Asian Clearing Union, whose membership extended all the way from Iran to Indonesia. The Clearing Union was more fiction than fact. But our meetings were very rewarding. A similar forum was the annual meeting of Sterling Area Governors in the Bank of England and a group of just four Governors organized by Paul Volcker which met once a year for one day—Governors from the US, Mexico, Switzerland and India. These meetings provided more valuable exchange of views then the annual meetings of the Bank and the Fund. I do not know if any of these groups exists now. But it would be a good idea if Governors from our region meet each year in different countries without any formal agenda.

* The draft of this paper was written in 2004; unpublished.

While I am happy to be here, I must admit that I do so with some trepidation. I belong to an age when "Communication Policy of Central Banks" sounded more like an oxymoron. Central Bank Governors then, like children, were supposed to be seen, not heard. Although they were allowed to smile in public, they had to emulate Mona Lisa and maintain an aura of mystery. This was not surprising in an age when much of the financial sector was publicly owned, interest rates were administered, credit was directed, reserve requirements were frequently changed, capital movements and indeed all foreign exchange transactions severely controlled and exchange rates fixed or pegged whether to one currency or a basket of currencies. As far as monetary policy and credit policy were concerned, the Governor did not have to communicate—he had to command and direct. At best, he had to explain the basis on which the credit plans were formulated. On the exchange front, Governors and Finance Ministers had to wear a brave face till the axe fell, and then too, they had to take care that it happened at a moment which would come as a surprise to most market participants. The world of financial markets has changed enormously over the past twenty years. Without any hands-on experience of this Brave New World, what can I say which might be of interest to the present generation? Despite my lack of operational experience, I am, however, encouraged to make a few remarks by Governor Reddy's assurance that I could speak around the subject so to speak and by the excellent background material prepared by the Reserve Bank. On more than one occasion in recent years I have acknowledged the progress made by the Reserve Bank in greatly expanding the range of its research and publications and making its actions more transparent. The underlying rationale of its policy is also explained simply. And all this is done without losing some of the mystique which must remain around Central Bank Governors. The credit for this goes largely to Governor Reddy and his two predecessors—Governor Jalan and Governor Rangarajan.

I am sure we can also agree with the broad conclusions drawn in the working papers. Central Banks should not confine their research and publications to areas of their special concern. They must publish their own assessment and forecasts relating to the economy as a whole. Communication is not just about transparency. It is also about education, guidance and steering things in the right direction. In this, the Central Bank can be an honest broker between the government and the public and even Parliament. Politicians have always an agenda of their own and their horizon is the next election. While research institutions can provide a more objective and long-term perspective, the Central Bank has an authority they cannot have. How to exploit this authority without being in the centre of political controversies is an art which Governors and their deputies have to have. They cannot cultivate in office the art of talking in coded language.

This aspect of communication becomes all the more relevant and tricky when coalition governments without any ideological or moral underpinning are at the helm.

One can also agree that one should err in the direction of transparency and simplicity, that communication should be based on sound analysis, should be selective in order to be effective and should keep the different target groups in mind. I do not wish to go over this ground which is well covered in the background papers. Instead, I would like to dwell a bit on three matters. Apart from communicating its own slant on national and international trends, there are three special areas which need attention. The first is the glamorous but elusive area of what the Central Bank communicates and how it does so in relation to its specific responsibility for monetary and foreign exchange policy; the second is communication on issues in regard to its regulatory functions; and the last is communication with the government of the day, including Parliament.

Let me take first the question of explicit targets in areas of direct concern to the Central Bank. There was a time when it was common for monetary authorities to set explicit targets for growth in money supply—with the emphasis shifting from M1 to M3. The methodology for setting the target was simple—you forecast the growth in real income, add to it an estimate for unavoidable inflation and allow for monetization. Somehow, the figure in India always came up to 14 or 15 per cent. This sort of reasoning was there in most of our early plans. I believe this has now gone out of fashion, maybe because of the tenuous relationship between money supply and prices. That is how direct inflation targeting became fashionable. I am not familiar with current international practice. But my impression is that inflation targeting is not the norm except perhaps in Europe. Even in the Mecca of inflation targeting, New Zealand, the concept no longer retains its virgin purity. I am not surprised. In most countries, Central Banks have only limited control over inflation. Oil prices, failure of monsoons and government deficits have a greater impact than unhealthy credit expansion to the private sector. If inflation targeting is to be made credible, adequate action must follow even in such eventualities. But what does a Central Bank do when oil prices rise sharply? Does it initiate recessionary policies to offset the rise in oil prices? This is hardly acceptable. One has no option but to allow price rises in important sectors to seep through the economy causing an increase in general prices. If the government monopolizes much of the scope for credit expansion, do we starve the rest of the economy? That would be like coming home and beating your wife because your boss gave you a drubbing in office.

But can we leave matters at that? Even if we have no single inflation target, we can have a range and revise it in the light of unavoidable circumstances. One can also stipulate a time period over which inflation will average around a certain level. The reason for doing this is that it will enable the Central Bank to act decisively at times and perhaps shame the government into mending its ways. The latter perhaps is problematic—and it is often not clear even to the Central Bank what effective and timely action it can take. Raising interest rates seldom reins in inflation unless the remedy is carried rather far.

And yet, the Central Bank cannot be passive or indifferent when inflation rises and threatens to be self-fuelling and cumulative. The Central Bank has to sound a warning, do some quiet diplomacy with the government on tariffs and imports and deferment of some expenditure, and do some preaching to the banks. Personally, I would not throw up the one instrument the Central Banks have for quick and effective action, viz., changes in cash reserve requirements. I would urge no changes in Statutory Liquidity Ratios and would hope that some day we would give up SLRs altogether. In the present circumstances in India when banks hold government securities far in excess of SLR requirements, even changes in cash reserves may not be effective. But this is no reason for throwing away the one weapon we have. And it must be communicated—by occasional use—that this weapon is not discarded.

All this does not mean that the Central Bank should never indicate what inflation rate is desirable and the limit beyond which it should not go over a period. But to say what is desirable only means that the Central Bank intends to play its part in making it happen. It does not mean that the Central Bank undertakes to make it happen. These are subtle distinctions, and I am afraid Governors in most countries have no option but to play it by the ear. This may often be a cover for inaction or for action only after the horse has bolted. But in seasoned hands, it need not be so. Playing it by the ear is only recognition of the fact that even Central Bank Governors are not omnipotent.

Can the Bank target interest rates? Here, I think the case is even weaker. In the present context of more or less free capital movements, interest rates everywhere converge towards some international trend. Governors in small countries or small economies can serve a useful purpose if they study these trends and bring their assessment to public notice in their countries. But it would be idle for them to pretend that they have much control over interest rates or that interest rates are all that decisive in macro-management. Even the rate at which the Central Bank lends to banks becomes effective only when banks push lending so far as to create a liquidity crunch for themselves. And government deficits have a decisive impact on interest rates. Barring sudden and large spurts in bank credit, the Central Bank can do the best by inflation through its influence on government policies.

What about the exchange rate? Should the Central Bank communicate simply and unequivocally what its exchange rate policy is? It is easy to do so if its exchange rate is pegged. Despite the consensus of the 1970s, the fascination for a pegged rate has not entirely vanished. One of the largest and the most successful economies in the world—China—has practised it for many years; and I suspect most managed currency managers have a bias towards a more or less fixed and undervalued exchange rate. The rationale offered for intermittent action may be "smoothing out changes". But the bias is for resisting appreciation more than depreciation. And this is for a good reason. The only rational argument I can find for China's behaviour is that it gives the highest priority to growth, employment and technical modernization of its economy. China is prepared to pay a price for it, be it lending abroad at low rates of interest and the prospect of loss in asset value. After all, it is better than digging holes and filling them up. And I suspect there is the fear that liberal import policies in richer countries may not continue forever so that it is better to hurry and make hay while the sun shines. At least the benefits of modernization will endure. This reasoning is not without appeal or relevance to other developing countries although most prefer to bend a little and avoid the danger of breaking. Once again, playing it by the ear and distributing one's risks seems to be the agenda—hidden or otherwise. I am afraid I see no alternative to this despite its many critics who ask for fluctuating rates and an end to reserve accumulation. The one thing common about these critics is that they all elaborate on what is wrong with reserve accumulation but do not spell out fully the consequences of what they recommend. Is it not likely that if we allow the rupee to appreciate freely, this trend will become cumulative fuelled by even greater inflow of funds? Can this not lead to less reliance on trade and more on capital inflows? Is it better to borrow than to sell? I do not know if any model can tell us what would be an optimum or ideal policy. But it is not necessarily true that a simple, transparent and inflexible policy will be the best—even if it is the easiest to communicate.

I am afraid we are in for some sort of international bickering on this front. Already, strong voices are heard that Asian currencies should appreciate significantly to ease the pressure on the euro and to bring about an orderly reduction in the US deficit. We will soon hear of beggar-my-neighbour policies, the IMF's mandate for orderly exchange rates and the Group of Eight or Ten or whatever it is now arguing for coordinated exchange rate changes. What will come out of this, I do not know. But in the meanwhile, we should seriously engage in a review of our asset management policy. This is one area where we need greater transparency and more open dialogue. Unfortunately, this is not the best time for an open dialogue as there is a serious possibility that diversification of assets will be resisted in the name of international cooperation. Such things have happened before in living memory.

I come now to the less glamorous—but in my view more important—role of the Central Bank, viz., the regulation of financial institutions, particularly commercial banks. As a Director of the State Bank of India, I have gained some familiarity with this aspect of the Central Bank's responsibility as seen from the other end. This regulatory function has become even more important and complex in this age of universal banking with banks embarking on merchant banking, term lending and even insurance. Economists like to say that a sound financial system is one which minimizes transaction cost, particularly the cost of financial intermediation. This may be so in terms of theoretical models. But I should have thought cost minimization is the function of competition and this objective would be achieved without regulation as long as maximum competition is permitted in financial markets. The trouble is, perfect competition in financial markets is seldom a reality. There is a tendency towards a few large operators dominating the scene and the danger is not so much of lack of competition but of excessive and blind competition among the banks. The dangers to ward off are a threat to the safety of depositors by aggressive and often infructuous investment which inhibits savings in the long run and speculative forces which threaten financial stability and create scams and crises. Much progress has been made in this regard in recent years through adoption of prudential norms and guidance on risk management and the like. But speculation, scams and bad investments continue. Action after the event is not much use. There has to be early detection of lapses through Bank supervision of individual banks and even large individual accounts. A balance has to be struck between thoroughness and quickness. Regulation which is too detailed and pervasive and invasive has to be avoided; and regulation which is quick to detect lapses and send out danger signals encouraged. The task is not easy. But I have the impression that Bank supervision by its very long history has become routine—going through the motion of observing timetables and checking merely compliance with rules and instructions and getting lost in minutiae, in short, bureaucratization. What one needs is a selective and sharp and focused system which is not routinized and standardized. We need some kind of intelligence system which can smell fraud and misbehaviour of managers and big borrowers, people who keep in touch with market operators and even market gossip and not just those who operate from their desk. Perhaps we can make better use of new techniques available now for devising ad hoc and well-directed disclosure requirements in individual cases. I am afraid I am not good at intelligence and we do not want to encourage gossip or indulge in espionage. But something needs to be done to make Bank supervision meaningful. This, I think, is a good subject for advice from persons with international management expertise.

The other urgent need is for cleaning up some of the debris left behind by the days of the command economy. As it is there are far too many reporting requirements of a routine nature emanating from past directives which are no longer necessary and far too many things which are to be reported to and approved by the Board of Directors—or even the government or the RBI. This puts a heavy and unnecessary burden on bank staff and in fact the internal data collection and distribution in banks is governed not so much by their management needs as by the requirements of reporting to the Board or to the RBI or the Ministry. I think we need a review of all such requirements to see what can be dispensed with. The issue goes beyond reporting and applies equally to instructions, institutional requirements as well as areas of prior permission.

One can quote many examples. But I will mention reporting on many schemes which need themselves to be wound up like the 20-point programme or the Indira Awas Yojana. Is there any justification now for the Lead Bank Scheme for each district in an age of free competition? This scheme only creates a lot of work for bank staff and opens doors for local political functionaries to exercise undue pressure. For the last several years, I have also been Chairman of the Gujarat Local Board of the State Bank of India—since I am the only Gujarati director and there were no other members of the Local Board for many months, I have yet to discover what purpose these Local Boards serve. Their approval is necessary only for writing off small debts, expenditure on furniture and repairs below a certain sum and opening of new ATMs away from bank branches. Much time and money is wasted and again, doors are opened for local political pressure. It may be too much to hope that everything in government should have a sunset clause. But surely, if economic reform has to have any meaning, there has to be a serious spring clearing of past cobwebs.

The two serious lacunae in bank regulation in India relate to cooperative banks and the so-called non-banking financial institutions. The problems here are well known and I do not wish to say more than to urge that, once again, these problems should not be swept under the carpet. Necessary legislative and other changes must be made soon. A related problem is the variety of regulatory agencies for different parts of the financial sector. The developments in the market for stocks and shares have serious repercussions on monetary and foreign exchange trends. And yet, the Reserve Bank has little control except through supervision of bank lending to the stock exchanges. It is not my purpose to suggest that there should be a single regulatory authority inside or outside the Reserve Bank. But surely, all the regulatory authorities should meet regularly and exchange notes.

Let me turn finally to the all-important and timely question of communication between the government and the Central Bank. In theory, this should not be difficult as most Governors are former officers of the Finance Ministry so that they know the ropes and often know the Minister as well. In practice, however, it is not enough always to let the Minister know your views. A good Governor is not content merely to have his say in private. He is interested in results as well. Often the Minister and the Governor are of the same mind and the Minister wants some help from the Governor in influencing his colleagues or political parties by creating some public opinion and debate. There is always a role for long-term watchdogs in a political climate of short-sighted opportunism. To put it more generously, politicians are often required to square circles, which forces them to embrace dubious ideas. How does the Governor go about his business in such situations? Again, there is no set roadmap. Personalities count, and the Governor has to have enough tact and guile to have his say without putting him at the centre of political controversies.

Take one current example. The proposal to use foreign exchange reserves to accelerate infrastructure development has received much public attention in India recently. Anyone who knows anything knows that the reference to foreign exchange reserves in this connection is only a red herring. It is to draw attention away from the real purpose: which is to indulge in greater deficit financing and even to monetize a part of the deficit in violation of solemn undertakings given to Parliament. If you say so openly, you will be shot down in no time. But if you bring in foreign exchange reserves which are useless and earn nothing and suggest using them for worthwhile purposes, you may hoodwink some people and get by. I have no doubt the proponents of the idea also know this—they are too intelligent not to know what you and I and everyone in the economic profession know. But politicians have to square the circle here and if they can get by, by diverting attention to something irrelevant, why not? They can always say the violation of past commitments is only temporary and once in a while and not a precedent for the future. All politicians always say that, for example, when they introduce amnesty schemes for laundering ill-gotten money which somehow crop up after every election. A former Governor can get by saying all these things openly. But a sitting Governor cannot. Nor can he keep quiet. If he has friends in the government, he can tell them what he thinks and hope it will reach the right ears. He can encourage think-tanks to debate the issue and create public opinion. In this case, perhaps he can even afford just to sit back and smile. The issue may well die of its own infirmity.

But the point is, when such vital questions arise, the Governor cannot just be inactive. He is a public servant with loyalty to the country and the Constitution—not just to a government in transit. And yet, he cannot behave as if every issue is of great import. He has to choose his ground and be discreet above all. Without offending the government he can start a debate and steer the argument in a certain direction. His ultimate defence is democracy and the tradition of free debate.

The relations between the Central Bank and Parliament pose more difficult questions. In the past, we used to resist any direct communication between the RBI and Parliament. Parliamentary Committees visited banks, but not the Central Bank. The Governor did not appear before Parliamentary Committees unlike Finance Ministry officials. Parliament had no say in the appointment of Governors. The Comptroller and Auditor General did not audit RBI accounts. The argument was that it is the Finance Minister who was answerable to Parliament for the affairs of the RBI. But the corollary—unspoken but understood—was that the Ministry controlled the Bank.

I do not know how much of the old practice survives. But it is worth asking if some departure from the past may not strengthen the independence of the RBI and the authority of the Governor. A meeting once a year between the Governor and some Parliamentary Committee may be a useful forum for the Governor to communicate his views more freely. My own experience of Parliamentary Committees as Economic Affairs Secretary is that these meetings were not at all confrontational or inquisitorial. The Members of Parliament were courteous and happy for some things to be explained. Perhaps times have changed. But I still think most politicians like to be taken seriously by those whom they consider experts. I would at least urge that even if Parliament has no role in the appointment of the Governor, there should be a convention that the appointment of a particular person should be discussed with the leader of the main opposition party. After all, Governors of Central Banks should be distinguished from Governors of other kinds!

Part II

Gold Policy

CHAPTER 7

India's Elasticity of Demand for Gold*

The purpose of this paper is to get some idea of the responsiveness of India's demand for gold to changes in its relative price. In Section I some general remarks on the nature of the demand for gold in India are made. This is followed up in Section II with an attempt to correlate the net flow of gold from (or into) private hoards during the years 1925–1942 with the relative price of gold and the consumption of sugar—the latter item being chosen as an indicator of real national income. In Section III we have tried to see what light the results of the multiple correlation analysis throw on the behaviour of India's demand for gold in recent months. Needless to say, any such statistical estimate is subject to a large number of limitations. But such limitations are clearly mentioned, wherever possible, so that the results can be appraised accordingly. The general conclusion seems to be that during the period studied the demand for gold was highly responsive to changes in the relative price of gold. But in view of the various limitations of our analysis and the peculiar nature of the current situation in India, such a high price elasticity of demand for gold is very unlikely to be operative at present. Nevertheless, our results are of some importance in suggesting the strength of the price factor insofar as this is the first attempt to measure it statistically.

General Remarks

The demand for gold in India has certain special features. Some general remarks on the nature of this demand are made, therefore, in this section

* Originally written as a research paper for the International Monetary Fund in 1950; subsequently published in the *Economic and Political Weekly*, Vol. 41, No. 6, 11 February 2006.

to serve as a preliminary guide to the interpretation of the statistical results obtained in Section II.

In India, gold is not merely a means of holding accumulated or new savings, but is also an article for direct consumption. A large part of the gold held is in the form of ornaments, the use of which is decreed by social and religious customs. The distinction between durable consumer goods and capital assets cannot, of course, be drawn rigidly. But in order to analyse the demand for gold in India properly, it is necessary to bear in mind the two sources from which it springs.

The demand for gold for consumption purposes would depend upon real income, the price of gold in relation to other consumer goods prices, and the changes in people's customary attitude. For a country where most people live at a subsistence level, a decline in per capita income would lead to dissaving rather than to a further cut in the standard of living; and a part of this dissaving would take the form of sale of gold. But the income elasticity of demand for gold is not likely to be greater than unity in the reverse case where per capita income increases. The point at which the proportion of income spent on luxuries increases comes late in the growth of standards of living; and this is particularly true in a society where rigid social and religious attitudes keep the demand for conventional luxuries high even at low levels of real income. If this is true, the demand for gold would be quite responsive to changes in the distribution of income also. On the other hand, it should be emphasized that in a country with a steadily growing population the demand for gold will increase with total real income, even if per capita real income remains the same. More people will demand more ornaments even if they remain at the same standard of living.

So far as price elasticity is concerned, normally we would expect the demand for gold to decline if its price rises faster than the prices of other commodities. But in the case of India, it is arguable that there are some limits beyond which the consumption of gold is not likely to be substituted by other forms of consumption. Being largely in the nature of ceremonial expenditure—say for the dowry of a daughter—gold can be substituted with other forms of ceremonial expenditure in the main—say on clothes or social feasting at a marriage. But the requirements of gold, clothes, or foodstuffs on such festive occasions are set down by conventional standards and cannot be altered very much. However, the gold required for this purpose is not bought in a single transaction; it is accumulated over time. And this means that there is considerable scope for varying the rate of purchase over time in response to the relative price of gold. A peasant can build a house when gold prices are too high, and buy gold when it is comparatively cheap. This responsiveness of the demand for gold to its relative price is, of course, a short-term phenomenon, based on an anticipation of a reverse movement of the relative price in future. But so long as people's ideas about the "normal" price of gold remain unchanged, the demand for gold for consumption purposes should be fairly responsive to price changes.

But it is not equally likely that a price movement by itself will make the demand for ornaments actually negative. For one thing, the conversion of ornaments into money and the repurchase of ornaments in future entail a loss which would neutralize some of the price effect. And secondly, most Indians have a sentimental attachment to ornaments, strong enough to resist the temptation of uncertain profits in the future. The situation is obviously different if the improvement in the price of gold comes about at a time when income is below the subsistence level.

What about the demand for gold as an embodiment of past and current savings? The influence of changes in real income on the demand for gold for this purpose is self-evident. But the more important factor is the substitution between various types of assets people hold in view of the changes in their relative profitability, riskiness and awareness and opportunity for investment. How will a change in the relative price of gold affect distribution of people's savings among the various types of assets—such as gold, local or foreign currency and the various interest-bearing or profit-yielding securities or equipment?

Obviously, there is no sense in converting gold into local or foreign currency if the rise in the relative price of gold is not deemed to be temporary. Much depends, therefore, on people's expectations about the future price. But in the case of savings, part of the resistance noted above in connection with ornaments does not apply; and this part of the demand can well be negative also. As regards conversion into interest-bearing or profit-yielding securities, this affects mainly a small part of the population which is aware of these movements and is accustomed to deal in the securities market. It is true that even the ignorant mass of peasants has an alternative outlet of investment on their own farms, but their share in the nation's savings must be quite small. And insofar as the large mass of people are ignorant of the niceties of substitution at the margin and keep their savings in the form of gold out of habit or due to a certain attachment to the yellow metal, demand for it may not be as responsive to price changes as we may expect *a priori*.

Apart from this, the demand for gold as an embodiment of savings depends on many accidental factors which far outweigh the effects of price changes. In other words, the demand for gold for this purpose is subject to such frequent shifts that the knowledge of the special factors causing such a shift at any moment is more pertinent than the effects of a movement along some "normal" demand curve. Thus, if savings are mainly a result of tax evasion, they are more likely to be embodied in gold rather than in securities or assets where the chances of detection are greater. And if a large amount of gold is hoarded for this purpose, any change in administrative practice conniving at past tax evasion will bring forth a substantial dishoarding even if the price of gold changes but little. The fear of war, political instability, or confiscation will produce similar results. These "accidental" elements in the situation have to be borne in mind particularly because they cannot be quantified and entered into any regression analysis.

Statistical Estimate of Price Elasticity

It should be obvious from the earlier discussion that the demand for gold in India depends on many factors other than the relative price of gold.[1] If we want to judge from experience how important the price effect has been, the influence of other factors must somehow be eliminated. An attempt was made to eliminate the effects of at least one important other variable, viz., income, by applying multiple regression analysis to the relevant series for the seventeen years from 1925–26 to 1941–42.

Table 7.1 gives the data about net flow of gold into or from private hoards, the total consumption of sugar and the ratio of the price of gold to wholesale prices in India for the years 1925–26 to 1941–42. A few remarks about the table may be made here.

During the 1920s there was a substantial flow of gold into private hoards. But during the 1930s gold began flowing out of private hoards largely due to the Great Depression. But throughout the period, the net flow of gold shows significant variations from year to year.

The reason why the consumption of sugar was chosen as an indicator of total real income needs elucidation. No reliable estimates of total real income for all the years studied here are available. R.C. Desai has computed the total consumption (in money and per capita real terms) in India for the years 1931–40. But apart from the fact that he makes no estimates for the 1920s, his figures seem prima facie unreliable. According to his estimates, the lowest point in per capita real consumption during the 1930s was reached in 1939—the figure for that year being 9 per cent below that reached in 1931 at the height of the Depression. A possible explanation may be that in 1931 consumption was high despite lower total income because of dissaving; but that once dissaving had gone on for years, the scope for further dissaving was reduced. It was, therefore, decided to take the consumption of a single commodity as an indicator of total real income. The question still remains whether sugar is a representative item: whether its income

[1] The demand for gold may mean one of two things: the demand for holding certain stocks of gold, or the demand for making additions to the existing stocks, i.e., demand for new gold. But in order to know the stocks at various dates we must know the actual stocks on any one date as well as the subsequent additions to or subtractions from these stocks. Since the only data we can compile are of changes in the stocks from year to year, the demand for gold in this paper refers throughout to demand for new gold.

elasticity is much greater or much smaller than unity, and whether factors other than income were affecting its consumption. This point is discussed a little later. But it may be noted at this stage that the actual figures of the consumption of sugar do show the type of fluctuation we would normally expect in total real income. It is quite high for the 1920s, but drops significantly in the early 1930s, and picks up again after 1935. The recession of 1937–38 is also reflected in this series. Some objections can always be made against any single commodity chosen as an indicator of total income. But sugar seems a good example insofar as it is not quite a necessity and yet not a luxury. It may be argued that insofar as dissavings affect consumption, the consumption of sugar will not reflect adequately changes in income, and our two series (of gold flow and consumption of sugar) would not be quite independent. But the fact that sugar is a semi-luxury reduces the significance of this error.

The relative price of gold is expressed in Table 7.1 in two alternative ways:

$$\text{as an index of } \frac{\text{Price of gold}}{\text{Wholesale prices}}$$

$$(X_3), \text{ or as an index of } \frac{\text{Wholesale prices } (X_3')}{\text{Price of gold}}$$

Now, if we treat the net flow of gold as the dependent variable (X_1), and the consumption of sugar (X_2), and the index of the relative price of gold (X_3 or X_3') as independent variables, we can fit two linear equations to our data:

$$X_1 = a + bX_2 + cX_3 \ldots \qquad \text{(Equation 7.1)}$$

or $$X_1 = a' + b'X_2' + c'X_3') \ldots \qquad \text{(Equation 7.2)}$$

Equations 7.1 and 7.2 are two alternative forms of the same relation—with the relative price of gold expressed differently in the two cases.[2]

The estimating equations work out as follows:

$$X_1 = 4990.6 + 12.6\, X_2 - 43.7\, X_3 \ldots \qquad \text{(Equation 7.1)}$$

The coefficient of correlations $R = 0.831$.

or $$X_1 = -20{,}088 + 12\, X_2 + 118.5\, X_3' \ldots \qquad \text{(Equation 7.2)}$$

The coefficient of correlation $R' = 0.871$.

[2] Two alternative linear equations were also fitted to two other sets of variables: (a) with box X_1 and X_2 deflated by population; and (b) with only X_2 deflated by population. But the fit in both these cases was poorer, and the size of the coefficients was not materially different from that revealed by neglecting population changes. These relations, therefore, are not included in this paper.

Table 7.1 Two Alternative Forms of Relative Price of Gold

Year	X_1	X_2	X_3	X'_3
1925–26	6,530	868	90	111
1926–27	3,770	1,030	100	100
1927–28	3,058	920	99	101
1928–29	3,924	1,026	103	98
1929–30	2,689	1,115	104	96
1930–31	2,562	1,151	128	78
1931–32	–8,920	778	171	59
1932–33	–8,920	768	217	46
1933–34	–6,364	768	251	40
1934–35	–5,377	838	275	36
1935–36	–3,692	1,180	266	38
1936–37	–2,678	1,145	259	39
1937–38	–1,436	900	231	43
1938–39	–2,066	976	253	40
1939–40	–3,841	894	252	40
1940–41	–725	900	236	42
1941–42	+103	1,032	218	46

Notes: X_1 = Net flow of gold into (+) or from (–) private hoards in 1,000 ounces.
X_2 = Consumption of sugar in 1,000 tonnes.

$$X_3 = \frac{\text{Price of gold}}{\text{Index of wholsale prices}} \text{ with 1926–27} = 100$$

$$X_3' = \frac{\text{Index of wholesale prices}}{\text{Price of gold}} \text{ with 1926–27} = 100$$

$X_1 = 4990.6 + 12.6X_2 - 43.7X_3$ (Equation 7.1)

$R = 0.831 \quad a = -4990.6 \quad b = 12.6 \quad c = -43.7 \quad B_{12.3} = 0.38 \quad B_{13.2} = -0.68$

or

$X_1 = -20{,}088 + 12X_2 + 118.5X_3'$ (Equation 7.2)

$R' = 0.871 \quad a' = -20.088 \quad b' = 12.0 \quad c' = +118.5 \quad B'_{12.3} = 0.36 \quad B'_{13.2} = 0.73$

where X_1 = Net flow of gold into or from private hoards in 1,000 ounces;
X_2 = Consumption of sugar in 1,000 tonnes;

$$X_3 = \text{Index of } \frac{\text{Price of gold}}{\text{Wholesale prices}} \text{ with } 1926 = 100;$$

and

$$X_3' = \text{Index of } \frac{\text{Wholesale prices}}{\text{Price of gold}} \text{ with } 1926 = 100.$$

Contd.

Table 7.1 Contd.

Explanatory Notes:

1. *Year*: Unless otherwise stated, all the figures relate to the fiscal year from 1 April to 31 March.

2. *Net flow of gold in private hoards*:

(a) This item is defined as:

(quantity of imports + domestic production of gold) –
(increase in official gold reserves + exports of gold).

(b) The figures for imports and exports are taken from *The Statistical Abstract for British India* for the years 1920–30 and from *The Reserve Bank of India Report on Currency and Finance* for the remaining years.

(c) Changes in official gold reserves are estimated from *The Banking and Monetary Statistics* of the Federal Reserve System, and they refer to the calendar year (31 December to 31 December). Thus, the year 1925–26, for example, in our table includes the change in official gold reserves from 31 December 1924 to 31 December 1925.

(d) Figures for gold production are taken from *The Statistical Abstract* and refer to calendar year; compare "c" above. This slight difference in the time period is not of much significance since the quantities involved and the variations therein are small.

3. *Consumption of sugar*: This item is defined as:

"Domestic production + imports – exports (including re-exports) for the years 1920–37". In other words, changes in stocks from year to year are disregarded as precise data about them are not available. But this procedure was not adopted for the years 1938–42 as estimates of consumption, including changes in stocks, are available for these years: compare *The Indian Sugar Industry Annual*, Vol. 12. Actually, this source estimates consumption for all the years after 1933, but changes in stocks become significant only after 1938. Figures for domestic production and imports for the years 1920–37 are taken from *A Statistical Study of India's Industrial Development*, and the data about exports and re-exports are taken from *The Statistical Abstract*. Unfortunately, the *Abstract* does not give figures for exports after 1927; but this is immaterial as exports had become negligible by 1925. For the years 1938–42, the consumption figures were taken from *The Sugar Industry Annual* as mentioned above, and they refer to the year period from November to October.

It should also be noted that not all types of sugar produced in India are included in the table. It is not possible to estimate the production of *khandsari* sugar for the years 1920–32; and hence, for the sake of comparability, this type of sugar was excluded throughout the time period studied. This is a rather serious omission as can be seen from the fact that in 1932–33, khandsari sugar accounted for some 40.1 per cent of India's sugar production although by 1941–42, this share had declined to only 11.1 per cent.

4 and 5. *Relative price of gold*:

The price of gold chosen is the average spot price of gold in the Bombay market. For the years 1920–25, an average of the prices at the end of each fortnightly period is taken; whereas for the remaining years, an average of the closing prices on each of the working day in the market is used. The wholesale price index used is that of prices in Calcutta, vide *Indian Trade Journal*.

It may be noted that the coefficient of correlation in both cases is large enough to be significant; and that both equations give an almost equally good fit. The coefficient for X_2 is virtually the same, and since the average value of X_3 was about three times as large as that of X'_3, the coefficients found for X_3 and X'_3 are virtually equivalent. This will also be seen in the two charts.

In Figure 7.1, $X_1{}^*$ represents the estimated amount of gold flow for each year on the basis of Equation 7.1; and in Figure 7.2, $X_1{}^*$ is the estimated amount of gold flow on the basis of Equation 7.2. By comparing $X_1{}^*$ with the actual gold flow (X_1 in the charts and Table 7.1) we get an idea of the goodness of the fit of our equations. The deviations of X_1 from $X_1{}^*$ indicate the variation in X_1 which is not explained by our equations. These deviations are shown in the charts by the curves $X_1 - X_1{}^*$; and it can be seen that

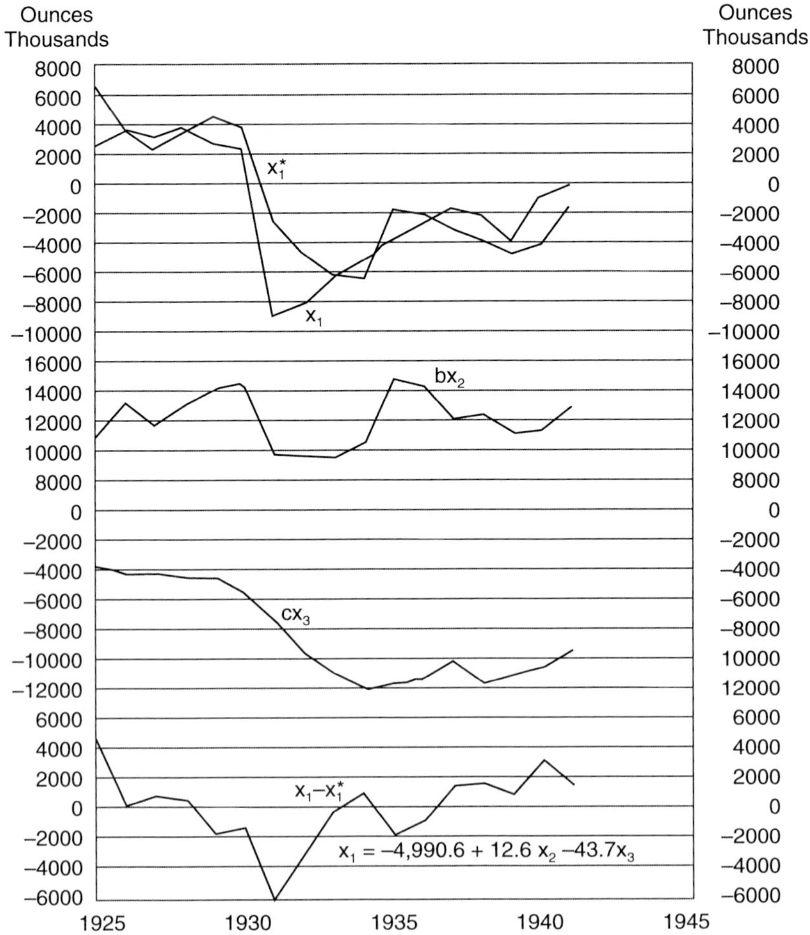

Figure 7.1 Demand for Gold in India: Correlation Chart (Equation 1)

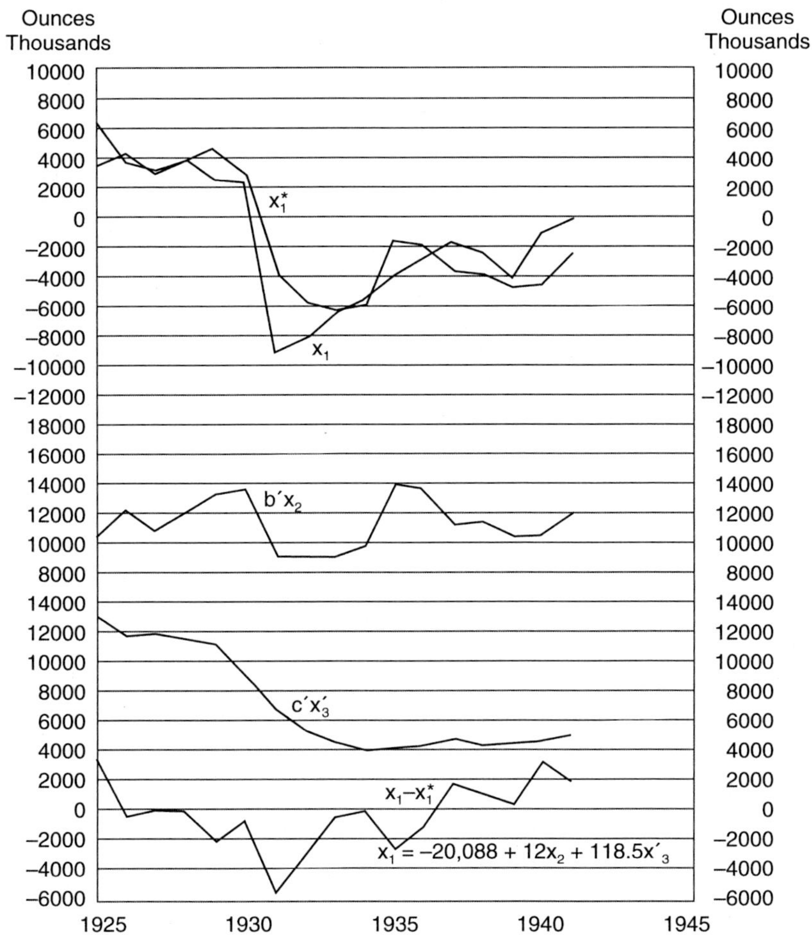

Figure 7.2 Demand for Gold in India: Correlation Chart (Equation 2)

the two curves are almost alike. The curves bX_2 and cX_3 indicate how much of the variation in X_1 is explained by variation in X_2 and X_3, respectively. And the fact that $b'X_2$ and $c'X_3'$ resemble closely bX_2 and cX_3, respectively, means that the significance assigned to the two variables (income and price) is roughly the same in both the equations (that is, irrespective of how the relative price of gold is expressed).

What can we infer from our estimating equations? It is clear that insofar as the consumption of sugar reflects changes in total real income, and inasmuch as other influences were non-operative in this period, the coefficients '*b*' and '*c*' (or b' and c') give us some idea of the significance of the income and price factor, respectively, in India's demand for gold during the period. Thus, we can say on the basis of Equation 7.1 that if total real income remained constant, but the index of the relative price of gold moved up one point, the demand for gold in India in the period 1926–41 declined roughly by 43,000 ounces.

Can we say anything from these results about the relative importance of the price and income effect? Unfortunately, when the dependent variable assumes negative values, computation of the traditional price and income elasticities is not possible. But we can still compare the absolute change in the demand for gold brought about by the same percentage change (say 1 per cent) in price and income, respectively. It is implicit in a linear relationship that the same percentage change in an independent variable will induce different absolute change in the dependent variable for different basic values of the independent variable considered. Thus, in the above relation, if the index of the relative price of gold moves from 100 to 101 (that is, by 1 per cent), the demand for gold will decline by 43,000 ounces; but if it moves from 200 to 202 (that is, also by 1 per cent), it will decline by (43,000 × 2) ounces. We can get around this difficulty by measuring the same percentage change in price and income from their respective average values during our period; and by comparing the induced change in the demand for gold, we can get some idea of the relative importance of these two factors. This is also important in view of the fact that the relative price of gold can be expressed in two different forms: X_3 and X_3'. It is obvious that when $X_3 = 200$, $X_3' = 50$. But suppose now the price of gold rises (or the wholesale prices decline), and X_3 moves to 250 and X_3' moves to 40. If we apply these values to Equation 7.1, we would expect the demand for gold to decline by (50 × 43.7) thousand ounces, that is, by 21,85,000 ounces; whereas if we use Equation 7.2, we would expect the demand for gold to decline by (10 × 118.5) thousand ounces, that is, by 11,85,000 ounces. If, however, we measure the absolute change in the demand for gold due to a 1 per cent change in the relative price of gold around the average relative price, we get virtually the same result whichever equation we use.

In our series, the average value of the consumption of sugar is 9,61,000 tonnes, and that of the index of the relative price of gold is 191 or 62, depending on whether we use X_3 or X_3'. It can be easily verified that a 1 per cent increase in price from this average value will bring about a decline of roughly 80,000 ounces in the demand for gold if Equation 7.1 is used, or a decline of about 73,000 ounces if Equation 7.2 is used. It can also be seen that a 1 per cent increase in "income" will induce an increase of 1,20,000 ounces in demand. Thus, we can say that on the average an increase in income is about one and a half times as important as a decline in the relative price of gold by the same percentage.[3]

[3] This does not mean, however, that during our period variations in the demand for gold were caused more by changes in income than by changes in price. This depends also on the relative variance of these two explanatory factors. Historically, price has been a more important factor since it has varied much more. This can be seen from the

Limitations of This Analysis

But before we proceed to apply these statistical results to the situation at present in India, we must note some of the limitations of our analysis. These limitations spring mainly from three sources: (a) the nature of the data used; (b) the type of analysis employed; and (c) the possible hazards of extrapolating the results obtained.

(a) So far as the data used for correlation are concerned, the estimates of the net flow of gold are least open to objection. But it can be doubted if the consumption of sugar reflects adequately the variations in total real income. For one thing, during the 1930s when real incomes declined, gold was being dishoarded precisely to supplement consumption—including that of sugar. In other words, the decline in real income must be greater than the decline in the consumption of sugar. Secondly, it is arguable that the decline in income during the 1930s affected mainly the agricultural classes which consume mainly *gur* or inferior kinds of sugar not included in our figures. The non-agriculturists who are the chief consumers of sugar did not suffer a similar decline in income. In other words, consumption of sugar underestimates the variations in total real income during our period. It is also arguable that our index of the relative price of gold overestimates the variations in the relative price or purchasing power of gold. The increase in this index during the 1930s is partly due to the fall in wholesale prices. But the index of the wholesale price used is based mainly on primary commodities which declined much more in price than industrial goods or services. These shortcomings of the data used tend, therefore, to overestimate the price effect and underestimate the income effect.

(b) Apart from this, fitting a linear equation to a given number of series implies that the underlying relation is linear and that over the period considered no factors other than price and income were changing. But both these assumptions are open to doubt. During the 1930s there was certainly one other factor that played an important part, viz., a change in the distribution of income. The change in the relative terms of trade between agriculture and other occupations brought about a shift in income, generally speaking, from the poor to the not-so-poor. And this had an important

---

values of the beta coefficients which are sometimes used as a measure of the individual importance of the variables.

$B_{123} = 38$ and $B_{13,2} = -0.68$ where

$$B_{123} = \frac{b \cdot \delta X_2}{\sigma X_1} \text{ (a measure of the relative importance of income)}$$

and $$B_{132} = \frac{c \cdot \sigma X_3}{\sigma X_1} \text{ (a measure of the relative importance of income)}$$

cf Table 7.1 also.

bearing on the dishoarding of gold. But by not including this factor in our equation, we overestimate the importance of the factors actually included. But apart from this, the period 1925–26 to 1941–42 seems to be reasonably free from accidental upsetting factors.

As for the linearity of the underlying relation, we have already suggested why the effect of a certain increase in income may not be the same as that of the same decline in income. It was also argued that a rise in the price of gold is not likely to depress the demand for gold beyond a point. Again, it is also implicit in our analysis that so long as income remains constant, a certain price change will have a certain fixed effect on demand irrespective of the level at which income happens to be constant. But this is not a reasonable assumption. When income is so low as to force people actually to dissave, a small rise in the price of gold may induce people to dissave mainly by selling gold. But when income is somewhat above subsistence levels, the same price change will have a smaller effect on demand. For most of the years included in our analysis, incomes were rather depressed and the relative price of gold was improving. This situation is rather unrepresentative of normal times when price changes would occur at a higher level of real income. It would seem, therefore, that an analysis based on our period would give an exaggerated picture of the importance of price movements. When we are dealing with a commodity like gold which is both an article of consumption and a means of holding savings, and with changes in real income around the subsistence level, the assumption of a linear functional relation is a rather tricky business.

(c) What about the dangers of extrapolating the results obtained to recent times? Since 1940, so many important changes in the psychology and the general economic situation have occurred that it is very unlikely that a relation which held good during 1925–40 will remain valid even now.

For one thing, during the years 1925–40, the Indian people had no experience of a serious inflation or a threat of political chaos in the country. But the generation which has lived through the 1940s has different memories and fears. During the inflation and the civil strife of recent years, the gold-hoarding classes proved wiser than the hoarders of local currency or investors in stocks and real assets. At the time of Partition, people had to leave behind their houses and land and farms; but most of them carried their gold with them. And people's psychological attitudes are governed more by such experiences than by anything else. With the threat of war and political chaos in the East, and the possibility of land redistribution in India, the price movements will not loom so large in people's minds, and their ideas about the "normal" price will become rather hazy.

Again since 1940, India is a divided country. A 1 per cent change in price in India today will have a smaller absolute effect on demand for this reason alone. Roughly speaking, this would make a difference of about 25 per cent in the demand.

On the other hand, during recent years people must have hoarded more gold than they normally do to conceal profits for tax evasion. If any change in the administrative attitude to past tax evasion were to occur, a small increase in price can bring a lot of this gold on the market for sale and profitable investment. It is also likely that the princes and zamindars whose economic position is a little adversely affected recently may want to dishoard some gold to keep up their standard of living. The inflation in recent years has brought a substantial class of the people to a point where they have to dissave in order to maintain their traditional standard of living. And an improvement in the price of gold may induce them to dissave primarily by selling gold.

But on the whole, it seems reasonable to assert that the demand for gold today would not be so responsive to changes in price as it was during 1925–40, and we have given reasons why even for the years 1925–40 our estimate errs on the side of exaggeration. This can be substantiated by two things: we can estimate the demand for gold in a recent year on the basis of our estimating equation, and see if it corresponds to the actual demand; and we can compare changes in demand with changes in the relative price of gold in the recent past, and see what this yields.

During 1949, the production of sugar in India was 10,50,000 tonnes and the index of the relative price of gold was roughly 210. Since our estimating equation applies to India and Pakistan, it is better to treat the entire production of sugar in India as the consumption for India and Pakistan. Prior to Partition, the sugar mills which met virtually all the demand for sugar in the subcontinent were almost all situated in present India. But to make allowance for error, we can put the consumption of sugar in India and Pakistan in 1949 at 11,00,000 tonnes.

Substituting these values in our equation, we get:

The demand for gold in India and Pakistan during 1949:

$$= -4990.6 + (12.6 \times 1100) - (43.7 \times 210)$$
$$= -307.6 \text{ thousand ounces.}$$

(If we use Equation 7.2 and substitute the relevant values, we get an estimated outflow of gold of about 2,00,000 ounces for the present year.)

That is to say, India and Pakistan should have been net exporters of gold in 1949 to the extent of roughly 3,00,000 ounces. But in point of fact, India alone was importing something like one million (1 million = 10 lakh) ounces of gold in that year. While the difference of about 1.3 million ounces is both considerable and understandable in view of the changes in the situation, it is well to remember that a discrepancy of that magnitude between the actual and the computed value occurred in half of the years for which the correlation was made. This piece of evidence, therefore, is not quite as decisive as it looks at first sight.

Let us look next at some of the recent data and see how responsive the demand for gold has been to changes in its relative price. Precise figures of changes in gold stock are not available since the suspension of gold import licences in 1947. But the off-take of gold from the Bombay market is a good indicator of changes in demand. In the early months of 1948, there was a sharp rise in wholesale prices and a consequent decline in the relative price of gold due to the policy of decontrol adopted in December 1947. But the demand for gold around these months does not show any great responsiveness to changes in the relative price of gold.

Application to the Current Situation

It has been emphasized in the foregoing discussion that due to the shortcomings in our data and statistical method and the changes in the situation since 1940, we would get an exaggerated idea of the responsiveness of India's demand for gold to changes in the price of gold if we apply our results automatically. Thus, if it is true even today that a 1 per cent increase in the relative price of gold will reduce the demand for gold by 80,000 ounces, this implies a price elasticity as high as eight[4] or, at least, of six if allowance is made for the fact that India is now smaller by approximately one-fourth its previous size. In other words, if the wholesale prices in India were to remain unchanged, and the price of gold were to rise about 16 per cent, the entire demand for gold in India would disappear, and something like a 20 per cent increase in the price of gold would make India a net exporter of gold. But in view of all the limitations pointed out above, we, at any rate, would be chary of drawing any such conclusions. What does seem reasonable to assert is that the demand for gold in India is fairly responsive to changes in its price, at least within a small range of price changes.

This discussion has a great bearing on the behaviour of gold prices in India after devaluation. One would normally expect the rupee price of gold to rise as a result of devaluation—the supply price of gold in terms of dollars being unchanged, it would rise in terms of rupees. But, in fact, the rupee price of gold has remained relatively stable. If we accept the validity of our statistical estimate to the recent situation without any reservation, we have here a complete explanation of this phenomenon. When the demand curve is highly elastic (with reference to price changes), an upward shift in the

[4] On the basis of the current demand for gold being put at one million ounces. Needless to say, this is merely an estimate. Some authorities have suggested a much smaller figure. It may be noticed that we are here using the relation which held good "on the average", and not applying a 1 per cent change in the relative price directly to the actual relative price at present. But this does not make much difference since the average value of the index of relative price (191) is not much different from the present value (about 210). In fact, we would get a still higher price elasticity if the actual value of the relative price index at present were used.

supply curve will raise the price but little. But it would be stretching the evidence too far to say that this, in fact, was the reason. Quite apart from the limitations of our analysis, such a conclusion does not square with the experience since devaluation. If demand is very elastic, price will not rise much despite a rise in the supply price; but the quantity demanded must decline significantly in this case. But if we look at the off-take of gold from the Bombay market, no such decline is in evidence.[5]

The explanation of the stability of gold price in India despite devaluation must be sought elsewhere. Various such explanations are possible.

For one thing, it may be argued that whereas devaluation shifted the supply curve (in terms of rupee prices) upwards, other factors simultaneously tended to push it downwards. One such factor was the sale of the Nizam of Hyderabad's gold by the Reserve Bank of India. But this could not have been of much importance; and it is well to remember that as against this we have the decision of the Bombay Bullion Association in early October 1949 to impose a margin of Rs 7 per *tola* of gold on all outstanding as well as fresh purchases. But the crash in premium prices, particularly in the East, due to the dishoarding of Chinese gold must have shifted the supply curve for India downwards. At present, the supply of gold in India consists of gold smuggled from outside markets. In view of the high price fetched by gold in India, a large part of this supply must have been bought at premium prices in other markets.

But there is another explanation possible also, viz., that due to the strict controls over the import of gold and the consequent insulation of the Indian market, the supply curve of gold is almost completely inelastic in the relevant range. The channels of smuggling being what they are, access to them is bound to be limited; and customs vigilance will not permit smuggling to exceed a certain limit. If the demand is high in relation to this limited supply, equilibrium will be reached at a price substantially above the price at which it is just worthwhile for the smugglers to put this supply on market. Under these circumstances, an increase in the price at which smugglers get their gold will not raise the market price. This factor will also explain why the Indian price should be stable in spite of a decline in the premium price of gold in other markets. This is illustrated in the diagram.

[5] The Average Daily Off-take of Gold from the Bombay Market (in *tolas*) was:

April 1949	6,800	November 1949	5000
May 1949	6,250	December 1949	4400
June 1949	5,550	January 1950	7500
July 1949	7,000	February 1950	6250
August 1949	4,250	March 1950	5600
September 1949	5,600	April 1950	7500
October 1949	5,200	May 1950	6000

Source: Computed from *Premchand Raychand Weekly Bulletins*.

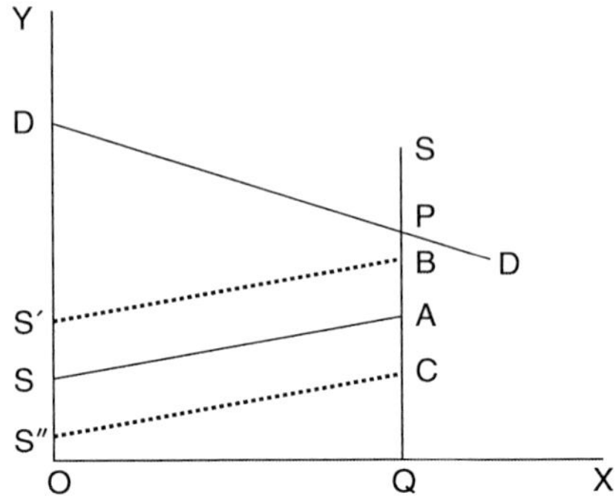

Point A corresponds to the rupee price at which the quantity *OQ* that can be normally smuggled can be sold by just covering the risk and cost of smuggling it. But the demand being high, the actual price would be *PQ*. As a result of devaluation, the supply curve SAS moves up to *S′BS*; but the price remains unchanged. The same is true if the crash in other premium markets pushes down the supply curve to *S″CS*. The rupee price of gold would remain pegged at *PQ* irrespective of the nature of the demand curve. Changes in the supply curve would only change the abnormal profits of the smugglers. The supply curve need not be completely inelastic as is shown in the diagram for the purpose of illustration. Our own guess is that the explanation of the stability of the Indian gold price should be sought in the crash in premium markets outside India and in the character of the Indian supply curve explained above rather than in the high elasticity of the Indian demand curve.

Admittedly, if the supply curve rises sufficiently (that is, above the point P) the demand curve will come into its own. This would also be the case if gold were to be freely admitted into India once again, pushing the supply curve downwards and making it more elastic. The rupee price of gold would be brought in harmony with premium prices in other markets, and the inflow of gold in India would increase depending on the elasticity of demand. But our own guess is that this elasticity would be found to be lower than that revealed by our statistical analysis. Needless to say, we cannot be dogmatic in such matters, lacking as we do the data for assessing the relative importance of the various qualitative considerations listed above. And any such conclusion is bound to remain largely a matter of individual judgement.

CHAPTER 8

On Turning Gold into Base Metal*

In prosperity as in the hour of need the thoughts of most Indians turn to gold. And with the steady drain on our foreign exchange reserves for over two years now, we have reached a stage as a nation when the question is being asked whether we could utilize the idle gold hoards of the people to see us through the critical years ahead. No less a person than the Prime Minister voiced this feeling at the recent meeting of the All India Manufacturers' Organization and the idea has received impetus after the publication by the Reserve Bank of India of its estimate of private gold hoards in the country. In a recent issue of its monthly bulletin, the Bank has ventured the estimate that the total private stocks of gold in the country would be around 1.5 million ounces, or Rs 1,750 crore (1 crore = 10 million) in value at the international price of gold of $35 an ounce. Needless to say, a sizeable part of this gold must be held in small quantities by thousands of people and the aggregate figure itself can only be indicative of the rough order of magnitude of private gold hoards. But the fact remains that a transfer to official reserves of even 10 or 15 per cent of the gold belonging to the people would add considerably to our external viability.

The transfer of private gold to official reserves can take place in one of the following ways:

(a) purchase in the open market by the government;
(b) issue of bonds redeemable in rupees against delivery of gold;
(c) issue of bonds to be subscribed as well as redeemed in gold; and
(d) acquisition by compulsion.

* Originally published in the *Economic Weekly*, Special Number, July 1958.

Open Market Purchase

The purchase of gold in the open market would seem to be ruled out as a practical step. As a member of the International Monetary Fund, the Government of India is debarred from buying gold at a price higher than the international price which works out at about Rs 62.50 per *tola*. It is obvious that with the internal price of gold around Rs 115 per tola, there would be no takers for any offer to buy gold at the international price. Even if we were to disregard the obligation to the Fund—and this can hardly be done lightly—there would be little gain in open market purchases of gold.

Apart from the inflationary consequences of large-scale monetization of idle gold, the purchase of gold by the government would make sense only if the supply of smuggled gold is extremely inelastic. Otherwise, the entry of government into the market would merely increase the scale of smuggling with the gain to official reserves in the form of gold more than offset by the indirect loss of foreign exchange, as each unit of smuggled gold must inevitably cost more in foreign exchange than its value in terms of the international price. But it would clearly be unwise to gamble with our dwindling reserves on the assumption that the worst is already happening in regard to gold smuggling so that the gold purchased by the government in the market could only come from existing internal supplies.

The second alternative of issuing rupee securities in exchange of gold is in a way already being adopted. It is open to anyone holding gold today to sell the gold in the market and to invest the proceeds in small savings or in rupee securities. The mere offer on the part of the government to exchange gold for rupee securities introduces no real change in the existing situation whereby the prevailing assets preference of the people could be modified. Nor does it alter the balance of advantage in favour of gold. It is therefore difficult to see how the mere offer of rupee securities in exchange of gold would induce people to part with even a small fraction of their gold. There is also the question of the valuation of the gold for determining the value of the security offered in return and the objection on the part of the IMF to valuation at anything other than the international price.

Gold Bonds

Would the situation alter materially if the securities offered in return of gold are also redeemable in gold? The issue of gold bonds would not involve any violation of IMF rules. If gold is to be returned for gold, it is obviously unnecessary to value gold unless the interest on gold bonds is to be paid in rupees. On this minor point, however, it should not be difficult to get a waiver from the Fund.

It is also clear that at a time when we are borrowing large sums from abroad, it is not entirely senseless to borrow gold on the promise of returning it, say, after fifteen or twenty years. The assumption in a foreign exchange borrowing must inevitably be that we expect our balance-of-payments position to improve in the years to come so that the debts incurred now could be paid back later without difficulty. On the same assumption, the gold borrowed now can be used for importing much-needed materials and machinery and can be replenished before the time comes for returning it to its rightful owners. Apart from this, in the present context, it would be useful to augment official gold reserves by transfer from private gold hoards even if the intention is not to use the gold so obtained for purchases abroad. A larger gold reserve now will strengthen confidence in the rupee and this is no mean advantage in the present state of our sterling balance.

Response Not Worthwhile

The real question is: Will the response to gold bonds be worthwhile? The demand for gold in India arises from many factors. In large part, it is decreed by social custom and it is doubtful if hoarders of jewellery or ornaments will be prepared to forgo the cost of workmanship in order to be able to purchase gold bonds. Equally, if the suggestion is that jewellery should be returned as such, it would make little sense on the part of the government to collect a large variety of small ornaments, value them, keep them in safe custody for fifteen or twenty years and pay interest on the same in the meanwhile. It is also clear that those who hold gold as insurance against political uncertainty would not be persuaded to part with their gold.

It is only that part of gold which is hoarded today as hedge against inflation or as a convenient way of concealing wealth obtained by illegal means which might come out in response to an offer of gold bonds—especially if the bonds are bearer bonds and no questions are asked of subscribers about the sources of their gold. A gold bond which can be purchased anonymously without fuss and which can be exchanged for gold at the end of a prescribed period would offer to its hoarders virtually all the economic advantages they enjoy today from the possession of gold with the additional attraction of being able to earn some interest on the hoarded wealth. On the other hand, the one advantage that will have to be given by exchanging gold for gold bonds is that of insurance against political and similar risks.

May Facilitate Tax Evasion

It will be seen that unlike bonds redeemable in rupees, gold bonds would introduce a real change in the prevailing assets preference of the people. But whether the response to gold bonds would be reasonably satisfactory or not is difficult to say in the absence of any knowledge about the extent to which different motives predominate in determining the demand for gold currently. All one can say is that to the extent that the motives for gold hoarding are likely to be mixed, even gold bonds would prove unattractive to most people.

There is also the question whether it would be advisable to introduce a new asset in the community where the main if not the sole attraction for it would lie in the superior facility it would offer for concealing illegally acquired wealth and for evading taxes. Indeed, to the extent that gold bonds prove attractive, they would also give an impetus to smuggling of gold into the country as it would clearly be to the advantage of people to acquire gold in the first instance in order to acquire gold bonds which are preferred to gold but which can be purchased only with gold. Admittedly, the gold smuggled for this reason would ultimately find its way into official reserves but this does not alter the fact that the country suffers, if anything, a loss in official foreign exchange reserves as a net result. The conclusion seems therefore inescapable that the introduction of gold bonds would either prove a flop or would make for a stronger entrenchment in the country of anti-social activities such as tax evasion and smuggling of gold.

Compulsory Acquisition

There remains then the alternative of compulsory acquisition of a part of privately held gold. One has only to mention this possibility to realize that short of a revolution, the gold held in the form of jewellery and ornaments can hardly be acquired by compulsion. The utmost one can think of adopting in the near future is a system of regulations such as those in the US which prohibit private ownership of gold except in the form of jewellery of certain specifications. But a regulation of this sort would serve little purpose in India where demand for gold is widespread and where the gold at present held privately is held in all sorts of forms, ranging from small ornaments to dinner sets and gold bars, so that the line of demarcation between jewellery and non-jewellery cannot be drawn easily. The only practicable alternative in India would be to prohibit private hoarding of gold in any form in excess of a certain limit per person. But politically and administratively, the time is hardly ripe for a solution of this nature.

Are we then to conclude that the search for a philosopher's stone which can turn gold into the sinews of India's economic growth is as much in vain as the more familiar search for an alchemy to convert base metals into gold? If the search is to yield fruit in the immediate future, when our balance-of-payments prospects appear particularly bleak, the answer to the question just raised is almost certainly in the affirmative. But for better or for worse, the habit of gold hoarding has a great deal of significance to India's economic future and it would be a pity if an attitude of utter helplessness is allowed to develop in regard to it. There is so much talk of perspective planning these days—talk of keeping the long-term goals in view even as we plan for the next year or two. But what is the perspective we should keep in mind in regard to private gold hoards in India? There can be little doubt that the development of the country requires that sooner or later ways must be found to eradicate the evil of gold hoarding which saps the vitality of the nation at many points. There can be even less doubt that the solution of the problem must lie, at least in part, in compulsion, for if we are to wait for the process of education to reduce the attraction of gold, we might as well wait for ever.

It is perhaps by means of a mixture of sustained propaganda, compulsion, incentives and a sort of war of nerves affecting people's expectations about the value of gold in future that the long-term objective of mobilizing private gold hoards and of reducing the attraction of gold can be achieved. But whatever the ultimate solution, the agenda for the dethronement of gold from the position it occupies today in India deserves more serious consideration at the hands of thinking people in the country than it has received so far.

Part III

Economic Development and Planning

CHAPTER 9

Exports by Countries in Process of Industrialization*

Balance-of-payments difficulties are by no means the prerogative of countries in the process of development. But unlike the difficulties encountered from time to time by industrially advanced countries, the payments problems of poorer nations are not amenable essentially to fiscal and monetary discipline. Inadequate savings and lack of an efficient and diversified economic structure, which are manifestations of poverty itself, are among the most important limiting factors in raising export earnings so that, in a fundamental sense, the surest and the best way of promoting export earnings of countries in the process of industrialization is to assist the process of growth and industrialization itself.

There is nevertheless justification for distinguishing policies for promoting export earnings from measures to promote growth as such for the following reasons:

(1) In the absence of deliberate measures to promote the export earnings of developing countries, their reliance on external capital will be that much greater. While the international community has shown increasing readiness to assist the development of the poorer nations, we have yet to accept unrequited and continuing transfers from the rich to the poor as a principle of international validity. For practical if not moral reasons, therefore, there is urgency about the task of promoting export earnings which stems from a realistic assessment of the possibilities of international aid. The urgency is

* Originally published in *New Directions for World Trade*, A Chatham House Report, Oxford University Press, London, 1964.

all the greater in view of the fact that such assistance as is available or likely to be available will in time create a sizeable and progressively growing burden of interest charges and debt repayment.

(2) While rapid growth provides the basis for growing exports, it cannot be taken for granted that in the absence of deliberate care, growth itself will proceed along lines where potential export opportunities are not frustrated. Either for lack of sufficient appreciation of the issues involved or for reasons inherent in their situation, the developing countries might need special effort if growth in general and increase in export earnings are to react favourably on each other.

(3) It is common knowledge that even such export opportunities as the developing countries have succeeded in creating for themselves are often frustrated by the policies of other countries so that growth in general cannot be translated into growing export opportunities without the cooperation of others.

(4) Given rational development policies on the part of the poorer nations and lack of restrictions in advanced countries, there may still be special handicaps which can be removed only by preferential arrangements or by measures of international assistance at least over a limited period. Thus the need to tap and cultivate export markets long before a country becomes fully competitive in a certain line and the difficulties of such a course for a country already beset by payments problems might call for arrangements which differ only slightly from direct aid. Aid through trade might, however, be justified if only because the urgency of a vigorous export drive on the part of the developing countries derives partly at any rate from the limitations on developmental assistance.

In keeping with the considerations just mentioned the main sections of this paper relate to policies of developing countries and those of advanced countries, and to measures of international preference and assistance. These sections are preceded by a brief account of the nature and magnitude of the problem. In view of their importance, relations between developing countries and those with socialist countries are dealt with separately. The emphasis throughout is on exports of semi-manufactures and manufactures, as problems of primary products are assumed to be the subject-matter of another paper. The focus again is on India. Tolstoy's dictum that happy families are all alike whereas the unhappy ones are unhappy each in their own way is true as much of nations as of families. There is nevertheless sufficient general validity in India's problems at this stage for the rest of the developing world. Relevant statistics for the developing countries as a whole have been presented in the *UN World Economic Survey, 1962*, and consequently, no elaborate attempt to quantify the problems has been made here.

The Nature and Magnitude of the Problem

There seems to be a consensus of opinion that the export earnings of developing countries should grow roughly at the rate of 7 per cent per annum so that they are virtually doubled over the current (or the next) decade. A 5 per cent per annum growth in national product for the poorer countries is now accepted as a minimum objective. Experience the world over indicates that import requirements grow with the growth of the economy and this is all the more so when growth is export oriented and requires as a consequence import of even sophisticated components and materials. While no generalization about the rate of growth of imports would be valid, it may be safe to assume that they will grow at the same rate as national income. Exports must grow even faster if only to bridge progressively the present gap in balance-of-payments as well as to provide for the growing requirements of debt servicing.

A 7 per cent per annum increase in export earnings is not altogether unknown in economic history; and it has, in fact, been exceeded in recent years by countries like Japan. For many of the developing countries, and particularly for India, however, it represents a very sharp improvement over recent trends. Although no firm targets for export earnings for 1970–71 or for 1975–76 are yet set officially, there is a feeling in many quarters in India that the objective of doubling the 1960–61 level of export earnings may have to be reached not by 1970–71 but by some date between 1970–71 and 1975–76 (that is, the end of the fourth and the fifth five-year plans, respectively). Whether a more modest target for exports implies greater emphasis on import substitution or/and an extension of the time required for reaching the stage of self-sustaining growth is a question that need not detain us here. But on any reckoning, a 5 per cent per annum increase in export earnings in the immediate future with prospects of an even higher rate of increase in the years to come appears to be a minimum objective even for a country like India where possibilities of import substitution are somewhat greater than in most developing countries.

Theoretically, an increase in export earnings could be secured to some extent by improvement in terms of trade. But whatever the justification for such a course in general, the chances for a significant improvement in terms of trade cannot be considered bright. The desired growth in exports, therefore, must be achieved essentially by an increase in the quantum of exports.

As for the nature of the products from which additional export earnings could or should be reasonably expected, perhaps the only generalization which can safely be attempted is that the problem is sufficiently urgent and complex to warrant the fullest exploitation of all the avenues for export—whether traditional or new, whether those related to primary products or manufactures or invisibles. No opportunity for increasing exports of primary products, whether by greater efficiency or cultivation of new uses and demands, could be neglected especially when an even modest percentage increase in primary exports (or traditional exports, which in India's case are not necessarily primary exports) would produce sizeable additional earnings. There is nevertheless a real sense in which it would be appropriate to look to newer products of industrialization for imparting a lasting dynamism to exports in most developing countries. Apart from questions of relative responsiveness of world demand, it is self-evident that exports of manufactures, whenever feasible, have a more beneficial effect on the growth of incomes and employment. Again, many of the primary products for which world demand is responsive, for example, iron ore, require such huge investment of capital and know-how in mining, transport, port facilities and the like that it is more meaningful to regard them as products of industrialization rather than as products akin to coca-beans or coffee or cotton.

By and large, the potential or actual ability to export products of industrialization even for countries in the process of industrialization arises from three factors: industrialization based on the processing of materials and minerals in the production of which they have a comparative advantage; industrialization which begins as an instrument for import substitution but which emerges in due course as a source for exports as a result both of development of skills and some intrinsic comparative advantage such as cheap labour (or convenient raw material supply); and industrial exports which are based on artistic skills in designing and the like which are not necessarily correlated with the degree of development. For India, a rough assessment of the likely avenues for additional export earnings is summarized in Table 9.1.

It is not necessary for our present purpose to comment in detail on the figures cited in Table 9.1. But a few points may be noted. As a matter of hope at any rate, considerable reliance is placed on primary products such as iron ore as well as on products of newer chemical and engineering industries. As for the nature of the engineering products for which export markets are visualized, the following enumeration from the report of a team which recently investigated the potential market for these products in Western Europe (in the non-insular sense of this term) is significant.

1. Iron and steel casting for machine tools and machine-building industries and other components and parts required.
2. Tools, dies, jigs arid fixtures as per specifications.
3. Free forgings.

Table 9.1 Projections of India's Exports
(Rs million)

	1960–61 (actual)	*1970–71 (est.)*
I. Major Traditional Exports	*3,160*	*4,000*
(a) Tea	1,236	1,550
(b) Jute manufactures	1,350	1,600
(c) Cotton textiles	574	850
II. Some Other Traditional Exports	*3,700*	*1,900*
(a) Spices	166	220
(b) Tobacco	157	250
(c) Vegetable oils & oilcakes	279	650
(d) Cashew kernel	189	300
(e) Raw cotton & cotton waste	108	200
(f) Leather, leather manufactures, & hides & skins	356	450
(g) Fish	46	300
(h) Manganese ore	140	140
(i) Coffee	72	140
(j) Coir yarn & manufacture	87	150
(k) Iron ore	300	900
III. Relatively New Exports of Manufactures	*390*	*1,500*
(a) Sugar	25	250
(b) Woollen manufactures	53}	200
(c) Art silk fabrics	26}	
(d) Other new manufactures, mainly engineering goods, metal products, chemicals & plastics	286	1,050
IV. Others (Mainly Miscellaneous Traditional)	*1,180*	*1,800*
Total	*6,630*	*11,000*

Source: *India's Foreign Trade*, Government of India; 1962.

4. Special purpose machines either for incorporation in a European product or for use as such, for example, lathe chucks, die-casting machines and hydraulic machines.
5. Fabrication of machine tools, plant and machinery of a less sophisticated nature where a European manufacturer is procuring them from elsewhere at present.
6. Wooden as well as metallic patterns according to the designs and specifications of European manufacturers.

7. Producer goods of the second degree such as diesel engines, electric motors, switchgear, sewing machines and small tools.
8. Consumer goods like steel folding furniture, specialized builders' hardware, coffers, ventilator fans, sanitary fittings, manhole covers and concrete reinforcing bars.
9. Special consumer items like musical boxes, tool kits, modern gift articles and domestic appliances.

The above quotation brings out an important fact about international trade in manufactures, viz., that much of it consists of bits and pieces of intermediate products which enter into different things, as distinguished from whole or final products which enter directly into consumption or investment not so much bicycles or sewing machines as a miscellany of products required by more sophisticated manufacturers in advanced countries. Trade in such products, which has a growing relevance to countries in the process of industrialization, requires a degree of contacts and collaboration among producers in different countries which is qualitatively different from normal notions of sales promotion and the like. We shall revert to this theme at a later stage.

As for the destination of additional exports, there is a prima facie case for increasing exports (of manufactures) to countries which are already industrially advanced. The present imbalance in India's payments position arises mainly in respect of its relations with the industrially advanced countries, particularly with members of the EEC; and the payment of debt charges will also need to be made to the same group of countries. Even allowing for substantial industrialization of an import-substituting character, total imports from advanced countries are bound to increase over the years especially when some of the advanced countries such as the United States and Canada are important producers of materials and primary products such as non-ferrous metals and food grains or cotton. There seems to be no escape, therefore, from the vital necessity of increasing exports to the countries already industrially advanced—whether capitalist or socialist.

Needless to say, there is need—and justification as we shall argue later—for increasing exports to other developing countries as well. But such exports (and the corresponding imports) are not likely to reduce the gap with the industrially advanced countries either by providing alternative sources of supply on a sufficiently large scale or by the emergence of a new triangular relationship in which India covers its gap with the richer nations by realizing a surplus with those among the developing nations which are still fortunate enough to have a surplus with the advanced nations. This kind of triangular-trade relationship has played an important part in world trade in the past; and it may still have a marginal role in the future in view of the inevitable differences in the stage of development reached by different developing nations at any given time, but the hinterland of underdeveloped nations ready to take the place of those who have moved up the ladder of development is fast disappearing; and the urge for development today is so ubiquitous that it is difficult to envisage that there would be many among the poorer nations who would continue to enjoy a payments surplus with the advanced nations. The experience of Japan, which has built its external viability on the solid foundation of a substantial increase in the exports of semi-manufactures and manufactures to more advanced countries, is instructive in this regard. Altogether, while multilateral trade relations are bound to exist and even perhaps grow in absolute terms, they are not likely to follow any standard pattern in which countries at the intermediate stage of development meet their deficits with more advanced nations by developing surpluses with those who are perched on an even lower rung of the ladder of industrialization.

In short, the heart of the problem in seeking to promote a rapid increase in the export earnings of countries in the process of industrialization is securing a rapid increase in the absorption of manufactured products from such countries on the part of the industrially advanced nations of Europe—East and West—North America and Japan.

Policies in Developing Countries

In the ultimate analysis the major part of the responsibility for promoting their exports must be borne by the developing countries themselves. This in turn requires on their part sufficient attention to the export sector in the allocation of investment and other scarce resources, an adequate measure of restraint on domestic consumption so as to release growing surpluses for export, the maintenance of a reasonable degree of financial stability (and failing that a promptness in adjusting the exchange rate to a realistic level) and, finally, a sustained promotional drive to exploit and cultivate markets abroad for the surplus it can export. So much in fact should command general agreement among economists of all persuasions and represents indeed the essential strategy for export promotion in all countries. Is there, then, something inherent in the situation of the developing countries which calls for special emphasis on any of these fundamental aspects of export policy?

A common feature of most developing countries is the very tight regime of import and exchange restrictions that they maintain in response to their chronic payments difficulties. It is arguable that this fact creates a bias in favour of import substitution as distinguished from export promotion which needs to be specifically corrected. In strict logic, import substitution and promotion of exports must be assigned equal priority as objectives as they have the same bearing on balance-of-payments.[1] Nor can one adduce any *a priori* reasons for readily assuming that the scope for import substitution for any country at a given stage of development must be necessarily greater than that for potential exports. The same conditions which create substantial opportunities for import substitution such as diversified resources and a population capable of mastering intricate techniques, should also augur well for sizeable new opportunities for export. At best one can only say that in some cases industrialization might proceed first from the above via import substitution and go on to create new export potential at a later stage. But as we have already argued, industrialization can also proceed in part at any rate along lines where exploitation of natural or cultural advantages is the decisive factor so that new export potential might be created without any previous phase of import substitution. In strict logic as well as a matter of practical necessity, therefore, export promotion and import substitution should receive equal emphasis unless there are strong reasons to the contrary. But the prevalence of import control imparts an obviousness to the need for import substitution which does not exist in regard to export promotion. And quite apart from possible distortions in policy or planning, the very existence of import controls increases the profitability of industries that compete with imports so that they are able to command an unduly high share of scarce resources.

If the industries which are thus favoured by import restrictions are in any ease those whose products are considered essential and which are likely to develop along efficient lines before long, there may not be anything objectionable in the bias imparted by import restrictions. A possible opportunity to export would be foregone in favour of replacing over a corresponding period of time an import which is considered essential and which would, therefore, have continued in the absence of the development under consideration. But quite often, the industries that grow behind tariff walls and quota restrictions produce less essential goods with little or no prospect of manufacture on a comparatively efficient basis for many years to come; and even when the goods produced are essential, import restrictions often encourage industrial progress on such a wide but thin front that it must be considered less beneficial than an alternative course which concentrates on the fullest exploitation of the opportunities for exports and import substitution in a few selected lines. The difficulties of operation on a small scale which are inherent in the early stages of industrialization are often compounded by the necessity to resort to high tariffs and import restrictions.

[1] One might, if one is inclined, apply a different risk factor to the potential for import substitution and export promotion; but the reasons for the difference must be established rather than assumed.

The dangers just outlined need to be avoided by a measure of control on the establishment and expansion of industries as well as by incentives—such as subsidies and preferential allocation of scarce resources including foreign exchange—for selected export industries and by fiscal disincentives by way of excise duties and the like for less essential activities which are made unduly profitable by restrictions. Indeed, a measure of preference for export industries is needed merely to redress the balance in their favour and to avoid an undue diversion of resources to other sectors. But it is doubtful if the restraint on the growth of inessential industries or on too diffused a growth of even essential import-substitution industries could be provided except by some form of direct control.

Given proper attention to exports in the allocation of investment and other scarce resources, there is little that is special about developing countries in the matter of exercising a restraint on domestic consumption so as to release reasonable export surpluses or about avoiding waste, inflation and unrealistic exchange rates. In the matter of sales promotion, however, the very fact that the developing countries have to make a desperate competitive effort in the midst of serious payments difficulties imposes certain handicaps. Promotion of exports is highly expensive in terms of foreign exchange expenditure, be it in terms of advertising, after-sale service, travel to maintain contacts, credit facilities, or demonstration and display. The difficulty is all the greater when developing countries have to export manufactures which have yet to establish a name and indeed to overcome prejudice, and when these manufactures are often in the nature of bits and pieces which meet the ancillary needs of more sophisticated producers abroad. While the developing countries might be urged to pursue a more forward-looking policy in these respects, there are limits to foresight on a limited budget, and we shall argue later that the handicap under consideration here provides perhaps one of the most fruitful fields for international assistance in promoting the export earnings of countries such as India.

Policies of Advanced Countries

The variety of ways in which the restrictive policies of advanced countries inhibit the growth of exports from poor countries even when the latter have developed comparative advantage in certain manufactures have been debated at great length in recent years. An admirable statement of the present position is given in the *World Economic Survey* for 1962. This is one area where despite all the talk and debate the distance between what is desirable and what actually prevails has remained as great as ever, and it is a sad commentary on statesmanship in the modern age that one still has to refute manifestly absurd arguments such as the unfairness of competition that derives its strength from general poverty and consequent low wages. Elimination of present restrictions—and the acceptance of a framework of commercial policy which would avoid the recurrence of similar restrictions in future—are by far the most important consequences that can flow from the United Nations Conference on Trade and Development. The danger here is that since this question of elimination and avoidance of restrictions has become so familiar, it is likely to inspire boredom or worse still, a desire to look for new remedies which might divert attention from the central task at hand.

What needs to be done in regard to the commercial policy of advanced countries is simple enough to state. The present tariff structure which discourages the imports of semi-processed and processed goods must be modified radically. By and large, the advanced countries must follow a policy of free trade, avoiding both high tariffs and quota restrictions. The proposed round of negotiations for reducing tariffs in the United States and Western Europe should include items of interest to the developing countries which must be formally and actively associated with these negotiations to ensure this outcome. One has also the suspicion that restrictionism is practised in many industrially advanced countries by indirect or administrative measures which are sometimes clothed as measures to protect public health and the like but are often kept carefully away from the public gaze. While simple to state, the tasks that lie in this field are by no means simple to achieve. The least that is needed is a firm declaration of what must be achieved in each specific field over a definite period of time with a regular international machinery for periodic consultations with all concerned to point up failures in performance and to make appropriate recommendations. It is again a curious commentary on our international institutional framework that while the IMF "consults" its poorer members every year with all the thoroughness of a judicial inquiry and with specific recommendations in regard to removal of exchange restrictions, no such machinery with the same authority exists for bringing about the necessary reform in the commercial policy of the advanced nations.

Apart from reform of commercial policy, the advanced countries could also assist the export drive of countries in the process of industrialization by suitable policies in regard to foreign investment, whether private or public. A greater flow of private foreign investment in export industries in the developing countries is one of the surest ways of promoting exports. Foreign private investment would command both greater knowledge of the needs of the home country (or the country of import) as well as greater power to exercise pressure for removing restrictions. Frozen shrimps, canned foods and a variety of specialized products which are produced and marketed by big concerns in advanced countries could be supplied more cheaply from developing countries in many cases. The recent measures adopted by the American administration for giving preferential treatment to private United States investment in developing countries are a step in the right direction, and it may not be difficult to evolve some international code in this regard. As it is, private foreign investment is often interested in merely getting entrenched behind tariff walls and import restrictions so as to preserve erstwhile markets rather than in creating abroad a base for world-wide markets. Indeed, till recently, most agreements pertaining to private foreign investment or collaboration in India used to include provisions prohibiting exports from India of the products of such investment. A measure of cooperation from advanced countries in limiting, if not outlawing, such blatantly market-sharing devices would also serve a very useful purpose.

Advanced countries are already providing considerable assistance from public funds to the developing nations and the question naturally arises if such assistance could not be made a basis for promoting exports from the developing countries. This is all the more imperative since aid at present takes the form of loans rather than grants. Unfortunately, there is still considerable prejudice against financing industrial ventures by aid, particularly if these ventures are not privately owned. This prejudice is bound to limit the scope for channelling aid in the direction of export creation. One could indeed argue again that since virtually all aid today is tied to purchases within the aid-giving countries, the payment of debt charges must similarly be tied to purchases within the country paying such charges. In equity as in logic, such a position would be fully justified. But even if one does not go so far, there is clear need for allocating a sizeable amount of aid to activities which are likely to lead to larger exports to the assisting country or to a group of assisting countries. Wherever possible, an element of long-term contracts could also be provided as in the case of Indo-Japanese collaboration for the development of Indian iron ore resources for export to Japan. The principle is capable of much wider application particularly in respect of a variety of metals and metal products such as aluminium or castings or even steel and standard structures. One advantage of such arrangements, apart from assurance of markets, would be the technical assistance that will go with it in assuring standards of quality and other specifications so as to evolve more enduring competitive capacity. In the case of assistance from the Soviet Union, India has received technical assistance for developing new export markets for items such as shoes, and the principle is sought to be extended in future to capital assistance as well. The capitalist countries which rely on private trade channels are somewhat at a disadvantage in this regard; but with conscious effort, some progress should not be difficult to achieve especially in major items such as iron ore, metal ingots and the like.

Preferences for the Underdeveloped World

It has been argued of late on a number of occasions that what the developing nations need for increasing their earnings from the exports of manufactures is not merely absence of restrictions in the advanced countries but a measure of preferential treatment as well. The argument rests on the contention that industries in developing countries suffer from a number of handicaps such as lack of adequate size, higher cost of imported equipment which is often purchased against tied aid, extraordinary fiscal burdens in countries struggling to raise revenues by all means at their command, and lack of adequate experience. This being the case, industries in developing countries can make an inroad in the markets in advanced countries if they are allowed to compete on preferential rather than equal terms. There is certainly every justification for developing countries compensating their industries against such unequal fiscal and other burdens as they may have to bear in their peculiar circumstances. Going beyond this, there is also a case for export subsidies for nascent industries which are in the process of developing their full competitive powers in the same way as there is a case for protecting infant industries in the initial stages from foreign competition. The present attitude to export subsidies (or selective undervalued exchange rates) which likens them to "dumping" and invokes countervailing measures is certainly out of place and there is need for educating public opinion in this regard in the developed countries.

But can we go beyond these propositions and urge that the burden of subsidizing nascent export industries in poorer countries should be borne by the advanced countries who should agree to admit the products of the developing nations on more favourable terms than similar products of other advanced countries? A case could certainly be made out for such a general proposition. But it is doubtful if this line of attack on the problem offers any scope for success, at least in the near future. There is considerable amount of work still to be done in removing restrictions and in eliminating what amounts to discrimination against the developing countries, so that there is little to be gained by diverting attention to more radical and less acceptable solutions. In any event, the theoretical argument for protection or preference requires discriminating action—more for some industries or countries and less for others, more for the same industry and country at one point of time and less at another. Such decisions, at any rate in matters of commercial policy, are more likely to be taken at a national rather than an international level so that there would be much to be said for leaving the argument with subsidization of exports rather than going on to plead for preferential treatment in respect of them.

Having said this, several examples could be cited where a measure of preference or at least non-reciprocity would be justified and conceded in respect of export of manufactures from developing countries. It is, for example, generally recognized that reductions in trade barriers need not be reciprocal in the sense that whereas advanced countries should move progressively towards freer trade, developing countries need tariffs and even quota restrictions—for a long time to come. Tariff reductions in General Agreement on Tariffs and Trade (GATT), therefore, should not take the form of bargaining between advanced countries on matters of mutual interest but should also embrace unilateral decisions on items of interest to the poorer nations. (The developing countries might also be released from past obligations to bind certain duties as such an obligation only perpetuates quotas and deprives public exchequers of much-needed revenues.) Similarly, if a single industrialized country or a group of countries wishes to accord preference to all developing countries without according most-favoured-nation treatment to other industrialized countries, it should be free to do so. Otherwise, strict insistence on non-discrimination would put a premium on restrictionism among the industrialized countries. Again, as we shall argue later, preferences accorded by developing countries to each other without extending them to advanced countries should be regarded as a legitimate exception to the principle of non-discrimination.

As for measures of international assistance in promoting exports of the developing countries, the most suitable field for such assistance clearly would be that of removing some of the common handicaps of all young industrial nations. It is again a sad commentary on our international institutions specifically charged with responsibility in the field of international trade that they are concerned more with policing trade relations rather than with actively promoting them. Perhaps the most fruitful approach would be to look to the World Bank for filling the lacunae that exist, both because it has shown awareness of the problem and because it commands resources to do what needs to be done. The Bank has built up sizeable reserves from past profits and is currently earning handsome profits which it is genuinely seeking to invest in the development of poorer nations along lines which go somewhat beyond its charter. It would not be unnatural, therefore, to expect the Bank or a suitable adjunct of the Bank to assume responsibility in the field of assistance for trade promotion.

One field for such assistance would be in regard to export credits. Poorer countries are naturally unable to compete with richer nations in the matter of promoting exports by foregoing payments for a while. While even poor nations ought to establish on their own export credit facilities of the pre-shipment variety, an international institution to refinance post-shipment credits by developing nations would serve a very useful purpose. With its long experience in developmental banking and international tendering, the World Bank should be in a very good position to promote the development of export-credit agencies in developing countries on healthy lines; and its refinance facilities would provide legitimate assistance to exporting nations in chronic payments difficulties.

There is no reason also why the World Bank could not establish regular facilities for market surveys, for assistance in maintaining quality and certifying it, for promoting vital trade displays and the like. A few centres in important advanced countries for promoting the exports of less developed countries in general, with periodic publications and activities including organization of seminars and trade fairs, as well as provision of office and other facilities for suitably sponsored visiting businessmen from poorer countries, could go a long way in removing the disadvantage that poorer countries face in matters of trade promotion as a result of their difficult payments position. International assistance of this kind is not easy to organize and it can perhaps grow only by stages in the light of experience. But the idea is at least worth further exploration.

Trade among Developing Countries

Generally speaking, trade among developing countries is no more and no less important than trade between advanced countries on the one hand and developing countries on the other. There are, however, valid reasons for special effort to promote trade among groups of developing countries. Since countries in the process of industrialization generally suffer from the disadvantage of small domestic markets which make for uneconomic scales of operation, they could overcome this difficulty by deliberate specialization and merging of markets. Again, with their payments difficulties, most developing nations are obliged to restrict less essential imports both from advanced countries as well as from other developing countries. If they could somehow embark on a process of mutual liberalization of trade without extending similar liberalization to advanced nations, they could benefit from the gains from trade without any additional pressure on their balance-of-payments.

How exactly a greater degree of specialization in industrial investment among developing nations is to be brought about is a matter more of practical statesmanship than of economic rationale. When one talks of the long-term future, economic rationale or comparative advantage is a highly uncertain quantity, so that decisions to specialize require a considerable measure of faith—as indeed of mutual good faith. On the prospects of regional groupings among developing nations in substance as well as in form—it would be fruitless to speculate here. The difficulties of coordination in investment even when considerable political homogeneity exists are demonstrated by the recent controversies in COMECON. But the case for making even a modest beginning wherever feasible is unexceptionable. Perhaps one approach which has not been tried so far deserves attention, viz., the approach of joint ownership of specified industrial projects by a group of countries with each country claiming its dividend in the form of an appropriate share in production. Thus it is self-evident that India, Ceylon, Burma and Indonesia, for example, would all need considerable amounts of steel, fertilizers, petroleum products including petro-chemicals, rubber tyres and non-ferrous metals in the years to come. These industries could in part at least be set up on the basis of joint ownership in different countries with relative shares in investment (and, therefore, output) so designed as to meet the requirements of all the participating countries at least partially without payments difficulties arising from this area of exchange for anyone. Details of such an approach can vary and difficulties can come to light as specific proposals are negotiated. But an approach along these lines offers reasonable prospects for success at least in regions where full-fledged free trade area arrangements are premature for some years to come.

As for mutual and beneficial liberalization of trade even in less essential items—and in travel—among developing nations, there is little that can be said about how this is to be secured as much would depend on their willingness to get together and take appropriate administrative decisions. In actual practice, some mutual liberalization of the kind envisaged here takes place by way of limited bilateral arrangements despite continuing strictures on such arrangements by the IMF. Mutual liberalization through bilateralism must legitimately guard against the genuine interests of other developing countries; and for this reason, more frequent contacts and discussions at a regional rather than a bilateral level would be helpful.

Trade with Socialist Countries

The socialist countries are either industrially advanced or in the process of development. In their trade relations with developing nations, therefore, they should follow the same general policies as have been outlined above. The institutional peculiarities of the socialist countries such as centralized investment and trade decisions as well as strict control over consumption both directly and by means of fiscal levies might make it difficult to assess whether and to what extent their policies frustrate or promote exports from developing countries. But in the ultimate analysis, figures must speak. There is welcome evidence of late that the Soviet Union and other East European countries have encouraged a significant growth in imports from developing countries, including in some cases, imports of manufactured consumer goods and simple capital goods. A great deal of further progress along these lines is envisaged and more should certainly be possible with growing willingness in socialist countries to respond to forces of international specialization and to permit a higher and discriminating standard of consumption for their people. By and large, the preference for balanced trade in socialist countries has served to quicken the pace of developing new trade relations between socialist countries and the developing nations, although departures from strict bilateralism would become more urgent and useful as the socialist countries trade more extensively with the developing countries.

On the whole, there is little distinctive that needs to be said about trade with socialist countries from the point of view of the problem at hand. For the developing countries struggling with their payments problem, trade with socialist countries which have hitherto developed on rather insular lines offers a welcome opportunity for alternative sources of supply as well as additional outlets for their export products. One can only urge that the recent tendency to respond to the trade needs of developing countries on the part of socialist countries would gather momentum in the years to come.

Summing Up

Some of the important issues raised in the preceding survey of the measures to promote the export earnings of countries in process of industrialization may be summarized as follows:

1. By far the soundest way of promoting the exports of developing countries is to promote the process of growth and industrialization. There are, however, reasons for emphasizing export policies as distinct from policies which promote growth in general.
2. If the developing countries are to reach the stage of self-sustaining and adequate growth in the foreseeable future, they would need to double their export earnings over ten to fifteen years. A sizeable part of this increase must be secured from exports of manufactures to countries already industrially advanced.
3. The major part of the responsibility for promoting exports of developing countries must be borne by these countries themselves. In their specific circumstances, which require resort to stringent import and exchange restrictions, there is need for special care to ensure that industries that compete with imports do not claim a disproportionate share of scarce resources to the detriment of export industries.
4. Perhaps the most important and difficult task before the international community at present is that of securing speedy elimination of the large variety of restrictions which advanced countries maintain against imports from poorer countries. Familiarity with this theme should not be allowed to divert attention to less significant issues.
5. Both foreign aid and private foreign investment could serve as important promoters of export potential. Policies in this field should take explicit account of this fact.
6. There is every need for developing countries to take measures to rectify some of the relative disadvantages to which their export

industries are subject. There is also justification for selective export subsidies for the same reasons that require protection for infant industries. But the case for preferential treatment for the manufactured exports of developing countries, while valid in theory, is not likely to command acceptance and insistence on it may well divert attention from more urgent issues. This is not to deny that there are specific cases where preference—or more correctly, a release from the obligation not to discriminate—would be both justified and practicable.

7. Given the difficulty of investing in export promotion on a sufficient scale in the face of acute payments difficulties for most developing nations, there is clear need for international assistance in forms such as re-finance facilities for export credits, establishment of international centres in selected advanced countries for promoting the exports of developing countries and the like.
8. Developing countries have much to gain by promoting trade among themselves both by specialization in creating new industries and by mutual liberalization of trade (on a discriminatory basis *vis-à-vis* more advanced countries) even in less essential items. The possibility of setting up new industries on the basis of joint ownership and sharing in production deserves further exploration.
9. The desire of the socialist countries to break away from their erstwhile isolation from world trade provides a welcome opportunity to developing nations to secure relief in their balance of payments and the present trend must be substantially accelerated in the years to come.

CHAPTER 10

The Challenge for the Newly Industrializing Countries*

It is a tribute to the remarkable progress achieved by Newly Industrializing Countries (NICs) that a whole session of this Symposium is devoted to their problems and prospects. But what exactly are we seeking to distinguish when we speak of NICs? If we adopt Dr Emmerij's admirable description of the theme for this Symposium, one can certainly say there is a group of countries now in the middle-income range which have been, for the most part of the last thirty or forty years at any rate, on the high-growth track. These are also countries for whom it matters a great deal whether the international environment is supportive and outward-looking or contentious and inward-looking. These countries also do not constitute—not as yet anyway—one of the poles of the multipolar world so that while their stake is great, their ability to mould the external environment is not all that great. But is there not some oversimplification in referring to all of them as industrializing—with perhaps more than a hint that manufactured exports do and will play a large part in their future? Would it not be appropriate to refer to newly modernizing countries to isolate those who, unlike the recently over-rich oil kingdoms, have a reasonably good infrastructure of modernity in the sense of skilled labour and other economic and financial infrastructure of a sophisticated character?

The question is not altogether academic. Even if we look at the two sets of countries discussed in the excellent papers before us the question arises why the Eastnics have managed a sustained economic growth better than the Latinics. The standard explanation—leaving aside for a moment the

* This paper was presented at the DAC Symposium, Paris, February 1989.

recent debt crisis—is bad economic policies. More precisely, that Eastnics followed an export-led strategy whereas the Latinics carried import substitution too far.

There is, I am sure, some truth in this conventional wisdom. But an added factor could well be that resource-rich countries are in a different position from labour-surplus countries. The former have the opportunity of earning high incomes in primary production which keeps real wages high and this might make it more difficult and less necessary for them to rely on export of manufactures. Of course, all high- or middle-income countries develop a sizeable industrial structure because it is natural for a great deal of industrial activity to be located at home—and the infant industry argument has some validity after all. My simple point is that the term NICs needs careful delineation if we are not to prescribe standard remedies that may not apply to all middle-income countries that have enjoyed high rates of growth in the past. After all, Australia and New Zealand and Canada may be closer models for Argentina or Chile or even Brazil than Korea or Taiwan.

I agree that resumption of sustained economic growth in the major Latin American countries requires both a reduction in the debt burden and a programme of reform towards greater equity which goes beyond what are often described as orthodox or heterodox approaches to stabilization and adjustment. We know that after a prolonged period of inflation, mere monetary and fiscal adjustment is not enough. Some unorthodox remedies like temporary wage and price fixation and currency reform may also be necessary. And the reverse is also true.

But even with the best programme containing orthodox and heterodox elements, success can only be guaranteed if it does not require the generation of too large an export surplus which is bound to be inflationary. This is the basic reason for debt reduction in terms of some reasonable figure of debt service beyond which payments should be postponed or written off—incidentally, this approach provides a guide for future prudence also as the debtor country would be expected not to transgress these limits in future. If a parallel is needed, it was provided as long ago as the Anglo-American loan agreement soon after the war. A general principle like this is also not inconsistent with a case-by-case approach.

A more important point which is seldom made is that for sustained growth we need in these countries some steps towards greater equity. Without that the discipline implicit in sound fiscal and monetary policy can at best be short-lived. A view is expressed here during discussion that these countries require the mobilization of a new multi-class majority, of a centre-left leaning, able to support a socially concerned project of modernization and development, based on a socially regulated free market economy, maximizing efficiency within the framework of social democracy. These words ring true to Indian ears. After all, we have been uttering them for a long time. But we are still awaiting a happy ending after several decades of lost or out-of-reach opportunities. The question is: how do we get there? And what exactly does a centre-left government do in detail? It is easy to say it will follow the Scandinavian model. But how long a road will it be before we can reach that goal? We do not also want mere redistributive equity. We want equity that equips the poor better with productive capabilities. How do we do it? Incidentally, can it not be—and this goes back to my first point—that unlike in India, there could be much greater scope in Latin America for land reform giving land to the poor who generate a new wave of more equitable growth through diversified agriculture?

I agree with the view expressed here that the US will not allow even a larger deficit with the Far East to develop. Nor can Japan take the place of the US as a market—and to the extent it does, the NICs will be under pressure to import more from the US and from the next generation of NICs in the Far East. Why then am I an optimist? First, because I believe the US will force the NICs to appreciate and open the doors wider even if it does not help the bilateral imbalance a great deal. Others can walk through the wider open door—and I am sure some agree that that is a good thing. The Eastnics, like Japan, have shown in the past a remarkable capacity to adjust to adverse shocks from abroad and they have even greater resilience now.

Second, I believe a better solution than the NICs increasing domestic consumption or investment is possible. After all, Hong Kong and Taiwan are only extensions of China, and with the Chinese policy of "one country, two systems" we can foresee huge investment by at least these two NICs in China—and there need be no return other than ownership of property in the motherland. For Korea also, similar opportunities may soon arise in North Korea and the Mekong region—not to speak of the Philippines and Indonesia, although obviously the relationship is different. Where the world is so hungry for capital, it is rather strange to think that we have to adjust by reducing savings anywhere rather than by diverting investment to where it is needed. If we are talking of shared international responsibility, there is surely much that the Eastnics can share in terms not just of capital but technology and management, at least with their immediate neighbours; and this need not be done on commercial terms only. The Eastnics can play a greater part in providing concessional finance also—particularly in respect of technical and managerial assistance.

My third reason for optimism is that if the Eastnics experience somewhat slower rates of growth after a long journey on the fast track, it is not really disaster for them or for anyone else. Japan too is slowing down. Maybe it is not so bad for the environment; and maybe it is good for the psychological health of the passengers on the slow train.

I have assumed that the Eastnics have no serious domestic equity problems which might justify more consumption at home and the fiscal and other reforms that may go with this approach. This may not of course be wholly true. It is certainly not true of Thailand, Malaysia or Indonesia, which are also resource rich. Does the lasting American remedy for equity have relevance for them?

I have refrained from commenting on China and India—but I hope this Symposium does not exhibit the same forgetfulness towards India which I have witnessed increasingly in so many international gatherings. But if you wish something else to divert your attention, I suggest we devote some attention to Eastern Europe. Here are the Socialnics who are also challenging the rest of us to make room for them in an interdependent world: will they find it in a European bloc as the Eastnics may find in a yen bloc and Latinics in an American bloc? I hope not. For where will South Asia and the Middle East seek their salvation then?

CHAPTER 11

Capital Formation in the Private Corporate Sector*

In a mixed economy like ours, the behaviour of capital formation in the private corporate sector is obviously a matter of importance. It is well to remember, however, that there is more to capital formation than what the private corporate sector accounts for. It is the trends in overall investment that are clearly the more meaningful variable we should be interested in; and here the factors affecting overall investment and its disposition are an epitome of the country's economic performance.

To revert, however, to the subject matter of this workshop, the authors of the study portray a generally depressing picture of the performance of the corporate sector in India in the last fifteen years. The performance perhaps has not been to expectations but it would be churlish to deny the fact that Indian industry today has certainly come of age, is more broad-based and diversified than ever before and provides the basis for further growth. This could not have happened without substantial capital formation and investment in industry. As I just mentioned, it is, of course, possible to take the view that the financial performance could have been better and this is what the authors of the study obviously believe. They suggest, both explicitly and otherwise, that what they regard as the somewhat uninspiring performance was the outcome of exogenous factors such as fiscal policy, price policy, monetary policy and the like. Among the exogenous factors, I would have thought the trends in public investment would also have figured prominently as this is a major determinant of private investment also.

* Comment on the Study of ASSOCHAM, Bombay on *Capital Formation*; unpublished.

Clearly, exogenous factors are important and, in the very nature of things, were bound to have affected the fortunes of the corporate sector but that is not all that there is to it. What is missing is adequate reference to factors endogenous to the corporate sector. Put more bluntly, did the performance of the corporate sector in managing, and in some cases mismanaging its affairs, not have something to do with this lacklustre performance? I will have more to say on this later, but for a start, let me leave this thought with you.

The report starts with a reference to the changing landscape of industrialization with a description, in picturesque phrase, of the emergence of "sunrise" industries and the decline of traditional ones. It is certainly true that in the *private* corporate sector, textiles, sugar and steel have not grown but this is not due only to the profitability in these sectors but clearly, as the authors would agree, it had something to do with deliberate policy in terms of which further development of textile production was to be largely in the decentralized sector, sugar industry development was to be largely in the cooperative sector while investment and growth in steel was in the public sector. One surely cannot equate the landscape of private corporate industry with that of industrialization as such. Again, the so-called sunrise industries naturally claimed a higher share in terms of capital employed but the industries, for instance chemical and aluminium, to mention but two of them, also happen to be capital-intensive industries as per the dictates of technology. It could not have been otherwise, therefore, than that their share in terms of capital employed rose. The authors point out that the contribution of organized manufacturing industry to the domestic product has declined. Incidentally, this is on the basis of current prices. If constant prices were the basis, the share of the manufacturing sector has increased. Let us, however, see what the implications of the calculations on the basis of current prices are. The investment in organized industry has not shown such a proportionate decline and I wonder whether there is not a point in this about the return to the economy on the investments made in this sector. I must also confess to some puzzlement at the reference to this decline in organized industry's contribution to GDP being contrary to the theory of economic development. In fact, our own experience has shown that we needed to give greater emphasis to the agricultural sector of our economy in terms of investment and thus to help it to contribute more to national income apart from its effects on employment.

I must also admit that I cannot agree with the authors of the study in identifying capital formation in the corporate sector with investment in plant and machinery. Capital formation, as is generally recognized, includes both investment in all fixed assets as well as inventory investment and the conceptual error in identifying capital formation with only investment in plant and machinery, apart from underestimating capital formation itself, disguises the fact that industry preferred, in highly inflationary years, to invest in inventory rather than in fixed assets. I shall have more to say later on this preference of industry to invest in inventory which was not unrelated also to increasing inflationary pressures.

Not merely is there this mistaken identity between capital formation and investment in plant and machinery but there is, I believe, a serious methodological flaw in the way investment trends have been analysed in terms of deflating this by the increase in prices of plant and machinery. What the authors of the study appear to have done is to take the book values, as given in the balance sheet, of the assets in the form of plant and machinery at the end of each of the fifteen-year periods and apply uniformly the price deflator on the basis of the price increase between 1961–62 and 1974–75. This is clearly wrong. The implicit assumption in this procedure is that in company balance sheets the valuation of plant and machinery is done at current prices. That this is not so is well known. The gross values of fixed asset items of a company recorded in its balance sheet are the aggregate of the purchase prices, except where they have been revalued, and of individual items acquired at different points of time. The aggregate gross value of plant and machinery of the companies in the Reserve Bank of India corporate studies is thus the aggregate of the balance sheet total of the historical costs of plant and machinery acquired at different periods. The price deflator series used in the Tata Economic Consultancy studies cannot reduce these costs to a uniform price basis. This major flaw in methodology has, in my view, vitiated the analysis and has led to misleading if not perhaps downright incorrect inferences about the decline in real investment. The whole thesis that there has been such a decline is the theme around which the authors have built up the spectre of an investment famine. That investment has not grown sufficiently is a fact which none would dispute but to suggest that investment in real terms has declined on so palpably wrong a base of calculation is misleading. I believe the correct method of estimating the gross capital stock at 1961–62 prices would have been to separate out the components according to the year of acquisition and applying the price deflators appropriate to the respective years and then aggregating the deflated value. If this exercise were done, even taking into account the fact that we could not apply this to the capital stock acquired before 1961–62, the results would be in sharp contrast to the dismal picture painted by the Tata Consultancy study. It would, indeed, show a steady growth in gross capital stock in the form of plant and machinery at 1961–62 prices throughout the period since then. I attach a great deal of importance to this point because, I believe, unless this central factor were appreciated, we would be tilting at imaginary windmills in assuming that there bas been a decline in investment in plant and machinery in real terms.

I am sorry if I sound critical but I believe I gave some forewarning of this earlier in my talk. Having started on this road, let me continue and make a reference now to that part of the study which talks about the average cost of borrowing and comparing this with the ratio of total borrowings to total liabilities and the ratio of interest paid to gross profits. I must confess I do not quite see the point of comparing these three ratios. A change in one need not necessarily affect the other. For example, an increase in the average cost of borrowing does not necessarily mean any variation in the ratio of total borrowings to total liabilities. This would depend on how other liabilities moved in this period. Any correlation between these ratios can only be coincidental and to inject a meaning into them could be hazardous. For obvious reasons, I do not wish to make any comments on the subject of interest-cost and its supposed impact on investments but I cannot help saying that I do not see the precise rationale of discussing the effective interest rates and the effective rates of corporate taxation together as, in a sense, one reduces the impact of the other.

While on the subject of effective rates of corporate taxation, I find the report once again committing what I regard as a conceptual error in that in including the effective rates of corporate taxation, it has taken the profits aggregated for 1,650 companies. In the process, the authors have apparently overlooked that this figure of aggregated profits includes also the losses of small companies and that corporate tax is germane only to the profit-making companies. The result of this is that the denominator is smaller than it would have been if only profit-making companies had been taken into account. Clearly the calculation of effective rates of corporate taxation on the basis of the profits of all the companies has tended to increase the effective rate of corporate taxation than is the case.

While on the subject of taxation and profitability, I am not impressed by the comparison of profitability rates in India and in countries like the USA or the UK only to disprove the point that sheltered market conditions in India have not made Indian industry any more profitable. This ignores the structure of industrial organization in the different countries apart from the efficiency dimension in India which may also have contributed to the profitability rates not being higher than what they were.

I now turn to the discussion in the report on the sources of funds for the corporate sector. The study brings out the important point that internal accruals, whether by way of depreciation or plough-back of profit has been an important element in financing capital formation in the corporate sector. I regard this as a good feature of the corporate financial performance, though in several sectors of industry the record is not as good as the aggregate increase might indicate. It is only natural that corporate savings should grow to finance an increasing share of corporate investment. The increased importance of internal generation of funds has its counterpart in reduced share of external source of finance. The study brings out the point that the share of household sector savings going into the private corporate sector as equity investment has been declining. This of course has its corollary in the increasing burden being cast on the public financial institutions to provide term loans and through underwriting also equity support. Incidentally, the reliance on RBI corporate data also has tended to depress the assistance rendered by the public financial institutions. As the RBI data cover only companies in regular production they miss out several newer companies to whom, of course, a good part of the assistance from the term-lending institutions has gone. The exclusion of the data on these companies also tends to underplay the extent of investment being undertaken.

On the more basic point of the smaller share of equity investment out of the total of household savings, perhaps parodying a phrase of Keynes, the report refers to the euthanasia of the stock market. I took the trouble of consulting the *Concise Oxford Dictionary* and I find that euthanasia has been defined there as "gentle and easy death, bringing about this, especially in case of incurable and painful disease". No one bas been bringing about a gentle and easy death of the stock market, though some may believe that it is subject to disease, how incurable or painful, one is not in a position to say. Let us, however, ponder as to what has brought this result about. Why is it that the discerning investor has chosen to move away from the stock market? It is not as if he has totally abandoned it as witness even now the fact that good companies with creditable performance are able to raise funds in the market though I myself do not attach too much importance to the phenomenon of over-subscription of some select issues. The investor clearly is choosy and if he has turned away from the stock market, industry might do well to turn its gaze inwards. What is the picture that we see? Instances are not unknown where the combination of speculative instinct, mismanagement and siphoning off of funds have transformed once flourishing companies into sick units and the shares of these companies from blue chips into a sickly ashen. Can you blame the investor if he, seeing his dividends being skipped, thinks twice before investing in the market, and prefers the safety and the security of contractual savings or the sanctuary of bank deposits and the Unit Trust? I venture to suggest that the lessons here are more than a mere comparative assets preference behaviour of the investor. It is also the psychological damage that has been inflicted on the market by the behaviour of some so-called industrial entrepreneurs. Even the good companies with a wholesome record and where this sort of damage to confidence has not taken place, seem to prefer to raise funds not through the issue of equity but through company deposits, partly presumably so as not to dilute the share-holding of the promoters and others in control. Company deposits obviously are preferred by the companies as they are a cheaper form of raising funds than borrowing from the banks with fewer questions asked and this obviously explains the preference of companies which are in a position to raise such funds for this means of doing so.

This brings me to that portion of the study dealing with the Tandon Committee norms. Much has been made in the para of the fact that far from short-term funds being used to finance fixed assets formation it may well have been the other way round. I see nothing wrong with this. After all, it is part of the logic of industrial finance that even in respect of what one might call the permanent or core-working capital, the funds should be of a long-term character. This indeed was the rationale of the Tandon Committee norms. On the other hand, the figures presented in the study are not entirely convincing. The increase in short-term assets in the latest period has, I believe, not been only due to the operation of the Tandon Committee norms—these came only recently—but reflect the fact that during periods of inflation the corporate sector found it of greater advantage to itself to prefer investing in inventory, presumably with an eye on speculative price movements, than in investing in long-term assets. In any case, the growth of these current assets was also matched by a considerable increase in current liabilities. It was, indeed, to correct this type of situation that the Tandon Committee norms have been brought into play. Certainly, the Tandon Committee norms have to be applied flexibly, but I do not believe that the essential logic of the system can seriously be questioned. The increase in the other liabilities and trade dues has been also the result presumably of the non-corporate, that is, unorganized, sector being made to provide credit to the organized sector, a feature which is not unrelated also to the growth of bank credit to the small-scale industrial sector who, in turn, may have been forced through presumably delayed payment of their bills to lend to the larger sector, who may thus have escaped the rigours of credit assessment and appraisal.

CHAPTER 12

Physical Planning*

There has been a great deal of discussion in recent months about the nature and content of the Second Five-Year Plan. It is now generally agreed that the Second Plan should represent a much greater developmental effort than what we have achieved in the last five years and that the emphasis in the Second Plan should be on the development of basic industries. Professor P.C. Mahalanobis has advanced an interesting thesis that the technique of planning itself should now undergo a change in emphasis in keeping with the declared objective of a quicker pace of development. The approach to planning in the First Five-Year Plan was essentially financial. That is to say, the emphasis was on the cost of the various developmental schemes included in the Plan and the methods of financing the total outlay on the Plan. The technique of physical planning which is now recommended seeks to emphasize the physical requirements of the Plan in terms of men, machines and materials and the need for securing a balanced increase in these requirements so as to ensure smooth implementation of the Plan.

"Physical planning" is a new expression. But the idea behind it is simple common sense. Planning for a better future implies essentially three things: taking a view of the future course of the economy as it would emerge in the absence of the Plan; influencing the future pattern of growth in accordance with certain socially desired priorities; and ensuring that, given the mechanics of growth and the order of priorities, the particular Plan or course of action chosen represents the maximum feasible rate of growth along desired lines. The last prerequisite of a rational plan may also be expressed by saying that a plan must be balanced in the sense that the relative rates of growth of different sectors of the economy must be so

* The draft of this paper was prepared around 1955–56; unpublished.

arranged as to prevent or forestall any avoidable shortages or surpluses in individual sectors. The productive process in a modern economy is highly interdependent. Unless care is taken in drawing up a plan to ensure that the rate of growth in any given sector takes into account the requirements of growth in other sectors, there would emerge shortages or surpluses which would impede the smooth and speedy implementation of the plan. The overall result achieved would not represent the maximum feasible effort in the event of wastage or delay arising from a lack of balance between different sectors. In the ultimate analysis, the determinants of production or growth are physical; that is to say, they are the men, machines and materials that make up the "inputs" in any line of production. A balanced plan therefore must necessarily take into account the physical requirements of each project or programme included in the plan and the interdependence of different sectors in physical terms.

The essential point is that an *overall* view of the physical requirements must be taken in advance. Each project authority has to start with knowledge of its own requirements of men, machines and materials even if the object is simply to estimate the cost of the project. What physical planning seeks to emphasize is that an overall view of the requirements of different projects and sectors must be taken by the planning authority in advance so as to determine both the constituents of the plan and the steps to be taken to ensure its smooth implementation.

While the case for physical planning as outlined above is self-evident, it is necessary to clarify certain preliminary points at the outset. No plan, however well construed, can make it possible to avoid shortages and surpluses altogether. This is so not only because of the imperfect instruments of predictions available to a planning authority and the uncertainties that inevitably exist in any society but also for the more fundamental reason that every society has to act within certain restraints during a given period ahead. These restraints are both physical and institutional. Were it not so, it would not be necessary to plan and order priorities and take deliberate policy decisions. It is clear that a society which is bent upon achieving a certain rate of investment, for example, or a certain pattern of investment, would necessarily find itself short of resources in some directions—say in the production of consumer goods. Similarly, it may not be possible to avoid surpluses in certain directions—say of manpower which cannot be fully employed. What is necessary is that the particular shortages or surpluses must be planned and foreseen—they must be inherent in the order of priorities first and not such as to throw the plan out of gear. All that can be hoped for is that the potential shortage of resources for some sectors or some purposes, which is implicit in any scheme of directing resources to more essential sectors, is prevented from appearing in the market as an effective shortage.

If physical planning cannot eliminate altogether the problem of shortages and surpluses, it cannot provide an escape from the necessity of financial planning either. In a money economy, finance or income flows are inseparable from the deployment of physical resources. Goods and services have to be purchased and sold. Incomes are generated in the process of production itself. The financial problem of ensuring that the resources in money terms are available to the authorities to whom the plan assigns certain functions of producing this or that cannot be waived aside simply by ensuring that the physical resources required for the particular task are available. Admittedly, the availability of finance is no guarantee that the job will necessarily be done. One has to plan and ensure that physical resources such as personnel are also made available as and when required. But the converse is equally true. The physical resources would remain idle or be misdirected in the absence of suitable demand in money terms at the right time and place and to the requisite extent. To argue that the physical requirements of a plan must receive greater emphasis is not to say that financial considerations can be disregarded or underplayed.

A distinction must also be drawn between the technique of drawing up a plan and the technique of implementing a plan. There has been a good deal of misunderstanding about the different meanings that can be assigned to the term "physical planning". It has been tacitly assumed in some quarters that physical planning implies necessarily a departure from the market economy or the price mechanism and reliance on physical or direct control. Planning implies essentially a direction of resources from the less desired channels to more desired channels. The basic purpose of a plan is to increase the rate of investment and to change the pattern of investment on desired lines. Given the decisions about investment, the pattern of production desired would also follow. In drawing up a plan we must have a clear idea of what pattern we want to see emerge. And for this purpose knowledge of the interrelationships between different sectors is essential. But this does not mean that the desired pattern of production or the use of resources must also be brought about exclusively or primarily by means of direct or physical controls. Even when a plan is drawn up so as to ensure a balance in physical terms, the necessary sanction for steering the course of the economy along desired lines may still remain primarily financial. Thus, if investment is to be raised and consumption is to be controlled accordingly, the policies to implement this may be largely financial, that is, in terms of taxation of incomes or differential excise duties rather than physical, that is, in terms of rationing or compulsory direction. The choice between the financial and direct instruments of regulation must depend on the judgement as to the relative effectiveness of these devices and the nature and extent of the particular change that is sought to be implemented. But in drawing up a plan there is really no choice between the physical and the financial approach. Both are essential and inseparable. As long as the money economy and the mechanism of a free market are retained to whatever extent, the balance to be achieved in a plan has to be in financial as well as physical terms.

So much for the meaning and rationale of physical planning. But given the need for thinking and planning in physical terms, how is such planning to be done? Since the purpose is to prepare a plan which is balanced in both physical and financial terms, perhaps a more meaningful question to ask would be: "How does one go about drawing up a balanced plan, and what does it entail?"

One technique, which is followed in the Soviet Union and other communist countries, is that of drawing up elaborate material or commodity balances. Let us assume that the basic objective of the plan is to produce a certain amount of investment goods. The investment goods to be produced may be used in the production of consumer goods or in the production of additional investment goods. Given the level of investment goods' output aimed at and its allocation between consumer goods' industries and investment goods' industries as well as the total amount of resources in the community, the total output of consumer goods that can be produced is also determined. The problem is to ensure that the targets of production for different consumer goods and intermediate goods are set in a manner consistent with the decisions about the amount and allocation of the output of investment goods. Starting from a certain hypothetical list of production in different lines we may prepare a balance sheet of the supply and disposal of a number of important commodities or services such as power, fuel, steel, cotton and so on, which are particularly likely to emerge as bottlenecks or surpluses. These balances of supply and demand will reveal the internal consistencies or inconsistencies in the original list of production which can be revised, within the framework of the priorities set by a process of successive approximations, till an internal balance in terms of the supply and demand for different commodities is achieved. In addition to key commodities, balances may also be drawn in respect of foreign exchange and labour including various specialized categories of it.

In addition to the plan and the balances in physical terms, it is also necessary to work out its counterpart in financial terms. The flow of incomes generated in the process of production, given assumptions about prices, wages and profits, would determine the total demand for consumer goods and the resources available to different investing authorities. Budgetary policies and policies in respect of prices, wages and profit must be so arranged that the total demand for consumer goods in money terms does not exceed or fall short of the supplies likely to be available (valued at appropriate prices). Apart from this overall balance, the demand for each consumer good must be consistent with the supply envisaged, and the resources available for investment to each investing authority must be in keeping with the investment it is expected to undertake. The overall and sector-wise balance between the flow of goods and the demand thereof in financial terms will not be achieved automatically. It is the result of the financial—or physical—policies envisaged in the plan. By making alternative sets of assumptions about these policies we may arrive, by successive approximations, at a picture of income and financial flows which is in harmony with the particular pattern of flow of goods and services which was deemed feasible. Since assumptions about policies cannot be made freely in a democratic society, it may become necessary to choose a pattern of production which, though less desirable than what physical possibilities permit, may be the optimum feasible in the light of the restraints on policies.

Various elaborations of the commonsense technique of drawing up balances of supply and demand for key commodities and materials are possible. One of these methods is what is called input–output analysis. Material balances for a few commodities do not take the entire economic system into account. It is also difficult, if not impossible, to take account of the whole chain of interrelationships between the products of different industries by means of the simple technique of drawing up balances. A more comprehensive method of analysis which can tell us how the whole system would be affected if the output of certain commodities is to be of the required order would be useful in that it would tell us at a glance what pattern of production is internally consistent. The input–output analysis essentially attempts to summarize the flow of products from one sector to the other over any given time in the form of equations which together define the inputs required for a unit of output in each sector or for each commodity. By giving certain predetermined values to certain outputs and by solving the system of simultaneous equations we can get the corresponding outputs in other sectors that would be required.

Another analytical device is what is called linear programming. This technique is an elaboration of the input–output analysis. It is also based on a translation of the input–output relations obtaining (or permissible) into a system of linear equations. But in addition, it attempts to take into account various possible alternative forms of production (or policies) and to work out an optimum solution in terms of certain defined objectives. In short, it aims at arriving at a solution or a pattern of production which is not only internally consistent but also conducive to the optimum realization of the objectives defined.

The present writer is not sufficiently familiar with the different techniques of ensuring a balance in a plan to which reference has been made in the earlier paragraphs. No attempt therefore is made here either at a full explanation or at any evaluation of the usefulness and limitations of these techniques.[1] What is important in the present context is to note certain implications of the kind of planning that is envisaged here.

Whatever the particular analysis chosen, an attempt to draw up a balanced plan requires far more information than is available at present in India. The kind and quantity of physical resources that enter into each activity, an accurate knowledge of the time and place where resources become available—this is what is wanted. But it requires much greater knowledge of the productive process than is brought together at any place at present. How much labour of each kind is needed for each activity? How will this relation differ from one enterprise to the other? As it is, even for such simple things as the employment given and the foreign exchange utilized in the projects completed already, we have hardly any information. What is more, if planning is to produce the maximum feasible result we must have a number of alternative projects worked out for each purpose so that a rational choice in the light of the overall resources may be made.

Even in the sphere of balancing in financial terms, our data or knowledge is extremely limited by how much will the consumption of different commodities go up at different levels of income and at different prices? What is the impact of a given budgetary or price and wage policy on the volume and pattern of savings and consumption in the economy?

These questions may be difficult; but they have to be asked and answered. Since the answers often depend on experience, we have to devise suitable ways of recording the experience. It is clear that a great deal of statistical work is needed to make planning more rational. But the kind of statistics needed are such that only scientists or technicians associated with the production process can furnish them. It is therefore essential that the technicians in various fields of production are associated with the process of collecting the data as well as with making use of the data in the preparation of a plan. Some of the questions such as the determination of the impact of the budget fall more in the province of economists. But since physical and financial planning are interrelated, what is needed is a much closer liaison and more frequent contacts among economists, statisticians, engineers and other technicians. Perhaps, a more composite type of technician who knows a little of all these disciplines would be the most useful one for purposes of detailed planning. "Multipurpose" technicians are an essential part in planning.

Another implication of the technique of planning outlined here is that planning must be continuous. We cannot plan in detail for five years

[1] Reference may be made in this connection to a forthcoming publication of the Indian Statistical Institute which brings together a number of papers on *Planning for National Development*. Refer also to Robert Dorfman, "The Nature and Significance of Input-Output", in *The Review of Economics and Statistics*, May 1954. This article gives an extensive list of references as well as a brief review of the analysis in question.

ahead; the experience on which it would be based might get out of date and circumstances may change. Whatever the balance postulated has to be realized in practice. There must therefore be a continuous review of the progress of the plan in physical terms and frequent alterations in a planned manner as circumstances warrant. In short, the technician and the project authorities must be in close contact with the planning authorities even after their projects are approved. The executive engineer is not merely executing a project; he is executing part of a plan.

CHAPTER 13

The Second Five Year Plan

*A Tentative Framework**

Introduction

This paper attempts to outline the general objectives and targets to be achieved in the Second Five Year Plan so as to serve as the first step towards the formulation of the plan as a whole. Without some idea of the overall aspirations and priorities to be observed in the plan, it is not possible to define clearly the schemes and policies necessary for their implementation. At the same time, the broad targets to be achieved in a plan period can be arrived at only after a careful scrutiny of the means and measures required for the fulfilment of the targets. The framework for the Second Plan given in this paper, therefore, is tentative and in the nature of a first approximation to what the final plan might look like.

The Second Plan must necessarily take its cue from the achievements and shortcomings of the First Plan. The targets we set ourselves in the First Plan were rather modest. At the time of its formulation, the country had to reckon with the dislocation caused by war and partition with the resurgence of inflationary pressure in the wake of the hostilities in Korea and with shortages of foodstuffs and essential raw materials. It was only natural, therefore, that we set our sights rather low and accorded high priority to the development of agriculture.

Nonetheless, the economy has gained considerable strength over the past three or four years. Inflation has been overcome. Shortages of foodstuffs and raw materials have disappeared. And there has been a considerable

* This framework prepared in early 1955 set a direction for the final version of the Second Five Year Plan; unpublished.

expansion in industrial production and in the provision of certain basic amenities such as health and education. These and other achievements of the First Plan have been recorded in great detail in the various Progress Reports and it is not necessary to make a detailed reiteration of the same here. But it may be claimed that the achievements of the First Plan give reason for hope that a bolder step ahead in the Second Plan is feasible.

At the same time, our experience in the past few years has focused attention on certain disquieting features of the economy. The continuing threat of unemployment, particularly in the urban areas, and the fall in agricultural prices have made it evident that the tempo of development in the economy must be stepped up with accent on industrialization. The shortfall in expenditure that occurred in the *initial stages of the First Plan* has emphasized the need for a detailed and timely formulation of schemes, for adequate administrative machinery and for the training of proper personnel at all levels.

Again, our experience with the First Plan does not give any ground for complacency about the financial resources needed for a greater rate of development. The budgetary position of the government is somewhat obscured by the extraordinary receipts in the first two years combined with a lower tempo of development; and the response of the people to government loans has been encouraging. But on the whole, the surplus from current revenue, receipts from railways and accumulations in various deposit funds have not come up to the targets set in the plan. This is due, in part, to the failure to tap additional incomes by suitable tax measures such as betterment levies and insufficient check over the expenditure outside the plan.

In short, if the experience with the First Plan suggests that a bolder approach in the Second Plan is both feasible and desirable, it also indicates the need for greater effort in realizing the financial and other resources essential for development.

Objectives of the Second Plan

The major objectives of the Second Plan may be set down in general terms as follows:

(a) a sizeable increase in national income so as to raise the level of living in the country;
(b) rapid industrialization;
(c) fuller employment; and
(d) social justice.

These objectives cannot be achieved fully in a matter of five or ten years. Indeed, in the short run, it may not be possible to reconcile fully the aims of social justice, greater production, fuller employment and a wider capital and industrial base for further progress. The central task in planning for a given period ahead is to define as precisely as possible the advance to be made in each desirable line and to ensure a certain optimum fulfilment of all the objectives.

National Income and Standard of Living

The First Plan contained an illustrative model of development over a period of some twenty-seven years. According to this model, our national income could be doubled in some twenty-two years, per capita income could be doubled in about twenty-seven years and per capita consumption could be increased by roughly 70 per cent in a little more than five plan periods (that is, between 1950–51 and 1977). The rate of progress envisaged was even more moderate for the first two plans—national income rising by some 11 per cent in the First and the Second plans. The increase in national income during the First Plan is likely to be greater than was anticipated and may amount to some 15 per cent over the five years. For the Second Plan, therefore, we may well aspire to an increase in national income higher than 15 per cent, say 25 to 27 per cent in five years, or 5 per cent per annum as a first approximation.

Table 13.1 shows that the national income of India increased by some 15 per cent in real terms during the five years 1948–49 to 1953–54. During the first three years of the First Plan, the increase was of the order of 12.5 per cent. Even when allowance is made for the provisional character of the estimate for 1953–54 and for the favourable monsoons in that year, it is reasonable to expect a 15 per cent increase in national income over the First Plan period.

On this basis, an increase in national income of about 5 per cent every year in the Second Plan is by no means unrealistic or ambitious. Even in advanced industrial countries a rate of increase in national income of 3 per cent per annum has been achieved over a period of years without any attempt at planning. In recent years, the socialist countries in Eastern Europe have achieved a rate of increase of some 10 to 12 per cent in national income every year (Table 13.2). We may accept, therefore, provisionally the target of a 5 per cent per annum increase in national income for the Second Plan. On this basis, it should be possible to advance the long-term targets outlined in the First Plan by some four to five years.

In order to step up the rate of growth in national income, the rate of savings and investment in the economy must also be increased. Without going into the details of the amount of savings and investment needed for the increase in national income postulated above, it may be stated that total consumption should increase roughly by 20 per cent during the Second Plan, and per capital consumption by 12 to 13 per cent.

One of the main objectives of the First Plan was to restore the pre-war consumption of the basic necessities of life in the country. There has been

Table 13.1 Net National Output of India at Current and Constant Prices

	*1953–54***	*1952–53*	*1951–52*	*1950–51*	*1949–50*	*1948–49*
Net output in R. abja*						
At current prices	106.0	98.6	99.9	95.3	90.1	86.5
At 1948–49 prices	99.5	95.2	91.6	88.5	88.2	86.5
Per capita net output in Rs						
At current prices	283.9	267.4	274.5	265.2	253.9	246.9
At 1948–49 prices	266.5	258.1	251.7	246.3	248.6	246.9
Index number of net output with 1948–49 as base						
At current prices	122.5	114.0	115.5	110.2	104.2	100.0
At 1948–49 prices	115.0	110.1	105.9	102.3	102.0	100.0
Index number of per capita net output with 1948–49 as base						
At current prices	115.0	108.3	111.2	107.4	102.8	100.0
At 1948–49 prices	107.9	104.5	101.9	99.8	100.7	100.0

Source: First Five Year Plan, Planning Commission, Government of India, 1955.
Notes: *abja = 100 crore = 10^9.
**preliminary.

a significant increase in the consumption of food grains, cloth and other items in recent years and the damage done by war and partition is all but repaired. However, the standard of nutrition, clothing, shelter, housing and education in the country are still inadequate and a sizeable increase in the basic amenities of life must be ensured during the Second Plan.

The minimum requirements of cereals in a balanced diet were estimated by the Nutrition Advisory Committee at 14 oz. per adult per day. The consumption of cereals in the country has already increased from less than 13 oz. per adult per day in 1950–51 to nearly 15 oz. in 1953–54. The availability of pulses and grams, however, still falls short of minimum nutritional requirements—2.5 against 3 oz. per adult per day. Thus, quite apart from the requirements of a growing population, the production of food grains needs to be increased in the Second Plan.

In the case of other foodstuffs such as milk, ghee, meat, fish, eggs, fats, fruits, vegetables and sugar the present level of consumption falls far short of minimum requirements. In the absence of dependable data on a

Table 13.2 Growth in National Income in Selected Countries

Country	*Period*	*Rate of Growth, Annual Average in per cent*
USA	1869–78—1904–13	4.5
	1869–78—1929	4.0
	1899–1908—1929	3.2
	1929–50	3.0
Canada	1903–29	2.6
Switzerland	1890–1929	2.7
Germany	1876–1913	2.8
Japan	1887–1913	3.0
	1914–30	6.7
	1914–37	6.7
Australia	1901–2003—1928–29	3.2
	1901–2003—1947–48	2.5
Soviet Union	1928–37 (official)	16
Poland	1947–53 (official)	14.5

Source: *Soviet Economic Growth*, (ed.) A. Bergson, 1954, pages 9 and 12.

continuing basis, it is not possible to indicate the recent trend in the consumption of these items. But it is self-evident that in planning for a higher standard of living, special attention must be devoted in the Second Plan to animal husbandry, fisheries, poultry farming, vegetable gardens and other branches of food production.

The consumption of cotton cloth in India is already restored to the pre-war standard of 15 yards per person. The Textile Enquiry Committee has recommended an increase in consumption of cotton cloth to 18 yards per person by 1960, and this modest objective must be achieved in the Second Plan.

During the war, an acute housing shortage developed in the urban areas. Urban population increased by 54 per cent during 1941–51, and the shortage of houses at the end of the decade was estimated at more than 18 lakh in addition to some 10 lakh houses required for displaced persons from Pakistan. There has been a substantial increase in urban construction in recent years, and it is reasonable to expect that the supply of houses in the urban areas would increase from some 102 lakh in 1950–51 to 115 to 120 lakh by the end of the First Plan. Even then, provision must be made in the Second Plan for the construction of an additional 30–40 lakh houses in the urban areas. The construction of houses in the rural areas is done largely by own labour with the use of locally available materials, and the housing problem is not as acute as in urban areas. But an effort must be made through the National Extension Service and similar channels to improve housing conditions in rural areas as well.

As regards education of the total population of children between the age of 6 and 14, only 23 per cent went to school in 1939–40 and some 32 per cent in 1950–51. It is expected that this proportion would increase to 40 per cent by the end of the First Plan. By 1960–61, we should provide school facilities for at least 75 per cent of the children between the age of 6 and 14. Correspondingly, the facilities for higher and technical education must also expand substantially. The combined expenditure of the Centre and state governments on education is likely to increase from Rs 61 crore (1 crore = 10 million) in 1950–51 to some Rs 100 crore by 1954–55, or from Re. l–11 annas per capita to Rs 2–10 annas per capita. It is reasonable to expect that this expenditure should be doubled by the end of the Second Plan.

Similarly, public expenditure (Centre and states) on health and medical facilities has also increased, from Rs 28 crore in 1950–51 to Rs 43 crore in 1954–55, that is, from 12 annas to 18 annas per capita. Nonetheless, the provision of hospitals, doctors, nurses, sanitation facilities, etc., in the country is far from adequate, and we should provide for a substantial increase in health and medical facilities during the Second Plan.

An increase in national product of some 25 per cent would be sufficient to ensure the increase in the average level of living envisaged above. But the standard of living of the people also depends on the distribution of income. The objectives of fuller employment and social justice are, therefore, an integral part of the attack on poverty in the Second Plan.

Rapid Industrialization

In addition to providing for a higher standard of living, the Second Plan must pave the way for a sustained and more rapid progress in subsequent plans. It was with this end in view that the First Plan laid great emphasis on the development of electric power in the country. In the Second Plan, we must accord a very high priority to the development of basic producer goods industries such as those producing iron and steel, machinery, electrical equipment and chemicals. From the long-term point of view, our endeavour must be to make a rapid advance in those sectors where the potentialities for further growth as well as the indirect benefits to other sectors are the greatest. Our natural resources put us at no serious disadvantage in the development of basic producer goods industries and it is self-evident that in an expanding economy these industries occupy the key to advance in other directions. Although we have made a beginning with the development of these basic industries, we rely on imports for the bulk of our requirements of machinery, equipment and chemicals. The development of these industries is also indispensable, therefore, to the economic independence of the country.

The major effort in the development of basic capital goods industries must come from the public sector schemes for setting up iron and steel plants and an electrical equipment plant in the public sector are already under way, and the possibility of taking up new schemes in this field must be further explored. Special attention needs to be given to the production of machinery to be employed in other producer goods industries and to the production of synthetic petrol. We are already planning to expand steel capacity in the country to 6 million tons by 1960–61 (1 million=10 lakh). There is no reason why this capacity should not increase to 10 or 20 million tons in the next ten or fifteen years. It is ordinary prudence to try and fabricate as much of the steel-making machinery as possible at home. Similarly, the development of synthetic petrol in the country would reduce our imports, provide a valuable use for our immense resources of low-grade coal and, at the same time, serve as a nucleus for the development of a chemical industry.

The private sector must also be encouraged to invest predominantly in the basic industries. A number of producer goods industries such as cement, chemicals and iron and steel are at present largely in private hands. Steps must be taken to divert private investment into basic industries by suitable tax and credit measures and by making a selective use of the powers to control capital issues and imports and by licensing of new enterprises.

The development of heavy industries would require a fuller exploitation of our mineral resources, extension of transport facilities and a rapid expansion in the number of trained personnel in the country. Concrete schemes for scientific training, mineral development and transport must, therefore, be worked out along with the projects for heavy industries.

In the ultimate analysis, all wealth is forged by human hands and brains with the help of such resources of minerals, land or water as are endowed by nature. The need for an extensive geological survey to discover additional mineral resources in the country can, therefore, be hardly exaggerated. At the same time, the comparative shortage of high-grade coal in the country makes it necessary to devise means for a more economical use of coal if the plans for a rapid expansion of basic industries are not to flounder on account of shortage of coal. Wherever possible, arrangements can be made with foreign countries, as in the case of recent steel negotiations, to make up the gap in skilled personnel in the country by practical training abroad.

In addition to raw materials, skilled personnel and transport, the development of capital goods industries requires large sums of investment, both directly and indirectly. The extent of such development is limited, therefore, by the feasibility of producing consumer goods on the scale required with the help of the residuary investment funds. The basic strategy in the Second Plan, therefore, must be to invest large sums in the development of basic industries, transport and mining at one end and to economize as much as possible in the capital requirements for other sectors without restricting the supply of consumer goods. This strategy requires all-out efforts for the maximum utilization of capacity in existing industries and for the development of additional production in the capital-light or small-scale sector of industries.

A great deal of unused capacity exists at present in organized industries. It is also possible to expand production on the basis of existing equipment by working additional shifts. A detailed survey of unused capacity in different industries should, therefore, be made as soon as possible and steps must be taken to ensure the fullest use of existing capacity before setting up new units.

The full utilization of existing capacity would naturally create problems of its own. Thus, private profits would increase substantively if existing equipment is worked for two or three shifts a day. If these higher profits are not to result in a speculative boom and a reinforcement of inflationary pressures, steps must be taken to encourage private investment in desirable lines.

The development of small-scale industries in the Second Plan is essential for a number of reasons. Apart from releasing scarce capital resources for the basic industries it would provide greater employment and incomes for the large number of persons engaged in small enterprises. Needless to say, a great deal of effort and organization would be required for resuscitating small-scale industries. Where these are not forthcoming the emphasis on capital-saving methods may well land us between two stools—the large-scale capital-using methods get discouraged without other methods filling in the gap. Again, with production organized on the basis of numerous units the problem of ensuring sufficient savings for further expansion becomes more difficult. If this difficulty is not resolutely faced, the attempt to husband scarce capital resources in the short run would only make capital scarcer still in the future.

It should also be recognized that the ultimate justification for developing producer goods industries lies in the need for modernizing the production of consumer goods and making it more efficient and capital-intensive. Although part of the output of capital goods may be exported or used for further expansion of producer goods industries, a part must be absorbed in the modernization of consumer goods industries. Thus, the development of heavy capital goods industries is not consistent with the fossilization of methods of production in other sectors over a longer period. The strategy of balancing the development of producer goods industries at one end with encouragement of capital-light methods of production at the other end is justified in the immediate future only because we hope that at a later date our savings would rise sufficiently to permit the adoption of capital-using methods over a larger area without starving the rest of the economy for capital and without creating much unemployment. It is perhaps just as well to recognize that the problem of tethering technological progress will remain with us for some time and that in deciding to develop heavy producer goods industries we are pitching our faith on the hope that the need for postponing capital-using methods of production will diminish over time as the economy develops.

Fuller Employment

The provision of adequate employment opportunities is an accepted objective of the Second Plan. The nature of unemployment in the country, however, is not easy to define and it may be useful to distinguish between different facets of the problem.

First, if there is to be no increase in unemployment, the entire increase in the adult population must be pressed into gainful occupation. With our population increasing by some 1.25 per cent every year, it would be necessary to create new employment opportunities for at least 9 or 10 million persons in the Second Plan.

Second, we must try and eradicate such unemployment as already exists in the country. It is easy to identify unemployment in an industrially advanced country where the large mass of adult persons is working for a wage or a salary. In such a situation, the problem of creating adequate employment opportunities can be conveniently expressed in terms of the number of jobs that must be created in order to absorb all the persons who are willing to offer their services in return of a wage. Such unemployment exists in India, particularly in the urban areas, and among the educated classes. There are at present some 6 lakh persons seeking jobs through Employment Exchanges in India. The creation of a certain number of jobs—say 1 to 2 million—in the strict sense of the term must be a part of any programme for adequate employment opportunities.

However, the bulk of our adult population is self-employed. For the large number of peasants, craftsmen, small traders and so on, unemployment comes in the form of lack of gainful work for a part of the year or the month. In this area, the task of creating more employment is not easily distinguishable from that of providing higher incomes per person employed. Indeed, it is arguable that as long as the incomes of our peasants and craftsmen are raised by providing better techniques, more irrigation and greater demand for their products, it is immaterial whether we find work for them all the year round or not. What is perhaps shocking about the state of most of our countrymen is not that they do not have work for a part of the year but that their back-breaking labour for a part of their time earns them only a miserable pittance. For those who have some gainful occupation of their own, the emphasis should lie on greater productivity and incomes rather than on employment over a greater part of the year. This is not to deny that in many cases, higher incomes and more employment may go together. Thus, raising of additional crops as a result of irrigation or greater production by craftsmen as a result of higher demand would bring both more work and more incomes.

There is yet another sense in which unemployment exists at present in India, particularly in agriculture, viz., the so-called disguised unemployment. It is often said that in an agricultural economy which has remained stagnant for years, a large number of persons remain attached to agriculture without really contributing anything to production. Since gainful occupation outside agriculture is not available to a sufficient degree the protective instincts of society give everyone some stake in economic activity even though their services are strictly redundant. If employment outside agriculture is available in the future, it would be possible to transfer a certain number of persons at present dependent on land to other jobs without affecting agricultural output. Although the existence of such disguised unemployment is often asserted no estimate of its amount is available, or indeed, is conceptually easy to make. Much depends on the techniques adapted in agriculture, and the problem here is essentially a long-term one. Nonetheless, we may set down the objective of keeping the numbers dependent on agriculture constant in the Second Plan. The income generated per employed person is, at present, lowest in agriculture. It is, therefore, particularly important to ensure that any increase in agricultural incomes does not go to support greater numbers.

On this basis, the employment target for the Second Plan may be expressed as "10–12 million persons pressed into gainful occupation outside agriculture". It may be noted that the target is for 10–12 million persons to be gainfully occupied and not for 10–12 million jobs. Although the target refers to additional persons to be absorbed outside agriculture, it does not rule out efforts to provide additional work or incomes to those already employed in agriculture or elsewhere. Nor does it imply that the 10–12 million persons are to be found work necessarily in the cities and towns.

It may also be emphasized that the target set is a *normative* one. It defines a state of affairs that would be desirable. It may, however, be that even if adequate employment opportunities outside agriculture are available, some additional persons may prefer to be absorbed in agriculture. After all, more than 6 million out of the 9 million additional persons in the labour force would be attached to farms or to agriculture to begin with. If incomes in agriculture are rising, some of them may prefer not to take up an alternative occupation even at a somewhat higher remuneration. This possibility cannot be ruled out in Indian conditions. It is not unlikely, therefore, that the total number of persons dependent on agriculture would increase by 2–3 million during the Second Plan in any case.

In the context of an employment-oriented plan, a word might be said about the possible conflict between greater production and greater employment. This conflict is generally represented in the form of the extent to which methods of production which require more capital but less labour should be encouraged.

However, from the national point of view this conflict is more apparent than real at least in the immediate future. For a single industry, the superiority of a capital-intensive method is easy to demonstrate. But a poor economy *as a whole* cannot be run on the basis of up-to-date capital-intensive methods for the simple reason that there is not that much surplus for investment to go round. Apart from this, we should not think too much in terms of "industries" only. There are a number of activities such as construction of houses, roads, dams and laying of railway tracks where "labour-using" methods may be just as economical as others. An increase in these activities can be a very useful source of additional employment.

Where the desire to provide more employment genuinely conflicts with greater production, it would be quite easy to provide reconciliation in theory. If the persons who benefit from greater production and those who suffer from the failure to keep or get jobs could be identified, we can work out some sort of compensation whereby no one would be worse off and someone would be better off. Schemes like unemployment insurance or relief can be a means of ensuring greater production for society as a whole without depressing too much the standard of living of the unemployed. But where greater production is associated with greater inequality of distribution and where any scheme of compensation is not feasible, the protection of the level of living at lower levels must take precedence over the raising of standards at a higher level. Needless to say, here also judgement cannot be based on an examination of a single industry or occupation. It may be that greater production and less employment in one industry does not imply a conflict between production and employment for the economy as a whole. Protecting the standard of living at lower levels does not imply protecting it in existing occupations.

Social Justice

The achievement of a "socialistic pattern of society" has already been declared as a basic objective of economic policy. A socialistic pattern is perhaps easy to recognize but not so easy to define. But it is clear that it implies the adoption of a plan which is in keeping with the requirements of social justice.

First, in raising the general level of living, the plan must give first priority to the claims of those whose incomes are among the lowest. The emphasis on employment opportunities as elaborated above is essentially dictated by considerations of social justice. Similarly, an inflationary rise in prices or distortions in relative prices which impair the well-being of the weak and unorganized sections of society must be avoided. A fair return to agriculturists and to industrial labour must be accepted as a basic part of the Second Plan. Among the poorer sections of society, the plight of agricultural labour is perhaps the worst and nothing short of a forthright land reform would give agricultural labour a secure position in society. The completion of land reforms by the end of the Second Plan must, therefore, be the first step towards a socialistic society.

Second, equality of opportunities, which is a basic element in social justice, requires that certain amenities must be provided to each and all irrespective of their ability to purchase the same. Among these amenities, education and health come first. In education, what is important is not merely the spread of schools and colleges but the assurance to the poorest parents that their children can get all the education that their faculties permit. This ideal obviously cannot be reached in five or ten years. But the Second Plan must pay special attention to the provision of free boarding, lodging and tuition facilities to poor and deserving students from the primary to postgraduate levels. Perhaps the best way of generating enthusiasm for education at the primary level is to have a network of free hostels in all districts so as to give hope of advancement for their children to all parents. Without multiplying examples, the State must endeavour to take the consumption of a number of things outside individual budgets and transfer them to the national budget. Such public consumption, so to speak, must form an increasing part of total consumption in the community in order to ensure greater equality of opportunities.

At the other end, glaring conspicuous consumption by the more privileged classes must be checked. This is not simply an emotional attitude of soaking the rich. In a poor country trying to lift itself by the bootstraps, a large number of sacrifices have to be imposed on the poor and the rich alike. Indeed, the self-denial of the poor who constitute the majority of people as well as incomes must provide, directly or indirectly, the major part of the resources for development. But such sacrifices cannot be justified in the midst of glaring inequality. Conspicuous consumption by a few persons also serves to dissipate the habit of thrift in others who follow suit in some measure or other for reasons of social prestige. Perhaps the best way of curbing conspicuous consumption by the few is a fairly stiff system of expenditure taxes on selected articles. Such a system of expenditure taxes would discourage extravagance and false standards without reducing unduly the incentive to effort or thrift. The Taxation Enquiry Commission has recommended that there should be a ceiling on net personal income after tax which, generally speaking, should not exceed approximately thirty times the prevailing average per family income in the country. This recommendation is intended to be implemented by steps over a period of time; and the first steps must be taken in the Second Plan.

A socialistic pattern of society also implies State ownership of the strategic means of production. With the rapid development of basic industries, largely in the public sector, the Second Plan would ensure for the State a significant increase in its share of the basic means of production.

The Second Five Year Plan in Outline

The concrete tasks to be performed in the course of the Second Plan are outlined in this section and an indication is given of the impact it would make on employment opportunities and the structure of the economy.

In fixing targets for the Second Plan, we have to take into account the socially determined norms of production and consumption in certain specified fields such as heavy industries, health and housing as well as the nature of consumer demand and the scope for international exchange. In addition, the production of intermediate goods has to be assured in keeping with the interdependence of different industries. The tentative targets for the Second Plan are fixed as far as possible, with these considerations in mind. But it is clear that no finality or complete consistency can be claimed for them at this stage. This can be done only after a detailed scrutiny of the projects and policies to be included in the plan. In the meanwhile, a tentative outline of the tasks to be performed in the next plan may throw some light on the decisions to be made by giving a rough measure of the effort involved in arriving at one set of results.

Industrial and Mineral Development

In order to achieve rapid development of basic industries in the country, the following major tasks must be performed in the Second Plan:

(1) The production of steel must be raised to 5 million tons and steel capacity to 6 million tons by the end of the plan. The capacity of existing plants must be expanded and three or four new steel plants must be established in the public sector.

(2) The State must set up a number of plants for producing the machine-tools required for fabricating the equipment in steel plants and in other producer goods industries.

(3) The production of heavy electrical equipment such as generators and turbines must be started by the State in order to make the country self-sufficient in the growing requirements arising from rapid electrification of the country.

(4) Steps must be taken to set up a synthetic petrol plant in the public sector with a capacity of one-quarter million tons.

(5) The production of locomotives, wagons, coaches and rolling stock must be increased as much as possible by working existing equipment to full capacity on a multi-shift basis. The same principle must be applied to other existing State enterprises.
(6) Three more companies must be established in the public sector in order to increase the production of fertilizers to four times the present level.
(7) The output of cement must be raised from 4.8 million tons at present to 10 million tons.
(8) The heavy chemical industry must expand to at least three times the present level.
(9) Steps must be taken to ensure full utilization of capacity in the existing units producing agricultural implements, diesel engines, light engineering goods and machineries for textiles, sugar and other consumer goods industries.
(10) The production of aluminium must be raised from some 4,000 tons at present to 40,000 tons by the end of the Second Plan in order to make up for the shortage of copper in the country.
(11) In order to make this development of heavy industries possible, the production of coal must be increased from 37 million tons to 60 million tons and of iron ore from 4 million to 13 million tons.
(12) The production of important minerals such as manganese and mica must increase in response to higher demand at home without curtailing the supplies available for exports. The output of manganese must increase from 2 to 3 million tons and of mica from 150,000 to 200,000 hundredweights.
(13) A comprehensive geological survey of the country must be undertaken in the next plan.

In the case of consumer goods industries, the following targets must be achieved.

(1) The production of mill-made cotton cloth must be stabilized at around 5,000 million yards and that of handlooms, improved handlooms and small power looms must be increased from 1,600 million yards to 32,000 million yards. These targets would provide for a domestic consumption of 8 yards per person per year while allowing for export of some 1,000 million yards every year.
(2) The production of woollen manufacture must be increased from 20 million lbs to 30 million lbs.
(3) In the case of sugar, production must be increased to 2.1 million tons in order to make the country self-sufficient while allowing for a 25 to 30 per cent increase in total consumption.

(4) The output of vegetable oils must be increased from 1.5 to 2 million tons.
(5) The production of footwear must be increased by 20 per cent mainly in the small-scale sector.
(6) In the case of the newer industries producing electrical goods, bicycles, sewing machines and glassware where there is a great deal of excess capacity and where export prospects are good, increases in production ranging from 60 to 100 per cent and even more must be achieved.
(7) A comprehensive effort must be made to ensure maximum utilization of existing capacity and to resuscitate production of consumer goods by small-scale labour-intensive methods.

The fulfilment of the targets for industrial and mineral development envisaged above would require concrete schemes for the training of personnel. These requirements, however, cannot be indicated at this stage.

The total investment required for achieving the targets in industries and mining may be roughly estimated at Rs 1,300–1,500 crore as given in Table 13.3.

Table 13.3 Estimated Total Investment Required for Achieving the Targets in Industries and Mining

Item	*Rs crore*
Iron and Steel	450 to 500
Synthetic Petrol	100
Electrical Equipment	50
Fertilizer	100
Aluminium	30
Marginal expansion of existing state enterprises	20
Machine tools for fabricating steel plants and similar equipment	200
Cement	50
Chemicals, Drugs & Paints	25 to 50
Agricultural Implements, Diesel Engines and Textiles	25 to 50
Sugar and similar machinery	
Development of Minerals and Geological Survey	100 to 150
Organized Consumer Goods Industries	50 to 100
Small-scale Industries (including credit, marketing and other facilities)	100
Total	1,300 to 1,500

The provision for investment made in Table 13.3 is, in the nature of things, rather generous inasmuch as allowance is made for a number of possibilities which still remain to be explored. On the other hand, these investment figures do not take into account the requirements of depreciation, replacement, working capital or the provision of housing for workers and the development of townships which may be associated with the establishment of new industries.

Of the total investment in industries and mining, the bulk must be in the public sector. A precise line of demarcation cannot be drawn at this stage between developments in the national and the private sector. But it may be estimated that private investment in this sector would be of the order of Rs 300–400 crore. Profits of existing enterprises constitute the main source of private investment; and since these profits are made largely in consumer goods industries where we do not envisage large increase in investment, it would be necessary to divert private investment to proper channels—by a well-defined and coordinated polity of control over imports of machinery, over capital issues and over the establishment of new units and by suitable tax incentives for investment in selected lines (including investment in government securities).

Transport and Power

Development of power and transport are essential preconditions for rapid industrial progress. The First Plan outlined a long-term programme for the development of power resources in the country over a period of fifteen to twenty years. It is expected that the generation of electricity would increase from 2.3 to 3.7 million kWt (capacity) over the First Plan. By the end of the Second Plan, this capacity must be increased to 7 million kWt, with an estimated outlay of some Rs 500 crore (including the cost of transmission).

In the case of railways, there is a considerable lag in the development of both goods and passenger traffic. However, the railways already have a tentative plan of expansion and re-equipment of some Rs 800 crore. This plan, which calls for an addition of 3,000 miles of railway lines among other things, may be accepted as the first approximation to the task in the Second Plan.

The long-term development of roads in the country has already been outlined in the Nagpur plan. An expansion of road building in the Second Plan is desirable from the point of view of providing both employment and the basic amenities of life in the rural areas. The planned outlay on roads in the public sector should be increased, therefore, from some Rs 108 crore in the First Plan to Rs 300 crore in the next plan so as to expand national highways from about 12,500 to 17,500 miles and state roads from about 20,000 to 35,000 miles.

Agriculture

Despite the general emphasis on industries in the Second Plan, we cannot afford to relax in our efforts to increase agricultural productivity in view of ever-increasing population, limited area, uncertain monsoons and low nutritional standards. It would also be necessary to provide for the raw materials needed in industries and for exports (or replacement of imports). The following major targets, therefore, must be achieved in the Second Plan:

(1) The production of food grains must be increased from some 66 million tons to 76 million tons by 1960–61. This would ensure the maintenance of self-sufficiency in food grains on an average on the basis of slightly higher standard of consumption than at present.

(2) The output of cotton must be increased from 4.2 million bales to 5.8 million bales. This target is related to the production of cotton textiles, and it is assumed that the country should cease to be a net importer of cotton by 1960–61.

(3) The total yield of sugarcane should increase from some 5 million tons (raw *gur*) to 7.5 million tons. The demand for sugar is highly income-elastic; and we are currently importing large amounts of sugar. We have been self-sufficient in the supply of sugar in the past, and it is not unreasonable to expect that we would revert to that position in the Second Plan.

(4) The production of oil-seeds must be increased from 5.6 to 7 million tons.

(5) The supply of protective foods such as milk, ghee, vegetables, meat, fish and eggs must be increased by some 25 per cent on an average by the end of the Second Plan.

(6) In the case of important export items such as tea and tobacco, exports must be maintained and increased as far as possible in spite of greater consumption at home. The production of tobacco must be increased from 250,000 to 300,000 tons and of tea from 650 to 750 million lbs.

(7) Apart from the important commercial crops like cotton and tobacco, attention must also be paid to others which are hitherto of only marginal significance. Some of the marginal items like wool are bound to increase in demand at home and have good export prospects. Wool also has special significance from the point of view of providing employment in some of the poorer areas such as Rajasthan, Saurashtra and Jammu and Kashmir.

(8) In order to achieve the targets outlined above, the total irrigated area in the country must be increased from 70 to 90 or 100 million acres.

(9) Special attention must be given to flood control.

The lines on which efforts must be made to raise agricultural production are already clearly established. The extension of NES blocks and community projects to cover the entire country by the end of the Second Plan are already contemplated, and the Rural Credit Survey has indicated the role of credit and warehousing facilities as the spearhead of rural uplift. Apart from this, the policy of ensuring an adequate return to agriculturists by price support, if necessary, has also been accepted. It is on the speedy implementation of a forthright system of land reforms that special emphasis needs to be placed at this stage.

Social Services

The provision of basic amenities such as schools, hospitals, housing, waterworks and drainage must respond primarily to the expression of popular needs. It is in this sphere that "planning from below" has real significance. The district plans under preparation now should give a fair measure of popular aspirations in this field. However, the following tentative targets may be set down:

(1) The total outlay on social services in the public sector must be increased to double its present size by 1960–61, that is, from some Rs 170–175 crore in 1954–55 (that is, Centre and states) to Rs 350–400 crore.

(2) The proportion of school-going persons to the total number between the age of six and fourteen must be increased from 50 per cent to 75 per cent. Correspondingly, the number of school teachers and school buildings must be raised. Facilities for higher education, with greater emphasis on vocational schools and on-the-job training must be expanded; and the state must bear an increasing proportion of the total cost of education by providing free boarding, lodging and tuition facilities.

(3) The total number of hospital beds in the country must be increased from 125,000 to 250,000. The number of registered physicians and of health workers in the country must be increased by 50 per cent.

(4) The total number of urban houses must be increased from 115–120 lakh to 150 lakh. In developing new industries, the housing of workers must be given due attention.

(5) A beginning has already been made in the country with the introduction of several social security schemes such as the employees' state insurance and provident fund schemes. Those schemes must be extended to other industries and areas and a scheme of unemployment insurance, combined with a network of active employment exchanges and training facilities must be introduced. In the context of an employment-oriented plan, some protection against

actual unemployment and facilities for a rapid re-absorption in the labour market are clearly indicated.

Investment and Priorities in the Plan

The basic targets to be achieved in the Second Plan have been indicated above, and these are summarized in the appendix to this chapter. Some indication is also given of the investment required in different sectors. In this section, the investment requirements of the plan are brought together so as to indicate the overall size and priorities in the plan. The concept of "investment", however, bristles with ambiguities; and in view of the variety of concepts in the field, it is necessary to specify clearly what is included in investment here so as to avoid unwarranted comparisons.

In the First Plan, two different concepts were used to denote the size of the plan, viz., net investment and developmental expenditure. Thus, the net investment in the public sector was expected to be of the order of Rs 1,600–1,700 crore; whereas the developmental expenditure which includes outlay of a capital as well as current nature was initially estimated at Rs 2,069 crore. Since outlay on the plan included only a portion of the outlay on certain developmental heads such as health and education, an additional concept of total developmental outlay as distinguished from that included in the plan has also been used at times to indicate the size of the plan. In the case of forty-two organized industries in the private and the private and public sector, the First Plan considered the requirements of gross rather than the net investment inasmuch as allowance was made for part of depreciation, replacement and modernization. Similarly, the requirements of working capital were taken account in the case of industries, but not for other sectors.

For the purposes of this paper, we speak of "net investment" when referring to the economy as a whole. If our idea in assessing the "investment cost" of a plan of certain size and character is to measure the effort of saving that is involved, it is more logical to consider gross income and gross investment. The entire gross product of the economy is, strictly speaking, available for consumption or investment. The allowance to be made for depreciation is in many cases notional in the sense that except in the case of repairs, maintenance or replacements no real resources are in fact required currently against the estimated amount of depreciation. Replacement itself is seldom a mere substitution of one machine or building with another of the same type. Nonetheless, since our national income statistics are expressed in net output terms, it is more convenient to relate them to net investment.

Non-monetized investment is not included in investment. In a community of self-supporting persons, a significant amount of investment must be done by the application of personal labour and by using locally available materials. With the efforts to mobilize voluntary labour for various nation-building activities such as flood control, investment in non-money terms must play an important part. It is also illogical not to include such investment when the income generating from it is included in national output. However, in view of the highly conjectural nature of the imputed value of such investment, it is proposed to disregard it at this stage.

As regards investment in working capital, that is, in stocks of goods and services waiting to be consumed or to be utilized in production, it is clear that any additional requirements here are indistinguishable from the requirements of fixed capital. Both require "savings" in real and financial terms; and as the Rural Credit Survey amply points out, provision of short-term capital has as much relevance to production as that of long-term capital. Indeed, unless increments in stocks of *all* goods are included in investment, it would be difficult to justify the inclusion of residential houses in investment. Construction of a house is investment not because it resembles a producer good more than a consumer good but because it represents a net addition to the stock of houses. Unfortunately, the requirements of additional working capital over a period are not easy to estimate, and only a rough allowance is made for them here.

Finally, in speaking of net investment for the economy as a whole, the cost of existing assets such as land is excluded. Although for a private individual or agency the cost of constructing a house must include the cost of land, for society as a whole the investment cost is net of the use of land which was already in existence.

Although it is more meaningful to speak of net investment when referring to the economy as a whole, it is useful to retain the concept of developmental expenditure in speaking of the public sector. Whether this developmental expenditure under the plan should include only a part or whole of the expenditure in certain specified heads is a moot question to which we return later. But at this stage, it may be emphasized that as long as we use more than one concept to indicate the size of the plan in the public sector, it would be essential to recast government budgets in a manner which would make explicit the magnitudes of all these concepts. Thus, net capital formation through the budget, total developmental outlay and the outlay on the plan must be all readily ascertainable from the budget statements.

The total amount of net investment required for achieving the targets outlined above may be estimated at about Rs 6,000 crore. This estimate is made up by aggregating, wherever possible, the capital requirements of the individual targets. However, this procedure cannot be adopted uniformly for two reasons. The targets do not cover all the items of production. And in several important sectors, particularly in agriculture, investment is multipurpose in the sense that only a complex of products can be related to a complex of investment.

Again, it is not as if all the investment in the community is strictly required for the achievement of the targets set. Residential construction, stockpiling and investment in gold and precious metals can take place irrespective of the requirements of the targets sought to be achieved. It is as well, therefore, to be clear in our minds as to how much allowance we make for such investment.

A tentative breakdown of the net investment of Rs 6,000 crore may be given as in Table 13.4.

Table 13.4 Tentative Breakdown of the Net Investment of Rs 6,000 crore

Item	*Rs crore*	*% of total*
Agriculture and Community Development (including irrigation and flood control)	1,100	18.3
Power (including transmission)	500	8.3
Transport and Communications	900	15
Industrial and Mineral Development	1,500	25
Construction (houses, shops, schools, hospitals, drainage, water-works, etc.)	1,500	25
Stocks, Miscellaneous and Adjustments	500	8.3
Total	6,000	100

In order to avoid any misunderstanding, it may be useful to relate these magnitudes to developmental outlay as conceived in the First Plan. For this purpose, we may assume that out of the total net investment of Rs 6,000 crore, some Rs 3,500 crore would be organized through government's budgetary and other operations and the remaining Rs 2,500 crore or so would represent private investment from private sources. Needless to say, this is only a tentative estimate.

The developmental expenditure under the plan in the public sector, corresponding to the net investment of Rs 3,500 crore, might amount to roughly Rs 4,200 crore. This figure is comparable to the outlay of Rs 2,069 crore initially proposed for the First Plan. In addition to capital formation proper, a part of the current expenditure on nation-building activities such as health and education may also be included in the plan in the public sector. If the entire expenditure on developmental heads is included in the plan, the total size of the plan in the public sector would amount to some Rs 5,100 crore. A tentative breakdown of the plan outlay of Rs 4,200 crore in the public sector might be as given in Table 13.5.

The total net investment of Rs 2,500 crore in the private sector might be distributed roughly as given in Table 13.6.

Table 13.5 Tentative Breakdown of the Net Investment of Rs 4,200 crore in the Public Sector

Item	*Rs crore*	*% of total*
Agriculture and Community Development (including irrigation and flood control)	900	21.4
Power	500	12
Transport and Communications	1,100	26
Industrial and Mineral Development	1,000	24
Social Services	700	16.3
Total	4,200	100

Table 13.6 Tentative Breakdown of the Net Investment of Rs 2,500 crore in the Private Sector

Item	*Rs crore*
Rural and Urban Construction	1,200–1,300
Industry, Mining, Power and Transport	400–500
Agriculture and Allied Pursuits	300
Working Capital in Trade and Industry and Miscellaneous	400–500
Total	2,400–2,600

It need hardly be emphasized that the pattern of investment outlined above is provisional and is intended to give only an approximate idea of the size and priorities in the plan.

National Income and the Structure of the Economy

One way of describing the achievements of the next plan would be to contrast the structure of production as it would emerge at the end of the plan (1960–61) with that prevailing on the eve of the plan (1955–56). This is done in the present section.

The latest available estimate of India's national income relates to the year 1953–54. At current prices, the national income of India in 1953–54 was approximately Rs 10,600 crore. In order to present a picture of the change in the economy over the Second Plan, it is necessary to have an estimate of national income for the year 1955–56. Even if we make allowance for the fact that national income in 1953–54 was somewhat unusually high on account of favourable monsoons, it is not unreasonable to expect that national income over the last two years of the First Plan would increase by some 4 per cent. On this basis, national income in 1955–56 should exceed Rs 11,000 crore at 1953–54 prices.

However, judged by recent trends, prices in 1953–54 were also high. In outlining the change in the economic structure over the Second Plan, we have necessarily to make all calculations at some constant prices. In one sense, it does not matter what particular prices we use. Nonetheless, since income estimates such as those of government receipts and expenditure are necessarily made at current prices, it is important that other calculations are also made at prices as near as possible to the prices current in the period under consideration. For the Second Plan, prices in 1955–56 may be taken as the nearest approximation. Since 1955–56 prices also have to be assumed at this stage, we have based our calculations on the assumption of 1952–53 prices inasmuch as they are nearer to current prices than those in any other recent year for which national income data are available. Table 13.7 presents the index of wholesale prices in India.

Table 13.7 Index of Wholesale Prices in India
(Year ended August 1939 = 100)

	Food Articles	*Industrial Raw Materials*	*Semi-manufactures*	*Manufactures*	*General Index*
1948–49	383	445	327	346	376
1949–50	391	472	332	347	385
1950	416	523	349	354	410
1951–52	399	592	374	401	435
1952–53	358	437	344	371	381
1953–54	384	467	359	367	398
1955, Jan. 22	309	431	345	377	363

Source: Government of India.

The national income of India in 1955–56 at 1952–53 prices may be estimated at Rs 10,800 crore. With a 5 per cent increase per annum it should amount to Rs 13,700 crore in 1960–61, that is, an increase of Rs 2,900 crore. This increase is consistent with the targets set as supplemented by assumptions about minor sectors not included in the targets.

The increase in national income would obviously not be uniform for different sectors. Table 13.8 illustrates the change in the economic structure envisaged for the Second Plan in terms of the sector-wise breakdown employed in national income statistics in India.

It is seen from Table 13.6 that the bulk of the increase in national income (Rs 2,900 crore) would still be in agriculture and allied pursuits (Rs 1,060 crore). Factory establishments would show an increase in net output of some Rs 550 crore, mines of Rs 50 crore and small enterprise of another Rs 40 crore. The rest of the additional output of about Rs 830 crore

Table 13.8 Domestic Product of India
(at 1952–53 prices)

	Product (Rs abja)			*Per cent of Total Product*		
	1950–51	*1955–56*	*1960–61*	*1950–51*	*1955–56*	*1960–61*
I. Agriculture and Allied Pursuits	45.2	52.8	63.4	49.2	49.0	46.3
II. Mining	0.8	1.0	1.5	0.9	0.9	1.0
III. Factory Establishments	5.8	8.0	13.5	6.3	7.4	9.6
IV. Small Enterprises	9.3	10.2	14.3	10.1	9.5	10.5
V. Railway, Communications, Banks, etc.	3.1	3.6	4.7	3.4	3.5	3.5
VI. Other Commerce and Transport	13.4	15.1	18.8	14.6	13.9	13.8
VII. Professions, Government Services, etc.	14.3	17.3	20.8	15.5	16.0	15.3
Total Product	91.9	108.0	137.0	100.0	100.0	100.0

Source: Government of India.
Note: Percentages are approximate.

would be generated in the tertiary sector. However, in relative terms, the increase in income generated would be greater in factory establishments (65 per cent), mining (50 per cent) and small enterprises (40 per cent) than in agriculture (20 per cent) or in the tertiary sector (23 per cent). On balance, the relative share of mines, factories and small enterprises in the national income would increase from 17.5 per cent in 1955–56 to 21.5 per cent in 1960–61, and that of agriculture would decline correspondingly from 49 per cent to 46.0 per cent. Thus, despite the seemingly high targets for industries, the structure of the economy would not show any marked change over the Second Plan.

The classification of domestic product by sectors given above does not reveal certain features of the development envisaged for the Second Plan. Thus, the development of heavy industries is obscured in the total of factory establishments. Similarly, the small enterprise sector is not identical with the small industries sector. It includes in addition workers employed in construction industries. A further breakdown of these sectors can be attempted only on rough lines. Thus, although the net output of factory establishments increases by two-third, the output of consumer goods industries is expected to increase by 20 to 25 per cent only, whereas that of producer goods by 150–175 per cent. In the case of small enterprises, as against a total increase of 40 per cent in net output, that of consumer goods is envisaged to increase by one-third, of producer goods by 50 per cent and of construction enterprises by some 60 per cent.

Similarly, the increase in agricultural output of 20 per cent comprises a 15 per cent increase in food grains and 25 per cent other foodstuffs and commercial crops.

In short, the structure of production envisaged here is in correspondence with the priorities dictated by the basic objectives outlined earlier. Heavy industries receive the greatest emphasis; in the production of additional manufactured consumer goods, small enterprises get a roughly equal share with factory establishments and the output in agriculture, on which the prosperity of the bulk of the people depends, shows a significant increase of 20 per cent.

The Pattern of Employment

The creation of adequate employment opportunities is one of the basic objectives of the Second Plan. Some of the implications of this policy have already been underlined earlier. In this section we may consider whether the target of 10–12 million additional persons to be pressed into gainful occupation outside agriculture can be realized in terms of the plan envisaged here. Unfortunately, our knowledge of the occupational distribution of the population on the eve of the Second Plan can only be based on an extrapolation of the picture revealed by the 1951 census. This is not very satisfactory; but a rough attempt is made to see where the additional persons might be absorbed.

In 1950–51, out of the total working force of 143.2 million persons, some 103.6 million were employed in agriculture and allied occupations. It is among the remaining 40 million persons—or say 42–43 million by 1955–56—employed in mines, factories, small enterprises, trade, transport, communications, professions and other salaried employees that some 10–12 million additional breadwinners have to be created in the Second Plan. The likely results of the plan outlined above may be analysed sector by sector.

Mining. In 1950–51, some 8 lakh persons were employed in mines. With output from mines increasing by some 50 per cent in the Second Plan, additional employment in mines may be of the order of 3–4 lakh.

Factory Establishments. Factory establishments employed some 30 lakh persons in 1950–51, of which roughly 24 lakh were in consumer goods industries and the remaining in producer goods industries. In the Second Plan the net output of factory-produced consumer goods is expected to increase by some 20 per cent and of producer goods by 150–175 per cent.

On this basis, additional employment in factories may be of the other of 12–14 lakh. (Total factory employment in 1955–56 may be a little higher than 30 lakh.)

Small Enterprises. In 1950–51, small enterprises employed some 115 lakh persons. The term "small enterprises" is, however, misleading. In addition to small-scale industries proper, it includes those engaged in construction of roads, buildings, irrigation works, carpenters, bricklayers, etc. This latter category accounted for as much as 44 lakh persons out of the total of 115 lakh in small enterprises. Among the rest, textiles and tailoring accounted for 32 lakh, metal-working and mechanical enterprises 12 lakh and food and tobacco industries another 15 lakh.

The Second Plan envisages an increase of about 40 per cent in the net output of small enterprises, ranging from 20 per cent in food industries and 25 per cent in leather products to 33 per cent in the metal group, 50 per cent in the textile and tailoring group and 60 per cent in the construction group. It is clear that incomes of persons employed in small enterprises are low and several of them do not have sufficient work. In this sector, therefore, employment should not increase as fast as production. Assuming that it increases, say by one-fourth as against a two-fifth increase in output, this sector would absorb about 30 lakh additional persons at the end of the Second Plan.

Railways, Communications, Organized Banks and Insurance. This sector provided employment to roughly 15 lakh persons in 1950–51. The Second Plan envisages considerable expansion in banking facilities, railways and communications. Additional employment of 3–4 lakh persons here may, therefore, reasonably be expected.

Other Commerce and Transport. This sector is a great employment provider, for some 95 lakh persons in 1950–51. Nearly two-third of this group is employed in retail trade, some 6 lakh in wholesale trade, 10–11 lakh in hotels and restaurants and about the same number in road transport. If net output of this sector increases by 20 to 25 per cent, as is envisaged, gainful occupation for some 20 lakh additional persons should reasonably be available in this sector. It is arguable that we should not rely on trade for additional employment inasmuch as this sector is already rather large in relation to the total size of the economy. However, in the absence of any scheme for the direction of labour and in the immediate future some expansion of employment in trade must be expected.

Government Administration. In 1950–51 there were 39 lakh persons employed in government administration, and additional employment in this sector during the Second Plan may be of the order of some 5 lakh.

Professions and Liberal Arts. This is another important sector from the point of view of employment. In 1950–51 some 64 lakh persons were employed in this sector including some 10 lakh teachers, 11 to 12 lakh barbers, 12 to 13 lakh dhobis, 7 lakh scavengers and 8 lakh medical practitioners and health workers. The juxtaposition of barbers and dhobis with teachers and doctors is rather curious; but it is retained here inasmuch as it corresponds to national income classification in India.

In view of the substantial increase in the expenditure on health, sanitation and education envisaged in the Second Plan and the increased demand for the services of barbers, dhobis, etc., an increase in employment by 15 lakh or more in this sector is not unlikely. It may not be unreasonable to expect a 50 per cent increase in the number of teachers, doctors and other health workers; and this in itself would create 10 lakh additional jobs.

The additional employment we may count on is given in Table 13.9.

Table 13.9 Additional Employment We May Count on in the Second Plan

Item	*In lakh*
Mines	3 to 4
Factories	12 to 14
Small Enterprises (including construction workers)	30
Railways, Communications, etc.	3 to 4
Other Commerce and Transport	20
Government Administration	5
Professions and Liberal Arts	15 to 20
Total	88 to 97

Source: Author's own.

Thus, the foreseeable employment potential of the plan is of the order of 9–9.5 million persons absorbed outside agriculture. Perhaps some 1–2 million persons would be added to those engaged in agriculture in any case in view of the natural immobility of persons in the face of rising standard of living in their existing occupations. Again, not all the persons employed in agriculture and allied pursuits depend on land. Some additional employment among those engaged in fishing, forestry or sheep-raising may not be undesirable.

It should be emphasized, however, that the increase in employment envisaged here will not take place automatically in the absence of suitable policies. It is clear that small enterprises, for example, which bear the brunt of the employment effort, will not expand on the scale envisaged without positive effort. Provision of employment also carries with it the implication that training facilities for the type of personnel needed could be provided for on the scale required. Again, in so many sectors we have assumed that additional output would mean a more or less proportionate increase in employment. This envisages some control over excessive rationalization, on concentration of units and on frittering away of higher demand in raising the remuneration of those already in employment to the detriment of the unemployed. The problem of unemployment, as has already been emphasized, can hardly be separated from that of distribution of income.

From this point of view, it may be of interest to note the following figures about the net output per person employed in different sectors. The figures must be interpreted with caution. Thus, figures in money terms do not take into account differences in cost of living or of the non-economic disabilities and advantages of certain occupations or places. Again, net output per employed person represents the earnings of labour as well as capital and does not take government draft into consideration. The differences among sectors are partly the result of different capital requirements per unit of output. What is more, the number of persons gainfully occupied per household varies from sector to sector, and the disparities in income per occupied person do not correspond to disparities in incomes per household. The occupational distribution envisaged for 1955–56 and 1960–61 is also largely conjectural. Nonetheless, Table 13.10 illustrates an important aspect of the Second Plan. It may be noted that the distribution of additional output and employment in the Second Plan is so designed, by and large, as to raise levels of living at lower levels.

Table 13.10 Occupational Pattern, India

	Working Force (in millions)			*Net Output per Occupied Person (Rs per year at 1952–53 prices)*		
	1950–51	*1955–56*	*1960–61*	*1950–51*	*1955–56*	*1960–61*
1. Agriculture and Allied Pursuits	103.6	109.5	111.0	446	482	572
2. Mining and Factory Establishments	3.8	4.0	5.7	1,737	2,250	2,630
3. Small Enterprises	11.5	12.0	15.0	810	850	955
4. Communications, Railways, Banks and Insurance	1.5	1.6	2.0	2,065	2,250	2,350
5. Other Commerce and Transport	9.5	10.0	12.0	1,410	1,500	1,566
6. Government Administration, Professions, Liberal Arts and the Rest	13.3	14.9	17.3	1,080	1,150	1,200
Total	143.2	152.0	163.0	642	710	845

Note: Calculations are provisional.

Net output per occupied person increases by only 4–5 per cent in the tertiary sector, where it is already high compared to the national average. In agriculture and small-scale industries, the increase is of the order of 20 and 13 per cent, respectively. Mining and factory establishments also show an increase in net output per employed person of some one-sixth. This increase reflects, however, the shift in favour of heavy industries where large amounts of capital are associated with a comparatively small employment of labour. Thus, by and large, the employment pattern envisaged here is in keeping with the basic objectives of fuller employment and social justice.

Mobilization of Resources for the Plan

If the economy is to develop along the lines indicated in the earlier sections, the resources needed for this development must be forthcoming in the right amount and at the right time. If the plan fails to gather momentum in the early stages or is thrown out of gear as a result of bottlenecks, the tempo of development in later years will also be retarded. The phasing of the plan over the five years and the phasing of the rate at which resources become available must, therefore, be carefully coordinated. No attempt is made at this stage to indicate this phasing, and the problem of resources is discussed in terms of the requirements for the five-year period as a whole.

The plan itself must make specific provision for creating such resources of skilled personnel, administrative cadre and intermediate goods as are needed for the fulfilment of the basic targets. A complete balance sheet of some of the key resources of personnel and materials must be prepared so as to ensure that adequate supplies become available as and when needed. Such balances are under preparation. But final commodity and personnel balances can only be arrived at after a study of concrete projects.

What is attempted in this section is an indication of the financial resources needed for the plan and the manner in which these might be mobilized. A tentative indication of the foreign exchange requirements of the plan is also given.

There are two distinct aspects to this question of raising the financial resources needed for the plan. First, the resources needed for the capital formation envisaged must be available in the aggregate. Second, the resources must be available and utilized by each sector and for each purpose in accordance with the priorities set in the plan. This second aspect requires a policy of regulating the direction of investment.

The broad order of effort needed for raising capital formation to some Rs 6,000 crore in the Second Plan is easy to indicate. The Taxation Enquiry Commission has estimated that aggregate savings and investment in 1953–54 amounted to Rs 730 crore or 7 per cent of national income. In order to achieve total investment of Rs 6,000 crore over the Second Plan savings must rise from 7 to 11 per cent of national income. To put it differently, some one-third of the additional incomes generated must be ploughed back into additional investment. It may be recalled that in the First Plan savings were expected to rise from 5 to 6.75 per cent of national income with 20 per cent of additional incomes devoted to additional investment. The savings target envisaged for the Second Plan is more difficult than it looks at first sight for two reasons. With the accent on raising incomes particularly at lower levels—in agriculture and small enterprises—it is not easy to raise savings. Again, a large part of the increased income is to take place in heavy producers' goods industries which are not likely to yield a surplus for investment in the initial stages. Nonetheless, an increase in the rate of savings to 11 per cent of national income by 1960–61 is not a very ambitious target.

Resources in the Public Sector

What is relevant from the standpoint of finding resources for the government is not the outlay on the plan but total outlay. What should be excluded from the plan has, therefore, an obvious significance to the realistic appraisal of the financing of the plan. It is suggested that the outlay on the plan should include all expenditure which results in the creation of new capital assets in the public or the private sector. In addition, it should include that part of the current expenditure on specific developmental heads which represents an increase over the level reached at the end of the First Plan. This would give a clear idea of the "lift" we are giving to the developmental effort during the next plan. This is the concept used in this paper in arriving at the plan outlay of Rs 4,200 crore.

An alternative would be to include all expenditure under specified developmental heads under the plan and leave out all expenditure on certain items like Defence and Civil Administration. In the First Plan, the outlay under the plan is running roughly at two-third of the total outlay on developmental heads. Consequently, although the inclusion of all expenditure on certain heads in the plan would greatly inflate the figures, it would facilitate a more realistic appraisal of the plan and its financing by ruling out the possibility of shifting of expenditure "under the plan" to that "outside the plan". It would also enable a quicker review of the progress under the plan from the budget itself. On the other hand, by narrowing the scope of the plan to the schemes deemed more essential to further effort, we are better able to scrutinize them. It may be useful, therefore, to highlight both the total expenditure under specified developmental heads and the outlay on the plan. As a rough approximation, the budgetary position of the Centre and the states combined may be outlined as given in Table 13.11.

Table 13.11 Rough Approximation of the Budgetary Position of the Centre and the States Combined

Rs crore

	1955–56	*1960–61*	*1956–57 to 1960–61*
(a) Total Outlay on Plan	600	1,150	4,200
(b) Total Outlay on Developmental Heads	750	1,150	5,100
(c) Total Government Outlay	1,400	1,950	8,500
(d) Total non-Plan Outlay (c–a)	800	900	4,300
(e) Total non-Developmental Outlay (c–b)	650	700	3,400

Source: Author's own.

It is assumed that outlay on the plan would increase by some 12 per cent per year and that outside the plan by a little over 2 per cent per year. However, the outlay on developmental heads which is not included in the plan would increase somewhat faster from Rs 150 crore in 1955–56 to Rs 200 crore in 1960–61, or by some 6 per cent per year. Non-developmental outlay not included in the plan would increase from Rs 650 crore to Rs 700 crore only in five years or by a little over 1 per cent every year. It is hardly necessary to emphasize that the assumption about the increase in the outlay outside the plan is rather optimistic. It is estimated that the expenditure outside the plan on revenue account alone has increased from about Rs 700 crore in 1951–52 to Rs 800 crore in 1954–55 (budget estimate).

How is a total government outlay of Rs 8,500 crore (Rs 4,300 crore outside the plan and Rs 4,200 crore on the plan) to be financed? Assuming that the government takes some 8.5 per cent of national income in taxes and in non-tax revenue as has been the case on an average over the past four or five years, the total revenue receipts would amount to about Rs 5,100 crore. After meeting the expenditure outside the plan, some Rs 800 crore would be available from current revenue to meet the expenditure on the plan. If borrowing from the public continues to yield roughly 1.5 per cent of national income, that is, as at present, another Rs 900 crore can be raised from this source (about Rs 550 crore from loans and Rs 350 crore from small savings). Our experience of the First Plan suggests that on balance we should not expect anything from deposits, funds and miscellaneous receipts and that the contribution from railways, at the present rate, would not amount to more than Rs 100 crore over five years. The budgetary position of the government over the Second Plan would, therefore, look somewhat as given in Table 13.12 on the basis of present trends.

Table 13.12 Budgetary Position over the Second Plan

Expenditure	*Rs crore*
(a) On the Plan	4,200
(b) Outside the Plan	4,300
	8,500
Receipts	
(a) On Revenue Account	5,100
(b) From Railways	100
(c) Loans from the People	900
	6,100
Deficit	2,400

Source: Author's own.

Before commenting on the deficit or gap of Rs 2,400 crore, we may recall the effort needed for fulfilling the assumptions made so far.

(1) Outlay outside the plan must increase from Rs 800 crore in 1955–56 to Rs 900 crore only by 1960–61. If it increases say to Rs 1,000 crore, an additional deficit of some Rs 300 crore will emerge over the five years as a whole.

(2) Although we have assumed revenue at 8.5 per cent of national income, it is running at a somewhat lower rate at present, about 8.35 per cent. After the collapse of the Korean boom, some revenues have declined. Thus, even to reach the level of revenue envisaged, some extra effort is needed.

(3) Nor should it be assumed that with the increase in national income during the Second Plan, revenues would automatically run at the proportionate rate postulated. With the increase in income at lower levels and in heavy producer goods' industries, some adjustments in tax structure and in the price and subsidy policy of government enterprises and activities must become essential even to maintain the present rate of government draft on private income. Apart from this, some of the structural changes such as greater import substitution (say in sugar) would necessitate a corresponding shift from import taxes to excise duties.

(4) The target of Rs 350 crore of small savings is reasonable; and there may even be an increase in the yield here of some Rs 50 crore or so. But public loans of Rs 550 crore are based on the rather optimistic experience of the current year which witnessed a somewhat sudden increase in national income. It should also be noted that during the

> Second Plan, loan maturities of some Rs 430 crore must be reckoned with.

To return to the gap or deficit of Rs 2,400 crore, we can take credit for some Rs 400 crore of foreign assistance, leaving about Rs 2,000 crore to account for. Over the First Plan, foreign assistance to the public sector is likely to be of the order of Rs 250 crore. Thus, we are assuming 60 per cent increase in the amount of external assistance utilized in the Second Plan.

It is clear that the entire gap of Rs 2,000 crore cannot be filled up by deficit financing or creation of money. As a first approximation, we may assume that we can take resort to such money creation to the extent of Rs 1,000 crore. Even this would increase money supply by some 50 per cent on account of government operations as against the 25 per cent increase in national income envisaged here. Allowance must also be made for credit creation for the needs of the private sector. It may be recalled that in the Second Plan we cannot hope to draw down our accumulated sterling balances to a significant extent in order to absorb the shock of deficit financing. Thus, even deficit financing on the scale of Rs 200 crore per year must be considered only as a provisional safe limit. In recent years, although we have budgeted for huge deficits, the shortfalls in expenditures have prevented the occurrence of deficits on the scale budgeted for. Our recent experience, therefore, is not a sure guide to what might happen if large deficits are in fact sustained over a number of years without a return to controls.

The safe limit of deficit financing can only emerge in the light of experience. Essentially, the limit to deficit financing lies in our capacity to provide the additional consumer goods needed by the people without an undue strain on the balance of payments. The extent to which the production of essential consumer goods like textiles or foodstuffs can be increased is not a matter on which we can be dogmatic. Much depends on organization rather than investment. If production responds more favourably than is assumed in the target of 25 to 27 per cent increase in national income with Rs 6,000 crore of investment, the scope for deficit financing would increase. On the other hand, it is also obvious that the elasticity of supply is not equally great in the case of all commodities. If our endeavour is to push ahead as far as possible, we should be prepared to "tackle" short supplies in some commodities as long as these are not of an essential character. The snag here is that even if some resources are released (say domestic servants employed by the rich) by restricting the consumption of the rich, the same may not be of much use in expanding the supplies of essential goods when the control over consumption is not socially desirable. In essence, if deficit financing is to be pushed to the limit, the endeavour must be to isolate the bottlenecks in the production of essential goods and try and remove them by making use of the resources released by the control over the consumption of other commodities. However, inasmuch as resources are not easily transferable—except in the case of foreign exchange—the scope for such selective handling of resources may not be large. Insofar as this is the case, deficit financing can be resorted to on an extensive scale only on the basis of controlling the consumption of essential goods and by building up latent inflation. If it is assumed that all-embracing controls, including those on the consumption of food grains and cloth, are not to be reintroduced and reliance is to be kept on only selective controls, deficit financing of Rs 1,000 crore may well be the safe limit unless our estimates of production potential and investment requirements are unduly pessimistic.

As a first approximation, therefore, an effort must be made to raise additional Rs 1,000 crore. It is doubtful if non-tax revenue can yield more than 1.5 per cent of the national income envisaged above without the government entering into profit-making activities such as state trading or running of consumer goods industries. Most of the economic activities of the government at present such as lending money or producing steel, fertilizers, locomotives and electrical equipment are not likely to yield significant profits in the early stages. It may be possible to raise some additional amount by way of loans or by intensive efforts, better terms and some compulsion. But on the whole, additional resources from these sources—loans and government profits—may only be of the order of Rs 200–300 crore. At least Rs 700–800 crore must come from additional taxes. An increase in the level of taxation from about 7 per cent to 9 per cent of national income by 1960–61 would ensure this. It is not necessary to go into the question of individual tax measures. But an increase in taxation from 7 to 9 or even 10 per cent of national income cannot be regarded as excessive if our aim is to have a bolder plan which requires an increase in the savings of the community from 7 to 11 per cent of national income.

The foregoing discussion of the resources for the public sector has been in terms of the receipts and tax expenditures of the Centre and the states combined. It is not possible at this stage to attempt a survey of the financial position of individual states during the Second Plan.

Finance for the Private Sector

In planning for a mixed economy, there is one question which needs special consideration. We may ensure that the resources needed for the government sector are somehow available. But how can we be sure that in raising additional resources for itself the public sector is not simply diverting savings to itself? Will not there be a corresponding decline in the savings available for the private sector even if there is no curtailment of the incentives to invest? Actually, the difficulty arises even a stage earlier.

For more than half of the plan expenditure government proposes to rely on the voluntary desire of the people to lend its savings—either in the form of loans or by holding the additional money the government creates; and there is no guarantee that additional taxation may not reduce the yield of public loans to some extent. The difficulty, in fact, is a general one. If development requires a rate of savings and investment higher than what the community voluntarily desires—and this must be the case if the plan hopes to improve upon what otherwise might be—it is necessary to provide some check to consumption. This check cannot be exercised by fiscal measures alone unless virtually all the investment is channelled through the budget—although fiscal measures may help indirectly in restricting the consumption of some items, say of luxuries. It must be assumed, therefore, that steps are taken to restrict the consumption of more dispensable articles in any case. Essentially, it is the absence of such steps and not the scale of operations of the government which might create difficulties for the private sector in raising resources. Part of the fiscal efforts must be devoted, therefore, not so much to raise revenue as to restrict consumption indirectly and this must be supplemented by direct control where necessary.

Again, the financial problem for the private sector is not simply one of the availability of resources in the aggregate. A plan implies priorities. It is essential, therefore, that steps are taken in any case to prevent too much investment in some lines and too little in others. As long as the investment in the high priority part of the private sector is assured, any shortfall in the availability of resources for other purposes need not cause much concern.

It may be recalled that of the total investment of Rs 2,500 crore in the private sector, Rs 1,200–1,300 crore was envisaged in construction, Rs 400–500 crore in industry, mining and transport, Rs 300 crore in agriculture and Rs 400–500 crore in working capital in trade and industry and in residual items. If the investment in industry and mining is regarded as more important, it is essential that too much of the available funds are not devoted to construction or stocks.

A selective credit and tax policy and licensing of construction are, therefore, necessary for the realization of investment in industries. Even for industrial investment, capital issued control, import control and licensing of new enterprises must follow a well-defined pattern.

In the First Plan, fixed investment in organized private industry was envisaged at Rs 233 crore and it is estimated that in 1954–55, such investment would be of the order of Rs 60 crore. At this rate, some Rs 300 crore of investment in private industry should be forthcoming in any case in the Second Plan. In view of the increased activity and greater coverage implied here, fixed investment in industry may well be around Rs 400 crore. However, it is not possible at this stage to be precise about the estimate in this sector. For one thing, for estimating financial resources, the concept of net investment is not very useful. The needs of replacement and modernization must also be provided for; and the provision for this as well as new investment is made from the same sources, viz., borrowing and profits.

As regards other investment in the private sector, provision of working capital is largely a question of bank accommodation and with deficit financing of Rs 1,000 crore, this should not raise much of a problem. Indeed, the problem would be one of preventing excessive bank accommodation for holding stocks.

Balance of Payments

A detailed picture of the balance of payments implications of the Second Plan cannot be put together at this stage. But it is clear that a plan for industrialization and development of transport must entail heavy imports of machinery and equipment. The balance of payments aspects of the plan are, therefore, of obvious significance.

Estimates in this field are particularly difficult. Terms of trade fluctuate widely and so does the state of demand abroad. However, a rough idea may be given on the basis of maintenance of exports at existing levels in the case of important items such as jute, tea, cotton textiles, tobacco, manganese and mica. There may be marginal increases in these as well as in some of the newer exports such as sewing machines, bicycles, electrical goods, etc. But these may be assumed to be offset by moderate increases in minor imports. Similarly, as a first approximation, the influx of private foreign capital may also be assumed to run at present levels on an average.

On the whole, the balancing should turn on the fate of major imports—the additional imports needed for some purposes and the reduction in other imports as a result of increased production at home. The figures for 1954 should serve as a good basis for forecasts inasmuch as we were roughly in balance in that year.

Imports of machinery and equivalent must remain the major concern. Of the total net investment of Rs 6,000 crore, only the investment in irrigation, power, railways, communications and industries is largely relevant for this purpose. This investment would come to some Rs 3,000 crore. Only a rough guess at the import content of this can be made. On an average, before one-third of net investment is assumed to be spent on imported equipment, the total needs would come to some Rs 1,000 crore. This does not take into account imports of machinery for replacement, which must take place to some extent in spite of greater production at home. Thus, imports of machinery may well average Rs 250–300 crore per year during the Second Plan. At present, these imports are not more than Rs 100 crore per year. Consequently, the extra strain on foreign exchange would be of the order of Rs 800–1,000 crore. We may look forward to some saving of foreign exchange on account of greater import substitution as in case of sugar, raw cotton, petroleum, and so on. But a gap of some Rs 700–800 crore may still remain. The foreign assets held by the Reserve Bank of India can be drawn down by perhaps another Rs 100–150 crore or so from their level at the end of the First Plan—that is, from their present level of about Rs 730 crore to Rs 550–600 crore after making allowance for some decline in the remaining period of the First Plan. There would thus be a problem of finding additional foreign exchange to the extent of Rs 600–700 crore over the Second Plan period.

Clearly, it is imperative to try and have additional foreign investment, loans or assistance. At present, foreign assistance to the public sector comes in at the rate of some Rs 50–60 crore per year, and there may be net private investment from abroad of the order of Rs 15–20 crore per year. If the entire gap of Rs 600–700 crore is to be filled by additional foreign assistance or investment, the present rate must be virtually trebled over the Second Plan. It is clear that control over imports to effect some savings in foreign exchange must also be maintained.

These remarks on the foreign exchange position during the Second Plan are tentative and are intended only to give an idea of the broad order of magnitudes involved. In the context of a bold plan for industrialization, the planning of our foreign exchange position would assume far greater importance than has been the case in the First Plan.

CHAPTER 14

The Role of the Public Sector in a Small Open Economy*

At the level of generalities, there is much that we economists can say which is right and can be useful; and as practitioners of the art, we can perhaps recount cautionary tales which can put you on guard against many a well-known but frequently recurring danger. But having been involved in the making of economic policy now for nearly thirty years, I have come to a few sobering conclusions which militate against the temptation to offer instant advice. I have come to realize that in the making of any economic policy decision, the knowledge you carry on general economic theory plays a very small part. The validity or otherwise of your policy prescription depends largely on how well you have been able to assess the relevant circumstances—social, political and economic—in which the prescription has to be applied. Economics, like politics, is the art of the possible and specifics are the essence of the matter. Outsiders are clearly at a disadvantage in this game.

The second conclusion I have come to is that given the complexity of life and the difficulty of correct assessment, most advisers settle down sooner or later to a particular stance—left or right, pro-market or pro-intervention, pro-public sector or otherwise, veering towards protection, towards an open economy and so on. In reality, most developing countries have a mixed economy, and policies that are needed and that work have to be a judicious blend of several strands. Economic history, even recent economic history, abounds in examples of something which has succeeded in one country but not in another, of something having succeeded for some

* Address at the seminar organized by UNIDO in Suva, Fiji Islands in March 1979; subsequently published by the Reserve Bank of India.

time in a country but not forever. Development is seldom a tree which springs forth from a single seed and proceeds to grow in a simple set pattern. Rather, it has to be bent and reshaped and pruned from time to time and infused with healthier grafts as circumstances and opportunities warrant. But what graft will stick and which will debilitate, which mixture is judicious and which is not are questions that have to be answered again and again and in the light of deep insight into the realities of the day and they cannot be answered by fly-by-night visitors who are here today and there tomorrow, who come with light luggage but with heavy overtones of preconceived notions.

You will appreciate, therefore, my difficulty in saying anything very concrete and with confidence on this occasion. My hesitation is all the greater because Fiji and India, while alike in many respects, are also very different one from the other. One is an island economy, the other a continental one; you have 600,000 people, we have 600 million (1 million = 10 lakh). The subject matter for this seminar, if I understand it right, is also one which is as sensitive as it is susceptible to preconceptions. The respective roles of the public and the private sectors, in the context of some signs of growing unemployment are, I believe, the desired focus for our deliberations, and this is an area where foreigners at least should fear to tread.

My first cautionary tale, therefore, is to urge that you should treat what we say at best as food for thought. This caution is all the more relevant in Fiji because Fiji is a going concern, a success story in virtually every way. There is much that you can be proud of, much that you have to conserve and preserve about your achievements in social, political as well as economic spheres. Here is a country with a per capita income of more than one thousand US dollars per year, a growth rate of more than 7 per cent per annum in real terms over the past decade, a record of sound economic management, considerable diversifications, of sources of income and success in even difficult areas such as family planning, social and economic harmony between various groups, domestic as well as foreign; and above all, a civilized and forward-looking political leadership which has nurtured and nourished a hardy plant of a viable democratic institution of acknowledged integrity. While you may need some reform or adjustment here and there you certainly do not need a radical departure or some bold new design or blueprint. A country in crisis may need a new turn; and in any event, it is easy to advise such a country just as it is relatively easy to assist a malnourished child. But in your case, you have amply demonstrated your ability to cope successfully with your problems. The most anyone from outside can do is to raise a few questions and to sound a few warnings.

Let me now proceed without any further protestations to make a few general observations on the role of the public sector and on the policies to promote employment. I do so in the hope that my remarks would serve as a basis for more detailed discussion during subsequent sessions of this seminar.

There are a number of activities that have of necessity to be undertaken by the government. These put a considerable strain on the available managerial and administrative talent which is limited in all countries. Thus, a considerable proportion of the educated manpower—and hopefully woman power—has to be absorbed in normal governmental functions including revenue collection, mobilization of savings, maintenance of law and order, provision of basic services such as education and healthcare, foreign relations, maintenance of a legal framework which makes contractual relations possible and a modicum of control over economic transactions such as licensing of production units or financial institutions and rationing of scarce resources including in most cases foreign exchange. Technical training, extension services and financial and marketing support to small but sizeable groups of producers such as farmers and artisans are also indispensable in every society. Taken together, these minimum economic functions place a disproportionate burden on available managerial and administrative talent in small countries, for no matter how small the size of a country, these minimum functions cannot be reduced below a certain workable level, with the result that the pool of managerial talent left for other purposes is comparatively limited. Other things being equal, therefore, countries like Fiji must have overwhelming justification before they embark on public ownership and management of economic enterprises.

This is not to say that the arguments generally advanced for public sponsorship and ownership of some kinds of economic enterprises by the government may not have validity even in a country like Fiji. But what is strongly implied is that these arguments must be weighed carefully in the light of the feasibility of efficient management and in comparison with other alternatives, imperfect as they may be. The choice in policymaking is always as between somewhat unsatisfactory alternatives and the fact that a particular situation is not wholly satisfactory should not lead us to the conclusion that it should be replaced with its theoretical opposite.

The reasons generally advanced for public sponsorship or ownership and management of an economic enterprise may be summed up under two broad heads:

(a) the activity is considered important for the nation, but is not likely to come up under private auspices; or
(b) that while the activity can be privately organized, this is likely to lead to exploitation of one kind or another.

It is, of course, conceivable that in a small island economy like that of Fiji, the habit of entrepreneurship may not be sufficiently developed. Consequently traditional agriculture and retail trade may account for virtually all private enterprise and there may not be much development of modern services or industry under local private initiative. Traditionally, the response to such a situation is to rely on imports for the bulk of the industrial requirements and to permit direct foreign investment in at least selected sectors. Quite rightly, this policy is usually supplemented by encouragement to private local enterprise in many ways—through tax concessions, cheaper credit facilities, a degree of protection against imports and the exclusion of foreign investment from certain relatively simple manufacturing activity. The experience of Fiji itself shows that a judicious mixture of promotion and protection can generate a significant amount of local industrialization.

But equally clearly, a small country should be particularly careful not to overprotect as in the nature of things it cannot sustain a very large range of industries on an economic basis. It would, for example, not make much sense for such a country to go in for heavy or capital-intensive industries which require a minimum size far beyond the absorptive capacity of the local market for efficient operations.

In such a situation, which perhaps corresponds to existing realities in many small countries, I can think of two legitimate circumstances which might warrant public initiative and ownership:

(a) First, because a certain degree of diversification of the economy is considered desirable in the long run but is not likely to be undertaken under private initiative. There are many investments for which the long-term social and economic benefits are considerable and which may not yet be attractive to private investors, whether domestic or foreign; and

(b) Second, even though foreign investment may be feasible while local investment is not, it is considered desirable on political and other grounds to keep foreign influence out of certain spheres.

Much of the economic activity undertaken by the government is in any case justified on the first ground just mentioned. The development of an irrigation network by harnessing rivers or programmes for reducing pollution or opening new forest areas by building roads, bridges, etc., are generally undertaken by governments everywhere. This is so because private investors generally have a relatively short-term horizon and thus discount long-term gains. Also, the benefits of such massive investments, while real and large in relation to cost, are not easily appropriable among individuals so that no private investor can recover his cost by a system of pricing which can be easily administered. It is easier and more appropriate to recover the cost from general taxation which is available only to the government.

From this, it is a short step to argue that since the government has spent large sums of public money on harnessing rivers or clearing forests or making them accessible, it might as well own and run the hydel power stations or even saw mills and paper plants that become feasible and profitable as a result of the initial public investment in creating the necessary infrastructure. Considerations of necessity and equity in the sense of not gifting away something to a few private parties, whether local or foreign, thus get intertwined. Much would depend, of course, on whether the government can command the necessary managerial personnel or whether it would be better advised to collect its legitimate share for pioneering efforts from future beneficiaries by suitable lease charges and licence fees and other forms of taxes that cannot easily be passed on to consumers.

A question which all small countries have to answer for themselves relates to areas where for social, political or cultural reasons they are not prepared to admit foreign investment. After all, there are many transnationals whose resources are several times larger then those of many countries. Given a chance, there is nothing they cannot develop on their own if they are given a long enough right to operate. Thus, even development of extensive forest areas with initial roads and all, or mining in remote areas or harnessing of rivers and exploration of the entire offshore areas and their exploitation for whatever resources that are found can be done by transnationals. Most countries, however, have the notion that certain areas are "sensitive" so that foreign investment should be kept out of them. This is the idea that underlies the notion of sovereignty over natural resources. Where exactly the line should be drawn between the "sensitive" and the not-so-sensitive is a decision which only the government of the country concerned can take.

The margin of social or political tolerance of the presence of vast islands of foreign money power in one's midst varies from country to country and certainly from time to time. But if history is any guide, public opinion sooner or later tends to be touchy about foreign ownership of land and mineral resources and about foreign control over economic activities on which the livelihood of large numbers directly or indirectly depends or which are otherwise highly visible. If such activities cannot be undertaken by private local enterprise, there may not be any choice left but for the government of the country to step in.

And here, it should also be remembered that it is not necessary, as things stand now, to choose between the classic type of colonial or imperialistic foreign investment on the one hand and complete ownership and management by government on the other. Many permutations and combinations of the two are possible. Apart from the fact that government can be a partner—even a major partner—along with foreign equity capital, it is also possible now to hire foreign management for limited periods either by entrusting the entire management to a group or by hiring individual managers and technicians. Indeed, either form of management assistance can now be had in most cases under various programmes of technical assistance, both bilateral and international. There are also many ways of borrowing even equity capital in part from international agencies. Hopefully, under the tripartite ownership of the national government, private foreign investors and international agencies, an acceptable degree of public confidence as well as sound management can be assured for long.

What about the argument that public ownership and management may be necessary to prevent exploitation of one kind or another? I have already referred to one aspect of this argument, viz., that if government has spent a lot of public funds to undertake the preliminary work, the subsequent opportunity for profitable investment should not be handed over on a platter to a private party. We have already noted that there may be alternatives available even under these circumstances such as suitable lease charges or licence fees. In any case, the argument should not be carried too far. In the ultimate analysis, all governmental activity, whether in the field of law and order or social and economic infrastructure, enlarges the opportunity for private profit. What needs to be ensured is that no particular group is unduly benefited. This aspect of undue concentration of economic power in a few private hands becomes politically sensitive, sooner or later; and care has to be taken to see that the benefits of government support, subsidies, protection etc., do not go primarily to a few favoured groups. But here again, the margin of social and political tolerance of pockets of private affluence triggered by government support of one kind or another will vary from country to country and time to time.

Where an economic activity by its nature is likely to be a monopoly, governmental ownership is often accepted as a means of avoiding exploitation. This is the rationale for government ownership of posts and telegraphs, railways, ports, etc. Here again, one has to remember that one can exploit as much by inefficiency and poor or discourteous service as by high profits which at least in part could end up in government coffers; and the experience of many countries, particularly parliamentary democracies, would suggest that organized labour is, if anything, more militant—and successfully—when it comes to dealing with public enterprises. In meeting consumer requirements of the kind where individual attention and specialized consumer service are important, for example, in tourism, some form of private management if not ownership is, therefore, generally desirable.

The danger of exploitation of sellers where there is likely to be only one buyer is often not recognized, but is very real indeed and can be a matter of great political sensitivity, particularly where the processing of products produced by a large number of poor peasants or artisans is involved. That is why it is often urged that sugar mills or cotton ginneries or rice mills should be either cooperatively or publicly owned. For the same reason, it is also often urged that wholesale trade in major agricultural commodities should be publicly controlled. But once again, the feasibility of efficient management must be emphasized. Per contra, the idea that since public ownership may be necessary to avoid exploitation, public enterprises should not make even reasonable profits must be strictly resisted. Even when public enterprises are efficiently run and are not bedevilled by militant trade unionism, public opinion often forces them to keep their prices unduly low. Such a policy amounts to conferring favours on the consumers of particular products at the expense of the community at large which would benefit by the alternative policy of insisting on appropriate pricing and reasonable rates of return.

A word is also in order about the paramount need of preventing excessive exploitation of a country's scarce resources of natural beauty, clean air and water and all the rest which distinguish say the Fiji islands from the Midlands or the North of England. Whether this calls for more public regulation rather than debarring private enterprise from certain activities altogether, is more than I can say. But the issue is clearly one of paramount importance for the future of these beautiful islands.

Lastly, on this subject of public ownership I should sound one more warning; and that is, that you do not fall prey to the temptation of acquiring sick industries out of fear of the unemployment that might result from the closing down of certain factories or establishments. Once you start on this road which seems sensible enough on the face of it, you soon find that sickness becomes almost attractive so that anyone can mulct a company for some time and leave it to the government to handle the mess at the end. This is not to say that there may not be cases of genuine sickness of industry requiring some assistance from the State for sustained recovery. But help is one thing, and taking over another. Sickness, death and regeneration are the law of life and some transitional unemployment in the interest of efficiency and mobility may be unavoidable.

I should now turn to offer a few remarks on the problem of unemployment which I believe has prompted this seminar at least to some extent. I am not familiar with the employment situation in Fiji, and what I have to say, therefore, is highly tentative and subjective—perhaps too much based on our experience in India. But for what it is worth, let me make a few general observations.

First of all, I am happy to know that despite your high standard of living and the relatively low density of population, the Government of Fiji has been laying great emphasis on family planning. It is a good augury for Fiji's future that birth rates have already started falling significantly. Death rates here are happily as low as in any advanced country and cannot fall much further. Population now grows at the rate of some 1.8 per cent per annum which is low in comparison with many developing countries. Even so the present population growth rate can and must be reduced. For such is the magic of geometric progression that even at the rate of growth of 1.8 per cent per annum, the total population will be doubled every forty years. The growth in numbers seeking work would be even faster what with the changing age composition and an increasing proportion of women wanting to work.

On similar reckoning and indeed for other pertinent reasons, I for one do not feel unhappy that a certain amount of emigration is taking place from these islands. I realize that this is controversial ground and that those who migrate are generally better trained than others. But for a small and relatively well-off country with good educational standards like Fiji, I should think that the possibility of migrating to more advanced countries like New Zealand, Australia, the UK and even Canada and the US forges new links through which modernizing influences and to some extent even capital can flow back. In my judgement, one of the greatest services that Fiji's affluent well-wishers, particularly in this region, can render is to permit a reasonable two-way flow of manpower between themselves and Fiji.

I should also think that agriculture would continue to provide additional employment for many years to come. Not only the schemes of diversification including cultivation of rice or raising of beef cattle and extension of cultivated area through more irrigation and the like, but also introduction of new technologies and crops and combination of farming with poultry-keeping and other subsidiary activities should keep more people on and around land. And this would be even more acceptable if there is rapid spread of civic and other amenities to the rural areas. Whether there are any inhibitory factors such as systems of land ownership is more than I can say. But it is the experience of many countries that the potential of agriculture for absorbing more people at higher levels of living is generally underestimated. So also is the potential of services and activities like fishing—which for Fiji with its growing success in attracting tourists and its splendid location are clearly more important than for most developing countries.

From the point of view of both income and employment generation, it may be worthwhile exploring ways of using by-products of the sugar industry, like manufacture of alcohol. Similarly, the practice of cultivation of short-duration vegetables in the ratoon crop of sugarcane has yielded good results in other countries. In general, in a country like Fiji, increasing the employment content of this kind should remain an important objective of development planning for many years to come.

I emphasize the development of agriculture and services not to underplay the importance of industrialization which is considerable in the longer run even for small island economies like that of Fiji. But industrialization ultimately has to thrive on a flourishing market which assumes maximum exploitation of the potential for growth in the primary and tertiary sectors. Industries feeding industries only and sustained largely by demand from industrial workers is not a feasible model and it is difficult to see Fiji emerging as a major exporter of industrial products except those based on processing of local produce and minerals. Nor can Fiji emulate countries like Singapore which thrive on entrepôt trade except to a limited extent. This being the case, there is need for caution against industrial growth promoted artificially by too much protection in the interest of short-term gains in employment, particularly in the urban areas where unemployment among the educated in particular tends to be both highly visible and vocal. Ultimately there is always a price to be paid; and it should not be paid at the expense of those in the rural areas who may not be less deserving just because they are less vociferous and visible.

CHAPTER 15

The First Five Year Plan of China (1953–1957)

An Appraisal[*]

In this note an attempt is made to bring forth the main features of China's First Five Year Plan and to appraise—so far as the material available permits—the size, pattern and economic import of that Plan relatively to India's First Five Year Plan and the proposed Second Five Year Plan as outlined in the Plan-frame papers.[1]

The major objective of Chinese economic policy during the three years 1949 to 1952 was the rehabilitation of national economic life. With the virtual completion of this task and with the restoration of economic stability in the country, the Chinese government embarked on its First Five Year Plan in 1953. The work of drawing up the Draft Plan had already begun in 1951. But it was only in February 1955 that the final Plan was worked out. There was thus a gestation period of almost four years. The delay in drawing up the Plan was on account of China's lack of experience in drawing up plans and the non-availability of adequate statistics. In the meanwhile, two annual plans for 1953 and 1954 have been worked out and implemented.

* The draft of this paper was prepared in late 1955; unpublished.

[1] Any comparison of China's Plan with India's plans necessitates a number of assumptions. It would be desirable to seek further clarification on some of the points if a more meaningful comparison is to be attempted. A list of such points is given in the Appendix.

The full text of China's First Five Year Plan is not available here. This note is based mainly on the Report[2] of the Chairman of the State Planning Commission, which outlines the major tasks before the country during 1953–1957 and surveys the progress made during the first two years of the Plan. The document is frank and sober in tone and the reasoning throughout is incisive. Although the statistics given are scrappy and inadequate and the concepts used are ambiguous at times—at least to an outside reader—it is possible to form a fairly clear picture of China's First Year Plan from the Report. Important aspects of the Plan are examined below under the following heads:

i. Size.
ii. Targets and Priorities.
iii. Major Policy Issues and Objectives.
iv. Progress in the First Two years.
v. Concluding Remarks.

Size

The size of China's Plan may be assessed in terms of the increase in national income and standard of living envisaged or with reference to the investment effort and the employment potential involved.

National Income

No estimates of the increase in national income over China's First Plan period are available. But the total value of the combined output of industries and agriculture is expected to increase by 43 per cent in five years, that is, at the average rate of 8.6 per cent per annum. This rate of increase may be compared with the increase in national income by 3 per cent per annum which is likely to be achieved over the First Plan period in India and the increase of 5 per cent per annum which is proposed for the Second Plan.

This comparison is, however, subject to a number of limitations. The growth of national economy in China is measured in terms of the increase in agricultural and industrial production whereas in India the tertiary sector of services is also included in national income. Further it would appear from the context that in reckoning the increase of 43 per cent in the combined output of industry and agriculture the Chinese measures take account of modern industry only. On a similar basis, the output of agriculture and

[2] Report on the First Five Year Plan by Li Fu-Chun, Chairman of the State Planning Commission, a speech delivered on 5 and 6 July 1955 at the Second Session of the First National People's Congress, as reproduced in the Supplement to *People's China* dated 16 August 1955.

industry together in India should increase by 19 per cent during the First Plan and by some 27 per cent during the Second Plan.

Apart from this, there is reason to believe that Chinese statistics give an unduly high weightage to industries in the initial period. Since industrial output is expected to increase much faster than agricultural output in both China and India, it is clear that a system which gives higher weightage to industries in the initial period would also show a higher percentage increase in the total output of industry and agriculture combined. Thus Chinese figures seem to refer to the increase in the *gross* value of output whereas Indian figures relate to the *net* increase in the value of output. The ratio of net output to gross output is substantially smaller for industries (and particularly for heavy industries) than for agriculture. It follows, therefore, that industries get a higher weightage in total production in terms of gross values than they would in terms of net values. Again, the percentage increase in the total output of industry and agriculture combined would also depend on the relative prices assumed initially for industrial and agricultural products. Although we have no precise information on relative prices in China, it is arguable that agricultural prices (relatively to industrial prices) are lower in China than in India. The system of compulsory levies on agriculture, the concentration of a large part of industries and trade in the hands of the State and the presumption that this concentration is utilized as a device for mobilizing savings are some of the reasons for assuming that the ratio of agricultural to industrial prices is lower in China. If the presumptions made in this paragraph are correct, it would follow that a large part of the difference between the percentage increase in the total output in China and in India would be statistical rather than real.

It may be noted that the share of modern industry in the total output of industry and agriculture in China in 1953 is claimed as 26.7 per cent. The corresponding share for India in 1950–1951 was only 12.7 per cent and it is estimated to be of the order of 14.5 per cent in 1955–1956. It cannot be said that the much higher share of modern industry in the total production of agriculture and industry in China was on account of the higher degree of industrialization reached in China even before the First Plan came into operation. The difference, therefore, must be ascribed to the factors analysed in the earlier paragraph. The significance of this consideration can be seen from the fact that if the share of (modern) industry in India is put at 25 per cent in 1950–1951 and 30 per cent in 1955–1956, the combined output of industry and agriculture would show an increase of 22 to 24 per cent over the First Plan and some 34 per cent over the Second Plan. Even these calculations do not compensate fully for the bias in favour of Chinese figures inasmuch as they do not compensate for the higher weightage given to heavy industries in a system of measuring output in gross terms.

The general impression that the difference between China's Plan and India's two plans is not as great as appears at first sight is also confirmed by the figures of the proposed increase in the output of different sectors. The output of agriculture and "subsidiary and rural production" is expected to increase by 23.3 per cent during China's First Plan. This rate of increase is not materially different from the 20 per cent increase in the output of agriculture and allied pursuits,[3] which is postulated for India's Second Plan. If account is taken of the fact that the progress of China's agricultural plan hitherto has not been according to schedule (see section on "Progress in the first two years" below), the rate of increase in Chinese agricultural production may not be very different from that expected over India's First Plan, viz., roughly of the order of 15 per cent.

China expects to increase industrial production by 98.3 per cent over the First Plan period. Industrial production in India is expected to increase by some 40 to 45 per cent over the First Plan period and an increase of 67 per cent is envisaged for the Second Plan. Here again, part of the difference in the rate of growth in China and in India is statistical rather than real inasmuch as it arises from the higher weightage to heavy industries in the initial period in China—a bias which is implicit in measuring output in gross terms. It is not possible to make any precise allowance for this factor with the help of available data. But it will be seen later that there is not much difference between the programme for heavy industries in China's First Plan and in India's Second Plan. The major difference is in regard to consumer goods' industries for which China's Plan envisages a greater rate of growth than India's Second Plan. It will be argued later that there are special reasons for this difference.

On the whole, the conclusion that emerges is that the rate of growth envisaged for the Chinese economy during its First Plan (1953–1957), though faster than that of India during the First Plan, is not materially different from the rate of expansion envisaged in India's Second Plan. If allowance is made for the various factors which vitiate a proper comparison, the proposed increase of 43 per cent in the combined output of industry and agriculture in China during 1953–1957 should be compared with a corresponding increase of some 23 to 25 per cent in India during 1951–1956 and with an increase of some 36 per cent envisaged during 1956–1961.[4]

[3] It is not clear whether "subsidiary rural production" in China includes rural handicrafts or not. If this is the case, there would hardly be any difference between the two targets.

[4] Some allowance is made for the higher weightage to heavy industry in the Chinese figures.

The Standard of Living

No indication is given of the proposed increase in the standard of living of the people in the Report of the Chairman. But it is claimed that the *production* of some of the main items of mass consumption is substantial and will increase as shown in Table 15.1.

Table 15.1 Increase in the Production of Mass Consumed Commodities

(percentage)

	China (1953–1957)	*India (1951–1956)*	*India (1956–1961)*
Grain*	13.3	20	15
Edible Vegetable Oil	65.9	25	33
Sugar	122.9	28	50
Cotton piece-goods	55.1	46	32
Rubber Shoes#	69.8	n.a.	25#
Machine-made Paper	89.2	23	43

Note: *There are certain anomalies in the Chinese figures. The increase in the production of grains at one place is given as 13.3 per cent and at another place as 17.6 per cent. Similar discrepancies are there in the case of sugar and cotton textiles. The figures mentioned here are quoted from page 36 of the Report where they are given specifically in support of the increase in consumption envisaged. They do not tally with figures given in Table 15.2 which are drawn from targets expressed in absolute terms. It would also be useful to know what is included under "grains" in China: the fact that China's grain output is placed at some 170 million tons (1 million = 10 lakh) as against 66 million tons in India would suggest that items such as potatoes are included in grains in China.

#Refers to all footwear.

Data on production are not a reliable guide to consumption inasmuch as allowance has to be made for exports and imports. Thus, although the production of cotton piece-goods is expected to increase by 32 per cent in India over the Second Plan period, consumption in the country is envisaged to increase by some 46 per cent over the same period, since the target for exports remains relatively low. On the other hand, the consumption of food grains in India would increase by less than 20 per cent over the First Plan period inasmuch as imports of food grains have declined over the past few years. Nothing is known, however, about imports and exports of consumer goods in China. It is also not clear whether the Chinese figures include the output of cottage and hand industries or not. Nonetheless, Table 15.1 suggests the general conclusion that whereas the percentage increase in the production (and therefore consumption) of food grains in China is expected to be somewhat smaller than in India (in both the First and Second Plans), China expects to increase the production and consumption of manufactured articles such as textiles, sugar and edible oils at a faster rate.

However, the relatively faster increase in the output of manufactured consumer goods in China seems to reflect, in the main, the low absolute level of production in the country in 1952. The output of edible oil or oilseeds in absolute terms is not known. China produces paper in much larger quantities than India (some 370,000 tons in 1952 as against roughly 140,000 tons in India now). But the production of sugar and cotton textiles in China appears to be substantially smaller than in India. The production of machine-processed sugar[5] in China amounted to some 2.5 lakh tons in 1952 as against roughly 16 lakh tons in India now. The Chinese production of cotton textiles in 1952 may be estimated at some 3,400 million yards[6] as against roughly 5,000 million yards of mill-made cloth and some 1,500 million yards of hand-woven cloth in India at present. It would appear, therefore, that although percentage increases in the production of manufactured consumer goods are expected to be greater in China than in India, the increase in production in absolute terms would be much larger in the case of India.

The percentage increase in the production of manufactured consumer goods in China should also be assessed with reference to the fact that China's population is 60 per cent larger than that of India and that it is estimated to be increasing at the rate of 2 per cent per annum as against the rate of increase of 1.25 per cent per annum in India.[7] The improvement in the standard of living of the Chinese people during the First Plan, therefore, is likely to be less striking than that of the Indian people during India's first or second plans. The consumption of food grains in China is not expected to increase as fast as in India; and the somewhat sharper increase in the consumption of manufactured commodities must be judged in the light of the much smaller level of per capita consumption in China at present.[8]

[5] Presumably, the output of cottage industries is excluded. It would be useful to know how important non-factory production is in the case of sugar.

[6] The Chinese figure of 111.6 million bolts is converted at the rate of 30 yards to a bolt. The dictionary defines a bolt as a roll of cloth of varying length, often 30 yards. It is not known whether this figure includes the production of the handloom sector and what the Chinese definition of a bolt is. One source, viz., *Problems of Communism*, May–June 1955, gives per capita production of cotton cloth in China as 3.2 metres only. This would suggest much smaller production than what we have estimated.

[7] *Jen-min Jib-pan* (*People's Daily*), 1 November 1954, quoted by *Problems of Communism*, May–June 1955.

[8] No account is taken here of the development of social services, which are an important part of the standard of living. But this omission is not likely to alter materially the conclusion reached here.

Investment Programme

The size of China's Plan may now be assessed with reference to the magnitude of the investment programme. The total outlay for China's economic construction and cultural and educational development during 1953–1957 is placed at 76,640 million yuan, that is, approximately Rs 15,000 crore (1 yuan is equal to Rs 2 roughly). Of this, 42,740 million yuan, or approximately Rs 8,500 crore (1 crore = 10 million), is for investment in what is called capital construction. These figures are substantially larger than the corresponding figures for India's first or second plans. The Report under consideration is not very clear about the concepts used.[9] Investment by the State in China accounts for virtually all the investment in the country and it would be more meaningful to compare the figure of Rs 8,500 crore mentioned above with the total investment in India rather than with the investment in the public sector. Even so, the proposed investment of Rs 8,500 crore in China is much larger than the total investment of Rs 3,600 crore and Rs 5,600 crore envisaged in India's first and second plans, respectively.

It is difficult to reconcile the size of China's investment programme with the proposed increase in production in general or with the production of investment goods. It has already been argued that the increase in the output of agriculture and industry in China, in percentage terms, is not materially different from that envisaged in India during the Second Plan. Although available information is rather limited, it would appear that the output of some of the basic investment goods in China is not expected to increase more than in India's Second Plan.[10] Thus the output of steel in China is expected to increase from 1.35 million tons in 1952 to 4.12 million tons in 1957; of cement from 2.9 to 6 million tons; and of coal from 63.5 million

[9] In India, Plan outlay in the public sector is divided into two parts: net investment or capital formation and current outlay. Thus, in the Plan-frame papers, the total Plan outlay of Rs 4,300 crore consists of Rs 3,400 crore of investment and Rs 900 crore of current outlay on education, etc. The Chinese figure of 42,740 million yuan for capital construction seems to correspond to the Indian concept of net capital formation. The remaining part of the outlay, that is, 33,900 million yuan, however, cannot be compared with the current outlay of Rs 900 crore. In India, only that part of the current outlay on social services, etc., which represents an increase over the level attained in the beginning of the Plan is included as Plan outlay. In China, on the other hand, the entire current expenditure on social services, etc., seems to be included in the figure of 33,900 million yuan. This figure, therefore, should be compared with total current developmental outlay of some Rs 2,000 crore over India's Second Plan. It would also appear that expenditure on prospecting, overhaul of equipment, trial manufacture of new products, etc., is included not in capital construction but in the remaining sum of 33,900 million yuan for which no detailed breakdown is available.

[10] Coal is the only exception to this statement. The greater use of coal per unit of output in China needs some scrutiny.

tons to 113 million tons. The production of steel in India is also expected to increase from some 1.3 million tons in 1956 to 4.5–5 million tons in 1961; of coal from 37 to 60 million tons; and of cement from 4.6 to 10 million tons. Such figures as are given of new railway mileage (2,000 miles) and of new shipping tonnage (4 lakh tons) or of additional road construction (3,500 miles to be built or *rebuilt*) are also not more ambitious than the proposals in India's Plan-frame papers.

The paradox of a much larger investment programme in China without a correspondingly larger increase in production (as compared with India's Second Plan) can be explained with reference to two factors.[11] A possible explanation is that the conversion of Chinese figures from yuan to rupees at the official rate of exchange exaggerates the real magnitude of China's investment programme. The official rate of exchange presumably does not reflect accurately the relative purchasing power of the two currencies in the respective countries.

In the second place, it is already felt that the level of investment or developmental expenditure envisaged in the Plan-frame may not be adequate in all cases for realizing the physical targets. The size of China's investment programme would seem to confirm this feeling to some extent.[12]

Unfortunately, it is not possible to say what proportion of national income is to be invested in China during the First Plan. Nor is it possible to indicate the extent to which the proposed investment of Rs 8,500 crore represents an increase over the rate availing before the Plan came into existence. But it may be noted that one estimate[13] of net investment in China during 1953 puts it at 7 per cent of national income, or roughly the rate as in India at present. It may also be noted that even at the official rate accepted for conversion, the per capita investment in China during the First Plan would not be very different from the corresponding amount proposed for India's Second Plan.

[11] A number of other explanations are, of course, possible. It may be that the absolute increase in China's production is greater. But this is true of grain and coal, in the main; the investment in agriculture is not larger even in absolute amount. Nothing precise is also known about the proportion of work done by unpaid labour and whether the imputed cost of such labour is included in the figures.

[12] A third reason for the paradox noted above may be that a much larger proportion of China's investment is obtained from foreign sources so that it is not reflected fully in China's production of investment goods. It will be seen later that it is difficult to form any judgement in this matter.

[13] Y.L. Wu in his forthcoming study of China's economic development, as quoted in *Problems of Communism*, May–June 1955.

Employment Potential

The size of China's Plan may also be judged in relation to its employment potential. It is interesting to note that China's First Plan does not stress employment as one of the major objectives. No mention is made in the Report under consideration of the need to create additional employment opportunities in the light of the increase in population and the extent of underemployment prevailing at present. It is explicitly stated that it will not be possible to eliminate unemployment completely and to make full use of surplus labour power by 1957. But no statistics are given to indicate the magnitude of the problem at present or at the end of the First Plan.

The only quantitative estimate of employment given in the Report is to the effect that 4.2 million more people will be employed in the five-year period. This strikes one as a very inadequate target in view of the fact that the total labour force in China should increase by at least 15–16 million in five years—or even more if it is assumed that China's population increases faster than in India. However, it would appear from the context that the figure of 4.2 million refers most probably to additional employment of factory and office workers only.[14] At any rate, it is safe to assert that this figure cannot be compared with the additional employment of 10–11 million persons which is commonly used in our country. Since the precise connotation of the 4.2 million figure is not available, it would be rather futile to attempt any comparison with the employment potential of India's Second Plan.

Targets and Priorities

Table 15.2 gives a comparative picture of the pattern of investment in China's First Plan and in India's Second Plan. Since a detailed breakdown of Chinese figures is available only in terms of the investment for construction, similar figures of investment (as distinct from developmental expenditure) are used for India also. Certain modifications,[15] however, are made in both the Chinese and the Indian figures to make them comparable. No

[14] The reference to employment is made only casually, thus: "In the five-year period, 4.2 million more people will find employment and there will be a 33 per cent rise in average money-wages for factory and office workers."

[15] Thus, investment for power generation is included under industries in the case of India inasmuch as it appears that this is what is done in the Chinese figures. Private investment in agriculture is excluded since this is explicitly stated to be the case in China's First Plan. On the other hand, the total investment in the economy is included in the case of industry and transport. Investment in private housing is disregarded as it does not seem to find a place in the Chinese figures. At the same time, the investment under public utilities and under cultural, educational and public health departments as well as investment in stocks are excluded in view of the difficulties involved in making meaningful adjustments.

comparison with India's First Plan is attempted in view of the lack of a comparable breakdown of figures and the difficulties in making suitable adjustments. But it will be seen that most of the conclusions that apply to India's Second Plan hold good—with even greater force—in the case of India's First Plan also.

Table 15.2 Pattern of Investment

	China—First Plan		*India—Second Plan*	
	Amount (Rs crore)	*%*	*Amount (Rs crore)*	*%*
Industries & Power	4,950	68.5	1,900	53.5
Agriculture (including irrigation)	650	9.0	750	21.1
Transport & Communications	1,630	22.5	900	25.4
Total	7,230	100.0	3,550	100.0

The broad picture that emerges is that although industries (including power and mining) claim the largest share of investment in both countries, the relative emphasis on industries in the Chinese Plan is greater whereas that on agriculture and to a smaller extent on transport and communications is greater in the case of India. Agriculture and allied occupations account for only 9 per cent of the total investment (in the three categories considered here) in China as against 21.1 per cent in India. In the case of transport and communications, the Chinese Plan devotes 22.5 per cent of "total investment" to this sector as against 25.4 per cent in India.

The somewhat lower priority given to transport and communications in the Chinese Plan is surprising in view of its greater emphasis on industrial development and on decentralization of industries. This is all the more so since the provision made for transport and communications in the Plan-frame papers in India is now regarded as inadequate. It has already been noted that the targets of new railway mileage, new shipping tonnage acquired and new roads built (or rebuilt) in China are also not as ambitious as the present proposals in India. This disparity cannot be explained in terms of better existing facilities for transport in the country. It would appear that greater reliance is placed in China on more efficient use of existing transport facilities.

The smaller emphasis on agriculture is explained in part by the fact that China does not propose to have many giant river valley projects such as we have under construction in India. It seems that greater reliance is placed on medium-size schemes of water conservancy, reclamation of wasteland and on small irrigation works built by the peasants themselves. China, however, is experiencing great difficulties at present in raising agricultural output. The output of grain in the country has increased by only 3.4 per cent in the first two years of the Plan as against the proposed increase of 13.4 per cent over five years.[16] Rationing, compulsory levies and similar devices have been introduced. It appears, therefore, that the lower priority given to agriculture has already led to difficulties in securing additional output from agriculture on the required scale (see section on "Progress in the first two years" below also).

Industries producing basic goods or means of production account for 88.8 per cent of the total investment in industries in China whereas investments in consumer goods industries make up only 11.2 per cent of the total. These figures illustrate the extent to which emphasis is placed in China's First Plan on the development of heavy or basic industries. This emphasis, however, is not very different from the one given in the Plan-frame papers in India. Even if we assume that the entire investment of Rs 200 crore on small-scale and cottage industries is for the development of consumer goods industries, the proportion of total investment in industries which is assigned to basic industries would amount to some 79 per cent in the case of India. This proportion will increase to 84 per cent if the investment in power is regarded as basic investment (as is probably done in China). It is interesting to note that the reasons given for devoting only a small part of investment to the production of consumer goods are the same in both cases. Thus the Report under consideration claims that the output of manufactured consumer goods can be increased considerably without additional investment in view of the fact that "there is considerable unused capacity in light industrial enterprises and that there are wide possibilities in handicraft production which can be called upon to serve as an important auxiliary to light industry".

Another point which may be noted in connection with the priorities in China's First Plan is that the development of social services is largely underplayed. Although repeated references are made to the need for increasing the cultural and educational facilities available to the people, it has also been stressed that this can only be done after laying the foundation of rapid industrial progress. It is not possible to say much about the proposed expenditure on social services in view of the fact that the figures given relate to construction which forms only a small part of the total outlay in this field. It was on account of difficulties involved in making a meaningful comparison that social services were excluded from Table 15.2. But it is noteworthy that such targets as are given of the increase in educational and medical facilities are not more ambitious than the corresponding targets for India. Thus it is claimed that over 70 per cent of the country's school-age children will be attending primary school in 1957 and

[16] It has already been noted that the percentage increase in the output of grain is given as 13.4 per cent in one place and 17.6 per cent in another.

that the number of hospital beds in China would increase by 77 per cent over the Plan period. In the case of India, the Plan-frame envisages that 75 per cent of the children between the ages of 6 and 11 will be going to school in 1961 and that the number of hospital beds would increase by 100 per cent over the Second Plan period. Indeed, it would appear that in the field of education, the emphasis is more on additional training for those who have already received some education rather than on providing the minimum basic education to the illiterate masses. Thus, enrolment in primary schools is expected to increase by only 18 per cent and that in junior middle schools by 78.6 per cent as against the proposed increase of 178.70 per cent in senior middle schools and of 127 per cent in higher educational institutions. The approach to education thus seems to be practical and utilitarian rather than idealistic. As regards housing, it is claimed that "46 million square metres of housing" will be built by the State for factory and office workers. But it is difficult to interpret this figure.

Major Policy Issues and Objectives

The Report under consideration does not spell out the policy measures to be adopted for implementing China's First Plan. Nothing is said, for example, about the manner in which the resources needed for the Plan are to be raised beyond the statement that it would be possible to raise funds on the required scale in view of the fact that the Chinese people no longer have to bear the burden of exploitation by landlords and by capitalists at home and abroad. Economic issues in a Communist State tend to be presented as a simple affair of exhorting the people to practise such virtues as the observance of strict economy in expenditure, cooperation and willing acceptance of sacrifices in the interest of the future. On the other hand, the whole institutional set-up is designed to extract from the system the savings needed. It is possible to give only a general idea of the Chinese attitude to some of the important problems that arise in implementing a bold plan for industrialization:

(1) *Stability of the Market.* The need for maintaining economic and financial stability which has been achieved in China over the last few years is strongly emphasized. It is, however, frankly recognized that for some time to come the supplies of many kinds of commodities would fail to meet demand. In the meanwhile, therefore, the State must continue with the programme of compulsory purchase and distribution of grain and similar other commodities which may be in short supply. This attitude is somewhat different from the current thinking in India which calls for planning without controls over the distribution of essential commodities except in the event of an emergency. Apparently, revenues and expenditures are to be balanced. The term "deficit financing" finds no place in Communist planning.

(2) *Training of Personnel.* It is recognized that a plan of industrial development cannot be put through without a rapid extension of training facilities. But it is also emphasized that shortage of trained personnel can be removed only by undertaking a lot of activities and by thus creating facilities for acquiring training on the job. ("Marking time will not add to our skill and knowledge. We cannot accept the proposition that everything we do we must undertake with previous knowledge".) It is also interesting to note that contrary to one's expectations, the emphasis is on raising the standards of technical knowledge rather than training a large number of persons quickly. Thus, for example, the four-year courses in engineering colleges are to be replaced with a five-year system and the two-year and three-year special courses are to be gradually abolished.

(3) *Economy.* The one aspect of practising strict economy in expenditure which has received the greatest emphasis is in relation to the standards of construction. The tendency to build massive structures with excessive regard for ornamentation and for providing amenities to workers which are far beyond the present capacity of the economy is decried in no uncertain terms. "We should criticize the idea that we must do everything at once. This is because to do everything at once means no priority for construction. We should criticize the idea that since we are building modern industrial enterprises, all non-productive buildings and amenities must also be modernized."

(4) *Foreign Assistance.* No figures are given of the amount of foreign assistance expected by China over the First Plan period. A generous tribute is, however, paid to the assistance received from other Communist countries, particularly from the Soviet Union. Of the 694 basic above-norm industrial projects as many as 156 are to be executed from the first to the last stage by the Soviet Union. Apparently, the Soviet Union is responsible for all the work connected with these projects, that is, for conducting geological surveys, selecting construction sites, designing, supply of equipment, directing the work of construction, installation, supply of technical information and for training of Chinese experts on the spot and in the Soviet Union. It is clear that whatever may be the amount of foreign assistance received by China, the quality of such assistance is much better than what is available to India.

It is not possible to say much about the amount of foreign assistance to be received by China. It would appear that the bulk of the assistance from the Soviet Union would be in connection with the 156 above-norm industrial projects. A project is defined as above-norm if the capital invested in it is above the "normal" figure, that is, above 10 million yuan in the case of iron and steel industries, 6 million yuan in the case of cement and chemicals and so on. But this definition does not permit even a rough calculation of the total Soviet assistance to be received in connection with these projects. In addition, China is receiving technical assistance from the Soviet Union, including that for the peaceful use of atomic energy. Assistance is also received from other People's Democracies such as Poland and Czechoslovakia. The Report under consideration gives no indication of the total foreign assistance China expects to receive from all these sources. It is also not known to what extent China is actually paying for the aid received (on a gross basis) with current exports.[17]

(5) *Population.* There is no mention in the report of any measures to check the growth in population or of the need for such measures. The fact that China has a population of 600 million is, however, underlined in arguing that the extra consumer goods which each person can get, for the time being, are limited.

(6) *Small-scale vs Large-scale Production.* It has already been noted that China's First Plan does not stress employment as one of the basic objectives. There is no reference either to the possible conflict between the objectives of employment and of increasing production and the measures that might be adopted for resolving this conflict. In keeping with this attitude, the Report suggests no special measures for protecting handicrafts or small-scale industries against competition from factory production. The important role played by the medium and small enterprises in increasing supplies is emphasized inasmuch as they can be built and put into operation in a comparatively short time, bringing quick returns to investment and adding to productive capacity. Attention is also drawn to the need for organizing handicrafts on a cooperative basis and it is argued that it would be a mistake to neglect this vital sector of the economy. Nonetheless, the accent is on the fact that unless handicrafts turn gradually from individual to cooperative management and equip themselves with modern techniques it will not be possible for handicraftsmen to free themselves from poverty and suffering.

The absence of any reference to the conflict between small-scale industries and large-scale industries—a conflict which looms so large in Indian economic planning—should be interpreted in the context of China's institutional arrangements. Since a substantial part of the trade in manufactured consumer goods is in the hands of the State, China has in fact the machinery for eliminating price competition between handicrafts and factory production. The fact remains, however, that no special significance

[17] *The Economist* (London) has argued recently that China is currently paying for virtually all the aid it receives. But it is not possible to form a judgement in this matter on the basis of available information.

is attached to small-scale and cottage industries from the point of view of employment.

(7) *Socialism*. The objective of a socialist society outlined in China's First Plan is different in coverage as well as in method from the Indian objective of a socialistic pattern of society. Although it is recognized that it would take perhaps fifteen years to attain a completely socialist society, it is made quite clear that socialism will eventually encompass all aspects of economic life in China. Collectivization of agriculture, the gradual transformation of private industries into socialist enterprises by State distribution of raw materials and finished products and similar other measures go far beyond current ideas on socialism in India. This is also evidenced by the fact that specific targets are set in China's First Plan for the proportion of trade to be handled by the State, for the proportion of total cultivated land to be brought under State farms, peasants' cooperatives and collective farms and for the extent to which private industry would be brought under various degrees of socialist control. "State Capitalism" rather than mixed economy is the operative philosophy of China's Plan; private enterprise is, in this context, of only marginal (and maybe transient) significance.

(8) *National Power*. The major justification for economic planning in India is in terms of the standard of living of the people. Although repeated references are made in the China Report to the importance of raising the cultural and material standards of the people, an almost equal emphasis is laid on strengthening China's defences and on increasing national power.

Progress in the First Two Years

Some indication is given in the Report of the progress made by China during the first two years of the Plan. The total gross value of industrial output increased by 53.7 per cent, of steel by 65 per cent, coal by 26 per cent, cement by 61 per cent and cotton piece-goods by 37 per cent. Industries, therefore, appear to have exceeded the rate of growth postulated in the Plan. However, the Report also lays considerable stress on the deterioration in the quality of industrial products; and it is doubtful if proper allowance has been made for this fact in assessing the growth of production.

The record of performance so far in relation to agriculture is not satisfactory. As has been noted earlier, the output of grain increased by only 3.4 per cent during the first two years of the Plan as against the target of an increase of 13.4 per cent over five years. As a matter of fact, the present target itself represents a considerable revision from the 30 per cent increase announced in 1953. Although it is stated that the yield of industrial crops such as sugarcane, oilseeds and tobacco has increased, no figures are given. The output of cotton actually declined during the first two years of the Plan. In view of this, the 37 per cent increase in the output of cotton textiles appears doubtful. It is, however, claimed that the failure of the Plan in agriculture is explained largely by unfavourable weather conditions in 1953 and 1954. On the whole, the improvement in transport and communications and in the educational and public health standards of the people during the first two years of the Plan appears to have been according to schedule.

Concluding Remarks

To sum up, the Report under consideration gives a fairly balanced picture of China's first Five Year Plan, of the tasks involved in achieving the targets set and of the progress made in achieving these targets so far. The statistical material provided in the Report, however, is not adequate and a definite assessment of the Plan cannot be attempted unless one could obtain clarification on the points mentioned in the Appendix.

On the whole, the picture that emerges is that the general dimensions of China's First Five Year Plan are similar to those of India's Second Five Year Plan as outlined in the Plan-frame papers. If the figures given in the Report are interpreted properly it would appear that judged by the criteria of the increase in production, the extent of industrialization and the relative emphasis on heavy industries, the Chinese Plan is no more ambitious than India's. The major difference in the rate of growth seems to be in organized consumer goods industries. But this is explained largely by the relatively smaller level of production in China in the initial period. If allowance is made for the fact that the Chinese population is 60 per cent larger than that of India, the level of prosperity and of economic potential that would be attained in China in 1957 should be somewhat below the corresponding level reached by India by 1961.

The conclusion just outlined, however, gives no ground for complacency. There is a difference of four years between 1957 and 1961. Even when allowance is made for a number of factors, China's investment programme may be larger than India's. An examination of India's Plan-frame estimates has revealed that India's investment programme will have to be expanded if the physical targets in the Plan-frame are to be realized. The institutional framework in China makes it easier to extract the necessary sacrifices from people. In view of these considerations, the possibility of China developing a higher economic potential than India in the course of the next five or ten years cannot be discounted. In fact, this would probably happen, since increases in current consumption can be kept down more easily in China and since, presumably, the techniques of mobilizing idle or unutilized resources are probably better in China.

Among those features of the Chinese Plan which stand out in sharp contrast to our Second Five Year Plan, mention may be made of the relatively smaller emphasis on transport and agriculture, the lack of any recognition of employment as a social problem or a basic objective and the absence of any special protection given to small-scale and cottage industries. The last point, perhaps, is not very significant inasmuch as the conflict between small-scale and large-scale production gets automatically resolved in the institutional framework of China where the State is responsible for a large part of trade. The Chinese Plan also recognizes the importance of small-scale industries (as well as of small- and medium-size projects in agriculture from the point of view of economizing on capital and of obtaining quick results).

The Report does not throw much light on the policies to be pursued for implementing the Plan. The Chinese conception of a socialist state is more far-reaching than the Indian one. The need for direct controls over distribution is also more explicitly stated in the Chinese Plan—perhaps as recognition of the lower priority given to agriculture. On the other hand, the quality if not the quantity of the foreign assistance given to China seems to be superior to what is available to India at present.

The programme for heavy industries has been completed successfully during the first two years of China's Plan. Chinese agriculture, on the other hand, has not shown satisfactory progress. This would have repercussions on consumer goods industries also. It would appear, therefore, that China's Plan would succeed in its basic objective of building up the economic potential of the country but with a smaller increase in the standard of living of the people than was envisaged in the early stages of the formulation of the Plan.

Appendix

Points for Clarification

1. The full text of China's First Five Year Plan, if available in English, would be useful.
2. Is it correct to assume that the increase in production—both industrial and agricultural—is measured in China in terms of the *gross* value of output ratter than the *net* value of output?
3. The prices of some of the major agricultural and industrial products may be obtained so as to give an idea of the relative price structure.
4. Is there any estimate of the output of heavy industries as a proportion of total industrial output?
5. What is the meaning of "agriculture and subsidiary rural production"? Are rural handicrafts and industries included in subsidiary rural production?
6. Is it correct to say that industrial production in China's Plan refers only to the modern sector of industry? Are there any estimates of industrial production in the unorganized or small-scale and cottage sector? In particular, what is the relative importance of the organized and the unorganized sectors in the production of sugar, paper, vegetable oils and cotton textiles?
7. The output of food grains in China is nearly three times that in India. What are the various things included in food grains in China? And to what uses is this grain output put?
8. What is the equivalent of a "bolt" of cloth in terms of yards?
9. Is it correct to assume that China's population is increasing at the rate of 2 per cent per annum?
10. Is it correct to assume that the official exchange rate between the yuan and the Indian rupee reflects accurately the purchasing power of the two currencies in their respective countries? The prices of a few standard commodities in terms of yuan in China would be useful in this connection. In particular, the prices of investment goods such as steel, cement and some of the machines may be obtained.
11. The output of coal in China is twice as large as in India. The greater dependence on coal in China needs some scrutiny.
12. Are there any estimates of the step-up in the rate of investment as a percentage of national income in China?
13. It is claimed that China's First Plan would create additional employment for 4.2 million persons. What categories of employment are included in this estimate? Is any account taken of the increase in the

number of self-employed persons? Are there any estimates of the volume of unemployment now or at the end of the First Plan?

14. How is it that the priority for transport and communications in China appears to be lower than that in India in spite of the fact that the emphasis on industrialization and on decentralization of industries is, if anything, greater in the case of China?
15. Is there any estimate of the amount of foreign assistance made available to China? Any data on China's trade with the Soviet Union and with other Communist countries would be useful in this connection.
16. Is there any estimate of the extent to which China's Plan depends on unpaid labour? Is the imputed value of such labour included in the cost of construction?
17. The total outlay on economic construction and cultural and educational development is given as 76,640 million yuan, of which 42,740 million yuan is for capital construction. A breakdown of the latter figure is available in terms of the sectors in which capital construction is to take place, for example, industry, agriculture, etc. Is it possible to get a similar breakdown for the remaining amount of 33,900 million yuan?

PART IV

Growth, Equity and Social Justice

CHAPTER 16

The Socialist Legacy*

For more than forty years Jawaharlal Nehru seized virtually every opportunity to preach the gospel of socialism to his countrymen. Before his death, he had the satisfaction of seeing this goal accepted officially not only by the Congress party of which he was the leader but by most other organs of public opinion in the country as well. And yet, anyone who looks closely at pronouncements on socialism in India in recent years including those of Panditji cannot fail to be impressed by a certain sense of unreality and vagueness, of ambivalence and evasiveness that surrounds them. "Not this, not that, not rigid, not doctrinaire", "not confiscation nor nationalization", "no negation of private initiative and enterprise, no violent overthrow of propertied classes, not Marxian, nor Russian"—the descriptions proceed in sonorous negations somewhat in the style of our ancient scriptures where the One is sought to be interpreted by emphasizing what it is not rather than by asserting what it is. The general impression created is also not dissimilar in the two cases: if the scriptures succeed in establishing that the Divine is present anywhere and everywhere, the current Indian vogue is to identify socialism with almost all that would be accepted as desirable in any society, whether capitalist or other. Is there any significance in this sense of vagueness about socialism in India? Has it always been so insofar as Panditji's advocacy of it is concerned? And what does it betoken for Indian society?

As things go, Panditji came into socialism somewhat late in his life. The *Autobiography* contains nothing to suggest that socialist thought or literature had any special impact on him during his student days. It is

* Originally published, anonymously, in the *Economic Weekly,* Special Number, July 1964.

only towards the middle of the 1920s (when he was about thirty-five) that he seems to have been drawn towards socialism. During the long visit to Europe in 1926–27 Panditji had come in touch with leftist movements there and was attracted by Communism.

> It was not a doctrinal adherence, as I did not know much about the fine points of Communism, my acquaintance being limited at the time to its broad features. These attracted me, as also the tremendous changes taking place in Russia. But Communists often irritated me by their dictatorial ways, their aggressive and rather vulgar methods, their habit of denouncing everybody who did not agree with them. (*Autobiography*, p. 163)

And a little later (pp. 182–3), writing of his activities about the time of the Great Depression, he says: "I was by no means a pioneer in the socialist field in India. Indeed I was rather backward and I had only advanced painfully, step by step, where many others had gone ahead blazing a trail."

Roots in Internationalism

One is inclined to say also, perhaps at the risk of drawing too sharp a contrast, that there was something unusual about Panditji's attraction to socialism, that its roots lay more in concern for peace and internationalism than in anger against exploitation, that it was the violence and vulgarity of capitalism that repelled him more than its inequity or inefficiency.

> I wanted to spread the ideology of socialism especially among Congress workers and the intelligentsia, for these people, who were the backbone of the national movement, thought largely in terms of the national movement, thought largely in terms of the narrowest nationalism. (*Autobiography*, p. 182)

Writing to Lord Lothian in 1936 (*Bunch of Letters*, pp. 138–40), we find him asserting that the anarchy of sovereign states with their hatreds, fears and conflicts cannot be ended and a world order created without a complete changeover from the capitalist system which stimulates acquisitiveness and the other deeper instincts which we must get rid of. Profit motive rather than profits is the villain of the peace; and while he is willing to disclaim understanding (and even validity) of the Marxian theory of value, he has nothing but the highest praise for Marx's interpretation of history (*Autobiography*, p. 591; *Letters*, p. 140).

But whether he came late to socialism or not and irrespective of the relative importance of what appealed to him in this doctrine, there is no trace of half-heartedness or evasiveness in Jawaharlal's concept of socialism before World War II. The Karachi Congress in 1931 had adopted a resolution on economic policy which advocated for the first time "nationalisation of key industries and services" and "various other measures to lessen the burden on the poor and increase it on the rich". Despite his vital role in getting this part of the resolution accepted, Panditji describes it as a "very short step in a socialistic direction" and goes on to say: "This was not socialism at all, and a capitalist State could easily accept almost everything contained in that resolution" (*Autobiography*, p. 267). When even this resolution began to give rise to misgivings among orthodox Congress leaders causing them to be evasive, Panditji thunders in his characteristic way in a letter to Gandhiji in 1934:

A strange way of dealing with the subject of socialism is to use the word, which has a clearly defined meaning in the English language, in a totally different sense. For individuals to use words in a sense peculiar to themselves is not helpful in the commerce of ideas. A person who declares himself to be an engine-driver and then adds that his engine is of wood and is drawn by bullocks is misusing the word engine-driver. (*Letters*, p. 116)

Concept Clear

As to the meaning of socialism in ordinary English, there was indeed little doubt in Panditji's mind at the time. In the 1936 letter to Lord Lothian already referred to, Panditji uses the following words—presumably a quotation—to describe the socialistic ideal: "a system whereby the earth and its fruits will be exploited for the benefit of all members of the community in proportion to the services they render to it and not according to the accident of private property." He goes on to refer even more explicitly to the crucial link between socialism and the elimination of private property in all forms:

How will socialism come? You say that it is not likely to be achieved by the universal nationalisation of the instruments of production and distribution. Must it not involve the ending of the profit and acquisitive motive and the replacement of it by a communal and co-operative motive? And does it not involve the building up of a new civilisation on a different basis from that of the present? It may be that a great deal of private initiative is left in some matters, cultural, etc., it must be left. But in all that counts, in a material sense, nationalisation of the instruments of production and distribution seems to be inevitable. There may be half-way houses to it, but one can hardly have two contradictory and conflicting processes going on side by side. The choice must be made and for one who aims at socialism there can be only one choice. (*Letters*, pp. 140–1)

Equally, there is insistence on socialism requiring a sharp or revolutionary, and often violent, break with the past.

Reformism was an impossible solution of any vital problem at a critical moment when the basic structure had to be changed, and however slow the progress might be *later on*, the *initial* step must be a complete break with the existing order ...In India, only a revolutionary plan could solve the two related questions of the land

and industry as well as almost every other major problem before the country. "There is no graver mistake", as Mr Lloyd George says, "than to leap the abyss in two jumps." (*Autobiography*, p. 362)

Consternation among Rightists

It is little wonder that socialism of this hue created consternation among the right-wing leaders of the Congress culminating among other things in a competition to identify socialism with things less radical and controversial. As in everything else in India at the time, Gandhiji's views remained the measuring rod for everything and it was natural to seek to dissolve the passion for socialism by alternatively identifying and contrasting it with Gandhism. But Panditji at any rate had no illusions about socialism or Gandhiji's adherence to it. Thus, in 1936 we see him observe in his *Autobiography* (p. 515):

> Sometimes he (Gandhiji) calls himself a socialist, but he uses the word in a sense familiar to himself, which has little or nothing to do with the economic framework of society which usually goes by the name of socialism. Following his lead, a number of prominent Congressmen have taken to the use of that word, meaning thereby a kind of muddled humanitarianism.

It is not perhaps without a touch of malice that he quotes in the same chapter the following rather remarkable statements by Ramsay MacDonald and Sardar Patel, respectively:

> The difficulties of the times make integration and concentration essential for every people. This is the true Socialism, as it is also the true Nationalism—and, for that matter, the true Individualism.
>
> True socialism lies in the development of village industries.

Summing up his general position on socialism in the *Autobiography* (pp. 587–93), Panditji reverts to the emphasis on its radical interpretation. He dwells on the necessity and even the propriety and prevalence of confiscation and on the impossibility of ushering in socialism by the sudden passing of a few laws. A clash of interests seems inevitable. There is no middle path. Each one of us will have to choose our side. He has, of course, no illusion that he had carried the country or the Congress appreciably towards socialism. In this respect, there had been little advance in the Congress movement beyond the Karachi resolution unless one calls a hardening of attitudes at the two rather vocal but narrow extremes an advance. There is more than a touch of wistful sadness, therefore, when he concludes:

> Coming back to India, communism and socialism seem a far cry, unless the rush of external events forces the pace here. We have to deal not with communism but, with the addition of an extra syllable, with communalism. And communally India is in a dark age.

The New 'Socialism'

The War, Independence and the holocaust of Partition naturally left little zest for reconstituting society. The Industrial Policy Resolution of 1948 marked the first attempt of free India to formulate economic policy in keeping with the Karachi resolution of 1931—a resolution, let us remember, which contained little which would not be acceptable in most capitalist countries. Neither the Constitution nor the First Five Year Plan makes any explicit reference to the socialist ideal. And it was only towards the end of 1954 that socialism asserts itself, almost inexplicably, as the goal in a parliamentary resolution. Since then, at Avadi and Bhubaneswar in the Second and the Third Plan and, indeed, in many a speech and statement by all and sundry, a great deal of homage has been paid to socialism. But the frequency with which the ideal has been reiterated is matched only by the variety of meanings assigned to it—or, more revealingly, by the meaning sought to be withheld from it.

No elaborate citations are perhaps necessary in proof of what was stated at the outset of this note and what has just been repeated. Consider, for instance, the following from the Second Plan report which was selected for endorsement in the Third Plan report:

> The socialist pattern of society is not to be regarded as some fixed or rigid pattern. It is not rooted in any doctrine or dogma... It is neither necessary nor desirable that the economy should become a monolithic type of organisation offering little play for experimentation either as to forms or as to modes of functioning. Nor should expansion of the public sector mean centralisation of decision-making and of exercise of authority... The accent of the socialist pattern of society is on the attainment of positive goals, the raising of living standards, the enlargement of opportunities for all, the promotion of enterprise among the disadvantaged classes and the creation of a sense of partnership among all sections of the community... Democracy, it has been said, is a way of life rather than a particular set of *institutional arrangements*. The same could well be said of the socialist pattern. (emphasis added.)

Not being content with these admirable sentiments, the authors of the Third Plan add their own contribution to the liturgy of socialism in India:

> Progress towards socialism lies along a number of directions, each embracing the value of the others. Above all, a socialist economy must be efficient, progressive in its approach to science and technology, and capable of growing steadily to a level at which the well-being of the mass of the population can be secured.

Not Doctrinaire, Not Rigid!

It would not be proper to pick out a few quotations from Panditji's speeches in recent years and suggest that they represent his full or final thinking on the subject. But the following extracts will serve to illustrate at least the change in emphasis from his earlier writings:

It does not matter what kind of resolution we pass and what kind of Government we have—Communist, Socialist, divine or semi-divine—ultimately, we have to achieve our objective by hard work (at Avadi Congress).

The slogans of yesterday have very little meanings in the present context, whether the slogans are capitalistic, socialistic or communistic. All these have to be fitted into the nuclear age. Not that they are all wrong. They have some elements of truth in them but they have to be refitted and rethought of (at the 1955 FICCI meeting).

I do not propose to define in precise terms what socialism in this context means, because we write to avoid any doctrinaire thinking, any rigid thinking, because even in my life time I have seen the world change so much, and I have seen so many other changes that I do not want to confine my mind to any rigid dogma. But, broadly speaking, what do we mean when we say our objective is a "socialist pattern of life"? Surely, we mean a society in which there is social cohesion, which is without classes, where there is equality of opportunity and the possibility for every one to live a good life. The essential thing is that there must be wealth and production. There is a good deal of talk about ceilings, and it is a talk with which one naturally tends to agree because you want to remove disparities. But one has to remember that the primary function of a growing society is to produce more wealth; otherwise it will not grow, and you will have nothing to distribute. We must not imagine that we have grown up because we have satisfied some textbook maxim of a hundred years ago. We talk of nationalisation as if it were some kind of a magic remedy to every ill. I believe that ultimately all the principal means of production will be owned by the nation, but I do not see why I should do something today which will hamper my progress, my increasing production, simply to satisfy some theoretical belief (initiating the debate on the Second Plan in the Lok Sabha).

Ends and Means

Here is, of course, still the faith in things turning out in a certain way in the ultimate analysis but it seems more by habit than by conviction and, in any case, it is not clear why something which in the immediate future is useful should give way ultimately to its opposite—and how. Nor do we find any clear and detailed expression of where exactly the slogans of yesterday have gone wrong and how they are to be refitted to suit the nuclear age. But almost unconsciously two important changes are brought about. First, socialism, which is essentially an argument about means and institutional arrangements, is elevated to the status of an end—or rather, a short-term expression for all desirable ends. And secondly, arguments about means, flexibility and relativity take the place of any definite judgements even about the near future. If one wants a version of present-day socialism in

India with its all-things-to-all-men generality and vagueness without even a trace of the ordinary meaning assigned to it in the English language—and in historical writings everywhere—one cannot do better than reread the Bhubaneswar resolution. It is perhaps not an accident that this—on the face of it unnecessary—attempt to redefine the socialist ideal after it was already endorsed in the Plans and elsewhere, carries the unmistakable mark of un-Nehru like draftsmanship. One is almost reminded of the transition from Jnana Yoga and Karma Yoga to Bhakti Yoga as one descends down the scale of human faculties.

Why the Change?

The change then is unmistakeable. But how to explain it? And what does it signify for the future? It would be easy to say that the change reflects essentially a shift in objective circumstances. But this hardly satisfies. The objective circumstances in India after 1947 were intrinsically no less propitious for socialism than in, say, 1946. Jayaprakashji has recently reminded us—and himself—that even at the level of personalities the field was left clear for Panditji by the death of the Sardar, the elevation of Rajenbabu and the desertion of C. Rajagopalachari. Nor could one seriously argue that socialism has gone further in Ceylon or Burma or Indonesia or Egypt because objective circumstances were more conducive to such an outcome there than in India. It is more to the man rather than to the environment that one must look for a deeper explanation.

It would be idle to pretend that at this stage an objective and full interpretation is at all easy and it would be more than absurd to seek refuge in reference to his bourgeois upbringing. But we might hazard a few suggestions. It has already been hinted that Panditji came to socialism rather late in life and that for him socialism was more an international and aesthetic virtue rather than a national or a moral one. As years advance, one comes to things intellectually rather than emotionally and the surer guide of intellect is not usually the steadier. As for war and peace and the brotherhood of man, it was difficult to believe after World War II and its aftermath of a cold war that only the capitalist system stood between chaos and world order. (In India, at any rate, even those who might have cherished such a hope were sadder but wiser after the events across the Himalayas in 1962.)

Unprepared for Austerity

What is more, the artist and the romantic in this world citizen with a boundless zest for life could not be the instrument for that measure of austerity and insularity which are the hallmark of transition towards socialism, whether revolutionary or reformist. At a practical level, socialism is nothing more and nothing less than substantive confiscation followed by sustained and enforced hard work and austerity. While Jawaharlal could talk of hard work with passion, he had little taste for austerity or insularity. Not the waste of wedding feasts so much as the laughter and joy it brings in the harshness of peasant life, not the national waste in smuggled gold so much as the possible loss of an ancient art—that is his emphasis; and even during the dire days when defence and development together claimed heavy sacrifices from the nation, the instruments of austerity did not, to all appearances, win his sustained or unstinted support. One detects the same lofty disregard of unpleasant necessities and attraction towards the elegant and orderly in his attitude to administration and to the civil service—a fascinating chapter in itself for future historians, but one which would speak more of continuity and stability than of change or revolution. And perhaps more important than everything else, there was the insidious influence of Gandhiji restoring to revulsion against violence the pride of place. It was easy enough to extol the violence of socialism as being less offensive than the violence of fascism or capitalism in theory, particularly before the War and Partition. But after the ghastly shame of Partition riots and the assassination of the Mahatma, it was not possible to countenance violence, much less to unleash it with a fine sense of calculation about the probable sum-total of evil along alternative routes.

Reasons for Revival

Indeed the real question, it would seem, is not why the revolutionary concept of socialism gave way to an eclectic and elusive one, but rather the opposite: why was the concept of socialism revived at all officially in 1954 after it had remained dormant for so many years! Once again, it would be irrelevant to invoke objective circumstances pressing towards this outcome; the atmosphere in 1954, despite its somewhat heavy crop of labour disputes, was hardly surcharged with revolutionary fervour. This too was the act of the man. Maybe the revival was for old times' sake. Maybe it was once again an aspect more of foreign rather than domestic policy, an instrument for retaining and enhancing the country's influence among the Afro-Asian non-aligned drifting progressively towards socialism or a means of holding one's head high and of resisting crude pressures from the aid-giving West. It seems most probable that the revival of the socialist idea was a calculated attempt to ensure that the Indian society did not drift too decisively towards the right, thus compromising its position as an honest broker between the Communist and the Capitalist camps. In short, when there were so many natural pressures pulling Indian society towards the right, one had to pitch the objective to left of the centre to be reasonably sure of remaining on the middle path. Whether valid or not as an interpretation of the past, this line of thought has certainly relevance for the after-Nehru era already upon us.

For the simple fact is that the socialist legacy of Jawaharlal Nehru is not that strong or substantial a plant as would withstand the prevailing winds from the right without further prop. It was Alfred Marshall who said that ideas were the most "real" of the gifts that each generation receives from its predecessors. But at the level of an idea, the socialism of the Nehru era has emerged as a rather weak and hollow reed in which one can blow almost any kind of music. In its concrete achievements, the socialism of the Nehru era can certainly lay claim to a respectable degree of public ownership of the means of production in the sphere of basic industries. But amidst the vast ocean of property in land, buildings, commerce, small industry and a major part of large industry as well, the prevailing tone of social behaviour is unmistakeably that of acquisitiveness and private profit. What is more, these erstwhile vices are increasingly—and rightly—acclaimed as necessary agents of progress. The future of the public sector even in large-scale industries, while reasonably assured, cannot certainly be guaranteed so far as being one of pre-eminence. The very fact that virtually all public industry has relied so far for finance on foreign aid and borrowing of the voluntary savings of the people—rather than on tax surpluses or profits or confiscation—is a pointer to an uncertain future. One can say, if one is so inclined, that socialism has come to stay in India. But so has capitalism. And in this uneasy coalition, irrespective of who presides officially, the strident voice is undoubtedly that of the capitalist majority.

Future of the Legacy

In a real sense then, the future of Indian society and with that the social legacy of Jawaharlal Nehru remain yet to be determined and defined. If the present generation brings off the rather difficult task of driving to the goal of plenty for the masses in the double harness of capitalism and socialism, future historians might well define Panditji's legacy as one essentially of saving democracy and capitalism in this ancient land. If we muff it all up and are unable to march decisively forward along any route, the blame perhaps will be rightly and entirely laid at our door. But it is only in the unlikely event of our exchanging smoothly the present double harness for an essentially socialist one without losing the momentum of progress towards mass plenty that history will speak of the Nehru legacy of a peaceful march towards socialism in India. And to complete the picture, let us add that in case socialism comes to India after a sharp break and violence, throwing things totally out of gear for a while till someone picks up the threads of hard work and austerity once again, the credit or discredit for it will surely belong to a leader who, if already born, has yet to force himself on public attention. For the truly great apparently, there is no escape from being judged at least in part by the wisdom or folly of succeeding generations!

CHAPTER 17

Growth, Modernization, Self-reliance and Social Justice*

I shall speak on the international environment and what it might mean for India. International environment is something which we have to contend with. It does shape us whether we like it or not, and it is something in which we have to find a place, however uncomfortable that place might be. I shall certainly speak on that but before that let me say that the international environment is changing rapidly in a complex manner and the ramifications it will have for India are mixed—some good and some not so good. The international environment could be divided into three separate compartments: the political environment, the ideological environment or the environment of economic perception and the environment of objective economic phenomena.

I don't want to speak on the political environment. We all know what a great relief it is that there are leaders like Gorbachev around who have really changed the entire psychological map of political vibrations around the world. It is obviously a good thing and helps us reduce our defence expenditure; and as we agree that we should, if big powers stop meddling with our affairs, our regional rivalries may be less acrimonious and we may be able to do with less defence expenditure. But I think there is also a danger in this very worthwhile development. Our bilateral relations with the Soviet Union are regarded as extremely important more or less on the same lines as in the past (minus defence, if you like). But I think we will have to take care to see that we are not so mesmerized by the new philosophy that this bilateral economic relationship is changed drastically. Russia is still

* This paper was presented at the National Conference on Indian Planning Experience, Planning Commission, February 1989.

the second-largest economic power in the world, not Japan. And Russia is going to grow and in that growth we can find a very important place internationally, provided some of the arrangements like the Rupee arrangements are continued. I hope we are not so progressive as to think that these things have not worked to our advantage. I remember some years ago how Yugoslavia wanted to change everything and regretted it very soon.

The changes in economic perception around the world are far-reaching and very important. If we think our people are not influenced by them we are mistaken. Our people are very much aware of what is going on around the world and the country at large is very much influenced by the ideological currents in the world. One of them is of course that people know more about markets than about planning. They believe more in free enterprise or private enterprise rather than any governmental intervention. They believe in lesser role for the State rather than for the individual. All over the world there is a belief that growth is not demand-led but supply-led. This certainly should not lead to any surprise for us: they are parameters of economic development. We have said that growth creates demand but demand does not create growth in the developing world. In this country growth comes from supply-side factors like investment and better technology; from motivation taking risk from enterprise. Growth leads to demand when the demand comes from exports. Demand coming from investment in the short run maybe all right but in the long run it is not. The rest of the world is accepting the rationale of developmental economics and in that sense they are also saying that they need to develop because they are also developing economies. All these things have relevance to us. I don't believe that we can privatize; therefore we should not emphasize privatization. Nobody will take over our power projects and sick units. I think it is enough if we de-politicize the public sector as well as the economic system as a whole. I think that is what the people will demand.

All over the world there is a need for depersonification or deprivatization of the political system and that goes side by side for depoliticization of the economic system. We are talking about socialism all the time, but we are not socialists; and we know it and everybody knows it. We say that we have a mixed economy, but we don't have one. We are a capitalist state for all practical purposes. And running a capitalist economy as if it is a socialist economy gets neither the good result of the one nor of the other. The sooner we realize this the better it would be. But there are two types of capitalism around the world and we have to ask what type of capitalist system we want. One is the Section model which we describe as the optimistic or Hedonistic kind of model where consumption is praised, and this leads to demand—optimistic in the sense that extreme competition is encouraged. The other model is the one we see in the Scandinavian countries, which is based on some kind of cooperatization where the state, industry and unions work together. It is a parsimonious concept or say of austerity. This is the kind of capitalist model that is succeeding today. Let us be honest and say we are not a socialist country and won't be anymore; that we have a capitalist system; and we have to choose which type of capitalist system we will have, whether based on the parsimonious model or the Hedonistic one.

Let me run very briefly through the major economic changes that are taking place in the world, which are again of very great significance and they have already been referred to. There is a very fast pace in technological change and technology is spreading to very different and new kind of fields, going beyond mere computer science or microchips and microbiology, material science, etc. The gap between a scientific discovery and its application is becoming increasingly narrower and is taking less and less time for the particular technology or the scientific achievement to be translated into some practical technology. All over the world economic progress is becoming technology led, making it competitive. The competitive power in international markets is now based more on technology rather than on labour surplus or capital surplus. It is not only driving economic progress, it is driving competitive power. That is the kind of world one has to live in. At the same time the world is becoming very interdependent: world trade has grown much faster than world income. It is only in India that it has not happened; even in the United States it has happened. Barring a few countries, everywhere trade has grown faster than the national income. Not only trade, capital movements are becoming international for all essential purposes. Even in our case capital movements are on a mass scale, and that itself has many repercussions.

The third change, which probably is not fully understood by everybody else, is that the multinational firms are becoming more and more international in character: they not only compete in the international market but draw their supplies of technologies, skilled manpower and capital from all over the world. They even locate themselves wherever they like, in terms of where it is convenient for them to produce in a manner that enables them to compete in the international market. They are no longer American, British or Swiss multinationals. Essentially they are becoming more and more international multinationals where anybody can hope to get employed and anybody can hope to get his money invested. This is also a very important change.

At the same time, while technology-led interdependence is becoming multipolar, there is no single country which can say: I am so powerful that I can do whatever I like. It is not just Japan, Europe and the United States that are becoming more or less equal partners and economically equally powerful nations, but even the newly industrialized countries are acquiring a great degree of strength. It also means that when we look at the outside world, we don't have to look only at the United States, Europe and Japan but at all the newly industrialized countries. We have got to look in many directions when we look at the world. Previously, if we had to go anywhere, we had to take a plane to the United States or London or sometimes to Russia, but seldom to any other part of the world. That will no longer do. So far as the world is concerned, it is multipolar. And unfortunately, if it is multipolar, it is also a two-track world. We think we are the only ones who talk in this country about growing inequalities between the rich and the poor, cities and villages. All over the world, I am afraid, unfortunately one part of the world is moving very fast and there are a large number of countries, including ours perhaps, which are on the slow track. Therefore the distances are growing and within countries also these distances are growing. This problem I think is partly a result of the growing adoption of technologies, and we will have to be aware of that fact internationally also.

Two cards are being played. There are very important trends in the world situation as far as demography is concerned. Population in large parts of the world—in Japan, Europe and the United States to a smaller extent—is ageing. The proportion of the older people is growing rapidly and will grow even more rapidly in the coming years. The proportion of the middle group would be smaller and the younger group would be much smaller, which I think is an important factor on the structure of world demand—to whom should we cater, who would be our customers?

The other point, mentioned earlier: in the world around the disparate tendencies of savings are growing. Japan, Korea, Taiwan, Germany, Scandinavian countries still save a very large proportion of their income. But in USA, UK and many Latin American countries savings rates are much lower than ours. It is important to remember that mere wealth does not give the capacity to save: it is something that is written in the social system. The result of this is that there is a very large imbalance in the world situation today. It is not just that the United States has a very big deficit; the UK is developing an almost equally big deficit. The richest countries in the world are having a very large balance-of-payments deficit. The United States has the largest debt that any country has encountered. It is not merely Japan that has tremendous surpluses; newly industrialized states like Korea, Taiwan and a few other countries have hundred billion dollar surpluses every year. This shows that even if we are progressing, we can develop imbalances and deficit in balance-of-payments. These imbalances also have a tendency towards protectionism/restrictionism; and we have the paradox of the world on the one hand becoming more interdependent—greater trade, greater capital movements, greater spread of technology—and at the same time everywhere protection is increasing and people try to find a compromise in this situation by dreaming of regional cooperation. It is not just a dream; in many ways it has become reality, as in Europe. The US has entered into a trade agreement—more or less free trade—with Canada and Israel; and I am sure it will try the same with Brazil and Mexico not before long. In the Pacific, Japan, Korea, etc., have already topped in the region.

The problem is, nobody talks of India as any part of the world. We are totally left out of any regional configuration. Thus regionalism is not becoming a reality for us. For our relations with the outside world we cannot pretend as if it is a free trade world and that therefore we should have totally free trade. No, we shouldn't. We shall have to play many cards. We shall have to play regional cards to the extent Japan played them. We also have to play bilateral cards to the extent we can. Of course, we must take optimum advantage of the multilateral situation.

As a result of these things—paradoxically again—the international institutions have become less and less relevant. One of the achievements of the post-world war era is that unlike in the previous centuries we in the twentieth century have a concept of global economy. Under global economic cooperation international institutions like the World Bank, IMF and General Agreement on Tariffs and Trade (GATT) were set up. None of them is really very effective. The World Bank lends less than it gets back in its command of lending. Even the IMF is withdrawing purchasing power from the poorer countries. It has very little influence on exchange rates and on the policies of countries except the very poor ones. Even GATT, in spite of the current negotiations, has not been able to make any effective contributions. So we have a paradox that the international institutions, in which we had great faith, have become, precisely at the time when the world economies are becoming interdependent and when no single world power can have its run rate, less and less relevant and less and less effective. We have a situation of uncertainty where we cannot rely on rules that the world community should observe. We have to take up rules that are imposed with a grain of salt; we cannot alone be bound by all rules while the rest of the world can go its own way. We have to try and put more power in such rules as can be accepted and enforced, at the same time looking over the shoulder to see that everybody observes these rules, as there is no rule-making authority today which is effective.

The final change, which is extremely important and which can be troublesome, is the great concern for environment. The concern about environment is obviously important. To my way of thinking there are three ways of looking at the problem. At the factory level, Bhopal has shown that there is a problem of environment; that is something we cannot be oblivious of. There is the environmental problem at the national level also, of avoiding degradation of soil, avoiding deforestation. We have to do whatever we can in this regard. But there is now the environmental problem which is getting a global term—ozone layer, greenhouse effect, global heating, etc. That is being turned increasingly—if you listen to the discussions at London, etc.,—into finger-pointing at developing countries. You, China, you are consuming a lot of coal, and that is causing more greenhouse effect than anybody else; as if the other non-fossil fuels do not create any kind of effect. But we are going to see a situation in which we are going to be told about international rules to control the global environment without necessarily asking whether the present standard of living in the West should be protected before our standard of living is prevented from rising fast. But this is again an international reality, just like the treaty on the non-proliferation of nuclear weapons is there. I think one of the coming problems will be how the global environmental problem, which is real enough, will be used as a counter argument to moderate our ambitions.

Let me say a few words about what some of this might mean to us. When we consider what the international environment means to India, we have essentially three things in mind: what it means in relation to capital environment, transfer of technology and trade.

As far as capital is concerned, I regret very much that we are increasing our dependence on overseas capital. On concessional terms it will not come through anyway—some amount will come—but it is not going to increase. India is no longer in anybody's good reckoning; the others are not particularly hostile to India, but indifferent. We are not reckoned as any kind of nuisance or strength, neither a case for charity nor fear. We are not going to get any more concessional rate. We should consider ourselves lucky if we continue to get whatever we are getting now.

On private capital again, the way private capital has burnt its fingers around the world—I am speaking of loan, capital—they may flatter us today but the moment we run into the slightest difficulty that capital will begin to move out. I hope we are not enamoured of the private capital market to borrow too much. Already our debt service ratio has soared. Out external debt service ratio is very high. It is no use laughing at Latin America and saying we overplay our difficulty and others do not. We are approaching very much that kind of a situation. The scope for borrowing from the private capital markets from the point of view of what the market will lend us is limited; and from the point of view of what we should borrow even if they want to lend us, the scope is even more limited.

I am not very hopeful about private foreign investment either, because we should have been open to it much earlier—more open thirty years ago as far as Japan was concerned. That was one of the mistakes I made along with everybody else. We simply did not understand the vast potential of Japan. If we had opened our doors to Japanese investment in the 1950s and early '60s—then we had an excellent relationship with them as we were among the few countries who did not ask for reparations from them; politically also we were at the highest rating as far as Japan was concerned. But today we will be competing with the rest of the world markets. Anyway, that is a missed bus—and once you miss a bus it may not come again. Today I don't see any country that is particularly going to want to invest in our country, because we are not going to be able to deregulate to the extent it is necessary to attract private foreign investment.

China has a tremendous advantage. China has put a part of its coastal region more or less in the international books. It can do so because it is not worried about the inequalities that are arising. The degree of inequality in China between a free trade zone in the East Coast and the rest of the country is staggering. China can manage it, we can't, short of giving a carte blanche like Korea or Taiwan can do. I don't think it is realistic to think that a great deal of private foreign investment and a great deal of available international technology will come to this country.

As regards technology transfer, the world is becoming a technology economy. From the economist's point of view, there are two problems. One is that no country can say that it can be totally self-reliant in technology. That is an absurd dream and becomes more absurd as we go along. But what do you import, what do you develop at home still remains a question. It is often said by the cognoscenti that even when we import something we have got to support it not only at the two sides, upstream and downstream, but in terms of technical manpower which understands it, so that we are not taken for a ride.

There is a real problem here for our country, because the introduction of the most modern technology is necessary to expand our export markets, to compete with others on equal terms. On the other hand, we are not rich enough yet to spread the technology of the highest kind over our entire population. Gandhiji used to say, "I am not against technology, I am only against that technology which can be used only for a few people. Find me a technology which can be applied to everybody, and I am in favour of that." That problem still remains with us: it is no use pretending that it has disappeared. We can undo the protection of handlooms but it illustrates a real problem for India. We haven't got the strength and the resources enough to apply the most modern technology all along the line. So some picking and choosing will have to be done, some degree of protection to the people who cannot otherwise be given high technology will have to be done.

It is being said that there could be some technology like the agriculture technology which poses no problem because it is based on nature and can be applied with very little capital, that it is not capital-intensive and can be applied to small farms as well as big farms. But not all technology comes in this form. Most technology comes in a double-edged way that it is good but it sometimes creates unemployment, and sometimes requires large amount of capital which we don't have. Scientists may know better to develop technologies which are appropriate to our needs and which do not cost much capital. Maybe biology-based technology, maybe other technologies of that kind in which we should specialize.

I am not a scientist. But barring areas where you have new technologies, in my opinion we should develop those technologies as the highest degree of scientific efforts which don't require much capital and could be generalized over people. This problem will remain with us. I for one do not believe this is a problem which we can overlook totally. The solution would not always be perfect. I think we have to reconcile ourselves to that.

The other problem from the economist's point of view is that when technological progress is as rapid as it is now, we will have a problem of obsolescence and consequent adjustment all round the world. This is becoming a most important and urgent problem. If we want to compete and if we want to grow, we have to be prepared to accept the obsolescence of capital. We have got to adjust and we have to be prepared to retrain our people. We have got to move out of one industry to another, which means really that we have to do a great deal about changing our labour legislation.

Nobody wants to talk about our labour legislation. But we have created in this country a kind of right of employment in the place of employment without any change. I do not think that in the modern world if you want to compete in the industrial sphere you can retain this kind of obsolescent rights for labour and yet maintain competitiveness. I agree that a certain amount of retraining is possible. But the way in which we take over any factory that does not work and then hope that somehow things would be all right has never worked and will not work. You cannot really expect to take advantage of technology. In the last analysis the only answer to poverty is through better technology, more investment, better motivation, more efficiency and more work. I have not discovered any economist who has found better answers to long-term growth than the worldly wisdom we have been taught in the course of our study of economics.

Let us not worry too much as to what is the great secret about the strategies of the next plan. How would the eighth plan strategy be different from the seventh plan? You would not find very much a new strategy. You find better ways of motivating people, better ways of balancing the objectives. But basically, the coexistence of technologies is a thing for which I at least do not find an answer. Unfortunately, when you are poor you have to find some way of coexistence of more than one kind of technology within your community. Everyone cannot travel by air. We need to find answers to our transport problems.

On trade, I think I have said enough. We cannot belong to any block, we cannot believe too much in things like GATT, so we have to be careful. We must provide as much regional cooperation as we can provide at least through investment. We would keep our options open.

The last point I would like to make is that in the final analysis there is no such thing as a trade policy which can deliver you out of bad internal policies. If we take care of our internal economy the balance of payments will take care of itself. We can do a little more by having a proper exchange rate. It would help a little more to have a more intelligent import policy. We can do a little more by giving some incentives here and there to export. But balance of payments is an effect; it is not something from which other things follow. We ultimately want to solve our problems, especially external problems, and increase our self-reliance. The only clue is to have an internal policy which is conducive to efficiency and higher savings, which results in having low rates of inflation. If you have high rates in savings and more efficiency, the inflation rate will automatically be low. Inflation would not be low since somehow we do print enough money.

When it comes finally to trade policy or external policy, basically you will have to improve the performance of the internal economy. That you can do only through finding a way of adopting better and better technology all along the line, even though it may be done in a manner where you have to take some areas for some time and more areas some other time, and keeping the incentives to saving. I agree with people when they talk about austerity but accept the fact that efficiency in the modern world will require adjustment, will require changes, will require some degree of dislocation and, therefore, discomfort for some people for some time. Without that, you really do not have progress. All these are old things; I don't think I have said anything new. I thank you, Chairman, for giving me an opportunity to present my views.

CHAPTER 18

Equity in a Modern Society*

I was struck by two things when I received the annoted agenda for our Conference. There is first an emphasis on "redefining" the good things of life. Normally, one assumes that things change and even life changes, but that good things remain the same. Even now, we go as far back as Ram-Rajya or Plato to picture a good society. Why then the need to redefine the good society? Do we need to reinterpret the good life or the good society in the modern context and wish to add some more ingredients to it in the light of our current needs and perceptions? I say "add" and not "subtract", because that is what we generally expect to happen with the passage of time at least in respect of desirable things. My second surprise, therefore, came when I saw that the first session on "liberty" was not to be followed by its usual companion "equality", but by a shorter and less felicitous word "equity". Could it be that the organizers of this Conference had the premonition that in the modern context, there is a move afoot to abridge the concept of equality—to have a narrower or less inclusive idea of how much equality is necessary or desirable in modern times?

This question is not as facetious as it may sound because there is a tendency nowadays to narrow the horizons of equality, at least in its economic aspects, for a variety of reasons. The welfare state is less popular now. Taxes are being reduced and made less progressive if not more regressive in rich and poor countries alike. Even in Sweden, unemployment benefits are being cut while unemployment is rising. Education and health are still considered vital ingredients of a good life, and the State is expected to provide for both to a significant extent. But there is backtracking even here despite a great

* This paper was presented at the 4th Indira Gandhi Conference, 'Redefining the Good Society', New Delhi, November 1993.

deal of public resistance. People everywhere now are expected to pay more for their education and health—at least more for education beyond the primary and the secondary stage and more for healthcare of a specialized or sophisticated nature. I single out employment, education and health as our agenda specifically refers to equity in respect of these three.

At the national level, the rhetoric is no longer about some abstract notion of economic equality but about basic needs and the abolition of poverty. There can be no questioning of first things first; and providing for the basic needs of all or for the eradication of poverty should certainly be the first priority in economic matters. But there is more than a suggestion in recent debates that beyond basic needs, everyone is on his or her own and that there is no obligation on the part of the State or others to worry about inequalities beyond this first priority. This is a far cry from the concern for inequality as such beyond a point because a high degree of inequality might lead to concentration of economic, social and political power in the hands of a few to the detriment of the many, or because it might impair social solidarity, be an affront to those at the bottom rung of the ladder and might even be demeaning for those at the top. Austerity is no longer a virtue to be actively preached. Doing without something or at least not flaunting something which one's neighbour does not have is no longer considered essential good manners. On the contrary, it is considered a legitimate reward for success to be able to exhibit it as an ornament for all to see. Even education and health and employment are to be valued not so much for themselves, being essential parts of a good life, as for their instrumental value to society—in raising productivity, or in lowering birth rates or in keeping criminals off the streets.

Internationally, there has certainly been a retreat from the earlier concern for the rapid development of the poorer societies. This fact is often clouded by the more visible concern for disasters and by the increase in humanitarian assistance to victims of natural or man-made calamities which television has made almost obligatory for all of us. But leaving aside such outbursts of generosity, there has certainly been greater apathy to the more enduring aspects of poverty and malnutrition and even hunger. Aid as a percentage of the gross domestic product of rich countries has remained stationary at less than half of the modest target of 0.7 per cent. And the most aid-weary are the least generous like the US in recent years where the corresponding ratio of aid to GDP is less than half of the overall average; and of even that amount of US aid, more than half goes to only two countries, viz., Egypt and Israel. The US represents only the extreme end of a trend which embraces all industrialized countries with the possible exception of Japan. The newly industrializing or middle-income countries are also none too anxious to help others less fortunate.

Let alone aid, even in trade we are witnessing the return of a more self-serving attitude on the part of the rich who are becoming more blatantly protectionist and try to justify such protectionism on dubious grounds of countering dumping or discouraging the use of child labour or combating lower wages or lower environmental protection in the poorer lands. In matters of trade, investment, services and intellectual property rights, one-sided standards are sought to be imposed on the poor under the threat of unilateral sanctions. The poor have a legitimate stake in environmental protection. But social protectionism and green protectionism in the richer countries—and even worse, green opposition to much developmental activity—often tend to become dangers to the poor all the greater because such causes are increasingly promoted by well-meaning but misguided civic groups with nothing more than a single agenda on their plate and no accountability to anyone.

At the risk of sounding alarmist, one can also point to a danger which though still somewhat distant is by no means just imagined. If in some way the capacity of our globe is strictly limited, one cannot avoid the question of sharing this capacity equitably. But the only really equitable way morally is the same share per person, that is, each one sharing equally. That this equal sharing is not likely to happen and that the poor and the less powerful will be kept back, if necessary by threats and token bribes, is already abundantly clear. There are already learned references to China and India not being allowed to be free riders in the matter of energy consumption when the greatest free ride in economic history has already taken place. We may still see revival of the invocation of the so-called brown or yellow or black peril. After all, it was only a few years ago, just before the advent of the green revolution, when voices were heard reminding us of the principle of triage, that is, on the need to throw off into the sea the weakest inmates of a sinking ship first. The reference was to those overpopulated countries which did not produce their own food, and were thus considered a net burden. They obviously had to be relieved of their misery soon and forever!

Even allowing for the fact that I have somewhat overdrawn the picture, there is little doubt that there has been a remarkable shift in the attitude towards equality or equity in recent years. Equality and even equity are no longer battle cries as they used to be. What is this due to?

There are, of course, good moral and economic grounds for moderating the appetite for equality—or for that matter, the penchant for opulence—at all times. Envy is a self-consuming passion, unless, of course, it spurs you to greater effort. Reliance on the State or the mentality of welfare creates a self-stultifying sense of dependency, and it is better to be self-reliant and poor than rich and dependent. If things go too far in one direction, as the welfare state presumably did, one has to restore the balance.

At least among the richer countries, the downplaying of equality by everyone can be regarded as a measure of their economic success. When almost everyone has enough and more and when virtually everyone eats and clothes and in essentials lives reasonably comfortably, no one really cares how much the other person may have tucked away in stocks and shares. This is really the major explanation for the growing and enduring popularity of conservative policies in richer countries despite very high rates of unemployment and the pauperization of a small but visible section of their society. Even so, the employed and the comfortable, who far outnumber the others, feel that they have earned what they have and see no reason why they should pay more taxes for what they consider to be the idle and the indigent or the selfish and the stubborn who would not actively look for a job or accept lower wages.

Economists underpin these anti-egalitarian arguments by their preoccupation with scarcity and incentives. Since resources are scarce, they have to be rationed; everyone cannot have all they want. The market is the best instrument for such rationing. Admittedly, markets ration best given the existing distribution of income and wealth. But any attempt to change this distribution through taxes or subsidies has serious limits in that it may destroy the incentive to save or work or invest and take risks. If we destroy these creative instincts to work and save and invest and take risks, we slow down growth which harms everyone in the long run and even postpones the day when poverty can be eradicated. Even death duties and inheritance taxes are now considered disincentives. The one tax that cannot be evaded and has, therefore, no distorting or disincentive effect is the poll tax; and it is an index of our age that such an inequitable and historically hated tax was actually tried in one of the most civilized countries in the world. In a modern society, clearly, equity is expected to be subordinated to efficiency and growth except in cases of extreme hardship so that equality or even a substantial reduction in the degree of inequality is no longer a goal that is considered appropriate.

Internationally, the indifference to the poverty of other nations has become more acceptable because of increased faith in the efficiency of good economic policies. There is now general support for a package of macroeconomic and microeconomic market-friendly policies which is conducive to efficiency and growth. If some countries remain poor, it is because they are mired in wrong interventionist policies so that it is policy reform and not aid that they really need. It may even be counterproductive to help those who refuse to help themselves. Such at least is the current conventional wisdom.

There is thus certainly some sense in noting that equity in a modern society means something much less than equality and is, in fact, currently advocated only in some minimalist sense. But can it not be that the pendulum is once again swinging too far in the other direction?

Whatever may be true of the rich countries, the poorer countries cannot afford to echo the latest fashions in countries more fortunately placed. We need to do more for the unemployed in India, for example, than we do today and not less. In education, the fashionable view that we neglect primary education because we spend too much on higher education is certainly wrong. We undoubtedly need to spend more than we do now on primary and secondary education and even more to increase the quality of such education. We may also agree that, unlike primary or secondary education, higher education cannot be considered the birthright of everyone. To be called "higher", higher education has to be of high quality, and that means restriction on entry by merit. But it also means spending much more per student than we do today in our colleges and universities. The same is true of health where we need to spend more on primary care as well as on research and on tackling complicated health problems. The poor, just because they are poor, may need to spend proportionately more on education and health than the rich, at least from the public exchequer if not in terms of total expenditure, both public and private. In general, the concern for equity or equality has certainly got to be greater in poorer lands than elsewhere both on grounds of social justice and efficiency, and one has to be careful in not aping the rich either in tax policy or in the policy on public expenditure.

Even internationally, the indifference to poverty in a great many countries cannot be explained away as good economics. While good economic policies are necessary for economic growth, they are by no means sufficient. There are many reasons other than wilful misbehaviour that explain entrenched poverty in large parts of Asia and Africa. It is only the people of the countries concerned who can overcome most of these difficulties. But this does not mean that we do not need a helping hand from those more fortunately placed. Surely, there could be greater debt relief for the poor, larger funds available to the International Development Association and to the soft windows of regional banks and the International Monetary Fund. In matters of transfer of technology, one cannot rely simply on direct foreign investment. Some direct forms of technical assistance and, even more, support for research of greater interest to the poor are needed. As it is, even institutions of higher learning in the rich countries are turning their face against students from poor countries as higher education is now considered increasingly an exportable commodity to be sold to the highest bidder.

Help apart, the poor at least should not be hindered by protection and one-sided international arrangements in a vain bid to protect the already high standards of living in the industrialized countries. The legitimate concern for environment cannot be allowed to become an excuse for holding back the poor. Where international equity is concerned thus, there is still a large deficit that needs to be cleared and efforts made to evolve a just and participatory as well as effective and efficient international economic order.

As far as economics is concerned, it is certainly true that we have to reckon with scarcity as well as incentives and that the best form of social organization is one which most effectively harnesses the strongest motives of people to the social good. But for an orderly and prosperous social order we need cooperation as much as competition and regard for self as well as for others. The noblest motives are undoubtedly weaker. But that makes it all the more necessary to emphasize them rather than to overlook them. One has to remember Rabbi Hillel's famous quandary: "If I am not for myself, then who is for me? And if I am not for others, then who am I? And if not now, when?"

We also have to ask: if the concept of equality needs now to be interpreted at least in its economic context in more modest or less grandiose terms, is it not also true that in some respects we have now to enlarge rather than abridge the concept? The concern for environment, for example, has brought another aspect of equity or equality under sharp focus. I refer to intergenerational equity. In a way, concern for intergenerational equity is deeply ingrained in our genetic inheritance. How else do we explain the enormous sacrifices that parents make for their children everywhere and at all levels of development? But the growing scientific evidence of the limited carrying capacity of planet earth adds an altogether new dimension to intergenerational equity in the sense that it forces us to think of the long line of generations yet unborn. As a minimum, it enjoins on us to follow the precautionary principle that even when there is some uncertainty as to the finiteness of some resources, it is prudent to cut their consumption to the utmost, particularly if such consumption is not strictly of a basic or essential nature. Austerity thus gets a new meaning and urgency. The growing concern for equality between men and women as economic agents and units of consumption and the attention to the deprivation of the female child add yet another dimension to equity in a modern society. Thus, if there is an abridgement of the concern for equity in some respects, there is also an enlargement of the scope of the concept in other respects.

Finally, our annoted agenda draws attention to equity from the point of view of groups rather than individuals. In a way, concern for the relative well-being of women is an aspect of equity for groups rather than individuals. Trade union rights are also a part of the scene for group rights. But the idea of equity for certain groups has a much wider connotation. It generally refers to some special or preferential treatment of handicapped or disadvantaged or historically maltreated groups or of religious and cultural minorities whose interests may not always be given due recognition by the majority. Positive discrimination is certainly a modern refinement of the concept of equity or equality and is based on the premise that strictly equal treatment meted out in inherently unequal situations can hardly be considered equitable.

But the concept of positive discrimination is by no means universally accepted. Apart from considerations of encouraging the dependency syndrome and, therefore, of effectiveness, there is the aspect of equity itself: how can every member of a group claim certain privileges simply as a member of that group and irrespective of his or her individual situation? Also, how can past injustice to one group by another in an earlier generation justify favouring or penalizing anyone in the present generation? And even if it does, how far in the past should we look for injustices to a group and how long in the future should the privileges continue? No precise answers to such questions are possible; and in practice, they will be answered in political rather than moral or philosophical terms and thus will always be a matter of public debate and dispute. All one can say is that there is here yet another dimension to the concept of equality or equity in modern societies which has to be kept in some sort of sensible balance.

More generally, group feelings about backwardness or past and present injustice or neglect are a reality and, if not properly addressed, they can create resentment and even violence borne out of righteous indignation. It is of such stuff that fundamentalism, harking back to some real or imagined golden past or obscurantism and blind hatred of and violence towards the more successful groups are born. One cannot overlook the fact, however, that minority or disadvantaged groups that seek special rights or protection have also the responsibility not to rupture the larger social fabric and indeed, an obligation to respect the interests and the integrity of the whole. Clearly, when questions of equity assume a "group" rather than an "individual" momentum, they can be divisive and can be constructively channelled and contained only by the utmost statesmanship. Mere philosophical or moral or logical considerations are of little avail.

In the ultimate analysis, equity, like liberty, in all modern societies that aspire to be democratic, has to be defined in the rough and tumble of the political arena. Economics and even philosophy or morality can only articulate the conflicting and pluralistic concerns among which statesmen must steer as best they can. Politics, they say, is the art of the possible. But statesmanship surely lies in stretching what is possible towards what we all know is desirable in the sense of being conducive to social solidarity as well as individual well-being.

CHAPTER 19

The Idea of India as an Ideal*

Rather than confine myself to my chosen professional subject of economics, I propose today to paint on an even wider canvas and reflect on "the idea of India as an ideal". Those of us who grew up in the decade or two before Independence had some definite views on what the freedom of India meant: what the idea of India stood for. Freedom for us was not a destination but a beginning, a necessary condition to create an India of our dreams. The India we cherished was not some reality, geographical or historical, and certainly not something rooted in the past or even in the present. It was the future that beckoned us. The flag we saluted was more like a flag-post: something to reach as soon as possible.

The idea, the ideal, the dream—if you like—was of course given to us by no less a person than Mahatma Gandhi, by common universal consent, the greatest man that the twentieth century produced. That dream was to some extent modified and extended by Pandit Nehru, arguably the most charismatic and sensible leader of that century. The two visions were largely coterminous. But there were some notable differences and the resultant dissonance in our minds and in the country has persisted and has influenced the course of our recent history. But consonant or not, Nehru was as much an author of our dreams as was Gandhiji.

Today, such is the cynicism and corruption in our society that it seems almost laughable even to speak of India as an ideal. But I honestly feel that our dreams are still relevant and can be realized to a great extent.

* The 8th D.T. Lakdawala Memorial Lecture, delivered posthumously at the Institute of Social Sciences, New Delhi, in November 2005; subsequently published by the Institue of Social Sciences.

The roadmap is clear by now. Not all has been black in our recent history. Without hope and the commitment to do whatever had to be done, nothing can happen. Dreams are never meant to be realized in full—they would cease to be dreams otherwise. But if we do not watch out, our dreams can turn into nightmares. We are at such a crossroads today. We can slowly drift into nightmarish chaos; or we can continue to march towards the goal with our heads held high. Both are possible. It is up to us to decide which road to take and what our future will be.

Both Gandhiji and Nehru wrote and spoke extensively. It is not easy to summarize what they taught us. But in the case of Gandhiji, I am helped by a play called "Mahadevbhai", which I saw recently. It is a remarkable play and I recommend that you see it with some younger members of your family if you get a chance. In that play, one actor acts out several episodes in Gandhiji's life as recorded in Mahadevbhai's diaries—like the Dandi march, for example. One episode depicts a Monday—Gandhiji's day of silence. Even on Monday, crowds came to see Gandhiji. They were not happy just to see him; they also wanted to hear his message. A method was devised to resolve the problem. Gandhiji would hold up one of his fingers, and one of his disciples would say what it stood for. His five fingers stood for: Hindu–Muslim unity, abolition of untouchability, equality of women, elimination of excesses like drunkenness or addiction to opium, and finally, the *charkha*. The fingers were held together by the wrist, which stood for non-violence.

I think it is permissible to enlarge on this metaphor of the hand and to interpret it to bring out its full significance. The crux of the matter is that it is the wrist of non-violence that nourishes and holds together everything else. One can perhaps add truth as distinct from non-violence, as something which stands for openness, transparency and willingness to accept one's own mistakes and faults. Similarly, non-violence is not just absence of violence. Gandhiji was keenly aware that in a society as unequal and differentiated as ours, differences and conflict of interests were bound to arise and the bargaining power of different groups would seldom be equal. Non-violence meant that all differences must be resolved by dialogue and discussion, by willingness to listen to and understand the other, with neither side feeling that it was humiliated or taken advantage of. There could be occasions when differences could not be resolved. It was possible then to resort to Satyagraha, which too had to be done in a non-confrontational manner and had to include self-punishment. Everything else followed from truth and non-violence so interpreted—democracy, rule of law, popular participation and amity among and equality across all divides—whether of caste, creed, race gender, intellect, class or language and culture and region. That is what would mould the amorphous and multilayered mass that was—and is—India into a common nationhood—not some garbled version of the past or a blind imitation of something which might exist somewhere in the present. Underlying all this was the conviction that means matter as much as ends. Both have to be pure and constructive. The best of ends achieved by corrupt or inappropriate means cannot endure, as that will generate resentment and reaction in one section or the other. The ends themselves will get corrupted.

The five fingers that the wrist holds should also be interpreted in a proper perspective. Hindu–Muslim unity stands for unity across all divides. The eradication of untouchability is not about atoning for or compensating for past injustice and cruelty. It is about abolishing current injustice and cruelty in all forms. It is also about the uplift of the weakest and the most deprived—as indeed about their dignity and self-respect. The same thought underlies the advocacy of equality of women. But here, there was also the intention of unleashing the creative energies of half of India. Gandhiji, as we all know, had a special concern for women, and he has been most responsible for the high position many women enjoy in our social, political and economic life today. Similarly, simply emphasizing prohibition does not do justice to Gandhiji's general insistence on moderation and restraint in all matters, and on austerity in both our personal and public lives. Austerity for Gandhiji was one of the pillars on which his economic vision for India stood.

The same applies to the charkha. It would be a travesty to reduce it to wearing khadi. The charkha stood for self-help, dignity of labour, decentralization of economic activity, narrowing of the gap between cities and villages—and above all, for ending the enslavement and joylessness of ordinary people without property or skills, who had only their hard physical labour to sell as a means of meagre livelihood. Gandhiji was against capitalism insofar as the capitalist system concentrated the means of production in a few hands. He wanted everyone to own his own means of production—a concept much wider than the current notion of empowerment through education and the like. He was against socialism as it concentrated all means of production in the hands of the State, which led to the enslavement of everyone. If everyone could have access to machinery, he was for it. Where large-scale production was inescapable as in the case of steel, he was for public ownership. If such a system of production was less efficient, so be it, for simple living is in any case desirable. But his system would be more equitable, and would give dignity and self-respect to even the poorest man and free him from the dependency syndrome. The inefficiency could also be modified to some extent if workers' cooperatives could be run by managers who acted as their trustees. Gandhiji did not perhaps outline his economic vision in the language of economics. But he had a clear vision of an economic system which encompassed every aspect of Indian society. We can ignore his vision only at our peril.

Where does Nehru fit into all this? I think we can all agree that Nehru would have no problem with Gandhiji's first three fingers of Hindu–Muslim unity, eradication of untouchability and equality of women. He would not quite preach austerity—but he too would revolt against ostentation, vulgar display of wealth and crude consumerism. As for non-violence, truth and the purity of means as well as ends, while Nehru may not have literally endorsed these ideals, he was in complete sympathy with their larger meaning as I have tried to analyse.

It is with regard to the economic system that Nehru departs most from Gandhiji. Nehru was not lacking in compassion or concern for the poor. But his focus was on India's economic power—India marching shoulder to shoulder with more advanced countries in technical excellence. He was not much of a socialist; and his socialism, such as it was, was eclectic: Russia, Gandhi and the Fabian welfare state all went into his crucible, as indeed did his liking for at least some pioneers of private enterprise. It is with regard to the economic vision and the economic system that we most need some introspection today. The process of economic change has begun in India. But we do not quite know what it is leading to. It is a moot point whether it can or should take a Gandhian turn.

Nehru contributed three distinct elements to our vision of an ideal India: the inculcation of the scientific temper, the revival of our rich cultural and historical heritage and our international outlook which sought to extend the idea of a rule of law to relations between nations and not just within nations. Gandhiji was not opposed to science or culture, or our international outlook. But these things were not central to his endeavour, whereas for Nehru they were almost the hallmark of his modernity and an integral part of his idea of India. We have much to be grateful for to Nehru in his own right and not just as a foil to Gandhiji.

Just imagine how lucky we have been to have as architects of our freedom movement two such towering personalities, who dared to think of the unthinkable about all aspects of life and had the gift of articulating their ideas in a language even illiterate persons could understand. It went straight to our hearts and we knew instinctively that what we heard was worth taking to heart.

How does the history of the past fifty years and more compare with our dreams? One is almost ashamed to ask the question. We have strayed very far and the drift is accelerating rather than coming to a halt. That at least is the situation with regard to some parts of our dream. The hand that Mrs Gandhi raised in 1969 as her symbol when the Congress party was split was not the hand of Gandhi, which proclaimed the sanctity of means as well as ends. It would not be much of a parody to state that the hand of Congress (I) has come to stand for: "whatever ends I choose justify whatever means I choose to achieve them." And that dictum has been embraced avidly by each party—national or regional. The result is progressive corruption and even criminalization of our politics with little prospect for stable governments, which would govern with an eye to the future rather than pander to the current prejudices of the voters. A fractured polity has given rise to an inefficient and corrupt bureaucracy and the cancer has spread even to the judiciary. About the police, the other arm of law and order, the less said the better.

We all accepted Partition with a heavy heart but with the hope that when two estranged brothers separate, they may live in greater harmony thereafter. That has not happened. Within the country, the distance between Hindus and Muslims has widened. Those who proclaim loudly to be secularists are concerned more with Muslim votes than with modern education for Muslim children, equality for Muslim women or acceptance of family planning by them as an essential means of self-improvement. After all, such ideas might cost them precious votes! Those who call others pseudo-secularists are at least not pseudo in one respect: they do not even hide their disrespect and hatred for our Muslim brothers and sisters. It is not any section of the Muslim community in India that continues to believe in the two-nation theory; it is the Sangh Parivar, which has created in a small section of the Hindu majority the vicious feeling that the Muslims are virtually a separate nation that must be assimilated by force, if necessary, or else exported. And what can you say of those leaders who call themselves secularists but think nothing of widening all other divides—between caste and creed, language and region, culture and race? Competitive politics has not just been a game of populism and handouts and the creation of a dependency syndrome. It has also been a suicidal process of trying to be popular by dividing the country and creating a variety of fault-lines.

We have all the institutions of a democratic society—a Constitution, elections, political parties, tomes of law, an active judiciary and so on. But we all know our democracy is flawed and somewhat in disarray. There is little enforcement of the rule of law or adherence to equality of access to justice. Popular participation in discussions that affect the people is not what it should be. Atrocities against women and scheduled castes are not uncommon. There is much greater addiction today to drugs, liquor and the like, which breed violence, malnutrition and crime. To blame it all on prohibition would be to shut our eyes to reality—the situation is no better in states without prohibition. As for consumerism and vulgar display of wealth and ostentation, nobody even offers an apology for such behaviour today and no one shows displeasure by non-participation. Recent economic reform measures have certainly reduced the scope for corruption and have given much more freedom to consumers. But it is a moot point whether the current concern for the poor takes into account Gandhiji's main objective, which was to give the poorest person the joy and dignity of creative work in his own rural environment. Our notions of economic progress are still Nehruvian rather than Gandhian—emphasizing grandeur and power over compassion and widespread participation. Acquiring nuclear bombs makes us feel good rather than sad. The idea of being the second- or third-largest economic power thrills us without anyone stopping to ask when the poorest man in India will be richer than the poorest in most other countries. There will always be poor people everywhere. Poverty is both an absolute and a relative concept. But in that ladder of the poor across nations, where will our poor stand?

I do not wish to go on with this sad tale of how far we have strayed from our dreams. My primary purpose is to argue that our record is not all that bad, that there are signs of hope, that there is also a roadmap of what has to be done and finally, that lack of outstanding success should not deter us. If the best is beyond our grasp, there is no reason why we should not strive for the good. If we do not do so, we may end up with the worst. I will now turn to this positive aspect of what I have to say—and I shall naturally be selective in dealing with such a vast subject.

Consider, for example, how often we have averted serious threats to national unity and integrity. The massacres that followed Partition could have easily spread around the country and destabilized the young republic. This was not allowed to happen and the Muslim community by and large was made to feel safe enough to stay on even in northern India and not uproot itself in an effort to escape to Pakistan. Some did. But imagine what would have happened if the anger of the refugees had not been calmed by quick action to restore peace followed by an equally determined action to rehabilitate them generously. India could have been easily divided along the fault-line of the princely states. But this was prevented by the Sardar's firm and statesmanlike action, which did not alienate the princes. Thanks again to the Sardar, the steel frame of administration was kept intact.

In the late 1950s, when regionalism and the linguistic divide raised their ugly heads, the spirit of discussion, dialogue, mutual accommodation and consensus prevailed again and the reorganization of states was done peacefully. Today, in Bombay, the fear that the Gujaratis would be on the streets if Bombay was made the capital of Maharashtra seems ridiculous and the two communities live happily together with mutual advantage. But in 1958, this fear was all too real. The same is true of the division of Punjab. Jharkhand, Chhattisgarh and Uttaranchal have been created only recently—and we feel as if they have always existed. Who could have thought that the opposition to Hindi as the national language in the South could have been overcome by accepting English—a foreign language—as the second language for national discourse? It speaks volumes of the spirit of accommodation and forgiveness in the country—and it has paid off immensely in this age of globalization. There are problems in Kashmir and the North–East, with attendant international complications. But there is increasing readiness to heal these festering wounds.

In our quest for rapid progress, we did make mistakes in the economic field initially. We indulged in a good deal of wishful thinking and wasted a tremendous amount of resources in pushing for rapid industrialization including heavy industries. The regime of controls we created was counterproductive and led to a lot of corruption and less of consumer choice. Much of nationalization was driven not by economics or even ideology but by electoral calculations. But with all that, the early era also laid some solid and sound foundations for future prosperity.

Panditji's insistence on setting up world-class institutions of higher learning in science and technology, agricultural research and management gave us the pillars on which our current success in a globalized world stands. The Petroleum Minister, Malaviyaji, was ridiculed for aspiring to a vibrant public sector oil industry. But that is a reality today and our hopes for energy security rest largely on the foundations laid then. Nationalization of banks may have led to weakening of credit norms at the behest of corrupt politicians; but that single act did much to encourage financial savings among ordinary people and to make bank credit available to hitherto neglected sectors of the economy and society. Even today, I would plead for a sizeable presence of the public sector in finance and petroleum industries, albeit with much greater autonomy and even some induction of private equity in public enterprises.

I would not dwell on the virtual cultural Renaissance that the country has achieved, greatly assisted by public effort. Despite the remarkable growth of private entertainment and cable television, it is only Doordarshan which still gives a lot of time to education and culture uncluttered by idiotic advertisements; and many among us yearn for something like the Public Broadcasting System of the US. I would actually go a step further and suggest that all television channels should be required to devote some time every day to cultural and educational programmes, with minimum encroachment of advertisements. If banks can be asked to devote a part of their credit to the priority sectors, what is so sacred about the media?

Let me turn to another area: the eradication of untouchability. We seldom stop to think how far this objective has been achieved. But it is a fact and we only have to look around to see it. It is true that there is still a good deal of violence against the scheduled castes in rural areas; but it is largely economically motivated and by castes only a shade higher in the social hierarchy. The credit for the widespread disappearance of untouchability goes entirely to the leaders of the scheduled castes themselves and to their supreme leader, Dr Ambedkar. It is he who refused to look to the past but focused instead on the future of his people. He had the foresight and wisdom to see that their future lay in education and not in self-imposed isolation from the mainstream of society. He was patriotic enough to work for a modern and united India and played a major part in devising a Constitution that would sustain his progressive vision. The community has wisely used the special treatment given to them. All political parties compete to claim them as their own, but they, by and large, keep their counsel, lift themselves up by self-help and education and join the mainstream whenever they can do so without rancour, and seldom with a chip on their shoulder. Their example has much to teach other communities which are or consider themselves to be handicapped in some respects.

A mere man, I would not venture to speak on how far we have come with regard to equality of women. Perhaps a fair statement would be—someway, but not far. The trend, however, is for the better, thanks mainly to the efforts of various voluntary organizations. Credit facilities for women's self-help groups are an important element of this voluntary effort. Two things are necessary if the progress of women in India is to be more rapid: education of the girl child must receive the highest attention. And as my friend Swaminathan Anklesaria Aiyer has rightly reminded us, assuring equal property rights to women is vital for their economic freedom, without which their other rights such as freedom from violence would always be insecure.

I would like to urge that the issue of women's rights should be taken out of the political agenda. Let us stop talking of the rights of Muslim women or the rights of Hindu women. That will inevitably set up a defensive reaction. God knows there is enough violence against women and violation of their dignity and self-respect in all communities and all classes. What is the difference between a girl child who becomes a burden to be avoided at all cost because of the dowry demands of in-laws and a young woman covered from head to foot and denied fresh air and sunlight? As I see it, both deprive women of their essential dignity and freedom. But by communalizing the issue for political reasons, we increase the resistance to change. This is particularly true when it comes to advocacy of family planning, so essential for the freedom of women. But if you use differences in fertility rates as something to accuse and attack a community with, in addition to hidden insinuations of ulterior motives, you only encourage resistance. Rather, it should be matter of cold analysis and determined appeal to self-interest. My observation is that the ingrained prejudice against women has something to property rights and in communities where property rights for women are more secure, the female–male ratio is nearer the normal. My point is not to compare communities with the intention of praising or blaming. My plea is that it is possible to go behind outward manifestations and that it is necessary to do so if we want to bring about change.

While I think our past record is not all that black, I agree that much remains to be done, and I do not feel very sanguine about some parts of our dream. I particularly have in mind Hindu–Muslim unity, moderation or austerity in consumption, an international system based on the rule of law for everyone and giving a Gandhian twist to the economic system. Even here, progress is possible and must be attempted—and I will turn to this soon. But we may have to be patient and be satisfied in the end with a less than acceptable situation for the foreseeable future.

Before I turn to these specific areas, let me turn to some general points. If we want real progress, we should stop demonizing particular groups or individuals and look more closely at the underlying systemic factors. Systems can be changed. Individuals and groups seldom change essentially—they only adjust to systems and circumstances. I have lived in and around politics now for some fifty years, and can honestly say that I have come across many honest, competent, conscientious, hard-working and patriotic politicians, civil servants and experts. If over time, some have learnt to be economical with truth, honesty and integrity, it is because of the rot in the political system, just as much of the corruption in the country was and still is the result of a faulty economic system. We have started modifying the economic system. It is time now to divert more attention to the political, administrative and legal systems. Laws are not enforced, justice is delayed and the corrupt and the criminals go scot-free, with many of them even enjoying the highest positions in the land. Before we demonize any particular group or class, we have to ask: how many times do we, ordinary citizens, have to resort to petty bribes or to using our influence with the authorities to get what is our due or avoid undue harassment? It is not because we are dishonest. It is because we have no choice. And so the vicious circle goes on. Let us not forget that some of those who are accused of corruption today were once idealistic young. It is the lure of power, compulsions of competitive politics and the general decline in moral standards that has made them the opposite of what they started as.

I am not an expert on politics, administration or law enforcement, and I do not want to propound solutions in these areas. I can only plead for concentrated attention on reform in all these areas. I do not subscribe to the view that politicians will not allow change as it might hurt their interests. They are shrewd enough to know when enough is enough and when their antics end up as zero-sum games. This situation has already arisen with regard to exploiting the secular or the caste cards. All parties have to now woo all communities. The same is the case with having to woo independents. If a consensus could be reached on how to tackle the so-called *ayarams* and *gayarams*, it is surely possible to arrive at a consensus on what Governors should do in a situation of a hung or fractured mandate. I think the power of independents to blackmail major parties can be curbed. A better system for financing elections can be devised. I am only giving a few examples; experts can suggest more far-reaching ones.

Again, on administration and law enforcement, one has to ask why civil servants have to have so much security against prosecution, why the vigilance machinery works so slowly as to be a mockery and why it is necessary to allow appeals in all cases that go on forever. Can there not be severe punishments or at least deterrence for not recording complaints, or for changing evidence and the like? No one is in favour of kangaroo courts, but some via media for ensuring speedier justice is necessary. And is it necessary for the highest court to declare someone a murderer or a blackmailer before he is denied high political position? It is time we stop condoning criminal behaviour in the name of natural justice. Again, an agreement on such issues should be possible.

The two other areas where we need systemic and far-reaching changes are education and economics. We have to raise our sights considerably with regard to universal education. It is no longer enough to talk of literacy or primary education. Emphasis has to shift to high quality. Everyone—boy or girl—should receive education up to the 12th standard, with good knowledge of English and Mathematics. Nothing less will serve the needs of our growing population in a globalized world. We have to set our sights on the other end also. It is not enough to have one or two world-class institutions of higher education. We need several—including some in the social sciences. We need first-class research laboratories for industries and universities, and as freestanding institutions. More imaginative partnership and coexistence of the public and private sectors will have to be evolved at all levels, including primary and secondary education. All this would mean a quantum jump in public and private expenditure on education. That is the main reason for the state selling off assets which can be better utilized by the private sector. It is also an important reason why we should strive ceaselessly for deriving a peace dividend from durable peace with all our neighbours.

As far as the economic system is concerned, the roadmap now is reasonably clear; and despite all the stops and starts, we will stay the course. The central theme of economic reform is competition and globalization, without which none of our dreams can be realized. I firmly believe that most of our problems—including the social and political ones—will become easier to tackle if we can secure sustained high rates of growth for the next generation. Differences tend to dissolve in an environment of enlarging economic opportunities. That is the moral of US history. That is what makes even the Dalai Lama plead for Tibet remaining a part of China. His disciples know which side offers them a better future.

Competition and globalization are not enough. But they are absolutely indispensable. Everyone agrees that they have to be supplemented by universal education, access to credit for all, a sound legal system to enforce contracts and direct action to alleviate poverty and other social ills.

Prosperity also requires a sense of private philanthropy to sustain it. But all this does not detract from the merits of competition and globalization.

There is one aspect of globalization which our Prime Minister rightly emphasizes and it is often neglected in public discourse. We need to pay special attention to removing all barriers to trade and investment between ourselves and our neighbours, and to creating a free trade and investment area from Samarkand to Jakarta. I for one would also encourage movement of people to the maximum extent with easy work permits in the entire region. Apart from the economic impact, it will reduce much of the social and political tension that exists in our region. The same argument applies to China also. Peace, prosperity and people-to-people interaction go well together.

We should be under no illusion that with the implementation of economic reforms—a distant dream anyway—we would be among the richest countries in per capita terms in one generation. Nor will there be an end to poverty or any significant reduction in inequality. But we can give everyone *roti*, *kapda*, *makan*, *sadak*, *bijli*, sanitation, safe drinking water and access to the literary treasures of the world, and eliminate malnutrition. That is a good enough dream to fulfil. Whether that means abolition of poverty or not will always remain a contentious subject as people raise the bar regarding what is the essential minimum for them. As for inequality, it might decline somewhat after a generation of good universal education and steady progress, but will not be eradicated. However, with full stomachs, a decent environment and proper education, people do not worry very much about what the other person has locked up in his vaults and bank accounts. Most people will be satisfied with a future for the working classes, about which Alfred Marshall, the doyen of British economics, wondered "whether progress may not go on steadily, till the official distinction between working man and gentleman has passed away, till, by occupation at least, every man is a gentleman".

The prospects are not bright for Gandhian notions of moderation, restraint and austerity. Human beings like to catch up with others and it is very easy to turn wants into needs. We have all experienced it and, like it or not, consumerism will prevail in India, by and large as it has in the US and Europe. And yet, can anyone deny that Gandhiji's ideas in this regard are worth emphasizing even more today? Savings and investments are vital for economic growth. Consumerism reduces savings—witness how the US rate of saving is much lower than that of India, let alone China. Global warming may or may not be around the corner. Science may stave off the exhaustion of scarce resources for some time. But we cannot be sure. Precaution demands restraint upon consumption. Vulgar display is demeaning; it reduces social solidarity and, at times, even creates violent resentment. Part of the fuel that propels fundamentalism today is the disgust that many well-meaning but conventional people feel at the indulgence they see spreading all around them. There may or may not be a clash of civilizations. But there is certainly a clash in each society between inner peace and limitless gratification; between civilized, compassionate and moderate behaviour and a self-centred rat race, which leaves you little time even to enjoy what you crave for. There is sense in what a young Chinese student told me some thirty years ago: "We do not believe in keeping up with the Joneses. We believe in not having something if our neighbours do not have it." I know it would be difficult to find such a Chinese student today. But he is not irrelevant or wrong.

What about giving the economy a Gandhian twist as I defined it? Here again, the prospects are not bright, but much can and should be done. Today, development with a human face largely means handouts, guarantees and subsidies—all of which lead to waste and intensify the dependency syndrome. That was not Gandhiji's dream. He was for empowerment in a much more fundamental sense. He was for self-help and individual responsibility. Decentralization of production may not be easy. But something needs to be done to prevent the relentless march to urban slums. With today's technology and with rural electrification and technical training, it should be possible to carry jobs where people live and not vice versa. Even in cities, many jobs can now be done from homes and small localities. Technology can devise simple tools. I believe in Swadeshi to the extent that as far as possible we should patronize the wonderful arts and crafts in which we excel, and which give creative and meaningful employment to poor people. Call it cultural protection or what you like, but it matters. One reason for Japan's success in the early years was that it borrowed technology from everywhere but retained its own cultural consumption patterns. The success of China in exporting labour-intensive products goes back to Mao's insistence that every commune should have some industry of its own. The Chinese had enough sense to modernize their rural industry. Trusteeship may not be a workable concept, but it is possible to ensure workers' participation in management and have stock options for workers. The work environment can be more democratic and participatory. Those who think Gandhi is economically irrelevant are only refusing to think on new and bolder lines, and can find no alternative to traditional notions of socialism and capitalism. Institutions evolve, and it is possible to imagine and create an economy which combines the best of Marx, Mohandas and Milton Friedman—to stick only to the Ms.

I am afraid I am not very sanguine about Gandhiji's first finger: Hindu–Muslim unity. It would take quite a while before his dream is realized. The past, particularly the recent past, is against us. I doubt if there ever was as much cultural synthesis and normal social discourse between these two communities as is often suggested—except perhaps in UP and around Delhi.

Social and cultural isolation was a reality even in my childhood. Today, the isolation is almost complete. What was trite and can still be true is peaceful coexistence and economic interdependence. In time, these will bring about greater warmth and normalcy in cultural and social relations. But much will have to be done by both communities if this is to happen. Hindu and Muslim fundamentalists will have to be fought and thwarted at all levels, and the law must be strictly enforced against all miscreants. If governments are unwilling to do this, NGOs must receive our wholehearted support in this task. Recent events give us hope that this can be done. I have every confidence that there is enough wisdom in the majority community to fight the communal passion instilled in some of them. Muslim society must find a path to modernity. *Madrassas* and *burqas* are not the way forward. One only hopes that some Dr Ambedkar among the Muslims will come forward to do what needs to be done in the interests of everyone. The media too should not inflame communal passions. It is possible to report facts without always talking of Hindus and Muslims. The economic ties between them are still strong and there is realization that violence hurts both communities, particularly the poorest families who live on their daily earnings. The ordinary Gujarati understands this. After all, there were no significant communal riots in Gujarat for almost a decade before 2002—and for most of this time, the BJP was in power. With patience and persistence on the right path, even this dream of Gandhiji will come true. But it will take some time.

Can peace with Pakistan help? To some extent yes, but not much. Both have to be dealt with on their own terms and both are important in their own right. The roadmap for peace with Pakistan is already there and both sides have travelled some distance on that. The groundswell of public support for peace in both countries is real. I think the solution to Kashmir is also not difficult to find. Any solution must be acceptable to some extent to Pakistan, India and the people of Kashmir on both sides of the line of control. Each must feel it has got something, but not everything. I think our Prime Minister was right when he drew the bottomline: we cannot have another partition of India and Kashmir should not be divided on religious lines. I can see only one solution along these lines: the present line of control as the international boundary, with some adjustments, if necessary, and the creation of an autonomous region of Kashmir around some part of the international boundary, including parts of Kashmir on both sides of the border. The unity and autonomy of Kashmiris would be respected. It is absolutely necessary that this autonomous region include both Jammu and the Kashmir Valley even if Ladakh and the northern regions in Pakistan are left out. Kashmiriat may have suffered a severe jot. But everything must be done to revive it. Once such an autonomous but not independent region is agreed upon, minor adjustments in the international order will not matter.

I know the fear of creating a precedent. All I can say is that no one can predict what can happen in future. The present cannot be held hostage to fears about the future. If a similar situation arises in the future, it will have to be dealt with in its own context.

I have left Nehru far behind and must return to him briefly before I end. The future is bright for his concerns, for the scientific temper of the nation and not cultural revival. As for his dream of a powerful India in the frontline of the nations of the world, I am more impressed by Gandhi. I was not happy when we acquired nuclear weapons. It has served no purpose; on the contrary, it has worsened matters.

I have some reservations with regard to India's membership of the Security Council also. If there are to be more than five permanent members, our claim is clear and we should not forsake it. But I would not spend much diplomatic capital on obtaining such a position. Similarly, on the veto—if other permanent members are to have it, we should have it too. But we should declare that we will surrender our veto if the majority of the other members are willing to do the same. After all, we are against all aristocracy in international affairs as we are for total nuclear disarmament. There is no other moral or Gandhian position.

I am not sanguine about the rule of law prevailing in international affairs. Power—economic and military—will still speak. But the point is that we are committed to containing power in the interests of what is right. Our commitment is to the poor and the powerless of the world. And I dare to say that we have succeeded a great deal in restraining power in the World Bank, IMF, WTO and even in the UN. But we cannot have it both ways—we cannot pretend to fight the rich and the powerful and seek to join them at the same time. I am glad we have had to give up the ambition of becoming leaders in the international arena—whether of the non-aligned movement or of the South. Let us not dream now of joining some other axis of power. Our international dharma has to be friendship and cooperation with all, and the democratization of international institutions to the maximum extent possible.

Part V

Economic Reform and Policy in India

CHAPTER 20

The Vision for a New India*

If I were to tell you what I have learnt from today's statements and repeat what has been said, you might accuse me of saying just "me too". I do believe that I can say yes to almost 90 per cent of the things that have been said. I think there is a certain amount of consensus which is building in the country about the new wave, the new atmosphere, the new policies.

But I think that is precisely the time when most people think alike that we should pause, we should halt, and somebody should say are these new policies all that new and is there nothing worthwhile in the old policies that you need to remember, implement better? Have the new policies gone as far as they should? Should we get into euphoria about the change that has taken place? Of course a lot of change has taken place. The new policies are not merely clichés about the magic of the marketplace and all that. Policies are supposed to have, and do have, an underlying economic rationale. What is that rationale? Will the reality reflect that rationale or will it be somewhat different? Unless we ask and answer such questions we are not likely to get as much out of the turmoil and the toil and the sacrifice and the bitterness that are bound to arise if these policies are carried forward as much as they should be and are implemented as honestly and sincerely as they should be.

If I sound as if I am saying something which is somewhat critical and at least somewhat qualifying what normally is being said these days, please forgive me. But I think some questioning is necessary.

I do not believe, for example, that we need to lay that much emphasis on a new vision for India. The vision for India has been expressed any number

* Valedictory remarks at the ASSOCHAM Annual Session, 24 September 1991.

of times: it is not new nor is it peculiar to India. We in India have a habit of thinking that we are a very special breed. None of the laws that apply to the world, whether they are the laws of economics or the laws of human nature, apply here, because we are a very special, very old, very ancient civilization. The objectives at the level of generalities and the vision are the same everywhere and have been for a long time. We all want that our children should have a better future than we have had. We all want that their future should be stable and not full of ups and downs. We don't want it only for ourselves. We are not all selfish. We want that better future for our neighbours, for everybody. I think it is a kind of special pride that some of us seem to take thinking that only we have social consciousness, or that we developed the concept of social justice. There are a few ostrich-like figures like Margaret Thatcher who think that there is no such thing as society. But the Germans don't believe it: they talk of social democracy. The Americans don't believe it: they talk of a caring democracy. The Japanese don't believe it. The Japanese capitalism is quite different from capitalism elsewhere: they believe that the consumers come first, workers come second, the shareholders come probably last. In many other countries, perhaps in America and England, they do think that the shareholders come ahead of the workers or the consumers but they have a very rich tradition of voluntary effort. They have percentage clubs which I am afraid I am not sure businessmen in this country do have. So there is nothing new about social justice.

Yes, sustainable development is perhaps something new. But there is nothing new about participatory development either. Democracy means participation. All of us also believe that economic well-being is not everything. Lord Keynes expressed his vision by saying that his vision was to see a day when economics will no longer be relevant, when economic growth will no longer be necessary and when we would have become all so prosperous that we will be able to spend the rest of our lives in living a good life of culture, art, what have you.

So let us not emphasize too much the fact that we need a new vision. What we need I think is something different. Yes, at the level of generalities, objectives, we all know what we want. We can put it in different words. But there is not the same agreement about the means, and I think it is true that as far as the means of achieving what we want is concerned there has been a change and there needs to be a change.

Even here I would like to remind you that there is a lot in the old style of thinking, a style of thinking which we in India may have overstretched and held up as an example to others, that there is some truth in that. I would like to remind you, just for the sake of reminding you, that not everything that needs to be done in the country is along new lines. There are many things which are outside economic policy and are still important. Mention was made of the population problem, the law and order problem, the problem of peace with our neighbours. These are very large problems which are outside economics and which would have a tremendous bearing on how successful we are in our quest for prosperity, social justice, participation and all the rest.

Not only that. Even in the economic sphere, we economists like to divide economics into macroeconomics and microeconomics. I think it is correct to say that as far as macroeconomic management is concerned our understanding in India has always been good. There never have been disputes in India about what is necessary to be done in order to avoid inflation. The social tolerance for inflation and the political tolerance for inflation in India are very low. I think our record in controlling inflation, and having good macroeconomic management, has been good except during the last few years where, I am afraid, politics took over everything, politics took care of everything. I won't go into that. The failure in macroeconomic management is comparatively recent.

Even as regards the exchange rate, since 1971 the way we have managed our exchange rate is sound. If we had to devalue by a big step I don't think it was because we did not follow the right policies regarding the exchange rate in the preceding twenty years. It was only because, again for political reasons, we allowed the situation to develop so badly so fast that we created a crisis of confidence to overcome which one thing we could do—it was under nobody's pressure. I am sure that a drastic step had to be taken—so that those who were holding back had to be told, "This is it. It is going to remain so for several months to come." I think that in a sense is what happened.

It is also fair to say that quite apart from macroeconomic management there is such a thing as economics of development which requires very special action by the government. It is no use pretending in this country that there are important activities in the economic sphere where we can generate growth without the involvement of the public sector. There are constraints on growth which cannot be removed simply by leaving everything free. I don't need to recount all these constraints. Savings is one constraint. Lack of agricultural output will be another constraint. You as businessmen would recognize that not having sufficient power, sufficient transport is a constraint and no matter how much you are invited to produce power on your own steam and develop transport on your own steam you can rest assured that for the next five or ten years at least you would always be telling the government to do more in those areas. So please do not think that you can take on these responsibilities on your shoulders. When it comes to the development of human resources, education—primary, secondary, tertiary—which is again the main constraint for development, we are far, far behind in this country. I think the greatest shame in independent India is that we still have only 40 to 55 per cent literacy in this country despite forty to fifty years of effort. Many talk about compulsion in family planning under law. I don't want to say anything about it. But we still do not have compulsory primary and secondary education. I think I would like to see compulsory education for our children till the age of 14 or 15. Family planning, population, many other things will take care of themselves thereafter.

Let us, therefore, not throw the baby out with the bath water. The reason why many things have gone wrong, and of course there are many reasons again, is I think that we neglected the importance of what the economists will call microeconomics. Growth depends not merely on removing the bottlenecks to growth that I mentioned. But it depends on making the most efficient use of existing resources because it is only from existing resources that you can start. It is only if you get a surplus out of them that you can go on to the next stage. I think in regard to the policies of investment, policies regarding control of production, pattern of investment, many mistakes have been made. Most of you are familiar with that and I am not going to take much time on that.

Basically, however, let me say a little bit about what I think went wrong, which goes much beyond neglect of the market or underestimating the private sector. Those things we have done. We have overestimated the calibre of government. We thought by definition government must be more knowledgeable than the private sector. It is not true. We thought that by definition government must be more objective, less selfish. That is not true. I am afraid we know to our cost that governments also can act as a vested interest, they can also act in an arbitrary, wayward way, they can even be corrupt. Unfortunately, it has to be said that that has been the case not entirely or even largely as a result of the controlled and command economy. Partly, yes, but in many ways for reasons that go beyond that. We also thought that government can be all powerful, that it simply has to say "this will be done" and it will be done. We never realized that people also have their ways, people also have their desires and they will find ways to circumvent government desires and government policies when they go against the grain of their self-interest. That is human nature, and I think in a basic sense we have underestimated the importance of incentives in stimulating growth.

Again, many people talk about luxuries these days and I was very pleased when Prime Minister Rao the other day said, "Are you against electric washing machines? You want the nation to remain a nation of maidservants for all time?" I think these things need to be said because no matter how important it may be to preach austerity to every section of society, every section of society wants the same things, if not today, tomorrow. I have only one simple test for people who rail against this luxury and that luxury. I ask them, "When you were a child, say, thirty, forty years ago, you were not consuming many things. You are now consuming many more things. What is it that you would like to do without? What is it you think you can do without? If you cannot do without it, then why do you think other people can do without it?" People work for their children, they work for things in which they have put their hearts, maybe a house, maybe something else, and I think we have to provide that.

The whole philosophy of handouts, reservations, government as a *sarkar ma baap*, populism, you name it, we have it. Even today what are our leaders preoccupied with? They want to extend reservations beyond 50 per cent. I think it is a matter of shame. We talk of a free economy, a liberal economy, no protection. What is reservation but protection? What is reservation for small industry but protection? I think we have to go a very long way in changing this attitude. Yes, protection will be necessary for a while. But like the protection to Indian industry against foreign competition, internally also protection will have to be time-bound. While you are protecting them, simply reservations won't do. You have to take effective steps to see that those who are being protected, whether certain classes or small people, are actually technologically upgraded so that beyond a point reservations are not necessary.

There are many shortcomings in our political life, in our public life which have nothing to do with wrong policies but have something to do with misuse of political power. I don't think the politicians alone are to blame. Our people also think that for everything they have a right to go to the government. They can demand that we all have a right to work. Somebody said they don't want to work, they only want a job. This is the kind of philosophy where a total change has to come about if we are to have a major role in the world market.

We have also been in some sense reading wrongly the signals about what is happening in the world. We have been taking pride in being non-aligned. But the fact is that we looked neither left nor right. We have developed a kind of blinkered vision. We look only inward. We don't see what is happening in the outside world. We didn't realize that the greatest force making for change nowadays is technological change. It is so rapid that to think of finding all technologies within India and being self-sufficient in it doesn't really make any sense. We remain suspicious of foreign investment because we thought that was an instrument of foreign power as if foreign investment was going to come only from America. Japan after the war was not going to be a big power trying to dominate anybody. If only we had realized the importance of Japan and Japanese investment and Japanese collaboration in the 1950s and 1960s, the future of India would have been very different. Even today the world is multipolar even in regard to investment. There is Korea here. There will be Indonesia tomorrow, Malaysia, Singapore. There are many countries from which investment can come.

We are not dependent only on the great powers. There are many countries to which we can go as investors. We do not have to be completely self-reliant before we can invest abroad. Two-way flow, it has got to begin in a two-way.

We do not want to allow foreign people to come in, we want to impress upon them that everything must be produced here, all components. There is now less and less of export of totally finished products from one place to another. The whole production system is being fragmented. When you have globalization, multinational firms become multinational in the real sense of the word. A firm is multinational today not merely in the sense that it sells its products in a large number of countries. It also derives its inputs of skills, components, spare parts and many other things also from production facilities in a large number of countries, its own and of other people. The whole nature of trade has changed and I think we haven't really been aware of what is happening.

One can go on mentioning many things. Even ideologically, we have been thinking in rather simplistic terms: socialism, capitalism. There is not one kind of capitalism. There is no pure capitalism anywhere. As I mentioned some time back, one can argue that Japanese capitalism, German capitalism, Swedish capitalism and American capitalism are substantially different one from the other. It depends on their national moorings. I think it could also be true that our own capitalism need not be of the same kind. It need not be of only one kind either. There are industrialists in this country who genuinely believe in Gandhiji's trusteeship, who have never had a strike in their factory, who believe that consumers and workers come first before themselves. There are others who believe in the hire-and-fire American way of life, and I think both have a place in this country. I would not say that only one should prevail and the other should not. Each according to the historical inheritance, each according to what they believe in. But the freedom must be there.

Let me say when we talk of hire-and-fire and the exit policy and various other things, that it is not only meant for labour. Business people always seem to think that the exit policy has something to do with industrial relations, workers being unemployed. Exit policy has everything to do with the big business also, it means that no one is going to say that nobody can take over the Tatas and the Birlas or anything like that and that they must be there forever. Then you are not talking of exit policy. You are talking of the same things of which you are blaming labour. Exit policy also means that small industry must also from time to time go out of existence. There is no such thing as saying that the small people must always survive. Yes, as I said, give them fiscal protection for a while, give them all the encouragement that you can technologically, but everything has to be time-bound. By all means, takeovers and mergers must be regulated and that is not an easy task. But I think we should not forget that a policy which talks of competition, which talks of the survival of the fittest, will have its impact on industry as much as it will have on labour, as much as it will have on anybody else.

I am not in the least bit saying that policy changes are not necessary, have not been necessary, or indeed that they have not taken place. I think there is no denying the fact that in the last two, three months economic policy in this country has taken a very sharp turn for the better, and as far as I am concerned I do not really believe that we are going to be able to go back to the bad old days. We may have reverses, we may have a little bit of a step back, we may have a little bit of difficulty but the internal logic is such that we are on a new path on which we shall have to go further and further. The logic will take us that way.

If I were to say what are the things that I consider important I personally think that the industrial licensing and changes in the Monopolies and Restrictive Trade Practice (MRTP) Act are the extremely important step forward. In your heart of hearts you must have sensed it that the government has probably gone even a step further than you would have expected it to do in the short course of time.

The linkage between imports and exports is an extremely important step. I subscribe to the view, which I think somebody mentioned, that if you really believe in exports you cannot always say that those who are importing should somehow earn their own requirements through export. That kind of linkage does not make sense forever. If that is the meaning of saying exports and imports have to be linked forever then I don't think it works. What the linkage between exports and imports really means is—today it is only partial but before long you will have to make a total linkage between imports and exports. A total linkage between imports and exports means that the dual exchange rate system implicit today cannot last forever. Sooner or later there will have to be one unitary exchange rate. All exporters will be free to sell all their export earnings in a free market and all importers will have to get their import requirements in that free market. And that free market will have to produce a stable exchange rate because if that free market produces a continually downgraded and devaluing exchange rate you will have a rollicking inflation before long. Nobody will believe in that system.

So the aim of the linkage system ultimately is a convertible rupee: that is the meaning of the convertible rupee. Sooner or later we will have to reach a stage when all exporters and all incoming monies as a matter of fact will all go in one free market from which everybody will have to meet the requirements. There may be some controls. I am not saying there will be no controls and the resultant exchange rate will have to be stable. That assumes we have a long distance to travel before we get to that point in terms of our export increase because nothing else is going to come to our aid.

You know by now that bilateral official aid is more or less going down in real terms. It is not going to go up. If anybody thinks that private capital from non-resident Indians or private foreign investment or, for that matter, the money that Indian business people are known to hold abroad will solve our immediate problems to any great extent, then we are very mistaken. Private capital is a fair-weather friend. It only comes when you have solved your problems to make you richer. When you have solved your problems more or less, when people are convinced that the fiscal adjustment has more or less been made, when they are convinced that exports are going up, when they are convinced that there is a fair prospect of the exchange rate remaining stable, when they are convinced that the liberalized regime on imports and other things will more or less be in place, then foreign investors will come to join the party, then people who are holding money abroad will come to join the party, and then non-resident Indians also will come to join the party. For you to think that they will come to solve your problems is wishful thinking. They will not. I think if you search in your heart of hearts you know that that is the case.

I am not saying that some money will not come. You can have this and that device, you can allow them to buy shares and some money which is not coming today may come. They will not take their money back, which I think is the utmost we can hope for today, for the next two, three years.

So the real solution of our problem has to come over a period in terms of increased exports. But if you ask Indian industry and say you must increase exports, with all that has gone on so far, all that has gone on in terms of whatever you like to name it, labour relations, habits of mind, how will that happen? For it to happen the reform process will have to go much farther. Businessmen will say: how can they export more unless we have a level playing field? If they want to compete in the global markets, then they must be on a level playing field. Level playing field with whom? Foreign competitors, both in the internal market and in the external market, because there is no question of saying freedom to compete means freedom to compete in the external market but not in the internal market. That is the meaning of free licensing. But to have the same advantages as the outside people are enjoying means having very little by way of import control, being free to import whatever capital or raw materials or spares that you want. It means having relatively low rates of customs duties because if the customs duties are high, no matter what the assistance or drawback may be, it will come in the way because that is the way it is. It means many other things. It means the burden of taxation is low. It means also not merely the liberty to hire and fire but lack of rigidity in the wage structure so that real wages can sometimes come down as they can go up.

I remember asking a Japanese friend—that was after the first oil shock—how come you could overcome the oil shock so quickly whereas you are so much dependent on oil? His reply was very simple. He said, we knew at that point of time that workers had a better deal in the preceding four, five years, their wages had grown rather rapidly, so we told them you have to take the rap, the profits have been very low, capital cannot take the rap; and they understood it. In 1980–81 I asked another Japanese. This time the situation was reversed, profits were high, the wages had taken a rap, so they decided to do it the other way around. There has to be that kind of understanding.

I remember asking Mr Demag, way back in the mid-1950s, in 1956 or 1957 when I was in Germany negotiating the Rourkela agreement—even then we were borrowing money—how come that within a very few years, from a rubble of your industry you could develop an industry of this magnitude? He said, "Mr Patel, you won't believe it. The answer is very simple. When the war ended I found on my doorsteps my old workers coming back, some maimed, some mutilated, some with nobody in their families; they all gathered together here as if it was my job to see that something was done for them. They didn't go to the government. I said it is my job to do something for them. I told them, 'Let us work, let us build a school for the children so that they have something to do, let us put the women in the kitchen so that they can cook for all of you. Let us start digging whatever it is and let us start doing whatever we can do.' After a year we found that we were making something, we were selling something. I found that my wage bill was equal to my profits. I told myself, what a wonderful deal, by simply bringing them back my profits are equal to the wage bill. But I told them, 'From now on I won't take any more profits and you won't take any more for your wages, everything that comes extra we will put into the business.' When you do that year in and year out, in ten years you can quadruple your production or whatever it is." It is that kind of spirit which I think we have to develop.

Level playing fields, as I said, rely on many more things, if you ask me. You have to allow imports, you have to lower your duties, have a reasonable tax system, you have to have your exit policy, you have to have an impartial and competitive financial system.

Let me say without mincing words. One of the worst things that happened, partly as a result of controls but not entirely, is the politicization of everything—politicization of the judiciary, politicization of the civil service, politicization of business. That habit is not going to die easily. Even now with our liberalized policies there is plenty of scope for mischief. Yes, only eighteen industries require industrial licensing now. But the list includes such juicy items as electronics, entertainment industry and motor cars. Do you think that that does not open some scope for malpractices? If you have got to avoid this, sooner or later these industries also have to be delicensed. Not all the eighteen but certainly these three will have to be, which means many other things. You will have to make imports of those things free because to delicense them and be strict with imports will only create excessive profits, and you will be back where you are.

A German friend asked, “Why are we not allowed to take advantage of the internal large market?” I think my answer is very simple. There is such a thing as sequencing of policies. The right sequence for foreign investment, to allow foreign investment to come into India even in the production of cars and refrigerators is when the imports of those items are free. To allow foreign investment in those items, or even for that matter domestic investments in those items, when you do not allow imports—the second may be unavoidable for a while—is really to invite trouble. There is sequencing also in terms of import liberalization. Unless you have set the fiscal house in order, to liberalize imports would be a mistake. Many people say that the import liberalization policy of the mid-1980s was wrong, that it admitted luxury goods. Yes it was wrong, not so much because it admitted luxury goods. It was wrong because you opened two floodgates at the same time. The fiscal tap was open wide, the import tap was open wide. Nobody in his right senses will do that. It is only when your fiscal system and the monetary system is tightly controlled that you can afford to liberalize imports.

The question was asked, why has the Reserve Bank tightened the monetary policy? The answer is very simple: not that they like it. But at the time when the Reserve Bank introduced the tight monetary policy on imports the government was entirely helpless. The only thing that could be done was monetary policies. So they used that instrument to the hilt because when you do not know what will happen next week, whether your reserves would be there or you would be able to pay your debts, you have got to do whatever you can do in order to restrict imports. That was not the best thing, but that was the only thing that was possible at that time. I am quite sure the moment we find our way to liberalize imports, we will have to do it, if we mean business, sooner or later. That is when, I am sure, the Reserve Bank will liberalize the restrictions on credit that you find irksome now.

I am not equally sanguine about lowering the rates of interest. That is something where I myself have felt that we have kept our interest rates by and large much too high. For some time while the inflation is high there is probably no choice. But even when the inflation comes down we have inbuilt inefficiency in the banking system, inbuilt inefficiency in the financial system, inbuilt populism in the financial system; and unless you remove them it will be very difficult to maintain the viability of the financial institutions and still bring the interest rates down.

As I mentioned earlier, there are goods still requiring licences and there is scope for mischief. Even if everything is free, please don't believe that even with all the reforms the Narasimhan committee might recommend for the financial institutions, that we are going to get rid of the incubus of publicly owned financial institutions for a long time to come. It is simply not possible. You can allow more competition but by and large the capital market, the banking system will depend on the public sector banks, public sector financial institutions at least for the next five, ten years. There is scope for enough mischief there. So what needs to be done there, it is not a question of the government not actively investing, it is a question of government desisting from interfering in economic policy even through financial institutions. Even the fiscal system we know jolly well can be perverted. That is why it is important not merely to say that taxes should be lower but that the categorization in taxes should be as limited as possible. There should not be too many brackets of customs duties, too many brackets of excise duties, too many brackets of income-tax rates, because by manipulating these brackets from time to time you can still play havoc with the economy, you can still have an arbitrary behaviour coming from certain people.

All I am trying to drive at is, when you remember all these things, how far controls still exist in the states sector, how much more needs to be done in the areas that I have mentioned, the difficulties of sequencing, I think it is still important for us to say, thank you very much for what has been done, you deserve two cheers but not yet three cheers. You have to go a fairly long way. Diwali is still many days away. It is not time to light all your lamps and let off all your crackers.

Much of what I have said is true as much of business as it is true of government. I have referred to government so many times. I have avoided referring to business so far. Let me ask you one question. Why did the Swatantra Party fail? They were advocating the same things as most of you are now courageous enough to say. Why did business not support it? Because most businessmen found it more convenient, cosier and cheaper to find favours from the existing government rather than to seek public support, to cultivate public opinion, to create political support for the right policies—that is what you will have to do in future. I am not sure that the spirit of sycophancy has died out from private business yet. There are many people in private business who think even now that rather than incur the displeasure and unpleasantness of opposing government policies and all that, it is much simpler, much cheaper, much more comfortable to be on its right side. But there is a tremendous job to be done in this country for cultivating public opinion. I personally believe that public opinion in this country is already 60, 70, 80 per cent in favour of the new policies. It understands that old policies had not worked and that it is time for a change. But there are still demands that the income-tax exemption limit should be raised, otherwise we won't support you, that fertilizer subsidy should not be removed, otherwise we will not support you. I sometimes despair. In fact I despair when even the government of the day promises that fertilizer subsidies will be increased but the procurement prices also will be suitably increased. The day after that the issue prices will be increased, then dearness allowance will be increased. So what have we done? We have only got one more dose of inflation. We have solved no budgetary problem. It is that way that we have tried to deal with the budgetary problem for the last several years, tokenism. We take one step to please one person, another step to please another person, a third step to please a third person. In the end we raise no resources, we please nobody. We only have one more upward twist of cost-push inflation. I think unless we are going to change all those habits—and they are very deeply ingrained—I must remain somewhat sceptical about whether we will achieve all that the new policies are capable of.

Having said that, let me conclude by saying that I am still optimistic. I am optimistic because, as I said, public opinion is now ready for a change—anybody who has to travel by Indian Airlines or anybody with a telephone connection, how can he be in favour of the public sector? There is a sea-change in the attitude of our people. They are not fools.

Let me also say that maladjusted as the Indian economy has been, our maladjustment has not been very grave. We are not a Soviet Union, we are not Eastern Europe, and again, with apologies to Latin Americans, we have not been Latin Americans either in the matter of inflation. Our maladjustment has been there but it is of the order of 2 per cent of GNP or something like that, not much more. The fiscal deficit, yes, you find it is 8.5 per cent—very bad. I think if we reduce it to 5 per cent, eliminate the revenue deficit altogether and create a surplus, we would have done a good job. I don't think we need to go any further than that for the simple reason that we have a good rate of private saving. We have a very poor rate of corporate saving, public and private, but we have a very good rate of private saving. If the private savings don't flow to government, which accounts for 50 per cent of the investment, where will they flow? It may be 50 per cent today, it may be 40 tomorrow but it will have to flow there. So let us not be too mesmerized by new words and new definitions. The problem is not as grave as many people imagine it to be. We have strength, strength in terms of our people, our industry, our labour, our agriculture. Our share in world exports is so small that I think that in itself is an advantage. Even if we quadruple it, or have eight times that share we will hardly create any ripples around the world. There are, as everybody reminds us, forces of protectionism, regional blocs and many other things. Pressures of many kinds will also be on us to exchange concessions. But for us to find our way round those pressures would be comparatively easy. I dare say it would be easier than for Korea—pressures on stronger competitors would probably be much stronger.

Then there is a lot of external goodwill for us. People underestimate that a nation of 830 million (1 million = 10 lakh) people has a position in the world. I really find it extremely difficult to understand when people talk about the International Monetary Fund as if it is some kind of a sinister, malevolent agency. The fact of the matter is that today nobody other than the IMF can help you. If you have a $7 billion current account deficit you won't be able to cover more than $3 million from official and multilateral aid. That was the figure in the past and you know that is the figure that is going to remain, if at all, in the next few years. The remaining 4 billion, which for a few years we got from private short-term commercial capital and NRI funds, it is not going to be there. It may be half of it, it may be one-third of it, it is certainly not going to be 4 billion. Where are we going to get the extra $2–3 billion from? The exports are not going to increase by $3 billion in a year or two. They may increase over three or four years.

People say why can't we contract our imports? They are contracted badly enough. There will be a real social revolution in this country if you try to cut the imports by $2 to 3 billion, because that will require rationing not just of petroleum products, it will require rationing of vegetable oils and many things besides. All you will end up with is a rollicking inflation and you will have to start all over again after a period of possibly having defaulted, possibly having a 100 per cent inflation, and you will have to start the same struggle again of creating confidence and borrowing from the IMF. There is no friend other than the Fund today. I think not to have faith in the Fund, which has stood by us very well in the past—I negotiated with it in 1981 5 billion Special Drawing Rights (SDRs) loan, the biggest then, and I can tell you there was no real conditionality to that loan. There were only two conditions attached to the loan and we negotiated it in no time, because of our goodwill, because our record was good, because we had borrowed in the past and paid back in time. The two conditions were very sensible. One was a degree of fiscal adjustment, bring the deficit somewhat into line; and the second was some regrouping of investment to show that our balance of payments was going to improve with a change in the investment policy. We did that at that time, it may be short-sighted but I think it was right at that time, to say, yes, we will expedite exploitation of the Bombay High, and we did it. I think we came out from that crisis very quickly. Unfortunately, for political reasons we gave up borrowing the last instalment because we were in a hurry to get out of the Fund discipline. We wanted to continue the fertilizer subsidies, we wanted to continue so many populist devices which we could not have done if we had remained under the Fund discipline. Here again, of course, if we borrow from the Fund and as soon as the Fund monies come through and are drawn, we revert to our bad old days, we will have $10 billion or $8 billion of more debt and nothing to show for it.

So I think it is important for us to remember that we have friends. They are our friends. They are not out to do us any damage. Yes, they will bring some pressure on us. Even the Americans and the Japanese and even the Germans will probably bring some pressure on us, not only on economic matters, on matters other than economic, our relations with our neighbours. That is a part of the world. We live in that kind of world. It is no use pretending that we can get out of the world and the pressures will disappear.

Let me say in conclusion, I started by saying that we don't need any vision and I think at the same time all of us have a vision. For my part I have no great ambitions for India to be a big player anywhere. Yes, we have to play our part internationally, we have got to live in this world, we have to live by our wits, our export ratio should grow. All the talk of major power, major role somehow frightens me. I am quite happy with a modest role. If in my lifetime I can say that there is nobody below the poverty line and I am going to live fairly long, at least another twenty-five years—it is good enough; beyond that let other people take care of what needs to be done. It is not that easy.

I was struck by three figures that were mentioned today. Our per capita income is $350 per annum. The per capital income of Malaysia and Thailand is $1,400. Our friends from Korea say their per capita income today is $5,600. It happens that 1,400 is four times 350 and 5,600 is sixteen times 350. So, to be where the Malaysians are or where the Thais are, no great nations, we have to double our income twice and to be where Korea is we have to double our income four times. That is what it amounts to. To do that in twenty-five years, which is, let us say, my lifetime, if you want to reach even the Malaysian standard in twenty-five years and if you want to increase your income fourfold in real terms, that means your per capita income must be doubled every twelve years, which means it must grow every year at 6 per cent, which means, given the population rise at 2 per cent your real income must grow at 8 per cent per annum. Nobody would say that is an easy job. So when I say that that is my dream, it is not a very small dream, it is a very large dream. But in relation to the rest of the world by then we probably will be having a per capita income of $22,000 and we will still be where we are relatively. But that is probably good enough for us. We are where we are, we start from where we are.

I will end by saying only one thing. I said there is such a thing as different forms of capitalism. At the end of the day, when you talk of any society, there is no escape from different groups having to live together. In political terms you talk of different groups with different languages, different religions, different regions. In economic terms, the different groups are consumers, the workers, the savers, the shareholders, the managers and, if you like, the government which ought to look after the interests of the poorest of the people. How you reconcile the interests of all these people and how all of us remember the interests of all these parties together, not just that the high remembers the interests of the low but also that the low remembers the interests of the high—that, I think is the test. Ultimately, inflation is the reflection of the struggle between social classes for a higher share in the national income. Money is only a medium through which inflation passes. But the driving force for inflation is the struggle between different classes to get a higher share in the national income than what the other classes are prepared to surrender. How do you find a way out of conflicting interests that retard growth, that create populism, that permit politicians to pervert economic policies, that generate envy and jealousy and the rivalry and the lack of care as between each other—that is the acid test. I hope Mr Mahindra does not mean that he does not care because if people like him do not care then there is no future for this country. The Indian business community played a remarkable part in getting India politically free. I think they will have to play the same part in making us economically free, to make India economically independent, truly self-reliant in the sense that within five or ten years we can say our foreign debt is not growing, it is going down. We will have to get there. The only way we can get there is by creating a certain amount of current account surplus. If you are aiming at current account balance in any case, then creating a little surplus is not that far behind.

By all means, we should have a dream but that dream will have to be to say we are all Indians, we have to live in this country, we have to prosper in this country, our children will have to live in this country. There is talk of freedom everywhere, of movement of goods, of movement of capital. Have you ever heard any talk about movement of people? Is anybody ready to admit Indian labour on the ground that economically it makes sense to say that labour also should move freely? Five, ten, hundred, ten thousand Indians can go abroad. For the millions of our people this is our land and this is where we have to make a living. We will make a good living only if we agree that we have to take care of each other, not through envy, not through jealousy, but through constructive, creative, wealth-building activities. I do not think that business can simply say that it exists only for itself.

CHAPTER 21

India's Economic Reforms and Development*

Felicitation volumes generally suffer from one weakness: since the contributors are specialists in diverse fields, the collection as a whole lacks coherence. Fortunately, this collection of fifteen essays to honour Dr Manmohan Singh on his sixty-fifth birthday is free from this infirmity. It was only natural for the editors to decide that the process of economic reforms initiated by Dr Singh in 1991 should provide the central focus and that contributions should be invited from among the many renowned economists who have known and admired Dr Singh and have commented on Indian economic policy over the years. If no radical critic of the reform process finds a place among the authors, it is surely understandable in a volume of this nature; and the omission, if one wants to call it so, is amply compensated by the fact that the contributors, while generous in their recognition of Dr Singh's personal and intellectual qualities, are objective enough to emphasize both the significance and the limitations of his achievement. The limitations are largely sins of omission rather than of commission and arise not from lack of awareness or will but of political muscle. Dr Singh himself has often acknowledged this. The fact that two years after he relinquished office, the agenda he left unfinished remains almost equally so tells its own tale.

The editors deserve our gratitude not just for assembling a very distinguished cast of authors. They have themselves provided a very useful introduction which summarizes succinctly the views and findings of each of the contributors. There is value added also in the few but very astute comments they have offered on their own. Thus, while commenting on

* Originally published in the *Economic and Political Weekly*, 30 May 1998.

Dr Rangarajan's essay, they wonder how monetary aggregates can affect short-run output and yet leave the long-term output unchanged. They provide their own tentative answer that the inflation accompanying the short-term positive impact perhaps takes its toll in the long run. Even on matters of detail, when something is striking, they draw our attention to it, for example, to Vijay Joshi's preference for a statutory ceiling on government borrowing rather than some illusory independence of the Central Bank, and Deepak Lal's radical suggestion that all foreign aid and domestic public expenditure on social programmes and safety nets should be channelled through NGOs.

Partly by design—and partly, I suspect, by happenstance—the essays are grouped in four sections. The ones on "Reform and Poverty" and "Centre-State Relations" and much of the second group dealing with sectoral problems must be specifically designed. But the one entitled "India's Development Strategy" seems more an attempt to cap important contributions. This reviewer would have preferred separate sections on macroeconomic management and sectoral reforms and missed essays on labour market and financial reforms and on privatization. But even our most resourceful editors could not, I presume, call all the tunes they might have wanted.

The first section on Development Strategy raises some interesting questions. Amartya Sen (and Srinivasan and others) recall Dr Singh's 1964 book and rightly give him credit for being one of the earliest Indian analysts to emphasize the importance of exports. But does this justify the editors' assertion that as Finance Minister in 1991 Dr Singh was "finally able to implement what his earlier research findings had told him was the right thing to do"? From an appreciation of the importance of exports as a means of obtaining imports needed for growth to a radical shift in the very paradigm of development policy is a long journey; and one hopes Dr Singh himself would some day tell us the story of how and when he travelled that distance. I suspect—as the editors also recognize a little later—that our own experience and that of East Asia must have played a crucial part; and I for one would give credit also to the much-maligned Mrs Thatcher for changing the mindset of so many people.

Bhagwati and Desai both refer to a labour-intensive strategy as a better alternative to what was followed in India. This is now generally accepted and was advocated even then by Vakil and Brahmananda. But we need, I think, to remind ourselves of a few things if what we seek is guidance for the present and the future and not just insight into the past. First, there were many powerful advocates of a labour-intensive strategy in Gandhiji's India then. Their focus was not on a different basket of goods to be produced, but on the same basket produced differently. Amartya Sen's discovery of inferior techniques as distinguished from alternate techniques put an end to that line of reasoning for most people and most purposes. I hope we will not revisit that largely infertile territory once again.

The alternative idea of a labour-intensive export drive as an engine of general growth had very few takers then. As Sen reminds us, even Dr Singh in his 1964 book accepted in broad outline Nurkse's thesis of sluggish demand for exports of developing countries and hence the need for balanced growth. It is the success of Korea, Taiwan and Hong Kong in exporting a wide range of labour-intensive products and the largely unanticipated openness of rich markets, particularly in the US, that changed that perception. That change in perception was beginning to take hold well before 1991 and we too had been struggling since the mid-1960s to export a wide range of goods, albeit in our usual confused ways.

But why did we not succeed as well, for example, as China let alone Korea or Taiwan? Surely the answers are not all or even primarily to be found in different development strategies pursued by the two countries. Srinivasan, who draws pointed attention to the contrast between China and India, argues that our failure to match China in quality, timeliness and reliability of supply is the main culprit and that this is due to infrastructural deficiencies such as those in ports. But what lies behind these differences and deficiencies? Surely not differences in development strategy where China and India are concerned. The main reasons why China scores are non-economic and have something to do with how they can encourage and enforce efficiency and discipline whereas we coddle our labour which is in any case mired in a non-economic mindset where social customs, religious practices and superstitions subtract from economic motivation and encourage a dependency syndrome.

What we need now is not some labour-intensive strategy. We need an all-out effort to increase labour efficiency and discipline everywhere. Labour-intensive exports will then follow and spread as they have done in China not just to textiles and clothing and shoes but a whole range of sophisticated consumer goods and even luxury processed foods. In our case, our artistic and skilled labour can add an extra and unique dimension. Economists have a way of monopolizing the agenda for reforms whereas reforms are needed in India in every walk of life. If we have to take some steps backward from socialism to capitalism or shift from an inward to an outward look, we also have to take several steps forward from feudalism and a medieval mentality towards modernity and capitalism.

There is another vital and practical problem we have to face. Rightly or wrongly, we have sunk a great deal of national substance in building a broad-based industrial structure. It would be suicidal to let our capital-goods industries wither away out of neglect, inefficiency and abject surrender to competition from abroad. The aftermath of the unfortunate Pokhran II adventure is a reminder that the external environment will not always remain open and hospitable. But apart from this, there is no reason why India cannot have a vibrant and competitive iron and steel industry or a machine-building capacity. All that is needed is a bold attempt to restructure all inefficient public enterprises and turn them over, if necessary, to private management or ownership, whether Indian or foreign or joint. What matters is not who owns these industries but that we have on our soil an internationally competitive presence in most departments of industry and trade as indeed of agriculture and other services. What is on Indian soil will be managed and operated by Indians essentially and remain Swadeshi in spirit irrespective of where the shareholders reside. So far, successive governments have chosen to let our public sector industries continue by and large to suffocate in avoidable inefficiency.

The dangers of a high rate of inflation are now commonly recognized. But trying to push inflation too far down can also be counterproductive. What rate of inflation then is appropriate? Dr Rangarajan hazards a guess of 6 per cent per annum, and Vijay Joshi of 5 per cent. I suppose the factor that is crucial in this guess is essentially psychological and has to do with when inflation tends to be self-accelerating through the expectations of most people. On such a matter, dogmatism is hardly warranted. But I should think inflation of 5 or 6 per cent per annum is on the high side and I would plead ideally for around 3 per cent as likely to stick and just necessary to offset a part of the risk to investors and to facilitate the transfer of resources from one sector to the other.

Of the sectoral essays in the second part of the volume those by Montek Ahluwalia (infrastructure), Ashok Gulati (agriculture) and Vijay Joshi (fiscal stabilization) are a fine blend of a lucid exposition of the relevant facts and issues and balanced judgement on policy conclusions that follow. My own prejudices are so much in line with theirs that my only reaction is to ask for more. From Ahluwalia, I would have liked to know what exactly are the lessons we have learnt, as he claims, about how to deal with problems of regulatory interface and risk mitigation? While we all agree on rational user charges, one needs a discussion of what these might be in our actual circumstances and whether those affected should be compensated and how. In theory, and indeed in justice, those who have long enjoyed undeserved rents should not be compensated. But in practice, one is forced to do so. Does this not negate much of the benefit of abolishing subsidies?

Some of us, I remember, were unhappy when Dr Singh lowered subsidies on fertilizers and followed this up by revising support prices. Vijay Joshi argues that in the case of agricultural subsidies, there would be no general need for compensation if concurrently external trade in agriculture was freed, as it should be, it will result in higher prices for agricultural commodities and provide compensation against the loss of subsidies. I cannot help feeling however that when one deals with major sectors like agriculture affecting millions of families, we need the whole scenario of liberalization to be laid out quantitatively and in detail and over time so as to reveal all the dimensions of policy and conflict of interests so that compromises, if politically unavoidable, are made with least damage to the whole process of liberalization. What one needs is a time and quantity profile of the major consequences as they might unfold themselves. If economists cannot provide such scenarios, they should not complain if the process of reform remains somewhat half-baked and driven more by faith and opportunity than anything else.

One of the more interesting pieces in this volume is that by Dr Ajit Singh on corporate governance, a subject not much discussed in India. In conventional wisdom, mergers and takeovers are seen as competitive instruments for weeding out weak corporate governance in favour of more efficient ones. Ajit Singh questions this. But it is not clear what conclusion follows from this. If he is right, no active steps should be taken to encourage a market in corporate governance. But I doubt if it also follows that active steps should be taken to discourage such a development. The model of Germany and Japan which he commends is not static and has come in of late for a great deal of criticism and pressure for change from within as well as without.

The editors have certainly showed sound judgement in inviting in the third section specific contributions to the debate on Reform and Poverty. This is an area where a great deal of righteous emotion and even indignation is invested, and it is of the utmost importance that we look at this vital problem of poverty eradication in the cool light of reason and experience. Deepak Lal is at his provocative best in his analysis of poverty and the best ways of mitigating it, and Kirit Parikh and Tendulkar have their feet firmly grounded in Indian realities.

Despite the air of controversy that surrounds this subject, I venture to think that most of us would endorse some propositions, for example, that growth is the best long-term answer to poverty, that the process of growth will leave some persons mired in poverty, that such persons need special help which in poor developing countries should be provided not by imitating ambitious and generalized welfare schemes in the richer countries but by more targeted provision, preferably through employment schemes. I for one would also agree that provision of finance through public sources should not necessarily require public provision of the services concerned, which in many cases could be better provided by private or voluntary organizations.

Differences will remain about the feasibility of targeting in special cases and about the scope for combining public finance with private provision. I doubt, for example, if the State should or would be able to vacate a large part of primary or secondary education. Even Deepak Lal, having made his radical suggestion about NGOs, is obliged to remark: "The only reservation I would have about such a scheme is the continuing economic illiteracy shown by so many NGOs." I am afraid the NGO s and the private sector, like all human institutions, are prone to the same infirmities we rightly bemoan in the public sector. In our disillusion with one, we should not romanticize about the others. Not a monopoly of anyone but competition, even imperfect competition, and coexistence with checks and balances is the right recipe for most human institutions.

The one area of controversy that will also remain is the need, scope and wisdom of a redistributive policy that goes beyond poverty eradication. I am inclined to agree that an active policy of redistribution is not likely to succeed much and can even be counterproductive—except in the case of provision of mass education and primary health and hygiene. But questions of redistribution going beyond poverty eradication are at the heart of all political activity and it would be foolish to think that we can simply laugh them out of court. The process of economic reform itself is essentially redistributive and we cannot avoid asking which part of the redistribution is unjust or harmful and needs to be remedied and which does not. Distributive justice is also an essential part of public finance and he would be a bold man who advocates abolishing government budgets altogether. Even much of private activity like pricing or wage bargaining or eviction from land and buildings is motivated by the desire to shift the distribution of income and property one way or another; and as long as human beings are what they are, the State will have to retain an active role in distribution at all levels even if this role is exercised sparingly and as indirectly as possible.

The final section on Centre-State Relations reminds us of the enormous debt we owe to Raja Chelliah and Amresh Bagchi and to the institute over which they presided not just for a better understanding of all aspects of public finance but also for a detailed blueprint for reform in this vital area. I would commend, in particular, Chelliah's reminder that in the general rush for decentralization, we should not forget that the Centre must be strong enough to be able to perform certain vital functions which it alone can do. These include not just defence, external relations and law and order but macroeconomic stability, retaining and reviving a common market, harmonizing essential economic policies to these ends even when such policies are within the state sphere and protecting the sanctity of the Constitution, in particular, by protecting the rights of all citizens and by mitigating regional inequalities. In the current phase of decentralization and coalition politics based on regional parties, we are all too likely to weaken the nation by weakening the Centre economically.

The final essay by Dr Pai Panandikar is a welcome reminder that the process of economic reform cannot be discussed meaningfully without reference to the political context. Although he focuses on the political economy of Centre-state relations, the points he raises have a much wider significance. Much of the advice on economic reform, particularly from international agencies, is perfectionist in nature and assumes that governments which are otherwise to be distrusted are omnipotent nevertheless. They can and must balance the budget, remove all subsidies, cause retrenchment, treat sons of the soil no better than outsiders, remove all distortions and preferential arrangements and scrap all controls. But the stark fact is that governments are neither omnipotent nor even objectively benevolent. While we must devote much more thought to political reform and indeed reform the polity to the extent we can, the fact would remain that economic policy will have to be shaped in an imperfect political and social context. Not perfectionist and extremist or simplistic and rigid rules and remedies but a dynamic search for the optimum, for the second and even the third best based on compromises and buying time, is of the essence of the political life, at least in a democracy which has vast differences to reconcile. I do not understand why so many of us are reluctant to concede that authoritarianism has much to do with the economic success of China, Taiwan, Korea and even Singapore and Indonesia and that democracy in India takes an economic toll. If we value democracy, we should be willing to accept that it is worth paying some economic price for it, at least for a generation or so.

Take, for example, the knotty problem of fiscal deficits. Vijay Joshi rightly argues that a ceiling on the monetary deficit may not deter governments from excessive borrowing from the market. He, therefore, recommends a statutory limit on the total fiscal deficit. But he has to qualify this by accepting that there would be need for override clauses to take care of emergencies. The trouble is that for politicians every difficulty is an emergency. The states in India have never had the right to run monetary deficits. But they have almost routinely been bailed out for political reasons. This does not mean that a ceiling on budget deficits may not serve a purpose. It only means that it serves a purpose not because of the simplicity of the rule but only as a check and balancing device which in real life will be honoured as much in breach as in observance.

All in all, this admirable volume brings to the fore most of the important issues that arise in the process of economic reforms. The areas of achievement as well as the unfinished agenda are well delineated. Of the unfinished agenda, I would like in particular to emphasize two which have not received much attention. We need a searching look at all our labour legislation. The issue is not just closures and retrenchment. Organized labour today follows restrictive policies in regard to day-to-day management which makes any pursuit of efficiency, integrity or discipline impossible. Our judges, arbitrators and even the general public encourage and tolerate this coercive behaviour. We need a complete change in mindset in this regard; and we need to consider fresh legislation on the lines of what prevails in Singapore and in post-Thatcher Britain. The second major and related lacuna is in regard to privatization. What is needed is not just sale of public shares to ease the budgetary position or even to reduce public stake to a minority. What is needed in most cases is to transfer management and sizeable ownership to a new private stakeholder of repute which should be left free to restructure and rationalize. It is high time we consider the best way of inviting bids and evaluating them from reputable private firms, domestic or foreign, for most public enterprises in industry and trade, if not in finance.

I have already referred to a better understanding and reforms of the political process as well as of social and religious norms and practices. Questions of distribution also cannot be confined merely to poverty eradication. Beyond this, there are many unanswered questions on which our understanding is still imperfect and needs to be refined. It is now recognized that deregulation and decontrol and indeed privatization (say, of infrastructure) should be accompanied by some regulatory framework to preserve competition and protect the public interest. This is all the more true of the financial sector. But we do not know much about how this should be done in different spheres without bringing back the ills of government activism. This is particularly true of environmental regulation where public agitation and the inherent difficulties in the measurement of costs and benefits further complicate the problem.

It is also now agreed that competition does not always emerge spontaneously. But it is not clear how best governments can encourage it. Take for instance the universal experience that financial markets are seldom perfect and tend to neglect the needs of the small and the weak and the new. The US dealt with this, perhaps inadvertently, by restricting banks to operate in only limited areas for decades. This forced them to be active in seeking all clients, whether small or weak or new. What is the answer in the present context?

The new global markets with increasing competition and technological change have also multiplied risks and uncertainty even if this has spurred profits and growth at the same time. We understand little about all the risks that are emerging and about whether and to what extent some of the risks could be anticipated and should be reduced or mitigated and how. But surely we cannot just say, "Let the chips fall where they may as regeneration through destruction is also the way of Lord Shiva and Mother Kali"!

The truth of the matter is that despite all the talk of a new consensus and a few simple rules that should guide economies towards prosperity, the task of economic management has become even more difficult and complex. We do have major guidelines and we have learnt much from the recent past. But in a fast changing and politically vibrant world, economic wisdom cannot be reduced to a few commandments which in any case will have to be interpreted, quantified and reconciled in actual practice. Economists at least should be grateful for this as otherwise they would soon be cast off as historical debris left behind by the very march of their discipline.

CHAPTER 22

Current Unease with Indian Economic Reform*

The latest Reserve Bank of India Report on Currency and Finance describes the success of Indian economic reforms in the following words:

> India is no longer an economy of scarcity and shortages: food stocks and foreign exchange reserves are plentiful; shortages and rationing of essential goods and materials are memories of the past. In the macroeconomic and financial spheres, inflation has been contained, external debt indicators have improved, exchange rate is flexible and the country is free of financial repression. The trade account is open and India has become much more integrated with the world economy. All this has been reflected in a relatively high rate of economic growth over the decade and a significant reduction in poverty in the country. The economy has also become more resilient to shocks, both domestic and external: the twin shocks of the drought and increasing oil prices in the past year have been absorbed with relative ease.

The author of this paragraph could have gone much further in the same vein. He could have dwelt, for example, on increased freedom of choice for the ordinary consumer and on the freedom for many from having to kowtow to petty clerks and peons and politicians—not for receiving any favours, but for getting their legitimate due. People in authority seldom appreciate what this freedom from indignity and humiliation means to honest citizens. I was myself reminded of this rather rudely several years ago when a young lady lecturer from Lucknow insisted on seeing me at my home one late evening. She had spent the whole day in the Ministry of Finance for getting permission to travel abroad to attend an academic conference. She had to stand for hours, leered at by every passing male.

* This paper was presented at the Stanford University Conference, June 2003.

At the end, she was asked to come the next day. She said she would not get into that office again and would rather return to Lucknow and forgo the first, and perhaps the only, opportunity she had to go abroad. Such freedom from indignity is not reflected in GDP figures. But that is what it is all about.

And yet, despite all these real and substantial achievements, I sense that twelve years on, the reform process has left many people with a sense of unease. I use the word "unease" advisably; I do not sense dissatisfaction or disenchantment, let alone opposition. I honestly believe that most persons are happy with economic reform. While reform may not figure prominently in any of the election manifestos this year or next, the process will go on. Maybe, limp along would be a better prediction. But it is unlikely to be reversed.

There are still people who rail against globalization and the multinationals. But even they no longer say that reform has marginalized or de-industrialized or enslaved India. There are not many who would say today that the poor have become poorer. If you ask me, the poor have not become poorer in India for the last forty years, let alone the last ten. The poor have become less poor, the rich have become richer and both have become more numerous for most of the time.

Why then the sense of unease? Who is uneasy? Is this unease justified? If it is, what can be done about it? As in everything else, only a few persons are seriously concerned with evaluating the reform process. By now, most ordinary persons are perhaps bored by the expression, even if they may not be indifferent to some or the other manifestation of the process.

The unease, I think, comes from several things and only a part of it is justified. There is unease that:

(a) microeconomic reform is accompanied by macroeconomic deterioration at least in its fiscal aspect;
(b) even in regard to microeconomic reform, there is a long unfinished agenda;
(c) some of the reform measures have misfired or not taken hold; and perhaps the most common among economists;
(d) there is not yet a decisive impact on growth and employment generation.

Personally, I would add:

(e) there is no decisive impact on corruption;
(f) we have frittered away our rich inheritance in higher education; and
(g) we have not enlisted the support of civil society in the service of reform.

Not all this unease is justified. But one can draw important lessons from all of them.

The point about macroeconomic deterioration, at least in the fiscal sphere, is both valid and vital. There are apologists who argue that budget deficits have not had their anticipated effect. Inflation has not risen, interest rates have not gone up, there is no foreign exchange crisis and no sign of crowding out of private investment. But there has been ruinous, continuing and increasing "crowding out", so to say, of useful public expenditure on health, education, irrigation, agricultural research and economic infrastructure. If budget deficits have not crowded out private investment despite hardly any increase in the rate of saving, surely the conclusion is inescapable and worrying that private investment is not buoyant.

Macroeconomic mismanagement, whether internal or external, does repress growth sooner or later. Micro reform and macro health work well together. One of the smartest things done in 1991 was that decontrol of industry and liberalization of foreign trade were accompanied by substantial devaluation. This is not often mentioned now. But it was that macroeconomic adjustment which gave industry time to adjust to more competition and made the capacity then legalized actually usable by opening better opportunities for export. The initial spurt in growth after 1991 is largely attributed to this macroeconomic reform rather than to microeconomic reforms which take time to produce growth. Without macroeconomic health, the efficiency gains of microeconomic reform cannot be large and cannot endure.

I am afraid I am not sanguine that a decisive impact on fiscal deficits will be made in the near- or the medium-term future. So far, reduction in interest rates and privatization are the only routes taken to show token improvements in the financial position of the government. Both have severe limitations. Without substantial cuts in subsidies and administration and some even in defence, there cannot be reduction in public expenditure. There are limits to better collection of taxes. Reduction in customs duties and in direct taxes does slow down the growth in revenues—at least in the short and the medium term. The industrially advanced countries dealt with this problem by a superb confidence trick. They introduced a very substantial and comprehensive Value Added Tax (VAT) which is nothing but a large and proportional income-tax without virtually any exemption limit. I am afraid even the VAT, if and when introduced in India, will be rather modest and shot through with exemptions and will, therefore, invite evasion and avoidance. Without a sea-change in the political climate, the fiscal situation will remain worrisome.

On the other hand, I do not share the unease of many persons about the unfinished agenda of microeconomic reform. Part of this agenda is not all that necessary in my judgement and I consider some suggested reforms unrealistic in a democracy. In a sense, the agenda for reform like the agenda for individual perfection will always be unfinished. For my part, I think we should now stop talking of an agenda of reform as if it is a laundry list. Reform rings a bell for five or ten years. After that, it is likely to ring hollow. That does not mean that we give up the fight on each individual front. By all means let us concentrate on individual tasks. But there is danger not just of creating boredom but even resentment by perfectionist sermons akin to the Ten Commandments. What we need now is concentration on individual sectors rather than on some comprehensive conceptual agenda. That is what I think this Conference seeks to address.

The democratic world is always untidy; and while untidiness must always be fought, some of it must be endured. There is much talk these days about plural societies, multicultural or multiracial societies. But all democratic societies are plural by definition as indeed they are secular by definition—even if they are not multiracial or multicultural. They are plural because they respect and recognize the rights of each individual and group. They have several objectives and several conflicting but legitimate interests to reconcile. Any peaceful reconciliation of divergent objectives and interests inevitably involves compromises.

Let me take three illustrations from what would figure on the unfinished agenda of most economists: agriculture, labour markets and privatization. Agriculture is the subject of a special session at this seminar. So let me be brief. I have never understood why no country has been able to abolish the special privileges of farmers even when they are so obviously in conflict with the interest of most consumers. At times, the farmers are denied their due to please consumers. I am afraid this seesaw game will continue in India as elsewhere. Onion exports will be freed and then controlled and freed again. Input subsidies will go up and down. Price support for major products will not disappear. The utmost one can hope for is more rational support, abolition of restrictions on movement and the like. But the success would be partial and there would be setbacks. There is no agenda to be finished here but a constant tug-of-war, hopefully with some durable advance.

On labour reform, I am more sanguine; not because I see much change in law but because competition will assert itself to some extent to clip the wings of militant unions. But trade unions will remain; and they are more powerful in India, because they are an integral part of political parties. Exit policy may be less stringent than it is now, but some restrictions will remain on the books. Contract labour will be protected one way or another. But reasonable solutions will be worked out by workers and employees in individual cases when the writing on the wall is clear. This is already happening.

On privatization, my views are somewhat different from those of many mainstream economists. In India, privatization is fuelled by a basically flawed rationale of making budget deficits look smaller. That leads to targetry, which makes for haste and, therefore, mistakes and consequently unease and even opposition. Selling government property is no different from selling bonds from the point of view of fiscal responsibility. Both crowd out private investment or encroach upon private saving. Some long-term fiscal gain would be there if the public assets sold earn less than the amount of interest saved. But this will not happen in every case and would in any event depend on the degree of sophistication in disinvestment, the availability of a large number of possible buyers and the calculations of potential buyers about their ability to restructure acquired businesses. What that means is a selective, measured, well-planned and unhurried approach and a willingness to open the bidding process to as large an area of competition as possible, including foreign competition. This is less likely, particularly after Iraq.

I also believe that some public sector presence is necessary in some areas to give competition to the private sector and serve some social interest. I would include major financial institutions in this category. If governments are not perfect, neither are private entrepreneurs. We have had enough financial scams of late to remind us of this truth. I fear that excessive emphasis on privatization has tended to turn attention away from much-needed autonomy of viable public enterprises.

As for mistakes made in the reform process, everyone would have their own preferred list. Mine includes three rather different kinds of examples. Telecommunications reform is more a muddle than a mistake, and to some extent, the muddle continues, but by and large, we have come through. The Centaur Hotel in Mumbai, which was resold at huge profits soon after disinvestment, is surely an embarrassment caused by haste. It is the failure in the power sector that is more damaging. The supreme folly of Enron where full recovery of costs plus profits was guaranteed in foreign exchange passes imagination; and the Enron story still continues to sour public sentiment. The disappointment with the Orissa experiment in privatization of electricity distribution—and the doubts concerning a similar experiment in Delhi—have thrown the whole question of reform in the power sector back to square one. We will have to start all over again with drawing up a new roadmap. Meanwhile, despite environmental concerns, exploitation of cheap coal by the public and the private sector for power generation to feed existing grids is likely to be the major source of relief. While some mistakes are inevitable in real life, there is clearly a lesson here for more careful planning, free from ideological or other haste.

Many economists feel uneasy about the Indian economic reform process because they feel that the slow pace of reform and, perhaps, wrong sequencing have come in the way of achieving rates of growth of 8 per cent per annum or even more. I am afraid all this talk of a 8 or 9 per cent per annum growth in real terms to be achieved on an average over decades is unrealistic and counterproductive. It makes the achievable good look bad by comparison with utopian dreams. Growth is such a seductive word that it makes most of us part with reason. All societies work within certain limits. There is also the experience of history. One swallow does not make a summer. Nor does one China make the world—even if you take it at its word.

We achieved 5.5 per cent per annum growth in real terms in the 1980s. We have achieved something similar in the 1990s, hopefully with some improvement in the quality of growth at least in regard to external finance. I would be happy if we can sustain this rate of growth in the first decade of this century with some further qualitative improvements—in public finance, in standards of health and education, in environmental care, in family planning and in employment generation. This would be no mean achievement. I wish we would stop deluding our people about 8 or 9 per cent growth. Let them applaud a 5.5 per cent or 6 per cent rate of growth of good quality rather than bemoan the lack of an even higher rate of growth.

As for the disappointment with the increase in unemployment, I have very little to say. The data are not good; and there are many factors at work. Definitive conclusions are not easy. I have reconciled myself to the view that some transitional unemployment is unavoidable and that a reduction in structural unemployment will come only after a decisive decline in population growth.

Let me now come to my own corner of concern. One of the greatest disappointments with the reform process is that it has not made much impression on corruption. Reform is widely advertised as an answer to corruption. To some extent this has happened. But we know now that corruption is a much tougher nut to crack and requires action beyond economics. Much more can be done, for example, by harnessing new technology. This has been done in respect of railway reservations. It can also be done for land records, both rural and urban. But a major feasible attack can only come from a detailed and painstaking review of all laws, regulations, administrative procedures and the like to eliminate much accumulated irrelevance and discretion. A review of all regulatory authorities particularly at the state level is also necessary. Even at the Centre, where decontrol has been followed by new regulatory authorities, there is still much confusion about what is intended and who can and cannot do what. Regulation, like control, also implies some discretion. All this creates fertile ground for corruption. That is why regulatory authorities also need continuous watch and vigilance.

Sometimes I feel that the margin of tolerance for corruption in India is very high. But it is the result of decades of adjustment to what appeared and indeed became inevitable. It is time that this vicious circle is broken and people's natural appetite for freedom from corruption is revived.

Another area of unease not often highlighted is the deplorable state of higher education. I am glad that this is a subject for a special session at this Conference. We are still living on the capital built up in the 1950s and the '60s in this field. Believe me, there is so much politicization and political control and populism in this area that it is a mockery to say that most Indian universities are providing anything approaching higher education. Once again, people are finding some way out of this by voluntary effort and resorting to private enterprise. But I do not believe that higher education which deserves the name can ever be wholly self-financing. If for no other reason, this is so because higher education must attract students of high merit. This cannot be done when admissions are ruled by money or political calculations or limited possibilities of cross-subsidization. A generous system of student support is the very foundation of higher education.

One more area that concerns me is the indifference and even the hostility of the voluntary or the NGO sector to economic reform. One would have thought that the voluntary sector would be concerned with issues of freedom, choice, reduction in corruption and consumer protection. Most consumer associations in India, however, worry only about petty cheating by retail traders. They are ignorant of or indifferent to the vast exploitation of consumers—both rich and poor—by lobbies of all kinds.

Let me give you only one example. In the state of Gujarat where I come from, vegetable oil prices are a very sensitive political issue. Governments have lost when vegetable oil prices have risen a great deal. We have now some redress as imports of vegetable oils and oilseeds have been made free. But they are subject to an import duty of 70 per cent—till recently it was more than 90 per cent. Is this not a fit case for consumer associations and voluntary agencies to agitate on behalf of the consumers? For fifty years, we sacrificed the consumer for the sake of grandiose notions of industrialization and of marching rapidly to join the ranks of more advanced nations. We now know that the fruits of development were largely monopolized by workers and producers who were organized and articulate. Should the consumers remain for ever unorganized and inarticulate?

I have spent a lot of time talking of unease and have perhaps created even more unease in this room by what I have said. But I hope I have made it clear that my own unease comes from my belief that reforms are necessary as much for freedom and justice as they are for efficiency and growth. Our achievements are considerable and we should not be disheartened if the pace of reform is slow by some standards or the rate of growth inadequate. Much remains to be done as it always will. But let us not create unnecessary unease by raising expectations to unrealistic levels. What is needed is to enlarge both the area and the constituency for reform. The time now is not for general preaching of reform but for more painstaking and detailed work on individual issues and sectors so that rapid corrective action can be taken whenever opportunity arises.

Part VI

Banking and the Financial System

CHAPTER 23

Role of Banks and Financial Institutions in Corporate Finance*

The role of financial institutions, and I include banks in this general category, is supposed to be that of bringing lenders and borrowers together, of serving as an intermediary between those who save more than they can invest themselves and those who are willing to invest more than their own capacity to save. Put thus, it may well appear that the expertise which bankers and financiers require is essentially of a financial type, that is, it is concerned mainly with the financial standing of potential savers and lenders. There is no doubt that for many long decades before Independence, financial institutions saw their task essentially in financial terms, that is, in terms of security offered, soundness of the borrower as revealed by certain ratios derived from balance-sheets and the like—and these ratios or criteria are still relevant although I should think seminars like this can well examine whether changing circumstances may not require changes in accepted financial or accounting norms.

In industrially advanced capitalist countries it may still be true that financial expertise is by and large all that is required to run financial institutions—although things are changing even in those countries. But any such assumption would be clearly inappropriate in a country like India where financial institutions are specifically charged with a developmental role and where they are expected to help implement the priorities and policies periodically laid down by the government in five-year plans and other policy statements.

* Address at the seminar organized by the Management Consultants' Association of India at Bombay, 26 October 1979; subsequently published in the *Reserve Bank of India Bulletin*, September–October 1979.

One major distinguishing feature of a developing economy is that savings as well as entrepreneurs with clearly defined investment propositions are not easy to come by; apart from bringing the two together, financial institutions have, therefore, to play their part in inducing and mobilizing more savings as well as in creating more investment opportunities by advising potential entrepreneurs. Indeed, since the entrepreneurial base is narrow and needs to be enlarged to include people of smaller and smaller means, very often, there are no balance-sheets of existing companies to examine but only technical data—often poorly grasped—regarding the processes proposed to be employed and markets expected to be tapped. It is in performing this creative or developmental role of taking the inchoate ideas of potential investors and giving them a more rational shape after a sound assessment from the technical as well as marketing and financial point of view—in short, the role of making more and more persons and propositions creditworthy and not just sitting in judgement on them—that financial institutions can benefit from advice from appropriate consulting firms.

To some extent, the technical and managerial or marketing expertise required will have to be developed in-house or organized in suitable institutions. But there should be plenty of scope here for tapping the talents available with consulting firms. I found the literature sent by your Association interesting in this connection although I must admit that when I read that your charges range from Rs 250 to Rs 1,600 per day per consultant, I had the uneasy feeling that you might be well out of reach, at least of the nationalized banks. Perhaps you might consider bankers as privileged clients entitled to free advice at least for some years; and I think it would be a fair exchange if you insist that this privilege would be reserved only for those bankers who have helped you financially towards your education or initial establishment expenses. I should remind you that most of you qualify for assistance under the category of the priority sector—although I am sorry to say that I was informed last week at the Indian Institute of Management in Ahmedabad that this privilege applied to graduates of technical institutes but not to graduates of management institutes. Perhaps you can persuade your banker friends to do away with this discrimination.

Let me add also that the services of management consultants may be useful to financial institutions not only at the initial stage of setting up an enterprise that is being financed but also at later stages if only because enterprises have a way of becoming sick or even of being deliberately made sick. The very large involvement of banks and other financial institutions in sick accounts implies that there is much that needs to be done at earlier stages which is not done, such as assessment of incipient sickness, judgement as to whether sickness is curable and how much would the cure cost, judgement as to whether sickness is the result of fraudulent practices requiring change in management, provision of new and competent and dedicated management, possible merger with other companies and the like. All these are areas where professional managers or management consultants can help.

They can help also in devising better management practices for the banks themselves which are constantly growing in size—and I hope sophistication as well—and as such require more rational and scientific management practices. I should think our training institutions such as the National Institute of Bank Management and the various colleges run by the banks can also benefit by cooperation with members of your Association.

As far as the subject matter of today's seminar is concerned, I do not think I need to dwell at any length before this audience on the role played by financial institutions and banks in corporate finance. Let me just recall for you a few facts and raise a few questions which I think deserve greater attention.

Let me remind you first of all that as far as financial institutions are concerned, we have adopted a different approach towards them from the approach adopted towards the corporate sector of Indian industry. In relation to industrial development, we have adopted by and large a policy of mixed economy so that there are major corporate entities today in both the public as well as the private sector and new ones are coming into being also in both sectors. But for quite some time we have regarded financial institutions as a part—indeed a vital part—of the commanding heights of the economy which have to be occupied by the public sector. Maybe the approach initially was to take measured steps to fill up known gaps in the institutional structure; and this was reflected in the nationalization of life insurance and the Imperial Bank and in the establishment of institutions like Industrial Development Bank of India (IDBI) and ICICI. But very soon, this policy developed into virtual public control over and ownership of all major financial institutions as a deliberate step to achieve certain positive national goals as well as to overcome some negative tendencies within the economy. True, even today, there are private banks—some of them of considerable size—and several financial institutions of medium size specializing in certain areas or lines of finance such as hire-purchase; and it is true also that corporate entities have direct access to savings not only through their own internally generated resources but also through direct acceptance of deposits or issue of shares and debentures.

But the growing preponderance of public financial institutions and the demands on them for serving a variety of public purposes are clearly irresistible; and it is this aspect which needs to be kept in view when we assess the role of financial institutions in India in corporate finance and the direction which we may like to give to these institutions for their future development. And let there be no mistake about it: there is often a real and unavoidable conflict at least in the short run between different desirable objectives and between these objectives and financial prudence which needs to be resolved—and not just wished away or swept under the carpet by popular rhetoric. In assessing the role of financial institutions, we must record their substantial achievements which derive in large measure from their public ownership and control. But let us note also the broader objective, which still remains largely unachieved. Let us also recognize the conflicts and shortcomings so that the best does not become the enemy of the good. In public policy there is always continuing need for clarification, assessment and modification in the light of changing needs and experience; and it is this aspect of looking to the future rather than harping on past achievements which should be the centre of attention at seminars like this.

As far as past achievements are concerned, the commercial banks have certainly succeeded to a considerable extent in mobilizing private savings, particularly after nationalization. Thus, the additional deposits mobilized by the banking system today, that is, some Rs 5,000 crore (1 crore = 10 million) in a single year, exceed the total of such deposits outstanding at the time of nationalization of major banks. The traditional approach, as described by the Shroff Committee in 1954, which was "largely based on the British tradition of commercial banking under which banks as a rule provide only the working capital requirements of industries, particularly on the security of floating assets and eschew long-term advances against fixed assets", has also changed. In the 1970s the share of term loans in total advances of scheduled commercial banks has been growing rapidly: from about 11 per cent in 1972 to some 16 per cent in 1977. In the case of term loans to large and medium industries, the share has increased from 8 per cent in 1972 to about 11.5 per cent in 1977. The investment of banks in company shares and debentures is, however, small—on an average some Rs 8 crore per annum between 1971 and 1978.

In keeping with the emphasis on smaller people and priority sectors such as agriculture, small industry and professionals, the relative share of large and medium industries in total advances of scheduled commercial banks has declined from about 60 per cent in 1968 to slightly less than 40 per cent in 1979. Judged in absolute amounts, however, advances to large and medium industries have been rising by about Rs 500 crore per year on an average during the past decade.

As far as financial institutions specifically designed to give term loans and to subscribe to equity capital are concerned, there is now a wide variety of them both at the national and state level. The share of these institutions in financing industrial investment in the private sector has been increasing at a rapid rate; from around 13 per cent in the early 1960s to about 19 per cent in late 1960s and further to about 30 per cent in the 1970s. What this means essentially is that there is hardly any major investment in the private corporate sector which takes place today without the explicit scrutiny and approval of public financial institutions.

While these are substantial achievements, there is clearly much that still needs to be done by the combined efforts of the state and the financial institutions in achieving many of our cherished national objectives, about which there is general consensus among all sections of society. There is no disagreement, for example, about giving special attention to agriculture and small industry, or about giving higher priority to backward regions or districts or to smaller and poorer parties in general, or about curtailing concentration of economic power in a few hands and in a few metropolitan areas, or indeed about reducing the prevalence of black money and unofficial money and capital markets. Nor is there much disagreement about the public sector having a major share in the development of basic or heavy industries. We have, however, to admit that while progress has been made on all these fronts by the financial institutions, there is much that remains to be done; and I have no doubt your seminar will discuss ways and means of accelerating progress.

But let me mention a few areas where conflicts or conflicting actions arise and where there is need for a clearer policy choice and a consistent approach. Take, for instance, the objective of reducing regional disparities which, let us admit without apportioning blame to anybody, has not been achieved to any great extent. Now it is certainly arguable that it would be desirable to reduce the rigours of industrial and other licensing procedures at least as far as small and medium industries are concerned and to give state governments a larger role in the promotion and regulation of small and medium industries. But as we all know, this would weaken our ability to shift industrial development towards the backward states. Indeed, the financially more viable states are able to offer various incentives by way of better infrastructure facilities, which militate against the objective of reducing regional disparities. Should we not then accept the need for some coordination of policies of state governments? And if this is not possible, should we not recognize that regional disparities are better dealt with by giving the backward regions higher priority in the development of agriculture and social and economic infrastructure where direct action by the State is vital?

To continue with the same area of concern, financial incentives which reduce corporate taxation for enterprises undertaking investment in designated backward regions are found particularly effective in many countries where the incentive is strong enough. In Brazil, for example, the actual tax liability is reduced to the extent of the investment in backward regions subject to certain limits and safeguards. But by and large the companies which benefit by such concessions will be large ones, generally managed and owned by established firms and families. A choice has, therefore, to be made between reducing regional disparities through strong financial incentives and reducing concentration of economic power.

That the choice is a real one and not easy to make can be seen from the policy which was adopted for some time of allowing large firms licences only for industries which were difficult to establish but which were of high priority. Thus the larger firms were encouraged to move away from consumer goods industries and to shift to capital-intensive industries such as fertilizers or basic metals. But this inevitably meant giving large loans from public financial institutions to the large firms and houses, thus blunting the thrust towards reduction of economic power and concentration. The dilemma has to be faced squarely by policymakers and not passed on to financial institutions.

This is not to deny that it is legitimate to ask whether the concern for concentration can be left to be met primarily by the financial institutions which might take upon themselves the responsibility of sharing the management of all large concerns financed by them and/or adopt a discriminatory policy of financing different-size firms to a differing extent. In other words, as an alternative—or supplement—to discrimination in industrial licensing one might consider whether involvement of financial institutions in the management of larger firms and houses or/and a general stipulation that larger houses and firms should find a larger part of their financial requirements from their own resources would serve the purpose.

Active involvement of financial institutions in the management of all large concerns is not easy to achieve and may well be counterproductive. Even today, it is a moot question whether appointment of a director or two serves any real purpose; and one has to ask whether and how a large cadre of knowledgeable and public-spirited professional directors can be assembled and put in place. One has also to consider whether such involvement of financial institutions does not frighten away potential borrowers and investors: this is perhaps happening to some extent, as is evidenced by the paradox of at least some financial institutions having more money than they can invest in their traditional spheres. There is resistance not only to observing the financial norms prescribed by financial institutions, but even more to active involvement in major decisions and perhaps most to the threat of conversion of loans into equity. A practical way has to be found out of this dilemma, with perhaps greater awareness of each other's needs and greater mutual confidence generated by familiarity with each other's ways and greater professionalization of management everywhere. It is in relation to the last that associations like yours can be most useful.

I mentioned a moment ago that to some extent the objective of reduction in economic concentration may be sought through forcing larger firms and houses to rely more on their own resources. Some of you are aware that we have been encouraging banks to follow such a policy as part of the current restrictive credit policy. But again, it has to be admitted that such a policy is not all that easy to implement; and that as a long-term policy such a prescription has limitations. Prima facie, it stands to reason that those who have been established for long should find resources for expansion and new ventures on their own without support from public financial institutions; and to some extent, such a policy is clearly rational and called for. But one must recognize that an enterprise which grows by investment of its own resources develops concentration of ownership in a few hands, whereas sizeable reliance on resources raised in the market would expose it to more democratic currents. Excessive reliance on internal resources also leads to an inefficient allocation of scarce investible resources. However, if larger houses are permitted to rely on the market also for their needs to overcome these objections, we must recognize that sooner or later they will compete with the financial institutions in regard to tapping voluntary savings; and if this competition in turn is restricted in every way we would not have followed any alternative consistently and to its logical conclusion.

It is not my intention to suggest what policy mix would be ideal, as this is partly a matter of what would be feasible in terms of both acceptability to public opinion and ease of implementation in practice. But I hope I have raised sufficient questions to provoke useful discussion and to underline that all policy choices entail a balancing of different considerations so that it is not possible to score heavily on every count.

Let me touch on just one more problem before I conclude. There is often a tendency to think that existing problems can be solved by setting up new institutions. I am not one of those who are opposed in principle to institutional innovation. It does happen that a new institution sometimes means greater concentration on a particular need, even if it does not create new resources and in fact makes an additional claim on scarce managerial resources. But whatever the need for a new institution, there cannot be any compromise with certain overriding principles. First, the overall control of the monetary authority on aggregate credit expansion cannot be diluted in any way. All financial institutions have, therefore, to operate within the general jurisdiction and guidelines of the Central Bank in this regard. Second, however urgent the need, there cannot be any sacrifice of the criterion of financial soundness or viability where credit is involved. Credit is not a gift or a subsidy; and it has to be repaid out of surpluses generated, as otherwise the expansion of credit, no matter how worthy the recipient or the cause, will only result in a waste of scarce national resources which a poor country cannot afford. To encourage any section of society to incur debts which it cannot possibly repay and, even worse, to let it get away with wilful non-repayment, would be to mock the very concept of development and elimination of poverty.

This is not to deny that when circumstances beyond one's control make it difficult to meet repayment schedules, relief must be given promptly whether by the State or the financial institutions depending on the nature of the disaster or the calamity. I think there is scope here for improvement in present arrangements by way of deliberately creating sizeable contingency reserves with the financial institutions. But in the ultimate analysis, resources will always be scarce and there is no escape from applying certain uniform standards laid down in advance to ensure relief where it is needed without jeopardizing the viability of the institutions and without encouraging financial indiscipline and wilful non-repayment on the part of borrowers, be they small or big. It may be—and I share this belief—that our present policies towards large industrial units which become or are made sick are perhaps too indulgent. But if this is so, the remedy lies in tightening discipline towards sick industrial units and not in permitting the malady to spread. Let us also recognize that if large industrial units that turn sick receive favourable assistance from financial institutions, it is not always because the financial institutions prefer it that way in their own interest. It is so because often they are under pressure of public opinion to try and avoid unemployment caused by the closure of inefficient factories. Here again, there is always a difficult choice to be made and the actual course adopted cannot serve all desirable purposes. All I am emphasizing is that there are nevertheless certain basic principles which should not be sacrificed in the interest of society at large.

CHAPTER 24

Capital Market Regulation*

The Indian capital market has gone through substantial changes in the recent past; and we are on the threshold of even more far-reaching changes yet to come. The number of shareholding households in the country is estimated to have increased from some 2 million (1 million = 10 lakh) in 1980 to 15 million in 1990. The total amount of resources raised from the market annually by way of shares and debentures has increased more than tenfold over the past ten years. At the same time, many institutional innovations have been made and policies have moved—albeit haltingly till recently—towards a greater play for market forces and private initiative. The establishment of the Discount and Finance House of India, of several venture capital funds, of new mutual funds, of a credit rating agency for the first time and, indeed, of the Securities and Exchange Board of India, our hosts today, are only some of the examples of recent innovations. With the delicensing of industries and changes in the Monopolies and Restrictive Practices Act, with more welcome attitude to foreign investment and removal or relaxation of interest ceilings and an invitation to the private sector, for example, to start mutual funds, we are certainly in for many more changes. Not all is well, of course, with the Indian capital market, and particularly with the stock exchanges as the Pherwani Committee has so aptly reminded us only recently; and as far as policies are concerned, the process of financial reform so far has been rather sketchy and ad hoc, and we are all eagerly awaiting the Report of the Narasimhan Committee for a blueprint of a more orderly and comprehensive reform.

* This paper was presented at the International Conference on Capital Market Regulations, Bombay, October 1991.

If international experience is any guide, the process of change will have many surprises and uncertainties. Some things will move much faster than we imagine and perhaps in an unexpected direction. Others will not. Institutional change, unlike zero-budgeting, cannot and indeed should not, therefore, disregard the past; and even zero-budgeting at best is a figure of speech more honoured in rhetoric than in reality. Let me, therefore, take as my starting point some distinctive features of the Indian capital market as they may have some significance for the future as well.

A sizeable part of the capital market in India is still unorganized or in the informal sector. A good part of private savings are invested in one's own business, no doubt reflecting in part the predominance and the vitality of the small sector in industry and trade as well as in agriculture. But it is also a measure of the weakness of the link between this sector and the organized markets. Even today, many people invest in the enterprises of their friends and relations, even distant ones, without the benefit of any paper work; and there is black money and wealth in abundance which travels almost freely between the organized and the unorganized markets. The promotional or the developmental role of financial institutions, therefore, has a great deal of scope yet; and this is true of Securities and Exchange Board of India (SEBI) as well.

Perhaps the most distinguishing feature of the Indian financial scene is the preponderance of the State which hardly needs to be documented. Government monopoly of Life Insurance and General Insurance, the ownership of most commercial banks and all mutual funds so far, public promotion and ownership of a number of term-lending institutions, cumbersome regulation of new issues, if not of the stock exchanges and indeed the pre-empting of a large sector of pension and provident funds by direct absorption in State budgets are some of the unique features of the Indian scene—although the Indian example has been followed in many developing countries which regarded India as a pioneer in development finance. And let it be said that the record of public financial institutions in India has been a very creditable one. The possible exceptions are the nationalized banks which have been caught between the jaws of covetous governments and quarrelsome employees. But even here, it is certainly arguable that the very substantial increase in private savings and in the productivity of the small farms and small industry owe a great deal to the nationalized banks.

It is this experience that still keeps alive the appetite in India for new specialized financial institutions with privileged access to resources—a Tourism Finance Corporation today and another for artisans and backward classes tomorrow. There is more than a touch of populism in this as well; and I for one would wish for rather drastic family planning here. But the demand will not go away—and we should at least ask whether we should not restructure and regroup our existing public financial institutions so that a part can compete effectively in deregulated and even globalized markets whereas the other continues its essential developmental thrust.

The preponderance of public sector in the Indian financial structure is also in fact a reflection of the ideology of the earlier years—so well summed up in the phrase "to occupy the commanding heights of the economy". There has been a definite shift here and a considerable loss of faith in the effectiveness or impartiality of successive governments. But the suspicion of the private sector—particularly of the Big Fish—remains active in the popular mind. This suspicion will keep regulatory authorities constantly on their toes—not a posture which makes for a clear vision of what is possible or a steady stance which refuses to be deflected by the trivial and concentrates on the essential. This suspicion has a kind of eternal life because, as I will soon argue, there are many reasons why financial institutions tend to develop on oligopolistic lines rather than become a showpiece of the neoclassical equilibrium.

I have a suspicion that there was perhaps also a hidden agenda—hidden even from the actors most of the time—behind the desire to occupy the commanding heights. The share of the public sector in total investment in India has been high now for several decades—around 50 per cent. The government-qua-government as a monopsonistic agent has, therefore, a vested interest in supervising where savings originate and where they flow. I doubt whether the share of public investment in India will decline very much for many years to come. How are we to guard against the dangers of a physician not healing himself? In the past, we all know, the Special Liquidity Requirements for banks were more or less continuously raised for fiscal rather than monetary reasons. Will this stop and even be reversed?

For that matter, should we not look carefully at the proposal in the Budget this year of selling shares of public sector enterprises for fiscal window-dressing? Can this not crowd out private borrowers as any other kind of public borrowings? Should we not at least ensure that the mutual funds—many of them in their infancy—are not coaxed or cajoled, and even worse, into absorbing these shares against their better judgement? Such questions are vital for all players in the capital market. A level playing field as between all borrowers, among all lenders and indeed as between all financial intermediaries or segments of the market is not easy to achieve, particularly when elements of monopsony or oligopoly exist and when the prime monopsonistic player commands many exclusive rights including those of taxation and ownership—and indeed of regulation. There is, of course, no such thing as a completely level playing field anywhere—not even at Wimbledon. But we do not allow umpires there to compete in the tournament. That is one reason why regulators have to be as free as humanly possible from governmental influence. Will the proposed legislation for SEBI ensure this?

While the future is always uncertain, we can, I think, safely make two predictions. Public Financial Institutions will play a very sizeable role in the Indian capital market for many years to come; and second, while private financial institutions will no doubt grow and prosper and the general picture will be a good deal more competitive and market-driven than at present, the financial scene will be characterized by the presence of relatively few and large competing entities, that is, by oligopolistic or monopolistic competition. The outcome, therefore, will not be exactly what we read in textbooks or in World Bank reports, which largely postulate a more perfectly competitive world which is, of course, not a sufficient reason for rejecting their advice.

Financial institutions are totally dependent on the confidence factor which, by and large, is positively correlated with size and established reputations. Does anyone really doubt that the first few private mutual trusts to be established in India will be those by some of our large industrial houses? This natural bias towards size and past performance, I suspect, encouraged by governments and regulators as their task is made easier when there are fewer players—including, of course, the task of twisting the arm for a consideration. There is also a certain mumbo-jumbo about systemic failure which must be prevented for the sake of everyone; and this argument in democracies easily proceeds from genuine systemic or general considerations to individual failure for reasons of individual infirmity, particularly when the individuals are big. If you are not bailed out in time, you are merged—not allowed to die and be decently buried. With this insurance against death, quite apart from the moral hazard it begets, the big tend to get bigger even if much of the bigness is excess fat.

Oligopolists compete more through quality and customer service rather than through price which they often fix "in harmony". One should not, therefore, blindly accept the argument that administered prices are a thing of the past. One does not need the authority of Adam Smith to prove that oligopolies collude in many other ways as well. They also compete essentially by keeping some information very close to their chest—as knowledge specific to them is the basis for their share of the turf. One should not, therefore, be easily beguiled by requirements of disclosure of all information for the sake of transparency. Norms can be prescribed. Standards for accounts or balance sheets can be laid down. But this has been done for decades and can become a mere routine. Maybe with computerization and more rapid communications, transparency becomes easier. But our stock exchanges and companies have miles to go in this direction, and I for one would urge SEBI to pay serious regard in this connection to the recommendations of the Pherwani Committee.

But with all that, the need for ferreting out crucial information on a selective basis by detailed scrutiny of a few cases will remain. It is not generalized procedures for regulation that matter so much in the end as the quality of judgement, analysis and research into emerging typical situations. This requires a very high quality of expertise which cannot all be found within the SEBI any more than in the Unit Trust of India, for example. The quality of training and research and consultancy in financial analysis in the universities and elsewhere as also the sophistication of the community of financial analysts are of vital importance; and SEBI should do everything in cooperation with others to promote this. When it comes to acting, it should have the competence and the courage to act fast and hit hard selectively rather than seek shelter behind masses of reporting requirements.

As for self-regulation, it is obviously necessary and all oligopolists are rather good at that. Care has, therefore, to be taken to see that self-regulation does not become a cloak for monopolistic and restrictive practices, particularly in regard to entry of new firms. If the example of universities is any guide, the quality of self-regulation improves greatly when there is a substantial presence of outsiders of competence and eminence in the Court of Governors.

If privileged information is the essence of an oligopolistic position, some degree of "insider trading" is in the nature of things. Financiers are a very sociable and clubbable lot and so are their major clients. In this charmed circle, some degree of you-scratch-my-back-and-I-scratch-yours is the hallmark of civilized behaviour. It is no use concentrating on petty dealers who might take petty advantage of the ignorance of individual customers. The real big insider deals occur during mergers and takeover bids and require inefficiency or connivance or collusion among one or more dealers, financiers, accountants, lawyers and company managers. The best safeguard against insider trading or abuse of privilege in general is the standard of integrity and vigilance of all these professions, including the fraternity of consultants and financial journalists. I am not suggesting that SEBI should be inactive in this field. I am simply saying that it should be aware of its own limitations and seek the cooperation of the wider financial fraternity; and selectively, it should come out hard on suspected cases of fraud.

The situation is somewhat similar to that in the political sphere. The existence of civic institutions such as the free press, free universities, churches and voluntary agencies is necessary for the preservation of a climate of freedom. Similarly, the existence of high professional standards among lawyers, managers, accountants and the like is essential for the safeguard of the rights of the individual investor. Consumer protection cannot be the exclusive or even the major responsibility of SEBI even if it is the executive arm for ultimate redress and restraint.

Having said that, I must add that I was particularly pleased to note that even in its short period of existence, SEBI has been active in receiving and pursuing complaints from individual investors. Most of the complaints may appear petty, but are not; and in any event, it is the confidence of small investors that makes financial markets bigger and more useful. I trust that SEBI will be even-handed in pursuing complaints whether they are against public or private companies or institutions.

The likely predominance of public financial institutions for many years to come has also serious implications for regulatory authorities. Can one part of the government —and not the most glamorous part at that—really regulate other parts of the government effectively? Or will such regulation suffer from the traditional hazards of shifting personal equations between ministers and civil servants and the chief executives of financial institutions of which the Board will be only one among many? The different segments of the capital market cannot now be easily rated by the nature of their specialization. Banks are involved in term lending and run mutual funds. Term-lending institutions are active in the securities market and so is the Life Insurance Corporation of India (LIC). The jurisdictions of the regulating authorities like the Reserve Bank or the Banking Department of the Ministry of Finance and of the Securities and Exchange Board are bound to overlap; and however clear the delineation of responsibility on paper, things will not be easy in practice. And do not forget that even non-regulatory authorities like mutual funds can claim to be self-regulated and accountable to others and, therefore, not in need of regulation by anyone else. What sphere the Board ultimately will be able to carve out for itself remains to be seen, and the leadership in the initial period has undoubtedly a very heavy responsibility. It must attempt neither too little nor too much, and nothing where it cannot bring special expertise in addition to statutory powers.

The current conventional wisdom of deregulation which would tend to reduce the degree of specialization among financial institutions by encouraging them to trespass on each other's traditional turf also needs to be questioned as long as public financial institutions predominate. If there are nationalized banks, should all of them be allowed to start mutual funds or for that matter engage in foreign exchange markets? Would it not be better to have a two-tier system with many small banks catering for internal business with social objectives as a major thrust whereas a few big banks could develop a diversified personality which can some day soon stand up to global competition? If there are public sector mutual funds, should the term-lending institutions be encouraged over time to divest themselves of shares in private companies except perhaps for promotional reasons? Should they specialize instead in financing and restructuring public sector enterprises? Such questions I am sure will become increasingly relevant and cannot be answered in terms of some theoretical competitive model or the example of countries differently situated.

The large presence of public financial institutions also raises some knotty questions in the context of takeover bids—and you can spell the word naughty either way you like. When public financial institutions own a substantial part of the equity in a company, the problem of takeover bids assumes a very interesting character, as everyone at least in Bombay knows by now. Normally, one would say that takeovers are a legitimate form of competition and indeed of an exit policy which gets rid of less efficient management in favour of a more efficient one. Takeover bids, therefore, should not be hindered as long as there is no financial or other irregularity (and all shareholders are offered the option of selling their shares at the same negotiated price. But when the shares are bought over a period in the market and management is attempted to be changed by counting heads among shareholders, can the financial institutions who have a major stake refuse to stand up and be counted? It is absurd to say that they must be neutral or side with the largest shareholder. As investors, they must make up their mind whether the proposed change in management is for the better or for the worse—and there is no reason why each of the financial institutions should have the same view in the matter. In principle, the matter is as simple as that. In practice, at least in India, politics often intervenes—whether by commission or omission, for an omission to make a judgement for fear of being accused of partiality is as much to blame as a positive act of commission for political rather than economic reasons. And as for a brave chief executive of a public financial institution who chooses to break ranks with his colleagues, he may well be reminded about fools rushing in or about safety in numbers. But once again, what we have in reality is not real competition, but some form of collusion or, if you prefer to be euphemistic, of collective institutional judgement!

Concern for insider trading or for an orderly management of takeover bids or mergers is only one aspect of the general suspicion, by no means unwarranted, of the private sector which has been one of the factors behind the active involvement of the State in India in the financial sector. This suspicion will not disappear merely because more private players are allowed in the market or the government removes some of the restrictions on the private sector. I think most of us would agree that the recent changes in industrial licensing and in the Monopolies and Restrictive Practices Act are welcome, particularly the removal of discrimination against the big merely because they are big. The freedom for private firms to set up their own mutual funds is also surely welcome. But there would, I am sure, be demands that this freedom should not be used to divert private savings to particular industrial groups—and this demand will have practical significance as new private mutual funds are likely to be set up by some of the big industrial houses in the first place. Chances are that some regulations will be imposed on the proportion of funds that can be invested in particular companies or groups of companies. But does this really make sense? A stipulation, for example, that not more than 1 per cent of total funds should be invested in the shares of any one company will have little impact on groups which have many companies. And the question may be asked: if the Tatas or the Birlas want to start a mutual fund to ensure that they get a certain proportion of private savings for their companies without the intrusion of other financial intermediaries, why is this wrong? Where does it contravene the rules of competition as long as the investment policy is an open book and investors in shares know the investment policy of all the funds? I am sure there are flaws in my argument. But I think a Conference like this at least needs some provocation.

There are, of course, other abuses to which the private sector is prone or assumed to be so—and these could be pressed into service by regulators for spreading their net. Prima facie, one would have thought that in a competitive environment, there is no need for any regulatory agency to interfere in the issue price of shares or in decisions to issue bonus shares or even in the determination of prices at which takeovers, mergers or sale of bulk shares take place. One could, of course, argue that prices could be jacked up or down to serve as a vehicle for laundering black money or for transferring funds abroad—in the case of a foreign purchaser or buyer—or some such abuse which may not always be hypothetical. But general presumptions of some possible abuse cannot be a basis for instituting generalized procedures for regulation. Formulae cannot encompass all situations and can at best be a guide to further scrutiny. Here again, my preference is for a select rather than a prescriptive approach. But I am least sure of my ground here and look forward to the conclusions of the session especially devoted to new issues.

There are many more questions that arise when we contemplate the future of the Indian capital market which I can hardly touch upon this morning. Freedom of markets means greater risk and, therefore, scope for innovation to protect investors from the risk, albeit at a cost. But do market-makers really understand the nature of all the risks that can arise in a fast changing and increasingly integrated world? I have my doubts whether the Yuppies were all that gifted; and we should train and test our players much more before we let them loose to play with other people's money. Will the cost of financial intermediation go down with competition or do oligopolies generally succeed in passing on their costs? In the ultimate analysis, the financial markets must not merely increase savings. They must direct them to the most productive uses. Are market prices of shares and debentures—or even the evidence of who-takes-over-whom—sure guides as to where investment is relatively more productive? Can anything be done to lift the veil of the transient and the speculative and to reveal the true face of performance? If the Indian capital market gets really deregulated and globally integrated in due course, what will really happen to monetary policy? You might think that I am raising these questions merely to suggest that SEBI invite us all to yet another Conference. If they take the bait, I at least would prefer to be asked to give the valedictory address next time. I can then sum up what others say and not offer myself as a sitting duck.

Part VII

International Aspects

CHAPTER 25

The Role of PL-480 Supplies in the Development of India*

Background

Planned economic development has been underway in India now for nearly ten years. The first five-year plan of development, which was implemented during 1951–56, was a comparatively modest attempt to initiate the process of growth by enlarging such basic social and economic facilities as irrigation, transport, communications and education. Some $7 billion were invested in the Indian economy during the plan period, representing an increase in the rate of investment from some 5 per cent of national income in 1950–51 to 7 per cent in 1955–56. Partly as a result of this investment and in part as a consequence of fuller utilization of capacity, total national income increased by some 18 per cent, thus outpacing the growth in population by more than 10 per cent.

Perhaps the most significant progress during the first plan was made in the field of agriculture where total production increased at the rate of 3 per cent per annum and the production of food grains at an even faster rate of 3.8 per cent per annum. This increase in production was reflected in a sharp reduction in food grain prices and in imports and it made it possible to lift most of the price control and rationing measures that had been in existence in India since the middle of World War II.[1] Imports of food grains, which were as large as 3 million (1 million = 10 lakh) tons per annum in 1948–50 and more than 4 million tons per year in the lean

* The draft of this paper was written in March 1961 for the Sub-Committee International on the use of US Agricultural Resources in Economic Development Abroad; unpublished.

[1] This brief experiment with decontrol in 1947–48 was such a conspicuous failure that it was reversed within only a few months.

seasons of 1951 and 1952, were only 844,000 tons in 1954 and 700,000 tons in 1955. There was a widespread feeling at the end of the first plan that the objective of self-sufficiency in food grains at rising levels of per capita consumption was all but achieved.

Accordingly, the second five-year plan, which began its term in April 1956 and which laid considerable emphasis on the development of basic industries, allowed for only 6 million tons of imports of food grains over the five years (1956–61) at a total estimated cost of $500 million. Imports of even this order were felt to be justified in part at any rate in view of the need to build up stocks in the hands of the government so as to neutralize the effects of year-to-year variation in supplies. Contrary to the opinion sometimes held, the second plan despite its emphasis on industrialization did not assign to agriculture a lower priority than it deserved—in the sense that agricultural output was expected to keep pace with—and even outpace—demand. In the event, however, imports of food grains during the second plan have been substantially larger than what was envisaged and this has been made possible to a large extent by the US PL-480 programme. In addition, India has also received significant quantities of cotton under PL-480 during the second plan period.

Clearly, PL-480 supplies were not arranged for consciously and in advance as an integral part of the strategy of the second plan. The plan, as has already been suggested, envisaged that domestic agricultural production would rise in full proportion to the additional demands generated by the investment programme. The actual investment likely to be undertaken during the period as a whole is estimated at some $14 billion and is not much different in financial terms from that envisaged originally; in real terms, it should be about one-sixth less than was anticipated. PL-480 supplies during the second plan period, therefore, cannot be associated with an additional programme of investment undertaken, in view of the availability of such supplies. The role of PL-480 supplies in India's second five-year plan is thus, strictly speaking, a matter of conjecture—conjecture as to what India would have been able to do if such supplies were not available. There can, however, be no doubt that no matter what alternative one poses to the availability of PL-480 supplies, these supplies have played a significant role in India's development over the past five years.

A long-term agreement covering the third plan period (1961–66) has already been concluded—this time assigning to PL-480 supplies a deliberate (not to say easily definable) role in India's development.

The following analysis of the role of PL-480 supplies in India's economic development will treat the second plan period separately from the third plan period. It will be assumed for the most part as if PL-480 supplies are just given to the Government of India (and sold by the latter to the Indian people); the significance, if any, of the financial arrangements associated with PL-480 transactions will be examined separately. The basic reality behind PL-480 transactions is the net injection of additional resources of wheat, cotton, etc., into the recipient country and the growing fascination with the myths, frictions and distortions associated with the particular financial vehicle employed for the transfer of real resources under PL-480 should not be allowed to obscure the real significance of PL-480 supplies. To round off the discussion, some remarks will be offered at the end on the possible role that US agricultural supplies can play in India beyond the third plan period.

PL-480 and the Second Plan (1956–61)

Altogether the US has entered into five agreements so far with India under Title I of PL-480. The first four of these agreements, signed during 1956–59 and involving supplies of agricultural commodities of the value of $923 million in all, were intended for meeting India's needs during the second five-year plan. The last agreement, signed in May 1960 and covering commodities (mainly wheat) worth $1.28 billion, is expected to cover the requirements during the third plan period (1961–66). The entire amount intended for the second plan has been imported already and virtually all of it has been pressed into consumption. Shipments under the latest agreement intended for the third plan have already begun and small amounts of these are also being currently released to the public. Altogether, therefore, imports of agricultural commodities under Title I of PL-480 may well be a little over $1 billion during the second plan period. In addition, small quantities have been imported from the US during the second plan period under PL-665 ($32 million) and under Titles II and III of PL-480 (some $125 million). Since the distinctions between PL-665 and PL-480 or between Title I of PL-480 and Titles II and III of PL-480 are not strictly relevant to our purpose, we may speak of PL-480 supplies to India during the second plan period as amounting to some $1.2 billion. The bulk of the PL-480 supplies has been in the form of wheat (about 11 million tons). Shipments of rice (about 0.5 million tons) and cotton (some 0.5 million bales worth $87 million) have also been significant.[2]

Before assessing the significance of these supplies, the following factual points[3] may be noted.

(a) Imports of food grains during the second plan are likely to be of the order of 17 million tons with a total value of nearly $1.4 billion as against the initial estimate of 6 million tons with a value of about

[2] The figures quoted here do not include another agreement for 400,000 bales of cotton worth $41.6 million, which was signed in July 1960.

[3] Since the last year of the plan (1960–61) is not yet over, data relating to the second plan period as a whole are rough estimates.

$500 million. The entire increase in requirements has been taken care of by PL-480 supplies which have accounted for about 70 per cent of India's food imports.

(b) In relation to total internal production on an average of 70 to 71 million tons per year, PL-480 supplies of food grains have meant an addition to total consumption of food grains by some 3 per cent beyond what would otherwise have been possible.

(c) Total investment in the Indian economy during the second plan period is estimated at $14 billion. PL-480 supplies of $1.2 billion thus represent 8.5 per cent of total net investment during the second plan period.

(d) Actual utilization of external assistance during the second plan from all sources may well be of the order of some $3 billion. PL-480 supplies, therefore, represent 40 per cent of total external assistance. In relation to total US assistance to India during the second plan, PL-480 supplies have played an even more prominent part amounting to more than two-thirds of the total since the actual utilization of assistance in other forms (that is, from the ICA, DLF and the Ex-Im Bank) is not likely to exceed $550 million.

(e) Despite the availability of PL-480 supplies and the increase in domestic production at the rate of about 2.9 per cent per annum, food prices have risen steadily over the plan period. The total increase in food prices between April 1956 and the end of 1960 has been of the order of 20 per cent.

What can we say about the role of PL-480 supplies in India's second five-year plan in the light of the above-mentioned facts? It is clearly not sufficient or accurate to say, as is sometimes said, that the availability of PL-480 supplies merely allowed a marginal increase in consumption of food grains. Such an assertion implies that in the absence of PL-480 supplies, India would have been willing and able to impose a corresponding cut in consumption—leaving everything else, that is, the level and pattern of investment, unchanged. While the marginal nature of PL-480 supplies lends credence to such a view, it is extremely unlikely that India would have reacted to the absence of PL-480 supplies simply by allowing or enforcing a corresponding cut in consumption by inflation or a reimposition of controls or by higher taxation. Inflation and reimposition of controls over basic necessities such as food grains are clearly untenable in India today, both socially and politically; and there is general acceptance of the view that even from the economic standpoint, inflation and controls over the supply of basic necessities are harmful to the process of development. To a certain extent, the scarcity of food grains and consequent inflationary pressure would certainly have been met by higher taxation if PL-480 supplies were not available. But considering that additional taxation worth $2.1 billion was introduced during the plan period, it is doubtful if still higher taxation leading to a cut in food grains consumption of as much as $1.2 billion could have been countenanced.

On the other hand, it would be equally misleading to assume that PL-480 supplies worth $1.2 billion made it possible for total investment during the plan period to be higher by that amount. Although sanctioned by the conventions of national income accounting, such a view errs equally in assuming that in the absence of PL-480 supplies total imports of food grains would have remained unchanged and the resultant strain on foreign exchange resources would have been relieved entirely by a cut in imports of investment goods. Since India's foreign exchange reserves fell sharply to the minimum level required for working balances during the early years of the plan, these sets of assumptions too have a certain air of plausibility. But in actual practice, it is quite certain that in the absence of PL-480 supplies India would have had to contend with a number of more or less adverse developments in varying degrees, that is, some inflation, some tentative and rather ineffective gestures at control of consumption, greater control over less essential imports, somewhat higher taxation and somewhat lower rates of investment with an attempt—again rather tentative and ineffective—at altering the pattern of investment midstream in favour of more immediate increases in food production.[4] Whether one tends to emphasize the freedom from inflation and controls or the higher levels of consumption or the higher levels of investment in assessing the role of PL-480 supplies is more a matter of taste and temperament than of anything else; and in any event, it is not possible to attempt any measurement of what would necessarily have happened to all these relevant magnitudes taken together. When so many alternative assumptions are possible, perhaps the facts mentioned earlier give the best possible indication of the role of PL-480 supplies inasmuch as they indicate the limit of such a role in any one direction, for example, in increasing consumption or investment.

The question is sometimes raised whether PL-480 supplies have had an adverse effect on Indian agriculture. To the extent that the progress of Indian agriculture depends on the efforts of the government to increase irrigation facilities, promote better methods and the like, we have already argued that there was no conscious diminution of these efforts simply because PL-480 supplies were available. The very fact that agricultural production has increased over the plan period—despite year-to-year variations—may be adduced as sufficient evidence that PL-480 supplies

[4] It is, of course, possible that in the absence of PL-480 assistance, assistance in other forms would have been increased. To that extent, the adverse effects noted here would not have materialized.

have not affected Indian agriculture adversely. The index of agricultural production as a whole is expected to increase by some 16 or 17 per cent over the five years (1956–61), with food grains production increasing by at least 15 per cent and cash crops such as cotton and oil-seeds by some 30 per cent. The production of wheat, the commodity most affected by PL-480 supplies, increased from 8.6 million tons in 1955–56 to 9.7 million tons in 1959–60 and is expected to be even larger in the current year. It could, of course, be argued that agricultural production would have increased even more in India if PL-480 supplies had not depressed prices internally. But as already noted, prices in general have increased over the plan period. Nor has the increase in food articles (21 per cent) or in agricultural fibres (40 per cent) or in oil-seeds (40 per cent) been less than the increase in the general price level (25 per cent) or in the prices of manufactures taken as a whole (23 per cent). Admittedly, within the agricultural group the prices of wheat and rice and cotton, where large imports have been possible under PL-480 or otherwise, have not advanced as much as those of pulses (legumes), raw jute, sugar or oil-seeds. Even allowing for limitations of substitution and the operation of many special factors (such as efforts to increase the export of oil-seeds and the depressed condition of jute supplies in both India and Pakistan currently), it is certainly arguable that in the absence of PL-480 supplies there would have been some shift in the composition of agricultural production in favour of commodities such as wheat and cotton and away from sugar or groundnut. Whether such a shift would have been significant, however, is doubtful and it is certainly unlikely that it would have been in the overall interest of the country.

Another criticism which is sometimes voiced against the availability of PL-480 supplies is that it has diverted attention in India from the paramount necessity of increasing savings. There is no doubt that the rate of savings in India has not picked up as fast during the past five years as was envisaged.[5] It is also arguable—and we have already touched on this—that in the absence of PL-480 supplies the Government of India would have been forced to attempt to curtail consumption beyond what it has already done. But the main point here is that any such attempt would have been extremely irksome and perhaps intolerable politically. One cannot, of course, be dogmatic in matters such as the tolerable limit of sacrifices that can be imposed in a democracy. More often than not, democracy is made an excuse for poor leadership in many less developed countries. But such

[5] While it would not be relevant here to discuss the reasons for this, it may be mentioned that among the factors responsible are the growth in population at a rate faster than was envisaged, the somewhat slower increase in production as such, the growth in current expenditures of the government such as defence beyond earlier expectations and the comparative non-availability of desired investment goods in view of the foreign exchange shortage, which has impaired the will to save.

has certainly not been the case in India, by and large. It is possible to argue that despite the substantial efforts already made, India could and should have gone a little further during the past few years than it actually did in regard to additional taxation. But there is something perverse about blaming PL-480 supplies for whatever weakness one feels inclined to attribute to the Indian tax effort. After all, any additional savings that could have been generated could well have been directed to additional worthwhile investment rather than towards a policy of self-denial in regard to PL-480 supplies.

A word may also be said here concerning the arguments often advanced about the "real" value of PL-480 supplies as distinguished from their nominal "money" value. Most of the discussion in this field fails to distinguish between the variety of contexts in which this question can be raised. If the context, for example, were to measure the sacrifice on the part of the American economy in making PL-480 supplies available to others, it would be relevant to inquire whether and at what price these supplies could have been disposed of abroad—and the answer may well be that the "real" cost to the US of PL-480 supplies is negative inasmuch as they save storage costs. If, on the other hand, the intention is to determine whether a dollar worth of PL-480 supplies are as valuable to the recipient country as a dollar worth of free aid (that is, aid untied to commodities and without stipulation as to origin of the goods to be financed by aid), a whole set of considerations such as the priorities of the recipient country and the comparative prices of different goods in different markets would be relevant.

Since our focus here is to determine what PL-480 supplies have contributed to Indian development, it would not be appropriate to go into questions such as those just posed. Even within the context of Indian development, one might regard the contribution to additional investment as in some sense more "real" than the contribution to additional consumption. Whether or not one regards such a view as somewhat artificial, we have already seen that it is not possible on *a priori* grounds to determine separately the contribution to investment and that to consumption.[6] That is why we have referred so far to PL-480 supplies in terms of the value put on them for purposes of depositing rupees in India in the US account. In this sense, the money values referred to above represent the value of the US commodities in question at prevalent US prices together with a part of the cost of ocean transportation.[7] If the idea is to measure the totality of real

[6] In a privately circulated memorandum, Professor P.N. Rosenstein-Rodan has argued that in countries with a well-worked-out development plan a reasonable assumption would be to consider two-thirds of surplus product sales as investment aid and the rest as consumption aid.

[7] The formula for including a portion of the cost of ocean transportation is a complicated one since it takes into account the higher cost of transport in US ships.

resources added to Indian consumption and investment, it would be appropriate to make at least two adjustments to the nominal values mentioned above. Since a part of the rupee proceeds are retained by US authorities for meeting Embassy expenditures and for purchasing Indian goods and services for assisting third countries, India loses some foreign exchange that it would have otherwise earned. Whereas the amounts of rupees so retained by the US have varied from 10 to 20 per cent of the total, the actual expenditures therefrom for Embassy and other purposes have been much less. The reduction in resources available to India on this account, therefore, has not been as large as might appear at first sight.[8] The second adjustment relates to the subsidy, if any, that the Government of India gives in selling PL-480 supplies to the Indian people. In the earlier years of the plan there was an element of subsidy in the sense that PL-480 supplies were sold at prices lower than what was paid for them. Unfortunately, since PL-480 supplies are merged with supplies domestically obtained by the government, it is not possible to determine the exact amount of subsidy involved in disposing of such supplies. There is reason to believe that in recent years, in view of the rise in Indian prices, the element of subsidy, if any, is nominal. All in all, therefore, the values referred to above do not significantly overstate the contribution of PL-480 supplies in "real" terms. Perhaps a total valuation of $1 billion (instead of $1.2 billion mentioned earlier) might reflect more "truly" the extent of such contribution.

PL-480 Supplies and India's Third Five Year Plan (1961–66)

In April this year India will begin its third five-year plan of development. This plan is a part of a larger plan (of ten to twelve years) whose main aim is to enable India to reach the stage of self-sustaining growth so that it could continue to grow thereafter at a satisfactory pace (of about 5 per cent per annum) without the help of extraordinary forms of government-to-government assistance. While private foreign capital and normal flow of capital through international agencies, in other words, will continue to be welcome, India hopes to eliminate its reliance on government-to-government aid by the early 1970s. The third plan, which marks an important stage in this process, aims at a total investment of some $22 billion spread over agriculture, industry, transport, education, health and the like. Investment of this order is expected to yield a rate of growth in national income of some 5 per cent per annum, thus outpacing the growth in population of some 2 per cent per annum by 3 per cent per annum. While the plan envisages substantial increases in agricultural production

[8] A sum of $22.7 million has been released for US aid to Nepal and Burma. Details of Embassy expenditure met out of PL-480 rupees are not available.

(30 to 33 per cent overall; and 33 to 44 per cent in food grains, 30 per cent in oil-seeds, 33 per cent in cotton and 25 to 28 per cent in sugarcane), it is recognized that imports of agricultural commodities will be necessary. Thus although the aim is to achieve virtual self-sufficiency in food grains by the end of the plan period, imports would be required in the first four years of the plan for consumption as well as for building up stocks for implementing an effective stabilization machinery in the face of year-to-year variations in domestic supplies.

As already noted, a long-term agreement has already been signed under Title I of PL-480 involving 16 million tons of wheat and one million tons of rice valued at $1,276 million. All the supplies are expected to be received during the first four years. While 12 million tons of wheat are expected to be pressed into consumption, the remaining 4 million tons of wheat and the entire quantity of rice are expected to go into a buffer stock. Limited quantities have already been shipped to India under this agreement. A long-term agreement regarding cotton worth $300 million is under negotiation; and if concluded, the total value of PL-480 supplies during the third plan may be of the order of $1.5 billion as against $1.2 billion in the second plan. It is hardly necessary to repeat the qualitative considerations already mentioned regarding the usefulness of these supplies. A few facts, however, may be noted to set the matter in proper perspective:

(1) At the probable level of $1.5 billion, PL-480 supplies would represent some 7 per cent of total investment during the third plan.
(2) Even disregarding the amounts intended for buffer stocks, PL-480 supplies of wheat would augment total availability of food grains during the first four years by a little over 3 per cent.
(3) There would undoubtedly be imports of food grains (particularly of rice) in addition to those under PL-480. While the magnitude of these cannot be ascertained at this stage, PL-480 supplies would certainly account for at least as large a proportion of India's food imports in the third plan as they did in the second (more than 70 per cent).
(4) The gross requirements of external assistance other than those under PL-480 are estimated at some $5.5 billion during the plan. Of this, some $1 billion will be required for debt repayment so that the net inflow of external resources (other than under PL-480) is expected to be of the order of $4.5 billion. PL-480 supplies, therefore, may well account for 25 per cent of the total net resources made available to India from external sources during the third plan period.

There is one question which is often raised: Cannot India absorb during the third plan PL-480 supplies in addition to those already contracted for? Essentially, the question is tantamount to asking whether India cannot really increase the size of its third plan or alter its priorities away from agriculture and in favour of other sectors. Clearly, the availability of PL-480 supplies would facilitate the adoption of a larger plan. But a larger investment outlay would increase the demand not only for wheat and cotton—which can be had under the PL-480 programme—but for other items of consumption as well; it would also call for additional domestic savings and additional external assistance for the importation of investment goods and their components. The feasibility of a larger plan would thus turn on the view one takes of the feasibility both of (a) obtaining additional assistance from abroad in forms other than PL-480 supplies; and of (b) raising the rate of domestic savings beyond what is now contemplated. Without commenting on (a), it is certainly very doubtful if the sizeable effort at saving already postulated in the third plan through taxation and otherwise could be improved upon. It is, of course, possible to suggest forms of additional investment such as those employing unemployed labour in the main which require little imported capital and which direct the bulk of the additional demand to food and clothing. One could even think of undertaking such investment in wheat-consuming rather than rice-consuming areas. But when all is said and done, additional investment, no matter what its form or location, will make some additional claim on domestic savings and external assistance other than PL-480 assistance. About the only thing one can reasonably say in regard to this matter is that the question should be left open for answering till the plan gets underway and we know more than we do now about the feasibility of the targets for savings and external assistance as envisaged now. This is not to say, of course, that additional PL-480 supplies may not become necessary irrespective of any change in investment plans. Nor does it rule out the possibility of absorbing more PL-480 supplies as at present constituted (that is, wheat, mainly) if the scope of the PL-480 programme is extended to include significant supplies of other commodities such as edible oils, tobacco, dairy products and the like, or if requirements of normal marketing are relaxed by agreement among all concerned. Given a broader PL-480 programme and greater cooperation from other food producing countries, additional resources could certainly be absorbed into India beyond the levels contemplated now.

As for altering the pattern of investment in the third plan, Indian opinion for the present is overwhelmingly in favour of achieving self-sufficiency in food grains as early as possible. In the short run, therefore, there is little likelihood of India altering its present plans in view of the availability of PL-480 supplies. The feasibility and desirability of a modification of this attitude in the somewhat longer run is discussed towards the end of this paper.

Monetary Aspects of PL-480 Supplies

In our analysis so far we have disregarded the fact that PL-480 supplies are not just given away but are "sold" for rupees which in turn are given or loaned back to the Government of India for financing specific developmental projects. There has been considerable discussion in recent months about the illusions created by the local currency counterpart of PL-480 transactions and the frictions that arise and can arise by virtue of the United States ownership of these counterpart funds.[9] Without repeating this discussion here, can we assign any significance from the point of view of Indian development to the fact that PL-480 counterpart rupees are given or loaned back to the Government of India for developmental purposes?

The answer to this question simply is that the financial procedures associated with PL-480 transactions are entirely devoid of any developmental content. The rupees held in United States account are no more resources than the rupee notes printed by the Government of India. The fact that they are transferred to the Indian exchequer for financing project A or B does not make it any the easier to find the real resources that go into the completion of these projects. Nor is the pattern of Indian development influenced by the fact that counterpart rupees are released for projects A and B rather than for projects C and D. The Government of India and the Government of the United States have agreed that the projects to be "financed" from PL-480 counterpart funds should be selected from among the projects in any case included in India's development plans. This being the case, it is entirely a matter of indifference from the point of view of the development of India whether United States authorities wish to associate PL-480 rupees with projects A and B rather than with projects C and D. The whole financial rigmarole is just a meaningless chasing of shadows.

It would be equally misleading to speak of PL-480 transactions exerting an inflationary influence in the case of India at any rate. The inevitable accounting of PL-480 transactions in the budget of the Government of India does result in economic "oddities". Thus, the gift or a loan of rupees from the United States account to the Government of India is shown in the Indian budget as "external assistance" rather than what it is in strict economic terms, viz., deficit financing. But instances of a hiatus between budgetary conventions and strict economic interpretation are not confined to PL-480 transactions. Up to a point, such a hiatus is inevitable bearing in mind the special uses that the budget has to serve. And Indian authorities and analysts are fully aware of the need to "interpret" budgetary transactions in order to bring out their correct economic significance. Nor does

[9] The fact that counterpart funds under the Marshall Plan were on a different footing from PL-480 counterpart funds in that unlike the latter the former were owned by recipient countries is only now beginning to be generally appreciated.

the "distortion" injected by PL-480 transactions in budgetary statistics operate only one way. To the extent that the initial "purchase" of wheat or cotton by the Indian Government appears in the budget as an expenditure, it gives the impression of a transaction leading to an injection of purchasing power in the economy. In point of fact, no such thing happens as the "expenditure" results merely in an idle deposit. The basic point is that PL-480 transactions have two different effects at two points of time: they are deflationary, other things being equal, when the wheat or the cotton is sold to the people and, other things being again equal, they are inflationary when the United States-held rupees are spent after being passed on to the Government of India. And these basic effects need not be obscured by budgeting conventions[10]—and even if they are, the blame surely should not be laid at the door of PL-480 transactions.

The foregoing remarks, absolving PI-480 financial transactions from some of the charges levelled against them, should not of course be understood to imply that the present financial procedures are satisfactory. That they most assuredly are not. Perhaps the greatest "demerit" of the present procedure is that by pushing what is an immensely beneficial transaction to both the giver and the receiver through an elaborate smokescreen of sales and purchases and local currencies, and agreeing for the use of such local currencies, the basic goodwill that ought to result from PL-480 supplies is given little chance to assert itself. It would be far simpler and in keeping with the spirit of the programme to give the supplies in question as a grant to begin with. The idea that somehow the United States gets more goodwill if PL-480 supplies are "sold", and the rupee proceeds are tagged on to some concrete projects, has little validity especially when the basic impact of PL-480 supplies gets lost in useless negotiations and the frictions attendant upon them.

Perhaps the worst of these frictions in the case of India relates to the insistence on audit by United States authorities of expenditures incurred by the Government of India from the counterpart rupees given or loaned to it. In a sense, this is the natural consequence of the fact that the ownership of these funds vests in the United States Government. But when the receiver feels, and rightly, that the rupees are as good as useless, detailed submission to the audit procedures of a foreign government clearly becomes irksome.

This is also true to some extent of the use of the so-called Cooley Funds. A part of the counterpart rupees are set apart and given over to the United States Export-Import Bank for being loaned to United States firms operating in India either on their own or in partnership with Indian firms. Apart from its obviously discriminatory nature which goes against the basic

[10] In actual practice, the scope for misleading impressions being drawn is much less in a continuing programme.

non-discriminatory approach of India to private foreign capital (which enjoys in India the same credit, fiscal and other facilities as Indian capital), it requires a whole set of new bureaucratic procedures to ensure that loans from Cooley Funds do not disturb conditions in the Indian capital market and are not given in cases where they might substitute for a fresh inflow of capital from abroad. None of these determinations can be clear-cut or non-controversial especially when so many different agencies including the borrower, the credit agencies in India, the Export-Import Bank and the Government of India have all to be satisfied about the fairness of the decisions reached. When it is remembered that India has well-established credit facilities, even the apparent incentive effect of the Cooley Funds in attracting United States capital to India disappears. Whatever the justification for the Cooley provision in countries without well-established money and capital markets, this provision has served little purpose in India and, indeed, has led to some avoidable resentment.

On all accounts, therefore, there is everything to be said for replacing the present system with straightforward grants. Till such time as the whole programme is put on a grant basis, the entire rupee proceeds of PL-480 sales should be given back to the recipient governments as a grant rather than as a combination of grants and loans so that the myths attached to local currencies are at least not perpetuated. In addition, the attempt to "audit" the use of local currencies should be given up and provisions such as those relating to Cooley Funds should be used very sparingly, if at all.

Prospects

Taking a somewhat longer view of things, can America's agricultural productivity be married to India's growing needs so as to permit a faster rate of growth in India than would otherwise be possible? We have already noted that as plans stand now, India intends to achieve self-sufficiency in food grains by the end of the third plan period. Given the availability of PL-480 supplies for at least another decade, it is certainly arguable that India should not be in a hurry to achieve self-sufficiency in food grains and that it should concentrate instead a little more on industrialization and on social and other aspects of growth. But clearly, if India is to give up or postpone the objective of self-sufficiency in food grains, it cannot be on the basis of an indefinite continuance of concessional supplies of agricultural commodities. In keeping with the objective of self-reliance, or freedom from the need for external assistance, India can afford to plan for continuing imports of food grains or cotton only if it were assured that its long-term balance-of-payments strength would permit it to pay for these supplies in a normal way, that is, by Indian exports. It can certainly be argued that in a proper international division of labour when most economies of the world are sufficiently developed, India's natural role would be that of an importer of food and fibre and America's that of an exporter of the same. Consummation of such a pattern of world trade, however, presupposes a considerable development of industries and industrial skills in India beyond what seems probable over the next ten or fifteen years. It assumes also that as soon as India begins to develop comparative advantage in the field of manufactures—and it has already such an advantage in regard to many manufactures—it would be allowed access to the markets of other countries, whether more or less industrialized than itself. The development of such a rational course of world trade, however, would put a considerable strain on the worlds resources of statesmanship—and all the more so since in an era of rapidly changing economies, the "rational" is not always easy to define and much less easy to accept. As far as one can tell, India will have to pass through a rather long period when it would have to be content with virtual self-sufficiency in food grains, and perhaps an inward-looking development over a wide front before it can begin to count on being able to let its economy go where the winds of international division of labour might take it. This is not to say that in the meanwhile India may not export and import a growing volume of agricultural products as well as manufactures. What is implied merely is that if ever India emerges as a significant net importer of agricultural products and a significant net exporter of manufactured products, it would be after passing through a phase—and perhaps not a very short phase—during which its external trade, while growing, will not assume a clear or definite character or trend. Such supplies as it is able to absorb of American or other agricultural supplies on strictly commercial terms are likely to be of a marginal nature for a long time to come.

CHAPTER 26

Trade and Payments Policy for a Developing Economy*

A great deal of attention has been devoted in recent years to the problems of the so-called less developed countries. While economic growth is by no means the exclusive concern of any particular group of countries, there can be little doubt that the task of developing the poorer societies is particularly urgent and difficult. Partly as recognition of the urgent and difficult nature of the task and in part in response to world-wide trends, the opinion seems to be crystallizing that the economic development of the less developed countries must be attempted on the basis of consciously directed plans or programmes and within a framework of international cooperation. Problems of trade and payments as they emerge in the process of growth among the less developed countries cannot, therefore, be divorced from the broader strategy of development as such nor is it necessary to study them without reference to the present and potential form of cooperation among nations for dealing with these problems. Accordingly, the present paper[1] seeks to explore the ingredients of a rational trade and payments policy in a developing economy on the assumption that such a policy would be part and parcel of a general programme of development which can or does command international support in a greater or smaller degree.

* This paper was presented at the Conference on Trade in Developing World, organized by the International Economic Association (IEA) at Brissago, Switzerland, September 1961; subsequently published in the volume on the Conference brought out by the International Economic Association.

[1] I am extremely grateful to Subimal Mookerjee for his valuable comments and suggestions for improvement of this paper. Mookerjee, of course, is not responsible for the views expressed here or for the errors and omissions that remain.

While the discussion aims at a measure of generality, it is clear that the problems and prospects of different developing countries would differ greatly. This is all the more so when the focus is on national trade where the "specifics" of a given situation are the essence of the matter. It will, therefore, be made clear at the outset that the distribution of emphasis in this paper is derived largely from the experience and circumstances of countries such as India.

The Setting

The basic task in a developing economy is that of initiating a progressive spiral of growing productivity, savings and external viability so as to achieve and sustain a satisfactory rate of growth in per capita incomes. Whatever view one takes of the relative importance of the technological, managerial, sociological, psychological, educational or biological attributes which endow a human being with productive efficiency, it is clear that economic progress requires a continuing increase in such efficiency; and more often than not, and most certainly over the long pull, the fullest development and exploitation of human productivity would require a growing capital base and rising savings to sustain such a base. To a certain extent, the deficiency in productivity and savings in the initial stages of growth can be overcome by external assistance; but for practical if not moral reasons, there is much to be said for achieving, as soon as possible, a rate of saving and an environment of efficiency which would permit a satisfactory rate of growth without extraordinary forms of external assistance. Thus understood, the objective of external viability would be subsumed under the other two objectives of higher savings and productivity.

There is, however, a real sense in which it is important to speak of external viability as a separate or distinct objective. Most of the poor nations of the world suffer from the lack of a diversified economic structure. Economic growth sets up demands for imports which are too large for the small export sector to meet, especially when this export sector is confined to a range of goods for which world demand is not particularly responsive. To put it differently, internal resources cannot always be converted into the machines or the materials or the consumer goods required in adequate quantities either directly by internal production or indirectly by providing large enough export receipts. The balance-of-payments barrier, to use an expression of Mrs Robinson, generally appears before the inflation barrier so that the balance-of-payments difficulties of developing countries are not necessarily a reflection of inadequate savings or of inflationary fiscal and monetary policies. This is not to say that inadequate savings are not a factor in the situation or that many if not most cases of balance-of-payments difficulties are not generally aggravated by inflationary policies. Nor does it deny that there are obvious cases among the less developed countries where even a single export product can earn more than sufficient foreign exchange to sustain all the development that is otherwise possible. Nevertheless, as a general rule, the less developed countries suffer from such a limited degree of manoeuvrability in their balance-of-payments that it is meaningful to refer to their balance-of-payments problems as something distinct from a mere manifestation of inadequate savings or inappropriate fiscal and monetary policies.

In any ex-post reckoning, of course, the level of investment will exceed domestic savings exactly by the deficit in the balance-of-payments, so that the actual deficit in external accounts may reasonably be referred to as signifying a net clam on resources from abroad. What is contended here simply is that, in such a situation, an effort to increase domestic savings in the relevant amount, while feasible, would not eliminate—though it would in all probability reduce—the deficit in payments.

Perhaps a simplified example might serve to define the scope of the argument attempted here. Let us assume that a poor country has attained equilibrium at a low rate of growth with savings equal to investment and with its single export product, tea, earning enough to pay for the machines and the motor cars it imports. Assume further that it decides to increase the level of productivity of its farmers by importing additional fertilizers for free distribution by the use in the first instance of its foreign exchange reserves which it hopes to recover by the improvement in the balance-of-payments resulting from additional tax on its rich people. The tax is expected to produce a revenue equal to the cost of the additional import of fertilizers so that there is no deterioration in the budgetary position of the government. If the response of the rich to higher taxation were to be an equivalent cut in the demand for imported motor cars, all would be well. But they may just as well respond by dismissing their chauffeurs or by curtailing their demand for personal service a bit in many directions. If the fertilizers were applied immediately to raise production and if the persons employed in services were in one way or another related to the farming community, the consumption of the "poor" may even increase despite visible unemployment for some of them. The higher "savings" of the rich—or more appropriately, their lower consumption—would be reflected in a disappearance of a part of the services from the national income stream and the initial dissaving in the form of a loss of foreign exchange reserves would remain with its counterpart in the availability of additional fertilizers.

The foregoing example, while tailored to provide an extreme illustration, is not altogether unrealistic. The general point it seeks to make, viz., the difficulty of creating or releasing specific resources by overall financial policies, is one which had relevance to the entire process of development. When we are dealing with "advanced" countries with a diversified economic structure and when the changes in question are small, it is a valid procedure to assume that real resources are easily interchangeable. But the real or physical aspects of the situation would require specific attention in a developing economy if neglect or inappropriate action at one point of time is not to create crippling bottlenecks at subsequent periods of time. In the context of balance-of-payments, two conclusions would seem to follow from the considerations under discussion. At any given time it may be necessary to take direct or specific action to reduce the pressure on balance-of-payments so as to exploit to the full the available savings potential. More important, the pattern of investment and of resource allocation in general over time should be such as to remove progressively the balance-of-payments constraint on further progress.

An investment pattern of the kind just suggested does not imply a disregard of the productivity criterion and its substitution entirely by some balance-of-payments criterion. Apart from the logical difficulty of trying to segregate those elements of growth which enter, over the long run, into the balance-of-payments potential and those which do not, the ultimate objective of achieving higher production per capita cannot be sacrificed in favour of what is after all a means to growth. What is necessary to emphasize simply is that it is not so much the immediate contribution to production but the consequences over time which should be relevant to investment priorities at any given time. And given the balance-of-payments constraint that generally operates in developing countries, a course of action designed to strengthen progressively the balance-of-payments may be preferable to any available alternative even if the immediate consequences of such a preference imply a smaller increase in production. Whether this is the case or not is not, of course, a matter for *a priori* judgement but for a detailed consideration of the likely consequences of alternative actions. And it is precisely the function of a proper development strategy to unravel the future pattern of alternative sets of consequences so as to give an advance warning, so to speak, to policymakers.

Reference may be made in this connection to an argument which is often advanced, viz., that the exchange rate is generally overvalued in most developing countries in the sense that it does not reflect the "true" value of imports and exports. The presumption in favour of this contention is based on the fact that the current exchange rate does not equate supply and demand for foreign exchange without the help of foreign aid or import restrictions. Given the overvaluation of the exchange rate in this sense, it is further argued that correct investment decisions require the assumption of a "true" or "equilibrium" exchange rate. This would clearly give to "import substitution" and "export promotion" a considerable weightage in relation to their direct contribution to production when valued at the current exchange rate. The significance of this argument is, however, difficult to see despite the air of plausibility given to it by the use of familiar concepts such as supply and demand and equilibrium. Even if one could arrive at an exchange rate which would equate the supply and demand for foreign exchange at any given time without foreign aid or import restrictions, there is no *a priori* reason why investment decisions based on this exchange rate would produce the most satisfactory result in the long run. The only sensible meaning one can assign to an equilibrium or accounting exchange rate would be a rate which if used as a basis for investment decisions would produce the optimum long-term result. But in this sense, the accounting rate will itself have to be determined on the basis of a comparison of the long-term consequences of alternative actions and there can be no presumption about the level of this rate or its deviation from the current rate except on the basis of a comparison of alternative concrete possibilities.

In actual practice, of course, decisions about an appropriate development strategy may have to be based not so much on a detailed consideration of a likely long-term consequence as on broad judgements based on experience or on such light as one might gather from overall models which must of necessity incorporate a number of assumptions. But given the outlines of a broad strategy, the question that arises in relation to international trade and payments is that of defining a policy which would be consistent with the development strategy and its objectives and which would, in fact, reinforce the developmental strategy over time. While the search for a rational trade and payments policy raises many related issues which must be taken into account in framing the developmental strategy as such, it may be convenient to group the discussion mainly around the import and export policy with a few remarks on the exchange rate policy as well as on foreign aid and private foreign investment.

Import Policy

The process of development inevitably sets in motion a growing demand for imports. If rising level of production and investment cannot be sustained without a steady increase in the demand for machinery, raw materials and consumer goods; and while some of these growing needs can be satisfied by growing domestic production and by imports financed by exports or foreign aid, the question naturally arises whether the demand for imports should not be kept in check with a view to supplying a somewhat larger part of total demand from domestic production. The case for developing such industries or activities as would reduce the potential demand for imports, if necessary by "protection" while the industries or activities to be developed achieve the necessary level of efficiency, has long been generally accepted by economists of all persuasion. But in a sense, the familiar infant industries argument is both too narrow and too broad. It is too narrow in the sense that the industries or activities that may have to be developed from the point of view of "import-saving"[2] are not necessarily those where demand is already established, for example, imported food or textiles or where it can be curbed at least temporarily without affecting growth. In many cases, if not most, it may be just as important to focus attention on potential domestic supply to meet a potential demand which cannot be curtailed without retarding growth (for example, fertilizers or oil); and in such cases, it is not the familiar protection of tariffs or quotas but the protection in the form of priority in investment and training which should receive attention.

The infant industries argument is also too broad in the context of development planning insofar as it says very little about how many "infants" should begin to be artificially nourished and how soon and in what sequence. For a country like India, for example, a case can be well made out that virtually every conceivable industry or activity would qualify for infant industries protection since there is no *a priori* reason why sooner or later India cannot develop any of these industries on efficient lines. Nor can the inevitable choice among the infants to be protected or promoted be made with reference simply to the pace at which protection could be dispensed with. As already indicated, a whole set of considerations involving alternative uses of resources and their implications over time would be relevant.

In particular, it must be emphasized that what needs to be economized (given judgements about potential export opportunities) is the level of imports over time and not just immediately. One cannot, therefore, just pick out the current import list and start encouraging import substitution in proportion to the importance of different items in current imports. Equally, the development of import-substituting industries in itself would set up additional demands for imports both for investment goods and for raw materials and components. And while this additional import demand is a relevant part of the total picture which should determine the choice of action, it cannot be assumed that a course of action which swells imports for a while may not yet be most import-saving over time. A clear instance in point is the development of heavy and basic industries such as those producing steel or machinery in situations where the resource pattern of the country and the amenability to training of its people would establish the presumption that those industries can be efficiently established. Despite the fact that the development of basic industries is likely initially to set up large demands for imports, it may still make sense to try and develop such industries comparatively early rather

[2] The term "import-saving" is rather misleading in the context of a developing economy where total imports and even the imports of particular categories of goods would increase in all probability and where all production in a sense is import-saving. Nevertheless, satisfaction of potential demand by domestic production rather than by exports and imports is a sufficiently distinct process to deserve a name.

than late in the process of development. Whether such a course is feasible or not even where the underlying comparative cost advantages exist is of course a different matter—for prospective saving of imports does nothing to relieve present or immediate shortage of foreign exchange. In actual practice, where most developing countries depend on foreign capital to supplement their resources, the feasibility of the course of action which is heavy on current imports and light on future imports would turn on the decisions of those who supply the capital from abroad as much as on the decisions of the developing country. But the fact remains that even from the point of view of minimizing foreign assistance over time, there might be a case for an intensive administration of such assistance over a limited period.

Needless to say, the drive for import saving cannot be carried to the point at which it defeats its purpose by cutting too deeply into efforts to promote exports. From the point of view of balance-of-payments strength, export promotion is just as important as saving on imports. Even the familiar argument that there is a greater degree of uncertainty in any assessment of chances for large exports than in an estimate of potential import saving has at least a limited validity when we speak of a comparatively long period of time where mistakes are as likely to be made in estimating domestic demand and supply as in gauging foreign demand and supply where at least the law of averages would apply with somewhat greater force. Similarly, the superiority of import substitution over export promotion cannot be established merely by reference to the fact that at any given time existing exports face a somewhat unresponsive international market. In the context of long-term growth, the resources that go into import substitution can equally be diverted to the creation of new export opportunities where domestic supply conditions or world market conditions are more favourable than in the case of existing exports. Whatever judgement, therefore, one arrives at about the balance to be struck between import substitution and export promotion in the light of long-term possibilities and potential would still be a relative judgement; and it certainly would not be divorced from considerations of comparative cost.

What is perhaps less obvious but equally valid is that beyond a point import substitution or saving would be harmful even if it is at the expense of domestically produced and consumed goods. Any undue retardation of the growth of the purely "domestic" sector—if there is such a sector—would have a repercussion on the growth of savings and productivity in general and, therefore, on the balance-of-payments at least to some extent.

The discussion so far has centred on the infant industries argument, about which there is little disagreement in economic literature. Nevertheless, this argument gives only a limited clue to the policy that ought to be pursued in any given situation.[3] There are, however, two other arguments in favour of some restrictions on import demand in a developing economy to which we may now turn. It is often argued that a developing country which urgently needs to increase investment should curtail the demand for inessential or luxury imports so as to allow for a larger import of machinery and other developmental goods. The argument is again reinforced by reference to the so-called demonstration effect. The availability of imported textiles creates new demands and reduces the saving potential of poorer societies especially where the consumption of imported goods enjoys an altogether unusual social prestige.

In their simple or bland versions the arguments for import restrictions just advanced are, of course, easy to demolish. It does not take much knowledge of economics—or even of simple logic—to show that by increasing the imports of machinery and reducing the imports of cars or refrigerators or air-conditioners, we do not necessarily produce the additional savings which alone can sustain additional investment. And terms such as demonstration effect can be countered by reference to inducement goods. Nevertheless, the arguments under consideration contain an essential core of truth.

If the basic thesis advanced earlier, viz., that the balance-of-payments barrier often comes before the inflation barrier is right, it is clear that a reduction in "luxury or inessential" imports would make it possible to raise both savings and investment beyond what would be otherwise possible. That measures to economize on less essential imports must be supplemented by conscious measures to raise savings is axiomatic but that does not mean that it would be impossible to raise savings. What may not be (and often is not) possible is to ensure that measures to promote savings get automatically reflected in a requisite improvement in balance-of-payments. Under the circumstances, direct measures to curtail the demand for luxury imports would be a necessary, if not a sufficient, part of an optimum developmental strategy. Similarly, the availability of

[3] Partly in response to this consideration and in part in view of the difficulty of making overall judgements of the kind suggested by a logically integrated policy, investment priorities in actual practice are often decided by rules of thumb which derive vague comfort from the familiar jargon of economics. Thus quite often investment priorities proceed from the necessity of having to allocate available foreign exchange. Once certain "inescapable" or "obviously preferred" demands are met, the rest of the foreign exchange available is allocated among competing claimants for expansion of capacity on the basis of how soon and how surely any particular line of investment would recoup its initial foreign exchange cost after allowing for the recurrent need for foreign exchange to employ fully the capacity created. Quite apart from considerations of validity, it is clear that a conscientious application of even a simple rule of thumb such as the one just mentioned would raise the same kind of general questions of alternative uses and their consequences that it seeks to avoid.

inducement goods has a definite place in any development strategy insofar as willingness to work, take risks and accept technical changes depends on what one can do with the rewards of such willingness. But that does not mean that the demonstration effect also does not operate or that the totally free exercise of demand is at all a feasible proposition where the essence of developmental planning lies in moderating and modifying the pattern of demand even when it may have nothing to do with imports. A conscious environment of austerity is as vital to economic progress in less developed countries as some evidence of the fact that such progress is worthwhile and where status-conscious consumption is involved, a situation where the lure of imported commodities is less prevalent as in early Japan would make for greater growth potential. While it may be difficult to strike a precise balance in matters such as these, a correct balance is certainly not struck by a policy of free imports.

Notwithstanding the controversy that often surrounds this issue, the importance of import restrictions in a developing economy is recognized both by common custom and international sanction. Import restrictions for so-called balance-of-payments reasons are recognized by General Agreement on Tariffs and Trade (GATT) which also provides that these reasons apply with special force to the developing countries. The Articles of Agreement of the International Monetary Fund (IMF) do not recognize the need for a similar differential regime as between the advanced and the poorer countries. The special dispensation of Article XIV of the IMF is not supposed to apply with special reference to the developing countries. But in actual practice, the shelter of Article XIV of the Fund's Agreement is now sought mainly by the developing countries and the jurisdictional difference between exchange restrictions and import restrictions is of little substantive significance in any case.

The argument against import restrictions often takes the form of advocating that such restrictions should be exercised by tariffs and general fiscal measures rather than by direct import quotas. In a sense, such an argument accepts the fundamental case for a restraint on less essential imports, for an argument about proper means to implement a policy does not deny the validity of the policy in question. As far as the choice between tariffs and quotas is concerned, there is no doubt that tariffs are generally to be preferred and that this point is not often fully appreciated by the less developed countries. The administrative complications of quotas and the corruption they give rise to may not be significant factors in some countries. But there is no justification for import quotas unsupported by higher tariffs when the benefit of such quotas in terms of higher domestic prices and profits goes to a few quota holders. Even if it is desired to make things doubly sure, the proper prescription would be a combination of higher tariffs and quotas.

The difficulty in levying high enough tariffs sometimes arises from earlier hasty and unwarranted binding of tariffs under GATT; and in such cases rectification of such a situation would represent a sensible form of international cooperation. The idea that in matters such as tariffs, the strict parity or quid pro quo ought to prevail even as between advanced and developing countries can only contribute to the proliferation of quotas with all their baneful effects on distribution of income in the poorer countries. Sometimes the preference for quotas arises from the legislative difficulty in making frequent changes in tariffs to suit changing circumstances. But it should not be impossible to obtain greater executive or administrative freedom in regard to tariffs. It is also arguable that far too frequent changes in quotas have themselves been a source of much instability and undesirable speculation in developing countries so that a regime of more or less stable restrictions which rides out minor fluctuations in the payments position has much to recommend itself.

The basic objection to the policy of import restrictions in developing economies is not against the policy as such but against the way in which this policy is often applied without a clear conception of the objective in view. If the rationale for restrictions against luxury imports is that such restrictions widen the balance-of-payments bottleneck and encourage savings by moderating the demonstration effect and thus permit a higher rate of growth than would be otherwise possible, it is clear that there should be no attempt to substitute the import of less essential items with greater domestic production of the same commodities. And yet, far too often restrictions on the import of cars or refrigerators or air-conditioners are allowed to be followed by greater domestic production of the same items. Even where domestic production of luxuries is not deliberately encouraged, it is certainly not discouraged; and the taxes that domestically produced luxuries bear are generally only a fraction of the duties to which they might have been subject when imported. More often than not, the domestic production is undertaken by the foreign suppliers of erstwhile imports; and the general clamour for encouraging private foreign investment, supported by foreign governments providing assistance, obscures the fact that "investment" of this kind represents a wasteful diversion of resources which prevents any dampening of the demonstration effect and nullifies directly or indirectly the original import saving that was intended. Often, the domestic production of erstwhile luxury imports is manufacture only in name in the sense that the bulk of the components are imported and the easy profits made in a sheltered market represent an additional burden on the balance-of-payments. Even if care is taken to ensure that the cost of imported components and profits sent abroad is less than the cost of importing the commodity in a fully manufactured form, it does not follow that the course of action chosen is not worse than the alternative of cutting down imports and not permitting their domestic production at the same time.

It may be argued that the domestic production of erstwhile luxury imports would be desirable in view of the unemployment which prevails in most developing countries. Insofar as domestic luxury production depends on the employment of domestic savings, the existence of unemployment is totally irrelevant since the same saving could be employed in a more worthwhile investment to produce the same or even larger improvement in employment. Even where luxury production is established by private foreign investment, one will still have to demonstrate that the investment in question could not have been induced to flow in a different direction; and even then, the undesirable consequences on the flow of savings in view of the continuance of the demonstration effect would remain. Nor is it clear that all the resources of skill and materials that foreign producers would employ represent no diversion of scarce resources. Once established, domestic luxury industries become vested interests claiming a share in growing production and investment opportunities so that their direct and indirect claims on the balance-of-payments and on available savings tend to grow. What starts out, therefore, as an import-saving and employment-giving activity often develops into a voracious trap for scarce resources. At any rate, it is evident that if there is a case for allowing domestic production to take the place of imported luxuries, it is a case that can be established only after much careful and detailed consideration of the likely chain of events over time. But in actual practice, high-cost domestic luxury industries are generally allowed to grow without question in the wake of restrictions on luxury imports.

The accent of the discussion so far has been on the development of import-saving industries and activities and on the suppression or curtailment of less essential imports. But if balance-of-payments acts as a special or distinct brake on development and if the circumstances are such as to warrant a margin of priority[4] for activities that improve the balance-of-payments, it would follow that the current exchange rate would not restrain imports in general as much as it should. It should, therefore, be necessary to restrain the demand for imports in general by a tariff on all imports. From this point of view, the normal tendency to exempt from tariff duties items such as machinery or raw materials or essential consumer goods is not appropriate. Insofar as the objective here is not so much protection or a specific restraint on demand but a general incentive to economize on imports, the generalized duty need not be high. How high it should be is difficult to say *a priori*. But the contention that all imports need to

[4] Over and above what would be indicated by considerations of immediate productivity.

be taxed may be as relevant as it is generally ignored. Apart from the consideration here in mind and the much-needed gain to public revenues, a general tax on imports including those of machinery would also correct what is sometimes referred to as the artificial relative cheapness of capital in most developing countries. The normal prescription for correcting the phenomenon of undervaluation of capital is a hike in interest rates which is seldom acceptable to the harassed fiscal authorities. An increase in the price of imported capital would serve the same purpose at least to some extent.

The policy of import restriction we have recommended so far takes no account of the repercussions on other countries and their reaction thereto. The general presumption in this field seems to be that the repercussions of restrictions on luxury imports would be mainly on the richer countries. The examples of motor cars, refrigerators and air-conditioners would support such a presumption. And it may be argued that for philosophical, if not moral, reasons the richer countries would not retaliate and at any rate that they should not retaliate. The double standard of morality that Professor Myrdal has been preaching in this regard is certainly not without an obvious appeal, but there are more than one developing countries and the policies of any one of these countries cannot be deemed rational if they fail to take account of the interests of other countries similarly struggling with their own balance-of-payments weakness. Iraqi dates or Zanzibar cloves or Burmese high-quality timber would be luxuries for most Indian consumers and therefore good targets for import restrictions in India. If similar restrictions existed in Iraq and Zanzibar and Burma on exports of luxuries such as carpets or fine cloth or cashew nuts from India, a simple and logical way out of the dilemma would be a mutual liberalization of restrictions. But in practice, such a course may not prove so simple. For one thing, the mutual liberalization of imports may have to be on a bilateral or discriminatory basis if the baby is not to be thrown out with the bath water. Wine is produced both in France and Tunisia; and if liberal imports of wine are to be permitted from Tunisia, there is no point in giving up restrictions on the import of wine altogether. If the current international dogma of non-discrimination were strictly adhered to, the only alternative before most developing countries would be to maintain restrictions against each other's imports to the detriment of all of them. At the same time, if the principle of some marginal discrimination, whether through bilateral and barter deals or otherwise, is accepted, it would be extremely difficult to apply such a principle rationally or equitably. The markets that different developing countries can provide to the products of other developing countries would vary so much in size and scope that it would be difficult to establish even an approximate degree of reciprocity and it may well be that the discrimination implicit in any bilateral arrangement is against some other developing country rather than against those who can well take it in their stride. The dilemma that is posed in these conflicting considerations is difficult to resolve, and in actual practice is likely to be resolved more by pressures and counter-pressures than by the application of any rational principle.

One way of resolving the dilemma which has become a practical reality in some areas is that of forming units of regional cooperation. But apart from the difficulty of forming such regional cooperation units in some areas, there would still remain the question of relations between different regional groups among the developing countries. The logical thing to do, if one follows this line of thought, would be for all developing countries to adopt a liberal import policy towards each other except insofar as the considerations of the infant industries argument apply. The exception just noted is clearly important in view of the fact that different developing countries are not at the same stage of development. Even so, a considerable part of the trade among developing countries could still be brought within the purview of liberal import policy to the mutual benefit of all of them. A general principle of this sort may produce better results all round than a congerie of bilateral arrangements arrived at after much bickering and bargaining. The implicit discrimination against advanced countries could also be justified as being not without precedent in recent history; and unlike the discrimination still practised in parts of Europe against non-dollar non-EEC (European Economic Community) countries, it would certainly not be perverse in the sense of being applied against weaker nations.

Export Policy

There can be no doubt that with all the emphasis on potential import saving, the total import bill of the developing countries will continue to grow if development itself is to be a continuing process. Sooner or later, therefore, the developing countries must increase their exports substantially. The magnitude of the problem that faces the developing countries in this regard may be illustrated with reference to Indian experience. During the last ten years when a vigorous development programme has been underway, India's total imports have increased steadily from some \$1.5 billion a year to about \$2.5 billion. During the same period, exports have increased only marginally and are running currently at about \$1.4 billion a year. In the meanwhile, the draft on reserves and the growth in foreign indebtedness has led to the disappearance of the sizeable surplus on invisible account and there may well be a sizeable deficit on this account in the years to come. While it is reasonable to expect that imports may not grow as fast as they have in the past, it would not be surprising if they do not reach the level of \$3–3.5 billion in another ten years. India's exports, therefore, must be at least doubled over the next ten years if reliance on external assistance is to be reduced. Even a more heroic effort to increase exports would not be out of place, considering that the very emphasis on exports would underline to some extent the need to increase imports since export markets must be nourished even if this requires the import of more and more sophisticated components, materials and machinery. A similar order of export performance should be required sooner or later on the part of other developing countries as well. Given these magnitudes, what kind of export policy would produce the necessary results?

Basically, of course, the first and foremost requirement for a rational export policy would be sufficient attention to the development of export industries in the allocation of investment and other scarce resources. Judgement as to the kind of industries and activities which are more likely to emerge as significant export industries or activities would vary from case to case. About the only generalization one can make is that the problem is sufficiently large to warrant the fullest exploitation of all the avenues for export—whether old or new, whether those relating to primary production or secondary production or invisible income. No developing country which refuses to forfeit its ambitions for continuing development can afford, for example, to neglect such natural advantages as it possesses in the supply of primary products. Much less can it resign itself from the growing sectors of world trade in manufactures and semi-manufactures unless it enjoys superabundance of some natural resources for which world demand promises to grow rapidly. Equally clearly, the policy of adequate investment in export industries must be buttressed by a policy of restraint in domestic consumption of exportable items, by vigorous market promotion and by a scrupulous regard for efficiency and standards. There should also be a determined effort to avoid inflation which cannot but hurt the export drive; and when a general price rise becomes unavoidable, there should be a prompt adjustment in the exchange rate. While so much would be—or should be—common ground among most economists, it is doubtful if a rational and adequate export policy for the developing countries can stop at the principles just outlined.

For one thing, vigorous and efficient export industries cannot be created overnight. At the same time, export markets must begin to be tapped and cultivated as soon as possible if they are to be fully exploited in due course. A deliberate policy of giving incentives to the export industries in the initial stages is, therefore, imperative. The case for export incentives is essentially the same as that for infant industries protection or for import restrictions with a view to widening the balance-of-payments bottleneck. Unfortunately, while the infant industries argument is generally accepted, its application is generally supposed to apply only to import policy, and the equally valid case for export incentives often gets branded with the emotive term "dumping". Here is one field where economic analysis and economic statesmanship have much to offer by way of a clarification on the basic issues involved. Without such a clarification, there is every danger that the export efforts of the developing countries would flounder, with the consequent perpetuation of economic stagnation or of foreign aid. More likely, there would be the alternative danger of a surreptitious growth of export incentives such as would ill serve the interest of the developing as well as the developed parts of the world. If the case of export incentives is generally accepted, the debate could shift to the more fruitful plane or the proper form that such incentives should take.

The developing countries cannot obviously compete with the richer countries in regard to export incentives in the form of cheap credits and the like. The general practice among the developing countries is to offer a variety of incentives such as remission of taxes, subsidized transport or power facilities or cheaper supply of raw materials or easier access to import licences for replacement of imported components. Some of these incentives such as remission of customs and excise duties and licences for the import of machinery and components are not really "incentives" in the strict sense of the term. In some cases, a system of retention quotas whereby exporters can retain a part of their earnings and import therewith goods which are in scarce supply has been in force. The profits made on imports subsidize the exports. From the point of view of equity as well as efficiency, indirect forms of export subsidization leave much to be desired. It would be far simpler and rational to give a straightforward subsidy to exports; and the main reason why this is not done as often as it might be is the one already referred to, viz., a lack of international appreciation of the legitimate case for export incentives in a developing economy.

A closely related, but more complex, issue arises in connection with bilateral arrangements for export promotion. The issue here is posed mainly but not entirely by the need to develop trade with state-trading economies, that is, with Eastern Europe, Soviet Union and China. The growing desire on the part of the Soviet Union and other allied countries to develop trade with the outside world presents a valuable opportunity to the developing (as well as the developed) countries. It is as if a new continent were suddenly to be discovered, a continent not virgin and unexploited but with a well-developed economic structure. Many of the developing countries, and particularly those who find that their traditional markets for their limited exports (for example, Ghana cocoa, India tea, Ceylon rubber) are not growing sufficiently rapidly, have been anxious to exploit the opportunity thus presented. Traditionally, the growing trade with state-trading countries has developed on bilateral lines. This is true to some extent even where the trade has been ostensibly on the basis of multilateral clearing of bilateral balances since by administrative and other methods net clearings in third currencies are often minimized.

The conventional attitude to such bilateral trade is that it might distort trade patterns: sooner or later one partner would find that it has sold more than it was able but willing to buy from the other partner so that it would be inclined to divert normal imports from other sources to the bilateral trading partner or to import more with a view to re-export. What might appear as a net gain to exports may be much less so and may be offset by higher prices for imports. Notwithstanding the need for caution dictated by the kind of considerations just mentioned, it is doubtful if they destroy totally the validity of growing trade with state-trading countries on a bilateral basis. If Ghana can produce cocoa beyond what the non-Soviet world could conceivably consume and if the Soviet authorities wish to permit an increase in cocoa consumption in the Soviet Union, it would make sense for Ghana to sell the cocoa to the Soviet Union in return for Soviet goods even if these goods were more expensive than similar goods that can be obtained from elsewhere. In actual practice, the normal vigilance of trading partners and the desire to establish enduring and mutually profitable trading relations would ensure that fears about unreasonable pricing and trade diversion do not materialize so that the hypothetical arguments against bilateralism in relations with state-trading countries may not be valid at all (except perhaps where the motivation is predominantly non-economic). In time, when the Soviet Union and allied countries trade with the rest of the world on a general rather than selective basis as at present, it may well be that strictly bilateral trading would then appear superfluous and even unduly complex. But in the meanwhile, profitable and growing bilateral trade with the state-trading countries cannot be eschewed by the developing countries on purely hypothetical grounds.

In the nature of things, however, the bulk of the trade of the developing countries would be with the industrialized and richer countries of the West and it is to those countries that one must largely look for the expanding export markets which are such a vital necessity for the developing countries if they are to cease to rely on external assistance. Virtually the whole of the current (and prospective) deficit in the balance-of-payments of the developing countries is with the industrialized countries of the West and the present lopsided trade relationship cannot continue unless one is to be reconciled with a continuing transfer of capital from the richer to the poorer nations. The problem that is inherent in the present pattern of world trade is perhaps the toughest one that international economic statesmanship has yet to face.

As it is, the industrialized nations discourage imports from the developing countries in a variety of ways, including tariffs that discriminate against imports of semi-manufactures and manufactures, quotas, administrative action, high internal excises and the like. Much attention has been focused on this problem in recent years. But the actual progress in freeing and encouraging imports from the developing countries has been only of minute proportions. As a matter of fact, there are grave possibilities of a setback—possibilities which are underlined by the formation of regional units of cooperation, by the frequent and open use of the oft-exploded "cheap labour" argument and by the recent tendency to "regulate" the exports of textiles from the poorer countries.

And yet, it should be obvious to anyone who looks at the orders of magnitude involved in the problem at hand that what is required is not merely a removal of the obstacles in the advanced countries to imports from the developing countries but a positive and sustained act of cooperation in this regard. Any reference to integration of investment policies or to a conscious programme in the advanced countries to provide growing room for the products of developing countries runs the risk nowadays of being summarily dismissed out of court. But this is the direction in which we will inevitably have to move if international economic cooperation is to have any real meaning.

To a certain extent, the export problem of the developing countries would be rendered easier if the so-called advanced countries themselves were to continue to enjoy a significant rate of growth. Apart from the normal growth of demand consequent upon rising levels of income, the task of adjusting the economic structure of the advanced countries so that it leans more heavily on the developing countries would become that much easier. From this point of view, what the world needs is not so much progress towards some abstract concept of equality among nations as rapid progress all round. A 5 per cent per annum growth in the United States, for example, would be all the more desirable if it facilitates a 5 per cent per annum rate of growth in India and if the consequence of, say, a 3 per cent rate of growth in the United States were to hold the Indian rate of growth to 4 per cent per annum.[5]

It may be argued that the developing countries need not look mainly to the advanced countries for their growing markets. If the suggestion is that the developing countries can develop surpluses with countries still not quite developed in order to meet their deficits with more advanced

[5] In passing it may be mentioned that from the point of view of the problem we are considering it would be desirable that the current discussions on a suitable international monetary and payments system get resolved in favour of a more liberal system allowing more automatic settlement of international credits and debits. The fear of irresponsible behaviour on the part of deficit countries has imparted a bias which often acts to the detriment of truly forward-looking and imaginative policies on the part of surplus countries. One has also the suspicion that a measure of bilateralism in foreign assistance—through tied loans—might contribute, albeit rudely, to the kind of awakening that is needed among the richer countries in respect of their trade relations with the poorer countries.

countries, it is hardly likely to square with the present mood and shape of the world. In the past, the triangular kind of exchange envisaged here has played an important part and in view of the inevitable differences in the stage of development among the poorer countries, it may still have a part to play. But the hinterland of undeveloped virgin lands ready to take the place of those who have graduated from that stage is fast disappearing, if it has not already disappeared altogether. And today, the surge for development has enveloped all the nations. This is not to say that the developing nations cannot trade more and more among themselves; whether they do so only absolutely or in relation to total world trade is as irrelevant as it is difficult to predict. But given the ubiquitous urge to develop and the inevitable growth in imports in order to satisfy this urge, there is no likelihood of a decline in the imports of the developing countries from those already advanced economically. There can consequently be no escape from the task of finding some way whereby the advanced countries increase fairly rapidly their absorption of the products of the developing countries.

Exchange Rate Policy

Reference has been made in the earlier pages to the fact that a developing country may need to impose general import duties to act as a damper on import demand and at the same time to subsidize exports till such time as export industries attain their maximum efficiency. The question naturally arises why the same results should not be achieved by a straightforward devaluation. To the extent that imports are generally taxed and exports are subsidized across the board, there is, of course, no substantive difference between a regime of import-duties-cum-export-subsidies and a devaluation of the exchange rate. Perhaps the only difference would be in terms of government revenues insofar as uniform rates of import duties and export subsidies would produce a net revenue where imports generally exceed exports. There may, however, be other considerations which argue against the alternative of devaluation. Apart from the psychological repercussions of devaluation, it should be remembered that a rational policy may well require a gradual reduction in import duties and export subsidies. Small and frequent upward revisions in exchange rates are not as convenient as modifications in import duties and export subsidies.

Again, the arguments we have advanced so far in favour of import duties and export subsidies would not dictate a uniform rate of duty or subsidy on all imports and exports. That being the case, devaluation will not be a complete substitute for a regime of import duties combined with export subsidies. Given the degree and pattern of restraint on imports and encouragement of exports, there would, of course, still be room for choice as to the level of exchange rate around which the additional restraints or incentives are to be organized. If the exchange rate is kept rather low, there would be comparatively little scope for import duties or export subsidies and perhaps a need for taxation of some exports and subsidization of some imports. With a somewhat higher rate, there would be no need for export taxes or import subsidies and a correspondingly greater range over which import duties and export subsidies should apply. There may be a net fiscal advantage in one or the other alternative course. But in actual practice, the choice is more likely to be a matter of historical accident, with the exchange rate within the lower range of the permissible spectrum whenever past inflation necessitates a devaluation and within the higher range on other occasions.

It cannot be gainsaid that the continuing balance-of-payments weakness of the developing countries carries within it the dangers of competitive devaluations of the beggar-my-neighbour variety among the developing countries. Each hard-pressed country may find it difficult to resist the temptation to attract a larger share of the existing market for the traditional and narrow range of exports as well as for some of the newer exports. Sooner or later, the competing countries will follow suit and the net advantage may belong mainly to the developed countries in the form of improved terms of trade. Whether the competition through depreciation takes the form of devaluations or unreasonable proliferation of export incentives makes little difference to the economics of the situation. Unfortunately, international cooperation in matters of this kind is exceedingly difficult; and the general presumption in favour of devaluation—engendered by the continuous history of inflation in most developing countries—deters any serious examination of the competitive and mutually destructive aspects of any particular act of devaluation.

External Assistance and Private Foreign Capital

A detailed discussion on external assistance and private foreign capital is not germane to the present discussion. Where appropriate, we have already referred to them incidentally. We may, however, refer here to some aspects of external assistance and private capital movements which have a bearing on trade and payments problems. The first point relates to tied assistance. From a general point of view, tied loans and grants represent an unwholesome departure from the principle of international division of labour. At the same time, when assisting countries suffer from acute balance-of-payments or unemployment problems, the desire to tie assistance becomes understandable. In a sense the principle of international division of labour can also hardly be applied rationally when the international responsibility for external assistance is not rationally divided. At the same time, the case for tied assistance is being accepted a little too uncritically nowadays.

For one thing, if the rationale for tied assistance is to bring about a more rational distribution of the responsibility for aid, the latter objective can and must be approached more directly. At any rate, as progress is made in that direction—as, indeed, it is being made—the scope of tied assistance must be progressively reduced. Again, even if a measure of tying or discrimination is deemed justifiable in cases of payments difficulties, such discrimination cannot be without discrimination itself. While aid from countries temporarily in deficit may not be utilized for purchases in surplus countries, there is no reason for a similar bar on purchases from deficit countries. As a rule, the tying of aid need not and should not apply to purchases from the developing countries who are themselves the recipients of aid unless one is to make good with one hand what the other destroys. Lastly, the waste implicit in tied aid is often compounded by further insisting on tying the use of the aid funds to certain kinds of purchases, mostly machinery or capital goods. The fallacy of misplaced concreteness which assumes that capital formation is assisted only by the importation of capital goods has led often to the creation of additional capacity when existing capacity cannot be fully utilized for want of raw materials and components. It often accentuates the bias against the import of consumer goods which cannot or need not all be dispensed with. In the context of tied aid, limiting the use of aid to purchase of capital equipment has the added disadvantage of not allowing the most competitive—or least non-competitive—purchases within the assisting country itself. If the object of tied aid is to subsidize or boost domestic production, there is no reason why producers of machinery ought to be subsidized more than the producers of drugs or metals or lubricants.

Throughout the preceding discussion we have assumed that sooner or later, the developing countries should eliminate their dependence on external assistance. The reasons for this are practical rather than moral. But this does not mean that sooner or later the developing countries should cease to be net importers of capital and much less that they should reverse the earlier capital inflow. There is no reason why private capital and even international capital mobilized through agencies such as the World Bank should not continue to flow to the developing countries till kingdom come. How sanguine one can be about the prospects of a continuing and substantial availability of international capital through normal private channels and through accepted international institutions is a matter of taste and mood. But to the extent that one can be so sanguine, the urgency of the task of developing balanced trade relations would be that much less acute and the consequent claims on economic statesmanship that much less baffling.

Some Concluding Remarks

The general drift of the argument developed in this paper may be noted briefly. The balance-of-payments position of the developing countries acts as a special and distinct constraint on the continuing growth of their economies. The policy implications of this phenomenon and the truly gigantic nature of the task of overcoming this bottleneck over a reasonable period are not generally appreciated. Many of the concrete measures required in this connection run counter to accepted norms of international trade and payments behaviour. Some would appear as establishing a double standard of morality among nations. But the double standard is also more apparent than real. Problems of international trade in the world as we find it, cannot, after all, be approached in terms of some abstract model which seeks to maximize some abstract concept of world welfare in which each nation has an equal claim to share. There exists already a will to cooperation in the development of the less developed countries; and while an extension of this cooperation in the field of international trade would not at all be easy, especially as it cannot be expressed through simple rules of thumb, the need for such cooperation is nonetheless vital. All this, however, does not amount to throwing overboard all the accepted norms in the field of commercial and payments policy—much less a retreat from economics in the planning and programming of development. The very fact that there are more than one developing countries would also dictate that the policies of any developing country cannot be divorced from the interest of others equally beset with difficulties; and this consideration would tend to restore the validity of many of the liberal principles of trade and payments at least insofar as relations between the developing countries are concerned.

CHAPTER 27

Lessons from the Monetary Events of 1971*

There are essentially two ways in which we can draw lessons from the monetary events of 1971. In a larger sense, we can treat the year 1971 as a sort of watershed where the international monetary system that had evolved over a quarter of a century after Bretton Woods took a decisive new turn. The lessons of 1971, then, would cover the entire field of the functioning and reform of the international monetary system. This is clearly how Professor Wallich, and to some extent Mr Morse, have chosen to interpret their mandate. For my part, however, I would like to focus first rather naturally on what actually happened in 1971. For one thing, it is by no means certain yet that 1971 would really be that much of a watershed year. Even if it is, the central question of fundamental reform is already on the agenda of the Fund; and I at any rate do not feel any urge to deliver myself of all I may have to say on the subject so early in the game. On the other hand, pointing the searchlight at what actually took place in 1971 has, I think, important lessons to offer, particularly with regard to the process of decision-making which may not be altogether irrelevant irrespective of whether or not there is a brand new Bretton Woods in the making at present.

The Events of 1971

The main events of 1971 were obviously two—suspension of convertibility and the realignment of parities. One can even say that realignment was the only significant event and that the suspension of convertibility was totally a non-event in the sense that even prior to August 1971, the right to convert was hardly really exercised as a matter of course.

* Originally published as *The Monetary Crisis of 1971: The Lessons to be Learnt*, in the form of a booklet by the Per Jacobsson Foundation, September 1972.

In fact, it is possible to agree, that contrary to what is often said, the Bretton Woods system was not asymmetrical or inequitable in regard to the privilege enjoyed by different members in obtaining finance for their payment deficits. It was the non-exercise by and large of the right of conversion of dollars into gold by other countries which really created the dollar exchange standard and the consequent asymmetry.

Apparently, whatever may be the aesthetic virtue of symmetrical rights and obligations, the world has long realized that when it comes to the disciplining of major powers, it cannot be done by a routine or automatic duplication of rules of the kind which would bring them instantly to a halt so to speak in the pursuit of their national objectives. The suspension of convertibility was thus a mere formalization of what was already in existence informally and would in any case have been tacitly agreed to if proposed by the United States.

Be that as it may, it is, I think, clear that the United States' decision to suspend convertibility was essentially a sort of invitation to other major currencies to seek a new relationship with the United States dollar.

The more substantive development of 1971 was certainly the realignment of parities which came to be enshrined in the Smithsonian agreement. But it is equally significant to note that this realignment of parities did not take place in the most natural or normal or economical way in terms of the need to take decisions. Normally, when a country comes to realize that its exchange rate is out of line, it proposes a change in its own parity. If the United States had proposed such a change to $38 or even $40 an ounce, the rest of the world including the International Monetary Fund (IMF) would have accepted it readily; 1971 would then have been just another year like 1958 when the French franc was devalued or like 1967 when the pound sterling was devalued.

What was set in motion instead was a prolonged bargaining process involving a number of countries which were all invited to contribute towards an improvement of a certain order in the United States balance-of-payments or towards a certain overall depreciation of the United States dollar which was in fact notified at the outset through the 10 per cent surcharge on imports.

Now I am aware that there are people who suggest that the realignment of parities that occurred in 1971 was the result of scientific calculations made in the Fund about how much the value of each major currency needed to be changed in relation to the other. Not having access to the calculations, one cannot be sure how far this is true—and, if true, how scientific the calculations really were. But the fact that the average devaluation of the dollar in terms of the major currencies turned out to be the same 10 per cent as was heralded in the import surcharge plus the fact that some parts of the Smithsonian package, like the rate for sterling, came apart rather soon would lend weight to the feeling that the realignment was more an exercise in collective bargaining than in objective economic forecasting.

If this version of Rashmond or the elephant and the three blind mice bears at least a reasonable resemblance to reality, what are the lessons we can draw from it?

The Process of Decision-making

First and foremost, the events of 1971 are I think a timely reminder that international monetary cooperation is essentially a matter of reconciling conflicting national objectives and this conflict, when it relates to major powers, can seldom be resolved by laying down certain precise rules of the game. Nothing can be more naive than to imagine that since the Bretton Woods system is supposed to have failed, all we need to do is to devise a new system with new rules. While a reform of the system may be and indeed is necessary and has, in fact, to be a continuing process, it is not the system alone but also the manner in which it is worked from day-to-day with an implicit or explicit process of negotiation or give-and-take among the major partners which can really deliver the goods.

This should have been fairly obvious for a long time as what finally collapsed in 1971 was not the Bretton Woods system but the patchwork that came to be evolved over the 1950s and '60s in deference to the wishes or the interests of a few major countries. The original Bretton Woods system was a finely calibrated one with a remarkable balance it sought to maintain between different members or between different remedial measures. Thus it recognized that each country must have adequate freedom to pursue its national objectives without being constantly overwhelmed by balance-of-payments difficulties; at the same time, the right to get finance for covering deficits was not unlimited for any member. As already mentioned, this symmetrical position got altered long before 1971 as no one would really dare involve the United States in an immediate financial crisis. On the other hand, paradoxically, the rights of automatic finance for members were further circumscribed by new rules and procedures which had little or no sanction in the Articles of Agreement, for example, by policy decisions on the precise discipline to be followed when a member draws on the Fund the equivalent of successive tranches of its quota.

The way in which the system was overburdened by insisting on freedom of capital movements and the manner in which the technique of the scarce currency clause was disregarded as a means of sharing the burden of adjustment equitably between surplus and deficit countries illustrate further how no system can long remain immune from the twists and turns which its stronger members would like to give to it. Here again, it is noteworthy that the same richer members which were generally in favour of freedom of capital movements were not prepared to carry this to a logical conclusion.

Thus, for example, the advocacy of freedom for capital movements did not extend to untying of official aid or even to unrestricted freedom for other monetary authorities to hold their reserves in any major currency they liked.

While we cannot dismiss the reality of unequal power and influence from the international monetary scene, the fact remains that we cannot allow the decision-making process to degenerate into periodic bargaining among whoever happen to be the largest members of a community. Apart from anything else, decisions reached in an atmosphere of crisis—and with emotional and political overtones which cannot be avoided when more or less equal parties negotiate in a sort of open arena—cannot always be rational and are apt to include some irrelevant, if not ill-advised, elements. We all, I am sure, have our own pet ideas about the rightness or wrongness of the many things that happened in 1971. For my part, I would classify the original import surcharge of 10 per cent as ill-advised, the decision to include the United Kingdom and perhaps some other countries in addition to Germany and Japan as candidates for appreciation vis-à-vis the dollar as not so well considered and the insistence on a change in the gold parity of the dollar as somewhat redundant at least economically once the straightforward path of just devaluing the currency in need of adjustment most was discarded. The point, however, is not whether any of these assertions is necessarily valid, but that these issues became sufficiently controversial to leave a rather long trail of dust behind.

What then is a practicable middle course which recognizes the need for great-power accommodation, negotiation and even bargaining and yet keeps their combined or conflicting vested interest from vitiating the objectives of the system as a whole? I do not pretend that I have any definite or precise answers, but I think the question does deserve to be discussed and answered.

I like to think that all major decisions regarding international monetary problems should be taken in the International Monetary Fund and not in any limited forum. The main reason is that it is only the active participation of comparatively disinterested smaller members and of the Fund management and staff that can lead to rational decisions on important issues. The newly set up Committee of Twenty would concern itself not only with specific issues of monetary reform but would convert itself soon into a sort of Standing Committee for informal consultation on important issues as they arise from time to time.

One of the major defects of the present system of decision-making in the Fund has been that mere contacts at the level of Executive Directors are not enough for establishing the kind of rapport that is necessary among policymakers from all parts of the world. The format and functioning of the annual meetings of Governors have not been such as to overcome this difficulty. Perhaps the meetings of the Committee of Twenty and of their deputies could be so structured as to provide this much-needed forum for informal contacts and discussion on a continuing basis.

The process of arriving at a consensus on important issues would also be greatly facilitated if the policymakers could be brought into greater personal contacts with the large number of academic and other persons who have devoted so much of their time to a consideration of basic monetary issues. There is perhaps no area of practical international cooperation which has benefited as much from the attention of the academics as this area of international monetary cooperation. Attempts have been made in the past to bring the academics, the members of the Fund staff and decision-makers from selected countries together; and having participated in some of these highly cross-fertilizing gatherings, I can say with confidence that if the Per Jacobsson Foundation is looking for some alternative format for its annual tribute, it can do no better then arrange every year—preferably away from the Annual meeting—an informal get-together of the kind I have suggested with a somewhat loose agenda covering more than one topic of current or prospective interest.

There is scope also for more informal and closer contacts between the Fund management and staff on the one hand and the highest policymaking authorities in important countries on the other. Whether this can be done best by changes in the present method of consultations with Article VIII countries or in any other way is more than I can say. Perhaps in matters like this, while it is easy to note the need, there can be no standard prescriptions which would work in all possible concatenation of circumstances, including above all the juxtaposition of different kinds of personalities. But it is well to remember that international monetary cooperation is a rather fragile substance which requires the support of many intangible factors if it is not to explode into an unnecessary crisis from time to time. In this connection, the story that Per Jacobsson was so fond of telling about how he finally persuaded General De Gaulle to devalue the French franc in 1958 is perhaps worth recalling. "Napoleon introduced a franc which served the needs of France for a hundred years. You, my General, have now a chance to give France a new franc which can stand the test of time for the next hundred years." This kind of touch has to be there somewhere in the picture.

So much for the lessons of 1971 as far as the process of decision-making is concerned. May I now turn to some of those glossier titles like Adjustment of Exchange Rates where I hope I will have some comments to make on what Professor Wallich and Mr Morse have already placed before you.

Adjustment of Exchange Rates

Perhaps the most difficult problem in international monetary cooperation is the determination of the extent to which exchange rate changes are necessary from time to time. One might be inclined to think that we have become a little wiser in this regard after 1971. But I am afraid it is difficult to share this optimism. I have already said that it is not easy to accept the claim, for reasons already hinted at, that the Fund acquired experience in 1971 of evolving scientific and objective criteria for determining appropriate exchange relationships between major currencies and that this experience was already reflected in the Smithsonian agreement. One has also the apprehension that excessive preoccupation with objective and precise criteria in this field will lead to pseudo-quantitative theorizing of the kind with which we are already too familiar. Much of the worldly wisdom on inflation today centres on the Quantity Theory of money; and one shudders to think that the Purchasing Power Parity theory might acquire the same pre-eminence in the determination of exchange rates. By all means let us have a good deal of discussion on how to go about deciding on appropriate exchange rate relationships between major currencies. But let us not jump to the conclusion—unless more evidence is produced than we have today—that some definite progress in this direction was made in 1971.

Much the same I think is true of the experience with floating rates in 1971 and with wider margins after December 1971. A brief period of floating rates is supposed to help in establishing realistic rates. Wider margins are expected to help in reducing speculative capital flows and thus to facilitate orderly changes in exchange rates in small steps. Both these propositions have obviously a grain of truth and it would be certainly a great step forward if some automatic or semi-automatic procedure for making small but not necessarily frequent changes in major exchange rates could be devised. But I am inclined to agree with Professor Wallich that recent experience with floating rates or wider margins is not so conclusive and requires at any rate a more detailed analysis of our experience so far before we can generalize on the practical usefulness of these two devices in arriving at more appropriate changes in exchange rates. Professor Wallich's own suggestion at the end of his remarks did not convince me instantly, so to speak. But maybe I have not sized up all the nuances of his suggestion. Perhaps all one can say with confidence is that exchange rate policy like all economic policy is a matter of trial and error and successive approximations to truth so that while one can and must be sure of the direction in which change is necessary, it is always desirable to retain a degree of scepticism regarding the magnitude of the change.

To me, the most important lesson to be drawn from 1971 in regard to exchange rate policy is that almost imperceptibly we have now entered a new era in which competitive devaluation is once again a real danger to watch out for. I think Mr Morse also shares this view—although perhaps for different reasons. Whatever may have been the truth in oft-repeated statements about the bias in favour of overvalued exchange rates—incidentally, the charge really has been that there is generally a bias in favour of not making a change in exchange rates irrespective of whether they were over-valued or undervalued and irrespective of whether there was any intrinsic difficulty for the United States in changing its exchange rates on its own, the fact remains that the United States was able to shake off its inhibitions with considerable ease. The forbidden fruit has now been tasted by all and the world is not likely to be the same again.

One of the most significant parts of Professor Wallich's analysis is the attempt to show that a country like the United States with a relatively small proportion of Gross National Product (GNP) entering foreign trade would find it very difficult to adjust its balance-of-payments through adjustment of income or demand levels and would, therefore, presumably be inclined to opt for a change in exchange rate unless it had continued access to financing facilities. Apart from the fact that there are many countries, including my own, which have a low proportion of foreign trade to GNP, this claim for a special dispensation is not likely to be overlooked by others who would also try to avoid income adjustments by resorting instead more frequently to exchange rate changes. Already, the psychology—and I think it is a misguided psychology—that freedom to vary exchange rates more frequently somehow enables a country to pursue its national objectives in a more unfettered way is gaining ground. But the central problem in the adjustment process for a country in deficit is to moderate its national ambitions (unless it can persuade others to finance the deficit). That being the case, before one accepts the need for a country to devalue its currency, it is all the more important to inquire whether it should not instead—or at least in addition—seek adjustment through measures which operate on incomes and demand. At any rate, it is difficult to avoid the feeling that the era of resistance to exchange rate changes has yielded place to one in which governments are likely to accept too readily that adjustment of exchange rates will save them from many unpopular decisions at home. Even speculative capital movements can be summoned into existence by a mere whisper to justify what is desired. In such a climate, a response from the Fund or the international community that any offer to devalue is so rare that it should be accepted without question like a gift-horse would provide only one more illustration of how often institutions respond to problems of the day in the light of their memory of days gone by.

Convertibility

On the question of convertibility, Professor Wallich's suggestion that there are special reasons why the full rigours of asset convertibility should not be insisted upon may not be convincing—and is not at any rate convincing to me. It can be argued that the United States is not all that unique as Professor Wallich would seem to suggest. Nevertheless, it is I think necessary to be clear about what is really sought to be achieved by insisting on restoring convertibility—some day and to some extent—of dollars into other reserve assets such as gold and SDRs (Special Drawing Rights). This is obviously going to be one of the most difficult questions to settle during the forthcoming discussions on international monetary reform and it is not my intention to suggest any rigid or final position on such a complex and controversial subject. But I think there are some questions that at least need to be answered or at any rate borne in mind in the consideration of this problem of convertibility.

First of all, does not the experience of 1971 remind us that no great power really places its vital national interests and objectives at the mercy entirely of any fixed rules? What guarantee is there then that any new rules of convertibility will not be set aside in future with or without the tacit approval of others? If the only force that can discipline the great is moral force or the power of public opinion, why make such a fetish of symmetry in rules when in real life there is no such ultimate parity among unequal partners? Would it not be better instead for the smaller members to suggest that since no precise limits can be put in practice on the extent to which the big powers can obtain finance from each other more or less automatically for covering their deficits, the financing facilities available to the weaker members should also be liberalized? It is I think a moot point that when so many things about the monetary system are questioned today, no one has yet questioned the wisdom or the validity of the policies that started in the 1950s and grew in the '60s regarding the standard discipline to be imposed on the smaller members when they come to borrow successive trenches of their quota. It is very much to be hoped that any discussion on symmetrical treatment of all members would include an examination of these practices so that in the name of formal a more far-reaching asymmetry is not perpetuated.

One has also got to ask if insistence on convertibility does not lead us into other kinds of problems. Thus the United States becomes inveterately opposed to any suggestion which might reduce in absolute terms its share in any SDR creation as it feels that some day, to meet its hitherto undefined convertibility obligations, it may need every SDR it can legitimately lay claim upon. At any rate, it is at least worth considering seriously whether a check on the United States running unduly large deficits cannot be exercised by means other than a formal restoration of convertibility and whether a less moralistic and more pragmatic approach to symmetry may not serve better the interest—if not the *amour propre*—of the majority of the Fund's members.

Developing Countries

Finally, one might ask: are there any special lessons that the developing countries can draw from the events of 1971? The most important lesson, viz., the need for their being fully involved in the decision-making process has, I think, been learned all round at least to some extent and one can earnestly hope that the actual functioning of the Committee of Twenty will genuinely strengthen the effective role of developing countries in international monetary cooperation on an enduring basis. It would also be well for the developing countries to remember that what matters ultimately is not just an opportunity to sit around the same table or even to get equal time for expounding their views. What the developing countries really require is that the world community should devote the same time, energy and statesmanlike effort in solving the problems of concern to the poorer nations as it does in overcoming the difficulties of the richer nations. When we find, for example, that the whole world is thrown into turmoil all of a sudden when problems of the richer countries are to be solved but that problems of concern to the poorer countries, like International Development Association (IDA) replenishment, take long to settle, one cannot but wonder whether sitting around the same table and having one's say is not really a substitute for problems of concern to all getting equal attention all round.

In monetary matters, the developing countries have generally a preference for a greater degree of fixity in exchange rates and for a somewhat liberal approach to financing of deficits as distinguished from premature remedial measures. There is nothing in the experience of 1971 which would suggest that the developing countries should be less vigilant in questioning the need for frequent changes in the exchange rates for major currencies or that they should be less opposed to suggestions that their modest investment programmes should be curtailed or abandoned at the first sign of payments difficulties. Indeed, as already suggested, there is more reason for them now to ensure that any proposed change in the exchange rates for a major currency is not just an easy exit out of internal discipline. At the same time, on questions relating to how much of financing of deficits—as distinct from reducing them—might be appropriate, the developing countries have everything to gain by the encouragement of a more liberal climate.

It may also be noted in passing that the tendency to link the settlement of monetary issues with changes in trade and other policies which came into evidence in 1971, while desirable in itself, needs to be handled with care as far as the developing countries are concerned. There is every danger that trade negotiations may once again proceed on the basis of the exchange of mutual concessions or reciprocity rather than in pursuit of truly multilateral objectives or principles which take existing inequalities into account and try to remedy them. Having not so many concessions to offer, the developing countries may well find that they are left in the lurch except on the basis of an alliance with one or the other of the big trading powers; and the greater the number of issues that get mixed up in any particular negotiation, the less the chances of the interests of the rest of the world being kept in mind. The spectre of the world being divided in four or five major power blocs—both political and economic—has been clearly raised and the main task before the developing countries is to ensure that economic colonialism does net get revived in a new garb in the name of creating a more manageable structure of international economic cooperation.

To Sum Up

To sum up the lessons to be learned from a particular set of events, like beauty, are generally in the eyes of the beholder and perhaps most of us seek in each passing year a vindication of our own prejudices and preconceptions. For my part, the most important lessons of 1971 relate to the process of decision-making. When it comes to issues of major significance both internally and as between nations, no system or set of rules can be a substitute for negotiations. And yet, if every important question that needs to be settled is not to erupt into a major bargaining contest with its inevitable quota of irrelevance and irrationality, many subtle and intangible bridges between decision-makers have to be built so that the contacts, discussions and exchange of views more or less informally and on a reasonably continuing basis enable the problems to be solved or settled long before they reach explosive proportions. As in marriage, so also in monetary cooperation, it is not so much the system or the guidelines but the mutual forbearance that comes out of being constantly exposed to each other which ultimately stands in good stead in resolving the inevitable conflicts of will, interest and even understanding.

The experience of 1971 is not conclusive about the merit of wider margins in discouraging speculation or of floating rates in serving as a guide to realistic or appropriate exchange rates. Nor can it be said that we have advanced far in establishing objective criteria for determining an appropriate exchange rate relationship between major currencies. It would be a good thing if some reasonably automatic procedure for making small but not necessarily frequent changes in exchange rates could be evolved. But it is doubtful if we have yet hit upon any such procedure which would be easily acceptable to all. At the same time, one has an uneasy feeling that the danger of competitive devaluation is now greater than ever so that some objective procedure for adjudicating on exchange rate changes is all the more necessary.

Without presuming to come to any final conclusion, there is reason to question whether a return to asset convertibility may be the best way of achieving as much symmetry between the big and small as may be really practicable in any case.

For the developing countries, the year 1971 led to a welcome recognition of the importance of their being fully involved in the discussion on international monetary reform. But there are enough pointers to further dangers to their interests which would require vigilance on their part. In the meanwhile, there is nothing in the events of 1971 to suggest that the developing countries should give up their general suspicion of frequent changes in the exchange rates for major currencies or of any Calvinistic attitude towards the financing of external deficits.

And finally, and this is a new point, if the most significant aspect of recent international history is the attempt to carry the torch of discussion, dialogue and even cooperation to hitherto ostracized but important parts of the world, is it really prudent to imagine that a new era in international monetary cooperation can be ushered in without making any serious effort to see if it cannot also embrace those large parts of the international community which have not yet been included in the membership of the International Monetary Fund? Is there not a danger here that if international monetary cooperation fails to reflect the same trends as in international cooperation in general, much of our labours in trying to reform the monetary system may prove to be in vain and we may have to start all over again in a few years to accommodate the needs of those who cannot merely be wished away? At any rate, should we not at least incorporate in our scheme of reform all those aspects, including the voting structure and the system of election or appointment of Directors, which may have a bearing on how easily we can enlarge and indeed universalize the area of monetary cooperation as represented in the only international institution established for that purpose?

CHAPTER 28

Indebtedness of Developing Countries*

The seriousness of the problem in terms of facts and figures relating to the developing countries as a whole is well known. When you have debt and debt service which grow at the rate of 14 per cent per annum, and when export earnings can hardly be expected to increase by more than say 6 or 7 per cent per annum, which has been the experience in the past, one point is clear that debt service repayment will increasingly absorb larger and larger proportions of export earnings and this is a situation which sooner or later is bound to reach rather uncomfortable proportions.

In our own case of India, it is only a very short period since 1958 when we started borrowing abroad in a significant manner and yet by about 1968–69 we had already reached the situation that something of the order of 30 per cent of our export earnings had to be devoted to the repayment of debt, both amortization and interest charges. And today also, if I may put it in another way, more than three-fourths of the aid we get in a given year is given back in terms of repayment. We get about $800 million (1 million = 10 lakh) of aid and our repayments are already of the order of $625 million. This is an indication of the magnitude of the debt problem which is something which calls for a solution.

How has this problem come about? Partly, it is of course the earlier loans having been contracted on terms which were not as concessional as one would have liked them to be. There was a certain urgency about going ahead with development and at that stage the need for concessional credit was not so well appreciated around the world, so that one had to contract debts at such terms as one could get then, and this has created partly the problem and I think it is one part of the problem.

* Address to the Colombo Plan Consultative Committee, November 1972.

What has also made the problem of debt relief as such rather important at the present juncture is the fact that there is a certain degree of what I might call disenchantment regarding the quantum of aid that can be mobilized from year to year. The subject matter of our discussion, rightly so, is the problem of indebtedness of developing countries including the terms and quantum of aid.

Let me explain. If you take a simple arithmetical example, let us say a country gets $100 million of aid. If the net transfer of $100 million is to be maintained, while debt charges begin to mount up, you will have to negotiate every year over $100 million worth of aid; the next year it will be still more and the year after it will be still more. In other words, if there is to be no debt relief and if debt repayments are to be made on schedule, and since debt payment including interest payment will mount up from year to year, you will have to mobilize more aid from year to year.

Now for some years it was possible for the developing countries to think that the climate was such that one could hopefully look forward to more and more of new aid every year in order to maintain the same net transfer of resources. But this is no longer possible because the sentiment for foreign aid around the world is not such that you could borrow more from year to year in order to maintain the same level of net transfer of resources. When that is not the case and the new aid that you can mobilize is not likely to increase, then either the net transfer of resources has to fall precipitately or something has to be done on the debt side.

I think this point needs to be emphasized that irrespective of the harshness and hardness of the terms in the past, when you reach a stage when the international goodwill or public opinion is not of an order that new aid mobilization can increase significantly from year to year, then the net transfer of resources will decline sharply unless separately something is done about the debt problem itself. This is one of the reasons why the problem of debt has become so urgent for countries like India. I mean for the last several years the level of gross aid to India has not only remained static, it in fact has come down and it comes down almost every year with the result that you cannot possibly maintain even the minimal net transfer of resources of $200 million or something like that unless something is done on the debt side.

There are two or three other factors which I would like to mention. It is not simply a question of need alone; there is also an equity aspect and that arises in this way. Virtually all the bilateral aid is tied. You have got to use it in the country from which you get the aid and you have to use it for the purposes which are prescribed from time to time. On the other hand, repayments, at least to the Western countries, are not tied. They have to be made in free foreign exchange. The aid (tied aid) prima facie is not equitable because any foreign currency you get in terms of aid, is worth less than what you have to earn in order to make repayment in the same currency.

This is the situation which has to be corrected sooner or later. That is to say, if for some reason we could not have an equitable situation regarding repayment being of the same nature as the aid, then sooner or later this inequity or lack of symmetry has to be rectified. In other words, there has to be an element of debt adjustment, debt reduction in the process of debt relief; it is not just a question of postponement of payments; and this, I think, we should not forget.

I would also mention one factor or two more factors, if you like. One, I think, is that we all had a perspective which was rather ambitious. As I said, aid around the world started gathering momentum only around the latter half of the 1950s or towards the end of the 1950 as a matter of fact and somehow in order to create a climate for aid, we all thought that in ten or fifteen years the developing countries should be free from the need for aid. Just as the Marshall Plan countries were free from the need for aid in four or five years, the developing countries, it was thought, would take ten or fifteen years. This, I think, is a much too narrow and optimistic perspective if you bear in mind the extreme poverty of the developing countries, and I think one has to accept that if you really believe in aid then the perspective over which the aid in the sense of net transfer of resources will have to continue is not a ten- or fifteen-year perspective, it is a much longer perspective. This is one more reason why the mechanism for net transfer of resources will have to include some element of debt relief.

Finally, I would say that there is also a problem of sheer practical wisdom in this matter. No country, not even the richest in the world, is going to give up its national objectives which are vital. As we say in India, you cannot get blood out of stone; if you want to get something out of the countries to whom you have given money, then you have to ensure that they earn money in a reasonable way; otherwise they cannot repay. And I think time and again history has shown that if the burden becomes intolerable, people will throw it off. They are not going to accept that the burden is something which somebody has contracted for and ordered us to pay.

We all talked of inequity of reparations at the time of World War I. Recently, we had the example of it being said that convertibility into gold cannot be maintained; the world community will have to accept the fact that it cannot be maintained and it need not be maintained. As for the remedies, I think Mr Wood was right in pointing out a number of things, saying that it is not merely directly a problem of postponement or reduction of debt payments; something must be done also to help the developing countries to earn larger amounts by way of exports. I would certainly agree with him that there is a problem also of, shall I say, a certain degree of restraint in the matter of contracting short-term debts. There has also to be improvement in terms of new aid. I would say that of all the concessional forms of aid, I regard the aid which carries no rate of interest as the most desirable. I am aware that there are formulae whereby you describe the concessional nature of aid in a certain standard form but I think they are all misleading. The aid which carries no rate of interest is the most desirable because it avoids that arithmetical monster of having to borrow more and more every year in order to maintain the same net inflow of resources.

If there is no rate of interest, then at least I am free from that anxiety of having to borrow more and more every year to maintain the same net flow of resources; and if we were thinking in terms of what kind of improvement in terms will be necessary, I would first of all make a pitch for only one improvement and say: "Please make all your loans interest-free and make all your past loans also interest-free." If you accept the principle that loans in future should be interest-free, I do not see why loans in the past should not be interest-free; otherwise, it would not be concessional aid. Let us not even use the word aid so freely because, as I said, there is a certain inequity in the basic arrangements for it.

I would not agree readily on one point—not that I have any serious disagreement, but I know from experience that things work differently. It is true that there must be discussion. It is true that all creditors must take counsel together. But I think if you ask for equality of treatment, you are asking for the moon. If you think of an arrangement for debt relief where all the creditors will make equal sacrifice, you are only asking for trouble. I have heard in the debate in the Consortium—and I hope my Japanese friends would not mind it—every time they have been told that your terms in the past were harder because you charge a higher rate of interest, they privately come to me and say, "Tell me, Mr Patel, did you find Japanese equipment better than other equipment or not? Did you find that we finish the job early enough than others or not? So what would you find expensive, Japanese money or other money?"

I would not wish to say that I accept this argument of the Japanese friends wholeheartedly. But there is some truth in it. What I am driving at is that the comparison of each form of aid, at how concessional a rate or at how much of a non-concessional rate it is given, is an extremely difficult job and we know from experience that some rough and ready degree of equity is all that should be attempted. To try to be fussy or finicky about too much equity when it cannot be established as to what would be equal terms for all the creditors, merely amounts to an undue postponement of the solution of the problem, merely amounts to more or less the lowest denomination being adopted; and I hope, therefore, that we do not insist on concepts of equity beyond a point when it comes to how much sacrifice would each creditor country make in the solution of a particular debt problem.

If I were to make one or two additional points, I think that whereas in individual cases under the leadership of the World Bank, the problem of debt has been at least taken in hand, there are, I think, improvements possible in one or two ways. I have already said that we have to specifically recognize that what we are after is a genuine reduction in the burden of debt and not merely a postponement of debt. Postponement itself is a reduction if it is on better terms than in the past, but there has to be willing acceptance that when a situation reaches a certain proportion, then you will have to accept a certain amount of debt burden reduction as an objective; otherwise, I do not see how the net transfer of resources can be maintained even at a minimal level, for a country like India, at $100 million or at even virtually nothing.

The second point is that the arrangements for debt relief today are from hand to mouth; they are from year to year and this is certainly no way of solving the problem. One of the major difficulties about aid has been that the promise that it would be given in advance over a fairly long period to enable a country to plan has never been fulfilled. I remember President Kennedy tried it hard and at the beginning of the Second Plan we thought we will get somewhere with this objective; for a year or so we got some indication for a period, but after that it just got bogged down to year-to-year basis.

I know that recently the British, for instance, have agreed to give on the project side commitments which extend over a number of years. But by and large, the parliamentary processes of budget appropriation, etc., are such that on the aid front we have not been able to advance beyond year-to-year commitments. I hope that at least on the debt side where the parliamentary problems are not of the same order one could have arrangements which could extend over three to five years. Unfortunately, that has not been the case. If there is to be real relief, the arrangement must extend over a fairly long period of at least three to five years and not on a year-to-year basis.

I do want to repeat that this is not a problem which arises simply because the terms of aid in the past were harsher or harder. I think that is an over-simplification. I think the ultimate goodwill that we wish to achieve around the world by international economic cooperation, including cooperation through aid, will be totally lost if country after country begins to feel that the burden of debt was so great that theoretical insistence on bearing it fully is merely retarding their progress. The poor pay their debts more honourably than others do. But it has happened time and again in history that you can get something out of the debtor–creditor situation only if everybody is progressing. If everybody is not progressing, you do not get much out of it, no matter how you define the aid relationship.

CHAPTER 29

A New International Economic Order?*

In Memory

It is customary to begin a memorial lecture by saying a few words in honour of the person whose life and work we wish to commemorate. But for some of us who knew Ramaswami well and received so much of his affection and friendship, it is difficult to think of him even now without recalling that gruesome morning some five years ago when he lay serene in his own bed, looking benevolent and kind as ever, but with the breath of life plucked away by clouds of smoke from a nearby chair. All else gets obliterated by the utter senselessness of that tragic accident; and the mind keeps asking: "how can such things ever be?"

But he *is* gone; and we are here to recall, as is the way of this world, something which transcends our purely personal sense of loss. I will not speak of Ramaswami's remarkable qualities of head and heart, or of his outstanding contribution to economic analysis and policy. Others in this series of lectures have done that already. But there are one or two things which I cannot help recalling whenever I think of him; and perhaps it is not without some general significance if I share with you these thoughts before I come to the subject matter I have chosen for this evening.

So much has been said throughout centuries about the scourge of poverty and about the scars that are left on a sensitive mind by the struggle to overcome the disadvantages of birth. But in our age and clime, perhaps the scars that are left on the minds of the sensitive among the well-born by the struggle to establish that they should be accepted on their own terms and

* Ramaswami Memorial Lecture of 1974, delivered under the auspices of the Delhi School of Economics and the Indian Statistical Institute; subsequently published in the *Indian Economic Review*, Vol. 9, No. 1, January–June 1974.

on the basis of their own merit are no less real. However brilliant or able, however generous or self-effacing and however scrupulous in their desire to eschew the fruits of parental influence and wealth, the sons and daughters of the well-to-do seldom get the benefit of doubt, seldom get credit for what they truly deserve in their own right. Sooner or later, perhaps they do. But often it is too late and not without too heavy a price in terms of hurt pride and a sense of insecurity. How often do we remember that the injunction for mercy, for consideration, for understanding and indeed for equality applies in respect of everyone—irrespective of birth as the phrase goes, but irrespective of birth whether low *or* high?

The other thought that keeps coming to me as I think of Ramaswami is whether his kind of virtues are really out of place in our rough and ready modern world. Ramaswami belonged to a world in which personal relations are at least as important as public duty, where public duty consists at least as much of sharpening intellectual tools as of public action, where public action consists at least as much of honest and purposeful administration as of periodic reform of policies and institutions, where institutional reform is something which you fashion with a chisel with care and bit by bit rather than with a few strong blows from a sledgehammer. It is a world, in short, of small canvas but exquisite detail. But the question is on everyone's mind: "Are not our problems at least in this subcontinent so formidable that this civilized and orderly world of a Rajput miniature, so to speak, should yield place to the rough hues and creative chaos of a modern painting?"

For my part, I like to believe that revolutions, however necessary or inevitable they may be at times, are never sufficient; and for long stretches of history, at any rate, mankind must settle down to the virtues which belong to the world of Ramaswami, a world which can never be irrelevant or out of date, however passé it may become from time to time.

Characteristic of the New Order

So much about a fond and unforgettable memory. And now I must turn to the subject I have chosen for my talk this evening, viz., the future of international economic cooperation, a subject which was very dear to Ramaswami's heart. Of late, and particularly after the recent Special Session of the General Assembly of the UN, there has been renewed optimism in regard to the future of international economic cooperation. And it is at least opportune and appropriate to ask: "Are we really witnessing the birth of a new international economic order? If so, what are likely to be the characteristic features of such a new order? And what challenges and opportunities is it likely to hold for a country like India?"

Now in a sense our vision of a new international economic order has been a relatively simple affair. Basically, what we have been trying to achieve since Bretton Woods, through the United Nations, United Nations

Commission on Trade and Development (UNCTAD), General Agreement on Tariffs and Trade (GATT) and the like is to translate into international economic relations the kind of objectives and policies which have become the accepted norm for relations between groups within nation states in all modern societies. No matter what a modern state describes itself to be, it pays at least lip-service to the same ideals and objectives in the economic sphere, viz.,

(a) a minimum standard of living and a modicum of economic security for all its citizens;
(b) to achieve these ends, acceptance of a deliberate policy of development as well as redistribution; and finally,
(c) irrespective of the needs of a basic minimum and economic security for all, to a certain restraint on economic power per se so that it does not become the instrument of political or cultural domination.

The search for a new international economic order over the past three decades since Bretton Woods has meant simply this: that the responsibility for achieving the goals of a basic economic minimum and of economic security and freedom from economic domination in any given country should not be that of the citizens of that country alone; it must be shared by the international community at large. What is even more important, this sharing of responsibility internationally should take the same concrete form as what has come to be accepted more or less universally in the context of national policy, viz., deliberate promotion of economic development, redistribution of income and wealth and a systematic democratization of all economic institutions.

Needless to say, the New International Economic Order, as just outlined, is not yet there and will never be there in all its glory; nor is it even fully perceived today. But it is important to ask: how far are we likely to proceed in the new directions in the near future and how can we in India, for example, take advantage of the new situation with a little foresight? This is what I propose to do during the rest of this talk. And for reasons of convenience, I shall organize my remarks around the following broad topics:

(a) prospects for the redistribution of international wealth;
(b) commitment to economic security;
(c) prospects for a minimum standard of living for all; and
(d) democratization of international economic relations.

In the course of the discussions, I shall also attempt to draw a few general lessons for us in India. But the scope of discussions on a subject like the New World Economic Order is so wide that I shall have to be selective and assume that most of you are reasonably familiar with the functioning of the present international economic system and with the discussions on how to reform it.

Redistribution

There is no doubt that both at the national and the international level, a better distribution of income and wealth has received of late much greater attention. But are the prospects for a significant redistribution of international wealth more promising now than they have been for some time?

Foreign aid is by no means the only or the main instrument of a deliberate policy of international redistribution of wealth; but it is certainly the one which has received the most attention. Ideally again, the total quantum of foreign aid and the manner in which its costs and benefits are distributed among different nations should be governed by the same principles which guide national policies of income-taxation and the distribution of expenditure among different groups and purposes. Up to a point, an attempt has already been made to apply these principles to the sources and flow of foreign aid. Thus, the prescription of the target of 1 per cent of Gross National Product (GNP), the attempt to define contributions to IDA not on a voluntary basis but in terms of rough equivalence with IMF quotas which at least to some extent reflect relative wealth or economic strength and the attempt—again in International Development Association (IDA)—to decide on objective criteria the countries which would be entitled to IDA financing as distinguished from World Bank financing, are at least deliberate efforts to devise a conscious policy of international redistribution.

More recently, United Nations Development Policy (UNDP) has carried this process an interesting step forward. It has attempted to define the share of each of its more than 125 recipient members in the total assistance likely to be available, over a coming five year period, viz., 1977–1981, on the basis of precise and objective criteria, primarily population and per capita income. Despite the unavoidable simplicity of precise functions and formulae which cannot take into account all relevant factors, a decision has been all but reached on the absolute as well as relative share of each recipient by agreement among all concerned. The assumptions regarding availability of resources over a five-year period themselves imply an exhortation to donors to increase their contributions at a certain rate. Something like an international parliamentary democracy has certainly been successfully at work in UNDP's efforts at arriving at what are called Five-Year Indicative Planning Figures for each recipient member.

Having said this, I hasten to add that the process of international redistribution through foreign aid or transfer of resources has hardly begun and has even failed to gather momentum. We are far from achieving even the 1 per cent of GNP target of aid, much less the 0.7 per cent of GNP target for official aid; and while most industrialized countries now subscribe at least in theory to this target, these do not include the most important countries, including both the US and USSR. When one recalls that in most countries today the process of resource transfer internally through taxation accounts for anywhere between 20 and 30 per cent of GNP, the failure to achieve even the 1 per cent of GNP target internationally is a grim reminder of how far removed we really are from anything like a World Government. Nor is there any significant trend towards either multilateralization of aid or to its commitment over a number of years. The recent experience of IDA denotes, if anything, a retrogression. The example of UNDP, while interesting, is not all that significant as the resources involved are sufficiently small to permit the luxury of an agreed rate of growth or an agreed pattern of distribution without serious impairment of any one's larger interest. It is doubtful if recipients on their own would agree on relative shares if what was involved was the distribution of not just $400–500 million (1 million = 10 lakh) per year of technical assistance but, of say $10–12 million of capital assistance. And even in UNDP there is no agreement among donors to define their relative and absolute contributions in accordance with some objective criteria.

Surprisingly, the recent oil crisis seems to have won over some strange converts to the cause of international redistribution. After the recent sharp increase in oil prices it became a fashion in some quarters to ask whether a few countries were entitled to monopolize strategic resources and whether such resources should not be exploited and controlled by international entities. I say these voices came from strange converts because they were not heard earlier to demand that the unequal distribution of land among nations, for example, should be mitigated by free migration or by international control over the produce of land. Be that as it may, there is no doubt that a new dimension has now been added to the urge for redistribution of international wealth. The demand now is not that just wealth in general should be shared, but also that particular forms of wealth representing good fortune or bounty of nature should also be shared. That is why the oil-producing nations are exhorted not merely to compensate the poorer countries affected by higher oil prices, but also to go beyond that in supporting the developmental efforts of the poorer nations. That is also why it makes sense to ask the US, Canada and Australia to contribute specifically to food security, or to insist on the resources of the sea to be exploited for the common good rather than for the benefit of those who are economically and technologically in a better position to exploit them. The Soviet Union's insistence on devoting a part of the savings from disarmament to developmental assistance is an aspect of the same urge.

More recently, this idea has also been incorporated in the UN Revolving Fund for Natural Resources, which was established early this year. Countries receiving assistance from the Fund for exploration of their natural resources will receive assistance neither by way of grants nor by way of loans. The terms, in fact, would be conditional ones. If the country fails to discover any commercially exploitable natural resources as a result of the assistance from the Fund, it will pay nothing to the Fund. If on the other hand it does discover something, it will share this good fortune with the developing countries in general by contributing to the Fund a certain percentage of the value of the additional production over a number of years.

Unfortunately, there is no reason to believe that an appeal to share a particular form of wealth or good fortune would be more successful than an appeal to share wealth in general. But perhaps there is something in continuing to knock at every door; and a country like India which is not all that rich in natural resources has certainly a great stake, for example, in ensuring that the wealth of the sea is not sequestered by powerful nation states, as has been the case with the wealth of the land.

Going beyond that, can one see in recent events the possibility of the poorer countries compelling the rich to part with some of their wealth rather than persuading them to do so? The example of the Organization of Petroleum Exporting Countries (OPEC) is already being followed by the aluminium producers. Cannot all raw material producers follow the same pattern of combining for monopolistic behaviour? I for one remain highly sceptical of the bargaining power of raw material producers being deployed as an instrument for international redistribution in the right direction. While one can get away with one or two commodities of crucial importance, the attempt to improve the terms of trade for all raw materials dramatically will only lead to corresponding adjustment in other prices and therefore in another upward twist to world inflation. Even within a nation, the attempt of any group to improve its relative position to any significant extent is almost always frustrated by the countervailing action of others and results only in inflation; and the same is true internationally as well. And we in India need hardly to be reminded that when it comes to the dividing line between wealth and poverty, it is certainly not coterminous with the dividing line between the abundance of strategic raw materials and their absence. It is tempting to think that even if this policy of raising the prices of raw material succeeds only in a few cases, it can bring about a significant redistribution from the rich to the poor. This can be so if the relatively poor who suddenly become rich share their good fortune more readily and extensively with others than the rich have done so far. But in this age and day Robin Hoods are hard to come by; and the quality of mercy is evenly and rather thinly distributed all over the world.

In short, any significant redistribution of the wealth of the world does not seem probable either through foreign aid or the sharing of particular good fortune or through the exercise of collective bargaining. If it comes about, it would be more through differential rates of growth and perhaps through the bonus that inflation gives to all debtors. But the fact that things are not likely to be much better does not mean that they cannot be much worse; and we in India are so particularly vulnerable that we cannot afford to let down our guard in any forum where issues germane to possible redistribution of income are discussed.

Economic Security

Coming now to economic security, internationally, the post-war search for economic security as distinguished from economic progress began with the establishment of the International Monetary Fund. The ability to create international reserves was intended primarily to enable nations to avoid deflationary policies or to slow down development plans in the face of temporary difficulties; and international surveillance over exchange rates, monetary and fiscal policy and exchange restrictions was intended to prevent essentially beggar-my-neighbour policies. In the event, the facility to create reserves proved to be of only marginal use at least to the developing countries; and the bias against flexible exchange rates as well as periodic surveillance of internal policies of debtor nations by the Fund themselves proved important sources of instability. Despite the recent efforts to reform the international monetary system, there is little evidence that developing countries as a whole will now have much greater or readier access to internationally created reserves. The change that has really taken place—and it is mainly a reflection of the change in the US position—is that flexible exchange rates have come to stay and the rather dogmatic and doctrinaire surveillance of internal policies of member countries by the Fund in case of need will not hold the same terrors at least for some time to come.

If there is any moral in this for us in India, I would say that the outcome of the recent attempt to reform the international monetary system emphasizes once again that there is no real substitute for owned reserves as against borrowed reserves—as our own experience during the Bangladesh crisis showed. On matters like what level of foreign exchange reserves we should have, we need to raise our sights considerably. Our objective, at least when times are good, should be to have foreign exchange reserves well in excess of say a billion dollars. And what is true of foreign exchange reserves is equally true of reserves in real terms, that is, of reserves of food and essential raw materials.

I would say also that we should emphasize more and more our need for flexibility when times are bad not in terms of our right to borrow more as in terms of our right to repay less. And let us not forget that when it comes to temporary relief through postponement of repayment, a part at least of the initiative rests with us rather than with others.

I think it is time also that we practise real exchange rate flexibility from time to time and learn how to let the rupee float and control the float as and when necessary. The present practice of a link either with sterling or the dollar does not let the rupee respond to the needs of our own economic situation; nor does it give the Reserve Bank or the commercial banks the opportunity to develop the kind of expertise and experience they need to cope fully with the age of flexible exchange rates which, as I said, are here to stay.

As far as international trade is concerned, the search for economic security has focused mainly on the instability of raw material prices or more generally on the declining terms of trade for primary producers. In a sense, the recent special session of the General Assembly had this as its main theme, viz., how to assure primary producers a reasonable price. But the fact of the matter is that there has been no progress made, nor is any significant progress likely, in regard to international action to support raw material prices in general. Commodity agreements are few and not waterproof; there is no stabilization fund internationally put together nor even a yardstick to determine what would be a reasonable price that can be stabilized. The fact of the matter seems to be that international support to raw material prices raises essentially questions pertaining to international distribution of wealth to which no serious answers have been or can be realistically attempted.

An aspect of international action to promote greater economic security, which has recently been receiving attention, may also be noted. Last year, when food production and food stocks were unusually low and when conditions of famine prevailed over large parts of the world, it became clear that the world needed on an average much greater stocks of essential food grains. There was a general feeling that the earlier policies of giving up price supports or restricting production in some countries may have to be abandoned. What is equally important, it became abundantly clear that in bad times at any rate, there must be some international supervision of commercial sales as well as resumption of food aid on a significant scale. When it comes to a basic necessity like food, it is not purchasing power or superior market intelligence alone that should decide the distribution of available supplies. Urgency of need should also prevail at least to a reasonable extent if mass starvation and deaths are to be avoided. Indeed, questions were asked last year whether we can afford to feed more and more grain to cattle in order to raise meat consumption in the richer countries, including the socialist countries, when millions of human beings are facing starvation and worse for want of adequate food grains. On similar reasoning, there is need for some machinery to ensure an equitable distribution of key materials like fertilizers in times of scarcity.

It is against this background that the UN decided to hold in the autumn of this year a World Food Conference. I would not like to anticipate the results of the Conference. In matters like this, it is always a good policy to work for the best and assume the worst in guiding one's own actions. But I would like to urge that, as a nation, we have a great stake in this Conference as indeed in continuing to keep this matter of food and fertilizer security on the international agenda even after the Conference. Insistence on our part on international action to promote food or fertilizer security should not be interpreted as a departure from our policy of self-reliance. By now it should be abundantly clear to everyone that for us there can be no real alternative to self-sufficiency in food grains or fertilizers. But recent experience also shows that when it comes to a basic necessity like food grains, there is really little or no scope for tightening belts and the supplies needed have to be imported at any cost. There is no reason why we should not endeavour to ensure that imports when needed, whether of food grains or anything else, are available on as favourable terms as possible. Nor is there any point in overlooking the fact that food and fertilizer diplomacy will be an important part of our external relations with a large number of countries over the next several years.

International conferences and resolutions, even when they do not result in concrete international action, have this merit at least that they facilitate our bilateral diplomacy. To my mind, this has also been the main gain of the recent Special Session of the General Assembly in regard to our requirements of petroleum products. While the Special Fund for the benefit of countries most affected by the energy crisis may or may not come about, there is no doubt that our bilateral diplomacy has been greatly assisted by the success of our international diplomacy at the Special Session; and the UN forum, from this point of view holds a special value for a country like India which is non-aligned not only politically or ideologically but also in terms of geography and religion.

There is yet another aspect of economic security which is coming into prominence of late. I am referring to the feeling among many countries, particularly those left behind in the race for economic progress, that they must somehow be protected against the danger of serious depletion or exhaustion of vital natural resources around the world before they have had time to achieve their real economic breakthrough. The fear is prompted by the impetus given by the Club of Rome to the idea that there are definite limits to growth. This is not the place to debate the merits of the thesis that non-renewable natural resources constitute a serious potential constraint on world economic growth. But the important point is that a growing number of influential people around the world are coming to believe in it. The Shah of Iran, for example, has repeatedly made it clear that what he is really after is conservation of the world's oil supply for really essential uses such as production of fertilizers as against excessive heating or air-conditioning. It is felt that without such conservation, countries like Iran will be confronted with a serious energy situation of their own before they have achieved even a modest standard of living for all their people.

It is difficult to see what action can be taken internationally to promote conservation or avoidance of waste. But I for one would advocate, for this and other reasons, that we create public opinion in favour of the richer countries moderating their standards of consumption. I am aware of the general belief that higher demand from the rich nations creates growth and employment opportunities among the poor nations. But it creates much else besides, including false standards and unfavourable terms of trade for countries deficient in natural resources.

In any event, ultimately, there is more economic security—and also growth—in science and technology than in anything else. So far, the efforts of the UN—mainly channelled through UNDP—have been by way of technical assistance narrowly interpreted, that is, by way of transfer of existing technology and building up of national technical institutions rather than assistance for the actual development of new or more appropriate technology. The emphasis is now changing, although slowly; and countries like India have a special interest in encouraging UN efforts to promote international action to harness science and technology from the point of view of developing countries. The traditional forms of technical assistance are becoming less and less relevant to countries like India, Egypt or Brazil; and unless they take the initiative in defining what new approaches are necessary to suit their needs, they would soon close one possible door of assistance that has been open to them so far.

So much for economic security. May I now turn to the prospects for achieving a minimum standard of living for all persons all over the world?

A Minimum Standard

It is now commonly recognized that it is not enough to describe our common economic and social goals in terms of a certain rate of growth in GNP per annum or even in terms of an overall GNP per capita. The requirement of civilized existence must be broken down into its essential constituents such as nutrition, health, hygiene, salutary environment, good drinking water, shelter, education and vocation in life, access to culture, leisure and so on; and each of these aspects must be assured to each individual not by inference or as an indirect consequence of a certain general rate of growth of the economy, but by conscious and direct action, if necessary.

Internationally also, this emphasis on the quality of life in its manifold splendour has been gaining renewed momentum. I say renewed momentum, because in a sense the United Nations itself began in a very creative and imaginative mould in the early post-war years when it created an Organization for Education, Science and Culture, another for children, one for Food and Agriculture, another for health and so on. Gradually, however, these specialized UN agencies lost in glamour and prestige in comparison with strictly economic agencies like the World Bank. But the pendulum is beginning to swing again. In the United Nations itself, the social and larger cultural and other aspects of a decent minimum standard of life are receiving greater attention. The World Bank itself is taking a more active interest in education, population, housing, rural and urban water supply, etc.; and under Mr McNamara's leadership, the Bank has come much closer intellectually and operationally to other UN agencies such as Food and Agricultural Organization (FAO), World Health Organization (WHO) and United Nations Economic, Social and Cultural Organization (UNESCO). UNDP, which has a kind of coordinating role in providing technical assistance within the UN system as a whole, now disburses a respectable amount of assistance per year among some 130 countries. And although neither the International Strategy nor the Programme of Action for the New International Economic Order defines concrete goals in the area of nutrition or health or education around the world, there is an intention at any rate that this should soon be done.

Having said this, one must regretfully add that notwithstanding the growing awareness of the importance of each aspect of civilized existence, there has been no real move so far to equip agencies such as UNESCO and FAO adequately to enable them to perform their highly valuable tasks all over the world. The financial resources available to them are meagre by any standard. Their role is artificially restricted to technical assistance; and with minor exceptions like the World Food Programme or UNICEF, none of the agencies has resources enough to undertake what may broadly be called capital or financial assistance. Even such resources as all the UN agencies put together have—and these do not add up to even a billion dollars per year—are contributed year by year by way of voluntary contributions with all the uncertainties they entail. Ideas such as levying particular taxes to support particular institutions, for example, a tax on tobacco to help WHO to help eradicate diseases around the world and to build hospitals, or a tax on liquor to provide better nutrition to children all over the world, or a property tax internationally levied to clear slums everywhere—these are not at all in the realm of practical politics in the near future; and the international commitment to a minimum standard of living so far is more in words than in deeds.

On the other hand, it is perhaps worth reminding ourselves that actual economic achievements around the world over the past twenty-five years have far surpassed our expectations; and the ancient enemies—of hunger, want, disease and malnutrition—are being decisively eliminated from country after country. In Europe, even Spain, Portugal and Turkey, let alone Italy or Eastern Europe, have all but assured a decent minimum to all their people; and it is only a matter of a few decades before this would be equally true of Latin America and large parts of Asia and Africa as well. Comparisons are always invidious; but the remarkable fact is that thanks to national determination, natural bounty, scientific progress and to some extent at any rate international assistance, there are only a few countries even in Asia and Africa where the outcome of the economic struggle is not clearly weighted already in favour of a distinct and not too distant hope. As far as the new international economic order, therefore, is concerned, I do not see much reason to be pessimistic, at least on this score of a minimum standard of living. But the reasons for this stem more from the record of economic achievement over the recent past than from a faith in accelerated economic cooperation among nations in the years to come.

Diffusion of Economic Power

What about the chances of the diffusion of economic power so that it does not remain a serious threat to the political and cultural independence of nations, particularly the small and weak ones? There has certainly of late been greater insistence on the democratization of our international institutions such as the World Bank, the IMF and even the UN. The general desire among the developing countries, evidenced at the recent Special Session of the UN, not to entrust any new special fund for assisting the most affected countries to the IDA or the IMF, is in reality a reflection of their dissatisfaction with the voting pattern and the decision-making process in the Bank and the Fund. This dissatisfaction is shared also by a growing number of industrialized countries, particularly the Scandinavian countries and the Netherlands. And the establishment recently of a Permanent Committee of Twenty to straddle over both the Bank and the Fund, and the growing tendency in the Bank, the Fund as well as the UN to take decisions by consensus rather than actual voting, would indicate that the struggle for democratization of our international economic institutions is not altogether in vain.

But it would be unrealistic to think that this process can ever go very far. At the national level, it was the democratization of the political institutions—and particularly the system of one-man-one-vote—that ultimately led to policies of growth, security, redistribution and restraint on the economic power of the few. At an international level we have no such political machinery with the power of compulsion. No matter how democratic the functioning of the World Bank or the IMF or the UN may become, that cannot change the decisions of the US Congress or of other legislative bodies. As long as the international economic institutions have to depend primarily on the voluntary support of the richer nations, they are bound to look over the shoulder to make sure that they do not offend the rich no matter what the rules of procedure say. This is true as much of the UN or UNDP as it is of the World Bank. Consensus often means a veto for the powerful and sometimes even for just the vociferous and the cantankerous: and even as a voting system, one-country-one-vote is not much more rational than a vote for every billion dollars worth of wealth.

At the same time, there is no use denying that the threat of the economic power of the few being used for cultural, political or even economic domination of the many has distinctly receded. This has happened, however, because economic power itself is shared now by many countries, because even the smallest and weakest nation has grown in its determination to uphold its freedom and dignity and, above all, because of the political climate of détente. One could not have imagined only a decade or so ago that the oil-producing countries could have secured what they now have without inviting retaliation and even perhaps military intervention. But Suez changed all that; and Bangladesh confirmed the change. At least in this respect, a new international economic order is already upon us.

The change is nowhere more in evidence than in the widespread acknowledgement that multinational corporations have to accept certain norms of behaviour and that they certainly are not beyond the jurisdiction of national sovereignty. The international oil companies have turned out to be mere paper tigers; and complete national sovereignty over natural resources, unless one means by it the right to expropriate without compensation, is no longer seriously disputed by any one.

But perhaps one should also add that in respect of multinational corporations, two other changes are also taking place simultaneously which would restore the balance, so to speak, and help in evolving a mutually more rewarding and comfortable relationship of ease. The first relates to the fact that while the role of the multinational corporations as providers of capital and as centres of economic power is being steadily undermined, their contribution to the evolution of management skills and better technology is being increasingly recognized, including recognition from the socialist countries. Secondly, the oil-rich countries with their new-found wealth are becoming important partners in multinational corporations and, in some cases, setting up their own giant corporations which operate in several nations. When it comes therefore to protecting their legitimate rights, such as those for reasonable compensation in the event of nationalization, the multinational corporations now will have new allies.

To a certain extent, the emergence of the oil-rich countries on the world financial scene will certainly make for a greater degree of democratization of our international institutions. Whether or not we have a new UN Special Fund for assistance to the countries most affected by the oil crisis, countries like Iran and Venezuela will soon gain a greater say in the affairs of the World Bank, the IMF and the regional banks. It is true that even when countries like Iran and Venezuela are, so to speak, given their due in international agencies, the power structure in them will still reflect relative wealth rather than anything else. But it is in the nature of power that the more widely it is shared even at the top, the less arbitrary it is likely to be. And for the developing countries there is certainly safety in the fact that the number of potential donors—and effective decision-makers—has now increased substantially.

The one major lacuna that still remains in our structure of international economic cooperation is that it still does not reflect the emerging importance economically of the socialist countries, notably of China and Russia. Neither of them is a member of the Bank or the Fund; and although both of them are now members of UNDP, for example, there are difficulties in absorbing them into what has hitherto been regarded as the necessary framework for a truly international or multinational assistance programme. The Russian contribution to UNDP, for example, is unutilized to a considerable extent; and similar difficulties are now being experienced in regard to China. The situation is by no means parallel in the two cases. But basically, the problem arises at least in part because as a multilateral agency UNDP has hitherto felt that it cannot give turnkey jobs to particular countries but must operate on the basis of an internationally assembled team of experts (and assortment of equipment) after giving everyone an equal chance to bid.

There is, however, something odd about insisting that a pattern of behaviour which somehow cannot absorb the characteristic mode of operation of almost one-fourth of the human race is still the truly international or multilateral pattern. A way can and must be found to enable Russia and China to play their part internationally without their violating the basic principles on which their societies are based. For example, if UNDP can subcontract a particular piece of work to a firm in the US or Germany, what is wrong with its so doing with a department or agency in China or Russia? In other words, even now experts and equipment are, so to speak, bulked together for purposes of international competition; and all that we need to do is to recognize that in the Chinese or the Russian—or for that matter the Indian context—a government agency or department is the exact counterpart of a subcontractor in the capitalist countries.

I mention this aspect of the involvement of China and Russia at some length as it is of crucial importance if there is to be a new international economic order, that we find a sensible way for these countries to take their place economically in the international order as they have now done politically. If UNDP can set an example in this regard, it will certainly pave the way for the socialist countries to join the Bank and perhaps even the Fund and the regional banks in due course. There was a time when it used to be thought that it is the discipline implicit in internal monetary and fiscal policy as also in trade and exchange policy under the IMF charter which inhibited socialist countries from joining the World Bank, as membership of the Fund is a precondition for membership of the Bank. But recent events would seem to suggest that the disciplining role of the Fund need not hold the same terrors as before; and in any case, the time has certainly come to break this prenatal bond between the Fund and the Bank. There is no reason why membership of the IMF should be a precondition for membership of the Bank. I would personally hope that a greater degree of separation of IDA from the Bank will also soon be a reality. Be that as it may, the so-called "bilateralism" of the socialist countries has also hitherto been regarded as an obstacle to their integration into existing international institutions like the Bank and the IDA. It is here that clear thinking and a practical demonstration of its workability, as indicated a little earlier on the part of UNDP, can earn much larger dividends for the cause of international economic cooperation in general.

This has been a rather long and somewhat rambling safari into terrain which I hope has not been altogether unfamiliar to you. At any rate, I earnestly hope that I have at least succeeded in conveying my main point, which is this: nothing remains static in national or international affairs; and whether there is a new wind blowing in new directions and heralding a new world order or not, there is certainly a great deal of change afoot and a great deal of effort internationally to give these forces of change a constructive and cooperative edge. We in India can be indifferent to this process of international change and reform only at our peril. Let others write the judgement of history on the efforts to establish a new international economic order. For us in India there is more gain and excitement in being an active participant in the process rather than a detached judge; for if I may paraphrase what I have already said a few moments ago, if there are limits beyond which nations cannot rise when it comes to mutual cooperation, there certainly are no limits below which they may not sink; and fortunately, trying to put others on their best behaviour wears off at least a little on ourselves.

CHAPTER 30

The Adjustment Problem*

It is now generally recognized that technological progress apart, economic growth is essentially a consequence of economic efficiency and that economic efficiency, in turn, depends largely on the ease with which resources can be shifted from one use to another. Traditional economic theory treats growth as a function (apart from technical change) of changes in the aggregate supply of resources such as labour or skills or savings and investment, whereas economic efficiency is generally construed in the static sense of the best possible use of a given quantum of resources. But it is efficiency, understood in this sense, that provides the surplus or the additional margin from which alone skills and savings—and indeed the sustenance for additional labour—can be created. And if economic efficiency entails the best possible use of resources, it has to be so not so much in the static sense of under given conditions, but even more so under changing conditions.

Change—whether in supply, demand, technology or the relative efficiency of competing suppliers—is a fundamental fact of modern life. Indeed, it is this changing economic environment that presents both the challenge and the opportunity for growing economic efficiency and, therefore, of sound and sustained economic growth. The challenge lies in responding to the change by allowing or inducing resources to shift where new opportunities for more efficient use are emerging. And the so-called adjustment problem is nothing but the problem of ensuring that the desirable shift in resources is not hindered (that is, rigidities are removed) and in fact induced, encouraged and expedited.

* Originally published in *Trade Policies for a Better Future: The Leutwiler Report, the GATT and the Uruguay Round*, Springer Science and Business Media and Martinus Nijhoff, Dordrecht, 1987.

If the above propositions are made in the purely internal or national context (say, in a closed economy), they would command ready acceptance. In fact, they embody the essence of economic wisdom, not just conventional or traditional wisdom but the wisdom enshrined in the most sophisticated modern theory. But the propositions are equally true in the international context, that is, in the context of trade between and among nations. By the same token, if there has to be any caveat or qualification in regard to these propositions, they have to have the same rationale whether one is speaking of internal trade and competition or international trade and competition. For the notion that any particular nation can score points at the expense of another nation by restricting trade has hardly any validity in theory or as a practical proposition. The consequences of restricting international trade are felt essentially internally and they affect both overall economic efficiency and *inter se* distribution of costs and benefits (that is, income) in much the same way as restricting competition between two purely domestic producers.

If the case for "adjustment", for allowing, inducing, encouraging and expediting shift in resources as dictated by the changing winds of competition—whether internal or external—is so obvious, strong, and indeed well accepted, why then is there resistance to such a process particularly when it comes to international competition, even on the part of the most prosperous and economically advanced countries? The familiar infant industry (that is, learning by doing) argument or balance-of-payments considerations or the need to restrain conspicuous consumption, which have relevance to most developing countries, hardly apply to the industrially advanced countries. And yet the logic of open trade frontiers is denied almost universally in actual practice.

Part of the reason, of course, is the mistaken notion already referred to, that the cost of restricting international competition is borne by other nations whereas the benefits belong to the country of restriction. Part also lies in an exaggerated notion of the degree of adjustment that may be needed in any case. Much harm has been done in the context by glib talk of small countries or groups of countries getting out of some lines of production altogether and making room for another. It has become fashionable and even commonplace to speak of industrially advanced countries having to be ready to yield ground after ground to developing countries as they industrialize. Nothing can be more grievously misleading than such an extreme picture of the ultimate international division of labour—and such a denouement is hardly warranted by experience.

Competition is felt by units of production and not by some vague entity called a country in the first place. Individual units can often survive internal or external competition by some degree of rationality or by selling out to others at a certain loss in capital value. Even when a large number of units in a particular industry in a country are exposed to external competition, it is possible to argue that if, instead of shielding them from such competition, they are threatened with extinction, they would be able to come up with reasonable answers to their own problems. Either existing waste or inefficiency or excessive factor cost will be quickly rectified or there would be other changes such as improvement of quality, new technology or specialization in another variety of the same or similar product which may not require much training or retooling. Adjustment, in other words, can and generally does take place within more or less same units and in the same general line of production; and constructive adjustment of this kind may require nothing more than some prompt financial assistance or new technical collaboration agreements and some alterations in the product mix. And such adjustment which would be viable would not even be attempted if protection is granted too readily; for protection only freezes existing units in their existing inefficiency forever. But the point needs to be emphasized that whole industries do not die out quickly in any country and the same so-called product or industry or activity has wide enough range to permit "shifting" within the same broad frontiers. After all, there are kinds of textiles which are produced efficiently in countries which restrict import of other kinds of textiles and it is arguable that absence of restrictions on textile trade would mean an international division of labour which would make all textile producers more efficient with only minor shifts in relative shares. This is true even of competition between different US automobile units and one need not create horror stories of the US or Europe without an industry such as automobiles or steel or even textiles to make room for Japan or Brazil or India.

As more and more countries industrialize, they can, will and do compete more or less all along the line (even in regard to foodstuffs) in all departments of industry rather than specialize in some extreme manner. The choice is only between being frozen in existing inefficiencies in each line or industry and continuing the search and struggle for maintaining competitive strength all along the line, knowing full well that success can only be limited in each sector with no defined frontiers or turf that can be preserved forever for any country or group of industries. Per contra, no country that continues to respond to change need fear being converted into an industrial desert even in particular sectors. On the other hand, refusal to change by erecting protecting walls around existing industrial structures or units is bound to convert it before long into a semi-arid industrial tract.

It will be seen that advocacy of a strong or constructive policy of adjustment is not a plea for laissez-faire or for letting things take care of themselves. It is a plea for enlightened and limited or selective intervention in support of competitive trends as opposed to myopic intervention of the purely negative type which tries to push back the incentive for efficiency forever. It does not say: "Thou shalt not fear competition" or even "Thou shalt not fear competition for the next few years." It simply says: "You are entitled to some financial relief and assistance for some period as long you push relief and assistance to constructive use which can make you viable over the long run on your own." What the nature and scale of assistance should be and what adjustment would be necessary as a quid pro quo can only be decided on a case-by-case basis; and let it be remembered that the principle is the same whether we are talking of internal or external competition.

There, of course, could be cases where there is no reasonable adjustment plan which could put a unit of an industry on a long-term viable path. In that event, there is no alternative but for the unit to phase out or for the industry to shrink. There is obviously no point in throwing good money after bad. But protection would amount in such a situation precisely to throwing good money after bad; and the providers of good money in either case (of misapplied financial assistance or protection) are the general public which would pay taxes either directly or by way of unwarranted higher prices. One could, in fact, argue that a sound adjustment policy in such cases would be to expedite death or shrinking to a reasonable size—say, by not putting the burden of compensating the retrenched labour on the particular unit or industry in question but on the community at large. Payment of retrenchment benefits is understandable on grounds of equity. But there could be cases where on grounds of efficiency as well as equity the cost is borne not by the afflicted unit or industry but by the economy as a whole.

Would the prescription be different if in some cases a whole group of industries in a region reaches the point of no return so that we are faced with the prospect of massive unemployment concentrated in particular regions? I would venture to assert, first of all, that such a prospect or danger is often brought about by past and prolonged protection rather than by the sudden emergence of competition from elsewhere. If timely and proper adjustment had been encouraged, the situation would not have reached such a pass. Even so, it is not an impasse that would be reached because what has got to be done ultimately has to be begun sooner or later. Even if one grants the case for some protection in such extreme cases, it has to be phased out rapidly and has to be accompanied by a vigorous programme of retraining, resettlement, etc. Unemployment benefits, instead of being automatic and everlasting, may have to be linked with willingness to restrain and resettle.

After all, thousands of poor villagers in developing countries constantly face this problem as dams are built on rivers and whole villages are flooded. The trouble seems to be that those who have attained a high standard of living somehow feel that they can afford the luxury of continuing to enjoy this high standard in the same place and in the same job for an entire lifetime. But when change is inevitable and indeed necessary anyway, such a luxury would constantly slip out of the hands of those who resist change. It is not a question of choosing efficiency or growth over equity. Considerations of equity must be recognized by adopting an active plan of adjustment and having it financed in a manner consistent with equity as well as prompt adjustment. If there is any conflict, it is likely to be between lethargy and the needs of the situation as misguided assistance and protection act in the same way as drugs—that is, by producing a false sense of tranquillity rather than healing and acting as a spur to permanent improvement. But human beings already know—and can devise—drugs of many different kinds.

The argument so far proceeds on the assumption that the resources, particularly labour, that have to be shifted out can be reabsorbed elsewhere even if it is at a somewhat lower standard for some time than what they have been artificially accustomed to so far. But what is the guarantee that such an assumption is valid? One can readily concede that an active and constructive programme of adjustment has a macro as well as a micro aspect. Overall demand management policies have to be such as to ensure as nearly full employment as is possible consistent with reasonable price stability. I for one would agree that the case for protection has been given impetus in the recent past by callous political attitudes towards unemployment in the name of fighting inflation. It should not be beyond the wits of man to devise more humane policies based on consensus and persuasion and mutual accommodation that would permit a better balance between unemployment and inflation than has been the case in the recent past and hence provide a better environment in which protection can be rolled back. Indeed, if protection is to be rolled back in reality, we would certainly need to arrive at a new and more enlightened consensus on the management of the macro aspects of the major economies of the world; and it is this which makes monetary, financial and trade issues so irrevocably intermixed.

One can also agree that we should not assume glibly that there would always be newer and more profitable avenues where resources rendered redundant elsewhere can be employed. After all, avenues like electronics or computer technology or robotics do not spring up at will. What this amounts to is that all nations have to spend sufficient resources on research and development to keep opening new avenues for more profitable or efficient use of resources. They also have to create adequate opportunities where the young and old alike can acquire new technical and professional skills. And the cost of such research, development and training must be borne at least to some extent by society at large. There also have to be adequate savings to provide the capital needed for new investment. In short, if the capacity to adjust and grow among the people at large is not being constantly enlarged as a part of general policy, any particular act of adjustment, when needed, is going to be that much more difficult. The industrial countries are fortunate in this respect; and it is the developing countries which have a limited economic and technical base that are handicapped by an inherently weak capacity to adjust. Hence their need for a net inflow of capital and skills till such time as they develop a reasonably diversified industrial structure, a satisfactory rate of savings and a reasonable level of technical competence and the infrastructure to sustain and enlarge it.

There is also one more precondition for prompt and efficient adjustment. Not all such adjustment should depend on the availability of domestic demand. It should be possible to have access to foreign markets as at least part of the process of adjustment for the economy as a whole. This is clearly all the more so when the adjustment is needed in response to competition from abroad. There could be a case in static theory in favour of unilateral free trade: "You do not erect barriers at your ports because others do it." But in a dynamic sense, there have ultimately to be markets for one's exports if one is to import more freely. And at least one condition for access to markets abroad—apart from competitive strength and sensible exchange rate policies—is that they should also be reasonably open. Exceptions to this very broad statement of reciprocity can and should be made. But they must have a clear and widely accepted justification and the practices embodying such exceptional treatment should be transparent in the sense of being known to all concerned and also to the maximum degree possible non-discriminatory and not violating the principle of multilateralism. This ultimately is the basic rationale for having some rules or common code of conduct in international trade.

The case for protection on grounds of security is in a class by itself because security somehow invokes images of cost being of no concern. But one can at least argue that in this age of nuclear weapons, even if one believes in being able to win a nuclear war, the time required to overpower the enemy would be so short that all the security one needs in supplies can be had by very modest expenditure on stocks rather than indulge in the permanent and much larger waste of inefficient production.

Since freedom from inflation is becoming almost as sacrosanct as security, it is also reasonable to note that openness to competition keeps costs and prices down just as much as it promotes efficiency and growth. Indeed, there is a virtuous circle here in that growth, efficiency, adjustment and control of inflation mutually reinforce each other. This is true not only of countries that have to subject themselves to IMF discipline but also—and even more so—of countries which may not need IMF assistance. Indeed, adjustment in all cases requires adequate finance—the former is not possible without the latter and the latter without the former would be infructuous. But adjustment and finance are not in any real sense substitutes one for the other as is often sought to be made out. If finance is not adequate, adjustment will be of the inefficient type and will set in motion a vicious circle of low growth, low demand, less resources for constructive adjustment, greater tendency to protect and so on.

The only difference between developed and developing countries is that the former must find the finance themselves out of their own savings while the latter can legitimately lay claim to the savings of others—to windfall gains such as those involved in international liquidity creation which would also, when encashed, involve a drawal on the savings of others. In this sense, low savings in developed countries and—perhaps as a consequence—less willingness to share them with developing countries may well be the main bottleneck in constructive adjustment leading to sound growth all round at the present juncture. This is true at least as long as one is talking within the parameters set by the capacity of the developing countries to invest wisely and manage the same comparatively efficiently.

CHAPTER 31

Protectionism
*Its Causes and Manifestations**

There has been growing disillusionment with government intervention in economic matters in recent years. It is now more generally accepted that a greater degree of freedom in the operation of market forces or a reduction in "rigidities" of all kinds is conducive to greater efficiency, higher growth and less inflation in the long run. This change in economic perception varies in degree from country to country. But it is shared by all groups of countries, including the developing and socialist countries as well. And yet, paradoxically, instead of being reflected both in internal as well as international policies, it has been accompanied by a revival of protectionist sentiment and, indeed, a proliferation of protectionist practices, most notably in the US and Western Europe, where the faith in more or less freely functioning markets has witnessed the most dramatic revival. Lip service to an open and multilateral international trading system continues to be paid; and leaders of public opinion declare, at the highest level, their resolve to halt protectionism and to start rolling it back as soon as possible. But protectionism continues its insidious march.

How does one explain this paradox? And what conclusions can we draw from the explanations if protectionism is indeed to be halted and eventually rolled back to some reasonable level? The impetus to protectionism in recent years may come from somewhat different factors in different countries. But together, their actions have set in motion a new trend which threatens to wipe out the very solid gains towards an open or liberal system of international trade that were made during the 1950s and 1960s and early 1970s.

* Unpublished.

A more sanguine view of recent trends may well be that they are a response to temporary or short-term factors which came into prominence just as faith in the market mechanism was gaining ground. The control of inflation, after years of excess, required policies which led to a severe recession and substantial unemployment in most industrialized countries. In some of these, the need to absorb the second oil shock necessitated more restrictive macroeconomic policies than would have been the case otherwise. Lack of coordination of macroeconomic policies among major industrial countries and the absence of an appropriate mix of monetary and fiscal policies have resulted in very high real rates of interest which inhibit investment and curtail the return on risk capital; the same factors have also led to misalignment of key exchange rates, and at least in the US, the appreciation of the dollar has encouraged protectionist sentiment. The combination of unemployment and low rates of profit makes for protectionist sentiment both among workers and businessmen.

The newly industrializing countries, particularly those in Asia, which also had to adjust to the second oil shock, had to continue and enlarge the scope of their vigorous efforts at export promotion while perhaps going slow on import liberalization on which they were embarked, however haltingly. For those developing countries, particularly in Latin America, which had borrowed heavily in international capital markets, the now familiar debt crisis—itself the result largely of the developments mentioned earlier—meant a severe curtailment of imports for unavoidable balance-of-payments reasons.

The new trend towards protectionism, it can be argued, is the result of the juxtaposition of all these factors. As these factors are brought under control, a more propitious climate for halting and reversing protectionism may be expected to emerge, the more so as the prevalent political and intellectual mood is in favour of the freer functioning of markets.

There is obviously some truth in the somewhat optimistic interpretation just outlined. If there were not, there would be little point in the labours of groups such as the present one. But even the temporarily adverse factors such as high real rates of interest, misaligned exchange rates, recessionary trends or inadequate recovery, lack of coordination of macro-policies among major nations, inappropriate mix of monetary and fiscal policies and major shocks like the oil shock will not disappear from the scene necessarily or on their own. In this sense, halting protectionism and reversing it would be facilitated by a general improvement in the functioning of major economies as well as improvements in present monetary and financial arrangements between nations. That is why in our analysis and recommendations we have gone beyond purely trade questions. But it also needs to be emphasized that halting and reversing protectionism cannot wait till all other problems are solved. In fact, movement towards a more open system of international trade is an essential part of the solution of current economic problems. This is self-evident in relation to the long-term or enduring solution of the debt problem of developing countries. But it is equally true in relation to other objectives such as accelerating growth even where without reviving inflation, what is needed is to set in motion a number of measures which will mutually reinforce each other in the right direction; and halting protectionism and eventually reversing the trend is an essential ingredient of the programmes and policies required for overcoming the difficulties that have overtaken the world economy since the second oil crisis.

It would, however, be a mistake to treat recent protectionist tendencies as merely a short-term deviation from a longer-term healthier trend. For one thing, protectionist tendencies were there even before the recent economic malaise. One has only to recall in this connection the protection to agriculture enshrined in the original provisions of General Agreement on Tariffs and Trade (GATT) and the restrictions on textiles which are now nearly a quarter century old. Even during recent months of recovery, additional protectionist measures have been adopted in the US and elsewhere. One has, therefore, to enquire whether there are not some deep-seated factors at work which generally encourage protectionist tendencies everywhere. Quite apart from this, we have at least to enquire whether some of the short-term factors, such as recession or low returns on risk capital, reflect really longer-term secular trends so that, if protectionist tendencies have to be fought back, we have to demonstrate that protectionism is no answer to those unfavourable longer-term or secular trends which might be emerging over the recent past.

The most important factor that reinforces protection everywhere is, of course, the still powerful force of nationalism which constantly encourages an attitude of "my country, right or wrong". Governments and makers of public opinion everywhere constantly encourage this in subtle ways: "Buy British", "Explore your own Country this Summer", "Swadeshi is swaraj" (the way to self-determination is to buy national products). Yes, there is also the subtle appeal of "imported" or "foreign" goods and this is confined not just to the developing world or to fashion goods and speciality items. But the appeal is that of the fruit which is forbidden, at least partly and indirectly. One never sees advertisements or slogans like: "You are a citizen of a free country. The whole world is your market"; if one did see such an advertisement, it would be in aid of some export drive which inadvertently failed to notice the other edge!

One particular manifestation of this nationalist fervour is the widespread belief that protectionism is about the well-being of your country as against that of another country. That trade is not a zero-sum game is vaguely understood but seldom remembered when it comes to restricting some import. It needs to be constantly emphasized, therefore, that the costs and benefits of protection are borne almost always by the protecting country and that it is not possible generally to shift the cost of protection to other countries. The question that public opinion should be constantly urged to consider should be: who in your country would gain by the proposed protectionist measure and in what way? Who will lose, how and by how much? Protectionism is ultimately about A versus B in the same country and not about country X versus country Y even though it is true that protectionism is doubly cursed so that the interests of the other country are also relevant.

Even when it is recognized that some people gain and others lose by protection, a certain asymmetry of public perception remains in that those who stand to gain, that is, workers and businessmen in a particular industry, are more vocal and influential than those who stand to lose, viz., the general body of consumers or taxpayers and the export industries affected by any external backlash. Apart from the fact that the "benefits" of protection are concentrated whereas the "costs" are spread widely over a large number of persons scattered all over the country so that it is easy for protection to have a strong and vociferous advocate whereas opposition to it is likely to be either absent or muted, the very structure of most governments makes them more open to protectionist influences than to their opposite. Ministers of Commerce and Industry and even Treasury Officials concerned with balance-of-payments are always there to listen to the pleas for protection of a particular industry whereas there is no Minister to whom consumers can go to urge more freedom of choice for them. Some internal structural changes which would emphasize the general economic interest of the country within governmental decision-making processes whenever sectoral interests are pressed would be helpful.

There is reason to believe, however, that even if consumers are asked whether they would pay a somewhat higher price, say, for shoes if this saves a few hundred jobs in the shoe industry, the general response would be in favour of protection. Why? Mostly, of course, because despite the recent experience of people supporting policies which lead to high unemployment in the interest of controlling inflation, there is still an understandable feeling that most people would not mind some cut in their living standards if it helps some of their countrymen to retain their jobs. That such a sentiment would weaken if the inroads on living standards were to be a repeated and continuing affair may be true. It is certainly true that those who vote in favour of higher prices for shoes in order to protect employment in the shoe industry would not desist from asking for higher wages sooner or later to compensate for their higher price of shoes. What I think needs to be emphasized is that in most public discussion, the wrong questions are asked—or at any rate, the right ones are not. Does willingness to pay higher prices protect employment in the long run? What we have learnt through bitter experience about inflation being harmful to growth and employment in the long run is equally true of protection. In fact, protection is one of the inbuilt factors that lead to inflationary pressures.

But the fact remains that not all the costs and benefits of protection are felt at the same time. They are spread over time, and unevenly. The apparent benefit to employment or profits in some industries is soon manifest. That this benefit may not last or that, over time, it will weaken employment and profits elsewhere may be true. But when it comes to comparing the short versus the long run, most people tend to be myopic. It is important, therefore, that correct questions are correctly posed and lessons of history clearly brought out so that people are not misled into believing that there is an easy trade-off between one public good and another. The fact also is that some of the costs—also to employment and profits if the economy is considered as a whole—are also felt at the same time as protection is given to one industry if only because loss of markets forces other countries to restrict imports. Once again, the myopia is not often about the short-term versus the long-term but about what is concentrated (benefits) as against what is diffused (costs).

Protectionist pressures become strong when there is actual danger of large-scale retrenchment or unemployment in the absence of protectionist measures. Paradoxically, most people who are prepared to accept arguments in favour of freer trade in respect of new goods or new industries or additional production, balk at carrying the same logic further when it comes to disturbing existing production. This is what gave rise to that seductive but dangerous concept of "market disruption": as if competition is anything but a fight for disturbing entrenched market interests! If protectionist tendencies have to be fought, we have to emphasize that market disruption—whether through internal or external competition—is an essential part of the process of healthy and enduring growth in a changing world; and that trying to shore up particular markets for particular firms, and maintaining the profits they earn or employment they provide by artificial protection or subsidies is a self-defeating process. It is self-defeating in most cases for the firms themselves, and certainly for the economy as a whole. It is possible to argue that acceptance of the validity of the concept of "market disruption" was the original sin leading to the proliferation of voluntary export restrictions and the like.

This is not to say that any society, particularly a democratic one, can be indifferent to large-scale and concentrated unemployment. But the relief to the persons affected has to come in other ways if it is to be effective in the long run; and this problem of giving relief in a manner which is not self-defeating but constructive in the long run is the real challenge for public policy in the area of what has come to be known as "adjustment assistance". Here again, caution is needed: adjustment assistance should not be such that it inhibits adjustment to underlying market phenomena. After all, protection is also a form of adjustment assistance, except that it is perverse in terms of market realities. As a general rule, one can say that those rendered surplus by external or internal competition should be encouraged to move out rather than stay put.

When faced with a difficult problem, it is also a natural weakness of human beings to imagine that the problem is likely to be short-lived and will go away if some temporary expedient for survival or assistance for overcoming a particular weakness is forthcoming. There is no full proof way of demonstrating that loss of competitive power for a particular industry in a particular country is permanent any more than there is for a unit suffering from purely internal competition. The temptation to protect or subsidize in the hope that soon the industry will be able to do away with such help is not easy to resist. And yet, no one has really applied the sunset theory to such a situation and limited the support strictly in terms of time or total subsidy. One may not know for certain and from the outset whether a patient is just sick or senile or whether the sickness is terminal. But the diagnosis need not remain in doubt for long if there are established procedures and indeed requirements for making a periodic diagnosis at least as a condition of treatment.

A similar difficulty is faced by developing countries when it comes to the application of the infant industry argument. Vague hopes, wishful thinking and inability to appreciate that everything has an opportunity cost—in the here and now, as well as over time—lead to much infructuous and expensive protection for infants that remain perpetually retarded. Some discipline which makes for discriminating decisions—discriminating not only in the binary sense but also as to duration, scale, etc., would be an advance over current procedures both nationally and internationally.

A somewhat related consideration is the readiness with which arguments about competition being unfair are accepted. This is perhaps only one manifestation of nationalism. But it is a remarkable fact that patently self-serving arguments about "cheap" labour or "low" wages being a kind of infection against which one is entitled to seek protection are so repeatedly advanced and so readily accepted. The poor, obviously, are for ever cursed and have no business to better their lot either by migration or honest labour. The somewhat more sophisticated version that seeks to argue that what is being objected to is not low wages but "exploitation" of labour only adds unction to what is in fact an unworthy endeavour. More or less the same is true of arguments about countries keeping their exchange rates artificially low, forgetting that, at least when it comes to exchange rates, it takes two to tango.

This is not to say that nation states do not try surreptitiously to score over others in trade as in other matters. This is done not just through subsidies or dumping or artificially cross-subsidized prices but increasingly through linked deals of a variety of nature. That is why transparency of trade regimes and multilateralism and most-favoured-nation treatment or non-discrimination were among the most fundamental principles under GATT which are even more relevant now than ever. These principles will have to be reinforced and indeed enforced if the present slide into surreptitious practices which ultimately benefit the strong at the expense of the weak is to be prevented. More often than not, when it comes to surreptitious practices and trying to outsmart others, the result is really indeterminate except that, sooner or later, everyone gets outsmarted and caught in the act to boot. While games played in the dark can be exciting, you cannot complain if something goes wrong—and generally, it does. And when everyone tries to keep everyone in the dark and information becomes sketchy and based often on rumours rather than realities, you never know who is the fairest of them all.

Some better machinery for bringing about greater transparency about what is going on is necessary. If GATT is not able to go beyond and behind what governments say, perhaps an independent but publicly financed institution—on the analogy of the recently set-up institute for better information on bank loans—could be thought of. In any event, surveillance machinery and prompt procedures for settling disputes are essential if protectionism is to be fought off on a long-term basis. There could also be greater use of internally set-up but judicial or impartial agencies which could look into specific complaints of unfair competition—with provision for the foreign parties also to present their case.

As far as exchange rates are concerned, we already have a surveillance machinery in the IMF if only we are allowed to make use of it. Perhaps as the most favoured among the international institutions—at least among the major countries it could be given the specific task of receiving complaints about artificially maintained low exchange rates and deciding on such complaints!

One hears less these days about the age-old reasons for protection, particularly of agriculture, viz., security considerations or essentiality considerations or even about the need to preserve a certain way of life. These arguments obviously wear thin in a nuclear age. Nor is the way of a farmer all that different or glamorous these days. But the emotional basis for protecting agriculture is still strong everywhere and it is necessary to ask why this sacred cow has to be treated so differently as to convert it almost everywhere into an altogether new species of white elephants.

It is also often argued that at least in Western Europe, North America and perhaps even in Australia and Japan, there has been so much economic progress that people now want stability more than anything else. They do not mind if there is some loss of efficiency or even of growth as long as they can end their days in comparative comfort in their present jobs and present surroundings. The great drive towards consumerism in imitation of America, it is argued, is over, because American standards of life are a reality in many countries. Is there not an old saying, as Professor Assar Lindbeck reminds us, that the first generation in a family builds up affluence, the second administers it and the third consumes it?

Prophecies about saturation of wants and the end of consumerism have often been made and have equally often been proven wrong. At this point in history when a new industrial revolution is being ushered in with electronics, computers and robotics producing a mind-boggling range of new products and an extraordinary leap in productivity of labour, it is rather difficult to talk of some economic nirvana having been already achieved. And heaven knows how much poverty and deprivation there are even in the US. Societies cannot stand still. They either keep rowing against the inevitable winds of change or drift down. Those who get easily satiated also get easily bored and get busy with ways of destroying themselves. At any rate, even if the developed world is set on a suicidal path and keeps saying "I am all right, Jack", it is at least time for the developing world to realize that they have no alternative but to trade more freely at least among themselves. The banner for freer trade has to be kept flying even if one has to hoist it from different places at different times.

There is another version of the stability argument. Not that the developed world is satiated and wants to resist change altogether. Only, changes are coming so rapidly, unexpectedly and from all directions that it is argued, it is difficult to adjust to all of them with a reasonable degree of smoothness. The very fact that international trade grew so rapidly in the 1950s and '60s means that interdependence has grown so much that everyone is exposed much more than before to winds of change that come from abroad. The oil shocks are a proof of the unexpected and severe nature of the jolts. And the fact that Japan's success is being followed so soon by so many countries who compete internationally even in respect of sophisticated manufactures means that the whole international environment has become so unstable and uncertain as to increase the risks of an open trade policy.

To put it differently, an open trade policy, it would seem, requires such frequent and far-reaching adjustments that it would be politically impossible for most democratic countries to undertake them. And the difficulty becomes all the greater because there is a secular trend, so the argument runs, towards a lower rate of growth or even virtual stagnation in countries hitherto industrially advanced. The reasons advanced for a low growth scenario are many: limited natural resources including environmental resources, wage rigidities and even excessively high wages and correspondingly low returns on risk capital, lack of innovations and the like.

Each of these arguments, even if valid, does not really argue in favour of protection. If natural resources are limited, it is so for everybody, and has always been so. That is an argument for getting the best out of them by better international division of labour. The same would be true if innovations were getting fewer—which is far from the case. And as for wage rigidities which reduce profit margins and investment and growth, they are bound to be self-defeating as in the absence of growth, unduly high real wages cannot be maintained, unless perhaps when populations are declining. Withdrawing into one's shell is hardly possible even for the richest nations unless they are embarked on a course of cumulative decline.

The stability-versus-growth argument ignores the lessons of history as also the two-sided nature of trade: if you deny markets, you lose them also. The developing countries which were first told to give up aid in favour of trade are likely to reverse their halting moves towards a more open trading system if they are now denied access to the markets of the rich. There are dangers also in trying to create a kind of international caste system. Neither the rich nor the poor or the not-so-rich and the not-so-poor are homogeneous categories so that caste barriers will be broken, special deals across caste barriers will be struck and attempts made to create blocs that run across caste barriers. The alternative to an open, transparent, multilateral and non-discriminating trading system is not some orderly process imposed from above or even an orderly process of categorized self-restraint based on some consensus. The alternative is chaos, catch-as-catch-can and a return to the beggar-my-neighbour days of the 1930s and all their inevitable consequences. The pity is that with the passage of time, the memories of the 1930s are fading.

Yet another family of arguments in favour of protection revolves round the thesis that once you make exceptions even for good reasons, they tend to proliferate for good reasons and bad and it becomes difficult to draw the line anywhere. The exceptions in favour of the developing countries, or in relation to free trade areas, or agriculture and market disruption have all been mentioned in this context. But one cannot make out a case for rigidity even if it is irrational. Reciprocity does not mean treating equals as equals. Arguments about protecting agriculture or market disruption are just wrong. Arguments about infant industries or free trade areas or transparency, multilateralism and non-discrimination are essentially sound even if they may be misused or not respected.

The argument that we cannot talk only of trade in a context where services are becoming increasingly more important is also valid. But advocacy of a universally liberal regime for services sounds hollow when it comes from people who are not prepared first to talk of dismantling the restrictions on textiles, clothing, footwear and the like. More often than not, such arguments are advanced as a sort of weak defence of what is done or not done in the trade field. And the developed countries generally have lost credibility with the developing countries because of the systematic tendency on the part of the former in the recent past to withdraw from well-established forms of international cooperation. Their motives are suspect and it is feared that thinking in terms of equation of power is once again replacing thinking in terms of common cooperative endeavours.

Perhaps confidence is lacking on the part of the developed countries also when it comes to the attitude of the developing countries. And the situation among developed countries, or among developing countries and even among socialist countries, is not much better. That there is an erosion of mutual credibility and confidence everywhere is clear enough; and without apportioning blame, the first step should be to reverse this process by an act of statesmanship all round so that there could be a meaningful dialogue on what can and should be done in trade as in monetary and financial matters. It does not necessarily mean that the present atmosphere of mutual distrust can be lifted only by some supreme effort to resolve all problems for all time. Even a few steps forward which forge a greater degree of confidence and credibility among all concerned would be welcome as we can build upon them step by step to erect eventually a more satisfactory and enduring structure. And it is in this spirit of "Let us begin" rather than in pursuit of some grand design or theoretical ideal that we turn to for a few concrete suggestions towards a more liberal, open and equitable system of international trade.

PART VIII

Miscellany

CHAPTER 32

Professor A.C. Pigou
*A Memoir**

It does not become a Cambridge man to claim too much for his university, nor am I much tempted to do so. But there is, I think, a certain type, rare, like all good things, which seems to be associated in some peculiar way with my alma mater,... It is a type unworldly without being saintly, unambitious without being inactive, warm-hearted without being sentimental. Through good report and ill such men work on, following the light of truth as they see it; able to be sceptical without being paralysed; content to know what is knowable and to reserve judgment on what is not. The world could never be driven by such men, for the springs of action lie deep in ignorance and madness. But it is they who are the beacon in the tempest, and they are more, not less, needed now than ever before.

—*Goldworthy Lowes Dickinson*

On 7 March 1959 there came to an end one of the most active and distinguished careers in the service of our science. From 1902, when he was elected a Fellow of King's College, Cambridge, till death claimed him at the ripe old age of 81 nearly a year ago, Professor Pigou continued to engage the eager expectation of economists all over the world. There has been hardly any aspect of economics on which Professor Pigou has not brought to bear his outstanding powers of sustained analysis and lucid exposition. A proper assessment of the score and more books, both big and small, and the numerous articles that resulted from this intense and devoted activity would require a familiarity with the whole range of these works such as is not possessed by the present writer whose sole justification for attempting this commemorative piece is the desire to discharge a debt of gratitude,

* Originally published in the *Economic Weekly*, 5 March 1960.

however meagrely, for the unstinting kindness and affection he received from Professor Pigou during his undergraduate days at King's.

One had felt, of course, the impact of Professor Pigou's mind and heart even before meeting him. The decision whether to specialize in economics or not had turned largely on the glow one felt on reading *The Economics of Welfare*, more particularly the earlier pages: "It is not wonder, but rather the social enthusiasm which revolts from the sordidness of mean streets and the joylessness of withered lives, that is the beginning of economic science" (Fourth edition, p. 5). In those early days when one's mind began to be troubled for the first time about the larger issues of social order, it was Socialism versus Capitalism which set the matter in a proper perspective by its teaching that the best under one system should not be compared with the worst or not-so-good under another, that what is not-so-good for the United Kingdom may still be good for Russia, that one can learn in part even from that which one rejects as a whole, that in matters of this kind the economist possesses no special qualifications for pronouncing final judgements, that refusal to deride is itself a decision and that even gradualness requires action—perhaps more sustained, widespread and astute rather than less so for being administered in small doses.

Of the other more weighty of Professor Pigou's books—*The Theory of Unemployment* (1933), *Industrial Fluctuations* (1927), *The Economics of Stationary States* (1935), to name but a few—one had no first-hand knowledge. From a cursory and half-understood reading of Keynes's *General Theory* one had acquired a faint impression that this part of Pigou was a bit out-of-date anyway. On reaching Cambridge and getting drawn avidly into the current Keynesian tide, the image of a "classical" Pigou took a somewhat firmer shape. But between this image and the reality of Professor Pigou's views as one came to know them gradually there was no correspondence. In supervision after supervision one trotted out 100 per cent Keynesian answers to problems of wages, interest and employment and one was met not with debate and discussion about the "classical" position, but with approval and encouragement. What was even more significant, as one read some of Professor Pigou's books—*Employment and Equilibrium* (first edition, 1941), *Income* (1945), *Lapses from Full Employment* (1945)—one found one's understanding of Keynes deepened and in some respects fortified by a more rigorous exposition than what one had encountered before. This was true, for example, of the emphasis on monetary policy or monetary behaviour as the essential link between changes in money wage rates and employment. Consider, for instance, the following passage from *Lapses from Full Employment* (pp. 16–17):

> If, however, it (i.e. the rate of interest) does stay put, the contraction in money wage rates not only may, but necessarily will, entail an equi-proportionate contraction

in money income and the money demand for labour. There is no reason for the amount of real investment to be altered; therefore no reason for real income to be altered; and, therefore, finally no reason for employment to be altered. Thus the level of employment will be what it will be irrespective of what happens to the money rate of wages.

Could there be a clearer presentation of the Keynesian scheme than this one? And how are we to reconcile the image of a "classical" Pigou with the conclusion in the preface to the *Lapses*, viz., that "in the present state of act and opinion", the problem of unemployment should be attacked not by the manipulation of wages but along the lines of approach suggested in the White Paper on Unemployment Policy?

Part of the reason for the divorce between the image one had formed and the reality as one came to know it is undoubtedly to be found in Professor Pigou's own generous words in his memorial piece on Keynes prepaid for the British Academy:

> To me personally, if I try to evaluate for myself Keynes's direct contribution to fundamental economic thought, there is a special difficulty. Those of us who disagree in part with his analysis have, nevertheless, undoubtedly been affected by it in our own thinking; and it is very hard to remember exactly where we stood before. Not a little of what we now believe ourselves to have known all along it may well be we really owe to him. (John Maynard Keynes, *Baron Keynes of Tilton*, p. 17.)

In part, no doubt, the answer lies in the fact that the classical and the Keynesian positions were not as far apart as one had imagined and far from being theoretically inconsistent one with the other were only special cases of a more general reality. But be that as it may, it would be hard to find many parallels in the annals of scientific controversies in any field for the selfless devotion to truth and truth alone with which Professor Pigou endeavoured over many years to sift the essential contribution of Keynes.

True, the first reaction to *General Theory* as seen in the review article in the *Economica* (1936) is a trifle emotional. But the emotion is aroused mainly by the justifiable annoyance at the attempt "to win attention for one's own ideas (by presenting) them in a matrix of sarcastic comment upon other people" and by the desire to defend the Great Master, Marshall, against what seemed to be unjustifiable criticism expressed in a patronising manner. Even at this early stage, the disarming modesty and scrupulousness of the man are transparent. "I may even have missed, as has happened before now to critics of new work, some vital and path-breaking contribution to thought." The preliminary skirmish over, there is no attempt in subsequent years to hark back to the past—only a systematic and painstaking endeavour in his own way to rebuild the structure of his own thoughts in the light of what he felt was valuable in Keynes. The final assessment when it came after Keynes's death has the true ring of greatness both of mind and heart.

> After Marshall's main work was finished economic thought on fundamental issues moved little, at all events in this country. We were pedestrian, perhaps, a little complacent. Keynes's *Treatise on Money* and later, his *General Theory*, broke resoundingly that dogmatic slumber. Whether in agreement or in disagreement with him, discussion and controversy sprang up and spread over the whole world. Economics and economists came alive. The period of tranquillity was ended.
>
> For this the credit is almost wholly due to Keynes.... Maybe too, had he been less ready to hoist the flag of intellectual revolution, stressing agreement more and disagreement less, he would have obviated some misunderstanding and some unfruitful debate, thus freeing himself to produce even more constructive work than he actually did. But there are two sides to this. Had he acted so, in a more Marshallian manner, not only would he have proved a less effective catalyst, but also—and this to him would have meant much—his influence upon immediate public policy in these times of urgency must inevitably have been far smaller than it was. (*Baron Keynes of Tilton*, p. 19)

If it was easy thus to reconcile the image of a "classical" Professor Pigou with the reality one came to know, there was another aspect of his personality which was less easy to comprehend. From a reading of *The Economics of Welfare*, of *Socialism versus Capitalism* and of *The Political Economy of War* (1939) one had expected not only a humane and practical interest in the problems of the day but—should one say it—a measure of passion in regard to these issues as well. Only a few yards away from Professor Pigou lived another great economist, C.F. Shove, almost equally cloistered and withdrawn from this world. But the glint one saw every now and then in Mr Shove's eyes as one talked of the Soviet Union or of the Labour Party was seldom noticeable in the case of his neighbour. Perhaps one was wrong to expect it—for had not Professor Pigou himself once cautioned in the words of Henry Sidgwick: "Enthusiasm is often a turbid issue of smoke and sparks. Culture must refine it to a steady glow"? But around Professor Pigou there was an air of remoteness which seemed to go deeper than mere academic habit. Here was a man who in his own time was the President of the Cambridge Union and who was schooled in the Marshallian tradition of economics being the handmaid to practice. His first two books, written before succeeding Marshall in the Chair of Political Economy at the age of 30, were on import duties and on industrial peace. In the early part of his career, Professor Pigou had been a member of a number of committees such as the Cunliffe Committee (1918–19), the Royal Commission on the Income Tax (1919–20) and the Chamberlin Committee (1924–25). The interest in practical problems continued throughout his life, as can be seen, for example, from *Essays in Economics* published in 1952 which reproduces several contributions including those on "The Food Subsidies", "Inflation" and "The Gold and Dollar Reserve"—to mention but a few.

Despite this long series of contributions on practical matters, the impression persists of a certain reserve in approaching these problems at least in the latter part of Professor Pigou's career. Somewhere along the line something seems to have changed or developed—perhaps an increasing awareness of the difficulty of reconciling his own analytical bent of mind with the somewhat diffuse and diverse requirements of a fruit-bearing science, perhaps a growing recognition of the inadequacy of economic analysis per se and a humane inclination to turn away from some of the harsher judgements of economic reasoning. Here and there, in Professor Pigou's writings one gets a glimpse of some such attitude. Thus we read towards the end of his Stamp Memorial Lecture on "Wage Statistics and Wage Policy" (1949):

> In this last sentence I have come, for an academic person, dangerously near to hinting an opinion about what practical men ought to do. It is fitting, therefore, that I should end with a word of caution alike to you and to myself. In this field students of economics, when they have stepped down from their ivory tower, have not always won or deserved honour. Not once nor twice in this our island story, the garment of economic jargon has been used to veil the body of Mephistopheles. Our subject in popular versions of it, sometimes even in the hands of distinguished writers, has furnished forth for the ungodly blunt instruments with which to bludgeon at birth useful projects of social betterment.

On an earlier occasion, in replying to Professor Clapham's "Of Empty Economic Boxes" (*Economic Journal*, 1922), Professor Pigou remarks:

> There is, indeed, a lion in the path: the fact that those people with the towering exception of Jevons, who have the qualities required for conducting a detailed intensive study of particular industries and writing monographs about them, are not usually well versed either in the more intricate parts of economic analysis or in modern statistical technique; while the "analytics" lack alike capacity and inclination for these detailed studies. For this there is only one remedy. We must endeavour to train up more men of the calibre of Jevons, who are equally at home in both fields.

In 1935 (or was it 1934?), while addressing the students of the London School of Economics, we find Professor Pigou saying:

> Now the academic economist discussing economic life often suffers from the same handicap. ... He cannot write realistically because he lacks the necessary personal experience; and if he does not attempt to write realistically, but confines himself to analysis of a general character from which detail is excluded, his task is only half accomplished. Therefore—I am giving now advice that I myself have notoriously failed to follow—it is up to the economist, when he is young and his mind is plastic,

to take whatever opportunities he can find for direct acquaintance with the life of men and women in factory and field; to understand machinery; to see for himself at first hand how businesses are organized and run. (*Economics in Practice*, 1935, p. 12)

But whatever view one takes about Professor Pigou's hesitancy in treating matters of practical import and of the struggles that might have lain behind it, what handsome amends has he made not only by the imposing array of his analytical works but also by his incessant effort to bring to the ordinary intelligent reader the substance of economic analysis in a series of superbly lucid monographs! To those which have already been mentioned earlier—such as *Income, Socialism versus Capitalism, The Political Economy of War*—one can add *The Veil of Money* (1919). Whether or not posterity will judge Professor Pigou's contribution to economics as harshly as he himself implicitly did in his assessment of Keynes quoted earlier, one thing is clear. No other Cambridge man has deserved or will deserve more truly Goldsworthy Dickinson's tribute to some of the noblest products of his alma mater. For the light that guided him we can perhaps find no better words than those which he himself used at the conclusion of his lecture to Cambridge students in memory of Marshall:

Whatever way you choose, choose it with your whole heart. Follow the star that leads you, follow without turning, whatever the toil, whatever the pain. Do not hoard your life: spend it; spend it on an aim outside yourselves, the worth of which you feel. It may be that that way you will save your life, it may be you will lose it. But, save it or lose it, you will have saved or lost it well.

References

Pigou, A.C. 1922. 'Of Empty Economic Boxes', *Economic Journal*, June.

_______. 1927. *Industrial Fluctuations*. London: Macmillan.

_______. 1932. *The Economics of Welfare*. London: Macmillan.

_______. 1933. *The Theory of Unemployment*. London: Macmillan.

_______. 1935. *The Economics of Stationary States*. London: Macmillan.

_______. 1935. *Economics in Practice*. London: Macmillan.

_______. 1936. 'Review of General Theory of Employment, Interest and Money by Keynes', *Economica*, March.

_______. 1937. *Socialism Versus Capitalism*. London: Macmillan.

_______. 1939. *Political Economy of War*. London: Macmillan.

_______. 1941. *Employment and Equilibrium*. London: Macmillan.

_______. 1945. *Lapses from Full Employment*. London: Macmillan.

_______. 1949. 'John Maynard Keynes, Baron Keynes of Tilton', A memorial lecture on Keynes delivered at the British Academy.

_______. 1949. 'Wage Statistics and Wage Policy', Stamp Memorial Lecture.

_______. 1949. *Veil of Money*. London: Macmillan.

Pigou, A.C. 1952. *Essays in Economics*. London: Macmillan.
———. 1999. *Income: Income Revisited*. Houndmills, Basingstoke, Hampshire: Macmillan Press.

CHAPTER 33

The Adam Smith Perspective*

Contrary to common misconceptions, Smith's was a protean spirit; and you find in his writings eloquent testimony not just to a grand design of steady economic progress unfolded by the pursuit of the ordinary and even selfish instincts of individual economic agents as long as their activities are unhindered by the arbitrary regulations of the State. Equally, you find in Smith the most incisive account of why the ordinary instincts of self-love, clouded as they often are by self-deceit, myopic vision and insufficient regard for others, need to be circumscribed by judicial or legal restraints as well as by higher moral sentiments of beneficence. The Invisible Hand works hand-in-hand with the Silent Man within; the economic system needs a legal and institutional framework and indeed a certain regulatory mechanism in order to function as it should; there is a dark side to division of labour as well as to economic progress in general; and a statesman as distinct from a mere economic agent has to act in a larger social and historical context of which the economic system is only a part. Indeed, so comprehensive is Smith's vision and such the beauty of his language and talent for an arresting phrase or expression, that it is easy to be mesmerized into thinking that he is relevant for all times and places and that one can find support in him for widely divergent views.

At a broad level of generality his views are, of course, almost universally relevant—moral instincts and rules are deeply ingrained as part of man's adjustment to life in society; while beneficence is beautiful, it is more like an icing on the cake and it is prudence or self-interest or self-preservation that sustains social life; concern for others and the need for their approval are parts of the prudent scheme which, in economic life, makes for effort,

* This paper was presented at The Wealth of Nations Colloquium at Edinburgh, June 1990.

innovation, division of labour and the eventual evolution of a market-based commercial and capitalist system where individual self-interest is generally transmuted into overall social benefit; and even so, you need justice—both in the positive and negative sense—inscribed through laws to sustain social and economic life on an even keel. Although Smith, to my knowledge, does not explicitly say so, he would agree that laws are likely to be more even-handed the more democratic the political process is.

But this rather bland summary of Smith's views on ethics, economics, jurisprudence and the nature of the social and political process—which is now part and parcel of the received wisdom of the liberal tradition—does not carry us very far in answering the most burning questions of today and tomorrow. The failure of the totalitarian model of a command economy tells us very little about what model to follow—let alone how to get there; and those who think that the exact opposite of a totalitarian model of a command economy, viz., a fully democratic polity and an economic system based on private property and complete freedom of perfectly rational and competitive global markets for everything is the recipe for the next millennium should ponder on the following long passage which I take the liberty of quoting—from *The Theory of Moral Sentiments* which in many ways makes for more enjoyable and rewarding reading for a generation which takes much of *The Wealth of Nations* as axiomatic—and I quote:

> The man whose public spirit is prompted altogether by humanity and benevolence, will respect the established powers and privileges even of individuals, and still more those of the great orders and societies into which the state is divided. Though he should consider some of them as in some measure abusive, he will content himself with moderating, what he often cannot annihilate without great violence. When he can not conquer the rooted prejudices of the people by reason and persuasion, he will not attempt to subdue them by force, but will religiously observe what by Cicero is justly called the divine maxim of Plato, never to use violence to his country, no more than to his parents. He will accommodate, as well as he can, his public arrangements to the confirmed habits and prejudices of the people, and will remedy, as well as he can, the inconveniencies which may flow from the want of those regulations which the people are averse to submit to. When he cannot establish the right, he will not disdain to ameliorate the wrong; but, like Solon, when he cannot establish the best system of laws he will endeavour to establish the best that the people can bear.
>
> The man of system, on the contrary, is apt to be very wise in his own conceit, and is often so enamoured with the supposed beauty of his own ideal plan of government, that he cannot suffer the smallest deviation from any part of it. He goes on to establish it completely and in all its parts, without any regard either to the great interests or to the strong prejudices which may oppose it: he seems to imagine that he can arrange the different members of a great society with as much ease as the

hand that arranges the different pieces upon a chess-board; he does not consider that the pieces upon the chess-board have no other principle of motion besides that which the hand impressed upon them; but that in the great chess-board of human society, every single piece has a principle of motion of its own, altogether different from that which the legislature might choose to impress upon it. If those two principles coincide and act in the same direction, the game of human society will go on easily and harmoniously, and is very likely to be happy and successful. If they are opposite or different, the game will go on miserably, and the society must be at all times in the highest degree of disorder.

You will note that Smith's objection here to the imposition of a completely rational "system" is not that it may not be just—in the sense in which markets not supported by social security or transfer of incomes may not be just. Nor is it based on the need to reconcile different objectives: the system is perfect. Only, individual human beings are not totally rational and see reality differently—and it may not be possible for any system of education or persuasion to provide a common perspective. This *is* the human condition—and the point is exemplified today not only by religious fundamentalism but by the barriers of racism and nationalism which have reduced North/South economic cooperation, for example, to a mere trickle after half a century of dedicated effort. The title of the celebrated book which has often been described as one of the most influential books in history is: *The Wealth of Nations*. Whatever may have been the justification for interpreting "Nations" as a collection of singulars in the eighteenth century, the twenty-first surely will require greater emphasis on the collective identity of the world as a whole.

What this really means is that grand designs of social and economic systems are of very little use. In practical terms, we have to be reconciled with compromises, less than perfect solutions and slower than desirable adjustments—unless you are prepared to resort to direct or indirect violence, whether physical or by way of financial pressure. Within a country, a democratic political process gives legitimacy to whatever compromises are struck from time to time; but in the nature of things, no single compromise can be for ever; so that the debate and the search for the best answer for the next election will continue. At an international level, we do not yet have any political process with sufficient legitimacy—so that very little happens; and what little happens is as much by the imperfect instrument of mutual education as by *force majeure*.

Practical economic policy—except in post-revolutionary periods—is concerned with changes at the margin, with fine-tuning, with responding to changes. We may be more sceptical now about fine-tuning. But are we prepared to banish all policy in favour of some simple monetary or other rule—or no rule at all? We may, or may not, have a perfectly sound theoretical answer as to what is an optimum combination of inflation and unemployment—and how to get there. But if there is even an approximation of an answer, it is not to be found in Adam Smith.

To return to the grand themes of growth and social justice and tranquillity, again, what are the major concerns of today and tomorrow even if we set aside for a moment North/South problems or problems of the irreducible differences in human perception? We all accept the need for some kind of a welfare state and most of us may agree with Smith—and indeed with Milton Friedman—that income transfers and a system of charging for services used are better, when feasible, than actual provision of the services by the State. But does this help much in settling today's controversies about the National Health Service and the like? Is there really any psychological or other law which can tell us when a tax level becomes counterproductive, when a subvention becomes debilitating, when a particular differential in remuneration is just right for reducing acute shortages? And surely, like excess profits, excessive differences in remuneration should disappear sooner or later—if one believes that markets for skills and attitudes are as amenable to price incentives as the market for onions or potatoes. The truth of the matter is that much of the talk of incentives and constants of human nature is mere rhetoric. The limits of today are neither fixed nor firm, the scarcities of today are not sacrosanct and ought to be changed, the fact that certain sentiments like self-interest, self-deceit, myopia, desire to please and fellow-feeling are universally present does not mean that the proportions in which they are brought to bear on particular or even general behaviour cannot be made to vary within wide limits. The highest priority in public expenditure surely should be for those areas of education and persuasion which make growth and equity more and more compatible over time, which make our different perceptions converge by conquering self-deceit, ignorance and myopia. Smith was not unaware of this: some of his modern-day admirers are.

At the end of the twentieth century, the concept of steady and sustained economic growth also does not sound as glamorous as it did towards the end of the eighteenth century. The glaring differences in levels of living around the world, the threat to the environment and the population growth still continuing in large parts of the world at least raise the question whether austerity for the sake of austerity—and not for earning compound interest in future—should not receive greater attention. Yes, there is poverty. But there is also conspicuous consumption. Should we now agree with Smith that one's esteem of oneself—and of others—should depend on differences in material well-being? I remember being told in China in 1977—before materialism became so irresistible—that the Chinese had a different view of keeping up with the Joneses. They did not believe in having something because the neighbours had it. They believed in not having something until the neighbours could afford it. It is no longer a question of what the neighbours can afford. It is now a question of what we as a global community can afford. Not Smith but Thomas Aquinas or Gandhi may have greater relevance today—however marginal and slow the impact of their thinking may be to begin with.

If competition is important, so is the firmness with which some people refuse to compete except in their narrowly chosen and often non-economic sphere of interest. If markets are the basis for economic progress, income transfers and non-competing groups are the twin pillars on which human tranquillity and civilization rest. Smith's life—its pursuits and priorities—is itself an eloquent example of this. And today, we need more and more people who would prefer to opt out of essentially material spheres of competition in favour of others.

Growth, of course, is still necessary and even vital in large parts of the world; and competition and division of labour and markets free from interference by and large are essential for realizing the growth potential. But the main engine of economic growth nowadays is technological transformation—and this process is vastly different from innovation in the Smithian age when small individual entrepreneurs and landowners introduced better practices or invented some more labour-saving gadgetry. Science—big science—has changed all that; and growth and technological change now are a response to a complex set of circumstances including the nature and spread of the educational system, the esteem in which scholars and scientists are held and the freedom they enjoy, the international climate for free and unfettered academic exchange and responsiveness to change of large sections of the population. "Leaving things alone" even in respect of scientific and industrial priorities—let alone the profile and soul of education at all levels—would be a parody of what the modern world demands. The implications of modern science and technology for international exchange and division of labour also raise questions which were not paramount towards the end of the eighteenth century.

It is not perhaps surprising—coming from someone associated with an institution of higher learning—that the word "education" has figured so often in my presentation. Adam Smith has a great deal to say about education in his writings, some very pertinent even today and some positively dangerous. There is more than a grain of truth when he says, and I quote:

> The endowments of schools and colleges have necessarily diminished more or less the necessity of application in the teachers. Their subsistence, so far as it arises from their salaries, is evidently derived from a fund altogether independent of their success and reputation in their particular professions.

But what can one make on the eve of the twenty-first century of the following—and I quote:

> Those parts of education, it is to be observed, for the teaching of which there are no public institutions, are generally the best taught. When a young man goes to fencing or dancing school, he does not indeed always learn to fence or to dance very well; but he seldom fails of learning to fence or to dance.

There is more to learning now than can be learnt from the analogy of fencing or dancing. Let us face it. Nostalgia for the past is never a good substitute for thinking about the future.

CHAPTER 34

Advising the Advisers*

W.A. Johr and H.W. Singer, *The Role of the Economist as Official Adviser* (London: George Allen & Unwin, 15 sh, pages 149).

Economists in government are, comparatively, a recent phenomenon. The Keynesian revolution in economic analysis came at a time when governments in most countries were expanding the range of their economic activities; and the economists were in a position to claim that they had developed an analytical framework which could embrace the economic system in its entirety and could unravel the full impact of economic policies in a manner which was not available to simple common sense. The old textbook maxim that the economic problem is distinct from a technical one—that technicians can tell you what happens to output under different assumptions but that you need an economist to decide the point of optimum returns—never really carried conviction as long as the realm of discourse was a firm or an industry. Even in those fields such as that of monetary management, where economic analysis has developed principles of generalized behaviour, the authority of the economist was diluted on all sides—by the interminable controversies among his tribe, by the bitterness of his prescriptions and, above all, by the very simplicity of his analytical framework which could be grasped by any Central Banker without specialized knowledge. But once economists were furnished with the multiplier, the consumption function, the inflationary gap, the national income accounts, the national budgets, the input–output tables and other emblems of aggregative models, they were able to confront the administrators and the politicians with something which they could not easily comprehend and which had all the appeal of the soothsayer's art.

* Originally published in the *Economic Weekly*, Annual, January 1956.

For more than a decade now, economists in almost all countries have had the unique opportunity of holding responsible positions in government, of testing and applying their theories and of judging for themselves the contribution they can make to economic policy. In more than one country the administrative set-up itself has been reorganized with a view to giving the economist full scope for making his rightful contribution. These are developments of great significance to economists as well as to others. A full-fledged book on *The Role of the Economist as Official Adviser*, therefore, arouses a great deal of interest.

Unfortunately, Professor Johr and Dr Singer have written a book which is quite different from what one is led to expect from its title. Part Two of the book, which deals with "The Problem of the Economic Order", is hardly relevant to the subject in hand. After a somewhat perfunctory treatment of the nature of major objectives in economic policy and of the comparative claims of different economic systems as devices for coordination, the conclusion is reached that "the solution to the problem of the economic order is a market economy guided by the state and supplemented by collective agreements".

The first part of the book is in the nature of a methodological investigation into the process of forming practical judgements on economic policy. We are solemnly told that those who instinctively set about tackling economic problems in the right way and are averse to methodology should keep off the book:

> ... after studying the methodology they become conscious of the numerous pitfalls and other dangers which are waiting for them. The result is that they lose their former sure touch, and are led astray or in unsuitable directions. Scholars of this type are warned off methodology and advised especially not to read the following treatise.

It can confidently be said that no reader, however ignorant of methodology, is likely to suffer from such dire consequences by reading the book.

In formulating economic judgements, the analyst must go through a number of stages. He must delimit the problem, size it up, establish the aims, determine the situation and decide what action has to be taken. At each stage, he must avoid certain dangers such as those of wishful thinking, of choosing the wrong concepts, of making faulty comparisons, of neglecting secondary effects and so on. Some of the advice is penetrating enough. Thus the official advisers are advised not to assume away all problems simply because their solution depends on the assumptions made about the whole hierarchy of social problems of which the problem in hand is a part. Everything depends on everything else in economics and economists have been brought up in the tradition that their analysis must keep clear of value judgements. But "economic policy must act" and the distinction between ends and means is a treacherous one where action is involved. Official advisers must also associate themselves actively with the legal, administrative and enforcement aspects of economic policy. All this is somewhat distasteful to economists who enjoy the comparative calm of the study. But we must remember the picturesque American phrase to which Sir Robert Hall has drawn our attention: "If you don't like the heat, stay out of the kitchen."

On the whole, Professor Johr and Dr Singer have not managed to avoid the obvious in an attempt to be exhaustive. We are told, for example, that if we are interested in analysing the causes of balance-of-payments crises we should not define balance-of-payments in such a manner "that it is necessarily balanced in every case". It is statements such as these—of which the book contains quite a few—which make one wonder whether the book is addressed to fellow economists or not. On the other hand, a number of problems of great interest hardly get as much as a mention. Much of what the book contains is relevant to a general discussion of judgements in economic policy. But the specific problems of official advisers do not get the attention they deserve. Official advisers are available to a number of government departments. Economists in government are called upon to perform a number of different functions—of advice, research and general reference work. What should be the organization to ensure that there is sufficient coordination in economic advice and that the day-to-day routine of servicing and briefing administrators and politicians leaves enough scope and time for the proper functions of advice and research? What should be the position of economists in the official hierarchy and how should economists be recruited for government? What is the practice in these respects in different countries? These and similar questions do not come within the scope of the book.

What is perhaps more important to economists than all these questions is an assessment of the extent to which economic analysis has proved itself useful in practice to official advisers. In several European countries and in America the tide is already turning against economists. The annual economic survey in the UK, for example, does not enjoy the same status as it did a few years ago. In part, this is only a manifestation of the general swing to the Right in many Western countries. But can it be that experience has shown that the distance between an able administrator's intuitive judgement and the answers of the economists is not as great as it was imagined a few years ago? Or is it that New Economics has become so much embedded in the routine of government departments that economists must now go out and fashion newer and more efficient tools before they can lay claim once again to a technique which is not an open book to others? Economists will always be needed in government for compiling statistics and for servicing the powers-that-be in a hundred small ways. Economic research can be carried on with official support, in universities as well as in government departments. Even advice can be had from outside as well as from inside. If economists are no longer needed for initiating government departments into new ways of thinking, what then is the purpose of full-time official advisers? Or is it that official advisers are useful precisely in this that they cease to be pure economists and emerge as multipurpose personalities with a flair for research, administration and politics? In India, where the tide is still in favour of the economists and where the available data permit very little of a systematic and comprehensive analysis of anything, these questions are of more than academic value. But we have to wait for another book for a systematic assessment of the experience of other countries in this field.

It is interesting to note in this connection that Professor Johr has attempted in an appendix a critical evaluation of Professor Tinbergen's *Theory of Economic Policy* which is based on the concept of "decision models" elaborated by Ragnar Frisch. What Professor Johr has to say about the superiority of "the method of mental experimentation" to that of "the equations system" is not very convincing. But it is equally true that the practical utility of the method of "decision models" to the larger problems of economic policy is yet to be established.

A word must be said about Dr Singer's responsibility for the book. It would appear that Dr Singer has provided only a running commentary on a book which is essentially Professor Johr's. Dr Singer has apparently inserted a few paragraphs here and there to emphasize the special functions and working experience of economists employed in international organizations. It is difficult to avoid the impression that a separate chapter on economists in international organizations would have made for a better book.

EPILOGUE*

Current Debates on Economic Policy and Salience of I.G. Patel's Thinking

Dr I.G. Patel's thinking on economic policies evolved over almost half a century because of his involvement in policymaking with a theoretical underpinning. The collection of his essays, mostly unpublished and written during this period traces his transition from being an exalted theorist to becoming a formidable economic policymaker. He observed from several vantage points the developments in the real economy to underlay his thinking of economic policy in India, and globally. He combined scholarship and a deep understanding of the world around him in designing economic policy. He was generally reticent, but expressed his views on a wide variety of subjects, often in the course of discharging his duties. In the later part of his life, he wrote and debated major policy issues as a public intellectual in conferences and academia.

He wrote several papers and delivered addresses in public forums. As mentioned in the 'Introduction', only two books containing some of his writings have been published by Macmillan, not to speak of his memoirs brought out by the Oxford University Press (India) which expatiated extensively on his encounter with economic policymaking in India. But several important papers and addresses remained as unpublished manuscripts. After a careful review of his writings some of the papers of enduring interest and contemporary relevance are included in this volume.

* This paper includes excerpts from I.G. Patel, *Economic Reform and Global Change*, Macmillan Publishers India, 1998; I.G. Patel, *Glimpses of Indian Economic Policy*, Oxford University Press, 2002; and I.G. Patel, *An Encounter with Higher Education*, Oxford University Press, 2004.

A reading of these essays provides a sense of evolution of thinking on economic policies over half a century. The value of the collection lies not only in providing a background of his thinking on various economic issues that India confronted during this period, but it also evokes reflections on global economy, contemporary theory, and current challenges for policymakers.

The crux of economic policy deals with the extent and nature of the role of the state or the government in economic activity. While political economy considerations dominate actions and technological advances drive economic activity, there is a continuous interactive process between these two forces and the economic thought. The second half of twentieth century witnessed ascendancy in the role of the state in economic activity relative to markets, followed by the ideology of free markets. The post-Second World War period till the onset of the global financial crisis in 2008 reflects what may be called the rise and fall of state activism in national economies. In developed economies it was rise and rollback of the welfare state, and in developing economies it was the rise and decline of planning for development. The management of crisis is making significant state activism inevitable in most economies.

Development economics as an important branch of economics witnessed a parallel rise with global trends in state activism in the post-War period. With the spread of the ideology of free markets, distinctive characteristics of development economics were diluted. However, consequent upon the crisis, the importance of the quality of intervention of the state, as also the institutional context, and the incentive structures in both the private and public sectors are being recognized. In a sense, there may be a revival of interest in development economics as a branch of economics, but equally important is the recognition that the boundaries between developing and advanced economies seem to be getting blurred as the post-crisis global economy unfolds. Incremental global economic activity is shifting away from advanced to developing economies, indicating some overlapping between the two.

The global financial crisis of 2008 has, in some ways, brought about a degree of uncertainty in the thinking on what constitutes sound economic policy. There is a revival of interest in several issues that were thought to have been settled. There has been considerable exploration by scholars and policymakers of the causes of the crisis and its impact on economic thinking. Most of the literature on the global financial crisis is essentially in the nature of a reaction to the crisis, and sometimes, as a byproduct of an analysis of the historical evolution or explicable patterns of economic cycles. More often than not, contributions by scholars and ideologues seek confirmation of their subjective judgment on economics. Dr I.G. Patel's essays, on the other hand, provide a panorama of thinking for the period that witnessed both the rise and decline of state activism before the crisis, and hence the thoughts at the time that they were articulated are not constrained by the need to relate the thinking to the crisis. At the same time, the essays open a window to thinking on economic policies in the past that could have relevance beyond the immediate crisis.

A reading of the essays in this book helps to appreciate the eclecticism (ideas, style, or taste derived from a broad and diverse range of sources) and pragmatism in Dr Patel's approach. One important fallout of the analysis of the causes and course of the global financial crisis is the respectability that is increasingly ascribed to pragmatism in public policy, as articulated by Dr Patel in many of his essays.

Deena Khatkhate, one of the co-editors of this volume has highlighted Dr Patel's versatility and insight which had a pervasive sweep with a vision and idealism in the Introduction. The Epilogue dwells on a range of current issues with regard to economic policy and relates some of them to Dr Patel's main themes as a tribute to his prescience and foresight.

Currently, there is an intense debate on the role of economics in the global financial crisis. Some economists hold that economics as a discipline failed in anticipating the crisis and is failing in providing an appropriate intellectual framework for managing the crisis. Others, however, view that it is not economics that is to be blamed for the crisis, but it is a particular ideology in economics that deserves to be blamed. The economic theology that dominated the policy in the years preceding the crisis is blamed for ignoring several institutional and behavioural aspects of economics. In any case, there is an intense debate on some of the theoretical foundations of economic analysis and also assumptions and working hypotheses that were driving the economic policy. These debates have significantly longer term and historical significance. At the same time, there are immediate dilemmas for policymakers. It is, therefore, useful to consider current debates with regard to both short-term and long-term economic policies.

Monetary and Credit Policy

One of the main reasons for the global financial crisis which originated in US was a sole focus on price stability by monetary authorities. In some countries the mandate of the monetary authority emphasized the predominance of maintaining price stability as in the case of United Kingdom and by the European Central Bank. Thus, inflation targeting in terms of a formal commitment to a stable level of inflation over a medium-term became the norm rather than an exception. In the case of many developing countries, inflation targeting was adopted to gain credibility or at the instance of the International Monetary Fund (IMF) and the World Bank. As price stability in a narrow range was achieved, many central banks took credit for successfully discharging the mandate, though there were a few dissenting voices who argued that greater trade openness, and to some extent immigration played a role in moderating the price level. However, in view of the main focus on price stability, monetary authorities were impervious to the ominous developments in their financial systems following the rampant use of assets-backed securities based on mortgages in the housing markets, figuring prominently in the balance sheets of banks globally. Financial instability and the resulting recession were the inevitable consequences.

The main instrument of monetary policy in most advanced economies was short-term interest rates. Money supply was monitored, but was rarely used as an instrument. Transparency in communication and managing expectations were considered important instruments. However, the experience with the global crisis has shown that transparency and forward guidance could lead to underestimation of risks by financial markets. It has also shown that the quantitative aspects of money cannot be ignored under certain circumstances. In brief, in the conduct of monetary policy, there is a movement from a single instrument to a wide range of instruments to meet multiple objectives based on several indicators.

The link between monetary policy, credit growth, and fiscal policy was virtually ignored during the years preceding the crisis. The function of managing public debt was left to governments, and independent central banks were expected to conduct their monetary policies without explicitly taking account of the management of public debt or, in some senses, fiscal policy. However, in avoiding a financial collapse, monetary authorities had to undertake significant open market operations with quasi-fiscal implications. Further, bailout of troubled financial institutions in some countries required huge fiscal support. In some cases, the banking crisis actually led to a fiscal crisis. In view of the fact that the public debt to GDP ratio has reached significant proportions in advanced economies, the close linkages between monetary and fiscal policies have come to the forefront with the emergence of the global financial crisis and may continue to persist for a long time.

Consequent upon the global crisis, there is an explicit recognition of the need to adopt countercyclical monetary policies. Such countercyclical monetary policies require coordinated action between fiscal and monetary authorities and financial sector regulations. A countercyclical policy generally warrants a full recognition of credit growth, which is a distinct departure from the approaches in the past.

The relative emphasis between fiscal and monetary policies, between various instruments of such policies, and the relative weights to be accorded to them when there are multiple objectives, are matters that are confronting policymakers at this juncture. In view of the divergent challenges being faced by different countries, both advanced and developing, the conduct of national policies in a globalized world becomes complex. Conventional wisdom with regard to monetary policy responses was found to be inadequate, and hence the recourse to unconventional measures by several monetary authorities, both in advanced and developing economies, became inevitable.

Dr I.G. Patel did recognize as early as 1950 the need for unconventional responses under special circumstances. In Chapter 1 'Demand for Money During Periods of Inflation and Stabilization' he specified the circumstances under which the expansionist monetary policy is appropriate to the stabilization of the price level in an inflation ridden economy. Such apparently unconventional responses may be warranted because of people's desire for holding a part of their income in the form of money during the different phases of inflation, and partly because of the peculiarities of the various economies which may be attempting to stabilize. Many of the factors that were taken into account in Dr I.G. Patel's analysis relate to expectations in determining the demand for money and the need for monetary authorities to respond with policies to take into account expectations. Many economies currently confront complex factors that influence consumer as well as investment behaviour. The analytical framework by Dr Patel provides an interesting case of possible policy responses that may appear paradoxical in such complex situations.

The importance of credit in determining the price level is explained in detail by Dr Patel in Chapter 2, 'Nature and Significance of Monetary Policy and its Instruments'. He argues there that the general level of credit may influence the price level and that the composition of credit growth is also important. Some of the recent policy initiatives that have been considered in the UK where monetary and fiscal authorities are working together illustrate the significance of using some form of selective credit controls. The following statement by Dr Patel is instructive and relevant:

> The techniques of monetary policy discussed so far influence the cost or availability of credit in general. But if, as was suggested earlier, the conditions in an economy are such that expansion in some directions is desirable even as credit in some fields needs to be curtailed, some degree of selectiveness must be introduced in monetary control. To put it differently, if the supreme test of monetary policy lies in its ability to prevent the growth of prices without retarding the growth in production, it may be necessary to control in different ways the supply of money to different sectors of the economy (Chapter 2).

Chapter 2, and Chapter 3 titled 'Selective Credit Controls in Underdeveloped Economies' provide an interesting list of instruments for monetary and credit policies. Some of them have been dormant over a long period but, in view of the extraordinary circumstances in global economy, they are being resurrected now. One instrument mentioned by Dr Patel which appears to have been forgotten is 'moral suasion', and one wonders whether the loss of effectiveness of this instrument is a reflection on the credibility of monetary authorities in financial markets, or is it a reflection on the globalization of financial markets.

The political economy considerations that influence the conduct of monetary policy have been ignored by analysts on the assumption that the independence of central banks from governments ensures a pursuit of policies that are somewhat apolitical and in the long-term interest of the economies. At the same time, the fact that monetary and credit policies will have to be the main and not the only instrument of maintaining price stability has been eloquently expressed by Dr Patel, and this can be of particular significance for the current situation in many developing countries:

> The war against inflation, of course, has to be fought on many fronts; on our farms and in factories in terms of higher production as well as greater productivity; around negotiating tables where wage agreements are arrived at; at meetings where guaranteed or minimum prices for agricultural commodities are settled; and in board rooms and elsewhere where administered prices, generally of industrial goods, are determined in a virtually oligopolistic market. But inflation cannot also be fought without an active monetary and credit policy (Chapter 4).

Till very recently, the issue of inequalities was considered totally irrelevant in the conduct of monetary policy. As the economic consequences of the global financial crisis are unfolding, there is an explicit recognition that monetary policy, credit policy, and regulation of the financial sector, may have some role in income inequalities. How should monetary policy in developing countries be designed, taking into account the recent experience of developed countries and their own unique circumstances? Dr Patel's observation made decades ago, is worth recalling at the present juncture:

> Developments in industrialized countries are of significance to developing countries and some of them may well be echoed with profit by them. At the same time, the policy mix in developed countries has not yet settled down. The rhetoric of policy does not always correspond with reality and there are luxuries of oversimplification that poor countries can ill afford (Chapter 5).

Central Banking

Central banks had built an aura around them which evaporated somewhat mainly in the advanced economies as a result of the crisis. Their concerted actions in avoiding a collapse have restored some confidence in them. However, there are discernible changes in approaches to central banking in terms of ideal structures and appropriate roles. Financial stability has been formally added to their mandates in many cases. Their position in matters of countercyclical policies has been strengthened; and in some cases, regulators of the financial sector have been brought closer to central banks, thus reversing a trend in the pre-crisis period set by UK. There are indications of a closer involvement of central banks in managing public debt, diluting the spirit of independent central banks. There are some debates about the need to review governance and accountability arrangements that should go with the independence of central banks.

There is virtually no change on account of the global crisis in the policies of central banks relating to transparency and communication. Some argue that the 'forward guidance' that was practiced during the boom period encouraged market participants to take excessive risks. Yet, due to the compulsions of reviving confidence in the economy, there is evidence of assurances on a new stance and even of some specific measures relating to monetary policies. Since January 2012, the US Federal Reserve has indicated a target for inflation in line with the observed rate in recent decades in the US, though at the upper end of the traditional range in the advanced economies to assure financial markets about commitments to maintain price stability despite the firm assurances of an ample liquidity over the long term.

Dr Patel advocates that the central bank's communication should go beyond communicating with markets:

> Apart from communicating its own slant on national and international trends, there are three special areas which need attention. The first is the glamorous but elusive area of what the Central Bank communicates and how it does so in relation to its specific responsibility for monetary and foreign exchange policy; the second is communication on issues in regard to its regulatory functions; and the last is communication with the government of the day, including Parliament (Chapter 6).

Some challenges to communication policy were faced in India in the boom period prior to the global financial crisis, and these have been expressed in a forthright manner by Dr Patel. He takes the issue of accountability of central banks to a somewhat unique position, beyond the government, when he says:

> But the point is, when such vital questions arise, the Governor cannot just be inactive. He is a public servant with loyalty to the country and the Constitution—not just to a government in transit. And yet, he cannot behave as if every issue is of great import. He has to choose his ground and be discreet above all. Without offending the government he can start a debate and steer the argument in a certain direction. His ultimate defense is democracy and the tradition of free debate (Chapter 6).

Regulation of the Financial Sector

The new thinking on economic policies is justifiably most striking in the area of the regulation of financial sectors. The assumption was that financial markets left to themselves ensured efficient mobilization and allocation of resources in the real sector, that they have inbuilt self-correcting mechanisms without cost in case of deviations from the competitive equilibria. This assumption is now questioned. The current thinking favours regulation to be strengthened to avoid booms, busts, and liquidity shocks. The regulatory ambit is being extended beyond the banks to other intermediaries, and also to trading in derivatives. Emphasis is placed on macro and micro-prudential regulations and systemic stability along with consumer protection. Also the infrastructure and ecosystems of the financial sector, comprising accounting standards and credit rating agencies, are being subjected to greater regulatory scrutiny than before.

The large financial conglomerates, considered 'too big to fail' are sought to be regulated more intrusively, negating a notion of a level playing field in regulation. Interestingly, the manner in which these 'too big to fail', come into existence accompanied by potential vulnerability, was foretold by Dr Patel more than two decades ago:

> This natural bias towards size and past performance, I suspect, encouraged by governments and regulators as their task is made easier when there are fewer players—including, of course, the task of twisting the arm for a consideration. There is also a certain mumbo-jumbo about systemic failure which must be prevented for the sake of everyone; and this argument in democracies easily proceeds from genuine systemic or general considerations to individual failure for reasons of individual infirmity, particularly when the individuals are big. If you are not bailed out in time, you are merged—not allowed to die and be decently buried. With this insurance against death, quite apart from the moral hazard it begets, the big tend to get bigger even if much of the bigness is excess fat (Chapter 24).

Global minimum standards of regulation are sought to be developed along with arrangements for review of national policies of systemically important economies through peer reviews. The banks that are mainly in retail banking are sought to be insulated, to the extent possible from high risk taking functions like investment banking.

Most of the reforms, consequent upon the experience with the crisis, in terms of regulatory philosophy, structures, and policies, are mainly relevant to a few advanced economies which have adopted excessive deregulation, enabling excessive financialization of their economies. The focus of changes is to avoid serious threats to financial stability primarily by revisiting the appropriateness of deregulation in the past. For most developing economies, however, the issue is not one of reregulation but one of redrawing the design of reforms of the financial sector that was originally envisaged in their economies. The redrawing of the design is intended to take account of the new and emerging global norms of what may be called the optimal size and composition of the financial sector as well as a regulatory regime appropriate to each country. In particular, developing economies recognize that the current thinking on the subject is dominated by the pursuit of stability in advanced economies, while developing economies have to give considerable weight to growth and equity in addition to stability.

In the context of complex tradeoffs involved in the process, and difficulties in identifying cyclical and structural factors in rapidly growing economies, a renewed case for selective credit controls may be expected. Such a revisit may not be irrelevant for advanced economies if the current disconnect between ample liquidity and lack of credit growth persists. Dr Patel's essay on selective credit controls in underdeveloped economies (Chapter 3) is very instructive, since he argues that selective credit controls can play a role both in managing the aggregate level of demand, and the components of such a demand:

> Selective credit controls are intended to encourage or discourage specific types of investment and expenditure by influencing the lending policy of banks and similar credit institutions. In evaluating the usefulness of these controls and of the different techniques for selectiveness, it is necessary first to define the basic objectives to be fulfilled (Chapter 3).
>
> In some cases, selective credit controls may be adopted as an economical way of influencing the general level of demand rather than as a means of influencing certain types of demand. If fluctuations in effective demand are concentrated in certain sensitive areas, and if these areas are particularly susceptible to changes in credit conditions, a decisive influence on aggregate demand may be exercised by controlling credit conditions in a few strategic fields only (Chapter 3).

Further, developing economies are conscious of the fact that actual regulatory changes that may be brought about in the most affected economies may fall short of the current intentions due to pressures of political economy, especially at the international financial centres.

There is a renewed interest in the merits of the presence of public sector banking, mainly in developing economies, at this juncture. This is particularly true in Latin America where Brazil has shown impressive growth, apart from the experience in the growth of the real sector in China and India. However, there is a need to recognize the possible undermining of regulation of publicly owned financial institutions and also diluting the standards of credit. Dr Patel's observations on this subject are worthy of note:

> In assessing the role of financial institutions, we must record their substantial achievements which derive in large measure from their public ownership and control. But let us note also the broader objective, which still remains largely unachieved (Chapter 23).

The lessons from the sub-prime crisis in the US are primarily in the nature of what constitutes sound management of credit conditions. Dr Patel's observations, though in an entirely different context, are interesting:

All financial institutions have, therefore, to operate within the general jurisdiction and guidelines of the Central Bank in this regard. Second, however urgent the need, there cannot be any sacrifice of the criterion of financial soundness or viability where credit is involved. Credit is not a gift or a subsidy; and it has to be repaid out of surpluses generated, as otherwise the expansion of credit, no matter how worthy the recipient or the cause, will only result in a waste of scarce national resources which a poor country cannot afford. To encourage any section of society to incur debts which it cannot possibly repay and, even worse, to let it get away with willful non-repayment, would be to mock the very concept of development and elimination of poverty (Chapter 23).

As a result of the global financial crisis, there is emphasis on ensuring that financial markets serve the real needs of the economy by mobilizing and directing financial resources in an optimal manner. In the process, the asymmetrical capacities of buyers and sellers of financial products cannot obviously be ignored on the assumption that insisting on transparency in the financial markets will reduce information asymmetry. There is a realization now that complexity may be injected into financial products by sellers to dilute the extent of transparency to the buyers. Dr Patel's observations in the context of regulation of securities in India are relevant in this regard:

> But do market-makers really understand the nature of all the risks that can arise in a fast changing and increasingly integrated world? I have my doubts whether the Yuppies were all that gifted; and we should train and test our players much more before we let them loose to play with other people's money. Will the cost of financial intermediation go down with competition or do oligopolies generally succeed in passing on their costs? In the ultimate analysis, the financial markets must not merely increase savings. They must direct them to the most productive uses. Are market prices of shares and debentures—or even the evidence of who-takes-over-whom—sure guides as to where investment is relatively more productive? Can anything be done to lift the veil of the transient and the speculative and to reveal the true face of performance? (Chapter 24).

Taxes on the Financial Sector

The global financial crisis has resurrected an idea that was generally confined in the past to academia, namely, Tobin Tax. Mainstream thinking among economists was that financial markets deliver efficiency and stability if they are integrated and they are subjected to minimal transaction costs. Tobin Tax was not favoured, since it is advocated as a tax on foreign currency transactions to curb excessive volatility or excessive speculation. The global financial crisis witnessed considerable interest in the levy of taxes on financial transactions, not only in currency markets, but among other financial transactions as well. The arguments in favour of such taxes are not confined to curbing excessive volatility or speculation, but also to reduce fiscal costs of past crises and possibly as insurance for future fiscal burden.

While there is no consensus on a global coordination for such taxation, levy of such taxes at the national level is being increasingly favoured. Taxes on financial intermediaries which were hitherto exempt and levy of new taxes on bonuses are also being debated widely.

Developing Countries' Perspectives

The overall economic performance of many developing countries has been impressive since the 1980s. However, the overall performance has not been uniform across the regions, with East Asia and China showing the most impressive growth. Latin America's performance was marked by volatility in output. Transition economies also performed well, some of them due to their economic integration with Europe. Many, though not all, of the developing countries, faced a series of crisis, the most acute of them being in Latin America and the one in Asia. Many of them experienced the perils of a series of crises encompassing financial, external, and fiscal sectors in different combinations across countries. Hence, they took several measures in terms of reforming the structures of the economy, consolidating their fiscal positions, strengthening their external payments particularly by building forex reserves, and improving the regulation of the financial sector. Many of their policies were directed at building defences against the crisis. These measures were by no means either universal or uniform. However, the beneficial impact of many of these measures taken independently or collectively by many countries were brought to light through their resilience at the time of the global financial crisis in 2008. In fact, some analysts describe the crisis of 2008 as a western crisis, comparable to the earlier Asian crises and the Latin American crises. They attribute the 2008 crisis to neglect of lessons of previous crises in developing economies by the advanced economies. The developing countries exhibited not only some resilience despite elements of contagion, but have also bounced back and contributed significantly to improvements in the global economy after the initial shock. These diverse experiences amongst developing countries have led to a considerable revamping of established beliefs with regard to appropriate economic policies that would contribute to both growth and stability.

During this period of high growth, the advantages of globalization of trade in goods and, to some extent in services, were exploited by many developing economies. The boom period in advanced economies and the accelerated growth in developing economies gave a fillip to commodity markets thus benefiting many developing countries. While some faced stress on their balance of payments, many of the developing countries were able to acquire competitive strength both in manufacturing and in services. Trade between developing countries increased significantly, particularly within Asia. Their stake in the globalization of trade increased relative to the earlier periods despite several downsides of such globalization, such as an adverse impact on the natural environment and inequalities.

The globalization of finance resulted in unintended consequences—the savings on an aggregate basis started moving uphill from poor countries to richer economies. The globalization of finance surged ahead of the globalization of regulation and resulted in excessive financialization in advanced economies. Those developing countries which demonstrated considerable resilience during the global crisis were conspicuous by the building up of significant forex reserves, while the orthodoxy was concerned with the high cost of building reserves till the global financial crisis erupted. Some of the developing countries, contrary to the orthodoxy, took recourse to managing their capital accounts actively. Hence, rationale of maintaining forex reserves and capital controls, has become more nuanced. Advanced economies, in particular the US, have also noted possible policy infirmities which possibly cannot ensure that the financial sector absorbs surges in capital flows in a non-disruptive manner.

Before the crisis, the IMF was concerned with the provision of global liquidity to developing countries, but that the advanced economies would require such facilities was not expected. The perception that advanced economies have sovereign debt obligations that are virtually credit-risk free has been questioned after the crisis in the Euro Zone, and arguably the downgrading of the sovereign rating of the US.

The role of the public sector in some of the large developing economies in ensuring growth as well as stability is being noticed after the crisis. Links between the financial sector and the fiscal position became very evident during the crisis and its current management. Those countries whose public debt was predominantly in domestic currency (other than the Euro Zone) were less affected by the crisis, and those countries where most of their debt was held by residents (including Japan), tended to be resilient to the crisis. The public debt to GDP ratio which was generally high in developing economies relative to advanced economies (Japan being an exception), has dramatically changed in view of the huge public debt incurred in many advanced economies to support the financial sector and to stimulate their economies. The aggregate public debt of all countries as a proportion of a global GDP has multiplied due to the crisis.

The cumulative impact of this experience is that the nature of the problems being faced by developing countries has changed. Empirical evidence of their policies and economic performance does not reinforce dominant beliefs in the global economic community on what constitutes sound economic policy for them. The divergence between advanced and developing economies in terms of economic strength is getting narrowed, and a significant shift is occurring in incremental economic activity from advanced economies to developing economies.

There is, perhaps, an emerging vacuum in the intellectual framework that should govern the economic policies of developing countries in facing the policy challenges ahead. Among the models that have been less than successful in delivering prosperity to developing economies are the socialist model, the planning model, and more recently the Washington consensus based model. The market capitalism mode as practiced in advanced economies is under stress, despite its impressive achievements. It is also necessary to recognize that there are many advanced economies which are continuing with free market capitalism with considerable success, such as the Scandinavian countries, Canada, and Australia. Among the developing economies, there is variety of capitalism with special characteristics, as for example China, with a considerable role for the state and others like India, Brazil, Russia, and many parts of Asia. In brief, while there is disenchantment with the globally advocated development models and some of the policy tools, both in some advanced economies, and to some extent in some developing economies, they are yet to be replaced by an acceptable and coherent intellectual framework.

It will be useful from a policy point of view to identify the emerging challenges to economic policies of developing countries. The short-term challenges arise out of fragilities in the multi-speed recovery of the global economy, volatilities in commodity markets, and heightened uncertainties in the outlook for financial markets. The developing countries are faced with continued recourse to unconventional policy responses by some advanced economies. Such responses do have the potential for spill-over effects on developing countries. Thus, over the short-term developing countries may be compelled to consider a full range of conventional and unconventional policy instruments to respond to these short-term challenges.

The longer term challenges to policy in developing countries may be significantly different from the mainstream challenges that were considered by them before the crisis. They may have to begin assessing what the new normal in the global economy post-crisis would be, and how they need to respond. It is not unreasonable to assume that the new normal rates of growth in the global economy after the crisis may be less than those in the boom period prior to the crisis; and the new normal rates of inflation in the global economy may be higher than those experienced during the period immediately preceding the crisis often described as 'Great Moderation'. More important, the economic environment during the post-crisis period is likely to be vastly different from what it was before the onset of the crisis.

The allocation of global capital will be governed in future by the increasing demands on such capital from advanced economies due to the debt they have incurred to manage the crisis, and the fiscal burden of ageing populations. Global trade may be under stress because of the downward pressure on wages and employment in advanced economies on account of competition from emerging economies which have demonstrated their strengths to acquire skills and to adopt technology. The challenges with regard to climate are particularly acute with millions of people from developing economies trying to emulate the lifestyles of advanced economies. Above all, institutional arrangements for global governance through IMF and World Bank are heavily loaded in favour of advanced economies, and correcting this course may not be smooth.

There are challenges to developing countries which are embedded in domestic economies. For some of the economies considerable rebalancing may be needed between domestic demand and export demand. What was thought to be a problem of high population is now converted into a demographic dividend—a source of strength in some economies over the medium term. However, if the new entrants to the workforce do not have adequate skills to compete globally, it could turn into a demographic curse. Imparting skills cannot be left entirely to the private sector. Rapid urbanization is yet another area which requires considerable public investments. Effective public policies are required to manage the environmental impact of rapid growth. Many of these initiatives have to be accompanied by improvements in governance, both in the private and public sectors, consistent with what may be described as a sustainable middle income country status for many developing economies.

In this background of emerging global and domestic challenges, and the huge impact that China and India are likely to have on the global economy, it is not surprising that considerable attention is being paid globally to China's Twelfth Five Year Plan of China (2011–15) and to India's Twelfth Five Year Plan (2012–16).

Dr Patel attempted a study of India's five year plans in Chapter 13 and China's five year plans in Chapter 15. This remained unpublished till now, but it provides interesting contrasts with the new and divergent challenges being faced by China and India. The study also gives an inkling of the progress that the two economies have made in about half a century. It is noteworthy that currently there is significantly more interest in global think tanks and intellectual forums in China's five year plan, while about 50 years ago India's planning experience which held centre stage.

The Indian Economy

In the context of current debates on economic reforms in India there are three vital themes in Dr Patel's essays that are worth reiterating. Dr Patel reflects on what the long-term goals of economic reform should be, and those thoughts appear to be very relevant after the experience with the global crisis:

Human beings like to catch up with others and it is very easy to turn wants into needs. We have all experienced it and, like it or not, consumerism will prevail in India, by and large as it has in the US and Europe. And yet, can anyone deny that Gandhiji's ideas in this regard are worth emphasizing even more today? Savings and investments are vital for economic growth. Consumerism reduces savings—witness how the US rate of saving is much lower than that of India, let alone China. Global warming may or may not be around the corner. Science may stave off the exhaustion of scarce resources for some time. But we cannot be sure. Precaution demands restraint upon consumption. Vulgar display is demeaning; it reduces social solidarity and, at times, even creates violent resentment. Part of the fuel that propels fundamentalism today is the disgust that many well-meaning but conventional people feel at the indulgence they see spreading all around them. There may or may not be a clash of civilizations. But there is certainly a clash in each society between inner peace and limitless gratification; between civilized, compassionate and moderate behaviour and a self-centred rat race, which leaves you little time even to enjoy what you crave for (Chapter 19).

There are hopes of India being an emerging economic power, but Dr Patel combines realism and optimism on this:

We should be under no illusion that with the implementation of economic reforms—a distant dream anyway—we would be among the richest countries in per capita terms in one generation. Nor will there be an end to poverty or any significant reduction in inequality. But we can give everyone *roti*, *kapda*, *makan*, *sadak*, *bijli*, sanitation, safe drinking water and access to the literary treasures of the world, and eliminate malnutrition. That is a good enough dream to fulfil (Chapter 19).

Those who think Gandhi is economically irrelevant are only refusing to think on new and bolder lines, and can find no alternative to traditional notions of socialism and capitalism. Institutions evolve, and it is possible to imagine and create an economy which combines the best of Marx, Mohandas and Milton Friedman—to stick only to the Ms (Chapter 19).

What should be India's dream? Dr Patel's answer is that India should dream of an India, by Indians and for Indians living in India:

By all means, we should have a dream but that dream will have to be to say we are all Indians, we have to live in this country, we have to prosper in this country, and our children will have to live in this country.... For the millions of our people this is our land and this is where we have to make a living. We will make a good living only if we agree that we have to take care of each other, not through envy, not through jealousy, but through constructive, creative, wealth-building activities. I do not think that business can simply say that it exists only for itself (Chapter 20).

International Aspects

The global financial crisis has drawn attention to some important aspects of the global economic system, namely, the international monetary system, global financial architecture, sovereign debt restructuring mechanisms, and regional groupings. These debates are taking place in the background of what has been described as large economic imbalances. They refer to the persistent current account deficits of some countries and current account surpluses of others and also stresses on the fiscal and financial stability in some countries. It is recognized that in history there have been cases of such imbalances over a prolonged period, but in the recent crisis the design of the global economic system has injected instability globally and intensely.

The international monetary system is characterized by the predominance of the US dollar as a reserve currency. The supply of US dollar to meet the liquidity requirements of the global economy is not subject to market forces because there is no effective competition to its status. Further, there are no global rules governing its supply, since the Federal Reserve is mandated to consider the interests of the US economy. The interests of the global economy will, therefore, be best served only if they happen to be coinciding with the interest of the US economy. This situation brings about what has been known as 'exorbitant privilege' or the unique privilege for the United States of America whereby the country has been able to borrow almost without limit. It can be argued that growing international trade and global finance warrant additions to supply of liquidity. How could the supply of reserve currency be enhanced if the US were not to have a current account deficit? However, according to some, persistent deficits also put downward pressure on the value of the US dollar and also a strain on the US economy.

Efforts to improve the monetary system and evolve either a global currency or a multi-country currency, such as Special Drawing Rights (SDR) or promoting several currencies to compete have not been successful so far. At the same time, there is a serious threat of the loss of status of the US dollar as a store of value. There are indications that the role of China's currency is expanding in the area of trade, with plodding by the state. Similar expansion in the area of global finance and a store of value may happen sometime in the future.

In brief, while the status of the US dollar as the predominant reserve currency is being challenged, there is no agreement on an alternative, and the transition to an alternative system appears to be prolonged. It is obvious that substituting one national currency (say, the US dollar) with another will not solve the fundamental problems associated with the current non-system. While competition among a few leading national currencies to be global reserve currencies may be envisaged, the network externalities tend to favour a drift to a single predominant currency. Further, there are little prospects of acceptance of a new global currency in the absence of an effective global governance that can support a truly global currency. SDRs, a unit of account based on a basket of select currencies currently being used by IMF is sought to be popularized, but participants in the global financial market are not enthusiastic about it. In order to minimize the risks arising out of the current non-system, prominent leaders of the world economy are making efforts to agree on some limits to persistent and large current account surpluses or deficits. Such efforts have not proved successful so far. To sum up, the problems of the international monetary system have been identified, a search for solutions has been continuing with no immediate prospects of any viable option emerging, and the debates are continuing on a framework that is both desirable and feasible. Problems relating to the international monetary system may get worse in future, warranting deeper intellectual exploration and credible statesmanship.

The global financial architecture rests on three pillars—the World Trade Organisation (WTO), the World Bank, and the International Monetary Fund (IMF). There is consensus that there is governance deficit in IMF and the World Bank which has to be corrected. There is a welcome beginning of changing the disproportionate representation of many advanced economies, especially Europe, in favour of developing economies. The pace of implementation of changes in governance and the adequacy of the proposed changes are being debated. There are elements of credibility deficit and lack of even-handedness in surveillance of countries by IMF, but there is some evidence of correctives in this regard. IMF is making conscious efforts in its research and in policy documents, and is continuously reviewing intellectual framework that governs its surveillance and its operations. There are some developing countries which hold that in reality the changes in IMF's approaches have been marginal, in its conditionality and in its lending operations. Some perceive that IMF has been soft in its conditionality with regard to Euro Zone countries, though it is possible to argue that their circumstances are different. In any case, despite recent increases in its resource base, IMF's lendable capacity is considered to be constrained. The World Bank's resources continue to decline with sharply increased capital flows to developing countries.

The G20 has been described as a fourth pillar of global economic governance. G20, unlike other pillars, is an informal body of heads of governments of 20 systemically important countries for the global economy. The grouping was in many ways based on self-selection, and there is no evidence of binding criteria for eligibility to be a member. Its operating arm is the IMF. Its legitimacy as well as its representative nature is questioned. G20 played a useful role in avoiding the collapse, but in ensuring cooperation for sustained recovery of the global economy its success is less than what was expected. It is often considered a convenient arrangement in a given context but the G20 is yet to stand the test of time.

Despite several intellectual exercises, it has not been possible to have an effective system of 'global lender of last resort' for sovereigns. IMF's role as a provider of some liquidity for countries in need of such support was confined to its operations in developing countries in recent decades. There are, as yet, no formal mechanisms for orderly sovereign debt restructuring. Sovereign debt restructuring mechanisms have in the past been debated almost wholly in the context of developing economies. The context has now shifted, and seems to be as relevant for advanced economies, in particular the Euro Zone, as for developing economies. It is also interesting to notice that the IMF was less than enthusiastic in cooperating with the group of Asian economies that tried to provide facilities akin to the International Monetary Fund at the regional level. However, with the onset of problems in the Euro Zone, IMF is revising its approaches to regional arrangements for provision of liquidity.

There are several regional groupings among countries, but the most significant of these for the global economy are the Chang Mai Initiative (comprising of ASEAN countries Plus Three) and the Euro Zone comprising countries that adopted Euro as their currency. The Chang Mai Initiative did not turn out to be as comforting at the time of financial crisis of 2008 as it was thought to be. Despite the availability of swap arrangements under the Chang Mai Initiative for liquidity at the time of the crisis, two of the countries that needed liquidity preferred to obtain it from the US Federal Reserve (which was the epicentre of the crisis). The Euro Zone has come under stress due to the lack of effective institutional arrangements to reconcile national fiscal autonomy and a currency union. Thus, there is a considerable degree of uncertainty about the nature of regional arrangements that are desirable and feasible, consistent with the prevailing global financial architecture. Dr Patel's views on regional arrangements were understandably ambivalent, with some justifiable concern for where India would be in regional blocks:

> I have refrained from commenting on China and India—but I hope this Symposium does not exhibit the same forgetfulness towards India which I have witnessed increasingly in so many international gatherings. But if you wish something else to divert your attention, I suggest we devote some attention to Eastern Europe. Here are the Socialnics who are also challenging the rest of us to make room for them in an interdependent world: will they find it in a European block as the Eastnics may find in a yen bloc and Latinics in an American bloc? I hope not. For where will South Asia and the Middle East seek their salvation then? (Chapter 10).

Inequalities

The approach to inequalities in the past has been generally in the context of reduction of poverty, and that is considered appropriate both on moral grounds and on the grounds of consistency with the goals of economic development. However, the global financial crisis has brought to the forefront additional dimensions of inequalities. First, it is held that income inequalities have contributed to instability in aggregate demand and this was one of the causes for the global financial crisis. Second, the contention of the 'Occupy Wall Street' movement has been that the operation of the financial sector and its regulation has exacerbated inequalities. Third, the threat to social cohesion in some of the economies is being attributed to inequalities in the income generated by the model of economic development that has been adopted as part of excessive dependence on market forces. Fourth, the fiscal policy, in particular the taxation policies, seem to have operated considerably in favour of the rich. This has generated, what may be known as fiscal regimes in favour of the 1 per cent against the 99 per cent population. Fifth, the inequalities are common to both developing and advanced economies, as illustrated by US, China, and India. The issue of income inequalities is global. Sixth, capitalism as currently preached and practiced is deeply worried about this development. The sight of some billionaires pleading that they be taxed more is a tell-tale sign of a crisis and eagerness of capitalism to reform itself. Finally, there is a perception that rising inequalities, even in societies where poverty does not prevail, have led to the capture of political influence by the richer segments. Consequently, public policies in most countries tended to benefit a few to the detriment of large segments that finally led to the crisis. Many believe that the crisis and its management have not changed these political economy factors. This could imply that the social tensions that are erupting, including the 'Occupy Wall Street' movement, may intensify in the future.

There is recognition of the broader implications of not only widespread poverty but also persisting inequalities, but embedding them in public policies and the intellectual framework for this purpose are tasks that perhaps have just begun to attract serious attention. Current thinking on economic policy is grappling with the impact of inequality as well as the perception of inequity on social cohesion and consequently on economic stability and well being. It is also concerned with the long-term impact on nature and the sustainability of lifestyles that prevail in some of the advanced economies which are sought to be emulated by several developing economies. Fundamentally, economic thinking is not able to replace growth for its own sake as the dominant objective of its approach to public policy. There is a felt need for an intellectual framework in economics that incorporates ultimate goals of finance and growth. Such goals may include a sense of security or absence of serious instability (in jobs, for example) for people; a reason for hope of a better future, and the absence of a serious threat to natural resources.

Dr Patel's thoughts on the subject have been much nuanced. They recognize several dimensions of equity and equality; they also note that the pendulum of thinking on economic policies often swings on this issue, and that poorer nations cannot simply afford to ape richer nations:

> There is thus certainly some sense in noting that equity in a modern society means something much less than equality and is, in fact, currently advocated only in some minimalist sense. But can it not be that the pendulum is once again swinging too far in the other direction? (Chapter 18).

Dr Patel seems to suggest that issues of equity, inequality, and social cohesion are too complex to be managed by economic thinking only; though appropriate economic thinking is necessary it is not a sufficient condition for addressing such issues:

> In the ultimate analysis, equity, like liberty, in all modern societies that aspire to be democratic, has to be defined in the rough and tumble of the political arena. Economics and even philosophy or morality can only articulate the conflicting and pluralistic concerns among which statesmen must steer as best they can. Politics, they say, is the art of the possible. But statesmanship surely lies in stretching what is possible towards what we all know is desirable in the sense of being conducive to social solidarity as well as individual well-being (Chapter 18).

Economics, Economists, and Public Policy

The global financial crisis of 2008 and the subsequent developments have led to several debates on the role of economics, economists, and public policy in general. It has been argued by some that economics as a discipline failed in preventing the crisis, predicting the crisis, or managing it satisfactorily when it happened. This has led to considerable introspection, particularly in terms of expanding the horizons of economics to include behaviourial sciences, sociology, neurology, and evolutionary biology. There is a recognition that the tools of analysis used by economists in recent years depended excessively on models which focussed more on internal consistency than on consistency with facts. Further, the thinking process was dominated by deductive methods, often ignoring complex realities and empirical evidence. Often theoretical models tended to be misunderstood for reality itself rather than as a tool for understanding reality. In the process, socio-cultural factors as well as institutional dynamics were not fully appreciated. Dr Patel makes interesting observations on the discipline in several of his essays; one illustration is given below:

I have come to realize that in the making of any economic policy decision, the knowledge you carry or general economic theory plays a very small part. The validity or otherwise of your policy prescription depends largely on how well you have been able to assess the relevant circumstances—social, political and economic—in which the prescription has to be applied (Chapter 14).

There are some economists who argue that there is nothing wrong with economic theory, it was the political economy that caused the crisis. There are some in the fraternity who blame the dominance of particular schools of thought for causing the crisis. These are often associated with Efficient Market Hypothesis and Rational Expectations. The simplified models virtually captured academic thinking. Academic recognition of contrarian views was hard to obtain due to the dominance of this school's thought, particularly in the US and in multilateral bodies. This situation encouraged a tendency towards intolerance to dissent. Consequent upon the crisis, a movement has started which is devoted to developing new economic thinking that could challenge the overwhelming dominance of what is generally described as a free market orthodoxy or belief in unfettered markets. Dr Patel's articulation of the need to view simple everlasting rules in economics with considerable disdain is best expressed in Chapter 21:

The truth of the matter is that despite all the talk of a new consensus and a few simple rules that should guide economies towards prosperity, the task of economic management has become even more difficult and complex. We do have major guidelines and we have learnt much from the recent past. But in a fast changing and politically vibrant world, economic wisdom cannot be reduced to a few commandments which in any case will have to be interpreted, quantified and reconciled in actual practice. Economists at least should be grateful for this as otherwise they would soon be cast off as historical debris left behind by the very march of their discipline (Chapter 21).

It is also noteworthy that the American Economic Association in its annual meeting in 2011 thought it fit to work on a code of ethics for economists. This initiative was prompted by revelations that several economists, particularly in the area of financial economics, were advising financial sector regulators while simultaneously providing consultancy to market-participants. More often than not, these conflicts of interests were not revealed.

There is a class of economists which holds that the political economy in the US needs to be blamed for the crisis, since they adopted policies for encouraging credit expansion and leverage. In their view, the participants in financial markets or the prevailing theories of finance or economics cannot be held responsible for the crisis. The fallout of this line of thinking is an increasing focus on interactions between the state and the market that could result in a crisis. In other words, the assumptions made in the past were that market failures could be avoided by the active intervention of the state and that state failures are best avoided by enabling markets to function freely. The recent experience shows that expansion of either of the two, the state or the market, may not necessarily compensate for the potential failures of the other.

In sum, there are several areas in which the current economic thinking is exploring parameters for rebalancing in light of the experience so far with the global financial crisis. First, the rebalancing of the state and the market is a subject that has been traversed for long and is being revisited. Second, the importance of governance and values in both the public and private sectors has come into prominence. Third, the rebalancing between the financial sector, economy, and social concerns is more complex, and the search is for new tools of analysis. Fourth, an area of concern in this regard is the path to be traversed to restore trust in the financial sector, particularly in advanced economies. Finally, increasing globalization that is mostly driven by technological progress has to be matched by appropriate arrangements for governance at the global level. A tell-tale example of the consequences of a disconnect between national considerations and global arrangements is the global financial crisis, caused in part, by the globalization of finance while its regulation remained national. Reconciling national interests with global interests is essentially in the realm of political economy though economic thinking may aid the process. Dr Patel's observations on this subject are:

> What this really means is that grand designs of social and economic systems are of very little use. In practical terms, we have to be reconciled with compromises, less than perfect solutions, and slower than desirable adjustments—unless you are prepared to resort to direct or indirect violence, whether physical or by way of financial pressure. Within a country, a democratic political process gives legitimacy to whatever compromises are struck from time to time; but in the nature of things, no single compromise can be for ever; so that the debate and the search for the best answer for the next election will continue. At an international level, we do not yet have any political process with sufficient legitimacy—so that very little happens; and what little happens is as much by the imperfect instrument of mutual education as by *force majeure* (Chapter 33).

Y.V. Reddy

About the Author and Editors

The Author

DR I.G. PATEL was one of the most distinguished economists and economic advisers. He had a dazzling academic career both at the University of Bombay and the Cambridge University, England where he had the rare honour of being inducted into the Political Economy Club by Keynes. He traversed all fields with great distinction as a professor of economics at the University in Baroda, as an economist in the International Monetary Fund and later a member of its Executive Board, Chief Economic Advisor and finance secretary to the Government of India, Governor of the Reserve Bank of India, Deputy Chief Administrator of the United Nations Development Programme (UNDP), Director of the London School of Economics and Political Science, Director of the Indian Institute of Management, Ahmedabad, Chairman of the think-tank, Indian Council for Research on International Economic Relations (ICRIER) and member of the Prime Minister's Economic Advisory Council.

Dr Patel's career qua economist was multidimensional. He wrote theoretical papers on money and trade and later moved on to the practical application of economic theory to the solution of the problems he faced in his professional tenure as an economic advisor. He published several articles later incorporated into two books, *Essays in Economic Policy and Economic Growth* and *Economic Reform and Global Change*, both published by Macmillan in London and New Delhi. In addition, his insights into economic policy and higher education were encapsulated in his two other books, *Glimpses of Indian Economic Policy: Insider's View* and *Encounter with Higher Education*, both brought out by the Oxford University Press, New Delhi.

The Editors

DEENA KHATKHATE, an alumnus of the University of Bombay and the Manchester University held a senior position in the International Monetary Fund and later was the Managing Editor of *World Development*, an academic journal. He authored several papers on money, finance and economic development which were published in internationally reputed journals like *The Quarterly Journal of Economics*, *The Review of Economics and Statistics* and *The Oxford Economic Papers*.

DR Y.V. REDDY, a member of the Indian Administrative Service and economist, held top positions, among others, as the secretary to the Government of India, Governor of the Reserve Bank of India, and a member of the Executive Board of the International Monetary Fund. In recognition of his contributions both as an administrator and economist, he was honoured by several universities in India and elsewhere by bestowing on him doctorates (*honoris causa*). He was elected as an Honorary Fellow of the London School of Economics and Political Science. He has been a member of the Commission of Experts of the President of the UN General Assembly on Reform of the International Monetary Fund and Financial System and a Guest of Committee on Global Thought, Columbia University, New York. He is currently Emeritus Professor at the Central University, Hyderabad.

He has authored numerous articles and books, such as *India and the Global Financial Crisis: Managing Money and Finance* and *Global Crisis, Recession and Uneven Recovery*.

Index

advanced countries xxi, 121–2, 126–7, 129–34, 136–7, 163, 198–9, 251, 291, 335, 345, 349–50, 386; policies in 129–31

advanced economies 424, 426, 428–31, 433–6, 439–41, 444

agricultural: development 199–200; production 172, 204, 320, 323–4, 326, 331; technology 238

agriculture: in Second Plan 171–2

Ahluwalia, Montek 283

aid 242; mobilization of 366–7

aid-giving countries 131

Ambedkar, B.R. 254–5

Anglo-American loan agreement 139

Anklesaria Aiyer, Swaminathan 255

annual budgetary plans 61

anti-inflationary effects 26, 52–3

Asian Clearing Union 85

ATMs 91

austerity 230, 234, 246; Gandhi on 250

Austria: hyperinflation of 22; inflation and stabilization of 19–23

Austro-Hungarian Empire 20

ayarams and *gayarams* 256

Bagchi, Amaresh 285

balance-of-payments xix, xxviii, 7, 36, 46, 52–3, 69–70, 73, 77–8, 115–16, 190–1, 235, 334–6, 339–44, 351, 355–6, 395, 420; causes for crises of 420; considerations 386; difficulties 7, 52, 53, 121, 334–6, 339–40, 342, 346; deficit 236; disequilibria 82; and GATT 341

bank credit 35–6, 38–9, 40–2, 45–9, 52, 54, 61, 63, 67, 78–9, 88, 147, 254, 398

bank-financed deficits 42

banking system 12, 35, 37, 41–2, 48, 52, 58–60, 63, 74–5, 78, 274–5, 302; and long-term financial provision 60

barter xviii, 8–9, 17, 29, 344

Belgian imports, rise in price 27

Belgium 4, 23, 26; cessation of Marshall aid in 28; employment situation in 27–8, 29–30; inflation and stabilization in 23–9; liquidation of stocks of 28; production increasing 26; retail prices in 27

Bernstein, E.M. xvi

Bhagwati, J. 281

Bhubaneswar resolution 229

Bilateralism 135, 348–9, 384; with Soviet Union 232–3

Bombay Bullion Association 111

borrowing 18, 22, 38, 42, 46, 52, 54, 66–7, 72, 75, 77, 114–15, 145–6, 185, 190, 277

Brahmananda 281
Brazilian innovation 82
Bretton Woods system 355–6; *see also* General Agreement on Tariffs and Trade (GATT)
budget deficit and Central Bank 74
budgetary deficits xix, 17, 20, 24, 27–8, 57–8, 74

capital 279; formation of 143–4; surplus of 234
capital goods industries 19, 161–2
capital market 307–8, 314
capital-intensive industries xxiii, 143, 195, 304
capitalism xxv, 215, 224, 230–1, 233, 250, 259, 266, 270, 278, 282, 406, 408, 410, 435, 441; *see also* Japan, capitalism of
"captive" investors 59
cash balances 4, 6, 20, 22, 26
cash credit system 60
cash reserve ratio 78; and statutory liquidity requirement 78
caste system xiv–xv, 400
central bank xix–xx, 18, 20, 22, 32, 35–9, 41–3, 48–53, 72, 74–6, 78–9, 83–8, 90–1, 93, 425, 428–9; bond market and 38; credit risk for financial agencies 76; credits of 18, 39; in developing countries 75, 78; and exchange rate 88–9; Governors of 85–6, 88, 93; and liquidity of banks 37; and rediscount facilities 38; and resources to credit institutions 72; and subsidies 40
Centre-State Relations 285
Chakravarty Committee 71, 72
Chandavarkar, Anand xx
Chiang Mai Initiative 440
charka 249–50
"cheap" labour 397; *see also* labour, surplus of
Chelliah, Raja 285
child labour 243
China xxiv, 89, 238; agricultural prices in 203; agricultural production in 202–3; and industrialization 212, 216; cultural and educational development of 207; economic policy 201, 204; economy of 213; employment in 209; exporting labour-intensive products of 259; first five year plan of 201–3, 204, 215; for consumer and luxury processed foods 282; foreign assistance and 213–14; industrial production and 202–4, 215; investment and 207–8, 209, 210, 216; market stability in 212; mass consumption products in 205–6; national income of 202; one country, two systems policy of 140; personnel training and 213; planning of xxiii–xxiv, 201–2, 204, 207, 209–10, 215–19; population and 206, 209, 214; production 214–15; production of basic goods and 211; purchasing power in 208; rural production and subsidiary 203–4; social services development in 211–12; socialism in 215; standard of living in 205–6
COMECON 134
Commercial banks 48–9, 69, 75, 90, 302, 308, 377
Committee of Twenty 357–8, 362, 381
commodity: agreements 377; balances 151
communal riots in Gujarat 260
compensatory credit 12
competition xvii, xxxi, 77, 79, 90–1, 214, 257–8, 271–2, 291–3, 312–14, 386–8, 396–8, 416, 438; in interest rates 77; and technological change 287
compulsory education 268
consumerism 251–2, 258, 399, 437
consumption xxiv, xxviii, 5–7, 80, 97–101, 103, 105–7, 109, 127, 129, 140, 157–9, 166, 168, 205–6, 268–9, 322–6; and investment 326–8; of "poor" 335; of sugar 100, 106, 107
contract labour 292
convertibility 360–1; Walch on 369

Cooley Funds 330–1
corporate governance 284
corporate taxation 145, 303
corruption xxvii–xxviii, 248, 252, 256, 290, 294
cost-push pressures 79, 276
countries in process of industrialization 134; and promotion of export earnings 136–7
creation of money 42–3
credit 48–50, 139, 187, 237, 277, 329, 305–6; to private organized industry 61
credit creation 11–13, 20, 22, 73, 187; means of 11
credit expansion 28, 46–7, 51, 54, 58–9, 87, 305, 432, 443
credit planning 61–2; component of 62
credit policy 13, 18–19, 22, 29, 42–8, 56–60, 62, 79, 86, 305
currency reform 24, 26, 82, 139

de Gaulle 358
debt xiv, xxi, xxx, 33–5, 37, 41, 50, 75, 122–3, 139, 237, 365–9, 393–4, 426, 434–5, 440, (*see also* credit; balance-of-payment); crisis 19; relief 245, 366–9
deficit financing xvi, xviii, 12, 59, 74, 92, 187–8, 190, 212, 329, 362
Dehejia Committee 61
Demag 273
Democracy 266
dependency syndrome 247, 250; *see also* Positive discrimination
Desai, R.C. 100, 281
devaluation 351; of dollar 355; of rupee xxvi
developed countries xvii, xxix, 53, 65–6, 69–70, 72, 79–82, 84, 132, 134, 324, 333–5, 341, 351, 401, 428
developing countries xvii, xxix, 72, 74, 76–7, 80–1, 123–4, 127, 192, 199, 336, 339, 343–4, 351, 353, 361–3, 365–6, 386, 433–6; and Central Bank 84; indebtedness of xxx; policies in 127–9
development 193; process of 47, 121, 135, 175, 322, 335, 337, 339
development economics 424
development strategy 281–2
direct credit controls 70, 79
Discount and Finance House of India 307
domestic product, classification of 178
domestic: luxury industries 343; production of erstwhile luxury imports 343; savings xxx, 328, 335, 343
dual exchange rate system 271

economic efficiency xxxi, 66, 385–6
economic policies 418, 419, 421, 424; Patel on 423
economic power, diffusion of 381–4
economic progress and technology 234
economic reforms xvi, 91, 257–9, 280, 285–6, 289–90, 295, 436–7; *see also* currency reform
economic security 372, 376–9
economic theory xiii–xvii, xxviii, 192, 385, 443
economics 442–4
Economics in Practice xv
Economics of Welfare, The xv, 409
economist xiii–xvii, xxi–xxii, 65–6, 238–9, 267–8, 292–3, 405–6, 408–9, 418–21, 442–3
education and health 242
egalitarianism 34
“emergency” or “mushroom” money 16
Emmerij 138
employment 5–6, 163–5, 242, 328, 389, 406, 410; in Second Five Year Plan 163–5, 179–83
Employment Exchanges 163
English coal strike 16
environmental, concern 236–7; protection 243
equality 243–4, 246–7; and equity xxv; of women 250, 255; *see also* Muslim women, rights of

Euro zone 434, 439–40
exchange policy 80–1; in developing countries 80–1
exchange rate accounting 336
Exchange Rate Policy 350–1
exchange rate xxvi, xxix, 5–6, 66–9, 80–1, 88–9, 271–2, 336–7, 350–1, 358–60; devaluing 271; and IMF 398; stability in 9
exit policy 270
"exorbitant privilege" 438
expansionist monetary policy 3, 28–9, 427
explicit targets 87
exploitation xxiv, 124, 128, 161, 194, 196–8, 200, 212, 224, 277, 293, 295, 334, 346, 397; of labour 397
export policy 127, 337, 345–50
export surplus 42–3, 139
exportable items, domestic consumption of 346; *see also* domestic luxury industries
external assistance 187, 322, 327–9, 331, 334, 348, 351–2; and private foreign capital 351–3

factory-produced consumer goods 179
fall in prices 3, 5, 10–11, 14, 22, 26, 28–9
family planning, advocacy of 255
fertilizer subsidies 276
finance for private sector 188–90
financial institutions 59, 61, 72, 77, 79, 83–4, 90–1, 146, 194, 274–5, 293, 299–306, 308–10, 312–13, 426, 431–2, (*see also under* individual names) role of 299–301; commercial banks 302; involvement in large concerns 304; and term loans 302
financial sector: regulation of 429–32; taxes on 432–3
financing elections, system for 256
fiscal deficits 286
fixed exchange rates 81
food grains scarcity of 322
Foreign aid xxviii, 136, 231, 281, 336–7, 347, 366, 373–5
foreign assistance 187, 191, 213–14, 217, 219, 339, 349
foreign exchange xxviii–xxx, 11–15, 17–18, 20, 22, 42–3, 52–3, 57–8, 72, 91–2, 113–16, 190–1, 323–4, 335–7, 339–40, 376; crisis of 291; reserves 12–13, 323; surpluses 58, 57–8, 323, 335, 376
foreign investment 269–70, 272
foreign loans 9, 12–13, 20
Frankfurter Zeitung 16
free trade 130, 135, 236, 238, 258, 390; areas 400
Friedman, Milton xxvii, 259, 415, 437
Frisch, Ragnar 421
fundamentalism 258–9

G20 439–40
Gandhi, Indira, hand symbol of 251
Gandhi, Mahatma 248, 249, 258; and economy 259; on poor 252–3
Gandhism 226
General Agreement on Tariffs and Trade (GATT) 133, 236, 341, 372, 394, 398
general deflationist psychology 10
General Insurance 308
George, Lloyd 226
German inflation: "emergency" or "mushroom" money 16; hyperinflation 16; price decline and 14; "Rentenbank" 16–17; and stabilization 14–19; use of pseudo-currencies 16; and velocity of circulation 15; "Wholesale Prices" 15
global economy xxx, 236, 424, 427, 433, 435–6, 438–40
global financial crisis 424–5, 433, 438, 442, 444
Global trade 435–6
globalization 257–8, 270, 290; of finance 434
gold standard, imbalances 81
gold: compulsory acquisition of 116–17; demand in India xvi, 97–8, 109, 115; elasticity of 98–9;

Gold bonds 114–15; prices in India 110–11; purchase in open market 114; tax evasion 115–16; and US prohibition 116
goods and income-earning assets 10
Gorbachev 232
Great Depression 100, 224
gross domestic product 242
Gulati, Ashok 283

Hall, Sir Robert 420
Hicks, J.R. xx
higher education and self-financing 295
Hillel, Rabbi 246
Hindu–Muslim unity 249–51, 256, 259–60
Hollond, Tapan xv
human resources 267
hyperinflation xviii, 7–8, 16, 19–20, 22–3, 29, 82; solution to 82

ICICI 301
"idle" and "active" balances 4
import policy 337–45; and domestic production 337; and "import-saving" 338, 339
import: liberalization policy for 274; licenses for 52; restrictions 128, 131, 336–7, 340–2, 344, 346: surplus 12–13, 26
import-substitution industries 129, 338
income distribution xx, xxv, 8, 98, 107, 160, 182, 244, 285, 342, 373
income spent on luxuries 98
income-tax exemption 275; *see also* taxation
Indian Economy 436–7; reforms in 289
Indo-Japanese collaboration 131
industrial and mineral development in second plan 167–70
industrial countries xxix–xxx, 64–70, 157, 390, 393
Industrial Development Bank of India (IDBI) 301
industrial entrepreneurs 146
Industrial Policy Resolution 227
industrial production 18, 26, 156, 202, 204, 218; agriculture and transport in India 210; in India 204; small-scale and cottage industries 217
industrialization xxi, xxiii, xxxi, 121, 124, 126–8, 130, 134, 136, 143, 156, 160–3, 190–1, 195, 199, 203, 254; in Second Five Year Plan 160–3
industrialized countries xxxi, 65–7, 84, 127, 133, 234–5, 242, 246, 348, 374, 381, 393, 428
inequalities 441–2
inflation 3–4, 8–9, 11, 283, 322, 351; consequences of 56; freedom from 390–1; as harmful to growth and employment 396; volume of investment during 13
instruments of production 7, 225
interest rates 18, 33–6, 40–1, 48, 59, 67–70, 74–81, 83, 86, 88, 145, 274, 291, 344, 368, 406; increase in 18
internal stability 26–7
international cooperation 89, 333, 342, 351, 358, 364, 401
International Development Association (IDA) 362, 373–4, 384
International *dharma* 261
international division of labour 386, 400
international economic cooperation 349, 363, 369, 371–2, 383–4
International environment 232
international institutions 76, 133, 236, 261, 352, 364, 381–2, 384, 398; democratization of 381–2
international markets xxxi, 234
international monetary cooperation 358–9
International Monetary Fund (IMF) xiv, xvi–xvii, xxix, 32, 44, 71, 81–2, 89, 114, 277, 341, 355, 381, 383–4, 425, 439–40; mandate for orderly exchange rates 89; membership in 384; mission to India 71
international monetary system and US Dollar 438

international trade xxviii–xxxi, 126, 133, 337, 353, 377, 386, 390, 392, 394, 399, 401, 438; open system of 394–5
investment 13, 45–6, 342; banking 430; and developmental expenditure 173–4; famine 144; goods 151; and nation-building activities 175; pattern of 328, 336; policy of 268–9, 277, 314, 349; in Second Plan 173–6; in working capital 174

Jacobsson, Per 358
Japan: investment and 237, 269; success of 259, 399
Japanese capitalism 266, 270
Johr 419–21
Joshi, Vijay 281, 283, 286

Kahn, Richard xv
kangaroo courts 257
Karachi resolution 227
Kashmir 260
Keynes, Lord xiv, 65, 146, 266, 406–8, 410
Khatkhate, Deena 425
Kornai, Janos xxiii

labour xxvii; legislation 239; markets and privatization 292–3; mobility of 11; mobilization of voluntary 174; reform of 292; rise in the price of 8; surplus of 234
labour-intensive export 282
labour-intensive strategy 281–2
Lal, Deepak 281, 284–5
large credit limits 61–2
latent deflation 11, 29
latent inflation 6, 11–13, 23, 30, 33–4, 40–1, 188; and velocity of circulation 40–2
Lead Bank Scheme 91
legal currency xviii, 8–9, 17, 29
less developed countries xxix, 134, 324, 333–5, 341, 353; problems of 333
liberalization xxi, xxvii, 83–4, 134–5, 137, 274, 284, 291, 344, 393
Life Insurance 308
Lindbeck, Assar 399
linkage system 271
liquidation of stocks 11, 28
liquidity xxi, 4–6, 14, 17–19, 26, 28, 36–7, 41–2, 52, 69, 78, 82, 88, 429–31, 438, 440
loan. *See* credit
local currency 8, 11–12, 30, 43, 52, 108, 329
longer-term: equilibrium 76; savings 78

MacDonald, Ramsay 226
machine-building capacity 283
Mahalanobis, P.C. xxii–xxiii, 148
Malaviyaji 254
malnutrition 242; elimination of 258
market capitalism 435
Marshall, Alfred xxiv, 231, 258
material balances 152
McNamara 380
modernization 89, 139, 173, 190; in China 89; of consumer goods industries 162; and unemployment 19
monetary policy xvi, xviii–xx, xxii, xxvi, 3–4, 9, 27–30, 32–6, 39–43, 59–60, 64–71, 73–5, 77–81, 334–5, 425–9; in developing countries 70–84; during stabilization 13–29; and investments 33; and supply shock 80; techniques of 34–5
monetary targeting 70–5; criticism of 71, 73–4
money balances 7–8, 14–15, 20, 22–3, 28, 30; real value of 5, 7–8, 14–15, 20, 22, 30
money circulation, velocity of xviii, 4–10, 14–16, 20, 24, 34, 40–1, 57, 71
money supply xviii, 3, 5–6, 9, 12–24, 26–30, 35, 38–42, 50, 57–8, 68, 71–4, 81, 87, 187, 426–7; change in real value of 15
money wage rates 18, 406
Monopolies and Restrictive Trade Practice (MRTP) Act 271, 307, 313
Morishima, Michio xvi
Morse 359–60

Most favoured nation treatment 133
multilateral international trading system 392
multilateral trade relations 127
multinational firms 234
"mushroom" money 16
Muslim community 252, 260
Muslim women, rights of 255
Myrdal, Professor 344

Nagpur plan 170
Narasimhan committee 274–5, 307
Narayan, Jayaprakash 229
National Bank of Belgium 28
national income 4, 15, 17, 23–4, 26–9, 71, 97, 156–7, 176–9, 183–8, 202, 208, 279, 319; money supply to 28; and standard of living 157–60
national resources, allocation of 84
nationalization of banks 59, 76, 254
Nehru, Jawaharlal xxiv, 261, 248, 249; and austerity 230; letter to Gandhiji 225; to Lord Lothian 224, 225; and socialism 223–6, 231
"net investment" 173
new international economic order 372–3
Newly Industrializing Countries (NICs) 138, 234–5; domestic consumption 140; pressure of import from US 140
NGOs 260, 281, 285; and economic reforms 295
1971, events of 354–6
non-monetized investment 173–4
non-resident Indians 272
non-violence 249, 251
nuclear acquisition 253
Nurkse 282

'Occupy Wall Street' movement 441
oil crisis 374
oil-rich countries 382
open economy 192
Organization of Petroleum Exporting Countries (OPEC) 375
organized labour 286–7
ornaments into money, conversion of 99
over-accumulation of stocks 7
overseas capital dependence 237; *see also* dependency syndrome

Pakistan and peace process 260
Panandikar, Pai 285
paper money 16–17
Parikh, Kirit 284
Partition 252–3
Patel, I.G. xiii–xxxi, 423–5, 427–8
Patel, Sardar 226
pauperization 244
Pherwani Committee 307
"Physical planning" 148–50
Pigou, A.C. xv, 405–10
Pitamber Pant xxii
PL-480 supplies xxviii, 319–31; monetary aspects of 329–31; and Second Plan 321–6; Third Five Year Plan 326–8
Polak, J.J. xvi
politicization 84, 273, 295
poorer countries 123, 132–4, 136, 236, 245, 341–2, 349–50, 362, 374–5
population 236
Populism 252, 269, 274, 279, 295, 308
positive discrimination 247
postponement of payments 367
post-war recession 33
poverty 242, 244, 245, 253; elimination of 305
preservation 269
price elasticity, estimation of 100–10
price level 5–6, 11–14, 324, 425, 427; of consumers' goods 11; of gold 99; increase in 5, 6–7, 8, 12, 13
price stability 389, 425–6, 428–9; goals of 73
primary education 245
private banks and loans 48–9
private capital 237, 272, 351–2; movements 351
private entertainment 254
private foreign capital 326

private foreign investment 130–1, 136, 237–8, 272, 337, 342–3
private gold hoards 113, 115–16
private initiatives 195
private property, elimination of 225
private savings 73, 276, 293, 302, 308, 313–14
privatization 83, 233, 281, 287, 291–3
production xvii–xviii, 3–7, 11–13, 16–18, 26–30, 56–9, 149–53, 161–5, 167–9, 202–8, 214–18, 322–4, 334–8, 342–3; decentralization 259
products of industrialization 124
profit-yielding securities 99
promoting export earnings 121–2, 123–4
protectionism xxxi, 235, 243, 276, 392–5, 398; in agriculture 398; and unemployment 396
public and private participation 257
Public Broadcasting System 254
public financial institutions 83–4, 146, 301, 303–5, 308–10, 312–13
public ownership 197
Public Policy 442–4
public sector, resources in the 184–8
purchasing power 21, 59, 107, 208, 218, 236, 330, 359, 377
Purchasing Power Parity theory 359

quality of life 379; *see also* national income, and standard of living

Ramaswami 370–1
Rangarajan 281, 283
recession in America 28
Reddy, Governor 86
Reddy, Prakash xxvii
redistribution 10, 108, 285, 372–6, 381
reformism 225–6
regionalism 236, 253–4
Reichsbank 16–18
Reserve Bank and bank lending to stock exchanges 91
resources mobilization 183–4; and balance of payments 190–1; for private sector 188–90; in public sector 184–8
rising prices 14
Robinson, Austin xv
Robinson, Joan xiii, xvii, 58, 72; "The Quantity Theory" of 58, 72
Role of the Economist as Official Adviser, The 419
Rosenstein-Rodan, P.N. xxviii, 325

satyagraha 249
savings 7; in disproportion 235; and investment 44, 46, 56, 73–4, 157, 183, 189, 258, 267, 340, 385; value of 6
Scandinavian model 140
Second Five Year Plan 155; mobilization of resources for 183–91; objectives of 156–7; outline of 167–83
Securities and Exchange Board of India 307, 308, 310–12
selective credit control 40, 44–8, 51; and balance-of-payments difficulties 46; and bank incentives 51; and bank loans 52, 54; as long-term objective 48–50; policy of 44–7; and process of stabilization 47; as short-term expedient 51–4; techniques of 47–8
"self-liquidating" loans 45
self-regulation 311
self-reliance 240
Sen, Amartya xxiv, 281–2
Singer 419–21
Singh, Ajit 284
Singh, Manmohan xxvi, 280–1, 283
SLR requirements 88
small-scale industries, employment in 180, 183; in Second Plan 162
Smith, Adam 310, 412–17
Smithsonian agreement 355, 359
social justice 165–7; and conspicuous consumption 166; in Second Five Year Plan 165–7
social order 246
social organization 246
social services 172–3
social solidarity 242
socialism, revival of 230

socialist pattern of society 227
Special Drawing Rights (SDR) 277, 361, 438
Special Liquidity Requirements 88, 309
stabilization 3–4, 10–14, 16, 19–20, 81–3; crisis and xviii, 10, 12–13, 16, 22, 26, 28–9; demand for money during 31; of German economy 18; and IMF 81–2; and monetary policy 9; new money and 3; of production increases 30; and velocity of circulation of money 9–13
subsidies on fertilizers 283
"sunrise" industries 143
surplus money xviii, 33–5, 41

Tandon Committee 147
tariffs under GATT 342
taxation 12–13, 31, 145, 150, 166, 183, 188–9, 195, 272–3, 303, 309, 322–3, 325, 328, 335, 373–4; evasion of 100
Taxation Enquiry Commission 166–7, 183
technical manpower 238
technological change 269
technology 238–9; Gandhiji on 238
technology economy 238; *see also* technology transfer
technology transfer 238
technology-led interdependence 234
telecommunications reform 293
Ten Commandments 292
Tendulkar 284
term deposits 59–60
Thatcher, Margaret 266
Theory of Economic Policy of Tinbergen 421
Tobin Tax 432
Tourism Finance Corporation 309
trade agreement 236; *see also* General Agreement on Tariffs and Trade (GATT)
trade policy 240
trade with state-trading countries 347–8
Trade: among developing countries 134–5; with state-trading countries 348; trade with socialist countries 135–6
transfer of resources 283, 366–7, 369, 373–4
transport and power: in First Plan 170; in Second Plan 170
Treaty of Versailles 14
treaty on non-proliferation of nuclear weapons 237

UN Revolving Fund for Natural Resources 374
underdeveloped world 131–4
unemployment xxvii, 5, 11, 14, 17–19, 26–30, 163–5, 172–3, 198, 241, 294, 343, 388–9, 393, 395–6, 406–7; in Belgium 27
UNICEF 380
United Nations Commission on Trade and Development (UNCTAD) 130, 371–2
United Nations Development Policy (UNDP) 373–4
United Nations, organizations of 379–80
United States 40, 54–5, 126, 130, 234–5, 329–31, 349, 355–6, 360–1, 438; and debt 235; and PL-480 transactions 329
universal education 257
untouchability, eradication of 254

Vakil 281
Value Added Tax (VAT) 291
Velocity of Circulation of Money during Inflation 5–9
vision for India 265–6
Volcker, Paul 85

wage-price inflation 8
wage-push pressures 79–80
wages 6, 73, 80, 82, 139, 151, 273, 400, 406–7, 436
Wallich, Professor 354, 359–60
welfare state 241

women: atrocities against 252; rights of 255
World Bank xxix, 71, 133–4, 236, 261, 310, 352, 369, 373, 380–4, 425, 436, 439
World Food Conference 378
World Food Programme 380
World Trade Organization xxxi

zero-budgeting 308